About Face 3

About Face 3

The Essentials of
Interaction Design

Alan Cooper, Robert Reimann, and Dave Cronin

Wiley Publishing, Inc.

About Face 3: The Essentials of Interaction Design

Published by

Wiley Publishing, Inc.

10475 Crosspoint Boulevard

Indianapolis, IN 46256

www.wiley.com

Published by Wiley Publishing, Inc., Indianapolis, Indiana

Published simultaneously in Canada

ISBN: 978-0-470-08411-3

Manufactured in the United States of America

10 9 8 7 6 5 4 3 2

For general information on our other products and services or to obtain technical support, please contact our Customer Care Department within the U.S. at (800) 762-2974, outside the U.S. at (317) 572-3993 or fax (317) 572-4002.

Library of Congress Cataloging-in-Publication Data:

Cooper, Alan, 1952-

  About face 3 : the essentials of interaction design / Alan Cooper, Robert Reimann, and Dave Cronin.

    p. cm.

  Includes bibliographical references.

  ISBN 978-0-470-08411-3 (pbk.)

  1. User interfaces (Computer systems) 2. Human-computer interaction. I. Reimann, Robert. II. Cronin, Dave, 1972- III. Title. IV. Title: About face three.

  QA76.9.U83C6596 2007

  005.4'38--dc22

                                2007004977

For Sue, my best friend through all the adventures of life.

For Maxwell Aaron Reimann.

For Gretchen.

And for Cooperistas past, present, and future;
and for those visionary IxD practitioners who
have helped create a new design profession.

About the Authors

Alan Cooper is a pioneering software inventor, programmer, designer, and theorist. He is credited with having produced "probably the first serious business software for microcomputers" and is well known as the "Father of Visual Basic." For the last 15 years his software design consulting company, Cooper, has helped many companies invent new products and improve the behavior of their technology. At Cooper, Alan led the development of a new methodology for creating successful software that he calls the Goal-Directed process. Part of that effort was the invention of personas, a practice that has been widely adopted since he first published the technique in his second book, *The Inmates are Running the Asylum*, in 1998. Cooper is also a well known writer, speaker, and enthusiast for humanizing technology.

Robert Reimann has spent the past 15 years pushing the boundaries of digital products as a designer, writer, lecturer, and consultant. He has led dozens of interaction design projects in domains including e-commerce, portals, desktop productivity, authoring environments, medical and scientific instrumentation, wireless, and handheld devices for startups and Fortune 500 clients alike. As director of design R&D at Cooper, Reimann led the development and refinement of many of the Goal-Directed Design methods described in *About Face*. In 2005, Reimann became the first President of IxDA, the Interaction Design Association (www.ixda.org), a global nonprofit professional organization for Interaction Designers. He is currently manager of user experience at Bose Corporation.

Dave Cronin is the director of interaction design at Cooper, where he's helped design products to serve the needs of people such as surgeons, museum visitors, marketers, investment portfolio managers, online shoppers, hospital staff, car drivers, dentists, financial analysts, manufacturing planners, the elderly, and the infirm. At Cooper, he has also contributed substantially to the ongoing process of developing and refining the Goal-Directed Design methods described in this book.

Credits

Executive Editor
Chris Webb

Development Editors
Sara Shlaer
Sydney Jones

Production Editor
Eric Charbonneau

Copy Editor
Foxxe Editorial Services

Editorial Manager
Mary Beth Wakefield

Production Manager
Tim Tate

**Vice President and Executive Group
   Publisher**
Richard Swadley

**Vice President and Executive
   Publisher**
Joseph B. Wikert

Project Coordinator
Erin Smith

Graphics and Production Specialists
Sean Decker, Brooke Graczyk,
Stephanie D. Jumper,
Jennifer Mayberry, Barbara Moore,
Ronald Terry

Quality Control Technician
Christy Pingleton

Book Designers
Rebecca Bortman and Nick Myers

Illustrators
Rebecca Bortman and Nick Myers

Proofreading and Indexing
Aptara

Anniversary Logo Design
Richard Pacifico

Cover Design
Rebecca Bortman and Nick Myers

Contents

Foreword: The Postindustrial World

The industrial age is over. Manufacturing, the primary economic driver of the past 175 years, no longer dominates. While manufacturing is bigger than ever, it has lost its leadership to digital technology, and software now dominates our economy. We have moved from atoms to bits. We are now in the postindustrial age.

More and more products have software in them. My stove has a microchip in it to manage the lights, fan, and oven temperature. When the deliveryman has me sign for a package, it's on a computer, not a pad of paper. When I shop for a car, I am really shopping for a navigation system.

More and more businesses are utterly dependent on software, and not just the obvious ones like Amazon.com and Microsoft. Thousands of companies of all sizes that provide products and services across the spectrum of commerce use software in every facet of their operations, management, planning, and sales. The back-office systems that run big companies are all software systems. Hiring and human resource management, investment and arbitrage, purchasing and supply chain management, point-of-sale, operations, and decision support are all pure software systems these days. And the Web dominates all sales and marketing. Live humans are no longer the front line of businesses. Software plays that role instead. Vendors, customers, colleagues, and employees all communicate with companies via software or software-mediated paths.

The organizational structures and management techniques that have worked so well in the past for manufacturing-based companies are failing us today in the postindustrial age. They fail because they focus on the transformation and movement of things made out of atoms. There are only finite amounts of desirable atoms and it takes lots of energy to transform and transport them. Software—made out of bits, not atoms—is qualitatively different. There is an infinite quantity of bits and virtually no energy is needed to transform, transport, or even replicate them.

The people who make software are different as well. The average computer programmer and the average assembly line worker are qualitatively different in their aptitude, attitude, training, language, tools, and value systems. The most effective ways of supervising, tracking, and managing programmers are dramatically different from those used so successfully with blue-collar workers of an earlier age. Getting programmers to do what is best for the company requires skills unknown to the industrial-age executive.

Reducing the cost of manufacturing was the essential contribution of industrialization. Thus the best and brightest minds of an earlier age applied themselves to reducing the amount of money spent creating products. In the postindustrial age, the costs of raw materials, product assembly, and shipping are equally low for all players. The only significant leverage to lower manufacturing costs comes through automation, planning, and business intelligence: that is, software. In other words, instead of saving a dollar on the construction of each widget, you save a million dollars by making the precisely needed quantity of the most desirable product.

Once a software program has been successfully written, it can be reproduced an unlimited number of times for virtually nothing. There is little benefit in reducing the cost of writing it. Reducing the amount one spends on software construction usually means compromising the quality, so the primary business equation of the industrial age is reversed today. The best and brightest minds of today apply themselves to increasing the effectiveness of software and the quality of its behavior. Keep in mind that all modern financial accounting systems focus on tracking manufacturing costs and no longer accurately represent the state of our software-dominated businesses. Making executive decisions on these erroneous numbers causes significant waste of time, money, and opportunity.

It's no wonder that companies struggle with software. Very capable executives find that their intentions are subtly but significantly altered somewhere along the path from conception to release. What appeared to be a sound plan turns out to be inadequate for shepherding the software construction process. It's time to let go of obsolete industrial-age management methods and adopt interaction design as the primary tool for designing and managing software construction.

Since *About Face* was first published in 1995, the practice of interaction design has grown and matured enormously. Dominated for so long by simple ex post facto, trial-and-error methods, interaction design—along with its many siblings and variants—has matured into a clear, dependable, effective tool for determining what behavior will succeed. The invention and development of personas, the refinement of written behavioral blueprints, and the entire practice of Goal-Directed™ Design, have made high-quality software behavior achievable by any organization with the will to create it.

What's more, interaction design has emerged as an incredibly powerful software construction management tool. Because it is a description of the software as it will be when it is finally written, it acts as a blueprint, not only helping programmers know what to build but also helping managers measure the progress of the programmers.

Interaction design has also shown its power as a marketing tool, communicating with great clarity and specificity about exactly whom will be using the product and why. Getting to the root of customer motivations is manna for marketers, and the qualitative research and analysis aspects of Goal-Directed Design provide significant market insight.

Especially since the Web revolution—when tossing common sense overboard seemed to be the path to instant riches—I've heard many intelligent people who really should know better say, "It is simply not possible to know what the user wants!" While this assertion certainly absolves them of not, in fact, knowing what the user wants, it is boldly, obviously, incredibly false. At my company, Cooper, clients bring our designers into the complex worlds of finance, health care, pharmaceuticals, human resources, programming tools, museums, consumer credit, and any number of disparate fields. Our teams, none of whom have any training in—or typically even any exposure to—the particular subject matter at hand, routinely become sufficiently expert in only a few weeks to astonish our clients. We can do this because our point of departure is relentlessly human-centered, rather than technology-centered.

Interaction design is a tool for "Knowing what the user wants." Armed with that knowledge, you can create better, more successful, bit-empowered products, and you can sell them for more money. What's more, you will reach your market with a loyalty-inducing, better solution. Time and time again we have seen feature-loaded products early to market get trounced by later entries whose behavior has been better thought out. Imagine getting that thinking done before the first release ever has a chance to commit you to a nonoptimal strategy.

Nothing succeeds like success, and the success of the practical application of the principles and methods put forth in this book—and others like it—are clearly demonstrating that software isn't really as soft as many people first thought, and that thorough user research and detailed planning are more necessary than ever in the postindustrial age.

If you are committed to improving the world by improving the behavior of digital products and services, then I welcome you to the world of *About Face*.

—*Alan Cooper*

Acknowledgments

We'd like to express our deepest gratitude to the following individuals, without whom this new edition of *About Face* would not have been possible: Chris Webb at Wiley, who saw the time was right for a new edition; Sue Cooper, who shared that vision; and Sara Shlaer at Wiley, who has patiently helped us shape multiple editions of this book.

We would also like to thank the following colleagues and Cooper designers for their contributions to this volume and the previous, for which we are greatly indebted: Kim Goodwin, who has contributed significantly to the development and expression of the concepts and methods described in these pages; Rebecca Bortman and Nick Myers who overhauled the book and cover designs, as well as the illustrations; Hugh Dubberly, for his help in developing the principles at the end of Chapter 8 and for his assistance in clarifying the Goal-Directed process with early versions of the diagrams found in Chapter 1; Gretchen Anderson, Elaine Montgomery, and Doug LeMoine for their contributions on user and market research in Chapter 4; Rick Bond for his many insights about usability testing featured in Chapter 7; Ernest Kinsolving and Joerg Beringer at SAP for their contributions on the posture of Web portals in Chapter 9; Chris Weeldreyer for his insights into the design of embedded systems in Chapter 9; Wayne Greenwood for his contributions on control mapping in Chapter 10; and Nate Fortin and Nick Myers for their contributions on visual interface design and branding in Chapter 14. We would also like to thank Elizabeth Bacon, Steve Calde, John Dunning, David Fore, Nate Fortin, Kim Goodwin, Wayne Greenwood, Noah Guyot, Lane Halley, Ernest Kinsolving, Daniel Kuo, Berm Lee, Doug LeMoine, Tim McCoy, Elaine Montgomery, Nick Myers, Chris Noessel, Ryan Olshavsky, Angela Quail, Suzy Thompson, and Chris Weeldreyer for their contributions to the Cooper designs and illustrations featured in this volume.

We are grateful to clients David West at Shared Healthcare Systems, Mike Kay and Bill Chang at Fujitsu Softek, John Chaffins at CrossCountry, Chris Twogood at Teradata, and Chris Dollar at McKesson for granting us permission to use examples from the Cooper design projects featured in this book. We wish also to thank the many other clients who have had the vision and the foresight to work with us and support us in their organizations.

We would also like to acknowledge the following authors and industry colleagues who have influenced or clarified our thinking over the years: Christopher Alexander, Edward Tufte, Kevin Mullet, Victor Papanek, Donald Norman, Larry Constantine, Challis Hodge, Shelley Evenson, Clifford Nass, Byron Reeves, Stephen Pinker, and Terry Swack.

Finally, it should be noted that the parts of Chapter 5 concerned with cognitive processing originally appeared in an article by Robert Reimann on UXMatters.com, and are used with permission.

Introduction to the Third Edition

This book is about **interaction design**—the practice of designing interactive digital products, environments, systems, and services. Like many design disciplines, interaction design is concerned with form. However, first and foremost, interaction design focuses on something that traditional design disciplines do not often explore: the design of *behavior*.

Most design *affects* human behavior: Architecture is concerned with how people use physical space, and graphic design often attempts to motivate or facilitate a response. But now, with the ubiquity of silicon-enabled products—from computers to cars and phones—we routinely create products that *exhibit* complex behavior.

Take something as basic as an oven. Before the digital age, the operation of an oven was quite simple—it involved turning a single knob to the correct position. There was one position for off, and one position for any oven temperature one might want to use. Every single time a person turned that knob to a given position, *the same thing happened*. One might call this "behavior," but it is certainly quite simple and mechanistic behavior. Compare this to our modern-day ovens with silicon chips and LCD screens. They are endowed with buttons that say non-cooking-related things like Start, Cancel, Program, as well as the more expected Bake and Broil. What happens when you press any one of these buttons is quite a lot less predictable than what happened when you turned the knob on your old gas range. In fact, the results of pressing one of the buttons is entirely dependent on the state of the oven and what other buttons you might have pressed previously. This is what we mean by *complex behavior*.

This emergence of products with complex behavior has given rise to a new discipline. Interaction design borrows theory and technique from traditional design, usability, and engineering disciplines. But it is greater than a sum of its parts, with its own unique methods and practices. And to be clear—it is very much a *design* discipline, quite different from science and engineering. While it should always be practiced in a rational and considered manner, interaction design is about synthesis and imagining things as they might be, not necessarily as they currently are.

Interaction design is also an inherently humanistic enterprise. It is concerned most significantly with satisfying the needs and desires of the people who will interact with a product or service. In this book we describe a particular approach to interaction design that we call the Goal-Directed method. We've found that when a designer focuses on people's goals—the reasons why they use a product in the first place—as well as their expectations, attitudes, and aptitudes, they can devise solutions that people find powerful and pleasurable.

As even the most casual observer of developments in technology must have noticed, interactive products can become very complex very quickly. While a mechanical device may be capable of a dozen visible states, a digital product may be capable of being in thousands of different states (if not more!). This complexity can be a nightmare for users and designers alike. To tame this complexity, we rely on a very systematic and rational approach. This doesn't mean that we don't also value and encourage inventiveness and creativity. On the contrary, we find that a methodical approach helps us clearly identify opportunities for revolutionary thinking, and provides a way of assessing the effectiveness of our ideas.

According to Gestalt Theory, people perceive a thing not as a set of individual features and attributes but as a unified whole in a relationship with its surroundings. As a result, it isn't possible to effectively design an interactive product by decomposing it into a list of atomic requirements and coming up with a design solution for each. Even a relatively simple product must be considered in totality and in light of its context in the world. Again, we've found that a methodical approach helps provide the holistic perspective necessary to create products that people find useful and engaging.

A Brief History of Interaction Design

In the late 1970s and early 1980s a dedicated and visionary set of researchers, engineers, and designers in the San Francisco Bay Area were busy inventing how people would interact with computers in the future. At Xerox Parc, SRI, and eventually Apple Computer, people had begun discussing what it meant to create useful and usable "human interfaces" to digital products. In the mid-1980s, two industrial designers, Bill Moggridge and Bill Verplank, who were working on the first laptop computer, the GRiD Compass, coined the term **interaction design** for what they were doing, but it would be another 10 years before other designers rediscovered this term and brought it into mainstream use.

At the time *About Face* was first published in August 1995, the landscape of interaction design was still a frontier wilderness. A small cadre of people brave enough to hold the title user interface designer operated under the shadow of software engineering, rather like the tiny, quick-witted mammals that scrambled under the shadows of hulking tyrannosaurs. "Software design," as the first edition of *About Face* referred to it, was poorly understood and underappreciated, and, when it was practiced at all, it was usually practiced by programmers. A handful of uneasy technical writers, trainers, and product support people, along with a rising number of practitioners from another nascent field—usability—realized that something needed to change.

The amazing growth and popularity of the Web drove that change, seemingly overnight. Suddenly, "ease of use" was a term on everyone's lips. Traditional design professionals, who had dabbled in digital product design during the short-lived popularity of "multimedia" in the early nineties, leapt to the Web en masse. Seemingly new design titles sprang up like weeds: information designer, information architect, user experience strategist, and interaction designer. For the first time ever, C-level executive positions were established to focus on creating user-centered products and services, such as the chief experience officer. Universities scrambled to offer programs to train designers in these disciplines. Meanwhile, usability and human factors practitioners also rose in stature and are now recognized as advocates for better-designed products.

Although the Web knocked interaction design idioms back by more than a decade, it inarguably placed user requirements on the radar of the corporate world for good. Since the second edition of *About Face* was published in 2003, the *user experience* of digital products has become front page news in the likes of *Time* magazine and *BusinessWeek*, and institutions such as Harvard Business School and Stanford have recognized the need to train the next generation of MBAs and technologists to incorporate design thinking into their business and development plans. People are tired of new technology for its own sake. Consumers are sending a clear message that what they want is *good* technology: technology that has been *designed* to provide a compelling and effective user experience.

In August 2003, five months after the second edition of *About Face* proclaimed the existence of a new design discipline called *interaction design*, Bruce "Tog" Tognazzini made an impassioned plea to the nascent community to create a nonprofit professional organization, and a mailing list and steering committee were founded shortly thereafter by Challis Hodge, David Heller, Rick Cecil, and Jim Jarrett. In September of 2005, IxDA, the Interaction Design Association (www.ixda.org) was officially incorporated. At the time of writing, it has over 2000 members in over 20 countries. We're pleased to say that Interaction Design is finally beginning to come into its own as both a discipline and a profession.

Why Call It Interaction Design?

The first edition of *About Face* described a discipline called software design and equated it with another discipline called user interface design. Of these two terms, user interface design has certainly had better longevity. We still use it occasionally in this book, specifically to connote the arrangement of widgets on the screen. However, what is discussed in this book is a discipline broader than the design of user interfaces. In the world of digital technology, form, function, content, and behavior are so inextricably linked that many of the challenges of designing an interactive product go right to the heart of what a digital product *is* and what it *does*.

As we've discussed, interaction designers have borrowed practices from more established design disciplines, but have also evolved beyond them. Industrial designers have attempted to address the design of digital products, but like their counterparts in graphic design, their focus has traditionally been on the design of static form, not the design of interactivity, or form that changes and reacts to input over time. These disciplines do not have a language with which to discuss the design of rich, dynamic behavior and changing user interfaces.

In recent years, a number of new terms have been proposed for this type of design. As the World Wide Web gained prominence, information architecture (IA) emerged as a discipline dedicated to solving problems dealing with navigation to and the "findability" of content, mostly (though not exclusively) within the context of Web sites. While clearly a close relative of interaction design, mainstream IA still retains a somewhat limited, Web-centric view of organizing and navigating content using pages, links, and minimally interactive widgets. However, recent industry trends such as Web 2.0 and rich Internet applications have begun to open the eyes of Web designers, causing them to look beyond archaic browser interaction idioms. We believe this awakening is bringing information architects' concerns ever more closely in alignment with those of interaction designers.

Another term that has gained popularity is *user experience* (UX). There are many who advocate for the use of this term as an umbrella under which many different design and usability disciplines collaborate to create products, systems, and services. This is a laudable goal with great appeal, but it does not in itself directly address the core concern of interaction design as discussed in this volume: how specifically to design the behavior of complex interactive systems. While it's useful to consider the similarities and synergies between creating a customer experience at a physical store and creating one with an interactive product, we believe there are specific methods appropriate to designing for the world of bits.

We also wonder whether it is actually possible to *design* an experience. Designers of all stripes hope to manage and *influence* the experiences people have, but this is done by carefully manipulating the variables intrinsic to the medium at hand. A graphic designer creating a poster uses an arrangement of type, photos, and illustrations to help create an experience, a furniture designer working on a chair uses materials and construction techniques to help create an experience, and an interior designer uses layout, lighting, materials, and even sound to help create an experience.

Extending this thinking to the world of digital products, we find it useful to think that we influence people's experiences by designing the mechanisms for interacting with a product. Therefore, we have chosen Moggridge's term, **interaction design** (now abbreviated by many in the industry as IxD), to denote the kind of design this book describes.

Of course, there are many cases where a design project requires careful attention to the orchestration of a number of design disciplines to achieve an appropriate user experience (see Figure 1). It is to these situations that we feel the term *experience design* is most applicable.

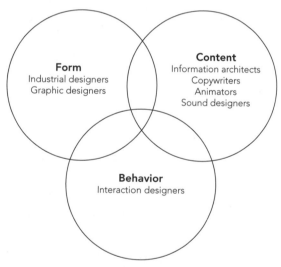

Figure 1 One can think of user experience design (UX) of digital products as consisting of three overlapping concerns: form, behavior, and content. Interaction design is focused on the design of behavior, but is also concerned with how that behavior relates to form and content. Similarly, information architecture is focused on the structure of content, but is also concerned with behaviors that provide access to content, and the way the content is presented to the user. Industrial design and graphic design are concerned with the form of products and services, but also must ensure that their form supports use, which requires attention to behavior and content.

Working with the Product Team

In addition to defining interaction design in terms of its primary concern with behavior and its relationships with other design disciplines, we also often find it necessary to define how interaction design should fit within an organization. We believe that establishing a rigorous product development process that incorporates design as an equal partner with engineering, marketing, and business management, and that includes well-defined responsibilities and authority for each group, greatly increases the value a business can reap from design. The following division of responsibilities, balanced by an equal division of authority, can dramatically improve design success and organizational support of the product throughout the development cycle and beyond:

- **The design team** has responsibility for users' satisfaction with the product. Many organizations do not currently hold *anyone* responsible for this. To carry out this responsibility, designers must have the authority to decide how the product will look, feel, and behave. They also need access to information: They must observe and speak to potential users about their needs, to engineers about technological opportunities and constraints, to marketing about opportunities and requirements, and to management about the kind of product to which the organization will commit.

- **The engineering team** has responsibility for the implementation and fabrication of the product. For the design to deliver its benefit, engineering must have the responsibility for building, *as specified,* the form and behaviors that the designers define, while keeping on budget and on schedule. Engineers, therefore, require a clear description of the product's form and behaviors, which will guide what they build and drive their time and cost estimates. This description must come from the design team. Engineers must also contribute to discussions of technical constraints and opportunities, as well as the feasibility of proposed design solutions.

- **The marketing team** has responsibility for convincing customers to purchase the product, so they must have authority over all communications with the customer, as well as input into the product definition and design. In order to do this, the team members need access to information, including the results of designers' research, as well as research of their own. (It's worth noting that, as we discuss further in Chapters 4 and 5, customers and users are often different people with different needs.)

- **Management** has responsibility for the profitability of the resulting product, and therefore has the authority to make decisions about what the other groups will work on. To make those decisions, management needs to receive clear information from the other groups: design's research and product definition, marketing's research and sales projections, and engineering's estimations of the time and cost to create the product.

What This Book Is and What It Is Not

In this book, we attempt to provide readers with effective and practical tools for interaction design. These tools consist of *principles*, *patterns*, and *processes*. Design *principles* encompass broad ideas about the practice of design, as well as rules and hints about how to best use specific user interface and interaction design idioms. Design *patterns* describe sets of interaction design idioms that are common ways to address specific user requirements and design concerns. Design *processes* describe how to go about understanding and defining user requirements, how to then translate those requirements into the framework of a design, and finally how to best apply design principles and patterns to specific contexts.

Although books are available that discuss design principles and design patterns, few books discuss design processes, and even fewer discuss all three of these tools and how they work together to create effective designs. Our goal with this volume has been to create a book that weaves all three of these three tools together. While helping you design more effective and useful dialog boxes and menus, this book will simultaneously help you understand how users comprehend and interact with your digital product, and understand how to use this knowledge to drive your design.

Integrating design principles, processes, and patterns is the key to designing effective product interactions and interfaces. There is no such thing as an objectively good user interface—quality depends on the context: who the user is, what she is doing, and what her motivations are. Applying a set of one-size-fits-all principles makes user interface creation *easier*, but it doesn't necessarily make the end result *better*. If you want to create good design solutions, there is no avoiding the hard work of really understanding the people who will actually interact with your product. Only then is it useful to have at your command a toolbox of principles and patterns to apply in specific situations. We hope this book will both encourage you to deepen your understanding of your product's users, and teach you how to translate that understanding into superior product designs.

This book does *not* attempt to present a style guide or set of interface standards. In fact, you'll learn in Chapter 14 why the utility of such tools is limited and relevant only to specific circumstances. That said, we hope that the process and principles described in this book are compatible companions to the style guide of your choice. Style guides are good at answering *what*, but generally weak at answering *why*. This book attempts to address these unanswered questions.

We discuss four main steps to designing interactive systems in this book: researching the domain, understanding the users and their requirements, defining the framework of a solution, and filling in the design details. Many practitioners would add a fifth step: *validation*, testing the effectiveness of a solution with users. This is part of a discipline widely known as *usability*.

While this is an important and worthwhile component to many interaction design initiatives, it is a discipline and practice in its own right. We briefly discuss design validation and usability testing in Chapter 7, but urge you to refer to the significant and ever-growing body of usability literature for more detailed information about conducting and analyzing usability tests.

Changes from the Previous Editions

Much in the world of interface design has changed since the first edition of *About Face* was published in 1995. However, much remains the same. The third edition of About Face retains what still holds true, updates those things that have changed, and provides new material reflecting not only how the industry has changed in the last 11 years but also new concepts that we have developed in our practice to address the changing times.

Here are some highlights of the major changes you will find in the third edition of *About Face*:

▶ The book has been reorganized to present its ideas in a more easy-to-use reference structure. The book is divided into three parts: The first deals with process and high-level ideas about users and design, the second deals with high-level interaction design principles, and the third deals with lower-level interface design principles.

▶ The first part describes the Goal-Directed Design process in much greater detail than in the second edition, and more accurately reflects current practices at Cooper, including research techniques, the creation of personas, and how to use personas and scenarios to synthesize interaction design solutions.

▶ Throughout the book, we attempt to more explicitly discuss visual interface design concepts, methods and issues, as well as issues related to a number of platforms beyond the desktop.

▶ Terminology and examples in the book have been updated to reflect the current state of the art in the industry, and the text as a whole has been thoroughly edited to improve clarity and readability.

We hope that readers will find these additions and changes provide a fresh look at the topics at hand.

Examples Used in This Book

This book is about designing all kinds of interactive digital products. However, because interaction design has its roots in software for desktop computers, and the vast majority of today's PCs run Microsoft Windows, there is certainly a bias in the focus our discussions—this is where the greatest need exists for understanding how to create effective, Goal-Directed user interfaces.

Having said this, most of the material in this book transcends platform. It is equally applicable to all desktop platforms—Mac OS, Linux, and others—and the majority of it is relevant even for more divergent platforms such as kiosks, handhelds, embedded systems, and others.

A good portion of examples in this book are from the Microsoft Word, Excel, PowerPoint, Outlook, and Internet Explorer, and Adobe Photoshop and Illustrator. We have tried to stick with examples from these mainstream applications for two reasons. First, readers are likely to be at least slightly familiar with the examples. Second, it's important to show that the user interface design of even the most finely honed products can be significantly improved with a Goal-Directed approach. We have included a few examples from more exotic applications as well, in places where they were particularly illustrative.

A few examples in this new edition come from now moribund software or OS versions. These examples illustrate particular points that the authors felt were useful enough to retain in this edition. The vast majority of examples are from contemporary software and OS releases.

Who Should Read This Book

While the subject matter of this book is broadly aimed at students and practitioners of interaction design, anyone concerned about users interacting with digital technology will gain insights from reading this book. Programmers, designers of all stripes involved with digital product design, usability professionals, and project managers will all find something useful in this volume. People who have read earlier editions of *About Face* or *The Inmates Are Running the Asylum* will find new and updated information about design methods and principles here.

We hope this book informs you and intrigues you, but most of all, we hope it makes you think about the design of digital products in new ways. The practice of interaction design is constantly evolving, and it is new and varied enough to generate a wide variety of opinions on the subject. If you have an interesting opinion or just want to talk to us, we'd be happy to hear from you at **alan@cooper.com**, **rmreimann@gmail.com**, and **dave@cooper.com**.

Part

I

Understanding Goal-Directed Design

1

Goal-Directed Design

This book has a simple premise: If we design and construct products in such a way that the people who use them achieve their goals, these people will be satisfied, effective, and happy and will gladly pay for the products and recommend that others do the same. Assuming that this can be achieved in a cost-effective manner, it will translate into business success.

On the surface, this premise sounds quite obvious and straightforward: Make people happy, and your products will be a success. Why then are so many digital products so difficult and unpleasant to use? Why aren't we all happy and successful?

Digital Products Need Better Design Methods

Most digital products today emerge from the development process like a creature emerging from a bubbling tank. Developers, instead of planning and executing with a mind towards satisfying the needs of the people who purchase and use their products, end up creating technologically focused solutions that are difficult to use and control. Like mad scientists, they fail because they have not imbued their creations with humanity.

Design, according to industrial designer Victor Papanek, is *the conscious and intuitive effort to impose meaningful order*. We propose a somewhat more detailed definition of human-oriented design activities:

▶ Understanding users' desires, needs, motivations, and contexts

▶ Understanding business, technical, and domain opportunities, requirements, and constraints

▶ Using this knowledge as a foundation for plans to create products whose form, content, and behavior is useful, usable, and desirable, as well as economically viable and technically feasible

This definition is useful for many design disciplines, although the precise focus on form, content, and behavior will vary depending on what is being designed. For example, an informational Web site may require particular attention to *content*, whereas the design of a chair is primarily concerned with *form*. As we discussed in the Introduction, interactive digital products are uniquely imbued with complex *behavior*.

When performed using the appropriate methods, design can provide the missing human connection in technological products. But clearly, most current approaches to the design of digital products aren't working as advertised.

The creation of digital products today

Digital products come into this world subject to the push and pull of two, often opposing, forces — developers and marketers. While marketers are adept at understanding and quantifying a marketplace opportunity, and at introducing and positioning a product within that market, their input into the product design process is often limited to lists of requirements. These requirements often have little to do with what users actually *need* or *desire* and have more to do with chasing the competition, managing IT resources with to-do lists, and making guesses based on market surveys — what people *say* they'll buy. (Contrary to what you might suspect, few users are able to clearly articulate their needs. When asked direct questions about the products they use, most tend to focus on low-level tasks or workarounds to product flaws.) Unfortunately, reducing an interactive product to a list of hundreds of features doesn't lend itself to the kind of graceful orchestration that is required to make complex technology useful. Adding "easy to use" to the list of requirements does nothing to improve the situation.

Developers, on the other hand, often have no shortage of input into the product's final form and behavior. Because they are in charge of construction, they decide exactly what gets built. And they, too, have a different set of imperatives than the product's eventual users. Good developers are focused on solving challenging technical problems, following good engineering practices, and meeting deadlines. They are often given incomplete, confusing, and sometimes contradictory instructions and are forced to make significant decisions about the user experience with little time or background.

Thus, the people who are most often responsible for the creation of our digital products rarely take into account the users' *goals*, needs, or motivations, and at the same time tend to be highly reactive to market trends and technical constraints. This can't help but result in products that lack a coherent user experience. We'll soon see why goals are so important in addressing this issue.

The results of poor product vision are, unfortunately, digital products that irritate, reduce productivity, and fail to meet user needs. Figure 1-1 shows the evolution of the development process and where, if at all, design has historically fit in. Most of digital product development is stuck in the first, second, or third step of this evolution, where design either plays no real role or it becomes a surface-level patch on shoddy interactions — "lipstick on the pig," as one of our clients once referred to it. The design process, as we will soon discuss, should *precede* coding and testing to ensure that products truly meet the needs of users.

In the dozen years since the publication of the first edition of this book, software and interactive products have certainly improved. Many companies have begun to focus on serving the needs of people with their products, and are spending the time and money to do upfront design. Many more companies are still failing to do this, and as they maintain their focus on technology and marketing data, they continue to create the kind of digital products we've all grown to despise. Here are a few symptoms of this affliction.

Digital products are rude

Digital products often blame users for making mistakes that are not their fault, or should not be. Error messages like the one in Figure 1-2 pop up like weeds announcing that the user has failed yet again. These messages also demand that the user acknowledge his failure by agreeing: OK.

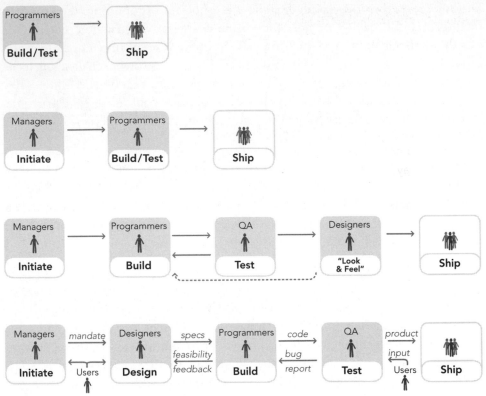

Figure 1-1 The evolution of the software development process. The first diagram depicts the early days of the software industry when smart programmers dreamed up products, and then built and tested them. Inevitably, professional managers were brought in to help facilitate the process by translating market opportunities into product requirements. As depicted in the third diagram, the industry matured, testing became a discipline in its own right, and with the popularization of the graphical user interface (GUI), graphic designers were brought in to create icons and other visual elements. The final diagram shows the Goal-Directed approach to software development where decisions about a product's capabilities, form, and behavior are made before the expensive and challenging construction phase.

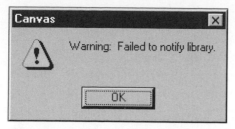

Figure 1-2 Thanks for sharing. Why didn't the program notify the library? What did it want to notify the library about? Why is it telling us? And what are we OKing, anyway? It is not OK that the program failed!

Digital products and software frequently interrogate users, peppering them with a string of terse questions that they are neither inclined or prepared to answer: "Where did you hide that file?" Patronizing questions like "Are you sure?" and "Did you really want to delete that file or did you have some other reason for pressing the Delete key?" are equally irritating and demeaning.

Our software-enabled products also fail to act with a basic level of decency. They forget information we tell them and don't do a very good job of anticipating our needs. For example, the feature-rich Palm Treo smartphone doesn't anticipate that a user might want to add the phone number of someone who has just called to an *existing* contact. It doesn't take a lot of research or imagination to deduce that this is something that many users will want to do, but nevertheless one is forced to go through a complicated maze involving copying the phone number, navigating to the contact in question, and pasting into the appropriate field.

Digital products require people to think like computers

Digital products regularly assume that people are technology literate. For example, in Microsoft Word, if a user wants to rename a document she is editing, she must know that she must either close the document, or use the "Save As..." menu command (and remember to delete the file with the old name). These behaviors are not consistent with the way a normal person thinks about renaming something; rather, they require that a person change her thinking to be more like the way a computer works.

Digital products are also often obscure, hiding meaning, intentions, and actions from users. Programs often express themselves in incomprehensible jargon that cannot be fathomed by normal users ("How many stop bits?") and are sometimes incomprehensible even to experts ("Please specify IRQ.").

Digital products exhibit poor behavior

If a 10-year-old child behaved like some software programs or devices, he'd be sent to his room without supper. Programs forget to shut the refrigerator door, leave shoes in the middle of the floor, and can't remember what you told them only five minutes earlier. For example, if you save a Microsoft Word document, print it, and then try to close it, the program once again asks you if you want to save it! Evidently the act of printing caused the program to think the document had changed, even though it did not. Sorry, Mom, I didn't hear you.

Programs often require us to step out of the main flow of tasks to perform functions that should fall immediately to hand. Dangerous commands, however, are often presented right up front where unsuspecting users can accidentally trigger them. The overall appearance of many programs is overly complex and confusing, making navigation and comprehension difficult.

Digital products require humans to do the heavy lifting

Computers and their silicon-enabled brethren are supposed to be labor-saving devices, but every time we go out into the field to watch real people doing their jobs with the assistance of technology, we are struck and horrified by how much work they are forced to do to manage the operation of software. This work can be anything from manually keying values from one window into another, to copying and pasting between applications that don't otherwise speak to each other, to the ubiquitous clicking and pushing and pulling of windows around the screen to access hidden functionality that people use every day to do their job.

Why are these products so bad?

So what, then, is the real problem? Why is the technology industry generally so inept at designing the interactive parts of digital products? There are three primary reasons: ignorance about users, a conflict of interest between serving human needs and construction priorities, and the lack of a process for understanding human needs as an aid to developing appropriate product form and behavior.

Ignorance about users

It's a sad truth that the digital technology industry doesn't have a good understanding of what it takes to make users happy. In fact, most technology products get built without much understanding of the users. We might know what *market segment* our users are in, how much money they make, how much money they like to spend on weekends, and what sort of cars they buy. Maybe we even have a vague idea what kind of jobs they have and some of the major tasks that they regularly perform. But does any of this tell us how to make them happy? Does it tell us *how* they will actually use the product we're building? Does it tell us *why* they are doing whatever it is they might need our product for, *why* they might want to choose our product over our competitors, or *how* we can make sure they do? Unfortunately, it does not.

We'll soon see how to address the issue of understanding users and their behaviors with products.

Conflicting interests

A second problem affects the ability of vendors and manufacturers to make users happy. There is an important conflict of interest in the world of digital product development: The people who build the products — programmers — are usually also the people who design them. Programmers are often required to choose between ease of coding and ease of use. Because programmers' performance is typically judged by their ability to code efficiently and meet incredibly tight deadlines, it isn't difficult to figure out what direction most software-enabled products take. Just as we would never permit the prosecutor in a legal trial to also adjudicate the case, we should make sure that the people designing a product are not the same people building it. Even with appropriate skills and the best intentions, it simply isn't possible for a programmer to advocate effectively for the user, the business, and the technology all at the same time.

The lack of a process

The third reason the digital technology industry isn't cranking out successful products is that it has no reliable *process* for doing so. Or, to be more accurate, it doesn't have a *complete* process for doing so. Engineering departments follow — or should follow — rigorous engineering methods that ensure the *feasibility* and quality of the technology. Similarly, marketing, sales, and other business units follow their own well-established methods for ensuring the commercial *viability* of new products. What's left out is a repeatable, predictable, and analytical process for *transforming an understanding of users into products that both meet their needs and excite their imaginations.*

When we think about complex mechanical devices, we take for granted that they have been carefully designed for use, in addition to being engineered. Most manufactured objects are quite simple, and even complex mechanical products are quite simple when compared to most software and software-enabled products that can be compiled from over one million lines of code (compare this to a mechanical artifact of overwhelming complexity such as the space shuttle, which has 250,000 parts, only a small percentage of which are *moving* parts). Yet most software has never undergone a rigorous design process from a user-centered perspective.

In the worst case, decisions about what a digital product will do and how it will communicate with users is simply a byproduct of its construction. Programmers, deep in their thoughts of algorithms and code, end up "designing" product behaviors and user interfaces the same way that miners end up "designing" the landscape with cavernous pits and piles of rubble. In unenlightened development organizations, the digital product interaction design process alternates between the accidental and the nonexistent.

Sometimes organizations do adopt a design process, but it isn't quite up to the task. Many programmers today embrace the notion that integrating customers directly into the development process on a frequent basis can solve human interface design problems. Although this has the salutary effect of sharing the responsibility for design with the user, it ignores a serious methodological flaw: a confusion of domain knowledge with design knowledge. Customers, although they might be able to articulate the problems with an interaction, are not often capable of visualizing the solutions to those problems. Design is a specialized skill, just like programming. Programmers would never ask users to help them *code*; design problems should be treated no differently. In addition, customers who *purchase* a product may not be the same people who *use* it from day to day, a subtle but important distinction.

This doesn't mean that designers shouldn't be interested in getting feedback on their proposed solutions. However, each member of the product team should respect the others' areas of expertise. Imagine a patient who visits his doctor with a horrible stomachache. "Doctor," he says, "it *really* hurts. I think it's my appendix. You've got to take it out as soon as possible." Of course, a responsible physician wouldn't perform the surgery without question. The patient can express the symptoms, but it takes the doctor's professional knowledge to make the correct diagnosis.

To better understand how to create a workable process that brings user-centered design to digital products, it's useful to understand a bit more about the history of design in manufacturing and about how the challenges of interactive products have substantially changed the demands on design.

The Evolution of Design in Manufacturing

In the early days of industrial manufacturing, engineering and marketing processes alone were sufficient to produce *desirable* products: It didn't take much more than good engineering and reasonable pricing to produce a hammer, diesel engine, or tube of toothpaste that people would readily purchase. As time progressed, manufacturers of consumer products realized that they needed to differentiate their products from functionally identical products made by competitors, so design was introduced as a means to increase user desire for a product. Graphic designers were employed to create more effective packaging and advertising, and industrial designers were engaged to create more comfortable, useful, and exciting forms.

The conscious inclusion of design heralded the ascendance of the modern triad of product development concerns identified by Larry Keeley of the Doblin Group: capability, viability, and desirability (see Figure 1-3). If any one of these three foundations is significantly weak in a product, it is unlikely to stand the test of time.

Now enter the computer, the first machine created by humans that is capable of almost limitless *behavior* when properly coded into software. The interesting thing about this complex behavior, or interactivity, is that it completely alters the nature of the products it touches. Interactivity is compelling to humans, so compelling that other aspects of an interactive product become marginal. Who pays attention to the black box that sits under your desk — it is the interactive screen, keyboard, and mouse to which users pay attention. Yet, the interactive behaviors of software and other digital products, which should be receiving the lion's share of design attention, all too frequently receive no attention at all.

The traditions of design that corporations have relied on to provide the critical pillar of desirability for products don't provide much guidance in the world of interactivity. Design of behavior is a different kind of problem that requires greater knowledge of *context*, not just rules of visual composition and brand. Design of behavior requires an understanding of the user's relationship with the product from before purchase to end-of-life. Most important of all is the understanding of how the user wishes to use the product, in what ways, and to what ends.

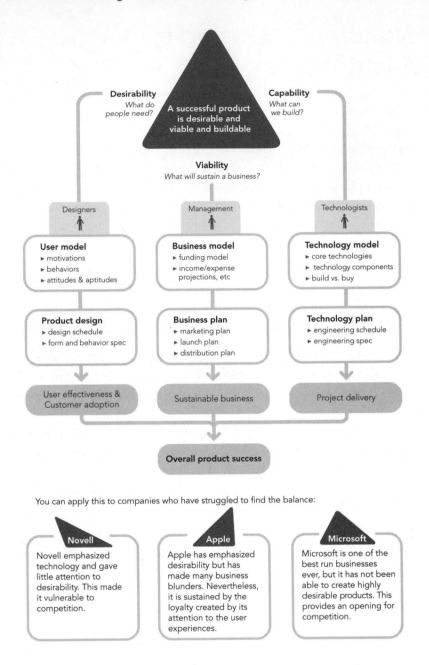

Figure 1-3 Building successful digital products. The diagram indicates the three major processes that need to be followed in tandem to create successful technology products. This book addresses the first and foremost issue: how to create a product people will desire.

Planning and Designing Behavior

The planning of complex digital products, especially ones that interact directly with humans, requires a significant upfront effort by professional designers, just as the planning of complex physical structures that interact with humans requires a significant upfront effort by professional architects. In the case of architects, that planning involves understanding how the humans occupying the structure live and work, and designing spaces to support and facilitate those behaviors. In the case of digital products, the planning involves understanding how the humans using the product live and work, and designing product behavior and form that supports and facilitates the human behaviors. Architecture is an old, well-established field. The design of product and system behavior — **interaction design** — is quite new, and only in recent years has it begun to come of age as a discipline.

Interaction design isn't merely a matter of aesthetic choice; rather, it is based on an understanding of users and cognitive principles. This is good news because it makes the design of behavior quite amenable to a repeatable process of analysis and synthesis. It doesn't mean that the design of behavior can be automated, any more than the design of form or content can be automated, but it *does* mean that a systematic approach is possible. Rules of form and aesthetics mustn't be discarded, of course, but they must work in harmony with the larger concern of achieving user goals via appropriately designed behaviors.

This book presents a set of methods to address the needs of this new kind of behavior-oriented design, which addresses the *goals* (Rudolf, 1998) and motivations of users: **Goal-Directed Design**. To understand Goal-Directed Design, we first need to better understand user goals and how they provide the key to designing appropriate interactive behavior.

Recognizing User Goals

So what are user goals? How can we identify them? How do we know that they are real goals, rather than tasks they are forced to do by poorly designed tools or business processes? Are they the same for all users? Do they change over time? We'll try to answer those questions in the remainder of this chapter.

Users' goals are often quite different from what we might guess them to be. For example, we might think that an accounting clerk's goal is to process invoices efficiently. This is probably not true. Efficient invoice processing is more likely the goal of the clerk's employer. The clerk is more likely concentrating on goals like appearing competent at his job and keeping himself engaged with his work while performing routine and repetitive tasks, although he may not verbally (or even consciously) acknowledge this.

Regardless of the work we do and the tasks we must accomplish, most of us share these simple, personal goals. Even if we have higher aspirations, they are still more personal than work related: winning a promotion, learning more about our field, or setting a good example for others, for instance.

Products designed and built to achieve business goals alone will eventually fail; personal goals of users need to be addressed. When the user's personal goals are met by the design, business goals are far more effectively achieved, for reasons we'll explore in more detail in later chapters.

If you examine most commercially available software, Web sites, and digital products today, you will find that their user interfaces fail to meet user goals with alarming frequency. They routinely:

- ▸ Make users feel stupid
- ▸ Cause users to make big mistakes
- ▸ Require too much effort to operate effectively
- ▸ Don't provide an engaging or enjoyable experience

Most of the same software is equally poor at achieving its business purpose. Invoices don't get processed all that well. Customers don't get serviced on time. Decisions don't get properly supported. This is no coincidence.

The companies that develop these products don't have the right priorities. Most focus their attention far too narrowly on implementation issues, which distract them from the needs of users.

Even when businesses become sensitive to their users, they are often powerless to change their products because the conventional development process assumes that the user interface should be addressed after coding begins — sometimes even after it ends. But just as you cannot effectively design a building after construction begins, you cannot easily make a program serve users' goals once there is a significant and inflexible code base in place.

Finally, when companies *do* focus on the users, they tend to pay too much attention to the *tasks* that users engage in and not enough attention to their *goals* in performing those tasks. Software can be technologically superb and perform each business task with diligence, yet still be a critical and commercial failure. We can't ignore technology or tasks, but they play only a part in a larger schema that includes designing to meet user goals.

Goals versus tasks and activities

Goals are not the same as tasks or activities. A goal is an expectation of an end condition, whereas both activities and tasks are intermediate steps (at different levels of organization) that help someone to reach a goal or set of goals.

Donald Norman describes a hierarchy in which activities are composed of tasks, which are in turn composed of actions, which are then themselves composed of operations. Using this scheme, Norman advocates "Activity-Centered Design" (ACD), which focuses first and foremost on understanding activities. His claim is that humans adapt to the tools at hand, and understanding the activities that people perform with a set of tools can more favorably influence the design of those tools. The foundation of Norman's thinking comes from Activity Theory, a Soviet-era Russian theory of psychology that emphasizes understanding who people are by understanding how they interact with the world, and which has in recent years been adapted to the study of human-computer interaction, most notably by Bonnie Nardi.

Norman concludes, correctly, that the traditional task-based focus of digital product design has yielded inadequate results. Many developers and usability professionals still approach the design of interfaces by asking, "What are the tasks?" Although this may get the job done, it won't produce much more than an incremental improvement: It won't provide a solution that differentiates your product in the market, and very often won't really satisfy the user.

While Norman's ACD takes some important steps in the right direction by highlighting the importance of the user's context, we do not believe that it goes quite far enough. While a method like ACD can be very useful in properly breaking down the "what" of user behaviors, it really doesn't address what should be the first question asked by any designer: *Why* is a user performing an activity, task, action, or operation in the first place? Goals motivate people to perform activities; understanding goals allows you to understand the expectations and aspirations of your users, which can in turn help you decide which activities are truly relevant to your design. Task and activity analysis is useful at the detail level, but only after user goals have been analyzed. Asking, "What are the user's goals?" lets you understand the *meaning* of activities to your users, and thus create more appropriate and satisfactory designs.

If you're still unsure about the difference between goals and activities or tasks, there is an easy way to tell the difference between them. Since goals are driven by human motivations, they change very slowly — if at all — over time. Activities and tasks are much more transient, since they are based almost entirely on whatever technology is at hand. For example, when traveling from St. Louis to San Francisco, a person's *goals* are likely to include traveling quickly, comfortably, and safely. In 1850, a settler wishing to travel quickly and comfortably would have made the journey in a covered wagon; in the interest of safety, he would have brought along his trusty rifle. Today, a businessman traveling from St. Louis to San Francisco makes the journey in a jet aircraft and, in the interest of safety, he is required to leave his firearms at home. The *goals* of the settler and businessman remain unchanged, but their activities and tasks have changed so completely with the changes in technology that they are, in some respects, in direct opposition.

Design based solely on understanding activities or tasks runs the risk of trapping the design in a model imposed by an outmoded technology, or using a model that meets the goals of a corporation without meeting the goals of their users. Looking through the lens of goals allows you to leverage available technology to eliminate irrelevant tasks and to dramatically streamline activities. Understanding users' goals can help designers eliminate the tasks and activities that better technology renders unnecessary for humans to perform.

Designing to meet goals in context

Many designers assume that making interfaces easier to learn should always be a design target. Ease of learning is an important guideline, but in reality, as Brenda Laurel notes, the design target really depends on the context — who the users are, what they are doing, and what goals they have. You simply can't create good design by following rules disconnected from the goals and needs of the users of your product.

Let us illustrate: Take an automated call-distribution system. The people who use this product are paid based on how many calls they handle. Their most important concern is not ease of learning, but the efficiency with which users can route calls, and the rapidity with which those calls can be completed. Ease of learning is also important because it affects the happiness and, ultimately, the turnover rate of employees, so both ease and throughput should be considered in the design. But there is no doubt that throughput is the dominant demand placed on the system by the users and, if necessary, ease of learning should take a back seat. A program that walks the user through the call-routing process step by step each time merely frustrates him after he's learned the ropes.

On the other hand, if the product in question is a kiosk in a corporate lobby helping visitors find their way around, ease of use for first-time users is clearly a major goal.

A general guideline of interaction design that seems to apply particularly well to productivity tools is that *good design makes users more effective*. This guideline takes into account the universal human goal of not looking stupid, along with more particular goals of business throughput and ease of use that are relevant in most business situations.

It is up to you as a designer to determine how you can make the users of your product more effective. Software that enables users to perform their tasks *without addressing their goals* rarely helps them be truly effective. If the task is to enter 5000 names and addresses into a database, a smoothly functioning data-entry application won't satisfy the user nearly as much as an automated system that extracts the names from the invoicing system.

Although it is the user's job to focus on her tasks, the designer's job is to look beyond the task to identify *who* the most important users are, and then to determine *what* their goals might be and *why*. The design process, which we describe in the remainder of this chapter and detail in the remaining chapters of Part I, provides a structure for determining the answers to these questions, a structure by which solutions based on this information can be systematically achieved.

The Goal-Directed Design Process

Most technology-focused companies don't have an adequate process for user-centered design, if they have a process at all. But even the more enlightened organizations, those that can boast of an established process, come up against some critical issues that result from traditional ways of approaching the problems of research and design.

In recent years, the business community has come to recognize that user research is necessary to create good products, but the proper nature of that research is still in question in many organizations. Quantitative market research and market segmentation is quite useful for *selling* products but falls short of providing critical information about *how people actually use products* — especially products with complex behaviors (see Chapter 4 for a more in-depth discussion of this topic). A second problem occurs after the results have been analyzed: Most traditional methods don't provide a means of *translating research results into design solutions*. A hundred pages of user survey data don't easily translate into a set of product requirements, and they say even less about how those requirements should be expressed in terms of a meaningful and appropriate interface structure. Design remains a black box: "A miracle happens here." This gap between research results and the ultimate design solution is the result of a process that doesn't connect the dots from user to final product. We'll soon see how to address this problem with Goal-Directed methods.

Bridging the gap

As we have briefly discussed, the role of design in the development process needs to change. We need to start thinking about design in new ways, and start thinking differently about how product decisions are made.

Design as product definition

Design has, unfortunately, become a limiting term in the technology industry. For many developers and managers, the word has come to mean what happens in the third process diagram shown in Figure 1-1: a visual facelift on the **implementation model** (see Chapter 2). But design, when properly deployed (as in the fourth process diagram shown in Figure 1-1), both identifies user requirements and defines a detailed plan for the behavior and appearance of products. In other words, design provides true **product definition**, based on goals of users, needs of business, and constraints of technology.

Designers as researchers

If design is to become product definition, designers need to take on a broader role than that assumed in traditional design, particularly when the object of this design is complex, interactive systems.

One of the problems with the current development process is that roles in the process are overspecialized: Researchers perform research, and designers perform design (see Figure 1-4). The results of user and market research are analyzed by the usability and market researchers and then thrown over the transom to designers or programmers. What is missing in this model is a systematic means of translating and synthesizing the research into design solutions. One of the ways to address this problem is for designers to learn to be researchers.

Figure 1-4 A problematic design process. Traditionally, research and design have been separated, with each activity handled by specialists. *Research* has, until recently, referred primarily to market research, and *design* is too often limited to visual design or skin-deep industrial design. More recently, **user research** has expanded to include qualitative, ethnographic data. Yet, without including designers in the research process, the connection between research data and design solutions remains tenuous at best.

There is a compelling reason for involving designers in the research process. One of the most powerful tools designers bring to the table is empathy: the ability to feel what others are feeling. The direct and extensive exposure to users that proper user research entails immerses designers in the users' world, and gets them thinking about users long before they propose solutions. One of the most dangerous practices in product development is isolating designers from the users because doing so eliminates empathic knowledge.

Additionally, it is often difficult for pure researchers to know what user information is really important from a design perspective. Involving designers directly in research addresses both issues.

In the authors' practice, designers are trained in the research techniques described in Chapter 4 and perform their research without further support or collaboration. This is a satisfactory solution, provided that your team has the time and resources to train your designers fully in these techniques. If not, a cross-disciplinary team of designers and dedicated user researchers is appropriate.

Although research practiced by designers takes us part of the way to Goal-Directed Design solutions, there is still a translation gap between research results and design details. The puzzle is missing several pieces, as we will discuss next.

Between research and design: Models, requirements, and frameworks

Few design methods in common use today incorporate a means of effectively and systematically translating the knowledge gathered during research into a detailed design specification. Part of the reason for this has already been identified: Designers have historically been out of the research loop and have had to rely on third-person accounts of user behaviors and desires.

The other reason, however, is that few methods capture user behaviors in a manner that appropriately directs the definition of a product. Rather than providing information about user goals, most methods provide information at the task level. This type of information is useful for defining layout, workflow, and translation of functions into interface controls, but is less useful for defining the basic framework of what a product *is*, what it *does*, and how it should meet the broad needs of the user.

Instead we need an explicit, systematic process to bridge the gap between research and design for defining user models, establishing design requirements, and translating those into a high-level interaction framework (see Figure 1-5). Goal-Directed Design seeks to bridge the gap that currently exists in the digital product development process, the gap between user research and design, through a combination of new techniques and known methods brought together in more effective ways.

A process overview

Goal-Directed Design combines techniques of ethnography, stakeholder interviews, market research, detailed user models, scenario-based design, and a core set of interaction principles and patterns. It provides solutions that meet the needs and goals of users, while also addressing business/organizational and technical imperatives. This process can be roughly divided into six phases: Research, Modeling, Requirements Definition, Framework Definition, Refinement, and Support (see Figure 1-5). These phases follow the five component activities of interaction design identified by Gillian Crampton Smith and Philip Tabor — understanding, abstracting, structuring, representing, and detailing — with a greater emphasis on modeling user behaviors and defining system behaviors.

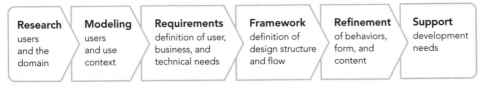

Figure 1-5 The Goal-Directed Design process.

The remainder of this chapter provides a high-level view of the five phases of Goal-Directed Design, and Chapters 4–7 provide more detailed discussion of the methods involved in each of these phases. See Figure 1-6 for a more detailed diagram of the process, including key collaboration points and design concerns.

Research

The Research phase employs ethnographic field study techniques (observation and contextual interviews) to provide qualitative data about potential and/or actual users of the product. It also includes competitive product audits, reviews of market research and technology white papers and brand strategy, as well as one-on-one interviews with stakeholders, developers, subject matter experts (SMEs), and technology experts as suits the particular domain.

One of the principal outcomes of field observation and user interviews is an emergent set of **behavior patterns** — identifiable behaviors that help categorize modes of use of a potential or existing product. These patterns suggest goals and motivations (specific and general desired outcomes of using the product). In business and technical domains, these behavior patterns tend to map into professional roles; for consumer products, they tend to correspond to lifestyle choices. Behavior patterns and the goals associated with them drive the creation of **personas** in the Modeling phase. Market research helps select and filter valid personas that fit business models. Stakeholder interviews, literature reviews, and product audits deepen the designers' understanding of the domain and elucidate business goals, brand attributes, and technical constraints that the design must support.

Chapter 4 provides a more detailed discussion of Goal-Directed research techniques.

Modeling

During the Modeling phase, behavior and workflow patterns discovered through analysis of the field research and interviews are synthesized into domain and user models. Domain models can include information flow and workflow diagrams. User models, or **personas**, are detailed, composite **user archetypes** that represent distinct groupings of behaviors, attitudes, aptitudes, goals, and motivations observed and identified during the Research phase.

Personas serve as the main characters in a narrative, scenario-based approach to design that iteratively generates design concepts in the Framework Definition phase, provides feedback that enforces design coherence and appropriateness in the Refinement phase, and represents a powerful communication tool that helps developers and managers to understand design rationale and to prioritize features based on user needs. In the Modeling phase, designers employ a variety of methodological tools to synthesize, differentiate, and prioritize personas, exploring different *types* of goals and mapping personas across ranges of behavior to ensure there are no gaps or duplications.

Specific design targets are chosen from the cast of personas through a process of comparing goals and assigning a hierarchy of priority based on how broadly each persona's goals encompass the goals of other personas. A process of designating persona types determines the amount of influence each persona has on the eventual form and behavior of the design.

A detailed discussion of persona and goal development can be found in Chapter 5.

Requirements Definition

Design methods employed by teams during the Requirements Definition phase provide the much-needed connection between user and other models and the framework of the design. This phase employs scenario-based design methods with the important innovation of focusing the scenarios not on user tasks in the abstract, but first and foremost on meeting the goals and needs of specific user personas. Personas provide an understanding of which tasks are truly important and why, leading to an interface that minimizes necessary tasks (effort) while maximizing return. Personas become the main characters of these scenarios, and the designers explore the design space via a form of role-playing.

For each interface/primary persona, the process of design in the Requirements Definition phase involves an analysis of persona data and functional needs (expressed in terms of objects, actions, and contexts), prioritized and informed by persona goals, behaviors, and interactions with other personas in various contexts.

This analysis is accomplished through an iteratively refined **context scenario** that starts with a "day in the life" of the persona using the product, describing high-level product touch points, and thereafter successively defining detail at ever-deepening levels. In addition to these scenario-driven requirements, designers consider the personas' skills and physical capabilities as well as issues related to the usage environment. Business goals, desired brand attributes, and technical constraints are also considered and balanced with persona goals and needs. The output of this process is a **requirements definition** that balances user, business, and technical requirements of the design to follow.

Framework Definition

In the Framework Definition phase, designers create the overall product concept, defining the basic frameworks for the product's behavior, visual design, and — if applicable — physical form. Interaction design teams synthesize an **interaction framework** by employing two other critical methodological tools in conjunction with context scenarios. The first is a set of general **interaction design principles** that provide guidance in determining appropriate system behavior in a variety of contexts. Chapters 2 and 3 and the whole of Part II are devoted to high-level interaction design principles appropriate to the Framework Definition phase.

The second critical methodological tool is a set of **interaction design patterns** that encode general solutions (with variations dependent on context) to classes of previously analyzed problems. These patterns bear close resemblance to the concept of architectural design patterns first developed by Christopher Alexander, and more recently brought to the programming field by Erich Gamma, et al. Interaction design patterns are hierarchically organized and continuously evolve as new contexts arise. Rather than stifling designer creativity, they often provide needed leverage to approach difficult problems with proven design knowledge.

After data and functional needs are described at this high level, they are translated into design elements according to interaction principles and then organized, using patterns and principles, into design sketches and behavior descriptions. The output of this process is an **interaction framework definition**, a stable design concept that provides the logical and gross formal structure for the detail to come. Successive iterations of more narrowly focused scenarios provide this detail in the Refinement phase. The approach is often a balance of top-down (pattern-oriented) design and bottom-up (principle-oriented) design.

When the product takes physical form, interaction designers and industrial designers begin by collaborating closely on various **input vectors** and approximate **form factors** the product might take, using scenarios to consider the pros and cons of each. As this is narrowed to a couple of options that seem promising, industrial designers begin producing early physical prototypes to ensure that the overall interaction concept will work. It's critical at this early stage that industrial designers not go off and create concepts independent of the product's behavior.

As soon as an interaction framework begins to emerge, visual interface designers produce several options for a **visual framework**, which is sometimes also referred to as a **visual language strategy**. They use brand attributes as well as an understanding of the overall interface structure to develop options for typography, color palettes, and visual style.

Refinement

The **Refinement phase** proceeds similarly to the Framework Definition phase, but with increasing focus on detail and implementation. Interaction designers focus on task coherence, using **key path** (walkthrough) and **validation scenarios** focused on storyboarding paths through the interface in high detail. Visual designers define a system of type styles and sizes, icons, and other visual elements that provide a compelling experience with clear affordances and visual hierarchy. Industrial designers, when appropriate, finalize materials and work closely with engineers on assembly schemes and other technical issues. The culmination of the Refinement phase is the detailed documentation of the design, a **form and behavior specification**, delivered in either paper or interactive media as context dictates. Chapter 6 discusses in more detail the use of personas, scenarios, principles, and patterns in the Requirements Definition, Framework Definition, and Refinement phases.

Development Support

Even a very well-conceived and validated design solution can't possibly anticipate every development challenge and technical question. In our practice, we've learned that it's important to be available to answer developers' questions as they arise during the construction process. It is often the case that as the development team prioritizes their work and makes trade-offs to meet deadlines, the design must be adjusted, requiring scaled-down design solutions. If the interaction design team is not available to create these solutions, developers are forced to do this under time pressure, which has the potential to gravely compromise the integrity of the product's design.

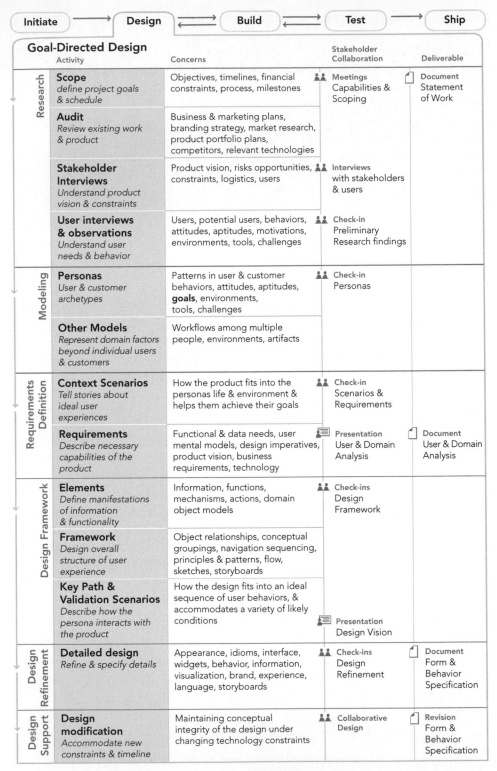

Figure 1-6 A more detailed look at the Goal-Directed Design process.

Goals, not features, are the key to product success

Developers and marketers often use the language of features and functions to discuss products. This is only natural. Developers build software function by function, and a list of features is certainly *one way* to express a product's value to potential customers (though this is clearly limiting, as well). The problem is that these are abstract concepts that only provide limited insight into how human beings can be effective and happy while using technology.

Reducing a product's definition to a list of features and functions ignores the real opportunity — orchestrating technological capability to serve human needs and goals. Too often the features of our products are a patchwork of nifty technological innovations structured around a marketing requirements document or organization of the development team with too little attention paid to the overall user experience.

The successful interaction designer must maintain her focus on users' goals amid the pressures and chaos of the product-development cycle. Although we discuss many other techniques and tools of interaction in this book, we always return to users' goals. They are the bedrock upon which interaction design should be practiced.

The Goal-Directed process, with its clear rationale for design decisions, makes collaboration with developers and businesspeople easier, and ensures that the design in question isn't guesswork, the whim of a creative mind, or just a reflection of the team members' personal preferences.

DESIGN
principle   Interaction design is not guesswork.

Goal-Directed Design is a powerful tool for answering the most important questions that crop up during the definition and design of a digital product:

> ► Who are my users?

> ► What are my users trying to accomplish?

> ► How do my users think about what they're trying to accomplish?

> ► What kind of experiences do my users find appealing and rewarding?

> ► How should my product behave?

> ► What form should my product take?

> ► How will users interact with my product?

> ► How can my product's functions be most effectively organized?

> ► How will my product introduce itself to first-time users?

- ► How can my product put an understandable, appealing, and controllable face on technology?

- ► How can my product deal with problems that users encounter?

- ► How will my product help infrequent and inexperienced users understand how to accomplish their goals?

- ► How can my product provide sufficient depth and power for expert users?

The remainder of this book is dedicated to answering these questions. We share tools tested by years of experience with hundreds of products that can help you identify key users of your products, understand them and their goals, and translate this understanding into effective and appealing design solutions.

2

Implementation Models and Mental Models

The computer industry makes frequent use of the term **computer literacy**. Pundits talk about how some people have it and some don't, how those who have it will succeed in the information economy, and how those who lack it will inevitably fall between the socioeconomic cracks. Computer literacy, however, is nothing more than a euphemism for forcing human beings to stretch their thinking to understand an alien, machine logic rather than having software-enabled products stretch to meet people's ways of thinking. In this chapter, we discuss how a poor understanding of users and the specific ways they approach digital products has exacerbated the computer-literacy divide, and how software that better matches how people think and work can help solve the problem.

Implementation Models

Any machine has a mechanism for accomplishing its purpose. A motion picture projector, for example, uses a complicated sequence of intricately moving parts to create its illusion. It shines a very bright light through a translucent, miniature image for a fraction of a second. It then blocks out the light for a split second while it moves another miniature image into place. Then it unblocks the light again for another moment. It repeats this process with a new image 24 times per second. Software-enabled products don't have mechanisms in the sense of moving parts; these are replaced with algorithms and modules of code that communicate with each other. The representation of how a machine or a program actually works has been called the **system model** by Donald Norman and others; we prefer the term **implementation model** because it describes the details of the way a program is implemented in code.

User Mental Models

From the moviegoer's point of view, it is easy to forget the nuance of sprocket holes and light-interrupters while watching an absorbing drama. Many moviegoers, in fact, have little idea how the projector actually works, or how this differs from the way a television works. The viewer imagines that the projector merely throws a picture that moves onto the big screen. This is called the user's **mental model**, or **conceptual model**.

People don't need to know all the details of how a complex mechanism actually works in order to use it, so they create a cognitive shorthand for explaining it, one that is powerful enough to cover their interactions with it, but that doesn't necessarily reflect its actual inner mechanics. For example, many people imagine that, when they plug their vacuum cleaners and blenders into outlets in the wall, the electricity flows like water from the wall to the appliances through the little black tube of the electrical cord. This mental model is perfectly adequate for using household appliances. The fact that the implementation model of household electricity involves nothing resembling a fluid actually traveling up the cord and that there is a reversal of electrical potential 120 times per second is irrelevant to the user, although the power company needs to know the details.

In the digital world, however, the differences between a user's mental model and the implementation model are often quite distinct. We tend to ignore the fact that our cellular telephone doesn't work like a landline phone; instead, it is actually a radio transceiver that might swap connections between a half-dozen different cellular base antennas in the course of a two-minute call. Knowing this doesn't help us to understand how to *use* the phone.

The discrepancy between implementation and mental models is particularly stark in the case of software applications, where the complexity of implementation can make it nearly impossible for the user to see the mechanistic connections between his actions and the program's reactions. When we use a computer to digitally edit sound or to create video special effects like morphing, we are bereft of analogy to the mechanical world, so our mental models are necessarily different from the implementation model. Even if the connections were visible, they would remain inscrutable to most people.

Represented Models

Software (and any digital product that relies on software) has a behavioral face it shows to the world that is created by the programmer or designer. This representation is not necessarily an accurate description of what is really going on inside the computer, although unfortunately, it frequently is. This ability to *represent* the computer's functioning independent of its true actions is far more pronounced in software than in any other medium. It allows a clever designer to hide some of the more unsavory facts of how the software is really getting the job done. This disconnection between what is implemented and what is offered as explanation gives rise to a *third* model in the digital world, the designer's **represented model** — the way the designer chooses to represent a program's functioning to the user. Donald Norman refers to this simply as the **designer's model**.

In the world of software, a program's represented model can (and often should) be quite different from the actual processing structure of the program. For example, an operating system can make a network file server look as though it were a local disk. The model does not represent the fact that the physical disk drive may be miles away. This concept of the represented model has no widespread counterpart in the mechanical world. The relationship between the three models is shown in Figure 2-1.

The closer the represented model comes to the user's mental model, the easier he will find the program to use and to understand. Generally, offering a represented model that follows the implementation model too closely significantly reduces the user's ability to learn and use the program, assuming (as is almost always the case) that the user's mental model of his tasks differs from the implementation model of the software.

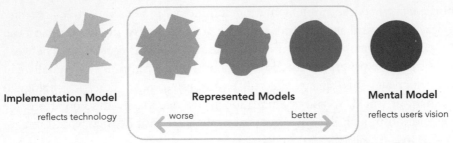

Implementation Model   **Represented Models**   **Mental Model**

reflects technology   worse   better   reflects user's vision

Figure 2-1 The way engineers must build software is often a given, dictated by various technical and business constraints. The model for how the software actually works is called the *implementation model*. The way users perceive the jobs they need to do and how the program helps them do it is their *mental model* of interaction with the software. It is based on their own ideas of how they do their jobs and how computers might work. The way designers choose to represent the working of the program to the user is called the *represented model*, which, unlike the other two models, is an aspect of software over which designers have great control. One of the most important goals of the designer should be to make the represented model match the mental model of users as closely as possible. It is therefore critical that designers understand in detail the way their target users think about the work they do with the software.

We tend to form mental models that are simpler than reality; so if we create represented models that are simpler than the actual implementation model, we help the user achieve a better understanding. Pressing the brake pedal in your car, for example, may conjure a mental image of pushing a lever that rubs against the wheels to slow you down. The actual mechanism includes hydraulic cylinders, tubing, and metal pads that squeeze on a perforated disk, but we simplify all that out of our minds, creating a more effective, albeit less accurate, mental model. In software, we imagine that a spreadsheet scrolls new cells into view when we click on the scrollbar. Nothing of the sort actually happens. There is no sheet of cells out there, but a tightly packed data structure of values, with various pointers between them, from which the program synthesizes a new image to display in real time.

Understanding how software actually works always helps someone to use it, but this understanding usually comes at a significant cost. One of the most significant ways in which computers can assist human beings is by putting a simple face on complex processes and situations. As a result, user interfaces that are consistent with users' mental models are vastly superior to those that are merely reflections of the implementation model.

DESIGN principle   User interfaces should be based on user mental models rather than implementation models.

In Adobe Photoshop, users can adjust the color balance and brightness of an illustration using a feature called Variations. Instead of offering numeric fields for entering color data — the implementation model — the Variations interface shows a set of thumbnail images, each with a different color balance (see Figure 2-2). A user can click on the image that best represents the desired color setting. The interface more closely follows his mental model, because the user — likely a graphic artist — is thinking in terms of how his image looks, not in terms of abstract numbers.

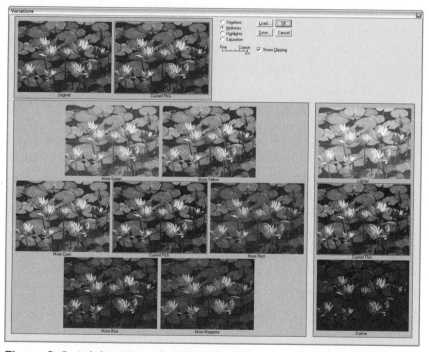

Figure 2–2 Adobe Photoshop has a great example of software design to match user mental models. The Variations interface shows a set of thumbnail images, varying color balance and brightness by adjustable increments. A user can click on the image that best represents the desired color setting. This image then becomes the new default for more varied thumbnails. The interface follows the mental model of graphic artists who are after a particular look, not a set of abstract numerical values.

If the represented model for software closely follows users' mental models, it eliminates needless complexity from the user interface by providing a cognitive framework that makes it evident to the user how his goals and needs can be met.

 DESIGN principle   Goal-directed interactions reflect user mental models.

A user's mental model doesn't necessarily have to be true or accurate, but it should enable him to work effectively. For example, most nontechnical computer users imagine that their video screen is the heart of their computer. This is only natural because the screen is what they stare at all the time and is the place where they see what the computer is doing. If you point out to a user that the computer is actually a little chip of silicon in that black box sitting under his desk, he will probably shrug and ignore this pointless (to him) bit of information. The fact that the CPU isn't the same thing as the video display doesn't help him think about how he interacts with his computer, even though it is a more technically accurate concept.

Most Software Conforms to Implementation Models

It is much easier to design software that reflects its implementation model. From the developer's perspective, it's perfectly logical to provide a button for every function, a field for every data input, a page for every transaction step, and a dialog for every code module. But while this adequately reflects the infrastructure of engineering efforts, it does little to provide coherent mechanisms for a user to achieve his goals. In the end, what is produced alienates and confuses the user, rather like the ubiquitous external ductwork in the dystopian setting of Terry Gilliam's movie *Brazil* (which is full of wonderful tongue-in-cheek examples of miserable interfaces).

User interfaces designed by engineers follow the implementation model

User interfaces and interactions designed by engineers, who know precisely how software works, quite often lead to a represented model that is very consistent with its implementation model. To the engineers, such models are logical, truthful, and accurate; unfortunately, they are not very intelligible or effective for users. The majority of users don't much care how a program is actually implemented.

A good example of a digital product that conforms to implementation models is the typical component home theater system, which requires the user to know exactly how all of the components are wired together in order to switch, say, between viewing a DVD and tuning a cable TV channel. In most products, users need to switch video sources, and sometimes even switch between multiple remote controls, to access the functions they need simply to watch their television. A more mental-model-centered alternative, adopted by some newer products, is to keep track of the component configuration in the remote, so that the user can simply pick "Watch TV," and the remote sends the appropriate commands to the TV, cable box, DVD player, and surround audio system without the user needing to know what's going on behind the scenes.

Even the Windows user interface slips into the implementation model sometimes. If you drag a file between directories on the same hard drive, the program interprets this as a MOVE, meaning that the file is removed from the old directory and added to the new directory, closely following the mental model. However, if you drag a file from hard drive C to hard drive D, the action is interpreted as a COPY, meaning that the file is added to the new directory but *not* removed from the old directory. This behavior is rooted in the implementation model — the way the underlying file system actually works. When the operating system moves a file from one directory to another on the same drive, it merely relocates the file's entry in the disk's table of contents. It never actually erases and rewrites the file. But when it moves a file to another physical drive, it must physically copy the data onto the new drive. To conform to the user's mental model, it should then erase the original even though that contradicts the implementation model.

This inconsistency in the computer's response to two seemingly similar user actions has the potential to create significant *cognitive dissonance* (confusion resulting from two contradictory images of reality) for users, which in turn makes this simple interaction difficult to learn. For a user to ultimately be able to achieve a desired result, he must understand that the computer's behavior depends on the physical nature of the particular storage devices.

Because treating the drag of a file from one disk to another as a COPY function can be desirable behavior, especially when copying files from a hard drive to removable media such as USB flash drives, many people aren't aware that it is an inconsistent side effect of the implementation model. As computers mature and logical volumes represent more than just physical drives, the side effects stop being useful and instead become irritating because we have to memorize the idiosyncratic behavior of each volume type.

Mathematical thinking leads to implementation model interfaces

Interaction designers must shield users from implementation models. Just because a technique is well suited to solving a problem in software construction doesn't necessarily mean that it is well suited to be a mental model for the user. Just because your car is constructed of welded metal parts doesn't mean that you must be skilled with a welding torch to drive it.

Most of the data structures and algorithms used to represent and manipulate information in software are logic tools based on mathematical algorithms. All programmers are fluent in these algorithms, including such things as recursion, hierarchical data structures, and multithreading. The problem arises when the user interface attempts to accurately represent the concepts of recursion, hierarchical data, or multithreading.

Mathematical thinking is an implementation model trap that is particularly easy for programmers to fall into. They solve programming problems by thinking mathematically, so they naturally see these mathematical models as appropriate terms for inventing user interfaces. Nothing could be further from the truth.

 DESIGN principle   Users don't understand Boolean logic.

For example, one of the most durable and useful tools in the programmer's toolbox is Boolean algebra. It is a compact mathematical system that conveniently describes the behavior of the strictly on-or-off universe inside all digital computers. There are only two main operations: AND and OR. The problem is that the English language has an **and** and an **or** and they are usually interpreted — by nonprogrammers — as the exact opposite of the Boolean AND and OR. If the program expresses itself with Boolean notation, the user can be *expected* to misinterpret it.

For example, this problem crops up frequently when querying databases. If we want to extract from a file of employees those who live in Arizona along with those who live in Texas, we would say to a human in English, "Find all my employees in Arizona and Texas." To express this properly to a database in Boolean algebraic terms, we would say, "Find employees in Arizona OR Texas." No employee lives in two states at once, so saying, "Find employees in Arizona AND Texas" is nonsensical. In Boolean, this will almost always return nothing.

Any application that interacts with users in Boolean is doomed to suffer severe user-interface problems. It is unreasonable to expect users to penetrate the confusion. They are well trained in English, so why should they have to express things in an unfamiliar language that, annoyingly, redefines key words.

Mechanical-Age versus Information-Age Represented Models

We are experiencing an incredible transformation from the age of industrial, mechanical artifacts to an age of digital, information objects. The change has only begun, and the pace is accelerating rapidly. The upheaval that society underwent as a result of industrialization will likely be dwarfed by that associated with the Information Age.

Mechanical-Age representations

It is only natural for us to try to draw the imagery and language of an earlier era that we are comfortable with into a new, less certain one. As the history of the industrial revolution shows, the fruits of new technology can often only be expressed at first with the language of an earlier technology. For example, we called railroad engines *iron horses* and automobiles were labeled *horseless carriages*. Unfortunately, this imagery and language colors our thinking more than we might admit.

Naturally, we tend to use old representations in our new environments. Sometimes, the usage is valid because the function is identical, even if the underpinning technology is different. For example, when we translate the process of typewriting with a typewriter into word processing on a computer, we are using a Mechanical-Age representation of a common task. Typewriters used little metal tabs to slew the carriage rapidly over several spaces until it came to rest on a particular column. The process, as a natural outgrowth of the technology, was called tabbing or setting tabs. Word processors also have tabs because their function is the same; whether you are working on paper rolled around a platen or on images on a video screen, you need to rapidly slew to a particular margin offset.

Sometimes, however, Mechanical-Age representations shouldn't be translated verbatim into the digital world. We don't use reins to steer our cars, or a tiller, although both of these were tried in the early days of autos. It took many years to develop a steering idiom that was appropriate for the car. In word processors, we don't need to load a new blank page after we fill the previous one; rather, the document scrolls continuously, with visual markers for page breaks.

New technology demands new representations

Sometimes tasks, processes, concepts, and even goals arise solely because new technology makes them possible for the first time. With no reason to exist beforehand, they were not conceived of in advance. When the telephone was first invented, for example, it was, among other things, touted as a means to broadcast music and news, although it was personal communication that became the most popular and widely developed. Nobody at the time would ever have conceived of the telephone as being a ubiquitous personal object that people would carry in their pockets and purses and that would ring annoyingly in the midst of theater performances.

With our Mechanical-Age mindset, we have a hard time seeing appropriate Information-Age representations — at first. The real advantages of the software products that we create often remain invisible until they have a sizable population of users. For example, the real advantage of e-mail isn't simply that it's faster than postal mail — the Mechanical-Age view — but rather that it promotes the flattening and democratization of the modern business organization — the Information-Age advantage. The real advantage of the Web isn't cheaper and more efficient communication and distribution — the Mechanical-Age view. Instead, it is the creation of virtual communities — the Information-Age advantage that was revealed only after it materialized in our grasp. Because we have a hard time seeing how digital products will be used, we tend to rely too much on representations from the past, Mechanical Age.

Mechanical-Age representations degrade user interaction

We encounter a problem when we bring our familiar Mechanical-Age representations over to the computer. Simply put, Mechanical-Age processes and representations tend to degrade user interactions in Information-Age products. Mechanical procedures are easier to perform by hand than they are with computers. For example, typing an individual address on an envelope using a computer requires significant overhead compared to addressing the envelope with pen and ink (although the former might look neater). The situation improves only if the process is automated for a large number of instances in batch — 500 envelopes that you need to address.

As another example, take a contact list on a computer. If it is faithfully rendered onscreen like a little bound book, it will be much more complex, inconvenient, and difficult to use than the physical address book. The physical address book, for example, stores names in alphabetical order by last name. But what if you want to find someone by her first name? The Mechanical-Age artifact doesn't help you: You have to scan the pages manually. So, too, does the faithfully replicated digital version: It can't search by first name either. The difference is that, on the computer screen, you lose many subtle visual cues offered by the paper-based book (bent page corners, penciled-in notes). Meanwhile, the scrollbars and dialog boxes are harder to use, harder to visualize, and harder to understand than simply flipping pages.

 DESIGN principle | Don't replicate Mechanical-Age artifacts in user interfaces without Information-Age enhancements.

Real-world mechanical systems have the strengths and weaknesses of their medium, such as pen and paper. Software has a completely different set of strengths and weaknesses, yet when mechanical representations are replicated without change, they combine the weaknesses of the old with the weaknesses of the new. In our address book example, the computer could easily search for an entry by first name, but, by storing the names in exactly the same way as the mechanical artifact, we deprive ourselves of new ways of searching. We limit ourselves in terms of capabilities possible in an information medium, without reaping any of the benefits of the original mechanical medium.

When designers rely on Mechanical-Age representations to guide them, they are blinded to the far greater potential of the computer to provide sophisticated information management in a better, albeit different, way. The use of a Mechanical-Age representation in a user interface can operate as a *metaphor* that artificially constrains the design. For further discussion of the pitfalls surrounding reliance on metaphors in user interfaces, see Chapter 13.

Improving on Mechanical-Age representations: An example

Although new technologies can bring about entirely new concepts, they can also extend and build upon old concepts, allowing designers to take advantage of the power of the new technology on behalf of users through updated representations of their interface.

For example, take the calendar. In the nondigital world, calendars are made of paper and are usually divided up into a one-month-per-page format. This is a reasonable compromise based on the size of paper, file folders, briefcases, and desk drawers.

Programs with visual representations of calendars are quite common, and they almost always display one month at a time. Even if they can show more than one month, as Outlook does, they almost always display days in discrete one-month chunks. Why?

Paper calendars show a single month because they are limited by the size of the paper, and a month is a convenient breaking point. Computer screens are not so constrained, but most designers copy the Mechanical-Age artifact faithfully (see Figure 2-3). On a computer, the calendar could easily be a continuously scrolling sequence of days, weeks, or months as shown in Figure 2-4. Scheduling something from August 28 to September 4 would be simple if weeks were contiguous instead of broken up by the arbitrary monthly division.

Similarly, the grid pattern in digital calendars is almost always of a fixed size. Why couldn't the width of columns of days or the height of rows of weeks be adjustable like a spreadsheet? Certainly you'd want to adjust the sizes of your weekends to reflect their relative importance in relation to your weekdays. If you're a businessperson, your working-week calendar would demand more space than a vacation week. The idioms are as well known as spreadsheets — that is to say, universal — but the Mechanical-Age representations are so firmly entrenched that we rarely see software publishers deviate from it.

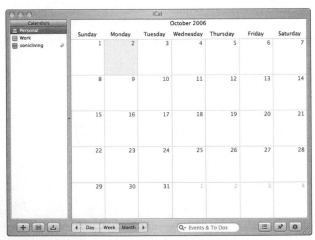

Figure 2-3 The ubiquitous calendar is so familiar that we rarely stop to apply Information-Age sensibilities to its design on the screen. Calendars were originally designed to fit on stacked sheets of paper, not interactive digital displays. How would you redesign it? What aspects of the calendar are artifacts of its old, Mechanical-Age platform?

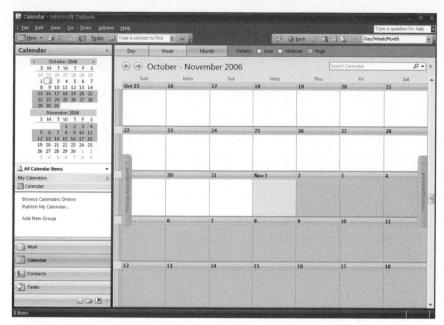

Figure 2-4 Scrolling is a very familiar idiom to computer users. Why not replace the page-oriented representation of a calendar with a scrolling representation to make it better? This perpetual calendar can do everything the old one can, and it also solves the mechanical-representation problem of scheduling across monthly boundaries. Don't drag old limitations onto new platforms out of habit. What other improvements can you think of?

The designer of the software in Figure 2-3 probably thought of calendars as canonical objects that couldn't be altered from the familiar. Surprisingly, most time-management software handles time internally — in its implementation model — as a continuum, and only renders it as discrete months in its user interface — its represented model!

Some might counter that the one-month-per-page calendar is better because it is easily recognizable and familiar to users. However, the new model is not that different from the old model, except that it permits the users to easily do something they couldn't do easily before — schedule across monthly boundaries. People don't find it difficult to adapt to newer, more useful representations of familiar systems.

DESIGN principle   Significant change must be significantly better.

Paper-style calendars in personal information managers (PIMs) and schedulers are mute testimony to how our language influences our designs. If we depend on words from the Mechanical Age, we will build software from the Mechanical Age. Better software is based on Information-Age thinking.

3

Beginners, Experts, and Intermediates

Most computer users know all too well that buying a new cell phone or opening the shrink-wrap on a new software product augurs several days of frustration and disappointment spent learning the new interface. On the other hand, many experienced users of a digital product may find themselves continually frustrated because that product always treats them like rank beginners. It seems impossible to find the right balance between catering to the needs of the first-timer and the needs of the expert.

One of the eternal conundrums of interaction and interface design is how to address the needs of both beginning users and expert users with a single, coherent interface. Some programmers and designers choose to abandon this idea completely, choosing instead to segregate the user experiences by creating wizards for beginners and burying critical functionality for experts deep in menus. Of course, no one wants to deal with the extra labor associated with moving through a wizard, but the leap from there to knowing what esoteric command to select from a series of long menus is usually a jump off a rather tall cliff into a shark-infested moat of implementation-model design. What, then, is the answer? The solution to this predicament lies in a different understanding of the way users master new concepts and tasks.

Perpetual Intermediates

Most users are neither beginners nor experts; instead, they are *intermediates*.

The experience level of people performing an activity tends, like most population distributions, to follow the classic statistical bell curve (see Figure 3-1). For almost any activity requiring knowledge or skill, if we graph number of people against skill level, a relatively small number of beginners are on the left side, a few experts are on the right, and the majority — intermediate users — are in the center.

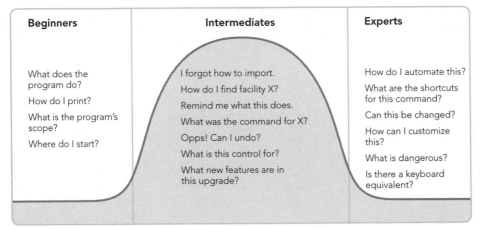

Figure 3-1 The demands that users place on digital products vary considerably with their experience.

Statistics don't tell the whole story, however. The bell curve is a snapshot in time, and although most intermediates tend to stay in that category, the beginners do not remain beginners for very long. The difficulty of maintaining a high level of expertise also means that experts come and go rapidly, but beginners change even more rapidly. Both beginners and experts tend over time to gravitate towards intermediacy.

Although *everybody* spends some minimum time as a beginner, *nobody* remains in that state for long. People don't like to be incompetent, and beginners, by definition, are incompetent. Conversely, learning and improving is rewarding, so beginners become intermediates very quickly — or they drop out altogether. All skiers, for example, spend time as beginners, but those who find they don't rapidly progress beyond more-falling-than-skiing quickly abandon the sport. The rest soon move off of the bunny slopes onto the regular runs. Only a few ever make it onto the double-black diamond runs for experts.

DESIGN principle   Nobody wants to remain a beginner.

Most occupants of the beginner end of the curve will either migrate into the center bulge of intermediates, or they will drop off of the graph altogether and find some product or activity in which they *can* migrate into intermediacy. Most users thus remain in a perpetual state of adequacy striving for fluency, with their skills ebbing and flowing like the tides depending on how frequently they use the product. Larry Constantine first identified the importance of designing for intermediates, and in his book *Software for Use*, he refers to such users as **improving intermediates**. We prefer the term **perpetual intermediates**, because although beginners quickly improve to become intermediates, they seldom go on to become experts.

Many popular ski resorts have a gentle slope for learning and a few expert runs to really challenge the serious skier. But if the resort wants to stay in business, it will cater to the perpetual intermediate skier, without scaring off the beginner or insulting the expert. The beginner must find it easy to matriculate into the world of intermediacy, and the expert must not find his vertical runs obstructed by aids for trepidatious or conservative intermediates.

In many cases, a well-balanced user interface takes the same approach. It doesn't cater to the beginner or to the expert, but rather devotes the bulk of its efforts to satisfying the perpetual intermediate. At the same time, it provides mechanisms so that both of its smaller constituencies can be effective.

Most users in this middle state would like to learn more about the product but usually don't have the time. Occasionally, the opportunity to do so will surface. Sometimes these intermediates use the product extensively for weeks at a time to complete a big project. During this time, they learn new things about the product. Their knowledge grows beyond its previous boundaries.

Sometimes, however, they do not use the product for months at a time and forget significant portions of what they knew. When they return to the product, they are not beginners, but they will need reminders to jog their memory back to its former state.

In some specialized products, it is appropriate to optimize the user experience for experts. In particular, tools that technically minded people rely on for a significant portion of their professional responsibilities should be inflected towards a high degree of proficiency. Development tools often fall into this category, as do scientific instrumentation and medical devices. We expect the users of those products to come to the table with the necessary technical knowledge, and to be willing to invest significant time and effort to mastering the application.

Similarly, there are other products, especially those used in a transient manner, or those used by people with certain disabilities, that must be optimized for beginners. Examples we have worked on include informational kiosks designed for public spaces like museums, or a device that helps elderly patients with diminished abilities take their blood pressure.

We are often asked whether consumer Web sites should be optimized for beginners or intermediates. Ultimately, we believe that the same considerations that we apply to other digital products should be used here. A well-designed Web site interface should help its user become quickly familiar and comfortable with navigation and functionality. Something worth considering here is that even a customer who has visited your site several times before and may be familiar with what you offer and with Web interaction idioms in general, may not visit your site frequently enough to memorize organizational constructs. This increases the importance of making interactions on your site as transparent and discoverable as possible. Also, as it has become increasingly popular to provide an adaptive experience by tracking user actions on a Web site, it is often useful to rely on cookies to identify a new visitor and to provide unobtrusive orientation assistance for the first few visits to the site.

Designing for Different Experience Levels

Now let's contrast our bell curve of intermediates with the way that software is developed. Programmers qualify as experts in the software they code because they have to explore every possible use case, no matter how obscure and unlikely, to create program code to handle it. Their natural tendency is to design implementation-model software with every possible option given equal emphasis in the interaction, which they, as experts, have no problem understanding.

At the same time, sales, marketing, and management often demonstrate the product to customers, reporters, partners, and investors who are themselves unfamiliar with the product. Because of their constant exposure to beginners, these professionals have a strongly biased view of the user community. Therefore, it comes as no surprise that sales and marketing folks lobby for bending the interface to serve beginners. They demand that training wheels be attached to the product to help out the struggling beginner.

Programmers create interactions suitable only for experts, while the marketers demand interactions suitable only for beginners, but — as we have seen — the largest, most stable, and most important group of users is the intermediate group.

It's amazing to think that the majority of real users are typically ignored, but more often than not that is the case. You can see it in many enterprise and commercial software-based products. The overall design biases them towards expert users, while at the same time, cumbersome tools like wizards and Clippy are grafted on to meet the marketing department's perception of new users. Experts rarely use them, and beginners soon desire to discard these embarrassing reminders of their ignorance. But the perpetual intermediate majority is perpetually stuck with them.

 Optimize for intermediates.

Our goal should be neither to pander to beginners nor to rush intermediates into expertise. Our goal is threefold: to rapidly and painlessly get beginners into intermediacy, to avoid putting obstacles in the way of those intermediates who want to become experts, and most of all, to keep perpetual intermediates happy as they stay firmly in the middle of the skill spectrum.

We need to spend more time making our products powerful and easy to use for perpetual intermediate users. We must accommodate beginners and experts, too, but not to the discomfort of the largest segment of users. The remainder of this chapter describes some basic strategies for accomplishing this.

What beginners need

Beginners are undeniably sensitive, and it is easy to demoralize a first-timer, but we must keep in mind that the state of beginnerhood is *never* an objective. Nobody wants to remain a beginner. It is merely a rite of passage everyone must experience. Good software shortens that passage without bringing attention to it.

As an interaction designer, it's best to imagine that users — especially beginners — are simultaneously very intelligent and very busy. They need some instruction, but not very much, and the process has to be rapid and targeted. If a ski instructor begins lecturing on snowpack composition and meteorology, he will lose his students regardless of their aptitude for skiing. Just because a user needs to learn how to operate a product doesn't mean that he needs or wants to learn how it works inside.

 Imagine users as very intelligent but very busy.

On the other hand, intelligent people always learn better when they understand cause and effect, so you must give them an understanding of why things work as they do. We use mental models to bridge the contradiction. If the represented model of the interface closely follows the user's mental model (as discussed in Chapter 2), it will provide the understanding the user needs without forcing him to figure out the implementation model.

Getting beginners on board

A new user must grasp the concepts and scope of the product quickly or he will abandon it. Thus, the first order of business of the designer is to ensure that the product adequately reflects the user's mental model of his tasks. He may not recall from use to use exactly which command is needed to act on a particular object, but he will definitely remember the relationships between objects and actions — the important concepts — if the interface's conceptual structure is consistent with his mental model.

To get beginners to a state of intermediacy requires extra help from the program, but this extra help will get in their way as soon as they become intermediates. This means that whatever extra help you provide, it must not be fixed into the interface. It must know how to go away when its services are no longer required.

Standard online help is a poor tool for providing such beginner assistance. We'll talk more about help in Chapter 25, but its primary utility is as a reference, and beginners don't need reference information; they need overview information, such as a guided tour.

A separate guide facility — displayed within a dialog box — is a fine means for communicating overview, scope, and purpose. As the user begins to use the product, a dialog box can appear that states the basic goals and tools of the product, naming the main features. As long as the guide stays focused on beginner issues, like scope and goals, and avoids perpetual intermediate and expert issues (discussed below), it should be adequate for assisting beginners.

Beginners also rely heavily upon menus to learn and execute commands (see Chapter 22 for a detailed discussion about why this is true). Menus may be slow and clunky, but they are also thorough and verbose, so they offer reassurances. The dialog boxes that the menu items launch (if they do so at all) should also be (tersely) explanatory, and come with convenient Cancel buttons.

What experts need

Experts are also a vital group because they have a disproportionate influence on less experienced users. When a prospective buyer considers your product, he will trust the expert's opinion more than an intermediate's. If the expert says, "It's not very good," she may mean "It's not very good for experts." The beginner doesn't know that, however, and will take the expert's advice, even though it may not apply.

Experts might occasionally look for esoteric features, and they might make heavy use of a few of them. However, they will definitely demand faster access to their regular working set of tools, which may be quite large. In other words, experts want shortcuts to everything.

Anyone who uses a digital product for hours a day will very quickly internalize the nuances of its interface. It isn't so much that they *want* to cram frequently used commands into their heads, as much as it is unavoidable. Their frequency of use both justifies and requires the memorization.

Expert users constantly, aggressively seek to learn more and to see more connections between their actions and the product's behavior and representation. Experts appreciate new, powerful features. Their mastery of the product insulates them from becoming disturbed by the added complexity.

What perpetual intermediates need

Perpetual intermediates need access to tools. They don't need scope and purpose explained to them because they already know these things. ToolTips (see Chapter 23) are the perfect perpetual intermediate idiom. ToolTips say nothing about scope and purpose and meaning; they only state function in the briefest of idioms, consuming the least amount of video space in the process.

Perpetual intermediates know how to use reference materials. They are motivated to dig deeper and learn, as long as they don't have to tackle too much at once. This means that online help is a perpetual intermediate tool. They use it by way of the index, so that part of help must be very comprehensive.

Perpetual intermediates establish the functions that they use with regularity and those that they only use rarely. The user may experiment with obscure features, but he will soon identify — probably subconsciously — his frequently used working set. The user will demand that the tools in his working set be placed front and center in the user interface, easy to find and to remember.

Perpetual intermediates usually know that advanced features exist, even though they may not need them or know how to use them. But the knowledge that they are there is reassuring to the perpetual intermediate, convincing him that he made the right choice investing in this product. The average skier may find it inspirational to know that there is a really scary, black-diamond, expert run just beyond those trees, even if she never intends to use it. It gives her something to aspire to and dream about, and it gives her the sense that she's at a good ski resort.

Your product's code must provide for both rank amateurs and all the possible cases an expert might encounter. Don't let this technical requirement influence your design thinking. Yes, you must provide those features for expert users. Yes, you must provide support for beginners. But in most cases, you must apply the bulk of your talents, time, and resources to designing the best interaction possible for your most representative users: the perpetual intermediates.

4

Understanding Users: Qualitative Research

The outcome of any design effort must ultimately be judged by how successfully it meets the needs of both the product user and the organization that commissioned it. No matter how skillful and creative the designer, if she does not have clear and detailed knowledge of the users she is designing for, the constraints of the problem, and the business or organizational goals that are driving design activities, she will have little chance of success.

Real insight into these topics can't be achieved by digging through the piles of numbers that come from a quantitative study like a market survey (though these can be critical for answering other kinds of questions). Rather, this kind of deep knowledge can only be achieved by *qualitative* research techniques. There are many types of qualitative research, each of which can play an important role in understanding the design landscape of a product. In this chapter, we focus on specific qualitative research techniques that support the design methods described in subsequent chapters. At the end of the chapter, we briefly discuss how quantitative research can, and cannot, be used to help support this effort.

Qualitative versus Quantitative Research

Research is a word that most people associate with science and objectivity. This association isn't incorrect, but it biases many people towards the notion that the only valid sort of research is the kind that yields the supposed ultimate in objectivity: quantitative data. It is a common perspective in business and engineering that numbers represent truth, even though we all know that numbers — especially statistics describing human activities — are subject to interpretation and can be manipulated at least as dramatically as words.

Data gathered by the hard sciences like physics are simply different from that gathered on human activities: Electrons don't have moods that vary from minute to minute, and the tight controls physicists place on their experiments to isolate observed behaviors are impossible in the social sciences. Any attempt to reduce human behavior to statistics is likely to overlook important nuances, which can make an enormous difference to the design of products. Quantitative research can only answer questions about "how much" or "how many" along a few reductive axes. Qualitative research can tell you about what, how, and why in rich detail that is reflective of the actual complexities of real human situations.

Social scientists have long realized that human behaviors are too complex and subject to too many variables to rely solely on quantitative data to understand them. Design and usability practitioners, borrowing techniques from anthropology and other social sciences, have developed many qualitative methods for gathering useful data on user behaviors to a more pragmatic end: to help create products that better serve user needs.

The value of qualitative research

Qualitative research helps us understand the domain, context, and constraints of a product in different, more useful ways than quantitative research does. It also helps us identify patterns of behavior among users and potential users of a product much more quickly and easily than would be possible with quantitative approaches. In particular, qualitative research helps us understand:

- ▶ Behaviors, attitudes, and aptitudes of potential product users
- ▶ Technical, business, and environmental contexts — the **domain** — of the product to be designed

- ▶ Vocabulary and other social aspects of the domain in question

- ▶ How existing products are used

Qualitative research can also help the progress of design projects by:

- ▶ Providing credibility and authority to the design team, because design decisions can be traced to research results

- ▶ Uniting the team with a common understanding of domain issues and user concerns

- ▶ Empowering management to make more informed decisions about product design issues that would otherwise be based on guesswork or personal preference

It's our experience that in comparison, qualitative methods tend to be faster, less expensive, and more likely to provide useful answers to important questions that lead to superior design:

- ▶ How does the product fit into the broader context of people's lives?

- ▶ What goals motivate people to use the product, and what basic tasks help people accomplish these goals?

- ▶ What experiences do people find compelling? How do these relate to the product being designed?

- ▶ What problems do people encounter with their current ways of doing things?

The value of qualitative studies is not limited to helping support the design process. In our experience, spending the time to understand the user population as human beings can provide valuable business insights that are not revealed through traditional market research.

In one particularly illustrative example, we were asked by a client to perform a user study for an entry-level consumer video-editing product for Windows users. An established developer of video-editing and -authoring software, the client had used traditional market research techniques to identify a significant business opportunity in developing a product for people who owned a digital video camera and a computer but hadn't connected the two yet.

In the field, we conducted interviews with a dozen users in the target market. Our first discovery was not surprising — that the people who did the most taping and had the strongest desire to share edited versions of their videos were parents. The second discovery, however, was quite startling. Of the 12 people whose homes we visited, only one person had successfully connected his video camera to his computer, and he had relied on the IT guy at work to set it up for him. One of the necessary preconditions of the success of the product was that people could actually get video onto their computers to edit, but at the time it was extremely difficult to get a FireWire or video capture card functioning properly on an Intel-based PC.

As a result of four days of research, we were able to help our client make a decision to put a hold on the product, which likely ended up saving them a considerable investment.

Types of qualitative research

Social science and usability texts are full of methods and techniques for conducting qualitative research, and readers are encouraged to explore this literature. In this chapter, we will focus specifically on techniques that have been proven effective in our practice over the last decade, occasionally drawing attention to similar techniques practiced in the design and usability fields at large. We will also try to avoid getting bogged down in theory, and instead will present these techniques from a pragmatic perspective. The qualitative research activities we have found to be most useful in our practice are:

- ▶ Stakeholder interviews
- ▶ Subject matter expert (SME) interviews
- ▶ User and customer interviews
- ▶ User observation/ethnographic field studies
- ▶ Literature review
- ▶ Product/prototype and competitive audits

Stakeholder interviews

Research for any new product design should start by understanding the business and technical context surrounding the product. In almost all cases, the reason a product is being designed (or redesigned) is to achieve one or several specific business outcomes (most commonly, to make money). It is the designers' obligation to develop solutions without ever losing sight of these business goals, and it is therefore critical that the design team begin its work by understanding the opportunities and constraints that are behind the design brief.

As Donald Schön so aptly puts it, "design is a conversation with materials"[1] This means that for a designer to craft an appropriate solution, he must understand the capabilities and limitations of the "materials" that will be used to construct the product, whether they be lines of code or extruded plastic.

Generally speaking, a **stakeholder** is anyone with authority and/or responsibility for the product being designed. More specifically, stakeholders are key members of the organization commissioning the design work, and typically include executives, managers, and representative contributors from development, sales, product management, marketing, customer support, design, and usability. They may also include similar people from other organizations in business partnership with the commissioning organization.

Interviews with stakeholders should occur before any user research begins because these discussions often inform how user research is conducted. Also, it is usually most effective to interview each stakeholder in isolation, rather than in a larger, cross-departmental group. A one-on-one setting promotes candor on the part of the stakeholder, and ensures that individual views are not lost in a crowd. (One of the most interesting things that can be discovered in such interviews is the extent to which everyone in a product team shares — or doesn't share — a common vision.) Interviews need not last longer than about an hour, though follow-up meetings may be called for if a particular stakeholder is identified as an exceptionally valuable source of information.

The type of information that is important to gather from stakeholders includes:

- ▶ **Preliminary product vision** — As in the fable of the blind men and the elephant, you may find that each business department has a slightly different and slightly incomplete perspective on the product to be designed. Part of the design approach must therefore involve harmonizing these perspectives with those of users and customers.

- ▶ **Budget and schedule** — Discussions on this topic often provide a reality check on the scope of the design effort and provide a decision point for management if user research indicates a greater (or lesser) scope is required.

- ▶ **Technical constraints and opportunities** — Another important determinant of design scope is a firm understanding of what is technically feasible given budget, time, and technology constraints. It is also often the case that a product is being developed to capitalize on a new technology. Understanding the opportunities underlying this technology can help shape the product's direction.

- ▶ **Business drivers** — It is important for the design team to understand what the business is trying to accomplish. This again leads to a decision point, should user research indicate a conflict between business and user needs. The design must, as much as possible, create a win-win situation for users, customers, and providers of the product.

▶ **Stakeholders' perceptions of the user** — Stakeholders who have relationships with users (such as customer support representatives) may have important insights on users that will help you to formulate your user research plan. You may also find that there are significant disconnects between some stakeholders' perceptions of their users and what you discover in your research. This information can become an important discussion point with management later in the process.

Understanding these issues and their impact on design solutions helps you as a designer to better develop a successful product. Regardless of how desirable your designs are to customers and users, without considering the viability and feasibility of the proposed solution there is no chance that the product will thrive.

Discussing these topics is also important to developing a common language and understanding among the design team, management, and engineering teams. As a designer, your job is to develop a vision that the entire team believes in. Without taking the time to understand everyone's perspective, it is unlikely that they will feel that proposed solutions reflect their priorities. Because these people have the responsibility and authority to deliver the product to the real world, they are guaranteed to have important knowledge and opinions. If you don't ask for it upfront, it is likely to be forced upon you later, often in the form of a critique of your proposed solutions.

Subject matter expert (SME) interviews

Early in a design project, it is often invaluable to identify and meet with several **subject matter experts** (SMEs) — experts on the domain within which the product will operate. Many SMEs were users of the product or its predecessors at one time and may now be trainers, managers, or consultants. Often they are experts hired by stakeholders, rather than stakeholders themselves. Similar to stakeholders, SMEs can provide valuable perspectives on a product and its users, but designers should be careful to recognize that SMEs represent a somewhat skewed perspective. Some points to consider about using SMEs are:

▶ **SMEs are often expert users.** Their long experience with a product or its domain means that they may have grown accustomed to current interactions. They may also lean towards expert controls rather than interactions designed for perpetual intermediates. SMEs are often not current users of the product and may have more of a management perspective.

▶ **SMEs are knowledgeable, but they aren't designers.** They may have many ideas on how to improve a product. Some of these may be valid and valuable, but the most useful pieces of information to glean from these suggestions are the causative *problems* that lead to their proposed solutions. As with users, when you encounter a proposed solution, ask "how would that help you or the user?"

▶ **SMEs are necessary in complex or specialized domains.** If you are designing for a technical domain such as medical, scientific, or financial services, you will likely need some guidance from SMEs, unless you are one yourself. Use SMEs to get information on industry best practices and complex regulations. SME knowledge of user roles and characteristics is critical for planning user research in complex domains.

▶ **You will want access to SMEs throughout the design process.** If your product domain requires use of SMEs, you should be able to bring them in at different stages of the design to help perform reality checks on design details. Make sure that you secure this access in your early interviews.

Customer interviews

It is easy to confuse users with customers. For consumer products, customers are often the same as users, but in corporate or technical domains, users and customers rarely describe the same sets of people. Although both groups should be interviewed, each has its own perspective on the product that needs to be factored quite differently into an eventual design.

Customers of a product are those people who make the decision to purchase it. For consumer products, customers are frequently users of the product; although for products aimed at children or teens, the customers are parents or other adult supervisors of children. In the case of most enterprise, medical, or technical products, the customer is someone very different from the user — often an executive or IT manager — with distinct goals and needs. It's important to understand customers and satisfy their goals in order to make a product *viable*. It is also important to realize that customers seldom actually use the product themselves, and when they do, they use it quite differently from the way their users do.

When interviewing customers, you will want to understand:

▶ Their goals in purchasing the product

▶ Their frustrations with current solutions

▶ Their decision process for purchasing a product of the type you're designing

▶ Their role in installation, maintenance, and management of the product

▶ Domain-related issues and vocabulary

Like SMEs, customers may have many opinions about how to improve the design of the product. It is important to analyze these suggestions, as in the case of SMEs, to determine what issues or problems underlie the ideas offered, because better, more integrated solutions may become evident later in the design process.

User Interviews

Users of a product should be the main focus of the design effort. They are the people who are personally utilizing the product to accomplish a goal (not their managers or support team). If you are redesigning or refining an existing product, it is important to speak to both current and **potential users**, that is, people who do not currently use the product but who are good candidates for using it in the future because they have needs that can be met with the product and are in the target market for the product. Interviewing both current and potential users illuminates the effect that experience with the current version of a product may have on how the user behaves and thinks about things.

Information we are interested in learning from users includes:

- ▶ The context of how the product (or analogous system, if no current product exists) fits into their lives or workflow: when, why, and how the product is or will be used

- ▶ Domain knowledge from a user perspective: What do users need to know to do their jobs?

- ▶ Current tasks and activities: both those the current product is required to accomplish and those it doesn't support

- ▶ Goals and motivations for using their product

- ▶ Mental model: how users think about their jobs and activities, as well as what expectations users have about the product

- ▶ Problems and frustrations with current products (or an analogous system if no current product exists)

User observation

Most people are incapable of accurately assessing their own behaviors,[2] especially when they are removed from the context of their activities. It is also true that out of fear of seeming dumb, incompetent, or impolite, many people may avoid talking about software behaviors that they find problematic or incomprehensible.

It then follows that interviews performed outside the context of the situations the designer hopes to understand will yield less-complete and less-accurate data. You can talk to users about how they think they behave, or you can observe their behavior first-hand. The latter route provides superior results.

Perhaps the most effective technique for gathering qualitative user data combines interviewing and observation, allowing the designers to ask clarifying questions and direct inquiries about situations and behaviors they observe in real time.

Many usability professionals make use of technological aides such as audio or video recorders to capture what users say and do. Interviewers must take care not to make these technologies too obtrusive; otherwise, the users will be distracted and behave differently than they would off-tape. In our practice, we've found that a notebook and a camera allow us to capture everything we need without compromising the honest exchange of information. Typically, we won't bring out the camera until we feel that we've established a good rapport with the interview subject, and then we use it to capture things about the environment that are difficult to jot in our notes. However, video, when used with care, can sometimes provide a powerful rhetorical tool for achieving stakeholder buy-in to contentious or surprising research results. Video may also prove useful in situations where note taking is difficult, such as in a moving car.

Literature review

In parallel with stakeholder interviews, the design team should review any literature pertaining to the product or its domain. This can and should include product marketing plans, brand strategy, market research, user surveys, technology specifications and white papers, business and technical journal articles, competitive studies, Web searches for related and competing products and news, usability study results and metrics, and customer support data such as call center statistics.

The design team should collect this literature, use it as a basis for developing questions to ask stakeholders and SMEs, and later use it to supply additional domain knowledge and vocabulary, and to check against compiled user data.

Product and competitive audits

Also in parallel to stakeholder and SME interviews, it is often quite helpful for the design team to examine any existing version or prototype of the product, as well as its chief competitors. Doing so gives the design team a sense of the state of the art, and provides fuel for questions during the interviews. The design team, ideally, should engage in an informal **heuristic** or **expert review** of both the current and competitive interfaces, comparing each against interaction and visual design principles (such as those found later in this book). This procedure both familiarizes the team with the strengths and limitations of what is currently available to users, and provides a general idea of the current functional scope of the product.

Ethnographic Interviews: Interviewing and Observing Users

Drawing on years of design research in practice, we believe that a combination of observation and one-on-one interviews is the most effective and efficient tool in a designer's arsenal for gathering qualitative data about users and their goals. The technique of **ethnographic interviews** is a combination of immersive observation and directed interview techniques.

Hugh Beyer and Karen Holtzblatt have pioneered an ethnographic interviewing technique that they call **contextual inquiry**. Their method has, for good reason, rapidly gained traction in the industry, and provides a sound basis for qualitative user research. It is described in detail in the first four chapters of their book, *Contextual Design*. Contextual inquiry methods closely parallel the methods described here, but with some subtle and important differences.

Contextual inquiry

Contextual inquiry, according to Beyer and Holtzblatt, is based on a **master-apprentice model** of learning: observing and asking questions of the user as if she is the master craftsman, and the interviewer the new apprentice. Beyer and Holtzblatt also enumerate four basic principles for engaging in ethnographic interviews:

- ▶ **Context** — Rather than interviewing the user in a clean white room, it is important to interact with and observe the user in her normal work environment, or whatever physical context is appropriate for the product. Observing users as they perform activities and questioning them in their own environments, filled with the artifacts they use each day, can bring the all-important details of their behaviors to light.

- ▶ **Partnership** — The interview and observation should take the tone of a collaborative exploration with the user, alternating between observation of work and discussion of its structure and details.

- ▶ **Interpretation** — Much of the work of the designer is reading between the lines of facts gathered about users' behaviors, their environment, and what they say. These facts must be taken together as a whole and analyzed by the designer to uncover the design implications. Interviewers must be careful, however, to avoid assumptions based on their own interpretation of the facts without verifying these assumptions with users.

> ► **Focus** — Rather than coming to interviews with a set questionnaire or letting the interview wander aimlessly, the designer needs to subtly direct the interview so as to capture data relevant to design issues.

Improving on contextual inquiry

Contextual inquiry forms a solid theoretical foundation for qualitative research, but as a specific method it has some limitations and inefficiencies. The following process improvements, in our experience, result in a more highly leveraged research phase that better sets the stage for successful design:

> ► **Shorten the interview process** — Contextual inquiry assumes full-day interviews with users. The authors have found that interviews as short as one hour can be sufficient to gather the necessary user data, provided that a sufficient number of interviews (about six well-selected users for each hypothesized role or type) are scheduled. It is much easier and more effective to find a diverse set of users who will consent to an hour with a designer than it is to find users who will agree to spend an entire day.
>
> ► **Use smaller design teams** — Contextual inquiry assumes a large design team that conducts multiple interviews in parallel, followed by debriefing sessions in which the full team participates. We've found that it is more effective to conduct interviews sequentially with the same designers in each interview. This allows the design team to remain small (two or three designers), but even more important, it means that the entire team interacts with all interviewed users directly, allowing the members to most effectively analyze and synthesize the user data.
>
> ► **Identify goals first** — Contextual inquiry, as described by Beyer and Holtzblatt, feeds a design process that is fundamentally task focused. We propose that ethnographic interviews first identify and prioritize user goals before determining the tasks that relate to these goals.
>
> ► **Looking beyond business contexts** — The vocabulary of contextual inquiry assumes a business product and a corporate environment. Ethnographic interviews are also possible in consumer domains, though the focus of questioning is somewhat different, as we describe later in this chapter.

The remainder of this chapter provides general methods and tips for preparing for and conducting ethnographic interviews.

Preparing for ethnographic interviews

Ethnography is a term borrowed from anthropology, meaning the systematic and immersive study of human cultures. In anthropology, ethnographic researchers spend years living immersed in the cultures they study and record. Ethnographic interviews take the spirit of this type of research and apply it on a micro level. Rather than trying to understand behaviors and social rituals of an entire culture, the goal is to understand the behaviors and rituals of people interacting with individual products.

Identifying candidates

Because the designers must capture an entire range of user behaviors regarding a product, it is critical that the designers identify an appropriately diverse sample of users and user types when planning a series of interviews. Based on information gleaned from stakeholders, SMEs, and literature reviews, designers need to create a hypothesis that serves as a starting point in determining what sorts of users and potential users to interview.

The persona hypothesis

We label this starting point the **persona hypothesis**, because it is the first step towards identifying and synthesizing personas, the user archetypes we will discuss in detail in the next chapter. The persona hypothesis should be based on likely behavior patterns and the factors that differentiate these patterns, not purely on demographics. It is often the case with consumer products that demographics are used as screening criteria to select interview subjects, but even in this case, they should be serving as a proxy for a hypothesized behavior pattern.

The nature of a product's domain makes a significant difference in how a persona hypothesis is constructed. Business users are often quite different from consumer users in their behavior patterns and motivations, and different techniques are used to build the persona hypothesis in each case.

The persona hypothesis is a first cut at defining the different kinds of users (and sometimes customers) for a product. The hypothesis serves as the basis for initial interview planning; as interviews proceed, new interviews may be required if the data indicates the existence of user types not originally identified.

The persona hypothesis attempts to address, at a high level, these three questions:

- ▶ What different sorts of people might use this product?
- ▶ How might their needs and behaviors vary?
- ▶ What ranges of behavior and types of environments need to be explored?

Roles in business and consumer domains

For business products, **roles** — common sets of tasks and information needs related to distinct classes of users — provide an important initial organizing principle. For example, for an office phone system, we might find these rough roles:

- ▶ People who make and receive calls from their desks
- ▶ People who travel a lot and need to access the phone system remotely
- ▶ Receptionists who answer the phone for many people
- ▶ People who technically administer the phone system

In business and technical contexts, roles often map roughly to job descriptions, so it is relatively easy to get a reasonable first cut of user types to interview by understanding the kind of jobs held by users (or potential users) of the system.

Unlike business users, consumers don't have concrete job descriptions, and their use of products may cross multiple contexts. Therefore, it often isn't meaningful to use roles as an organizing principle for the persona hypothesis for a consumer product. Rather, it is often the case that you will see the most significant patterns emerge from users' attitudes and aptitudes, as manifest in their behaviors.

Behavioral and demographic variables

In addition to roles, a persona hypothesis should be based on variables that help differentiate between different kinds of users based on their needs and behaviors. This is often the most useful way to distinguish between different types of users (and forms the basis for the persona-creation process described in the next chapter). Despite the fact that these variables can be difficult to fully anticipate without research, they often become the basis of the persona hypothesis for consumer products. For example, for an online store, there are several ranges of behavior concerning shopping that we might identify:

- ▶ Frequency of shopping (from frequent to infrequent)
- ▶ Desire to shop (from loves to shop to hates to shop)
- ▶ Motivation to shop (from bargain hunting to searching for just the right item)

Although consumer user types can often be roughly defined by the combination of behavioral variables they map to, behavioral variables are also important for identifying types of business and technical users. People within a single business-role definition may have different needs and motivations. Behavioral variables can capture this, although often not until user data has been gathered.

Given the difficulty in accurately anticipating behavioral variables before user data is gathered, another helpful approach in building a persona hypothesis is making use of *demographic variables*. When planning your interviews, you can use market research to identify ages, locations, gender, and incomes of the target markets for the product. Interviewees should be distributed across these demographic ranges in the hope of interviewing a sufficiently diverse group of people to identify the significant behavior patterns.

Domain expertise versus technical expertise

One important type of behavioral distinction is the difference between technical expertise (knowledge of digital technology) and domain expertise (knowledge of a specialized subject area pertaining to a product). Different users will have varying amounts of technical expertise; similarly, some users of a product may be less expert in their knowledge of the product's domain (for example, accounting knowledge in the case of a general ledger application). Thus, depending on who the design target of the product is, domain support may be a necessary part of the product's design, as well as technical ease of use. A relatively naive user will likely never be able to use more than a small subset of a domain-specific product's functions without domain support provided in the interface. If naive users are part of the target market for a domain-specific product, care must be taken to support domain-naive behaviors.

Environmental considerations

A final consideration, especially in the case of business products, is the cultural differences between organizations in which the users are employed. At small companies, for example, workers tend to have a broader set of responsibilities and more interpersonal contact; at huge companies, workers tend to be highly specialized and there are often multiple layers of bureaucracy. Examples of these environmental variables include:

- Company size (from small to multinational)
- Company location (North America, Europe, Asia, and so on)
- Industry/sector (electronics manufacturing, consumer packaged goods, and so on)
- IT presence (from ad hoc to draconian)
- Security level (from lax to tight)

Like behavioral variables, these may be difficult to identify without some domain research, because patterns do vary significantly by industry and geographic region.

Putting a plan together

After you have created a persona hypothesis, complete with potential roles and behavioral, demographic, and environmental variables, you then need to create an interview plan that can be communicated to the person in charge of coordinating and scheduling the interviews.

In our practice, we've observed that each presumed behavioral pattern requires about a half-dozen interviews to verify or refute (sometimes more if a domain is particularly complex). What this means in practice is that each identified role, behavioral variable, demographic variable, and environmental variable identified in the persona hypothesis should be explored in four to six interviews (sometimes more if a domain is particularly complex).

However, these interviews can overlap. If we believe that use of an enterprise product may differ, for example, by geographic location, industry, and company size, then research at a single small electronics manufacturer in Taiwan would allow us to cover several variables at once. By being clever about mapping variables to interviewee-screening profiles, you can keep the number of interviews to a manageable number.

Conducting ethnographic interviews

After the persona hypothesis has been formulated and an interview plan has been derived from it, you are ready to interview — assuming you get access to interviewees! While formulating the interview plan, designers should work closely with project stakeholders who have access to users. Stakeholder involvement is generally the best way to make interviews happen, especially for business and technical products.

If stakeholders can't help you get in touch with users, you can contact a market or usability research firm that specializes in finding people for surveys and focus groups. These firms are useful for reaching consumers with diverse demographics. The difficulty with this approach is that it can sometimes be challenging to get interviewees who will permit you to interview them in their homes or places of work.

As a last alternative for consumer products, designers can recruit friends and relatives. This makes it easier to observe the interviewees in a natural environment but also is quite limiting as far as diversity of demographic and behavioral variables are concerned.

Interview teams and timing

The authors favor a team of two designers per interview, one to drive the interview and take light notes, and the other to take detailed notes (these roles can switch halfway through the interview). One hour per user interviewed is often sufficient, except in the case of highly complex domains such as medical, scientific, and financial services that may require more time to fully understand what the user is trying to accomplish. Be sure to budget travel time between interview sites, especially for consumer interviews in residential neighborhoods, or interviews that involve "shadowing" users as they interact with a (usually mobile) product while moving from place to place. Teams should try to limit interviews to six per day, so that there is adequate time for debriefing and strategizing between interviews, and so that the interviewers do not get fatigued.

Phases of ethnographic interviews

A complete set of ethnographic interviews for a project can be grouped into three distinct, chronological phases. The approach of the interviews in each successive phase is subtly different from the previous one, reflecting the growing knowledge of user behaviors that results from each additional interview. Focus tends to be broad at the start, aimed at gross structural and goal-oriented issues, and more narrow for interviews at the end of the cycle, zooming in on specific functions and task-oriented issues.

> **Early interviews** are exploratory in nature, and focused on gathering domain knowledge from the point of view of the user. Broad, open-ended questions are common, with a lesser degree of drill-down into details.

> **Middle interviews** are where designers begin to see patterns of use and ask open-ended and clarifying questions to help connect the dots. Questions in general are more focused on domain specifics, now that the designers have absorbed the basic rules, structures, and vocabularies of the domain.

> **Later interviews** confirm previously observed patterns, further clarifying user roles and behaviors and making fine adjustments to assumptions about task and information needs. Closed-ended questions are used in greater number, tying up loose ends in the data.

After you have an idea who your actual interviewees will be, it can be useful to work with stakeholders to schedule individuals most appropriate for each phase in the interview cycle. For example, in a complex, technical domain it is often a good idea to perform early interviews with the more patient and articulate interview subjects. In some cases, you may also want to loop back and interview this particularly knowledgeable and articulate subject again at the end of the interview cycle to address any topics that you weren't aware of during your initial interview.

Basic methods

The basic methods of ethnographic interviewing are simple, straightforward, and very low tech. Although the nuances of interviewing subjects takes some time to master, any practitioner should, if they follow the suggestions below, be rewarded with a wealth of useful qualitative data:

- Interview where the interaction happens
- Avoid a fixed set of questions
- Focus on goals first, tasks second
- Avoid making the user a designer
- Avoid discussions of technology
- Encourage storytelling
- Ask for a show and tell
- Avoid leading questions

We describe each of these methods in more detail in the following sections.

Interview where the interaction happens

Following the first principle of contextual inquiry, it is of critical importance that subjects be interviewed in the places where they actually use the products. Not only does this give the interviewers the opportunity to witness the product being used, but it also gives the interview team access to the environment in which the interaction occurs. This can give tremendous insight into product constraints and user needs and goals.

Observe the environment closely: It is likely to be crawling with clues about tasks the interviewee might not have mentioned. Notice, for example, the kind of information they need (papers on desks or adhesive notes on screen borders), inadequate systems (cheat sheets and user manuals), the frequency and priority of tasks (inbox and outbox); and the kind of workflows they follow (memos, charts, calendars). Don't snoop without permission, but if you see something that looks interesting, ask your interviewee to discuss it.

Avoid a fixed set of questions

If you approach ethnographic interviews with a fixed questionnaire, you not only run the risk of alienating the interview subject but can also cause the interviewers to miss out on a wealth of valuable user data. The entire premise of ethnographic interviews (and contextual inquiry) is that we as interviewers don't know enough about the domain to presuppose the questions that need asking: We must learn what is important from the people we talk to. This said, it's certainly useful to have *types* of questions in mind. Depending on the domain, it may also be useful to have a standardized set of *topics* that you want to make sure you cover in the course of your interview. This list of topics may evolve over the course of your interviews, but this will help you make sure that you get enough detail from each interview so that you are able to recognize the significant behavior patterns.

Here are some **goal-oriented questions** to consider:

- ▶ **Goals** — What makes a good day? A bad day?
- ▶ **Opportunity** — What activities currently waste your time?
- ▶ **Priorities** — What is most important to you?
- ▶ **Information** — What helps you make decisions?

Another useful type of question is the **system-oriented question**:

- ▶ **Function** — What are the most common things you do with the product?
- ▶ **Frequency** — What parts of the product do you use most?
- ▶ **Preference** — What are your favorite aspects of the product? What drives you crazy?
- ▶ **Failure** — How do you work around problems?
- ▶ **Expertise** — What shortcuts do you employ?

For business products, **workflow-oriented questions** can be helpful:

- ▶ **Process** — What did you do when you first came in today? And after that?
- ▶ **Occurrence and recurrence** — How often do you do this? What things do you do weekly or monthly, but not every day?
- ▶ **Exception** — What constitutes a typical day? What would be an unusual event?

To better understand user motivations, you can employ **attitude-oriented questions**:

- ▶ **Aspiration** — What do you see yourself doing five years from now?
- ▶ **Avoidance** — What would you prefer not to do? What do you procrastinate on?
- ▶ **Motivation** — What do you enjoy most about your job (or lifestyle)? What do you always tackle first?

Focus on goals first, tasks second

Unlike contextual inquiry and the majority of other qualitative research methods, the first priority of ethnographic interviewing is understanding the *why* of users — what motivates the behaviors of individuals in different roles, and *how* they hope to ultimately accomplish this goal — not the *what* of the tasks they perform. Understanding the tasks is important, and the tasks must be diligently recorded. But these tasks will ultimately be restructured to better match user goals in the final design.

Avoid making the user a designer

Guide the interviewee towards examining problems and away from expressing solutions. Most of the time, those solutions reflect the interview subject's personal priorities, and while they sound good to *him*, they tend to be shortsighted, idiosyncratic, and lack the balance and refinement that an interaction designer can bring to a solution based upon adequate research and years of experience. That said, a proposed design solution can be a useful jumping off point to discuss a user's goals and the problems they encounter with current systems. If a user blurts out an interesting idea, ask "What problem would that solve for you?" or "Why would that be a good solution?"

Avoid discussions of technology

Just as you don't want to treat the user as a designer, you also don't want to treat him as a programmer or engineer. Discussion of technology is meaningless without first understanding the purpose underlying any technical decisions. In the case of technical or scientific products, where technology is always an issue, distinguish between domain-related technology and product-related technology, and steer away from the latter. If an interview subject is particularly insistent on talking about how the product should be implemented, bring the subject back to his goals and motivations by asking "How would that help you?"

Encourage storytelling

Far more useful than asking users for design advice is encouraging them to tell specific stories about their experiences with a product (whether an old version of the one you're redesigning, or an analogous product or process): how they use it, what they think of it, who else they interact with when using it, where they go with it, and so forth. Detailed stories of this kind are usually the best way to understand how users relate to and interact with products. Encourage stories that deal with typical cases and also more exceptional ones.

Ask for a show and tell

After you have a good idea of the flow and structure of a user's activities and interactions and you have exhausted other questions, it is often useful to ask the interviewee for a show and tell or **grand tour** of artifacts related to the design problem. These can be domain-related artifacts, software interfaces, paper systems, tours of the work environment, or ideally all the above. Be careful to not only record the artifacts themselves (digital or video cameras are very handy at this stage) but also pay attention to *how* the interviewee describes them. Be sure to ask plenty of clarifying questions as well.

Avoid leading questions

One important thing to avoid in interviews is the use of *leading questions*. Just as in a courtroom, where lawyers can, by virtue of their authority, bias witnesses by suggesting answers to them, designers can inadvertently bias interview subjects by implicitly (or explicitly) suggesting solutions or opinions about behaviors. Examples of leading questions include:

- ▶ Would feature X help you?

- ▶ You like X, don't you?

- ▶ Do you think you'd use X if it were available?

After the interviews

After each interview, teams compare notes and discuss any particularly interesting trends observed or specific points brought up in the most recent interview. If they have the time, they should also look back at old notes to see whether unanswered questions from other interviews and research have been properly answered. This information should be used to strategize about the approach to take in subsequent interviews.

After the interview process is finished, it is useful to once again make a pass through all the notes, marking or highlighting trends and patterns in the data. This is very useful for the next step of creating personas from the cumulative research. If it is helpful, the team can create a binder of the notes, review any videotapes, and print out artifact images to place in the binder or on a public surface, such as a wall, where they are all visible simultaneously. This will be useful in later design phases.

Other Types of Research

This chapter has focused on qualitative research aimed at gathering user data that will later be used to construct robust user and domain models that form the key tools in the Goal-Directed Design methodology described in the next chapter. A wide variety of other forms of research are used by design and usability professionals, ranging from detailed task analysis activities to focus groups and usability tests. While many of these activities have the potential to contribute to the creation of useful and desirable products, we have found the qualitative approach described in this chapter to provide the most value to digital product design. Put simply, the qualitative approach helps answer questions about the product at both the big-picture and functional-detail level with a relatively small amount of effort and expense. No other research technique can claim this.

Mike Kuniavsky's book *Observing the User Experience* is an excellent resource that describes a wide range of user research methods for use at many points in the design and development process. In the remainder of this chapter, we discuss just a few of the more prominent research methods and how they fit into the overall development effort.

Focus groups

Marketing organizations are particularly fond of gathering user data via **focus groups**, in which representative users, usually chosen to match previously identified demographic segments of the target market, are gathered together in a room and asked a structured set of questions and provided a structured set of choices. Often, the meeting is recorded on audio or video media for later reference. Focus groups are a standard technique in traditional product marketing. They are useful for gauging initial reactions to the *form* of a product, its visual appearance, or industrial design. Focus groups can also gather reactions to a product that the respondents have been using for some time.

Although focus groups may appear to provide the requisite user contact, the method is in many ways not appropriate as a design tool. Focus groups excel at eliciting information about products that people own or are willing (or unwilling) to purchase but are weak at gathering data about what people actually do with those products, or how and why they do it. Also, because they are a group activity, focus groups tend to drive to consensus. The majority or loudest opinion often becomes the group opinion. This is anathema to the design process, where designers must understand all the different patterns of behavior a product must address. Focus groups tend to stifle exactly the diversity of behavior and opinion that designers must accommodate.

Market demographics and market segments

The marketing profession has taken much of the guesswork out of determining what motivates people to buy. One of the most powerful tools for doing so is market segmentation, which typically uses data from focus groups and market surveys to group potential customers by demographic criteria (such as age, gender, educational level, and home zip code) to determine what types of consumers will be most receptive to a particular product or marketing message. More sophisticated consumer data also include psychographics and behavioral variables, including attitudes, lifestyle, values, ideology, risk aversion, and decision-making patterns. Classification systems such as SRI's VALS segmentation and Jonathan Robbin's geodemographic PRIZM clusters can add greater clarity to the data by predicting consumers' purchasing power, motivation, self-orientation, and resources.

These market-modeling techniques are able to accurately forecast marketplace acceptance of products and services. They are an invaluable tool in assessing the *viability* of a product. They can also be powerful tools for convincing executives to build a product. After all, if you know X people might buy a product or service for Y dollars, it is easy to evaluate the potential return on investment.

However, understanding whether somebody wants to buy something is not the same thing as actually defining the product. Market segmentation is a great tool for identifying and quantifying a market opportunity, but an ineffective tool for defining a product that will capitalize on that opportunity.

It turns out, however, that data gathered via market research and that gathered via qualitative user research complement each other quite well. Because market research can help identify an opportunity, it is often the necessary starting point for a design initiative. Without assessing the opportunity, you will be hard pressed to convince a businessperson to fund the design. Also, as already discussed, ethnographic interviewers should use market research to help them select interview targets, and finally, as the video-editing story earlier in this chapter illustrates, qualitative research can shed critical light on the results of quantitative studies. We will discuss the differences between segmentation models and user models in more detail in Chapter 5.

Usability and user testing

Usability testing (also known, somewhat unfortunately, as "user testing") is a collection of techniques used to measure characteristics of a user's interaction with a product, usually with the goal of assessing the usability of that product. Typically, usability testing is focused on measuring how well users can complete specific, standardized tasks, as well as what problems they encounter in doing so. Results often reveal areas where users have problems understanding and utilizing the product, as well as places where users are more likely to be successful.

Usability testing requires a fairly complete and coherent design artifact to test against. Whether you are testing production software, a clickable prototype, or even a paper prototype, the point of the test is to validate a product design. This means that the appropriate place for usability testing is quite late in the design cycle, after there is a coherent concept and sufficient detail to generate such prototypes. We discuss evaluative usability testing as part of design refinement in Chapter 7.

A case could certainly be made for the appropriateness of usability testing at the beginning of a redesign effort, and the technique is certainly capable of finding opportunities for improvement in such a project. However, we find that we are able to assess major inadequacies of a product through our qualitative studies, and if the budget is limited so as to allow usability testing only once in a product design initiative, we find much more value in performing the tests after we have a candidate solution, as a means of testing the specific elements of the new design.

Because the findings of user testing are generally measurable and quantitative, usability research is especially useful in comparing specific design variants to choose the most effective solution. Customer feedback gathered from usability testing is most useful when you need to validate or refine particular interaction mechanisms or the form and expression of specific design elements.

Usability testing is especially effective at determining:

- ▶ **Naming** — Do section/button labels make sense? Do certain words resonate better than others do?

- ▶ **Organization** — Is information grouped into meaningful categories? Are items located in the places customers might look for them?

- ▶ **First-time use and discoverability** — Are common items easy for new users to find? Are instructions clear? Are instructions necessary?

- ▶ **Effectiveness** — Can customers efficiently complete specific tasks? Are they making missteps? Where? How often?

As suggested previously, it is also worth noting that usability testing is predominantly focused on assessing the first-time use of a product. It is often quite difficult (and always laborious) to measure how effective a solution is on its 50th use — in other words, for the most common target: the perpetual intermediate user. This is quite a conundrum when one is optimizing a design for intermediate or expert users. One technique for accomplishing this is the use of a *diary study*, in which subjects keep diaries detailing their interactions with the product. Again, Mike Kuniavsky provides a good explanation of this technique in *Observing the User Experience*.

Finally, when usability testing, be sure that what you are testing is actually measurable, that the test is administered correctly, that the results will be useful in correcting design issues, and that the resources necessary to fix the problems observed in a usability study are available. Jakob Nielsen's *Usability Engineering* is the classic volume on usability and provides excellent guidance on the subject.

Card sorting

Popularized by information architects, card sorting is a technique to understand how users organize information and concepts. While there are a number of variations on the technique, it is typically performed by asking users to sort a deck of cards, each containing a piece of functionality or information related to the product or Web site. The tricky part is analyzing the results, either by looking for trends or using statistical analysis to uncover patterns and correlations.

While this can undoubtedly be a valuable tool to uncover one aspect of a user's mental model, the technique assumes that the subject has refined organizational skills, and that the way that they sort a group of abstract topics will correlate to the way they will end up wanting to use your product. This is clearly not always the case. One way to overcome these potential challenges is to ask the users to sequence the cards based upon the completion of tasks that the product is being designed to support. Another way to enhance the value of a card sort study is to debrief the subject afterwards to understand any organizational principles they have employed in their sort (again, attempting to understand their mental model).

Ultimately, we believe that properly conducted open-ended interviews are quite capable of exploring these aspects of the user's mental model. By asking the right questions and paying close attention to how a subject explains his activities and the domain, you can decipher how he mentally associates different bits of functionality and information.

Task analysis

Task analysis refers to a number of techniques that involve using either questionnaires or open-ended interviews to develop a detailed understanding of how people currently perform specific tasks. Of concern to such a study is:

- ▶ Why the user is performing the task (that is, the underlying goal)
- ▶ Frequency and importance of the task
- ▶ Cues — what initiates or prompts the execution of the task
- ▶ Dependencies — what must be in place to perform the task, as well as what is dependent on the completion of the task
- ▶ People who are involved and their roles and responsibilities
- ▶ Specific actions that are performed
- ▶ Decisions that are made

- ► Information that is used to support decisions

- ► What goes wrong — errors and exception cases

- ► How errors and exceptions are corrected

Once the questionnaires are compiled or the interviews are completed, tasks are formally decomposed and analyzed, typically into a flow chart or similar diagram that communicates the relationships between actions and often the relationships between people and processes.

We've found that this type of inquiry should be incorporated into ethnographic user interviews. Further, as we'll discuss in the next chapter, the analysis activities are a useful part of our modeling activities. It should be noted, though, that while task analysis is a critical way of understanding the way users currently do something, as well as a way of identifying pain points and opportunities for improvement, we want to reiterate the importance of focusing first and foremost on the users' goals. The way people do things today is often merely the product of the obsolete systems and organizations they are forced to interact with, and typically bear little resemblance to the way they would like to do things or the way they would be most effective.

User research is the critical foundation upon which your designs are built. Take the time to plan your user research and match the appropriate technique to the appropriate place in your development cycle. Your product will benefit, and you'll avoid wasting time and resources. Putting a product to the test in a lab to see whether it passes or fails may provide a lot of data, but not necessarily a lot of value. Using ethnographic interviews at the beginning of the process allows you, as a designer, to truly understand your users, their needs, and their motivations. Once you have a solid design concept based on qualitative user research and the models that research feeds, your usability testing will become an even more efficient tool for judging the effectiveness of design choices you have made. Qualitative research allows you to do the heavy lifting up front in the process.

Notes

1. Schön, D., and Bennett, J., 1996

2. Pinker, 1999

5

Modeling Users: Personas and Goals

Having gone out into the wide world to understand your users' lives, motivations, and environs, a big question arises: How do you use this research data to come up with a design that will result in a successful product? You have notebooks full of conversations and observations, and it is likely that each person you spoke to was slightly different from the others. It is difficult to imagine digging through hundreds of pages of notes every time you have to make a design decision, and even if you had the time to do this, it isn't entirely obvious how these notes should inform your thinking.

We solve this problem by applying the powerful concept of a **model**. Models are used in the natural and social sciences to represent complex phenomena with a useful abstraction. Much as economists create models to describe the behavior of markets, and physicists create models to describe the behavior of particles, we have found that using our research to create descriptive models of our users is a uniquely powerful tool for interaction design. We call these user models **personas**.

Personas provide us with a precise way of thinking and communicating about how users behave, how they think, what they wish to accomplish, and why. Personas are not real people, but they are based on the behaviors and motivations of real people we have observed and represent them throughout the design process. They are *composite archetypes* based on behavioral data gathered from the many actual users encountered in ethnographic interviews. Personas are based upon *behavior patterns we observe* during the course of the Research phase, which we then formalize in the Modeling phase. By using personas, we can develop an understanding of our users' goals in specific contexts — a critical tool for using user research to inform and justify our designs.

Personas, like many powerful tools, are simple in concept but must be applied with considerable sophistication. It is not enough to whip up a couple of user profiles based upon stereotypes and generalizations, nor is it particularly useful to attach a stock photograph to a job title and call it a "persona." For personas to be effective tools for design, considerable rigor and finesse must be applied to the process of identifying the significant and meaningful patterns in user behavior and turning these into archetypes that represent a broad cross-section of users.

While there are other useful models that can serve as tools for the interaction designer, such as workflow models and physical models, we've found that personas are the strongest, and it is possible to incorporate the best from other modeling techniques into a persona. This chapter focuses on personas and their goals. Other models are considered briefly at the end of the chapter.

Why Model?

Models are used extensively in design, development, and the sciences. They are powerful tools for representing complex structures and relationships for the purpose of better understanding, discussing, or visualizing them. Without models, we are left to make sense of unstructured, raw data, without the benefit of any organizing principle. Good models emphasize the salient features of the structures and relationships they represent and de-emphasize the less significant details.

Because we are designing for users, it is important that we can understand and visualize the salient aspects of their relationships with each other, with their social and physical environments, and of course, with the products we hope to design.

Just as physicists have created models of the atom based on observed data and intuitive synthesis of the patterns in their data, so must designers create models of users based on observed behaviors and intuitive synthesis of the patterns in the data. Only after we formalize such patterns can we hope to systematically construct patterns of interaction that smoothly match the behavior patterns, mental models, and goals of users. Personas provide this formalization.

Personas

To create a product that must satisfy a diverse audience of users, logic might tell you to make it as broad in its functionality as possible to accommodate the most people. *This logic, however, is flawed.* The best way to successfully accommodate a variety of users is to design for *specific types of individuals with specific needs.*

When you broadly and arbitrarily extend a product's functionality to include many constituencies, you increase the cognitive load and navigational overhead for all users. Facilities that may please some users will likely interfere with the satisfaction of others (see Figure 5-1).

Figure 5-1 A simplified example of how personas are useful. If you try to design an automobile that pleases every possible driver, you end up with a car with every possible feature, but that pleases nobody. Software today is too often designed to please too many users, resulting in low user satisfaction. Figure 5-2 provides an alternative approach.

The key to this approach is first to choose the right individuals to design for — those users whose needs best represent the needs of a larger set of key constituents (see Figure 5-2) — and then to prioritize these individuals so that the needs of the most important users are met without compromising our ability to meet the needs of secondary users. Personas provide a powerful tool for communicating about different types of users and their needs, then deciding which users are the most important to target in the design of form and behavior.

Since they were introduced as a tool for user modeling in *The Inmates are Running The Asylum,*[1] personas have gained great popularity in the user experience community, but they have also been the subject of some misunderstandings. We'd like to clarify and explain in more depth some of the concepts and the rationale behind personas.

Alesandro's goals
► Go fast
► Have fun

Marge's goals
► Be safe
► Be comfortable

Dale's goals
► Haul big loads
► Be reliable

Figure 5-2 A simplified example of how personas are useful. By designing different cars for different people with different specific goals, we are able to create designs that other people with similar needs to our target drivers also find satisfying. The same holds true for the design of digital products and software.

Strengths of personas as a design tool

The persona is a powerful, multipurpose design tool that helps overcome several problems that currently plague the development of digital products. Personas help designers:

▶ **Determine** what a product should do and how it should behave. Persona goals and tasks provide the foundation for the design effort.

▶ **Communicate** with stakeholders, developers, and other designers. Personas provide a common language for discussing design decisions and also help keep the design centered on users at every step in the process.

▶ **Build consensus and commitment** to the design. With a common language comes a common understanding. Personas reduce the need for elaborate diagrammatic models; it's easier to understand the many nuances of user behavior through the narrative structures that personas employ. Put simply, because personas resemble real people, they're easier to relate to than feature lists and flowcharts.

▶ **Measure** the design's effectiveness. Design choices can be tested on a persona in the same way that they can be shown to a real user during the formative process. Although this doesn't replace the need to test with real users, it provides a powerful reality-check tool for designers trying to solve design problems. This allows design iteration to occur rapidly and inexpensively at the whiteboard, and it results in a far stronger design baseline when the time comes to test with actual people.

▶ **Contribute** to other product-related efforts such as marketing and sales plans. The authors have seen their clients repurpose personas across their organization, informing marketing campaigns, organizational structure, and other strategic planning activities. Business units outside of product development desire sophisticated knowledge of a product's users and typically view personas with great interest.

Personas also can resolve three design issues that arise during product development:

▶ The elastic user

▶ Self-referential design

▶ Edge cases

We discuss each of these briefly in the following sections.

The elastic user

Although satisfying the users of our products is our goal, the term *user* causes trouble when applied to specific design problems and contexts. Its imprecision makes it dangerous as a design tool — every person on a product team has his own conceptions of who the user is and what the user needs. When it comes time to make product decisions, this "user" becomes *elastic*, conveniently bending and stretching to fit the opinions and presuppositions of whoever's talking.

If the product development team finds it convenient to use a confusing tree control containing nested, hierarchical folders to provide access to information, they might define the user as a computer-literate "power user." Other times, when it is more convenient to step through a difficult process with a wizard, they define the user as an unsophisticated first-time user. Designing for the elastic user gives a product-development team license to build what it pleases, while still apparently serving "the user." Of course, our goal should be to design products that appropriately meet the needs of *real* users. Real users — and the personas representing them — are not elastic, but rather have specific requirements based on their goals, capabilities, and contexts.

Even focusing on user roles or job titles rather than specific archetypes can introduce unproductive elasticity to the focus of design activities. For example, in designing clinical products, it might be tempting to lump together all nurses as having similar needs. However, if you have any experience in a hospital, you know that trauma nurses, pediatric intensive-care nurses, and operating room nurses are quite different from each other, each with their own attitudes, aptitudes, needs, and motivations. A lack of precision about the user can lead to a lack of clarity about how the product should behave.

Self-referential design

Self-referential design occurs when designers or developers project their own goals, motivations, skills, and mental models onto a product's design. Many "cool" product designs fall into this category. The audience doesn't extend beyond people like the designer, which is fine for a narrow range of products and completely inappropriate for most others. Similarly, programmers apply self-referential design when they create implementation-model products. *They* understand perfectly how the data is structured and how software works and are comfortable with such products. Few nonprogrammers would concur.

Edge cases

Another syndrome that personas help prevent is designing for edge cases — those situations that might possibly happen, but usually won't for the target personas. Typically, edge cases must be designed and programmed for, but they should never be the design *focus*. Personas provide a reality check for the design. We can ask, "Will Julie want to perform this operation very often? Will she ever?" With this knowledge, we can prioritize functions with great clarity.

Personas are based on research

Personas, like any models, must be based on real-world observation. As discussed in the preceding chapter, the primary source of data used to synthesize personas should be in-context interviews borrowing from ethnographic techniques, contextual inquiry, or other similar dialogues with and observation of actual and potential users. The quality of the data gathered following the process (outlined in Chapter 4) directly impacts the efficacy of personas in clarifying and directing design activities. Other data that can support and supplement the creation of personas include (in rough order of effectiveness):

- ▶ Interviews with users outside of their use contexts
- ▶ Information about users supplied by stakeholders and subject matter experts (SMEs)
- ▶ Market research data such as focus groups and surveys
- ▶ Market-segmentation models
- ▶ Data gathered from literature reviews and previous studies

However, none of this supplemental data can take the place of direct user interviews and observation. Almost every aspect of a well-developed persona can be traced back to a user statement or behavior.

Personas are represented as individual people

Personas are user models that are represented as specific, individual human beings. They are not actual people but are synthesized directly from observations of real people. One of the key elements that allow personas to be successful as user models is that they are *personifications*.[2] This is appropriate and effective because of the unique aspects of personas as user models: They engage the *empathy* of the design and development towards the human target of the design.

Empathy is critical for the designers, who will be making their decisions for design frameworks and details based on both the cognitive *and* emotional dimensions of the persona, as typified by the persona's goals. (We will discuss the important connections between goals, behaviors, and personas later in this chapter.) However, the power of empathy should not be quickly discounted for other team members. Not only do personas help make our design solutions better at serving real user needs, but they also make these solutions more compelling to stakeholders. When personas have been carefully and appropriately crafted, stakeholders and engineers begin to think about them as if they are real human beings and become much more interested in creating a product that will give this person a satisfying experience.

We're all aware of the power of fictional characters in books, movies, and television programs to engage viewers. Jonathan Grudin and John Pruitt have discussed how this can relate to interaction design.[3] They note, as well, the power of **method**

acting as a tool that actors use to understand and portray realistic characters. In fact, the process of creating personas from user observation, and then imagining and developing scenarios from the perspective of these personas, is, in many ways, analogous to method acting. (We've even heard our Goal-Directed use of personas referred to as the Stanislavsky Method of interaction design.)

Personas represent groups of users

Although personas are depicted as specific individuals, because they function as archetypes, they *represent* a class or type of user of a *specific* interactive product. A persona encapsulates a distinct set of **behavior patterns** regarding the use of a particular product (or analogous activities if a product does not yet exist), which are identified through the analysis of interview data, and supported by supplemental quantitative data as appropriate. These patterns, along with specific motivations or goals, define our personas. Personas are also sometimes referred to as **composite user archetypes** because personas are in a sense composites assembled by grouping related usage patterns observed across individuals in similar roles during the Research phase.[4]

Personas and reuse

Organizations with more than one product often want to reuse the same personas. However, to be effective, personas must be context specific — they should be focused on the behaviors and goals related to the specific domain of a particular product. Personas, because they are constructed from specific observations of users interacting in specific contexts, cannot easily be reused across products even when those products form a closely linked suite.[5]

For a set of personas to be an effective design tool for multiple products, the personas must be based upon research concerning the usage contexts for all of these products. In addition to broadening the scope of the research, an even larger challenge is to identify manageable and coherent sets of behavior patterns across all of the contexts. Clearly, it is a fallacy to believe that just because two users exhibit similar behaviors in regard to one product, that those two users would behave similarly with respect to a different product. Thus, as focus expands to encompass more and more products, it becomes increasingly difficult to create a concise and coherent set of personas that represents the diversity of real-world users. We've found that, in most cases, personas should be researched and developed individually for different products.

Archetypes versus stereotypes

Don't confuse persona archetypes with **stereotypes**. Stereotypes are, in most respects, the antithesis of well-developed personas. Stereotypes represent designer or researcher biases and assumptions, rather than factual data. Personas developed by drawing on inadequate research (or synthesized with insufficient empathy and sensitivity to interview subjects) run the risk of degrading to stereotypical caricatures. Personas must be developed and treated with dignity and respect for the people whom they represent. If the designer doesn't respect his personas, nobody else will either.

Personas also bring issues of social and political consciousness to the forefront.[6] Because personas provide a precise design target and also serve as a communication tool to the development team, the designer much choose particular demographic characteristics with care. Ideally, persona demographics should be a composite reflection of what researchers have observed in the interview population, modulated by broad market research. Personas should be *typical* and believable, but not stereotypical. If the data is not conclusive or the characteristic is not important to the design or its acceptance, we prefer to err on the side of gender, ethnic, age, and geographic diversity.

Personas explore ranges of behavior

The target market for a product describes demographics as well as lifestyles and sometimes job roles. What it does not describe are the ranges of different behaviors exhibited by members of that target market regarding the product and related situations. Ranges are distinct from *averages*: Personas do not seek to establish an average user, but rather to express *exemplary* or definitive behaviors within these identified ranges.

Because products must accommodate *ranges* of user behavior, attitudes and aptitudes, designers must identify a **persona set** associated with any given product. Multiple personas carve up ranges of behavior into discrete clusters. Different personas represent different correlated behavior patterns. These correlations are arrived at through analyzing research data. This process of identifying behaviors is discussed in greater detail later in this chapter.

Personas must have motivations

All humans have motivations that drive their behaviors; some are obvious, and many are subtle. It is critical that personas capture these motivations in the form of goals. The goals we enumerate for our personas (discussed at length later in this chapter) are shorthand notation for motivations that not only point at specific usage patterns but also provide a reason why those behaviors exist. Understanding *why* a user performs certain tasks gives designers great power to improve or even eliminate those tasks yet still accomplish the same goals.

Personas can also represent nonusers

While the users and potential users of a product should always be an interaction designer's primary concern, it is sometimes useful to represent the needs and goals of people who do not use the product but nevertheless must be considered in the design process. For example, it is commonly the case with enterprise software (and children's toys) that the person who purchases the product is not the same person who uses it. In these cases, it may be useful to create one or more **customer personas**, distinct from the set of user personas. Of course, these should also be based upon behavior patterns observed through ethnographic research, just as user personas are.

Similarly, for many medical products, patients do not directly interact with the user interface, but they have motivations and objectives that may be very different than the clinician using the product. Creating a **served persona** to represent patients' needs can be useful in these cases. We discuss served and customer personas in greater depth later in this chapter.

Personas and other user models

There a number of other user models commonly employed in the design of interactive products, including user roles, user profiles, and market segments. These are similar to personas in that they seek to describe users and their relationship to a product. However, personas and the methods by which they are created and employed as a design tool differ significantly from these in several key aspects.

User roles

A user role or role model, as defined by Larry Constantine, is an *abstraction*, a defined relationship between a class of users and their problems, including needs, interests, expectations, and patterns of behavior.[7] As abstractions (generally taking the form of a list of attributes), they are not imagined as people, and do not typically attempt to convey broader human motivations and contexts.

Holtzblatt and Beyer's use of roles in consolidated flow, cultural, physical, and sequence models is similar in that it attempts to abstract various attributes and relationships abstracted from the people possessing them.[8]

We find these methods limiting for several reasons:

- ▶ It is more difficult to clearly communicate human behaviors and relationships in the abstract, isolated from people who possess them. The human power of empathy cannot easily be brought to bear on abstract classes of people.

- ▶ Both methods focus on *tasks* almost exclusively and neglect the use of goals as an organizing principle for design thinking and synthesis.

- ▶ Holtzblatt and Beyer's consolidated models, although useful and encyclopedic in scope, are difficult to bring together as a coherent tool for developing, communicating, and measuring design decisions.

Personas address each of these problems. Well-developed personas describe the same type of behaviors and relationships that user roles do, but express them in terms of goals and examples in narrative. This makes it possible for designers and stakeholders to understand the implications of design decisions in human terms. Describing a persona's goals provides context and structure for tasks, incorporating how culture and workflow influence behavior.

In addition, focusing on user roles rather than on more complex behavior patterns can oversimplify important distinctions and similarities between users. It is possible to create a persona that represents the needs of several user roles (for example, in designing a mobile phone, a traveling salesperson might also represent the needs of a busy executive who's always on the road), and it is also possible that there are several people in the same role who think and act differently (perhaps a procurement planner in the chemical industry thinks about her job very differently from a procurement planner in the consumer electronics industry). In consumer domains, roles are next to useless. If you're designing a Web site for a car company, "car buyer" is meaningless as a design tool — different people approach the task in very different manners.

In general, personas provide a more holistic model of users and their contexts, where many other models seek to be more reductive. Personas can certainly be used in combination with these other modeling techniques, and as we'll discuss at the end of the chapter, some other models make extremely useful complements to personas.

Personas versus user profiles

Many usability practitioners use the terms **persona** and **user profile** synonymously. There is no problem with this if the profile is truly generated from ethnographic data and encapsulates the depth of information the authors have described. Unfortunately, all too often, the authors have seen user profiles that reflect Webster's definition of **profile** as a "brief biographical sketch." In other words, user profiles often consist of a name and a picture attached to a brief, mostly demographic description, along with a short, *fictional* paragraph describing the kind of car this person drives, how many kids he has, where he lives, and what he does for a living. This kind of user profile is likely to be based on a stereotype and is not useful as a design tool. Although we give our personas names, and sometimes even cars and family members, these are employed sparingly as narrative tools to help better communicate the real underlying data. Supporting fictional detail plays only the most minor part in persona creation and is used just enough to make the persona come to life in the minds of the designers and the product team.

Personas versus market segments

Marketing professionals may be familiar with a process similar to persona development because it shares some process similarities with market definition. The main difference between market segments and design personas is that the former are based on demographics, distribution channels, and purchasing behavior, whereas the latter are based on usage behavior and motivations. The two are not the same and don't serve the same purpose. Marketing personas shed light on the sales process, whereas design personas shed light on the product definition and development process.

However, market segments play a role in persona development. They can help determine the demographic range within which to frame the persona hypothesis (see Chapter 4). Personas are segmented along ranges of usage behavior, not demographics or buying behavior, so there is seldom a one-to-one mapping of market segments to personas. Rather, market segments can act as an initial filter to limit the scope of interviews to people within target markets (see Figure 5-3). Also, we typically use the prioritization of personas as a way to make strategic product definition decisions (see the discussion of persona types later in this chapter). These decisions should incorporate market intelligence; an understanding of the relationship between user personas and market segments can be an important consideration here.

When rigorous personas aren't possible: Provisional personas

Although it is highly desirable that personas be based upon detailed qualitative data, there are some occasions when there simply is not enough time, resources, or corporate buy-in to perform the necessary fieldwork. In these cases, *provisional* personas (or, as Don Norman refers to them, "ad hoc" personas) can be useful rhetorical tools to clearly communicate assumptions about who the important users are and what they need, and to enforce rigorous thinking about serving specific user needs (even if these needs are not validated).

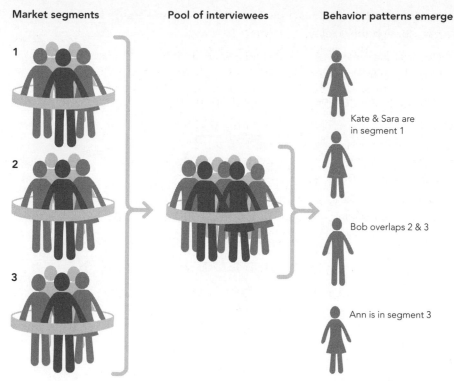

Figure 5-3 Personas versus market segments. Market segments can be used in the Research phase to limit the range of personas to target markets. However, there is seldom a one-to-one mapping between market segments and personas.

Provisional personas are structured similarly to real personas but rely on available data and designer best guesses about behaviors, motivations, and goals. They are typically based on a combination of stakeholder and subject matter expert knowledge of users (when available), as well as what is understood about users from existing market data. Provisional personas are, in fact, a more fleshed-out persona hypothesis (as described in Chapter 4).

Our experience is that, regardless of a lack of research, using provisional personas yields better results than no user models at all. Like real personas, provisional personas can help focus the product team and build consensus around product features and behaviors. There are, however, caveats: Provisional personas are called this because they should be recognized as stand-ins for personas based on definitive qualitative data. While provisional personas may help focus your design and product team, if you do not have data to back up your assumptions you may:

- ► Focus on the wrong design target
- ► Focus on the right target, but miss key behaviors that could differentiate your product

> ► Have a difficult time getting buy-in from individuals and groups who did not participate in their creation

> ► Discredit the value of personas, causing your organization to reject the use of personas in the long term

If you are using provisional personas, it's important to:

> ► Clearly label and explain them as such

> ► Represent them visually with sketches, not photos, to reinforce their provisional nature

> ► Try to make use of as much existing data as possible (market surveys, domain research, subject matter experts, field studies, or personas for similar products)

> ► Document what data was used and what assumptions were made

> ► Steer clear of stereotypes (more difficult to do without field data)

> ► Focus on behaviors and motivations, not demographics

Goals

If personas provide the context for sets of observed behaviors, **goals** are the drivers behind those behaviors. A persona without goals can still serve as a useful communication tool, but it lacks utility as a design tool. User goals serve as a lens through which designers must consider the functions of a product. The function and behavior of the product must address goals via tasks — typically, as few tasks as absolutely necessary. Remember, tasks are only a means to an end; goals are that end.

Goals motivate usage patterns

People's or personas' goals motivate them to behave the way they do. Thus, goals not only provide an answer to why and how personas desire to use a product but also can serve as a shorthand in the designer's mind for the sometimes complex behaviors in which a persona engages and, therefore, for their tasks as well.

Goals should be inferred from qualitative data

You usually can't ask a person what his goals are directly. Either he won't be able to articulate them, or he won't be accurate or even perfectly honest. People simply aren't well prepared to answer such questions accurately. Therefore, designers and researchers need to carefully reconstruct goals from observed behaviors, answers to other questions, nonverbal cues, and clues from the environment such as the titles of books on shelves. One of the most critical tasks in the modeling of personas is identifying goals and expressing them succinctly: Each goal should be expressed as a simple sentence.

User goals and cognitive processing

Don Norman's book *Emotional Design* introduced the idea that product design should address three different levels of cognitive and emotional processing, which he has called visceral, behavioral, and reflective. Norman's ideas, based on years of cognitive research, provide an articulated structure for modeling user responses to product and brand and a rational context for many intuitions long held by professional designers.

Norman's three levels of cognitive processing are:

- ▶ **Visceral** — The most immediate level of processing, in which we react to visual and other sensory aspects of a product that we can perceive before significant interaction occurs. Visceral processing helps us make rapid decisions about what is good, bad, safe, or dangerous. This is one of the most exciting types of human behavior, and one of the most challenging to effectively support with digital products. Malcolm Gladwell explores this level of cognitive processing in his book *Blink*. For even more in-depth study of intuitive decision making, see Gary Klein's *Sources of Power* or *Hare Brain, Tortoise Mind* by Guy Claxton.

- ▶ **Behavioral** — The middle level of processing that lets us manage simple, everyday behaviors, which according to Norman, constitute the majority of human activity. Norman states — and rightly so — that historically, interaction design and usability practices have nearly exclusively addressed this level of cognitive processing. Behavioral processing can *enhance* or *inhibit* both lower level visceral reactions and higher-level reflective responses, and conversely, both visceral and reflective processing can enhance or inhibit behavioral processing.

- ▶ **Reflective** — The least immediate level of processing, which involves conscious consideration and reflection on past experiences. Reflective processing can enhance or inhibit behavioral processing but has no direct access to visceral reactions. This level of cognitive processing is accessible only via memory, not through direct interaction or perception. The most interesting aspect of reflective processing as it relates to design is that, through reflection, we are able to integrate our experiences with designed artifacts into our broader life experiences and, over time, associate meaning and value with the artifacts themselves.

Designing for Visceral Responses

Designing for the visceral level means designing what the senses initially perceive, before any deeper involvement with a product or artifact occurs. For most of us, that means designing visual appearance and motion, though sound can also play a role — think of the distinctive Mac power-up chord. Those of us designing devices may design for tactile sensations as well.

A misconception often arises when discussing visceral-level design: that designing for visceral response is about designing *beautiful* things. Battlefield software and radiation-therapy systems are just two examples where designing for beauty may not be the proper focus. Visceral design is actually about designing for affect — that is, eliciting the appropriate psychological or emotional response for a particular context — rather than for aesthetics alone. Beauty — and the feelings of transcendence and pleasure it evokes — is really only a small part of the possible affective design palette. For example, an MP3 player and an online banking system require very different affects. We can learn a great deal about affect from architecture, the cinema and stage, and industrial design.

However, in the world of consumer products and services, attractive user interfaces *are* typically appropriate. Interestingly, usability researchers have demonstrated that users initially judge attractive interfaces to be more usable, and that this belief often persists long after a user has gained sufficient experience with an interface to have direct evidence to the contrary.[9] Perhaps the reason for this is that users, encouraged by perceived ease of use, make a greater effort to learn what may be a challenging interface and are then unwilling to consider their investment ill spent. For the scrupulous designer, this means that, when a user interface promises ease of use at the visceral level — or whatever else the visceral promise of an interaction may be — it should then be sure to deliver on that promise at the behavioral level.

Designing for Behavior

Designing for the behavioral level means designing product behaviors that complement a user's own behaviors, implicit assumptions, and mental models. Of the three levels of design Norman contemplates, behavioral design is perhaps the most familiar to interaction designers and usability professionals.

One intriguing aspect of Norman's three-level model as it relates to design is his assertion that behavioral processing, uniquely among his three levels, has direct influence upon and is influenced directly by both of the other two levels of processing. This would seem to imply that the day-to-day behavioral aspects of interaction design should be the primary focus of our design efforts, with visceral and reflective considerations playing a supporting role. Getting design of behavior right — assuming that we also pay adequate attention to the other levels — provides our greatest opportunity for positively influencing the way users construct their experience with products.

Not following this line of reasoning can lead to the problem of users' initial impressions being out of sync with reality. Also, it is difficult to imagine designing for reflective meaning in memory without a solid purpose and set of behaviors in place for the here and now. The user experience of a product or artifact, therefore, should ideally *harmonize elements of visceral design and reflective design with a focus on behavioral design.*

Designing for Reflection

Reflective processing — and, particularly, what it means for design — is perhaps the most challenging aspect of the three levels of processing that Norman discusses. What is clear is that designing for the reflective level means designing to build long-term product relationships. What isn't clear at all is the best way to ensure success — if that's even possible — at the reflective level. Is it chance that drives success here — being in the right place at the right time — or can premeditated design play a part in making it happen?

In describing reflective design, Norman uses several high-concept designs for commodity products as examples — such as impractically configured teapots and the striking Phillipe Starck juicer that graces the cover of his book. It is easy to see how such products — whose value and purpose are, in essence, the aesthetic statements they make — could appeal strongly to people's reflective desire for uniqueness or cultural sophistication that perhaps may come from an artistic or stylish self-image.

It is more difficult to see how products that also serve a truly useful purpose need to balance the stylistic and the elegant with the functional. The Apple iPod comes very close to achieving this balance. Although its click-wheel navigation scheme is perhaps less than optimal in some respects, users' visceral reaction to the product is tremendous, due to its elegant industrial design. Its reflective potential is also significant, because of the powerful emotional connection people experience with their music. It's a winning combination that no competitor has yet been able to challenge.

Few products become iconic in people's lives in the way that, say, the Sony Walkman or the iPod has. Clearly there are some products that stand little chance of ever becoming symbolic in peoples lives — like Ethernet routers, for instance — no matter how wonderful they look or how well they behave. However, when the design of a product or service addresses users' goals and motivations — possibly going beyond the product's primary purpose, yet somehow connected to it via personal or cultural associations — the opportunity for the creation of reflective meaning is greatly enhanced.

The three types of user goals

In *Emotional Design*, Norman presents his three-level theory of cognitive processing and discusses its potential importance to design. However, Norman does not suggest a method for systematically integrating his model of cognition and affect into the practice of design or user research. In our practice, we've found that the key to doing so lies in properly delineating and modeling three specific types of user goals as part of each persona's definition.[10]

Three types of user goals correspond to Norman's visceral, behavioral, and reflective processing levels:

> ▶ Experience goals
>
> ▶ End goals
>
> ▶ Life goals

We describe each of these in detail in the following sections.

Experience goals

Experience goals are simple, universal, and personal. Paradoxically, this makes them difficult for many people to talk about, especially in the context of impersonal business. Experience goals express how someone *wants to feel* while using a product or the quality of their interaction with the product. These goals provide focus for a product's visual and aural characteristics, its interactive feel — such as animated transitions, latency, and the snap ratio (clickiness) of a physical button — and its physical design by providing insights into persona motivations that express themselves at the visceral level. For example:

> ▶ Feel smart or in control
>
> ▶ Have fun
>
> ▶ Feel cool or hip or relaxed
>
> ▶ Remain focused and alert

When products make users feel stupid or uncomfortable, their self-esteem drops and their effectiveness plummets, regardless of their other goals. Their level of resentment also increases. Enough of this type of treatment and users will be primed to use any chance to subvert the system. Any product that egregiously violates experience goals will ultimately fail, regardless of how well it purports to achieve other goals.

Interaction, visual, and industrial designers must translate persona experience goals into form, behavior, motion, and auditory elements that communicate the proper feel, affect, emotion, and tone. Visual language studies, as well as mood or inspiration boards, which attempt to establish visual themes based on persona attitudes and behaviors, are a useful tool for defining the tonal expectations of personas.

End goals

End goals represent the user's motivation for performing the tasks associated with using a specific product. When you pick up a cell phone or open a document with a word processor, you likely have an outcome in mind. A product or service can help accomplish such goals directly or indirectly. These goals are the focus of a product's interaction design, information architecture, and the functional aspects of industrial design. Because behavioral processing influences both visceral and reflective responses, end goals should be among the most significant factors in determining the overall product experience. End goals must be met for users to think that a product is worth their time and money.

Examples of end goals include:

- ▶ Be aware of problems before they become critical
- ▶ Stay connected with friends and family
- ▶ Clear my to-do list by 5:00 every day
- ▶ Find music that I'll love
- ▶ Get the best deal

Interaction designers must use end goals as the foundation for a product's behaviors, tasks, look, and feel. Context or day-in-the-life scenarios and cognitive walkthroughs are effective tools for exploring users' goals and mental models, which, in turn, facilitate appropriate behavioral design.

Life goals

Life goals represent personal aspirations of the user that typically go beyond the context of the product being designed. These goals represent deep drives and motivations that help explain *why* the user is trying to accomplish the end goals he seeks to accomplish. Life goals describe a persona's long-term desires, motivations, and self-image attributes, which cause the persona to connect with a product. These goals form the focus for a product's overall design, strategy, and branding. For example:

- ▶ Live the good life
- ▶ Succeed in my ambitions to . . .

▶ Be a connoisseur of . . .

▶ Be attractive, popular, or respected by my peers

Interaction designers must translate life goals into high-level system capabilities, formal design concepts, and brand strategy. Mood boards and context scenarios can be helpful in exploring different aspects of product concepts, and broad ethnographic research and cultural modeling are critical for discovering users' behavior patterns and deeper motivations. Life goals rarely figure directly into the design of specific elements or behaviors of an interface. However, they are very much worth keeping in mind. A product that the user discovers will take him closer to his life goals, and not just his end goals, will win him over more decisively than any marketing campaign. Addressing life goals of users makes the difference (assuming that other goals are also met) between a satisfied user and a fanatically loyal user.

User goals are user motivations

In summary, it's important to remember that understanding personas is more about understanding motivations and goals than it is about understanding specific tasks or demographics. Linking up persona goals with Norman's model, top-level user motivations include:

▶ Experience goals, which are related to visceral processing: how a user wants to *feel*

▶ End goals, which are related to behavior: what a user wants to *do*

▶ Life goals, which are related to reflection: who a user wants to *be*

Using personas, goals, and scenarios (as you'll learn in upcoming chapters) provides the key to unlocking the power of visceral, behavioral, and reflective design, and bringing these together into a harmonious whole. While some of our best designers seem to understand and act upon these aspects of design almost intuitively, consciously designing for all levels of human cognition and emotion offers tremendous potential for creating more satisfying and delightful user experiences.

Types of goals

User goals are not the only type of goals that designers need to take into account. Customer goals, business goals, and technical goals are all nonuser goals. Typically, these goals must be acknowledged and considered, but they do not form the basis for the design direction. Although these goals do need to be addressed, they must not be addressed at the expense of the user.

Customer goals

Customers, as already discussed, have different goals than users. The exact nature of these goals varies quite a bit between consumer and enterprise products. Consumer customers are often parents, relatives, or friends who often have concerns about the safety and happiness of the persons for whom they are purchasing the product. Enterprise customers are typically IT managers, and they often have concerns about security, ease of maintenance, and ease of customization. Customer personas also may have their own life, experience, and especially end goals in relation to the product if they use it in any capacity. Customer goals should never trump end goals but need to be considered within the overall design.

Business and organizational goals

Businesses and other organizations have their own requirements for products, services, and systems, which should also be modeled and considered when devising design solutions. While the goals of businesses, where users and customers work, are typically captured in user and customer personas, it is often useful to define the business goals of the organization commissioning the design and developing and selling (or otherwise distributing) the product. Clearly, these organizations are hoping to accomplish something with the product (which is why they are willing to spend money and effort on design and development),

Business goals include the following:

- Increase profit
- Increase market share
- Retain customers
- Defeat the competition
- Use resources more efficiently
- Offer more products or services

You may find yourself designing on behalf of an organization that is not necessarily a business, such as a museum, nonprofit, or school (though all organizations are increasingly run as businesses these days). These organizations also have goals that must be considered, such as:

- Educate the public
- Raise enough money to cover overhead

Technical goals

Most of the software-based products we use everyday are created with technical goals in mind. Many of these goals ease the task of software creation, which is a programmer's goal. This is why they typically take precedence at the expense of the users' goals. Technical goals include:

- ▶ Run in a variety of browsers
- ▶ Safeguard data integrity
- ▶ Increase program execution efficiency
- ▶ Use a particular development language or library
- ▶ Maintain consistency across platforms

Technical goals in particular are very important to the development staff. It is important to stress early in the education process that these goals must ultimately serve user and business goals. Technical goals are not terribly meaningful to the success of a product unless they are derived from the need to meet other more human-oriented goals. It might be a software company's *task* to use new technology, but it is rarely a *user's goal* for them to do so. In most cases, users don't care if their job is accomplished with hierarchical databases, relational databases, object-oriented databases, flat-file systems, or black magic. What we care about is getting our job done swiftly, effectively, and with a modicum of ease and dignity.

Successful products meet user goals first

"Good design" has meaning only for a person using a product for some purpose. You cannot have purposes without people. The two are inseparable. This is why personas are such an important tool in the process of designing behavior; they represent specific people with specific purposes or goals.

The most important purposes or goals to consider when designing a product are those of the individuals who actually use it, not necessarily those of its purchaser. A real person, not a corporation or even an IT manager, interacts with your product, so you must regard her personal goals as more significant than those of the corporation who employs her or the IT manager who supports her. Your users will do their best to achieve their employer's business goals, while at the same time looking after their own personal goals. A user's most important goal is always to retain her human dignity: not to feel stupid.

We can reliably say that we make the user feel stupid if we let her make big mistakes, keep her from getting an adequate amount of work done, or bore her.

Don't make the user feel stupid.

This is probably the most important interaction design guideline. In the course of this book, we examine numerous ways in which existing software makes the user feel stupid, and we explore ways to avoid that trap.

The essence of good interaction design is devising interactions that achieve the goals of the manufacturer or service provider and their partners without violating the goals of users.

Constructing Personas

As previously discussed, personas are derived from patterns observed during interviews with and observations of users and potential users (and sometimes customers) of a product. Gaps in this data are filled by supplemental research and data provided by SMEs, stakeholders, and available literature. Our goal in constructing a set of personas is to represent the diversity of observed motivations, behaviors, attitudes, aptitudes, mental models, work or activity flows, environments, and frustrations with current products or systems.

Creating believable and useful personas requires an equal measure of detailed analysis and creative synthesis. A standardized process aids both of these activities significantly. The process described in this section, developed by Robert Reimann, Kim Goodwin, and Lane Halley at Cooper, is the result of an evolution in practice over the span of hundreds of interaction design projects, and has been documented in several papers.[11] There are a number of effective methods for identifying behavior patterns in research and turning these into useful user archetypes, but we've found the transparency and rigor of this process to be an ideal way for designers new to personas to learn how to properly construct personas, and for experienced designers to stay focused on actual behavior patterns, especially in consumer domains. The principle steps are:

1. Identify behavioral variables.

2. Map interview subjects to behavioral variables.

3. Identify significant behavior patterns.

4. Synthesize characteristics and relevant goals.

5. Check for redundancy and completeness.

6. Expand description of attributes and behaviors.

7. Designate persona types.

We discuss each of these steps in detail in the following sections.

Step 1: Identify behavioral variables

After you have completed your research and performed a cursory organization of the data, list the distinct aspects of observed behavior as a set of **behavioral variables**. Demographic variables such as age or geographic location may also seem to affect behavior, but be wary of focusing on demographics because behavioral variables will be far more useful in developing effective user archetypes.

Generally, we see the most important distinction between behavior patterns emerge by focusing on the following types of variables:

> **Activities** — What the user does; frequency and volume

> **Attitudes** — How the user thinks about the product domain and technology

> **Aptitudes** — What education and training the user has; capability to learn

> **Motivations** — Why the user is engaged in the product domain

> **Skills** — User capabilities related to the product domain and technology

For enterprise applications, behavioral variables are often closely associated with job roles, and we suggest listing out the variables for each role separately. Although the number of variables will differ from project to project, it is typical to find 15 to 30 variables per role.

These variables may be very similar to those you identified as part of your persona hypothesis. Compare behaviors identified in the data to the assumptions made in the persona hypothesis. Were the possible roles that you identified truly distinct? Were the behavioral variables (see Chapter 4) you identified valid? Were there additional, unanticipated ones, or ones you anticipated that weren't supported by data?

List the complete set of behavioral variables observed. If your data is at variance with your assumptions, you need to add, subtract, or modify the roles and behaviors you anticipated. If the variance is significant enough, you may consider additional interviews to cover any gaps in the new behavioral ranges that you've discovered.

Step 2: Map interview subjects to behavioral variables

After you are satisfied that you have identified the set of significant behavioral variables exhibited by your interview subjects, the next step is to map each interviewee against each variable. Some of these variables will represent a continuous range of behavior (for instance, from a computer novice to a computer expert), and a few will represent multiple discrete choices (for example, uses a digital camera versus uses a film camera).

Mapping the interviewee to a precise point in the range isn't as critical as identifying the placement of interviewees in relationship to each other. In other words, it doesn't matter if an interviewee falls at precisely 45% or 50% on the scale. There's often no good way to measure this precisely; you must rely on your gut feeling based on your observations of the subject. The desired outcome of this step is to accurately represent the way multiple subjects cluster with respect to each significant variable (see Figure 5-4).

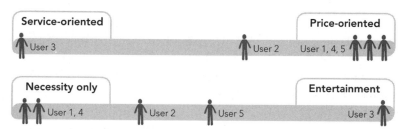

Figure 5-4 Mapping interview subjects to behavioral variables. This example is from an online store. Interview subjects are mapped across each behavioral axis. Precision of the absolute position of an individual subject on an axis is less important than its relative position to other subjects. Clusters of subjects across multiple axes indicate significant behavior patterns.

Step 3: Identify significant behavior patterns

After you have mapped your interview subjects, look for clusters of subjects that occur across multiple ranges or variables. A set of subjects who cluster in six to eight different variables will likely represent a significant **behavior pattern** that will form the basis of a persona. Some specialized roles may exhibit only one significant pattern, but typically you will find two or even three such patterns.

For a pattern to be valid there must be a logical or causative connection between the clustered behaviors, not just a spurious correlation. For example, there is clearly a logical connection if data shows that people who regularly purchase CDs also like to download MP3 files, but there is probably no logical connection if the data shows that interviewees who frequently purchase CDs online are also vegetarians.

Step 4: Synthesize characteristics and relevant goals

For each significant behavior pattern you identify, you must synthesize details from your data. Describe the potential use environment, typical workday (or other relevant context), current solutions and frustrations, and relevant relationships with others.

At this point, brief bullet points describing characteristics of the behavior are sufficient. Stick to observed behaviors as much as possible. A description or two that sharpens the personalities of your personas can help bring them to life. However, too much fictional, idiosyncratic biography is a distraction and makes your personas less credible. Remember that you are creating a design tool, not a character sketch for a novel. Only concrete data can support the design and business decisions your team will ultimately make.

One fictional detail at this stage *is* important: the personas' first and last names. The name should be evocative of the type of person the persona is, without tending toward caricature or stereotype. We use a baby name book as a reference tool in creating persona names. You can also, at this time, add in some demographic information such as age, geographic location, relative income (if appropriate), and job title. This information is primarily to help you visualize the persona better as you assemble the behavioral details. From this point on, you should refer to the persona by his or her name.

Synthesizing goals

Goals are the most critical detail to synthesize from your interviews and observations of behaviors. Goals are best derived from an analysis of the behavior patterns comprising each persona. By identifying the logical connections between each persona's behaviors, you can begin to infer the goals that lead to those behaviors. You can infer goals both by observing actions (what interview subjects in each persona cluster are trying to accomplish and why) and by analyzing subject responses to goal-oriented interview questions (see Chapter 4).

To be effective as design tools, goals must always directly relate, in some way, to the product being designed. Typically, the majority of useful goals for a persona are *end goals*. You can expect most personas to have three to five end goals associated with them. Life goals are most useful for personas of consumer-oriented products, but they can also make sense for enterprise personas in transient job roles. Zero or one life goal is appropriate for most personas. General experience goals such as "don't feel stupid" and "don't waste time" can be taken as implicit for almost any persona. Occasionally, a specific domain may dictate the need for more specific experience goals; zero to two experience goals is appropriate for most personas.

Persona relationships

It sometimes makes sense for the set of personas for a product to be part of the same family or corporation and to have interpersonal or social relationships with each other. The typical case, however, is for individual personas to be completely unrelated to each other and often from completely different geographic locations and social groups.

When considering whether it makes sense for personas to have business or social relationships, think about:

1. Whether you observed any behavioral variations in your interview subjects related to variations in company size, industry, or family/social dynamic. (In this case, you'll want to make sure that your persona set represents this diversity by being situated in at least a couple of different businesses or social settings.)

2. If it is critical to illustrate workflow or social interactions between coworkers or members of a family or social group.

If you create personas that work for the same company or have social relationships with each other, you might run into difficulties if you need to express a significant goal that doesn't belong with the preestablished relationship. While a single social relationship between your set of personas is easier to define than several different, unrelated social relationships between individual personas and minor players outside the persona set, it can be much better to put the initial effort into development of diverse personas than to risk the temptation of bending more diverse scenarios to fit a single social dynamic.

Step 5: Check for completeness and redundancy

At this point, your personas should be starting to come to life. You should check your mappings and personas' characteristics and goals to see if there are any important gaps that need filling. This again may point to the need to perform additional research directed at finding particular behaviors missing from your behavioral axes. You might also want to check your notes to see if there are any political personas that you need to add to satisfy stakeholder assumptions or requests.

If you find that two personas seem to vary only by demographics, you may choose to eliminate one of the redundant personas or tweak the characteristics of your personas to make them more distinct. Each persona must vary from all others in at least one significant behavior. If you've done a good job of mapping, this shouldn't be an issue.

By making sure that your persona set is complete and that each persona is meaningfully distinct, you ensure that your personas sufficiently represent the diversity of behaviors and needs in the real world, and that you have as compact a design target as possible, which reduces work when you begin designing interactions.

Step 6: Expand description of attributes and behaviors

Your list of bullet point characteristics and goals arrived at in Step 4 points to the essence of complex behaviors, but leaves much implied. Third-person narrative is far more powerful at conveying the persona's attitudes, needs, and problems to other team members. It also deepens the designer/authors' connection to the personas and their motivations.

A typical persona description should be a synthesis of the most important details observed during research, relevant to this persona. This becomes a very effective communication tool. Ideally, the majority of your user research findings should be contained in your persona description. This will be the manner in which your research directly informs design activities (as you will see in the upcoming chapters).

This narrative should be no longer than one or two pages of prose. The persona narrative does not need to contain every observed detail because, ideally, the designers also performed the research, and most people outside the design team do not require more detail than this.

The narrative must, by nature, contain some fictional situations, but as previously discussed, it is not a short story. The best narrative quickly introduces the persona in terms of his job or lifestyle, and briefly sketches a day in his life, including peeves, concerns, and interests that have direct bearing on the product. Details should be an expansion of your list of characteristics, with additional data derived from your observations and interviews. The narrative should express what the persona is looking for in the product by way of a conclusion.

Be careful about the precision of detail in your descriptions. The detail should not exceed the depth of your research. In scientific disciplines, if you record a measurement of 35.421 meters, this implies that your measurements are accurate to .001 meters. A detailed persona description implies a similar level of observation in your research.

When you start developing your narrative, choose photographs of your personas. Photographs make them feel more real as you create the narrative and engage others on the team when you are finished. You should take great care in choosing a photograph. The best photos capture demographic information, hint at the environment (a persona for a nurse should be wearing a nurse's uniform and be in a clinical setting, perhaps with a patient), and capture the persona's general attitude (a photo for a clerk overwhelmed by paperwork might look harried). The authors keep several searchable databanks of stock photography available for finding the right persona pictures.

We have also found it useful to create photographic collages for each persona to convey more emotional and experiential forces that drive the persona (see Figure 5-5). Numerous small images juxtaposed have the potential to convey things that are difficult to describe in words. There are also times that we find it useful to create models of the personas' environments (for example, in the form of a floorplan). Again, this helps to make these environmental considerations more tangible.

When creating such communication aides, it's important to remember that personas are design and decision-making tools, not an end in themselves. While there can be a lot of power in creating a holistic image of a persona, too much embellishment and theatre can run the risk of making personas seem a fluffy waste of time. This can ultimately reduce their usefulness as user models.

Figure 5-5 Collages such as this, combined with carefully written narratives, are an effective way to convey the emotional and experiential aspects of a persona.

Step 7: Designate persona types

By now, your personas should feel very much like a set of real people whom you know. The final step in persona construction finishes the process of turning your qualitative research into a powerful set of design tools.

Design requires a target — the audience upon whom the design is focused. Typically, the more specific the target, the better. Trying to create a design solution that simultaneously serves the needs of even three or four personas can be quite an overwhelming task.

What we then must do is *prioritize* our personas to determine which should be the primary design target. The goal is to find a single persona from the set whose needs and goals can be completely and happily satisfied by a single interface without disenfranchising any of the other personas. We accomplish this through a process of designating **persona types**. There are six types of persona, and they are typically designated in roughly the order listed here:

- ▶ Primary
- ▶ Secondary
- ▶ Supplemental
- ▶ Customer
- ▶ Served
- ▶ Negative

We discuss each of these persona types and their significance from a design perspective in the following sections.

Primary personas

Primary personas represent the primary target for the design of an interface. There can be only one primary persona per *interface* for a product, but it is possible for some products (especially enterprise products) to have multiple distinct interfaces, each targeted at a distinct primary persona. For example, a health-care information system might have separate clinical and financial interfaces, each targeted at a different persona. It should be noted that we use the term *interface* in an abstract sense here. In some cases, two separate interfaces might be two separate applications that act on the same data; in other cases, the two interfaces might simply be two different sets of functionality served to two different users based upon their role or customization.

A primary persona will not be satisfied by a design targeted at any other persona in the set. However, if the primary persona is the target, all other personas will not, at least, be dissatisfied. (As you'll see below, we will then figure out how to satisfy these other personas without disturbing the primary.)

 DESIGN principle   Focus the design for each interface on a single primary persona.

Choosing the primary persona is a process of elimination: Each persona must be tested by comparing the goals of that persona against goals of the others. If no clear primary persona is evident, it could mean one of two things: Either the product needs multiple interfaces, each with a suitable primary persona (often the case for enterprise and technical products), or the product is trying to accomplish too much. If a consumer product has multiple primary personas, the scope of the product may be too broad.

Secondary personas

A **secondary persona** is mostly satisfied with the primary persona's interface but has specific additional needs that can be accommodated without upsetting the product's ability to serve the primary persona. We do not always have a secondary persona, and more than three or four secondary personas can be a sign that the proposed product's scope may be too large and unfocused. As you work through solutions, your approach should be to first design for the primary, and then adjust the design to accommodate the secondary.

Supplemental personas

User personas that are not primary or secondary are **supplemental personas**. Their needs are completely represented by a combination of primary and secondary personas and are completely satisfied by the solution we devise for one of our primaries. There can be any number of supplemental personas associated with an interface. Often political personas — the ones added to the cast to address stakeholder assumptions — become supplemental personas.

Customer personas

Customer personas address the needs of customers, not end users, as discussed earlier in this chapter. Typically, customer personas are treated like secondary personas. However, in some enterprise environments, some customer personas may be primary personas for their own administrative interface.

Served personas

Served personas are somewhat different from the persona types already discussed. They are not users of the product at all; however, they are *directly affected by the use of the product*. A patient being treated by a radiation therapy machine is not a user of the machine's interface, but she is very much *served* by a good interface. Served personas provide a way to track second-order social and physical ramifications of products. These are treated like secondary personas.

Negative personas

Negative personas are used to communicate to stakeholders and product team members that there are specific types of users that the product is *not* being built to serve. Like served personas, they aren't users of the product. Their use is purely rhetorical: to help communicate to other members of the team that a persona should definitely *not* be the design target for the product. Good candidates for negative personas are often technology-savvy early adopter personas for consumer products and IT specialists for business-user enterprise products.

Other Models

Personas are extremely useful tools, but they are certainly not the only tool to help model users and their environment. Holtzblatt and Beyer's *Contextual Design* provides a wealth of information on the models briefly discussed here.

Workflow models

Workflow or **sequence models** are useful for capturing information flow and decision-making processes inside organizations and are usually expressed as flow charts or directed graphs that capture several phenomena:

- ▸ The goal or desired outcome of a process
- ▸ The frequency and importance of the process and each action
- ▸ What initiates or prompts the execution of the process and each action
- ▸ Dependencies — what must be in place to perform the process and each action, as well as what is dependent on the completion of the process and each action
- ▸ People who are involved and their roles and responsibilities
- ▸ Specific actions that are performed
- ▸ Decisions that are made

- ▶ Information that is used to support decisions
- ▶ What goes wrong — errors and exception cases
- ▶ How errors and exceptions are corrected

A well-developed persona should capture individual workflows, but workflow models are still necessary for capturing interpersonal and organizational workflows. Interaction design based primarily on workflow often fails in the same way as "implementation model" software whose interaction is based primarily on its internal technical structure. Because workflow is to business what structure is to programming, workflow-based design typically yields a kind of "business implementation model" that captures all of the functionality but little of the humanity.

Artifact models

Artifact models represent, as the name suggests, different artifacts that users employ in their tasks and workflows. Often these artifacts are online or paper forms. Artifact models typically capture commonalities and significant differences between similar artifacts for the purpose of extracting and replicating best practices in the eventual design. Artifact models can be useful later in the design process, with the caveat that direct translation of paper systems to digital systems, without a careful analysis of goals and application of design principles (especially those found in Part II of this book), usually leads to usability issues.

Physical models

Physical models, like artifact models, endeavor to capture elements of the user's environment. Physical models focus on capturing the layout of physical objects that comprise the user's workspace, which can provide insight into frequency of use issues and physical barriers to productivity. Good persona descriptions will incorporate some of this information, but it may be helpful in complex physical environments (such as hospital floors and assembly lines) to create discrete, detailed physical models (maps or floorplans) of the user environment.

Personas and other models make sense out of otherwise overwhelming and confusing user data. Now that you are empowered with sophisticated models as design tools, the next chapter will show you how to employ these tools to translate user goals and needs into workable design solutions.

Notes

1. Cooper, 1999
2. Constantine and Lockwood, 2002
3. Grudin and Pruitt, 2002
4. Mikkelson, N., and Lee, W. O., 2000
5. Grudin and Pruitt, 2002
6. Grudin and Pruitt, 2002
7. Constantine and Lockwood, 1999
8. Beyer and Holtzblatt, 1998
9. Dillon, 2001
10. Goodwin, 2001
11. Goodwin, 2002, 2002a

6

The Foundations of Design: Scenarios and Requirements

In the two previous chapters, we talked about how to gather qualitative information about users and create models using that information. Through careful analysis of user research and synthesis of personas and other user models, we create a clear picture of our users and their respective goals. This brings us, then, to the crux of the whole method: how we use this understanding of people to create design solutions that satisfy and inspire users, while simultaneously addressing business goals and technical constraints.

This chapter describes the first part of a process for bridging the research-design gap. It employs personas as the main characters in a set of techniques that rapidly arrive at design solutions in an iterative, repeatable, and testable fashion. This process has four major activities: developing stories or *scenarios* as a means of imagining ideal user interactions, using those scenarios to define *requirements*, using these requirements in turn to define the fundamental *interaction framework* for the product, and filling in the framework with ever-increasing amounts of design detail. The glue that holds the processes together is *narrative*: using personas to create stories that point to design.

Scenarios: Narrative as a Design Tool

Narrative, or storytelling, is one of the oldest human activities. Much has been written about the power of narrative to *communicate* ideas. However, narrative is also one of our most powerful creative methods. From a very young age, we are accustomed to using stories to think about possibilities, and this is an incredibly effective way to *imagine* a new and better future for our users. Imagining a story about a person using our product leverages our creativity to a greater power than when we just imagine a better form factor or configuration of screen elements. Further, because of the intrinsically social aspect of narrative, it is a very effective and compelling way to share good ideas among team members and stakeholders. Ultimately, experiences designed around narrative tend to be more comprehensible and engaging for users because they are structured around a story.

Evidence of the effectiveness of narrative as a design tool is all around us. The famous Disney Imagineers would be lost without the modern-day myths they use as the foundation for the experiences they build. Much has been written about this idea: Brenda Laurel explored the concept of structuring interaction around dramatic principles in her 1991 book *Computers as Theater*, where she urges us to "...focus on designing the action. The design of objects, environments, and characters is all subsidiary to this central goal."[1] John Rheinfrank and Shelley Evenson also talk about the power of "stories of the future" for developing conceptually complex interactive systems,[2] and John Carroll has created a substantial body of work about scenario-based design, which we discuss later in this chapter.

Narrative also lends itself to effective visual depictions of interactive products. Because interaction design is first and foremost the design of behavior that occurs over time, a narrative structure, combined with the support of fast and flexible visualization tools (such as the humble whiteboard), is perfectly suited for motivating, envisioning, representing, and validating interaction concepts.

Interaction design narratives are quite similar to the comic-book-like sequences called storyboards that are used in the motion picture industry. They share two significant characteristics: plot and brevity. Just as storyboards breathe life into a movie script, design solutions should be created and rendered to follow a plot — a story. Putting too much detail into the storyboards simply wastes time and money and has a tendency to tie us to suboptimal ideas simply because drawing them consumes significant resources.

In the initial requirements definition phase we are free to focus only on the "plot points," allowing us to be fluid as we explore design concepts. Because they are enough to convey the action and the potential experience, many millions of Hollywood dollars have been invested on the basis of simple pencil sketches or line drawings. By focusing on the narrative, we are able to quickly and flexibly arrive at a high-level design solution without getting bogged-down by the inertia and expense inherent to high-production-value renderings (though such renderings are certainly appropriate once a working design framework is in place).

Scenarios in design

In the 1990s, substantial work was done by the HCI (Human-Computer Interaction) community around the idea of use-oriented software design. From this work came the concept of the **scenario**, commonly used to describe a method of *design problem solving by concretization*: making use of a specific story to both construct and illustrate design solutions. These concepts are discussed by John Carroll, in his book, *Making Use*:

> *Scenarios are paradoxically concrete but rough, tangible but flexible . . . they implicitly encourage "what-if?" thinking among all parties. They permit the articulation of design possibilities without undermining innovation . . . Scenarios compel attention to the use that will be made of the design product. They can describe situations at many levels of detail, for many different purposes, helping to coordinate various aspects of the design project.[3]*

Carroll's use of **scenario-based design** focuses on describing how *users accomplish tasks*. It consists of an environmental *setting* and includes *agents* or *actors* that are abstracted stand-ins for users, with role-based names such as Accountant or Programmer.

Although Carroll certainly understands the power and importance of scenarios in the design process, we've found two shortcomings with scenarios as Carroll approaches them:

▶ Carroll's concept of the actor as an abstracted, role-oriented model is not sufficiently concrete to provide understanding of or empathy with users. It is impossible to design appropriate behaviors for a system without understanding the users of the system in specific detail.

▶ Carroll's scenarios jump too quickly to the elaboration of tasks without considering the user's goals and motivations that drive and filter these tasks. Although Carroll does briefly discuss goals, he refers only to *goals of the scenario*. These goals are circularly defined as the completion of specific tasks. In our experience, user goals must be considered before user tasks can be identified and prioritized. Without addressing the motivation of human behavior, high-level product definition can be difficult and misguided.

The missing ingredient in Carroll's scenario-based design methods is the use of personas. A persona provides a tangible representation of the user to act as a believable agent in the setting of a scenario. In addition to reflecting current behavior patterns and motivations, personas enable the exploration of how user motivations should inflect and prioritize tasks in the future. Because personas model *goals* and not simply tasks, the scope of the problems addressed by scenarios can be broadened to include those related to product definition. They help answer the questions, "What should this product *do*?" and "How should this product look and behave?"

Using personas in scenarios

Persona-based scenarios are concise narrative descriptions of one or more personas using a product to achieve specific goals. They allow us to start our designs from a story describing an ideal experience from the persona's perspective, focusing on people, and how they think and behave, rather than on technology or business goals.

Scenarios can capture the *nonverbal dialogue*[4] between the user and a product, environment, or system over time, as well as the structure and behavior of interactive functions. Goals serve as a filter for tasks and as guides for structuring the display of information and controls during the iterative process of constructing the scenarios.

Scenario content and context are derived from information gathered during the Research phase and analyzed during the Modeling phase. Designers role-play personas as the characters in these scenarios,[5] similar to actors performing improvisation. This process leads to real-time synthesis of structure and behavior — typically, at a whiteboard — and later informs the detailed look-and-feel. Finally, personas and scenarios are used to test the validity of design ideas and assumptions throughout the process.

Different types of scenarios

The Goal-Directed Design method employs three types of persona-based scenarios at different points in the process, each with a successively more interface-specific focus. The first — the **context scenario** — is used to explore, at a high level, how the product can best serve the needs of the personas. (We used to call these "day-in-the-life scenarios," but found that term excessively broad.) The context scenarios are created before any design is performed and are written from the perspective of the persona, focused on human activities, perceptions, and desires. It is in the development of this kind of scenario that the designer has the most leverage to imagine an ideal user experience. More detail about the creation of this type of scenario can be found later in this chapter, under Step 4 in the Requirements Definition process.

Once the design team has defined the product's functional and data elements, and developed a Design Framework (as described in Chapter 7), a context scenario is revised to become a **key path scenario** by more specifically describing user interactions with the product and by introducing the vocabulary of the design. These scenarios focus on the most significant user interactions, always maintaining attention on how a persona uses the product to achieve their goals. Key path scenarios are iteratively refined along with the design as more and more detail is developed.

Throughout this process, the design team uses **validation scenarios** to test the design solution in a variety of situations. These scenarios tend to be less detailed and typically take the form of a number of "what if . . ." questions about the proposed solutions. More detail about development and use of key path and validation scenarios can be found in Chapter 7.

Persona-based scenarios versus use cases

Scenarios and use cases are both methods of describing a user's interaction with a system. However, they serve very different functions. Goal-Directed scenarios are an iterative means of defining the *behavior* of a product from the standpoint of specific users (personas). This includes not only the functionality of the system, but the priority of functions and the way those functions are expressed in terms of what the user sees and how she interacts with the system.

Use cases, on the other hand, are a technique based on exhaustive descriptions of functional requirements of the system, often of a transactional nature, focusing on low-level user action and accompanying system response.[6] The precise *behavior* of the system — precisely *how* the system responds — is not typically part of a conventional or *concrete* use case; many assumptions about the form and behavior of the system to be designed remain implicit.[7] Use cases permit a complete cataloguing of user tasks for different classes of users but say little or nothing about how these tasks are presented to the user or how they should be prioritized in the interface. In our experience, the biggest shortcoming of traditional use cases as a basis for interaction design is their tendency to treat all possible user interactions as equally likely and important. This is indicative of their origin in software engineering rather than interaction design. They may be useful in identifying edge cases and for determining that a product is functionally complete, but they should be deployed only in the later stages of design validation.

Requirements: The "What" of Interaction Design

The Requirements Definition phase determines the *what* of the design: what information and capabilities our personas require to accomplish their goals. It is absolutely critical to define and agree upon the *what* before we move on to the next question: *how* the product looks, behaves, operates, and feels. Conflating these two questions can be one of the biggest pitfalls in the design of an interactive product. Many designers are tempted to jump right into active design and render possible solutions. Regardless of how creative and skillful you are, we urge you not to do this. It runs the risk of turning into a never-ending circle of iteration; proposing a solution without clearly defining and agreeing upon the problem leaves you without a clear method of evaluating the fitness of the design. In lieu of such a method, you, your stakeholders, and your clients are likely to resort to taste and gut instinct, which have a notoriously low success ratio with something as complex as an interactive product.

DESIGN principle   Define *what* the product will do before you design *how* the product will do it.

It's important to note that our concept of a "requirement" here is much different from the way the term is commonly misused in the industry. In many product-development organizations, "requirement" has come to be synonymous with "feature" or "function." While there is clearly a relationship between requirements and functions (which we leverage as a key part of our design process, as you will see in the next chapter), we suggest that you think of requirements as synonymous with *needs*. Put another way, at this point, you want to rigorously define the human and business needs that your product must satisfy.

Another critical reason not to conflate requirements with features is that in figuring out the best way to meet a particular human need, an interaction designer has an extraordinary amount of leverage to create a powerful and compelling product. Think, for example, about designing a data analytics tool to help an executive better understand the state of his business. If you jump right to the *how* without understanding the *what*, you might assume that the output of the tool should be reports. It would be easy to come to this conclusion; if you went out and performed user research, you probably would have noticed that reports are a very widespread and accepted solution. However, if you imagine some scenarios and analyze your users' actual requirements, you might realize that your executive actually needs a way to recognize exceptional situations before opportunities are missed or problems arise, as well a way to understand emerging trends in the data. From here, it isn't difficult to see that static, flat reports are hardly the best way to meet these needs. With such a solution, your executive has to do the hard work of scrutinizing several of these reports to find the significant data underlying such exceptions and trends. Much better solutions might include data-driven exception reporting or real-time trend monitors.

A final reason to separate problem and solution is that such an approach provides the maximum flexibility in the changing face of technological constraints and opportunities. By clearly defining the user need, designers can then work with technologists to find the best solutions, without compromising the product's ability to help people achieve their goals. Working in this manner, the product definition is not at risk when the implementation runs into problems, and it becomes possible to plan long-term technology development so that it can provide increasingly sophisticated ways of meeting user needs.

As we've mentioned briefly, these requirements come from several sources. Personas' previous experiences and mental models often result in some baseline expectations of the product. We derive the bulk of the user requirements from analyzing ideal usage scenarios, and understand business and technical requirements from our stakeholder interviews. Our Goal-Directed process for defining product requirements is described below.

Requirements Definition Using Personas and Scenarios

As discussed briefly in Chapter 1, the translation from robust models to design solutions really consists of two major phases: **Requirements Definition** answers the broad questions about what a product is and what it should do, and **Framework Definition** answers questions about how a product behaves and how it is structured to meet user goals. In this section, we'll discuss Requirements Definition in detail, followed by a discussion of the Framework Definition in Chapter 7. The methods described are based upon the persona-based scenario methodology developed at Cooper by Robert Reimann, Kim Goodwin, Dave Cronin, Wayne Greenwood, and Lane Halley.

The Requirements Definition process comprises the following five steps (which are described in detail in the remainder of this chapter):

1. Creating problem and vision statements

2. Brainstorming

3. Identifying persona expectations

4. Constructing context scenarios

5. Identifying requirements

Although these steps proceed in roughly chronological order, they represent an iterative process. Designers can expect to cycle through Steps 3 through 5 several times until the requirements are stable. This is a necessary part of the process and shouldn't be short-circuited. A detailed description of each of these steps follows.

Step 1: Creating problem and vision statements

Before beginning the process of ideation, it's important for designers to have a clear mandate for moving forward. While the Goal-Directed method aims to comprehensively define the product through personas, scenarios, and requirements, it is often useful at this point to define what direction these scenarios and requirements should be headed in. At this point in the process, we already have a sense of which users we're targeting and what their goals are, but lacking a clear product mandate, there is still room for considerable confusion. Problem and vision statements provide just such a mandate and are extremely helpful in building consensus among stakeholders before the design process moves forward.

At a high level, the **problem statement** defines the purpose of the design initiative.[8] A design problem statement should concisely reflect a situation that needs changing, for both the personas *and* for the business providing the product to the personas. Often a cause-and-effect relationship exists between business concerns and persona concerns. For example:

> Company X's customer satisfaction ratings are low and market share has diminished by 10% over the past year because users don't have adequate tools to perform X, Y, and Z tasks that would help them meet their goal of G.

The connection of business issues to usability issues is critical to drive stakeholders' buy-in to design efforts and to frame the design effort in terms of both user and business goals.

The **vision statement** is an inversion of the problem statement that serves as a high-level design objective or mandate. In the vision statement, you lead with the user's needs, and you transition from those to how business goals are met by the design vision:

> *The new design of Product X will help users achieve G by giving them the ability to perform X, Y, and Z with greater [accuracy, efficiency, and so on], and without problems A, B, C that they currently experience. This will dramatically improve Company X's customer satisfaction ratings and lead to increased market share.*

The content of both the problem and vision statements should come directly from research and user models. User goals and needs should derive from the primary and secondary personas, and business goals should be extracted from stakeholder interviews.

Problem and vision statements are useful both when you are redesigning an existing product and for new technology products or products being designed for unexplored market niches, when formulating user goals and frustrations into problem and vision statements helps to establish team consensus and attention on the priorities of design activity to follow.

Step 2: Brainstorming

At the early stage of Requirements Definition, brainstorming assumes a somewhat ironic purpose. At this point in the project, we have been researching and modeling users and the domain for days or even months, and it is almost impossible to avoid having developed some preconceptions about what the solution looks like. However, we'd ideally like to create context scenarios without these prejudgments, and instead really focus on how our personas would likely want to engage with the product. The reason we brainstorm at this point in the process is to get these ideas out of our heads so that we can record them and thereby "let them go" for the time being.

The primary purpose here is to eliminate as much preconception as possible, allowing designers to be open-minded and flexible as they use their imagination to construct scenarios, and use their analytic minds to derive requirements from these scenarios. A side benefit of brainstorming at this point in the process is to switch your brain into "solution mode." Much of the work performed in the Research and Modeling phases is analytical in nature, and it takes a different mindset to come up with inventive designs.

Brainstorming should be unconstrained and uncritical — put all the wacky ideas you've been considering (plus some you haven't) out on the table and then be prepared to record them and file them away for safekeeping until much later in the process. It's not necessarily likely any of them will be useful in the end, but there might be the germ of something wonderful that will fit into the design framework you later create. Karen Holtzblatt and Hugh Beyer describe a facilitated method for brainstorming that can be useful for getting a brainstorming session started, especially if your team includes nondesigners. [9]

Don't spend too much time on the brainstorming step; a few hours should be more than sufficient for you and your teammates to get all those crazy ideas out of your systems. If you find your ideas getting repetitious, or the popcorn stops popping, that's a good time to stop.

Step 3: Identifying persona expectations

As we discussed in Chapter 2, a person's **mental model** is their own internal representation of reality — the way they think about or explain something to themselves. Mental models are deeply ingrained and are often the result of a lifetime of experience. People's expectations about a product and the way it works are highly informed by their mental model.

Returning to our discussion in Chapter 2, it's absolutely critical that the **represented model** of the interface — how the design behaves and presents itself — should match the user's mental model as closely as possible, rather than reflecting the implementation model of how the product is actually constructed internally.

In order to accomplish this, we must formally record these expectations. They will be an important source of requirements. For each primary and secondary persona, you must identify:

- ▶ Attitudes, experiences, aspirations, and other social, cultural, environmental, and cognitive factors that influence the persona's expectations
- ▶ General expectations and desires the persona may have about the experience of using the product
- ▶ Behaviors the persona will expect or desire from the product
- ▶ How that persona thinks about basic elements or units of data (for example, in an e-mail application, the basic elements of data might be messages and people)

Your persona descriptions may contain enough information to answer these questions directly; however, your research data will remain a rich resource. Use it to analyze how interview subjects define and describe objects and actions that are part of their usage patterns, along with the language and grammar they use. Some things to look for include:

- ▶ What do the subjects mention first?

- ▶ Which action words (verbs) do they use?

- ▶ Which intermediate steps, tasks, or objects in a process *don't* they mention? (Hint: These might not be terribly important to the way they think about things.)

Step 4: Constructing context scenarios

While all scenarios are stories about people and their activities, context scenarios are the most storylike of the three types we employ. The focus is on the persona's activities, as well as her motivations and mental model. **Context scenarios** describe the broad context in which usage patterns are exhibited and include environmental and organizational (in the case of enterprise systems) considerations. [10]

As we discussed above, *this is where design begins.* As you develop context scenarios, you should be focusing on how the product you are designing can best help your personas achieve their goals. Context scenarios establish the primary touch points that each primary and secondary persona has with the system (and possibly with other personas) over the course of a day or some other meaningful length of time.

Context scenarios should be broad and relatively shallow in scope. They should not describe product or interaction detail but rather should focus on high-level actions from the user's perspective. It is important to map out the big picture first so that we can systematically identify user requirements. Only then will we be able to design appropriate interactions and interfaces.

Context scenarios address questions such as the following:

- ▶ In what setting(s) will the product be used?

- ▶ Will it be used for extended amounts of time?

- ▶ Is the persona frequently interrupted?

- ▶ Are there multiple users on a single workstation or device?

- ▶ With what other products will it be used?

- ▶ What primary activities does the persona need to perform to meet her goals?

- ▶ What is the expected end result of using the product?

- ▶ How much complexity is permissible, based on persona skill and frequency of use?

Context scenarios should *not* represent system behaviors as they currently are. These scenarios represent the brave new world of Goal-Directed products, so, especially in the initial phases, focus on the goals. Don't yet worry about exactly *how* things will get accomplished — you should initially treat the design as a bit of a magic black box.

In most cases, more than one context scenario is necessary. This is true especially when there are multiple primary personas, but sometimes even a single primary persona may have two or more distinct contexts of use.

Context scenarios are also entirely *textual*. We are not yet discussing form, only the behaviors of the user and the system. This discussion is best accomplished as a textual narrative.

An example context scenario

The following is an example of a first iteration of a context scenario for a primary persona for a personal digital assistant (PDA) type phone, including both the device and its service. Our persona is Vivien Strong, a real-estate agent in Indianapolis, whose goals are to balance work and home life, close the deal, and make each client feel like he is her *only* client.

Vivien's context scenario:

1. While getting ready in the morning, Vivien uses her phone to check her e-mail. It has a large enough screen and quick connection time so that it's more convenient than booting up a computer as she rushes to make her daughter, Alice, a sandwich for school.

2. Vivien sees an e-mail from her newest client, Frank, who wants to see a house this afternoon. The device has his contact info, so now she can call him with a simple action right from the e-mail.

3. While on the phone with Frank, Vivien switches to speakerphone so she can look at the screen while talking. She looks at her appointments to see when she's free. When she creates a new appointment, the phone automatically makes it an appointment with Frank, because it knows with whom she is talking. She quickly enters the address of the property into the appointment as she finishes her conversation.

4. After sending Alice off to school, Vivien heads into the real-estate office to gather some papers for another appointment. Her phone has already updated her Outlook appointments, so the rest of the office knows where she'll be in the afternoon.

5. The day goes by quickly, and she's running a bit late. As she heads towards the property she'll be showing Frank, the phone alerts her that her appointment is in

15 minutes. When she flips open the phone, it shows not only the appointment, but a list of all documents related to Frank, including e-mails, memos, phone messages, and call logs to Frank's number. Vivien presses the call button, and the phone automatically connects to Frank because it knows her appointment with him is soon. She lets him know she'll be there in 20 minutes.

6. Vivien knows the address of the property but is a bit unsure exactly where it is. She pulls over and taps the address she put into the appointment. The phone downloads directions along with a thumbnail map showing her location relative to the destination.

7. Vivien gets to the property on time and starts showing it to Frank. She hears the phone ring from her purse. Normally while she is in an appointment, the phone will automatically transfer directly to voicemail, but Alice has a code she can press to get through. The phone knows it's Alice calling, and uses a distinctive ring tone.

8. Vivien takes the call — Alice missed the bus and needs a pickup. Vivien calls her husband to see if he can do it. She gets his voicemail; he must be out of service range. She tells him she's with a client and asks if he can get Alice. Five minutes later the phone makes a brief tone Vivien recognizes as her husband's; she sees he's sent her an instant message: "I'll get Alice; good luck on the deal!"

Notice how the scenario remains at a fairly high level, without getting too specific about interfaces or technologies. It's important to create scenarios that are within the realm of technical possibility, but at this stage the details of reality aren't yet important. We want to leave the door open for truly novel solutions, and it's always possible to scale back; we are ultimately trying to describe an *optimal*, yet still feasible, experience. Also notice how the activities in the scenario tie back to Vivien's goals and try to strip out as many tasks as possible.

Pretending it's magic

A powerful tool in the early stages of developing scenarios is to *pretend the interface is magic*. If your persona has goals and the product has magical powers to meet them, how simple could the interaction be? This kind of thinking is useful to help designers look outside the box. Magical solutions obviously won't suffice, but figuring out creative ways to technically accomplish interactions that are as close to magical solutions as possible (from the personas' perspective) is the essence of great interaction design. Products that meet goals with the minimum of hassle and intrusion seem almost magical to users. Some of the interactions in the preceding scenario may seem a bit magical, but all are possible with technology available today. It's the goal-directed behavior, not the technology alone, that provides the magic.

DESIGN principle   In early stages of design, pretend the interface is magic.

Step 5: Identifying requirements

After you are satisfied with an initial draft of your context scenario, you can analyze it to extract the personas' needs or requirements. These **requirements** can be thought of as consisting of *objects*, *actions*, and *contexts*.[11] And remember, as we discuss above, we prefer not to think of requirements as identical to features or tasks. Thus, a need from the scenario above might be:

Call (action) a person (object) directly from an appointment (context).

If you are comfortable extracting needs in this format, it works quite well; otherwise, you may find it helpful to separate them into data, functional, and contextual requirements, as described in the following sections.

Data requirements

Personas' data needs are the objects and information that must be represented in the system. Using the semantics described above, it is often useful to think of data requirements as the objects and adjectives related to those objects. Common examples include accounts, people, documents, messages, songs, images, as well as attributes of those such as status, dates, size, creator, subject, and so on.

Functional requirements

Functional needs are the operations or actions that need to be performed on the objects of the system and which are typically translated into interface controls. These can be thought of as the *actions* of the product. Functional needs also define places or containers where objects or information in the interface must be displayed. (These are clearly not actions in and of themselves but are usually suggested by actions.)

Other requirements

After you've gone through the exercise of pretending it's magic, it's important to get a firm idea of the realistic requirements of the business and technology you are designing for (although we hope that designers have some influence over technology choices when it directly affects user goals).

▶ **Business requirements** can include development timelines, regulations, pricing structures, and business models.

► **Brand and experience requirements** reflect attributes of the experience you would like users and customers to associate with your product, company, or organization.

► **Technical requirements** can include weight, size, form factor, display, power constraints, and software platform choices.

► **Customer and partner requirements** can include ease of installation, maintenance, configuration, support costs, and licensing agreements.

Having performed these steps, you should now have a rough, creative overview of how the product is going to address user goals in the form of context scenarios, and a reductive list of needs and requirements extracted from your research, user models, and the scenarios. Now you are ready to delve deeper into the details of your product's behaviors, and begin to consider how the product and its functions will be represented. You are ready to define the framework of the interaction.

Notes

1. Laurel, *Computers as Theater*, 134

2. Rheinfrank and Evenson, 1996

3. Carroll, 2001

4. Buxton, 1990

5. Verplank, et al, 1993

6. Wirfs-Brock, 1993

7. Constantine and Lockwood, 1999

8. Newman and Lamming, 1995

9. Holtzblatt and Beyer, 1998

10. Kuutti, 1995

11. Shneiderman, 1998

7

From Requirements to Design: The Framework and Refinement

In the previous chapter, we talked about the first part of the design process: developing **scenarios** to imagine ideal user interactions, and then defining **requirements** from these scenarios and other sources. Now we're ready to **design**.

The Design Framework

Rather than jump into the nuts and bolts right away, we want to stay at a high level and concern ourselves with the overall structure of the user interface and associated behaviors. We call this phase of the Goal-Directed process the Design Framework. If we were designing a house, at this point, we'd be concerned with what rooms the house should have, how they should be positioned with respect to each other, and roughly how big they should be. We would not be worried about the precise measurements of each room, or things like the doorknobs, faucets, and countertops.

The **Design Framework** defines the overall structure of the users' experience, from the arrangement of functional elements on the screen, to interactive behaviors and underlying organizing principles, to the visual and form language used to express data, concepts, functionality, and brand identity. In our experience, form and behavior must be designed in concert with each other; the Design Framework is made up of an interaction framework, a visual design framework, and sometimes an industrial design framework. At this phase in a project, interaction designers use scenarios and requirements to create rough sketches of screens and behaviors that make up the **interaction framework**. Concurrently, visual designers use visual language studies to develop a **visual design framework** that is commonly expressed as a detailed rendering of a single screen archetype, and industrial designers execute form language studies to work towards a rough physical model and **industrial design framework**. Each of these processes is addressed in this chapter.

When it comes to the design of complex behaviors and interactions, we've found that focusing on pixel-pushing, widget design, and specific interactions too early can get in the way of effectively designing a comprehensive framework that all of the product's behaviors can fit within. By taking a top-down approach, concerning ourselves first with the big picture and rendering our solutions without specific detail in a low-fidelity manner, we can ensure that we and our stakeholders stay initially focused on the fundamentals: serving the personas' goals and requirements.

Revision is a fact of life in design. Typically, the process of representing and presenting design solutions helps designers and stakeholders refine their vision and understanding of how the product can best serve human needs. The trick, then, is to render the solution only in enough detail to provoke engaged consideration, without spending too much time or effort creating renderings that are certain to be modified or abandoned. We've found that sketchlike storyboards, accompanied by narrative in the form of scenarios, are a highly effective way to explore and discuss design solutions without creating undue overhead and inertia.

Research about the usability of architectural renderings supports this notion. A study of people's reactions to different types of CAD images found that pencil-like sketches encouraged discourse about a proposed design, and also increased understanding of the renderings as representing work-in-progress.[1] Carolyn Snyder covers this concept at length in *Paper Prototyping*, where she discusses the value of such low-fidelity presentation techniques in gathering user feedback. While we believe that usability testing and user feedback is often most constructive during design refinement, there are certainly cases where it is useful as early as the Framework phase. (More discussion of usability testing can be found at the end of the chapter.)

Defining the interaction framework

The interaction framework defines not only the high-level structure of screen layouts but also the flow, behavior, and organization of the product. The following six steps describe the process of defining the interaction framework:

1. Define form factor, posture, and input methods

2. Define functional and data elements

3. Determine functional groups and hierarchy

4. Sketch the interaction framework

5. Construct key path scenarios

6. Check designs with validation scenarios

While we've broken the process down into numerically sequenced steps, this is not typically a linear effort, but rather occurs in iterative loops. In particular, Steps 3–5 may be swapped around, depending on the thinking style of the designer (more on this later). The six steps are described in the following sections.

Step 1: Define form factor, posture, and input methods

The first step in creating a framework is to define the **form factor** of the product you'll be designing. Is it a Web application that will be viewed on a high-resolution computer screen? Is it a phone that must be small, light, low-resolution, and visible in both the dark and bright sunlight? Is it a kiosk that must be rugged to withstand a public environment while accommodating thousands of distracted, novice users? What are the constraints that each of these imply for any design? Each of these form factors has clear implications for the design of the product, and answering this question sets the stage for all subsequent design efforts. If the answer isn't obvious, look to your personas and scenarios to better understand the ideal usage context and environment. Where a product requires the design of both hardware and software, these decisions also involve industrial design considerations. Later in the chapter we discuss how to coordinate interaction design with industrial design.

As you define the form, you should also define the basic **posture** of the product, and determine the **input method(s)** for the system. A product's posture is related to how much attention a user will devote to interacting with the product, and how the product's behaviors respond to the kind of attention a user will be devoting to it. This decision should be based upon usage contexts and environments as described in your context scenario(s) (see Chapter 6). We discuss the concept of posture in greater depth in Chapter 9.

The input method is the way users will interact with the product. This will be driven by the form factor and posture, as well as by your personas' attitudes, aptitudes, and preferences. Choices include keyboard, mouse, keypad, thumb-board, touch screen, voice, game controller, remote control, dedicated hardware buttons, and many other possibilities. Decide which combination is appropriate for your primary and secondary personas. In cases where it may be appropriate to use a combination of input methods (such as the common Web site or desktop application that relies on both mouse and keyboard input), decide upon the *primary* input method for the product.

Step 2: Define functional and data elements

Functional and data elements are the representations of functionality and data that are revealed to the user in the interface. These are the concrete manifestations of the functional and data requirements identified during the Requirements Definition phase. Where the requirements were purposely described in general terms, from the personas' perspective, functional and data elements are described in the language of user-interface representations. It is important to note that these elements must each be defined in response to specific requirements defined earlier. This is how we ensure that every aspect of the product we are designing has a clear purpose that can be traced back to a usage scenario or business goal.

Data elements are typically the fundamental subjects of interactive products. These objects, such as photos, e-mail messages, customer records, or orders, are the basic units to be referred to, responded to, and acted upon by the people using the product, and ideally should fit with the personas' mental models. At this point, it is critical to comprehensively catalog the data objects, because the product's functionality is commonly defined in relation to them. We are also concerned with the significant attributes of the objects (for example, the sender of an e-mail message or the date a photo was taken), but it is less important to be comprehensive about the attributes at this point, as long as you have an idea whether the personas care about a few attributes or a lot.

It's useful to consider the relationships between data elements. Sometimes a data object may contain other data objects; other times there may be a more associative relationship between objects. Examples of such relationships include a photo within an album, a song within a playlist, or an individual bill within a customer record.

Functional elements are the operations that can be done to the data elements and their representations in the interface. Generally speaking, they include tools to act upon data elements and places to put data elements. The translation of functional requirements into functional elements is where we start making the design concrete. While the context scenario is the vehicle to imagine the overall experience we will be creating for our users, this is where we make that experience real.

It is common that a single requirement will necessitate multiple interface elements. For example, Vivien, our persona for a smartphone from Chapter 6, needs to be able to telephone her contacts. Functional elements to meet that need include:

- Voice activation (voice data associated with contact)
- Assignable quick-dial buttons
- Selecting a contact from a list
- Selecting a contact from an e-mail header, appointment, or memo
- Auto-assignment of a call button in appropriate context (for example, upcoming appointment)

Again, it is imperative to return to context scenarios, persona goals, and mental models to ensure that your solutions are appropriate to the situation at hand. This is also the place in the process where design principles and patterns begin to become a useful way to arrive at effective solutions without reinventing the wheel. You also must exercise your creativity and design judgment here. In response to any identified user requirement, there are typically quite a number of possible solutions. Ask yourself which of the possible solutions is most likely to:

- Accomplish user goals most efficiently?
- Best fit our design principles?
- Fit within technology or cost parameters?
- Best fit other requirements?

Pretend the product is human

As you saw in Chapter 6, pretending a tool, product, or system is *magic* is a powerful way to imagine the ideal user experience to be reflected in concept-level context scenarios. In the same way, pretending the system is *human* is a powerful tool to structure interaction-level details. This simple principle is discussed in detail in Chapter 12. In a nutshell, interactions with a digital system should be similar in tone and helpfulness to interactions with a polite, considerate human.[2] As you determine the interactions and behavior along with the functional elements and groupings, you should ask yourself: What would a helpful human do? What would a thoughtful, considerate interaction feel like? Is the primary persona being treated humanely by the product? In what ways can the software offer helpful information without getting in the way? How can it minimize the persona's effort in reaching his goals?

For example, a mobile phone that behaves like a considerate person knows that, after you've completed a call with a number that isn't in your contacts, you may want to save the number, and provides an easy and obvious way to do so. An inconsiderate phone forces you to scribble the number on the back of your hand as you go into your contacts to create a new entry.

Apply principles and patterns

Critical to the translation of requirements to functional elements (as well as the grouping of these elements and the exploration of detailed behavior in scenarios and storyboards) is the application of general interaction principles and specific interaction patterns. These tools leverage years of interaction design experience. Neglecting to take advantage of such knowledge means wasting time on problems whose solutions are well known. Additionally, deviating from standard design patterns can create a product where the users must learn every interaction idiom from scratch, rather than recognizing behaviors from other products and leveraging their own experience (we discuss the idea of design patterns in Chapter 8). Of course, sometimes it is appropriate to invent new solutions to common problems, but as we discuss further in Chapter 14, you should obey standards unless you have a darn good reason not to.

Scenarios provide an inherently top-down approach to interaction design. They iterate through successively more detailed design structures, from main screens down to tiny subpanes or dialogs. Principles and patterns add a bottom-up approach to balance the process. Principles and patterns can be used to organize elements at all levels of the design. Chapter 8 discusses the uses and types of principles and patterns in detail, and the chapters of Parts II and III provide a wealth of useful interaction principles appropriate to this step in the process.

Step 3: Determine functional groups and hierarchy

After you have a good list of top-level functional and data elements, you can begin to group them into functional units and determine their hierarchy.[3] Because these elements facilitate specific tasks, the idea is to group elements to best facilitate the persona's flow (see Chapter 10) both within a task and between related tasks. Some issues to consider include:

- Which elements need a large amount of video real estate and which do not?
- Which elements are *containers* for other elements?
- How should containers be arranged to optimize flow?
- Which elements are used together and which aren't?
- In what sequence will a set of related elements be used?

► What interaction patterns and principles apply?

► How do the personas' mental models affect organization?

At this point it's important to organize data and functions into top-level container elements, such as screens, frames, and panes. These groupings may change somewhat as the design evolves (particularly as you sketch out the interface), but it's still useful to provisionally sort elements into groups as this will speed up the process of creating initial sketches.

Consider which primary screens or states (which we'll call **views**) the product requires. Initial context scenarios give you a feel for what these might be. If you know that a user has several end goals and needs where data and functionality don't overlap, it might be reasonable to define separate views to address them. On the other hand, if you see a cluster of related needs (for example, to make an appointment, your persona needs to see a calendar and contacts), you might consider defining a view that incorporates all these together.

When grouping functional and data elements, consider how they should be arranged given the product's platform, screen size, form factor, and input methods. Containers for objects that must be compared or used together should be adjacent to each other. Objects representing steps in a process should, in general, be adjacent and ordered sequentially. Use of interaction design principles and patterns is extremely helpful at this juncture; Part III of this book provides many principles that can be of assistance at this stage of organization.

Step 4: Sketch the interaction framework

Now we're ready to sketch the interface. This visualization of the interface should be extremely simple at first. Around the studio, we often refer to this as "the rectangles phase" because our sketches start out by subdividing each view into rough rectangular areas corresponding to panes, control components (such as toolbars), and other top-level containers (see Figure 7-1). Label the rectangles, and illustrate and describe how one grouping or element affects others.

You may want to sketch different ways of fitting top-level containers together in the interface. Sketching the framework is an iterative process that is best performed with a small, collaborative group of one or two interaction designers and a visual or industrial designer. This visualization of the interface should be extremely simple at first: boxes representing each functional group and/or container with names and descriptions of the relationships between the different areas (see Figure 7-1).

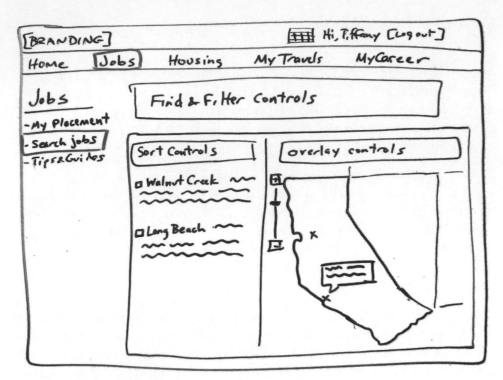

Figure 7-1 Example of an early framework sketch from designs Cooper created for Cross Country TravCorps, an online portal for traveling nurses. Framework sketches should be simple, starting with rectangles, names, and simple descriptions of relationships between functional areas. Details can be visually hinted at to give an idea of contents, but don't fall into the trap of designing detail at this stage.

Be sure to look at the entire, top-level framework first; don't let yourself get distracted by the details of a particular area of the interface (although *imagining* what goes into each container will help you decide how to arrange elements and allocate real estate). There will be plenty of time to explore the design at the widget level later; trying to do so too soon may risk a lack of coherence in the design as you move forward. At this high-level, "rectangle phase," it's very easy to explore a variety of ways of presenting information and functionality and to perform radical reorganizations, if necessary. It's often useful to try several arrangements on for size, running through validation scenarios (see Step 6, below), before landing on the best solution. Spending too much time and effort on intricate details early in the design process discourages designers from changing course to what might be a superior solution. It's easier to discard your work and try another approach when you don't have a lot of effort invested.

Sketching the framework is an iterative process that is best performed with a small, collaborative group of one or two interaction designers (or ideally an interaction designer and a "design communicator" — someone who thinks in terms of the narrative of the design) and a visual or industrial designer. We haven't found a better tool for initial sketches than a simple whiteboard. Working at a whiteboard promotes collaboration and discussion and, of course, everything is easy to erase and redraw. A digital camera provides a quick and easy means to capture ideas for later reference.

Once the sketches reach a reasonable level of detail, it becomes useful to start rendering in a computer-based tool. Each has its strengths and weaknesses, but tools commonly used to render high-level interface sketches include Adobe Fireworks, Adobe Illustrator, Microsoft Visio, Microsoft PowerPoint, and Omni Group's Omni-Graffle. The key here is to find the tool that is most comfortable for you, so you can work quickly, roughly, and at a high level. We've found it useful to render Framework illustrations in a visual style that suggests the sketchiness of the proposed solutions (recall that rough sketches tend to do a better job promoting discourse about design). It is also critical to be able to easily render several related, sequential screen states to depict the product's behavior in the key path scenario (the "Frames" construct in Fireworks makes it a particularly good tool for doing this).

Step 5: Construct key path scenarios

A **key path scenario** describes how the persona interacts with the product, using the vocabulary of the interaction framework. These scenarios depict the primary pathways through the interface that the persona takes with the greatest frequency, often on a daily basis. Their focus is at the task level. For example, in an e-mail application, key path activities include viewing and composing mail, not configuring a new mail server.

These scenarios typically evolve from the context scenarios, but here we specifically describe the persona's interaction with the various functional and data elements that make up the interaction framework. As we add more and more detail to the interaction framework, we iterate the key path scenarios to reflect this detail in greater specificity around user actions and product responses.

Unlike the goal-oriented context scenarios, key path scenarios are more task oriented, focusing on task details broadly described and hinted at in the context scenarios. This doesn't mean that we can ignore goals — goals and persona needs are the constant measuring stick throughout the design process, used to trim unnecessary tasks and streamline necessary ones. However, **key path scenarios** must describe in exacting detail the precise behavior of each major interaction and provide a walkthrough of each major pathway.

Storyboarding

By using a sequence of low-fidelity sketches accompanied by the narrative of the key path scenario, you can richly portray how a proposed design solution helps personas accomplish their goals. This technique of **storyboarding** is borrowed from filmmaking and cartooning, where a similar process is used to plan and evaluate ideas without having to deal with the cost and labor of shooting actual film. Each interaction between the user and the product can be portrayed on one or more frames or slides. Advancing through them provides a reality check for the coherence and flow of the interactions (see Figure 7-2).

Process variations and iteration

Because creative human activities are rarely a sequential, linear process, the steps in the Framework phase shouldn't be thought of as a simple sequence. It is common to move back and forth between steps and to iterate the whole process several times until you have a solid design solution. Depending on how you think, there are a couple different ways to approach Steps 3–5. You may find that one works better for you than another.

Figure 7-2 An example of a more evolved Framework rendering from the Cross Country TravCorps job search Web application.

Verbal thinkers may want to use the scenario to drive the process and approach Steps 3–5 in the following sequence (as described above):

1. Key path scenarios
2. Work out the groupings verbally
3. Sketch

Visual thinkers may find starting from the illustration will help them make sense of the other parts of the process. They may find this easier:

1. Sketch
2. Key path scenarios
3. See if your groupings work with the scenarios

Step 6: Check designs with validation scenarios

After you have storyboarded your key path scenarios and adjusted the interaction framework until the scenario flows smoothly and you're confident that you're headed in the right direction, it is time to shift focus to less frequent or less important interactions. These **validation scenarios** are not typically developed in as much detail as key path scenarios. Rather, this phase consists of asking a series of "what if . . ." questions. The goal here is to poke holes in the design and adjust it as needed (or throw it out and start over). There are three major categories of validation scenarios that should be addressed in the following order:

▶ **Key path variant scenarios** are alternate or less-traveled interactions that split off from key pathways at some point along the persona's decision tree. These could include commonly encountered exceptions, less frequently used tools and views, and variations or additional scenarios based upon the goals and needs of secondary personas. Returning to our smartphone scenario from Chapter 6, an example of a key path variant would be if Vivien decided to respond to Frank by e-mail in Step 2 instead of calling him.

▶ **Necessary use scenarios** include those actions that *must* be performed, but only infrequently. Purging databases, configuring, and making other exceptional requests might fall into this category. Necessary use interactions demand pedagogy because they are seldom encountered: Users may forget how to access the function or how to perform tasks related to it. However, this rare use means that users won't require parallel interaction idioms such as keyboard equivalents, nor do such functions need to be user-customizable. An example of a necessary use scenario for the design of a smartphone is if the phone was sold second-hand, requiring the removal of all personal information associated with the original owner.

▶ **Edge case use scenarios**, as the name implies, describe atypical situations that the product must nevertheless be able to handle, albeit infrequently. Programmers focus on edge cases because they often represent sources of system instability and bugs, and typically require significant attention and effort. Edge cases should never be the focus of the design effort. Designers can't ignore edge case functions and situations, but the interaction needed for them is of much lower priority and is usually buried deep in the interface. Although the *code* may succeed or fail on its capability to successfully handle edge cases, the *product* will succeed or fail on its capability to successfully handle daily use and necessary cases. Returning once again to Vivien's smartphone (in Chapter 6), an example of an edge case scenario would be if Vivien tried to add two different contacts with the same name. This is not something she is likely to want to do, but something the phone should handle if she does.

Defining the visual design framework

As the interaction framework establishes an overall structure for product behavior, and for *the form as it relates to behavior*, a parallel process focused on the visual and industrial design is also necessary to prepare for detailed design unless you're working with a well-established visual style. This process follows a similar trajectory to the interaction framework, in that the solution is first considered at a high level and then narrows to an increasingly granular focus.

The **visual design framework** typically follows this process:

1. Develop visual language studies
2. Apply chosen visual style to screen archetype

Step 1: Develop visual language studies

The first step in defining a visual design framework is to explore a variety of visual treatments through **visual language studies** (see Figure 7-3). These studies include color, type, and widget treatments, as well as the overall dimensionality and any "material" properties of the interface (for example, does it feel like glass or paper?).

These studies should show these aspects abstractly and independently of the interaction design, because our goal here is to assess the overall tone and suitability for general interactions, and we want to avoid running the risk of distracting our stakeholders with highly rendered versions of rough interaction designs.

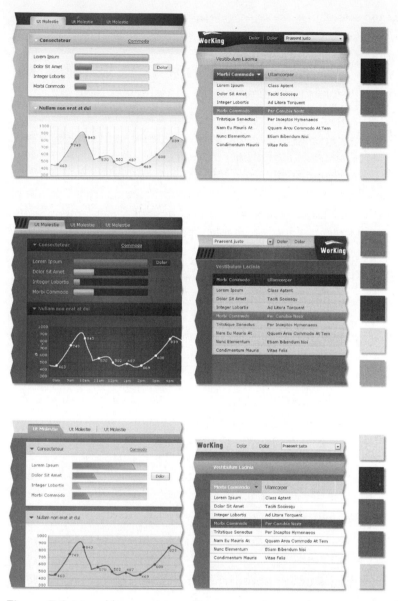

Figure 7-3 Visual language studies are used to explore a variety of visual styles abstractly and somewhat independently of the interaction design. This is useful because it allows us to have initial discussions about visual language without getting hung up on interaction design details. Of course, eventually visual design and interaction design must be conducted in lockstep.

Visual language studies should relate to the experience goals of the personas, as well as any experience or brand keywords that were developed in the Requirements Definition phase. Commonly, a company's brand guidelines form a good starting point for this activity, but it should be noted that brand guidelines rarely consider the interactive experience. "Brand guidelines" commonly consist of a document explaining how a company's brand identity should be visually and textually conveyed.

Substantial work is often required to translate a style guide for marketing collateral into a meaningful look-and-feel for an interactive product or Web site. It's also important to consider environmental factors and persona aptitudes when devising visual styles. Screens that must be visible under bright lights or from a distance require high contrast and more saturated colors. The elderly and other sight-impaired users require larger and more readable type faces.

We typically show between three and five different approaches during our initial review with stakeholders. This is a little different from our approach to interaction design, where there is usually one optimal behavioral framework for a product. Visually, there can be several different styles that are all consistent with experience keywords and goals. And of course, "beauty is in the eye of the beholder." We've found many stakeholders to have quite unpredictable taste for which colors should be used in the interface.

It is often useful to develop one or two extreme options that push the look-and-feel a bit too far in one direction. Doing this makes it easier to differentiate between the various approaches and helps stakeholders to decide upon an appropriate direction. There is ample opportunity later in the process to tame a particularly extreme visual style. That said, all the choices you present to your stakeholders should be reasonable and appropriate. It's almost an unwritten rule that if there's one direction that you don't want your client or stakeholders to choose, that's the one that they're guaranteed to like.

 DESIGN principle   Never show a design approach that you're not happy with; stakeholders just might like it.

Once you've developed a good spectrum of visual language studies reflecting persona experience goals and brand and experience keywords, it's time to present them to stakeholders for feedback. It's important to contextualize them in terms of these goals and keywords, and to describe the rationale for each direction and its relative merits. We ask stakeholders to first give us their initial emotional reaction and then talk through things in a more rational fashion. By the end of this presentation, we usually have consensus to move forward with some aspects of several of the visual styles, and it is common to iterate the visual language studies before moving forward to the next step.

Step 2: Apply the chosen visual style to the screen archetype

The next step is to apply one or two selected visual styles to key screens. We typically coordinate our visual and interaction design efforts so this step is performed close to the end of the interaction framework, when the design has begun to stabilize and there is sufficient specific detail to reflect the visual style. This further refines the visual style so that it reflects key behaviors and information. By making the design more concrete, you can better assess the feasibility of the proposed solution without the overhead of updating numerous screens for each minor change. Additionally, it's easier to elicit feedback from stakeholders.

Defining the industrial design framework

We develop the **industrial design framework** in much the same manner as the visual design framework, but because the form factor and input method have significant implications for both the industrial and interaction design, it's useful to collaborate early to identify relevant issues.

The industrial design framework typically follows this process:

1. Collaborate with interaction designers about form factor and input methods
2. Develop rough prototypes
3. Develop form language studies

Step 1: Collaborate with interaction designers about form factor and input methods

If the product you are designing relies upon custom hardware (as with a cell phone or medical device), it is important for interaction designers and industrial designers to agree upon a general physical form and input methods. While the course of the design framework will certainly help to refine the design, decisions should be made at this point about the general size and shape of the product, the screen size (if any), the number and general orientation of hard and soft buttons, and if it has a touch screen, keyboard, voice recognition, and so on. This collaboration typically starts with a couple of days at the whiteboard and a condensed set of scenarios.

Important things to consider when making these decisions include persona experience goals (refer to Chapter 5), attitudes, aptitudes, and environmental factors, as well as brand and experience keywords, market research, manufacturing costs, and pricing targets. Because the cost of a hinge can make or break the margin on hardware, and because internal components (such as a battery) can have a tremendous impact on form, an early sanity check with mechanical and electrical engineers is critical.

There is only one user experience, and it comes from the combination of the physical form and the interactive behavior of the product. The two must be designed in concert, and according to the old adage of Modern architecture: form should follow function. The demands of interaction must guide the industrial design, but concerns about fabrication and cost will also impact the possibilities available to interaction design.

 DESIGN principle There is only one user experience — form and behavior must be designed in concert with each other.

Step 2: Develop rough prototypes

It is often the case that even after the overall form and input methods are defined, there are still a variety of approaches that the industrial designers can take. For example, when we've designed office phones and medical devices, there's often been the question of whether the screen angle should be fixed or if it should be adjustable, and if so, how that will be accomplished. Industrial designers sketch and create rough prototypes from foam board and other materials. In many cases, we'll show several to stakeholders because there are different cost and ergonomic considerations with each.

Step 3: Develop form language studies

In a fashion similar to the visual language studies described above, the next step is to explore a variety of physical styles. Unlike the visual language studies, these are not abstract composites but rather represent various looks applied to the specific form factors and input mechanisms determined in Steps 1 and 2. These studies include shape, dimensionality, materials, color, and finish.

As with visual style studies, form language studies should be informed by persona goals, attitudes, aptitudes, experience keywords, environmental factors, and manufacturing and pricing constraints. Typically these studies require several rounds of iteration to land upon a feasible and desirable solution.

Refining the Form and Behavior

When a solid, stable framework definition is reached, designers see the remaining pieces of the design begin to smoothly fall into place: Each iteration of the key path scenarios adds detail that strengthens the overall coherence and flow of the product. At this stage, a transition is made into the **Refinement** phase, where the design is translated into a final, concrete form.

In this phase, principles and patterns remain important in giving the design a fine formal and behavioral finish. Parts II and III provide useful principles for the Refinement phase. It is also critical for the programming team to be intimately involved throughout the Refinement phase; now that the design has a solid conceptual and behavioral basis, programmer input is critical to creating a finished design that will be built, while remaining true to concept.

The Refinement phase is marked by the translation of the sketched storyboards to full-resolution screens that depict the user interface at the pixel level (see Figure 7-4).

Figure 7-4 Full-resolution bitmap screens for Cross Country TravCorps based on the Framework illustration from Figure 7-2. Note that there are minor changes to the layout that naturally result from the realities of pixels and screen resolution. Visual and interaction designers need to work closely together at this stage to ensure that visual changes to the design continue to reinforce appropriate product behaviors and meet the goals of the primary personas.

The basic process of design refinement follows the same steps we used to develop the design framework, this time at deeper and deeper levels of detail (though, of course, it isn't necessary to revisit the form factor and input methods unless an unexpected cost or manufacturing issue crops up with the hardware). After following Steps 2–6 at the view and pane levels, while incorporating the increasingly refined visual and industrial designs, use scenarios to motivate and address the more granular components of the product.

Address every primary view and dialog possible. Throughout the refinement phase, visual designers should develop and maintain a visual style guide. Programmers use this guide to apply visual design elements consistently when they create low-priority parts of the interface that the designers typically don't have time and resources to complete themselves. At the same time, industrial designers work with engineers to finalize components and assembly.

While the end product of the design process can be any one of a variety of outputs, we typically create a printed form and behavior specification. This document includes screen renderings with callouts sufficiently detailed for a programmer to code from, as well as detailed storyboards to illustrate behaviors over time. It can also be valuable to produce an interactive prototype in HTML or Flash that can augment your documentation to better illustrate complex interactions. However, keep in mind that prototypes alone are rarely sufficient to communicate underlying patterns, principles, and rationale, which are vital concepts to communicate to programmers. Regardless of your choice of design deliverable, your team should continue to work closely with the construction team throughout implementation. It requires vigilance to ensure that the design vision is faithfully and accurately translated from the design document to a final product.

Design Validation and Usability Testing

In the course of an interaction design project, it's often desirable to evaluate how well you've hit the mark by going beyond your personas and validation scenarios to put your solutions in front of actual users. This should be done once the solution is detailed enough to give users something concrete to respond to, and with enough time allotted to make alterations to the design based upon your findings.

In our experience, user feedback sessions and usability tests are good at identifying major problems with the interaction framework and at refining things like button labels and activity order and priority. They're also essential for fine-tuning such behaviors as how quickly a screen scrolls in response to turning a hardware knob. Unfortunately, it's difficult to craft a test that assesses anything beyond first-time ease of learning. There are a number of techniques for evaluating the usability of a product for intermediate or expert users, but it can be quite time consuming, and is imprecise at best.

There are a variety of ways to validate your design with users, from informal feedback sessions where you explain your ideas and drawings and see what the user thinks, to a more rigorous *usability test* where users are asked to complete a predetermined set of tasks. There are advantages to each approach. The more informal style can be done spontaneously and requires less preparation. The downside to this approach is that the designer is often guilty of "leading the witness" by explaining things in a persuasive manner. In general, we've found this approach to be acceptable for a technical audience that is capable of imagining how a few drawings might represent a product interface. It can be a useful alternative to usability testing when the design team doesn't have time to prepare for formal usability testing.

Given sufficient time, we prefer more formal usability testing. Usability tests determine how well a design allows users to accomplish their tasks. If the scope of a test is sufficiently broad, it can also tell you how well the design helps users reach their end goals.

To be clear, usability testing is, at its core, a means to *evaluate*, not to *create*. It is not an alternative to interaction design, and it will never be the source of that great idea that makes a compelling product. Rather, it is a method to assess the effectiveness of ideas you've already had and to smooth over the rough edges.

Usability testing is also not the same as user research. For some practitioners, "tests" can include research activities such as interviews, task analyses, and even creative "participatory design" exercises. This is conflating a variety of needs and steps in the design process into a single activity.

User research must occur *before* ideation, usability testing *following* it. In fact, when project constraints force us to choose between ethnographic research and usability testing, we find that time spent on research gives us much more leverage to create a compelling product. Likewise, given limited days and dollars, we've found that spending time on design provides more value to the product design process than testing. It's much more important to spend time making considered design decisions based upon a solid research foundation than to test a half-baked design created without the benefit of clear, compelling models of the target users and their goals and needs.

When to test: Summative and formative evaluations

In his 1993 book *Usability Engineering,* Jakob Nielsen distinguished between *summative evaluations,* which are tests of completed products, and *formative evaluations,* conducted during design as part of an iterative process. This is an important distinction.

Summative evaluations are used in product comparisons, to identify problems prior to a redesign, and to investigate the causes of product returns and requests for training and support. Summative studies are generally conducted and thoroughly documented by professional, third-party evaluators. In some cases, particularly in competitive product comparisons, summative studies are designed to yield quantitative data that can be tested for statistical significance.

Unfortunately, summative evaluations are often used as part of the quality assurance process near the end of the development process. At this point, it's usually too late to make meaningful design changes; that train has left the station. Design should be evaluated before the coding begins (or at least early enough that there is time to change the implementation as designs are adjusted). However, if you need to convince stakeholders or programmers that there *is* a usability problem with the current product, nothing beats watching real users struggle through basic tasks.

Formative evaluations do just this. These quick, qualitative tests are conducted during the design process, generally during the Refinement phase. When effectively devised and moderated, a formative evaluation opens a window to the user's mind, allowing the designers to see how their target audience responds to the information and tools they've provided to help them accomplish their tasks.

Though summative evaluations have their uses, they are product- and program-management activities conducted to inform product lifecycle planning. They can be useful "disaster checks" during development, but the costs of changes at this point — in time, money, and morale — can be high. Formative evaluations are conducted in the service of design, during the design process.

Conducting formative usability tests

There are a wide variety of perspectives on how to conduct and interpret usability tests. Unfortunately, we've found that many of these approaches either presume to replace active design decision making, or are overly quantitative, resulting in non-actionable data about things like "time to task." A good reference for usability testing methods that we've found to be compatible with Goal-Directed interaction design methods is Carolyn Snyder's *Paper Prototyping*. It doesn't discuss every testing method or the relationship between testing and design, but it covers the fundamentals well and provides some relatively easy-to-use techniques for usability testing.

In brief, we've found the following to be essential components to successful formative usability tests:

- Test late enough in the process that there is a substantially concrete design to test, and early enough to allow adjustments in the design and implementation
- Test tasks and aspects of the user experience appropriate to the product at hand
- Recruit participants from the target population, using your personas as a guide
- Ask participants to perform explicitly defined tasks while thinking aloud
- Have participants interact directly with a low-tech prototype (except when testing specialized hardware where a paper prototype can't reflect nuanced interactions)
- Moderate the sessions to identify issues and explore their causes
- Minimize bias by using a moderator who has not previously been involved in the project
- Focus on participant behaviors and their rationale
- Debrief with observers after tests are conducted to identify the reasons behind observed issues
- Involve designers throughout the study process

Designer involvement in usability studies

Misunderstanding between the designer and the user is a common cause of usability problems. Personas help designers understand their users' goals, needs, and points of view, creating a foundation for effective communication. A usability study, by opening another window on the user's mind, allows designers to see how their verbal, visual, and behavioral messages are received, and to learn what users intend when interacting with the designed affordances.

Designers (or, more broadly, design decision makers) are the primary consumers of usability study findings. Though few designers can moderate a session with sufficient neutrality, their involvement in the study planning, direct observation of study sessions, and participation in the analysis and problem-solving sessions are critical to a study's success. We've found it important to involve designers in the following ways:

▸ Planning the study to focus on important questions about the design

▸ Using personas and their attributes to define recruiting criteria

▸ Using scenarios to develop user tasks

▸ Observing the test sessions

▸ Collaboratively analyzing study findings

Notes

1. Schumann et al.

2. Cooper, 1999

3. Shneiderman, 1998

Part

II

Designing Behavior and Form

8

Synthesizing Good Design: Principles and Patterns

In the last four chapters, we discussed how to appropriately sequence the decisions to define and design a desirable and effective product. But how do we make these decisions? What makes a design solution good? As we've already discussed, a solution's ability to meet the goals and needs of users while also accommodating business goals and technical constraints is one measure of design quality. But are there recognizable attributes of a good solution that enable it to accomplish this successfully? Can we generalize common solutions to apply to similar problems? Are there universally applicable features that a design must possess to make it a "good" design?

The answers to these questions lie in the use of interaction design principles and patterns. Design **principles** are guidelines for design of useful and desirable products, systems, and services, as well as guidelines for the successful and ethical practice of design. Design **patterns** are exemplary, generalizable solutions to specific classes of design problems.

Interaction Design Principles

Interaction design principles are generally applicable guidelines that address issues of behavior, form, and content. They encourage the design of product behaviors that support the needs and goals of users, and create positive experiences with the products we design. These principles are, in effect, a set of rules based upon our values as designers and our experiences in trying to live up to those values. At the core of these values is the notion that technology should serve human intelligence and imagination (rather than the opposite), and that people's experiences with technology should be structured in accordance with their abilities of perception, cognition, and movement.

Principles are applied throughout the design process, helping us to translate tasks and requirements that arise from scenarios into formalized structures and behaviors in the interface.

Principles operate at different levels of detail

Design principles operate at several levels of granularity, ranging from the general practice of interaction design down to the specifics of interface design. The lines between these categories are fuzzy, to say the least, but interaction design principles can be generally thought of as falling into the following categories:

- ▶ **Design values** describe imperatives for the effective and ethical practice of design. These principles inform and motivate lower-level principles and are discussed later in this chapter.

- ▶ **Conceptual principles** help define *what a product is* and how it fits into the broad context of use required by its users. Chapters 3, 9, and 10 discuss conceptual-level design principles.

- ▶ **Behavioral principles** describe *how a product should behave*, in general, and in specific situations. Chapters 8–20 discuss general behavior-level principles.

- ▶ **Interface-level principles** describe effective strategies for *the visual communication of behavior and information*. Principles in Chapters 13 and 14 are focused on this level of interaction design, which is also touched upon in many chapters in Parts II and III.

Most interaction and visual design principles are cross-platform, although some platforms, such as mobile devices and embedded systems, require special consideration because of constraints imposed by factors like screen size, input method, and use context.

Behavioral and interface-level principles minimize work

One of the primary purposes principles serve is to optimize the experience of the user when she engages with a product. In the case of productivity tools and other non-entertainment-oriented products, this optimization means *minimizing work*.

Types of work to be minimized include:

▶ **Cognitive work** — Comprehension of product behaviors, as well as text and organizational structures

▶ **Memory work** — Recall of product behaviors, command vectors, passwords, names and locations of data objects and controls, and other relationships between objects

▶ **Visual work** — Figuring out where the eye should start on a screen, finding one object among many, decoding layouts, and differentiating among visually coded interface elements (such as list items with different colors)

▶ **Physical work** — Keystrokes, mouse movements, gestures (click, drag, double-click), switching between input modes, and number of clicks required to navigate

Most of the principles in this book attempt to minimize work ,while providing greater levels of feedback and contextually useful information to the user.

It should also be mentioned that certain kinds of entertainment products (such as games) are able to engage as a result of requiring users to do just the right amount of a certain kind of work and rewarding them for doing so. Recall the Tamagotchi craze from the late 1990s: People became addicted to the work required to take care of their handheld virtual pet. Of course, too much work or too little reward would turn the game into a chore. This kind of interaction design requires a fine touch.

Design Values

Principles are rules that govern action, and are typically based at their core on a set of values and beliefs. The following set of values was developed by Robert Reimann, Hugh Dubberly, Kim Goodwin, David Fore, and Jonathan Korman to apply to any design discipline that aims to serve the needs of humans.

Designers should create design solutions that are:

▶ **Ethical** [*considerate, helpful*]
Do no harm
Improve human situations

- **Purposeful** [*useful, usable*]
  Help users achieve their goals and aspirations
  Accommodate user contexts and capacities

- **Pragmatic** [*viable, feasible*]
  Help commissioning organizations achieve their goals
  Accommodate business and technical requirements

- **Elegant** [*efficient, artful, affective*]
  Represent the simplest complete solution
  Possess internal (self-revealing, understandable) coherence
  Appropriately accommodate and stimulate cognition and emotion

The following subsections explore each of these values.

Ethical interaction design

Interaction designers are faced with ethical questions when they are asked to design a system that has fundamental effects on the lives of people. These may be direct effects on users of a product, or second-order effects on other people whose lives the product touches in some way. This can become a particular issue for interaction designers because, unlike graphic designers, the product of their design work is not simply the persuasive communication of a policy or the marketing of a product. It is, in fact, the means of executing policy or the creation of a product itself. In a nutshell, interactive products *do things*, and as designers, we must be sure that the results of our labor do *good* things. It is relatively straightforward to design a product that does well by its users, but the effect that product has on others is sometimes more difficult to calculate.

Do no harm

Products shouldn't harm anyone, or given the complexities of life in the real world, should, at the very least, *minimize harm*. Possible types of harm that interactive systems could be a party to include:

- **Interpersonal** harm (loss of dignity, insult, humiliation)

- **Psychological** harm (confusion, discomfort, frustration, coercion, boredom)

- **Physical** harm (pain, injury, deprivation, death, compromised safety)

- **Environmental** harm (pollution, elimination of biodiversity)

- **Social and societal** harm (exploitation, creation, or perpetuation of injustice)

Avoiding the first two types of harm requires a deep understanding of the user audience, as well as buy-in from stakeholders that these issues are within a scope that can be addressed by the project. Many of the concepts discussed in Parts II and III can help designers craft solutions that support human intelligence and emotions. Avoiding physical harm requires a solid understanding of ergonomic principles and appropriate use of interface elements so as to minimize work. See Part III for guidance on this. Obviously, the last two types of harm are not issues for most products, but you can surely imagine some examples that are relevant, such as the control system for an offshore oil rig or an electronic voting system.

Improve human situations

Not doing harm is, of course, not sufficient for a truly ethical design; it should be improving things as well. Some types of situations that interactive systems might improve broadly include:

- **Increasing understanding** (individual, social, cultural)
- **Increasing efficiency/effectiveness** of individuals and groups
- **Improving communication** between individuals and groups
- **Reducing sociocultural tensions** between individuals and groups
- **Improving equity** (financial, social, legal)
- **Balancing cultural diversity with social cohesion**

Designers should always keep such broad issues at the back of their minds as they engage in new design projects. Opportunities to do good should always be considered, even if they are slightly outside the box.

Purposeful interaction design

The primary theme of this book is purposeful design based on an understanding of user goals and motivations. If nothing else, the Goal-Directed process described in the chapters of Part I should help you to achieve purposeful design. Part of purposefulness, however, is not only understanding users' goals but also understanding their limitations. User research and personas serve well in this regard. The behavior patterns you observe and communicate should describe your users' strengths *as well as* their weaknesses and blind spots. Goal-Directed Design helps designers to create products that support users where they are weak and empower them where they are strong.

Pragmatic interaction design

Design specifications that gather dust on a shelf are of no use to anyone: A design must get built to be of value. Once built, it needs to be deployed in the world. And once deployed, it needs to provide benefits to its owners. It is critical that business goals and technical issues and requirements be taken into account in the course of design. This doesn't imply that designers necessarily need to take everything they are told by their stakeholders and programmers at face value: There must be an active dialog among the business, engineering, and design groups about where there are firm boundaries and what areas of the product definition are flexible. Programmers often state that a proposed design is *impossible* when what they mean is that it is *impossible given the current schedule*. Marketing organizations may create business plans based upon aggregated and statistical data without fully understanding how individual users and customers are likely to behave. Designers, who have gathered detailed, qualitative research on users, may have insight into the business model from a unique perspective. Design works best when there is a relationship of mutual trust and respect among Design, Business, and Engineering.

Elegant interaction design

Elegance is defined in the dictionary as both "gracefulness and restrained beauty of style" and "scientific precision, neatness, and simplicity." We believe that elegance in design, or at least interaction design, incorporates both of these ideals.

Represent the simplest complete solution

One of the classic elements of good design is *economy of form*: using less to accomplish more. In interface design, this means using only the screens and widgets necessary to accomplish the task. This economy extends to behavior: a simple set of tools for the user that allows him to accomplish great things. In visual design, this means using the smallest number of visual distinctions that clearly conveys the desired meaning. Less is more in good design, and designers should endeavor to solve design problems with the fewest additions of form and behavior, in conformance to the mental models of your personas. This concept is well known to programmers, who recognize that better algorithms are clearer and shorter.

Yvon Chounard, famed outdoorsman and founder of outdoor clothing company Patagonia, puts it best when he quotes French writer and aviator Antoine de St. Exupéry, who said, "in anything at all, perfection is finally attained not when there is no longer anything to add, but when there is no longer anything to take away."

Possess internal coherence

Good design has the feeling of a unified whole, in which all parts are in balance and harmony. Products that are poorly designed, or not designed at all, often look and feel like they are cobbled together from disparate pieces haphazardly knit together. Often this is the result of implementation model construction, where different development teams work on different interface modules without communicating with each other, or where hardware and software are designed independently of each other. This is the antithesis of what we want to achieve. The Goal-Directed Design process, in which product concepts are conceived of as a whole at the top level and then iteratively refined to detail, provides an ideal environment for creating internally coherent designs. Specifically, the use of scenarios to motivate and test designs ensures that solutions are unified by a single narrative thread.

Appropriately accommodate and stimulate cognition and emotion

Many traditionally trained designers speak frequently of *desire* and its importance in the design of communications and products. They're not wrong, but we feel that in placing such emphasis on a single (albeit, complex) emotion, they may sometimes be seeing only part of the picture.

Desire is a narrow emotion to appeal to when designing a product that serves a purpose, especially when that product is located in an enterprise, or its purpose is highly technical or specialized. One would hardly wish to make a technician operating a radiation therapy system feel desire for the system. We, instead, want her to feel cautious and perhaps reverent of the rather dangerous energies the system controls. Therefore, we do everything we can as designers to keep her focus on the patient and his treatment. Thus, in place of what we might call *desire*, the authors believe that elegance (in the sense of gracefulness) means that the user is stimulated and supported both cognitively and emotionally in whatever context she is in.

The remaining chapters of this book enumerate what we view as the most critical interaction and visual interface design principles. There are, no doubt, many more you will discover, but this set will more than get you started. The chapters in Part I provided the process and concepts behind the practice of Goal-Directed interaction design. The chapters to come provide a healthy dose of design insight that will help you to transform this knowledge into excellent design, whatever your domain.

Interaction Design Patterns

Design patterns are a means of capturing useful design solutions and generalizing them to address similar problems. This effort to formalize design knowledge and record best practices can serve several vital purposes:

- ▶ Reduce design time and effort on new projects
- ▶ Improve the quality of design solutions
- ▶ Facilitate communication between designers and programmers
- ▶ Educate designers

Although the application of patterns in design pedagogy and efficiency is certainly important, we find the development of interaction design patterns to be particularly exciting because they can represent optimal interactions for the user and the class of activity that the pattern addresses.

Architectural patterns and interaction design

The idea of capturing interaction design patterns has its roots in the work of Christopher Alexander, who first described architectural design patterns in his seminal work *A Pattern Language* and *The Timeless Way of Building*. By defining a rigorous set of architectural features, Alexander sought to describe the essence of architectural design that creates a feeling of well-being on the part of the inhabitants of structures.

It is this last aim of Alexander's project that resonates so closely with the needs of interaction designers, and it is the focus on the human aspects of each pattern that differentiates architectural and interaction design patterns from engineering patterns, which are primarily intended as a way to reuse and standardize programming code.

One important difference between interaction design patterns and architectural design patterns is the concern of interaction design patterns not only with structure and organization of elements but also with dynamic behaviors and changes in elements in response to user activity. It is tempting to view the distinction simply as one of change over time, but these changes are interesting because they occur in response to both application state and human activity. This differentiates them from preordained temporal transitions that can be found in mechanical products and broadcast and film media (which each have their own distinct set of design patterns).

Recording and using interaction design patterns

Patterns are always context specific: They are defined to be applicable to common design situations that share similar contexts, constraints, tensions, and forces. When capturing a pattern, it is important to record the context to which the solution applies, one or more specific examples of the solution, the abstracted features common to all of the examples, and the rationale behind the solution (why it is a good solution).

For a set of patterns to be useful, they must be meaningfully organized in terms of the contexts in which they are applicable. Such a set is commonly referred to as a *pattern library* or *catalog*, and if this set is rigorously defined and specified, and sufficiently complete to describe all the solutions in a domain, then it is referred to as a *pattern language* (though considering the pace of innovation in all types of digital products, it seems unlikely that such a language will stabilize anytime soon).

Design patterns are *not* recipes or plug-and-play solutions. In her book *Designing Interfaces*, which is a broad and useful collection of interaction design patterns, Jenifer Tidwell provides us with the following caveat: "[Patterns] aren't off-the-shelf components; each implementation of a pattern differs a little from every other."[1]

There is some temptation in the world of software design to imagine that a comprehensive catalogue of patterns could, given a clear idea of user needs, permit even novice designers to assemble coherent design solutions rapidly and with ease. Although we have observed that there is some truth to this notion in the case of seasoned interaction designers, it is simply never the case that patterns can be mechanically assembled in cookie-cutter fashion, without knowledge of the context in which they will be used. As Christopher Alexander is swift to point out, architectural patterns are the antithesis of the prefab building, because context is of absolute importance in defining the manifest form of the pattern in the world. The environment where the pattern is deployed is critical, as are the other patterns that compose it, contain it, and abut it. The same is true for interaction design patterns. The core of each pattern lies in the relationships between represented objects and between those objects and the goals of the user. (This is one reason why a general style guide can never be a substitute for a context-specific design solution.) The precise form of the pattern is certain to be somewhat different for each instance, and the objects that define it will naturally vary from domain to domain, but the relationships between objects remain essentially the same.

Types of interaction design patterns

Like most other design patterns, interaction design patterns can be hierarchically organized from the system level down to the level of individual interface widgets. Like principles, they can be applied at different levels of organization (and as with design principles, the distinctions between these different levels are sometimes quite fuzzy):

- ▶ **Postural** patterns can be applied at the conceptual level and help determine the overall product stance in relation to the user. An example of a postural pattern is "transient," which means that a person only uses it for brief periods of time in service of a larger goal being achieved elsewhere. The concept of product posture and its most significant patterns are discussed at length in Chapter 9.

- ▶ **Structural** patterns solve problems that relate to the arrangement of information and functional elements on the screen. They consist of views, panes, and element groupings discussed briefly in Chapter 7.

- ▶ **Behavioral** patterns solve wide-ranging problems relating to specific interactions with functional or data elements. What most people think of as widget behaviors fall into this category, and many such lower-level patterns are discussed in Part III.

Structural patterns are perhaps the least documented patterns, but they are nonetheless in widespread use. One of the most commonly used high-level structural patterns is apparent in Microsoft Outlook with its navigational pane on the left, overview pane on the upper right, and detail pane on the lower right (see Figure 8-1).

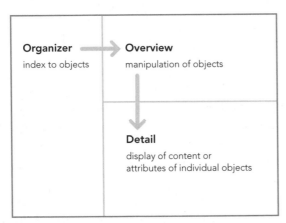

Figure 8-1 The primary structural pattern used by Microsoft Outlook is widely used throughout the industry, across many diverse product domains. The left-vertical pane provides navigation and drives the content of the overview pane in the upper right. A selection in this pane populates the lower-right pane with detail or document content.

This pattern is optimal for full-screen applications that require user access to many different kinds of objects, manipulation of those objects in groups, and display of detailed content or attributes of individual objects or documents. The pattern permits all this to be done smoothly in a single screen without the need for additional windows. Many e-mail clients make use of this pattern, and variations of it appear in many authoring and information management tools where rapid access to and manipulation of various types of objects is common.

Building up a mental catalog of patterns is one of the most critical aspects of the education of an interaction designer. As we all become aware of the best parts of each other's work, we can collectively advance the interaction idioms we provide to our users, and by leveraging existing work, we can focus our efforts on solving new problems, rather than reinventing the wheel.

Notes

1. Tidwell, 2006, p. xiv

9

Platform and Posture

As you'll recall from Chapter 7, the first question to answer as you begin to design an interactive product is, "What platform and posture are appropriate?" The **platform** can be thought of as the combination of hardware and software that enables the product to function, in terms of both user interactions and the internal operations of the product.

You're undoubtedly familiar with many of the most common platforms for interactive products, including desktop software, Web sites and Web applications, kiosks, in-vehicle systems, handhelds (such as cameras, phones, and PDAs), home entertainment systems (such as game consoles, TV set-top boxes/tuners, and stereo/home theater systems), and professional devices (such as medical and scientific instruments). Looking at this list, you also may notice that "platform" is not an entirely well-defined concept. Rather, it is shorthand to describe a number of important product features, such as the physical form, display size and resolution, input method, network connectivity, operating system, and database capabilities.

All of these factors have a significant impact on the way the product is designed, built, and used. Choosing the right platform is a balancing act, where you must find the sweet spot that best supports the needs and context of your personas and fits within the business constraints, objectives, and technological capabilities.

A product's **posture** is its behavioral stance — the way it presents itself to users. Posture is a way of talking about how much attention a user will devote to interacting with the product, and how the product's behaviors respond to the kind of attention a user will be devoting to it. This decision, too, must be based upon an understanding of likely usage contexts and environments.

Posture

Most people have a predominant behavioral stance that fits their working role on the job: The soldier is wary and alert; the toll collector is bored and disinterested; the actor is flamboyant and bigger than life; the service representative is upbeat and helpful. Products, too, have a predominant manner of presenting themselves to users.

A program may be bold or timid, colorful or drab, but it should be so for a specific, goal-directed reason. Its manner shouldn't result from the personal preference of its designer or programmer. The presentation of the program affects the way users relate to it, and this relationship strongly influences the usability of the product. Programs whose appearance and behavior conflict with their purposes will seem jarring and inappropriate, like fur in a teacup or a clown at a wedding.

The look and behavior of a product should reflect how it is used, rather than the personal taste of its designers. From the perspective of posture, look-and-feel is *not* solely an aesthetic choice: It is a behavioral choice. Your program's posture is part of its behavioral foundation, and whatever aesthetic choices you make should be in harmony with this posture.

The posture of your interface dictates many important guidelines for the rest of the design, but posture is not simply a black-and-white issue. Just as a person may present herself in a number of slightly different ways depending on the context, some products may exhibit characteristics of a number of different postures. When reading e-mail on a Blackberry during a train ride, a user may devote concentrated attention to interactions with the device (and expect a commensurate experience), whereas the same user will have significantly less attention to devote if she is using it to look up an address while running to a meeting. Similarly, while a word processor should generally be optimized for concentrated, devoted, and frequent user attention, there are tools within the word processor, like the table construction tool, that are used in a transient and infrequent manner. In cases like this, it is worthwhile both to define the predominant posture for a product as a whole and to consider the posture of individual features and usage contexts.

Platform and posture are closely related: Different hardware platforms are conducive to different behavioral stances. An application running on a mobile phone clearly must accommodate a different kind of user attention than an educational program running on a game console.

In this chapter we discuss appropriate postures and other design considerations for several platforms, including desktop software, Web sites and applications, kiosks, handhelds, and appliances.

Designing Desktop Software

We use the term "desktop software" as a catchall phrase referring for applications that run on a modern PC. Generally speaking, interaction design has its roots in desktop software. While historically there have been designers grappling with issues related to complex behaviors on a variety of technical platforms, it has been the personal computer that has brought these complex behaviors to every desktop. As a result, much of what you'll find in this book is grounded in what it takes to effectively serve human needs with desktop software. In more recent history, this understanding has been expanded to encompass the Web, large and small devices, and other embedded systems, which we discuss later in the chapter.

When defining the platform of your product, clearly you must go beyond the term "desktop" to consider what the appropriate operating system, database, and user-interface technology are for your product. While it is considerably outside the scope of this book to assess each of these technical aspects of the desktop platform, it is absolutely critical that these decisions be analyzed in regard to whether they will support the needs of users. Furthermore, as all design is a conversation with materials, it is also important to understand the limitations and opportunities associated with each of these fundamental technologies.

In many organizations, platform decisions, particularly those regarding hardware, are unfortunately still made well in advance of the interaction designer's involvement. It is important to inform management that platform choices will be much more effective if made after interaction designers complete their work.

 DESIGN principle   Decisions about technical platform are best made in concert with interaction design efforts.

Desktop applications fit into four categories of posture: **sovereign**, **transient**, and **daemonic**. Because each describes a different set of behavioral attributes, each also describes a different type of user interaction. More importantly, these categories give the designer a point of departure for designing an interface. A sovereign posture program, for example, won't feel right unless it behaves in a "sovereign" way.

Sovereign posture

Programs that monopolize users' attention for long periods of time are **sovereign posture** applications. Sovereign applications offer a large set of related functions and features, and users tend to keep them up and running continuously, occupying the full screen. Good examples of this type of application are word processors, spreadsheets, and e-mail applications. Many vertical applications are also sovereign applications because they are often deployed on the screen for long periods of time, and interaction with them can be very complex and involved. Users working with sovereign programs often find themselves in a state of flow. Sovereign programs are usually used *maximized* (we'll talk more about window states in Chapter 20). For example, it is hard to imagine using Microsoft Outlook in a 3-x-4-inch window — at that size it's not really appropriate for its main job: creating and viewing e-mail and appointments (see Figure 9-1).

Figure 9-1 Microsoft Outlook is a classic example of a sovereign posture application. It stays onscreen interacting with a user for long, uninterrupted periods, and with its multiple adjacent panes for navigation and supporting information, it begs to take up the full screen.

Sovereign products are characteristically used for long, continuous stretches of time. A sovereign product dominates a user's workflow as his primary tool. Power-Point, for example, is open full-screen while you create a presentation from start to finish. Even if other applications are used for support tasks, PowerPoint maintains its sovereign stance.

Users of sovereign applications are typically intermediates

Because people typically devote time and attention to using sovereign applications, they often have a vested interest in getting up the learning curve to become inter-mediate users, as discussed in Chapter 3. Each user spends time as a novice, but only a short period of time *relative to the amount of time he will eventually spend* using the product. Certainly a new user has to get over the initial learning curve, but seen from the perspective of the entire relationship between a user and the product, the time he spends getting acquainted with the program is small.

From the designer's point of view, this often means that the program should be optimized for use by perpetual intermediates and not be aimed primarily at begin-ners (or experts). Sacrificing speed and power in favor of a clumsier but easier-to-learn idiom is out of place here, as is providing only sophisticated power tools. Of course, if you can offer easier or more powerful idioms without compromising the interaction for intermediate users, that is often best. In any case, the sort of user you're optimizing for is determined by your choice of primary persona and your understanding of their attitudes, aptitudes, and use contexts.

Between first-time users and intermediate users there are many people who use sovereign applications only on occasion. These infrequent users cannot be ignored. However, the success of a sovereign application is still dependent on its intermedi-ate, frequent users until someone else satisfies both them *and* inexperienced users. WordStar, an early word processing program, is a good example. It dominated the word processing marketplace in the late '70s and early '80s because it served its intermediate users exceedingly well, even though it was extremely difficult for infrequent and first-time users. WordStar Corporation thrived until its competi-tion offered the same power for intermediate users, while simultaneously making it much less painful for infrequent users. WordStar, unable to keep up with the com-petition, rapidly dwindled to insignificance.

Be generous with screen real estate

Because a user's interaction with a sovereign application dominates his session at the computer, the application shouldn't be afraid to take as much screen real estate as possible. No other application will be competing with yours, so don't waste space, but don't be shy about taking what you need to do the job. If you need four toolbars to cover the bases, use four toolbars. In an application of a different posture, four toolbars may be overly complex, but the sovereign posture has a defensible claim on the pixels.

In most instances, sovereign applications run maximized. In the absence of explicit instructions from the user, your sovereign application should default to maximized or full-screen presentation. The application needs to be fully resizable and must work well in other screen configurations, but the interface should be optimized for full-screen use, instead of the less common cases.

 Optimize sovereign applications for full-screen use.

Use a minimal visual style

Because users will stare at a sovereign application for long periods, you should take care to mute the colors and texture of the visual presentation. Keep the color palette narrow and conservative. Big colorful controls may look really cool to newcomers, but they seem garish after a couple of weeks of daily use. Tiny dots or accents of color will have more effect in the long run than big splashes, and they enable you to pack controls together more tightly than you otherwise could.

 Sovereign interfaces should feature a conservative visual style.

The user will stare at the same palettes, menus, and toolbars for many hours, gaining an innate sense of where things are from sheer familiarity. This gives you, the designer, freedom to do more with fewer pixels. Toolbars and their controls can be smaller than normal. Auxiliary controls such as screen-splitters, rulers, and scrollbars can be smaller and more closely spaced.

Rich visual feedback

Sovereign applications are great platforms for creating an environment rich in visual feedback for users. You can productively add extra little bits of information into the interface. The status bar at the bottom of the screen, the ends of the space normally occupied by scrollbars, the title bar, and other dusty corners of the product's visible components can be filled with visual indications of the application's status, the status of the data, the state of the system, and hints for more productive user actions. However, be careful: While enriching the visual feedback, you must be careful not to create an interface that is hopelessly cluttered.

The first-time user won't even notice such artifacts, let alone understand them, because of the subtle way they are shown on the screen. After a period of steady use, however, he will begin to see them, wonder about their meaning, and experimentally explore them. At this point, a user will be willing to expend a little effort to learn more. If you provide an easy means for him to find out what the artifacts are, he will become not only a better user but also a more satisfied user, as his power over the application grows with his understanding. Adding such richness to the interface is like adding a variety of ingredients to a soup stock — it enhances the entire meal. We discuss this idea of **rich visual modeless feedback** in Chapter 25.

Rich input

Sovereign applications similarly benefit from rich input. Every frequently used aspect of the application should be controllable in several ways. Direct manipulation, dialog boxes, keyboard mnemonics, and keyboard accelerators are all appropriate. You can make more aggressive demands on a user's fine motor skills with direct-manipulation idioms. Sensitive areas on the screen can be just a couple of pixels across because you can assume that the user is established comfortably in his chair, arm positioned in a stable way on his desk, rolling his mouse firmly across a resilient mouse pad.

 DESIGN principle   Sovereign applications should exploit rich input.

Go ahead and use the corners and edges of the application's window for controls. In a jet cockpit, the most frequently used controls are situated directly in front of the pilot; those needed only occasionally or in an emergency are found on the armrests, overhead, and on the side panels. In Word, Microsoft has put the most frequently used functions on the two main toolbars (see Figure 9-2). They put the frequently used but visually dislocating functions on small controls to the left of the horizontal scrollbar near the bottom of the screen. These controls change the appearance of the entire visual display — Normal view, Page Layout view, and Outline view. Neophytes do not often use them and, if accidentally triggered, they can be confusing. By placing them near the bottom of the screen, they become almost invisible to new users. Their segregated positioning subtly and silently indicates that caution should be taken in their use. More experienced users, with more confidence in their understanding and control of the application, will begin to notice these controls and wonder about their purpose. They can experimentally select them when they feel fully prepared for their consequences. This is a very accurate and useful mapping of control placement to usage.

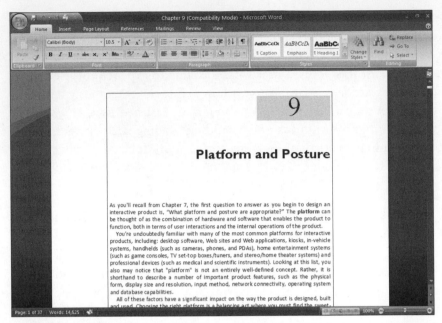

Figure 9-2 Microsoft Word has placed controls at both the top and the bottom of the application. The controls at the bottom are used to change views and are appropriately segregated because they can cause significant visual dislocation.

Document-centric applications

The dictum that sovereign applications should fill the screen is also true of document windows within the application itself. Child windows containing documents should always be maximized inside the application unless the user explicitly instructs otherwise, or the user needs to simultaneously work in several documents to accomplish a specific task.

DESIGN principle   Maximize document views within sovereign applications.

Many sovereign applications are also document-centric (i.e., their primary functions involve the creation and viewing of documents containing rich data), making it easy to believe that the two are always correlated, but this is not the case. If an application manipulates a document but only performs a simple, single function, such as scanning an image, it isn't a sovereign application and shouldn't exhibit sovereign behavior. Such single-function applications have a posture of their own, the transient posture.

Transient posture

A product with a **transient** posture comes and goes, presenting a single function with a constrained set of accompanying controls. The application is invoked when needed, appears, performs its job, and then quickly leaves, letting the user continue her normal activity, usually with a sovereign application.

The defining characteristic of a transient application is its temporary nature. Because it doesn't stay on the screen for extended periods of time, users don't get the chance to become very familiar with it. Consequently, the product's user interface should be obvious, presenting its controls clearly and boldly with no possibility of confusion or mistakes. The interface must spell out what it does: This is not the place for artistic-but-ambiguous images or icons — it *is* the place for big buttons with precise legends spelled out in a large, easy-to-read typeface.

 Transient applications must be simple, clear, and to the point.

Although a transient application can certainly operate alone on your desktop, it usually acts in a supporting role to a sovereign application. For example, calling up Windows Explorer to locate and open a file while editing another with Word is a typical transient scenario. So is setting your speaker volume. Because the transient application borrows space at the expense of the sovereign, it must respect the sovereign by not taking more space onscreen than is absolutely necessary. Where the sovereign can dig a hole and pour a concrete foundation for itself, the transient application is just on a weekend campout. It cannot deploy itself onscreen either graphically or temporally. It is the taxicab of the software world.

In cases when the entire computer system is fulfilling a transient role in the real world of atoms, it is not necessarily appropriate to minimize the use of pixels and visual attention. Examples of this include process monitors in a fabrication environment, or digital imaging systems in an operating theatre. Here, the entire computer screen is referred to in a transient manner, while the user is engaged in a sovereign mechanical activity. In these cases, it is critical for information to be obvious and easily understood from across the room, which clearly requires a bolder use of color and a more generous allotment of real estate (see Figure 9-3).

Figure 9-3 Yahoo! Widgets and iTunes are good examples of transient applications. They are referred to or interacted with briefly before a user's attention turns to an activity in a sovereign application. The use of rich dimensional rendering gives them an appropriate amount of visual gravity.

Bright and clear

Whereas a transient application must conserve the total amount of screen real estate it consumes, the controls on its surface can be proportionally larger than those on a sovereign application. Where more forceful visual design on a sovereign application would pall within a few weeks, the transient application isn't onscreen long enough for it to bother the user. On the contrary, bolder graphics help the user to orient himself more quickly when the application pops up.

Transient applications should have instructions built into their surface. The user may only see the application once a month and will likely forget the meanings and implications of the choices presented. Instead of a button captioned Setup, it's better to make the button large enough to caption it "Set up user preferences." The verb/object construction results in a more easily comprehensible interface, and the results of clicking the button are more predictable. Likewise, nothing should be abbreviated on a transient application, and feedback should be direct and explicit to avoid confusion. For example, a user should be easily able to understand that the printer is busy, or that a piece of recently recorded audio is five seconds long.

Keep it simple

After the user summons a transient application, all the information and facilities he needs should be right there on the surface of the application's single window. Keep the user's focus of attention on that window and never force him into supporting subwindows or dialog boxes to take care of the main function of the application. If you find yourself adding a dialog box or second view to a transient application, that's a key sign that your design needs a review.

DESIGN principle   Transient applications should be limited to a single window and view.

Transient applications are not the place for tiny scrollbars and fussy mouse interactions. Keep demands on the user's fine motor skills down to a minimum. Simple pushbuttons for simple functions are good. Direct manipulation can also be effective, but anything directly manipulable must be discoverable and big enough to interact with easily. You should also provide keyboard shortcuts, but they must be simple, and all important functions should also be visible on the interface.

Of course, there are some rare exceptions to the monothematic nature of transient applications. If a transient application performs more than just a single function, the interface should communicate this visually and unambiguously and provide immediate access to all functions without the addition of windows or dialogs. One such application is the Art Directors Toolkit by Code Line Communications, which performs a number of different calculator-like functions useful to users of graphic design applications (see Figure 9-4).

Keep in mind that a transient application will likely be called upon to assist in the management of some aspect of a sovereign application (as in the Art Directors Toolkit in Figure 9-4). This means that the transient application, as it is positioned on top of the sovereign, may obscure the very information that it is chartered to work on. This implies that the transient application must be movable, which means it must have a title bar or other obvious affordance for dragging.

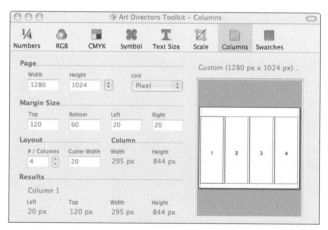

Figure 9-4 Art Directors Toolkit by Code Line Communications is another example of a transient application. It provides a number of discrete functions such as calculating dimensions of a layout grid. These functions are designed to support the use of a sovereign layout application such as Adobe InDesign. While this application provides a number of different functions, they are organized into tabs and are all directly accessible at all times.

It is vital to keep the amount of management overhead as low as possible with transient applications. All the user wants to do is perform a specific function and then move on. It is completely unreasonable to force the user to add nonproductive window-management tasks to this interaction.

Remember user choices

The most appropriate way to help users with both transient and sovereign apps is to give the applications a memory. If a transient application remembers where it was the last time it was used, the chances are excellent that the same size and placement will be appropriate next time, too. It will almost always be more apt than any default setting might chance to be. Whatever shape and position a user morphed the application into is the shape and position the application should reappear in when it is next summoned. Of course, this holds true for its logical settings, too.

DESIGN principle   A transient application should launch to its previous position and configuration.

No doubt you have already realized that almost all dialog boxes are really transient applications. You can see that all the preceding guidelines for transient applications apply equally well to the design of dialog boxes (for more on dialog boxes, see Chapters 24 and 25).

Daemonic posture

Programs that do not normally interact with the user are **daemonic posture** applications. These applications serve quietly and invisibly in the background, performing possibly vital tasks without the need for human intervention. A printer driver or network connection are excellent examples.

As you might expect, any discussion of the user interface of daemonic applications is necessarily short. Where a transient application controls the execution of a function, daemonic applications usually manage processes. Your heartbeat isn't a function that must be consciously controlled; rather, it is a process that proceeds autonomously in the background. Like the processes that regulate your heartbeat, daemonic applications generally remain completely invisible, competently performing their process as long as your computer is turned on. Unlike your heart, however, daemonic applications must occasionally be installed and removed and, also occasionally, they must be adjusted to deal with changing circumstances. It is at these times that a daemon talks to a user (or vice versa). Without exception, the interaction between a user and a daemonic application is transient in nature, and all the imperatives of transient application design hold true here also.

The principles of transient design that are concerned with keeping users informed of the purpose of an application and of the scope and meaning of the available choices become even more critical with daemonic applications. In many cases, users will not even be aware of the existence of the daemonic application. If you recognize that, it becomes obvious that reports about status from that application can be quite dislocating if not presented in an appropriate context. Because many of these applications perform esoteric functions — such as printer drivers or communications concentrators — the messages from them must take particular care not to confuse users or lead to misunderstandings.

A question that is often taken for granted with applications of other postures becomes very significant with daemonic applications: If the application is normally invisible, how should the user interface be summoned on those rare occasions when it is needed? One of the most frequently used methods in Windows is to represent the daemon with an onscreen application icon in the system tray. Putting the icon so boldly in a user's face when it is almost never needed is a real affront, like pasting an advertisement on the windshield of somebody's car. Daemonic icons should only be employed persistently if they provide continuous, useful status information. Microsoft solved this problem in Windows XP by hiding daemonic icons that are not actively being used to report status or access functionality (see Figure 9-5).

Figure 9-5 The status area of the taskbar in Windows XP. The mouse cursor is pointed at an icon representing a daemonic process that monitors the network. The icon provides modeless visual status information, as the icon changes if there is no network access. Hovering over the icon provides more information, and right-clicking on it provides access to various functions related to the network connection.

Both Mac OS and Windows employ **control panels** as an effective approach to configure daemonic applications. These launchable transient applications give users a consistent place to go to configure daemons. It is also important to provide direct, in-line access to daemonic applications any time there is an issue with them that prevents a person from accomplishing what he aims to. (Of course, standard disclaimers apply: Don't interrupt users unnecessarily.) For example, if a taskbar icon indicates a problem with a printer, clicking on that icon should provide a mechanism to troubleshoot and rectify the problem.

ng for the Web

e World Wide Web was both a boon and a curse for interaction
haps the first time since the invention of graphical user interfaces,
makers began to understand and adopt the language of user-
n the other hand, the limitations and challenges of Web interac-
are a natural result of its historical evolution, set interaction design
back several years. Designers of Web applications are only now beginning to take
advantage of the many desktop interaction idioms (such as drag-and-drop) that
were old news years before the first Web sites went online.

In the early days of the Web boom, the industry was flooded with fresh design
school graduates, traditional graphic designers, and young enthusiasts who saw the
Web as an exciting and lucrative opportunity to create compelling communication
through new forms of interactive visual expression. The biggest challenges involved
working around the tight constraints of the medium (originally created to share
scientific papers and attached diagrams) to produce a user experience with even a
rudimentary level of interactivity and visual organization.

Even then, the people designing and building Web sites recognized that a new
design issue resulted from the support of hyperlinks in documents: the design,
organization, and structuring of content. *Findability*, a term coined by Peter
Morville, is an apt way to describe the design issue in a nutshell. A new breed of
designers, the *information architects*, built a discipline and practice to address the
nonvisual design problems of logical structure and flow of content.

Some of today's browser-based applications (often collectively referred to as *Web
2.0*, a term credited to Tom O'Reilly) blur many of the distinctions between desktop and Web applications, and even offer the opportunity to define new interaction
idioms that better support the people we are designing for. With the rise of so-
called "rich Internet applications" supported by technologies such as AJAX, Macromedia Flash, Java, and ActiveX, the design of Internet-enabled software demands
much greater attention to sophisticated product *behavior* than is required of simpler page-based Web sites. While findability remains a significant issue, it can be
eclipsed by the classic interaction problems of PC-based applications.

This newly available ability to deliver complex behavior in a browser demands
application-quality interaction design. The visual designer's focus on look-and-feel
and the information architect's focus on content structure are not sufficient to create effective and engaging user experiences with this new generation of the Web.

Before we get into different postures that emerge on the Web, we'll first discuss the
different kinds of services and products that are typically offered through a Web

browser: informational Web sites, transactional Web sites, and Web applications. As with many of the categorizations we offer in this book, the lines between these can be fuzzy. Consider them to represent a spectrum upon which any Web site or application can be located.

Informational Web sites

Web browsers were originally conceived of as a means of viewing shared and linked documents without the need for cumbersome protocols like File Transfer Protocol (FTP), Gopher, and Archie. As a result, the Web was originally made up solely of collections of these documents (or *pages*) referred to as **Web sites.** We continue to use the term to refer to informational services on the Web whose level of interaction primarily involves searching and clicking on links. Web sites, as described, can easily be conceived of as sets of pages or documents organized sequentially or hierarchically, with a navigation model to take users from one page to another, as well as a search facility to a provide more goal-directed location of specific pages. Plenty of Web sites still exist out there, in the form of personal sites, corporate marketing and support sites, and information-centric intranets. In such informational Web sites, the dominant design concerns are the visual look-and-feel, the layout, navigational elements, and the site structure (information architecture). Web sites do not typically exhibit complex behavior (where the result of a user interaction is dependent on application state), and therefore don't often require the services of interaction designers.

As this book is focused on interaction design, we won't attempt to address the many aspects of designing Web sites that have been covered in great detail in many other volumes. Steve Krug's *Don't Make Me Think!*, Louis Rosenfeld and Peter Morville's *Information Architecture*, and Jeffrey Veen's *The Art and Science of Web Design*, in particular, cover the essential elements of Web design in a clear and straightforward manner. Jakob Nielsen's *useit.com* Web site is also an excellent resource.

Postures for informational Web sites

Sites that are purely informational, which require no complex transactions to take place beyond navigating from page to page and limited searching, must balance two forces: the need to display a reasonable density of useful information and the need to allow first-time and infrequent users to learn and navigate the site easily. This implies a tension between sovereign and transient attributes in informational sites. Which stance is more dominant depends largely on whom the target personas are and what their behavior patterns are when using the site: Are they infrequent or one-time users, or are they repeat users who will return weekly or daily to view content?

The frequency with which content is updated on a site does, in some respects, influence this behavior: Informational sites with real-time information will naturally attract repeat users more than a site updated once a month. Infrequently updated sites may be used more for occasional reference (assuming that the information is not too topical) rather than for heavy repeat use and should thus be given more of a transient stance than a sovereign one. What's more, the site can configure itself into a more sovereign posture by paying attention to how often a particular user visits.

Sovereign attributes

Detailed information display is best accomplished by assuming a sovereign stance. By assuming full-screen use, designers can take advantage of all the space available to clearly present the information as well as navigational tools and wayfinding cues to keep users oriented.

The only fly in the ointment of sovereign stance for the Web is choosing which full-screen resolution is appropriate. (To a lesser degree, this is an issue for desktop applications, though it is easier for creators of desktop software to dictate the appropriate display.) Web designers need to make a decision early regarding what resolution to optimize the screen designs for. While it is possible to use a "liquid layout" to flexibly display content in a variety of browser window sizes, your designs should be optimized for common display sizes and should accommodate the lowest common denominator appropriate for the primary persona. Quantitative research is helpful in determining this: Among people similar to your personas, how many really have 800x600 screens these days?

Transient attributes

The less frequently your primary personas access the site, the more transient a stance the site needs to take. In an informational site, this manifests itself in terms of ease and clarity of navigation and orientation.

Sites used for infrequent reference might be bookmarked by users: You should make it possible for them to bookmark any page of information so that they can reliably return to it at any later time.

Users will likely visit sites that are updated weekly to monthly only intermittently, so navigation must be particularly clear. If the site can retain information about past user actions via cookies or server-side methods and present information that is organized based on what interested them previously, this could dramatically help less frequent users find what they need with minimal navigation (assuming that a user is likely to return to similar content on each visit to the site).

Transactional Web sites

Some Web sites go beyond simple clicking and searching to offer transactional functionality that allows users to accomplish something beyond acquiring information. Classic examples of transactional Web sites are online stores and financial services sites. These are typically structured in a hierarchical page-based manner, similar to an informational Web site, but in addition to informational content, the pages also contain functional elements with complex behaviors. In the case of the online store, these functional elements include the shopping cart, check-out features and the ability to save a user profile. Some shopping sites also have more sophisticated and interactive tools as well, such as "configurators," which allow users to customize or choose options related to their purchases.

Designing transactional Web sites requires attention to both information architecture to organize the pages and to interaction design to devise appropriate behaviors for the more functional elements. Of course, visual design must serve both of these ends, as well as the effective communication of key brand attributes, which is often particularly important considering the commercial nature of most transactional sites.

Postures for transactional Web sites

Online shopping, banking, investment, portal, and other transactional sites must, like informational sites, strike a balance between sovereign and transient stances. In fact, many transactional sites have a significant informational aspect — for example, online shoppers like to research and compare products or investments. During these activities, users are likely to devote significant attention to a single site, but in some cases (such as comparison shopping), they are also likely to bounce around among several sites. For these types of sites, navigational clarity is very important, as are access to supporting information and efficient transactions.

Search engines and portals like Google and Yahoo! are a special kind of transactional site designed to provide navigation to other Web sites, as well as access to aggregated news and information from a variety of sources. Clearly, performing a search and navigating to resulting sites is a transient activity, but the information aggregation aspects of a portal like Yahoo! sometimes require a more sovereign stance.

The transient aspects of users' experiences with transactional sites make it especially important that they not be forced to navigate more than necessary. While it may be tempting to break up information and functions into several pages to reduce load time and visual complexity (both good objectives), also consider the potential for confusion and click fatigue on the part of your audience. In a landmark usability study conducted in 2001 by User Interface Engineering about user perception of page load time for e-commerce sites like Amazon.com and REI.com, it turned out that *user perception of load time is more closely correlated to whether a user is able to achieve her goal than to actual load time.*[1]

Web applications

Web applications are heavily interactive and exhibit complex behaviors in much the same way that a robust desktop application does. While some Web applications maintain a page-based navigation model, these pages are more analogous to views than they are to Web documents. While many of these applications are still bound by the archaic server query/response model (which requires users to manually "submit" each state change), technology now supports robust asynchronous communication with the server and local data caching, which allows an application delivered through a browser to behave in much the same way as a networked desktop application.

Examples of Web applications include:

- ▸ Enterprise software, ranging from old school SAP interfaces duplicated in a browser to contemporary collaborative tools such as Salesforce.com and 37Signals' Basecamp

- ▸ Personal publishing tools, including blogging software such as SixApart's MoveableType, photo-sharing software such as Flickr, and of course the ubiquitous Wiki

- ▸ Productivity tools such as Writely, a browser-based word processor, and Google Spreadsheets

These Web applications can be presented to users very much like desktop applications that happen to run inside a browser window, with little penalty as long as the interactions are carefully designed to reflect technology constraints. While it certainly can be challenging to design and deliver rich and responsive interactions that work in a number of different browsers, the Web platform is very conducive to delivering tools that enable and facilitate collaboration. The Web browser is also a good method for delivering infrequently used functionality for which a user may not want to install a dedicated executable. And of course, a Web application enables users to access their information and functionality from anywhere they have Internet access. This is not always appropriate or necessary, but given the mobility of today's workforce and the popularization of telecommuting, it can certainly be of significant value to allow people to access the same tools and functionality from several different computers.

There are a number of popular misconceptions about Web applications worth mentioning. For one, they are not easier or faster to build. In our experience, building an application to be delivered through a browser takes just as much (if not more) planning, engineering, and programming as building it to be delivered through standard desktop technologies. Second, Web applications are not inherently more usable or comprehendible. It is a common assumption that because many users are familiar with some Web interactions based upon their experience with online stores and informational Web sites that they will be able to leverage this familiarity to more easily understand applications delivered through a browser. While there may be a small amount of truth in this, the fact of the matter is that designing a good user experience for any platform requires careful consideration and hard work. Delivering the product through a browser certainly doesn't get you this for free.

Postures for Web applications

Web applications, much like desktop applications, can have sovereign or transient posture, but since we use the term to refer to products with complex and sophisticated functionality, by definition they tend towards sovereign posture.

Sovereign posture Web applications strive to deliver information and functionality in a manner that best supports more complex human activities. Often this requires a rich and interactive user interface. A good example of such a Web application is Flickr, an online photo-sharing service that provides for things like drag-and-drop image sorting and in-place editing for text labels and annotation (see Figure 9-6). Other examples of sovereign posture Web applications include a multitude of enterprise software delivered through a browser.

Unlike page-oriented informational and transactional Web sites, the design of sovereign Web applications is best approached in the same manner as desktop applications. Designers also need a clear understanding of the technical limitations of the medium and what can reasonably be accomplished on time and budget by the development organization. Like sovereign desktop applications, most sovereign Web applications should be full-screen applications, densely populated with controls and data objects, and they should make use of specialized panes or other screen regions to group related functions and objects. Users should have the feeling that they are in an environment, not that they are navigating from page to page or place to place. Redrawing and re-rendering of information should be minimized (as opposed to the behavior on Web sites, where almost any action requires a full redraw).

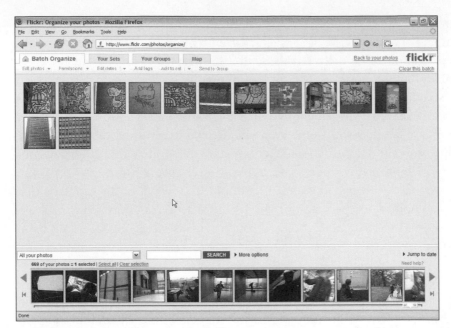

Figure 9-6 Flickr's Organize tool allows users to create sets of photos and change their attributes in a batch, in one place, without navigating through countless Web pages to do so.

The benefit of treating sovereign Web applications as desktop applications rather than as collections of Web pages is that it allows designers to break out of the constraints of page-oriented models of browser interaction to address the complex behaviors that these client-server applications require. Web sites are effective places to get information you need, just as elevators are effective places to get to a particular floor in a building. But you don't try to do actual work in elevators; similarly, users are not served by being forced to attempt to do real, interaction-rich transactional work using page-based Web sites accessed through a browser.

One advantage to delivering enterprise functionality through a browser-based user interface is that, if done correctly, it can provide users with better access to occasionally used information and functionality without requiring them to install every tool they may need on their computers. Whether it is a routine task that is only performed once a month or the occasional generation of an ad hoc report, **transient posture Web applications** aim to accomplish just this.

When designing transient posture Web applications, as with all transient applications, it is critical to provide for clear orientation and navigation. Also keep in mind that one user's transient application may be another user's sovereign application. Think hard about how compatible the two users' sets of needs are — it is commonly the case that an enterprise Web application serves a wide range of personas and requires multiple user interfaces accessing the same set of information.

Internet-enabled applications

Two of the most exciting benefits to emerge from the continued evolution of the Internet are the instant access to immense amounts of information and the ease of collaboration. Both of these benefits depend on the World Wide Web, but that does not mean your product must be delivered through a Web browser to capitalize on them.

Another excellent approach is to abandon the browser entirely and, instead, create a non-browser-based, *Internet-enabled* application. By building an application using a standard desktop platform such as .NET or Java/Swing so that it communicates with standard Internet protocols, you can provide rich, clean, sophisticated interactions without losing the ability to access data on the Web. The recent development of data interfaces like RSS and Web application programming interfaces (APIs) allows products to deliver the same information and content from the Web that a browser could, but presented with the far superior user experience that only a native application can deliver.

A good example of this is Apple iTunes, which allows users to shop for and download music and video, retrieve CD information, and share music over the Internet, all through a user interface that's been optimized for these activities in a way that would be next to impossible in a Web browser.

Another example where this is a useful approach is with PACSs (picture archiving and communication systems) used by radiologists to review patient images like MRIs (magnetic resonance imaging). These systems allow radiologists to quickly navigate through hundreds of images, zoom in on specific anatomy, and adjust the images to more clearly identify different types of tissue. Clearly these are not interactions well suited to a Web browser. However, it is very useful for radiologists to be able to review imagery from remote locations. For example, a radiologist at a big research hospital may provide a consultation for a rural hospital that doesn't have the expertise to diagnose certain conditions. To facilitate this, many PACSs use Internet protocols to enable remote viewing and collaboration.

Intranets

Intranets (and their cousins, the extranets) are usually hybrids of a Web site and Web application. An **intranet** is a private version of the Web that is only accessible to employees of a company (and its partners, clients, or vendors in the case of an extranet), typically including both a significant number of informational pages about the company, its departments, and their activities, as well as components of richer functionality ranging from timesheet entry and travel arrangements to procurement and budgeting. Designing for the informational portion requires information architecture to create a strong organizational structure, whereas designing for the application portion requires interaction design to define critical behaviors.

Other Platforms

Unlike software running on a computer, which has the luxury of being fairly immersive if need be, interaction design for mobile and public contexts requires special attention to creating an experience that coexists with the noise and activity of the real world happening all around the product. **Handheld devices, kiosks, and other embedded systems**, such as TVs, microwave ovens, automobile dashboards, cameras, bank machines, and laboratory equipment, are unique platforms with their own opportunities and limitations. Without careful consideration, adding digital smarts to devices and appliances runs the risk that they will behave more like desktop computers than like the products that your users expect and desire.

General design principles

Embedded systems (physical devices with integrated software systems) involve some unique challenges that differentiate them from desktop systems, despite the fact that they may include typical software interactions. When designing any embedded system, whether it is a smart appliance, kiosk system, or handheld device, keep these basic principles in mind:

- ▶ Don't think of your product as a computer.
- ▶ Integrate your hardware and software design.
- ▶ Let context drive the design.
- ▶ Use modes judiciously, if at all.
- ▶ Limit the scope.
- ▶ Balance navigation with display density.
- ▶ Customize for your platform.

We discuss each of these principles in more detail in the following sections.

Don't think of your product as a computer

Perhaps the most critical principle to follow while designing an embedded system is that what you are designing is *not* a computer, even though its interface might be dominated by a computer-like bitmap display. Your users will approach your product with very specific expectations of what the product can do (if it is an appliance or familiar handheld device) or with very few expectations (if you are designing a public kiosk). The last thing that you want to do is bring all the baggage — the idioms and terminology — of the desktop computer world with you to a "simple" device like a camera or microwave oven. Similarly, users of scientific and other technical equipment expect quick and direct access to data and controls within their domain, without having to wade through a computer operating system or file system to find what they need.

Programmers, especially those who have designed for desktop platforms, can easily forget that even though they are designing software, they are not always designing it for computers in the usual sense: devices with large color screens, lots of power and memory, full-size keyboards, and mouse pointing devices. Few, if any, of these assumptions are valid for most embedded devices. And most importantly, these products are used in much different contexts than desktop computers. Idioms that have become accepted on a PC are completely inappropriate on an embedded device. "Cancel" is not an appropriate label for a button to turn off an oven, and requiring people to enter a "settings" mode to change the temperature on a thermostat is preposterous. Much better than trying to squeeze a computer interface into the form factor of a small-screen device is to see it for what it is and to then figure out how digital technology can be applied to enhance the experience for its users.

Integrate your hardware and software design

From an interaction standpoint, one defining characteristic of embedded systems is the often closely intertwined relationship of hardware and software components of the interface. Unlike desktop computers, where the focus of user attention is on a large, high-resolution, color screen, most embedded systems offer hardware controls that command greater user attention and that must integrate smoothly with user tasks. Due to cost, power, and form factor constraints, hardware-based navigation and input controls must often take the place of onscreen equivalents. Therefore, they need to be specifically tailored to the requirements of the software portion of the interface as well as to the goals and ergonomic needs of the user.

It is therefore critical to design the hardware and software elements of the system's interface — and the interactions between them — simultaneously, and from a goal-directed, ergonomic, and aesthetic perspective. Many of the best, most innovative digital devices available today, such as the TiVo and iPod, were designed from such a holistic perspective, where hardware and software combine seamlessly to create a compelling and effective experience for users (see Figure 9-7). This seldom occurs in the standard development process, where hardware engineering teams regularly hand off completed mechanical and industrial designs to the software teams, who must then accommodate them, regardless of what is best from the user's perspective.

Figure 9-7 A Cooper design for a smart desktop phone, exhibiting strong integration of hardware and software controls. Users can easily adjust volume/speakerphone, dial new numbers, control playback of voicemail messages with hardware controls, and manage known contacts/numbers, incoming calls, call logs, voicemail, and conferencing features using the touch screen and thumbwheel. Rather than attempt to load too much functionality into the system, the design focuses on making the most frequent and important phone features much easier to use. Note the finger-sized regions devoted to touchable areas on the screen and use of text hints to reinforce the interactions.

Let context drive the design

Another distinct difference between embedded systems and desktop applications is the importance of environmental context. Although there can sometimes be contextual concerns with desktop applications, designers can generally assume that most software running on the desktop will be used on a computer that is stationary and located in a relatively quiet and private location. Although this is becoming less true as laptops gain both the power of desktop systems and wireless capabilities, it remains the case that users will, by necessity of the form factor, be stationary and out of the hubbub even when using laptops.

Exactly the opposite is true for many embedded systems, which are either designed for on-the-go use (handhelds) or are stationary but in a location at the center of public activity (kiosks). Even embedded systems that are mostly stationary and secluded (like household appliances) have a strong contextual element: A host juggling plates of hot food for a dinner party is going to be distracted, not in a state of mind to navigate a cumbersome set of controls for a smart oven. Navigation systems built into a car's dashboard cannot safely use "soft-keys" that change their meaning in different contexts because the driver is forced to take her eyes off the road to read each function label. Similarly, a technician on a manufacturing floor should not be required to focus on difficult-to-decipher equipment controls — that kind of distraction could be life-threatening in some circumstances.

Thus the design of embedded systems must match very closely the context of use. For handhelds, this context concerns how and where the device is physically handled. How is it held? Is it a one-handed or two-handed device? Where is it kept when not in immediate use? What other activities are users engaged in while using the device? In what environments is it being used? Is it loud, bright, or dark there? How does the user feel about being seen and heard using the device if he is in public? We'll discuss some of these issues in detail a bit later.

For kiosks, the contextual concerns focus more on the environment in which the kiosk is being placed and also on social concerns: What role does the kiosk play in the environment? Is the kiosk in the main flow of public traffic? Does it provide ancillary information, or is it the main attraction itself? Does the architecture of the environment guide people to the kiosks when appropriate? How many people are likely to use the kiosk at a time? Are there sufficient numbers of kiosks to satisfy demand without a long wait? Is there sufficient room for the kiosk and kiosk traffic without impeding other user traffic? We touch on these and other questions shortly.

Use modes judiciously, if at all

Desktop computer applications are often rich in modes: The software can be in many different states in which input and other controls are mapped to different behaviors. Tool palettes (such as those in Photoshop) are a good example: Choose a tool, and mouse and keyboard actions will be mapped to a set of functions defined by that particular tool; choose a new tool, and the behavior resulting from similar input changes.

Unfortunately, users are easily confounded by modal behavior that is less than clearly obvious. Because devices typically have smaller displays and limited input mechanisms, it is very difficult to convey what mode the product is in, and often requires significant navigational work to change modes. Take, for example, mobile telephones. They often require navigation of seemingly countless modes organized into hierarchical menus. Most cell phone users only use the dialing and address book functionality and quickly get lost if they try to access other functions. Even an important function such as silencing the ringer is often beyond the expertise of average phone users.

When designing for embedded systems, it's important to limit the number of modes, and mode switches should ideally result naturally from situational changes in context. For example, it makes sense for a PDA/phone to shift into telephone mode when an incoming call is received and to shift back to its previous mode when the call is terminated. (Permitting a call while other data is being accessed is a preferable alternative.) If modes are truly necessary, they should be clearly accessible in the interface, and the exit path should also be immediately clear. The four hardware application buttons on most Palm OS handhelds are a good example of clearly marked modes (see Figure 9-8).

Limit the scope

Most embedded systems are used in specific contexts and for specific purposes. Avoid the temptation to turn these systems into general-purpose computers. Users will be better served by devices that enable them to do a limited set of tasks more effectively, than by devices that attempt to address too many disparate tasks in one place. Devices such as Microsoft Windows Mobile handhelds, which of late have attempted to emulate full desktop systems, run the risk of alienating users with cumbersome interfaces saturated with functions whose only reason for inclusion is that they currently exist on desktop systems. While many of us are reliant on our "smart" phones (such as Treos and BlackBerries), I think most would agree that the depth of functionality included on these devices does somewhat compromise their efficacy as telephones.

Figure 9-8 The Palm Treo 650 provides hardware buttons for switching between modes (notice the calendar and e-mail buttons on either side of the four-way rocker).

Many devices share information with desktop systems. It makes sense to approach the design of such systems from a desktop-centric point of view: The device is an extension or *satellite* of the desktop, providing key information and functions in contexts where the desktop system isn't available. Scenarios can help you determine what functions are truly useful for such satellite systems.

Balance navigation with display density

Many devices are constrained by limited display real estate. Whether limited by hardware cost, form factor, portability, or power requirements, designers must make the best use of the display technology available while meeting the information needs of users. Every pixel, segment, and square millimeter of display are significant in the design of display-constrained embedded systems. Such limitations in display real estate almost always result in a trade-off between clarity of information displayed and complexity of navigation. By appropriately limiting the scope of functions, you can ameliorate this situation somewhat, but the tension between display and navigation almost always exists to some degree.

You must carefully map out embedded systems' displays, developing a hierarchy of information. Determine what is the most important information to get across, and make that feature the most prominent. Then, look to see what ancillary information can still fit on the screen. Try to avoid flashing between different sets of information by blinking the screen. For example, an oven with a digital control might display both the temperature you set it to reach and how close it is to reaching that temperature by flashing between the two numerical values. However, this solution easily leads to confusion about which number is which. A better solution is to display the temperature that the oven has been set to reach and next to that, to show a small bar graph that registers how close to the desired temperature the oven currently is. You must also leave room in the display to show the state of associated hardware controls, or better yet, use controls that can display their own state, such as hardware buttons with lamps or hardware that maintains a physical state (for example, toggles, switches, sliders, and knobs).

Minimize input complexity

Almost all embedded systems have a simplified input system rather than a keyboard or desktop-style pointing device. This means that any input to the system — especially textual input — is awkward, slow, and difficult for users. Even the most sophisticated of these input systems, such as touch screens, voice recognition, handwriting recognition, and thumb-boards, are cumbersome in comparison to full-sized keyboards and mice. Thus, it's important that input be limited and simplified as much as possible.

Devices such as RIM's BlackBerry make effective use of a thumbwheel as their primary selection mechanism: Spinning the wheel very rapidly scrolls through possible choices, and pressing the wheel (or a nearby button) selects a given item. Both of these devices also make use of thumb-boards when text data entry is necessary.

In contrast, the Palm Treo makes use of a touch screen and a thumb-board. This would be effective if you could adequately activate everything on the Treo screen by the touch of a finger. However, most Palm screen widgets are too small and require users to rely on a stylus for accurate interactions. This means that users must switch between stylus and thumb-board, making for considerably awkward input interactions. Palm has attempted to compensate for this in recent models by adding a five-way (left, right, up, down, and center) D-pad between the touch screen and thumb-board, which allows users to navigate to and activate screen widgets without actually touching the screen (see Figure 9-8).

Kiosks, whose screens are usually larger, should nonetheless avoid complex text input whenever possible. Touch screens can display soft keyboards if they are large enough; each virtual key should be large enough to make it difficult for the user to accidentally mistype. Touch screens should also avoid idioms that involve dragging; single-tap idioms are easier to control and more obvious (when given proper affordance) to novice users.

Designing for handhelds

Handheld devices present special challenges for interaction designers. Because they are designed specifically for mobile use, these devices must be small, lightweight, economical in power consumption, ruggedly built, and easy to hold and manipulate in busy, distracting situations. Especially for handhelds, close collaboration among interaction designers, industrial designers, programmers, and mechanical engineers is a real necessity. Of particular concern are size and clarity of display, ease of input and control, and sensitivity to context. This section discusses, in more detail, these concerns and useful approaches to address them. The following are the most useful interaction and interface principles for designing handheld devices:

▶ **Strive for integration of functionality to minimize navigation.** Handheld devices are used in a variety of specific contexts. By exploring context scenarios, you can get a good idea of what functions need to be integrated to provide a seamless, goal-directed experience.

Most *convergence* devices run the risk of pleasing nobody by attempting to do too much. Communicators such as the Treo are at their best when they integrate functionality for a more seamless experience of communication-related functions. These devices currently do a reasonable job of integrating the phone and address book: When a call arrives, you can see the full name from the address book and, by tapping on a name in the address book, you can dial it. However, this integration could be taken a step further. Clicking on a name in an address book could show you *all* documents known to the communicator that are associated with that person: appointments, e-mails, phone calls from the log, memos including the caller's name, Web sites associated with him, and so on. Likewise, clicking on the e-mail address in the address book could launch the mail application. Some recent applications for communicators, such as iambic Inc.'s Agendus, are beginning to take this approach to integrating what were once different applications into a more seamless flow that matches users' goals.

▶ **Think about how the device will be held and carried.** Physical models are essential to understanding how a device will be manipulated. The models should at least reflect the size, shape, and articulation (flip covers and so on) of the device, and they are more effective when weight is also taken into account. These models should be employed by designers in context and key path scenarios to validate proposed form factors. Labels on buttons have very different contextual needs depending on where and when they will be used. For example, the labels on a package-delivery tracking tool don't need to be backlit like those on a cell phone or TV remote control.

▶ **Determine early on whether the device or application will support one-handed or two-handed operations.** Again, scenarios should make it clear which modes are acceptable to users in various contexts. It's okay for a device that is intended primarily for one-handed use to support some advanced functions that require two-handed use, as long as they are needed infrequently. A handheld inventory tool, for example, that allows all counting to be done single-handedly, but then requires two hands to submit the entered data confers no advantage because the submit function is part of a frequent-use scenario.

▶ **Consider whether the device will be a satellite or a standalone.** Most handheld data devices are best designed as *satellites* of desktop data systems. Palm and Windows Mobile devices both succeed best as portable systems that communicate with desktop systems or servers. Rather than replicate all desktop functions, they are geared primarily towards accessing and viewing information and provide only lightweight input and editing features. The latest handheld models extend the idea of a tethered satellite into the realm of wireless connectivity, making the idea of the satellite device even more powerful and appropriate.

On the other hand, some devices, such as standard cell phones, are truly designed to be standalone. It's possible to upload phone numbers from PCs to many cell phones, but most users never try to do so because of the interaction complexity. Such standalone devices are most successful when they focus on a narrow set of functions, but provide world-class behaviors for those functions.

▶ **Avoid use of pluralized and pop-up windows.** On small, low-resolution screens, floating windows typically have no place. Interfaces, in this regard, should resemble sovereign posture applications, taking the full-screen real estate. Modeless dialogs should be avoided at all cost, and modal dialogs and errors should, whenever possible, be replaced using the techniques discussed in Chapters 24 and 25.

Postures for handheld devices

Designing for handheld devices is an exercise in hardware limitations: input mechanisms, screen size and resolution, and power consumption, to name a few. One of the most important insights that many designers have now realized with regard to some handheld devices is that handhelds are often not standalone systems. They are, as in the case of personal information managers like Palm and Windows Mobile devices, satellites of a desktop system, used more to view information than perform heavy input on their own. (Despite the fact that many handhelds have thumb-boards or detachable fold-up keyboards, they are still hardly fit for input-intense interactions.) These satellite devices usually take a transient posture. In a typical interaction, a user quickly refers to his daily calendar or adds an item to his to-do list while sitting at a stop light.

Cellular telephones are an interesting type of handheld device. Phones are *not* satellite devices; they are primary communication devices. However, from an interface posture standpoint, phones are also transient. A user places a call as quickly as possible and then abandons the interface in favor of the conversation. The best interface for a phone is arguably nonvisual. Voice activation is perfect for placing a call; opening the flip lid on a phone is probably the most effective way of answering it (or again using voice activation for hands-free use). The more transient the phone's interface is, the better.

In our work we routinely hear about ideas to create sovereign applications for handheld devices, such as a product that allows radiologists to review medical imaging such as x-rays and MRIs while at the golf course. Clearly portable display technology has a long time to go before these products are ready for the market, and it remains to be seen how appropriate handhelds can be for sovereign applications (aside from for entertainment products like portable game devices and portable DVD players).

Designing for kiosks

On the surface, kiosks may appear to have much in common with desktop interfaces: large, colorful screens and reasonably beefy processors behind them. But as far as user interactions are concerned, the similarity ends there. Kiosk users, in comparison with sovereign desktop application users, are at best infrequent users of kiosks and, most typically, use any given kiosk once. Furthermore, kiosk users will either have one very specific goal in mind when approaching a kiosk or no readily definable goal at all. Kiosk users typically don't have access to keyboards or pointing devices, and often wouldn't be able to use either effectively if they did. Finally, kiosk users are typically in a public environment, full of noise and distractions, and may be accompanied by others who will be using the kiosk in tandem with them. Each of these environmental issues has a bearing on kiosk design (see Figure 9-9).

Transaction versus exploration

Kiosks generally fall into two categorical types: **transactional** and **explorational**. Transactional kiosks are those that provide some tightly scoped transaction or service. These include bank machines (ATMs) and ticketing machines such as those used in airports, train and bus depots, and some movie theaters. Even gasoline pumps and vending machines can be considered a simple type of transactional kiosk. Users of transactional kiosks have very specific goals in mind: to get cash, a ticket, a Tootsie Roll, or some specific piece of information. These users have no interest in anything but accomplishing their goals as quickly and painlessly as possible.

Figure 9-9 The GettyGuide, a system of informational kiosks at the J. Getty Center and Villa in Los Angeles, designed by Cooper in collaboration with the Getty and Triplecode.

Explorational kiosks are most often found in museums. Educational and entertainment-oriented kiosks are typically not a main attraction, but provide additional information and a richer experience for users who have come to see the main exhibits (though there are certainly a few museums, such as the Experience Music Project in Seattle, where interactive kiosks form the basis for some exhibits). Explorational kiosks are somewhat different from transactional kiosks in that users typically have open-ended expectations when approaching them. They may be curious, or have the desire to be entertained or enlightened, but may not have any specific end goals in mind. (On the other hand, they may also be interested in finding the café or nearest restroom, which are goals that can be supported alongside the more open-ended experience goals.) For explorational kiosks, it is the act of exploring that must engage the user. Therefore, the kiosk's interface must not only be clear and easy to master in terms of navigation, but it must also be aesthetically pleasing and visually (and possibly audibly) exciting to users. Each screen must be interesting in itself, but should also encourage users to further explore other content in the system.

Interaction in a public environment

Transactional kiosks, as a rule, require no special enticements to attract users. However, they do need to be placed in an optimal location to both be obviously visible and to handle the flow of user traffic they will generate. Use wayfinding and sign systems in conjunction with these kiosks for the most effectiveness. Some transactional kiosks, especially ATMs, need to take into account security issues: If their location seems insecure, users will avoid them or use them at their own risk. Architectural planning for transactional kiosks should occur at the same time as the interaction and industrial design planning.

As with transactional kiosks, place explorational kiosks carefully and use wayfinding systems in conjunction with them. They must not obstruct any main attractions and yet must be close enough to the attractions to be perceived as connected to them. There must be adequate room for people to gather: Exploration kiosks are more likely to be used by groups (such as family members). A particular challenge lies in choosing the right number of kiosks to install at a location — companies employing transactional kiosks often engage in user flow research at a site to determine optimum numbers. People don't linger long at transactional kiosks, and they are usually more willing to wait in line because they have a concrete end goal in mind. Explorational kiosks, on the other hand, encourage lingering, which makes them unattractive to onlookers. Because potential users have few expectations of the contents of an explorational kiosk, it becomes difficult for them to justify waiting in line to use one. It is safe to assume that most people will only approach an explorational kiosk when it is vacant.

When designing kiosk interfaces, carefully consider the use of sound. Explorational kiosks seem naturals for use of rich, audible feedback and content, but volume levels should be chosen so as not to encroach on the experience of the main attraction such kiosks often support. Audible feedback should be used sparingly for transactional kiosks, but it can be useful, for example, to help remind users to take back their bankcard or the change from their purchases.

Also, because kiosks are in public spaces, designing to account for the needs of differently-abled users is especially important. For more about designing for accessibility, see Chapter 26.

Managing input

Most kiosks make use either of touch screens or hardware buttons and keypads that are mapped to objects and functions on the screen. In the case of touch screens, the same principles apply here as for other touch screen interfaces:

▶ **Make sure that your click targets are large enough.** Touchable objects should be large enough to be manipulated with a finger, high contrast, colorful, and well separated on the screen to avoid accidental selection. A 20mm click target is a typical minimum if users will be close to the screen and not in a hurry — this size should be increased for use at arm's length or when in a rush. A good low-tech trick to make sure that your click targets are large enough is to print the screens at actual size, ink the end of your finger with a stamp pad, and run through your scenarios at a realistic speed. If your fingerprints are overlapping the edges of your click targets, you probably should increase their size.

▶ **Use soft-keyboard input sparingly.** It may be tempting to make use of an onscreen keyboard for entering data on touch screen kiosks. However, this input mechanism should only be used to enter very small amounts of text. Not only is it awkward for the user, but it typically results in a thick coating of fingerprints on the display.

▶ **Avoid drag-and-drop.** Drag-and-drop can be very difficult for users to master on a touch screen, making it inappropriate for kiosk users who will never spend enough time to master demanding interaction idioms. Scrolling of any kind should also be avoided on kiosks except when absolutely necessary.

Some kiosks make use of hardware buttons mapped to onscreen functions in lieu of touch screens. As in handheld systems, the key concern is that these mappings remain consistent, with similar functions mapped to the same buttons from screen to screen. These buttons also should not be placed so far from the screen or arranged spatially so that the mapping becomes unclear (see Chapter 10 for a more detailed discussion of mapping issues). In general, if a touch screen is feasible, it should be strongly considered in favor of mapped hardware buttons.

Postures for kiosks

The large, full-screen nature of kiosks would appear to bias them towards sovereign posture, but there are several reasons why the situation is not quite that simple. First, users of kiosks are often first-time users (with some obvious exceptions, such as ATM users and users of ticket machines for public transport), and are in most cases not daily users. Second, most people do not spend any significant amount of time in front of a kiosk: They perform a simple transaction or search, get the information they need, and then move on. Third, most kiosks employ either touch screens or bezel buttons to the side of the display, and neither of these input mechanisms support the high data density you would expect of a sovereign application. Fourth, kiosk users are rarely comfortably seated in front of an optimally placed monitor, but are standing in a public place with bright ambient light and many distractions. These user behaviors and constraints should bias most kiosks towards transient posture, with simple navigation, large, colorful, engaging interfaces with clear affordances for controls, and clear mappings between hardware controls (if any) and their corresponding software functions. As in the design of handhelds, floating windows and dialogs should be avoided; any such information or behavior is best integrated into a single, full screen (as in sovereign-posture applications). Kiosks thus tread an interesting middle ground between the two most common desktop postures.

Because transactional kiosks often guide users through a process or a set of information screen by screen, contextual orientation and navigation are more important than global navigation. Rather than helping users understand where they are *in the system*, help them to understand where they are *in their process*. It's also important for transactional kiosks to provide escape hatches that allow users to cancel transactions and start over at any point.

 DESIGN principle   Kiosks should be optimized for first-time use.

Educational and **entertainment kiosks** vary somewhat from the strict transient posture required of more **transactional kiosks**. In this case, exploration of the kiosk environment is more important than the simple completion of single transactions or searches. In this case, more data density and more complex interactions and visual transitions can sometimes be introduced to positive effect, but the limitations of the input mechanisms need to be carefully respected, lest the user lose the ability to successfully navigate the interface.

Designing for television-based interfaces

Television-based interfaces such as TiVo and most cable and satellite set-top boxes rely on user interaction through a remote control that is typically operated by users when they are sitting across the room from the television. Unless the remote control uses radio-frequency communications (most use one-way infrared), it also means that the user will need to point the remote towards the TV and set-top boxes. All of this makes for challenges and limitations in designing effective information display controls for system navigation and operation.

> ▶ **Use a screen layout and visual design that can be easily read from across the room.** Even if you think you can rely on high-definition television (HDTV) screen resolutions, your users will not be as close to the TV screen as they would be to, say, a computer monitor. This means that text and other navigable content will need to be displayed in a larger size, which will in turn dictate how screens of information are organized.

▸ **Keep onscreen navigation simple.** People don't think about their TV like they do a computer, and the navigation mechanisms provided by remotes are limited, so the best approach is one that can be mapped easily to a five-way (up, down, left, right, and center) controller. There may be room to innovate with scroll wheels and other input mechanisms for content navigation, but these will likely need to be compatible with other set-top devices in addition to yours (see the next point), so take care in your design choices. In addition, visual wayfinding techniques such as color-coding screens by functional area and providing visual or textual hints about what navigational and command options are available on each screen (TiVo does a particularly good job of this) are important for ensuring ease of use.

▸ **Keep control integration in mind.** Most people hate the fact that they need multiple remotes to control all the home entertainment devices connected to their TV. By enabling control of commonly used functions on other home entertainment devices besides the one you are designing for (ideally with minimal configuration), you will be meeting a significant user need. This will mean that your product's remote control or console will need to broadcast commands for other equipment and may need to keep track of some of the operational state of that equipment as well. Logitech's line of Harmony universal remote controls does both of these things, and the remotes are configured via a Web application when connected to a computer via USB.

▸ **Keep remote controls as simple as possible.** Many users find complex remote controls daunting, and most functions available from typical home entertainment remotes remain little used. Especially when remote controls take on universal functionality, the tendency is to cram them with buttons — 40, 50, or even 60 buttons on a universal remote is not unusual. One way to mitigate this is to add a display to the remote, which can allow controls to appear in context, and thus fewer buttons are available in any one source. These controls can be accessible via a touch screen or via soft-labeled physical buttons that lie adjacent to the screen. Each of these approaches has drawbacks: Most touch screens do not provide tactile feedback, so the user is forced to look away from his TV to actuate a touch screen control. Soft-labeled buttons address this problem, but add more buttons back to the surface of the remote. The addition of a display on your remote may also tempt you to allow navigation to multiple "pages" of content or controls on the display. While there are instances where this may be warranted, any design choice that divides the user's attention between two displays (the TV and the remote) runs the risk of creating user confusion and annoyance.

▸ **Focus on user goals and activities, not on product functions.** Most home entertainment systems require users to understand the topology and states of the system in order to use it effectively: For example, to watch a movie, a user may need to know how to turn the TV on, how to turn the DVD player on, how to switch input on the TV to the one that the DVD player is connected to, how to turn on surround sound, and how to set the TV to widescreen mode. Doing this may require three separate remote controls, or half a dozen button presses on a function-oriented universal remote. Remote controls like Logitech's Harmony take a different approach: organizing the control around user activities (such as "watch a movie"), and using knowledge the user provides (at setup time) on what is connected to what to perform the appropriate sequence of device-level commands. While this is much more complex to develop, it is a clear win for the user if implemented well.

Designing for automotive interfaces

Automotive interfaces, especially those that offer sophisticated navigation and entertainment (telematics) functionality, have a particular challenge around driver safety. Complex or confusing interactions that require too much attention to accomplish can put all on the road at risk, and such systems require significant design effort and usability validation to avoid such issues. This can be a challenge, given the spatial limitations of the automobile dashboard, center console, and steering wheel.

▶ **Minimize time that hands are off the wheel.** Commonly used navigation controls (e.g., play/pause, mute, skip/scan) should be available on the steering wheel (driver use) as well as on the center console (passenger use).

▶ **Enforce consistent layout from screen to screen.** By maintaining a very consistent layout, the driver will be able to keep his bearings between context shifts.

▶ **Use direct control mappings when possible.** Controls with labels on them are better than soft-labeled controls. Touch screen buttons with tactile feedback are also preferable to soft-labels with adjacent hard buttons, because again it requires fewer cognitive cycles on the part of the driver operating the system to make the mapping.

▶ **Choose input mechanisms carefully.** It's much easier for drivers to select content via knobs than a set of buttons. There are fewer controls to clutter the interface, knobs protrude and so are easier to reach, and they afford (when properly designed) both rough and fine controls in an elegant and intuitive way.

▶ **Keep mode/context switching simple and predictable.** With its iDrive system, BMW mapped most of the car's entertainment, climate control, and navigation into a single control that was a combination of a knob and a joystick. The idea was to make things simple, but by overloading the control so extremely, BMW created a danger for users by requiring them to navigate an interface in order to switch contexts and modes. Modes (e.g., switching from CD to FM, or climate control to navigation) should be directly accessible with a single touch or button press, and the location of these mode buttons should be fixed and consistent across the interface.

► **Provide audible feedback.** Audible confirmations of commands help reduce the need for the driver to take his eyes off the road. However, care needs to be taken to ensure that this feedback is itself not too loud or distracting. For in-car navigation systems, verbal feedback highlighting driving directions can be helpful, as long as the verbal instructions (e.g., turning instructions and street names) are delivered early enough for the driver to properly react to them. Speech *input* is another possibility, using spoken commands to operate the interface. However, the automobile environment is noisy, and it is not clear that verbalizing a command, especially if it needs to be repeated or corrected for, is any less cognitively demanding than pressing a button. While this kind of feature makes for great marketing, we think the jury is still out on whether it makes for a better or safer user experience in the automobile.

Designing for appliances

Most appliances have extremely simple displays and rely heavily on hardware buttons and dials to manipulate the state of the appliance. In some cases, however, major appliances (notably washers and dryers) will sport color LCD touch screens allowing rich output and direct input.

Appliance interfaces, like the phone interfaces mentioned in the previous section, should primarily be considered transient posture interfaces. Users of these interfaces will seldom be technology-savvy and should, therefore, be presented the most simple and straightforward interfaces possible. These users are also accustomed to hardware controls. Unless an unprecedented ease of use can be achieved with a touch screen, dials and buttons (with appropriate tactile, audible, and visual feedback via a view-only display or even hardware lamps) may be a better choice. Many appliance makers make the mistake of putting dozens of new — and unwanted — features into their new, digital models. Instead of making it easier, that "simple" LCD touch screen becomes a confusing array of unworkable controls.

Another reason for a transient stance in appliance interfaces is that users of appliances are trying to get something very specific done. Like users of transactional kiosks, they are not interested in exploring the interface or getting additional information; they simply want to put the washer on normal cycle or cook their frozen dinners.

One aspect of appliance design demands a different posture: Status information indicating what cycle the washer is on or what the VCR is set to record should be presented as a daemonic icon, providing minimal status quietly in a corner. If more than minimal status is required, an auxiliary posture for this information then becomes appropriate.

Designing for audible interfaces

Audible interfaces, such as those found in voice message systems and automated call centers, involve some special challenges. Navigation is the most critical challenge because it is easy to get lost in a tree of functionality with no means of visualizing where one is in the hierarchy, and bad phone tree interactions are a common way to erode an otherwise strong brand identity. (Almost all voice interfaces are based upon a tree, even if the options are hidden behind voice recognition, which introduces a whole other set of problems.)

The following are some simple principles for designing usable audible interfaces:

- **Organize and name functions according to user mental models.** This is important in any design, but doubly important when functions are described only verbally, and only in context of the current function. Be sure to examine context scenarios to determine what the most important functions are, and make them the most easily reachable. This means listing the most common options first.

- **Always signpost the currently available functions.** The system should, after every user action, restate the current available activities and how to invoke them.

- **Always provide a way to get back one step and to the top level.** The interface should, after every action, tell the user how to go back one step in the function structure (usually up one node in the tree) and how to get to the top level of the function tree.

- **Always provide a means to speak with a human.** If appropriate, the interface should give the user instructions on how to switch to a human assistant after every action, especially if the user seems to be having trouble.

- **Give the user enough time to respond.** Systems usually require verbal or telephone keypad entry of information. Testing should be done to determine an appropriate length of time to wait; keep in mind that phone keypads can be awkward and very slow for entering textual information.

In conclusion, it's important to keep in mind that the top-level patterns of posture and platform should be among the first decisions to be made in the design of an interactive product. In our experience, many poorly designed products suffer from the failure to make these decisions consciously at any point. Rather than diving directly into the details, take a step back and consider what technical platform and behavioral posture will best meet the needs of your users and business, and what the implications of these decisions might be on detailed interactions.

Notes

1. Perfetti and Landesman, 2001

10

Orchestration and Flow

If our goal is to make the people who use our products more productive, effective, and engaging, we must ensure that users remain in the right frame of mind. This chapter discusses a kind of mental ergonomics — how we can ensure that our products support user intelligence and effectiveness and how we can avoid disrupting the state of productive concentration that we want our users to be able to maintain.

Flow and Transparency

When people are able to concentrate wholeheartedly on an activity, they lose awareness of peripheral problems and distractions. The state is called **flow**, a concept first identified by Mihaly Csikszentmihalyi in *Flow: The Psychology of Optimal Experience*.

In *Peopleware: Productive Projects and Teams*, Tom DeMarco and Timothy Lister describe flow as a "condition of deep, nearly meditative involvement." Flow often induces a "gentle sense of euphoria" and can make you unaware of the passage of time. Most significantly, a person in a state of flow can be extremely productive, especially when engaged in constructive activities such as engineering, design, development, or writing. To state the obvious, then, to make people more productive and happy, it behooves us to design interactive products to promote and enhance flow, and for us to go to great pains to avoid any potentially flow-disturbing behavior. If the application consistently rattles a user and disrupts her flow, it becomes difficult for her to maintain that productive state.

In most cases, if a user could achieve his goals magically, without your product, he would. By the same token, if a user needs the product but could achieve his goals without messing about with a user interface, he would. Interacting with a lot of software will never be an entirely aesthetically pleasing experience (with many obvious exceptions, including things like games, creative tools like music sequencers, and content-delivery systems like Web browsers). For a large part, interacting with software (especially business software) is a pragmatic exercise.

 DESIGN principle   No matter how cool your interface is, less of it would be better.

Directing your attention to the interaction itself puts the emphasis on the side effects of the tools and technology rather than on the user's goals. A user interface is an artifact, not directly associated with the goals of a user. Next time you find yourself crowing about what cool interaction you've designed, just remember that the ultimate user interface for most purposes is no interface at all.

To create a sense of flow, our interaction with software must become **transparent**. When a novelist writes well, the craft of the writer becomes invisible, and the reader sees the story and characters with clarity undisturbed by the technique of the writer. Likewise, when a product interacts well with a person, interaction mechanics disappear, leaving the person face to face with his objectives, unaware of the intervening software. The poor writer is a visible writer, and a poor interaction designer looms with a clumsily visible presence in his software.

 DESIGN principle   Well-orchestrated user interfaces are transparent.

To a novelist, there is no such thing as a "good" sentence in isolation from the story being told. There are no rules for the way sentences should be constructed to be transparent. It all depends on what the protagonist is doing, or what effect the author wants to create. The writer knows not to insert an obscure word in a particularly quiet and sensitive passage, lest it sound like a sour note in a string quartet. The same goes for software. The interaction designer must train himself to hear sour notes in the **orchestration** of software interaction. It is vital that all the elements in an interface work coherently together towards a single goal. When an application's communication with a person is well orchestrated, it becomes almost invisible.

Webster defines orchestration as "harmonious organization," a reasonable phrase for what we should expect from interactive products. Harmonious organization doesn't yield to fixed rules. You can't create guidelines like, "Five buttons on a dialog box are good" and "Seven buttons on a dialog box are too many." Yet it is easy to see that a dialog box with 35 buttons is probably to be avoided. The major difficulty with such analysis is that it treats the problem *in vitro*. It doesn't take into account the problem being solved; it doesn't take into account what a person is doing at the time or what he is trying to accomplish.

Designing Harmonious Interactions

While there are no universal rules to define a harmonious interaction (just as there are no universal rules to define a harmonious interval in music), we've found these strategies to be effective at getting interaction design moving in the right direction:

1. Follow users' mental models.

2. Less is more.

3. Enable users to direct, don't force them to discuss.

4. Keep tools close at hand.

5. Provide modeless feedback.

6. Design for the probable; provide for the possible.

7. Provide comparisons.

8. Provide direct manipulation and graphical input.

9. Reflect object and application status.

10. Avoid unnecessary reporting.

11. Avoid blank slates.

12. Differentiate between command and configuration.

13. Provide choices.

14. Hide the ejector seat levers.

15. Optimize for responsiveness; accommodate latency.

Each principle is discussed in detail below.

 DESIGN principle   Follow users' mental models.

We introduced the concept of mental models in Chapter 2. Different people have different mental models of a given activity or process, but they rarely imagine them in terms of the detailed mechanics of how computers function. Each user naturally forms a mental image about how the software performs its task. The mind looks for some pattern of cause and effect to gain insight into the machine's behavior.

For example, in a hospital information system, the physicians and nurses have a mental model of patient information that derives from how they think about patients and treatment. It therefore makes most sense to find patient information by using names of patients as an index. Each physician has certain patients, so it makes additional sense to filter the patients in the clinical interface so that each physician can choose from a list of her own patients, organized alphabetically by name. On the other hand, in the business office of the hospital, the clerks there are worried about overdue bills. They don't initially think about these bills in terms of who or what the bill is for, but rather in terms of how late the bill is (and perhaps how big the bill is). Thus, for the business office interface, it makes sense to sort first by time overdue and perhaps by amount due, with patient names as a secondary organizational principle.

 DESIGN principle   Less is more.

For many things, more is better. In the world of interaction design, the contrary is true. We should constantly strive to reduce the number of elements in user interfaces without reducing the capabilities of the products we are creating. To do this, we must do more with less; this is where careful orchestration becomes important. We must coordinate and control the power of the product without letting the interface become a gaggle of windows and dialogs, covered with a scattering of unrelated and rarely used controls.

It is very common for user interfaces to be complex but not very powerful. Products like this typically segregate functionality into silos and allow a user to perform a single task without providing access to related tasks. When the first edition of this book was published in 1995, this problem was ubiquitous. Something as common as a "Save" dialog in a Windows application failed to provide the ability for users to also rename or delete the files they were looking at. This required users to go to an entirely different place to accomplish these very similar tasks, ultimately requiring applications and operating systems to provide *more interface*. Thankfully, contemporary operating systems are much better at this sort of thing. Because they have started to offer appropriate functionality based upon a user's context, users are less often required to shuffle off to various places in the interface to accomplish simple and common tasks.

We have, however, a rather long way to go. In our work we see a lot of enterprise software where each function or feature is housed in a separate dialog or window, with no consideration for the way people must use these functions together to accomplish something. It is not uncommon for a user to use one menu command to open a window to find a bit of information, copy that information to the clipboard, and then use a different menu command for a different window, merely to paste that bit of information in a field. Not only is this inelegant and crude, but it is error-prone and fails to capitalize on a productive division of labor between humans and machines. Typically, products don't end up this way on purpose — they have either been built in an ad hoc manner over years, or by several disconnected teams in different organizational silos.

Motorola's popular Razr phone is an example of the problem: while the industrial design of the phone is deservedly award-winning for its elegance, the software was inherited from a previous generation of Motorola phones, and appears to have been developed by multiple teams who didn't coordinate their efforts. For example, the phone's address book uses a different text-entry interface than its calendar application. Each software team must have devised a separate solution, resulting in two interfaces doing the job that one should have done — both a waste of development resources and a source of confusion and friction to Motorola's users.

Mullet and Sano's classic *Designing Visual Interfaces* includes a useful discussion of the idea of **elegance**, which can be thought of as a novel, simple, economical, and graceful way of solving a design problem. Because the software inside an interactive product is typically so incredibly complex, it becomes all the more important to value elegance and simplicity; these attributes are crucial for technology to effectively serve human needs.

A minimalist approach to product design is inextricably tied to a clear understanding of purpose — what the user of a product is trying to accomplish using the tool. Without this sense of purpose, interactive products are just a disorganized jumble of technological capabilities. A model example where a strong sense of purpose has driven a minimal user interface is the classic Google search interface consisting of a text field, two buttons ("Google Search," which brings the user to a list of results, and "I'm Feeling Lucky," which brings the user directly to the top result), the Google logotype, and a couple of links to the broader universe of Google functionality (see Figure 10-1). Other good examples of minimal user interfaces include the iPod Shuffle, where by carefully defining an appropriate set of features to meet a specific set of user needs, Apple created a highly usable product with one switch and five buttons (and no screen!), and Hog Bay Software's WriteRoom, an incredibly simple text editor with no user interface aside from an area in which to write text, which is automatically saved, eliminating the need to even interact with files.

Figure 10-1 The celebrated Google search interface is a classic example of minimalist interface design, where every screen element is purposeful and direct.

It's worth noting that the quest for simplicity can be taken too far — reduction is a balancing act that requires a good understanding of users' mental models. The iPod hardware interface mentioned as an example of elegance and economy in design is also at odds with some users' expectations. If you're coming from the world of tape decks and CD players, odds are it feels a bit weird to use the iPod's Play/Pause toggle to shut the device off, and the Menu button to turn the device on. This is a classic case of visual simplicity leading to cognitive complexity. In this situation, these idioms are simple enough to learn easily, and the consequences of getting it wrong are fairly small, so it's had little impact on the overall success of the product.

 DESIGN principle   Enable users to direct, don't force them to discuss.

It seems that many developers imagine the ideal interface to be a two-way conversation with a user. However, most people don't see it that way. Most people would rather interact with the software in the same way they interact with, say, their cars. They open the door and get in when they want to go somewhere. They step on the accelerator when they want the car to move forward and the brake when it is time to stop; they turn the wheel when they want the car to turn.

This ideal interaction is not a dialogue — it's more like using a tool. When a carpenter hits nails, she doesn't discuss the nail with the hammer; she directs the hammer onto the nail. In a car, the driver gives the car direction when he wants to change the car's behavior. The driver expects direct feedback from the car and its environment in terms appropriate to the device: the view out the windshield, the readings on the various gauges on the dashboard, the sound of rushing air and tires on pavement, and the feel of lateral g-forces and vibration from the road. The carpenter expects similar feedback: the feel of the nail sinking, the sound of the steel striking steel, and the heft of the hammer's weight.

The driver certainly doesn't expect the car to interrogate him with a dialog box, nor would the carpenter appreciate one (like the one in Figure 10-2) appearing on her hammer.

Figure 10-2 Just because programmers are accustomed to seeing messages like this, it doesn't mean that people from other walks of life are. Nobody wants his machine to scold him. If we guide our machines in a dunderheaded way, we *expect* to get a dunderheaded response. Sure, they can protect us from fatal errors, but scolding isn't the same thing as protecting.

One of the reasons interactive products often aggravate people is that they don't act like cars or hammers. Instead, they often have the temerity to try to engage us in a dialogue — to inform us of our shortcomings and to demand answers from us. From a user's point of view, the roles are reversed: It should be the person doing the demanding and the software doing the answering.

With direct manipulation, we can point to what we want. If we want to move an object from A to B, we click on it and drag it there. As a general rule, the better, more flow-inducing interfaces are those with plentiful and sophisticated direct manipulation idioms.

 DESIGN principle   Keep tools close at hand.

Most applications are too complex for one mode of direct manipulation to cover all their features. Consequently, most applications offer a set of different tools to users. These tools are really different modes of behavior that the product enters. Offering tools is a compromise with complexity, but we can still do a lot to make tool selection and manipulation easy and to prevent it from disturbing flow. Mainly, we must ensure that information about tools and application state is clear and present and that transitions between tools are quick and simple.

Tools should be close at hand, commonly on palettes or toolbars for beginner and intermediate users, and accessible by keyboard command for expert users. This way, a user can see them easily and can select them with a single click or keystroke. If a user must divert his attention from the application to search out a tool, his concentration will be broken. It's as if he had to get up from his desk and wander down the hall to find a pencil. Also, he should never have to put tools away.

DESIGN principle   Provide modeless feedback.

When users of an interactive product manipulate tools and data, it's usually important to clearly present the status and effect of these manipulations. This information must be easy to see and understand without obscuring or interfering with a user's actions.

There are several ways for an application to present information or feedback to users. Unfortunately, the most common method is to pop up a dialog box on the screen. This technique is modal: It puts the application into a special state that must be dealt with before it can return to its normal state, and before the person can continue with her task. A better way to inform users is with **modeless feedback**.

Feedback is *modeless* whenever information for users is built into the structures of the interface and doesn't stop the normal flow of activities and interaction. In Microsoft Word, you can see what page you are on, what section you are in, how many pages are in the current document, and what position the cursor is in, modelessly just by looking at the status bar at the bottom of the screen — you don't have to go out of your way to ask for that information.

If you want to know how many words are in your document, however, you have to call up the Word Count dialog from the Tools menu, from there you can open a persistent Word Count toolbar, but even this requires users to click Recount to see accurate information (see Figure 10-3). For people writing magazine articles, who need to be careful about word count, this information would be better delivered modelessly. Even though many people don't use it, there's plenty of space on the bottom of the screen in the status bar to deliver such statistics.

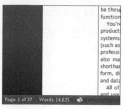

Figure 10-3 In Word 2003, if you want to know the number of words in your document, you must choose Word Count... from the Tools menu. This opens a dialog box. To get back to work, you must first click the Close button on the Word Count dialog. This behavior is the opposite of modeless feedback, and it hampers flow. In Word 2007, Microsoft has improved the situation considerably: The number of words in the document is modelessly displayed on the lower-left edge of the window, next to the page count, a similar bit of information.

Jet fighters have a heads-up display, or HUD, that superimposes the readings of critical instrumentation onto the forward view of the cockpit's windscreen. The pilot doesn't even have to use peripheral vision but can read vital gauges while keeping her eyes glued on the opposing fighter. Applications can use the edges of the display screen to show users information about activity in the main work area of applications. Many drawing applications, such as Adobe Photoshop, already provide ruler guides, thumbnail maps, and other modeless feedback in the periphery of their windows. We will further discuss these types of rich modeless feedback in Chapter 25.

 DESIGN principle   Design for the probable; provide for the possible.

There are many cases where interaction, usually in the form of a dialog box, slips into a user interface unnecessarily. A frequent source for such clinkers is when an application is faced with a choice. That's because programmers tend to resolve choices from the standpoint of logic, and it carries over to their software design. To a logician, if a proposition is true 999,999 times out of a million and false one time, the proposition is false — that's the way Boolean logic works. However, to the rest of us, the proposition is overwhelmingly true. The proposition has a *possibility* of being false, but the *probability* of it being false is minuscule to the point of irrelevancy. One of the most potent methods for better orchestrating your user interfaces is segregating the possible from the probable.

Programmers tend to view possibilities as being the same as probabilities. For example, a user has the choice of ending the application and saving his work, or ending the application and throwing away the document he has been working on for the last six hours. Either of these choices is possible. Conversely, the probability of this person discarding his work is at least a thousand to one against, yet the typical application always includes a dialog box asking the user if he wants to save his changes, like the one shown in Figure 10-4.

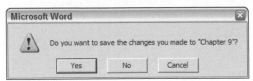

Figure 10-4 This is easily the most unnecessary dialog box in the world of GUI. Of course, we want to save our work! It is the normal course of events. *Not* saving it would be something out of the ordinary that should be handled by some dusty dialog box. This single dialog box does more to force users into knowing and understanding the useless and confusing facts about RAM and disk storage than anything else in their entire interaction with their computer. This dialog box should never be used.

The dialog box in Figure 10-4 is inappropriate and unnecessary. How often do you choose to abandon changes you make to a document? This dialog is tantamount to your spouse telling you not to spill soup on your shirt every time you eat. We'll discuss the implications of removing this dialog in Chapter 17.

Programmers are judged by their ability to create software that handles the many possible, but improbable, conditions that crop up inside complex logical systems. This doesn't mean, however, that they should render that readiness to handle offbeat possibilities directly into a user interface. The obtrusive presence of edge case possibilities is a dead giveaway for user interfaces designed by programmers. Dialogs, controls, and options that are used a hundred times a day sit side by side with dialogs, controls, and options that are used once a year or never.

You *might* get hit by a bus, but you probably *will* drive safely to work this morning. You don't stay home out of fear of the killer bus, so don't let what might possibly happen alter the way you treat what almost certainly will happen in your interface.

DESIGN
principle

Contextualize information.

The way that an application represents information is another way that it can obtrude noisily into a person's consciousness. One area frequently abused is the representation of quantitative, or numeric, information. If an application needs to show the amount of free space on disk, it can do what the Microsoft Windows 3.x File Manager did: give you the *exact* number of free bytes, as shown in Figure 10-5.

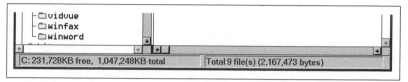

Figure 10-5 The Windows 3.x File Manager took great pains to report the exact number of bytes used by files on the disk. Does this precision help us understand whether we need to clear space on the disk? Certainly not. Furthermore, is a seven-digit number the best way to indicate the disk's status? Wouldn't a graphical representation that showed the space usage in a proportional manner (like a pie chart) be more meaningful? Luckily, Microsoft Windows now uses pie charts to indicate disk usage.

In the lower-left corner, the application tells us the number of free bytes and the total number of bytes on the disk. These numbers are hard to read and hard to interpret. With more than ten thousand million bytes of disk storage, it ceases to be important to us just how many hundreds are left, yet the display rigorously shows us down to the kilobyte. But even while the application is telling us the state of our disk with precision, it is failing to communicate. What we really need to know is whether or not the disk is getting full, or whether we can add a new 20 MB application and still have sufficient working room. These raw numbers, precise as they are, do little to help make sense of the facts.

Visual presentation expert Edward Tufte says that quantitative presentation should answer the question, "Compared to what?" Knowing that 231,728 KB are free on your hard disk is less useful than knowing that it is 22% of the disk's total capacity. Another Tufte dictum is, "Show the data," rather than simply telling about it textually or numerically. A pie chart showing the used and unused portions in different colors would make it much easier to comprehend the scale and proportion of hard disk use. It would show us what 231,728 KB really means. The numbers shouldn't go away, but they should be relegated to the status of labels on the display and not be the display itself. They should also be shown with more reasonable and consistent precision. The meaning of the information could be shown visually, and the numbers would merely add support.

In Windows XP and Vista, Microsoft's right hand giveth, while its left hand taketh away. The File Manager shown in Figure 10-5 is long dead, replaced by the Explorer dialog box shown in Figure 10-6. This replacement is the properties dialog associated with a hard disk. The Used Space is shown in blue and the Free Space is shown in magenta, making the pie chart an easy read. Now you can see at a glance the glad news that GranFromage is mostly empty.

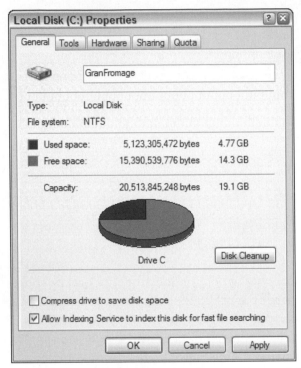

Figure 10-6 In Windows XP and Vista, Microsoft has replaced the electric chair with lethal injection. Instead of long, inscrutable numbers at the bottom of the File Manager, you can request a Properties dialog box from Windows Explorer. The good news is that you can finally see how your disk is doing in a meaningful, graphic way with the pie chart. The bad news is that you have to stop what you're doing and open a dialog box to see fundamental information that should be readily available. In Windows 2000, this graph was automatically displayed on the left side of the Explorer window when a disk was selected; XP's solution represents a step backwards.

Unfortunately, that pie chart isn't built into the Explorer's interface. Instead, you have to seek it out with a menu item. To see how full a disk is, you must bring up a modal dialog box that, although it gives you the information, takes you away from the place where you need to know it. The Explorer is where you can see, copy, move, and delete files, but it's not where you can easily see if things need to be deleted. That pie chart should have been built into the face of the Explorer. In Windows 2000, it was shown on the left-hand side when you selected a disk in an Explorer window. In XP, however, Microsoft took a step backwards, and the graphic has once again been relegated to a dialog. It really should be visible at all times in the Explorer, along with the numerical data, unless a user chooses to hide it.

DESIGN
principle   Provide direct manipulation and graphical input.

Software frequently fails to present numerical information in a graphical way. Even rarer is the capability of software to enable graphical input. A lot of software lets users enter numbers, then, on command, it converts those numbers into a graph. Few products let a user draw a graph and, on command, convert that graph into a vector of numbers. By contrast, most modern word processors let you set tabs and indentations by dragging a marker on a ruler. Someone can say, in effect, "here is where I want the paragraph to start," and let the application calculate that it is precisely 1.347 inches in from the left margin instead of forcing a user to enter **1.347**.

This principle applies in a variety of situations. When items in a list need to be reordered, a user may want them ordered alphabetically, but he may also want them in order of personal preference; something no algorithm can offer. A user should be able to drag the items into the desired order directly, without an algorithm interfering with this fundamental operation.

DESIGN
principle   Reflect object and application status.

When someone is asleep, he usually looks asleep. When someone is awake, he looks awake. When someone is busy, he looks busy: His eyes are focused on his work and his body language is closed and preoccupied. When someone is unoccupied, he looks unoccupied: His body is open and moving, his eyes are questing and willing to make contact. People not only expect this kind of subtle feedback from each other, they depend on it for maintaining social order.

Our applications and devices should work the same way. When an application is asleep, it should look asleep. When an application is awake, it should look awake, and when it's busy, it should look busy. When the computer is engaged in some significant internal action like performing a complex calculation and connecting to a database, it should be obvious to us that it won't be quite as responsive as usual. When the computer is sending a fax, we should see a small representation of the fax being scanned and sent (or at least a modeless progress bar).

Similarly, the status of user interface objects should be apparent to users. Most e-mail programs do a good job making it obvious which messages have not been read and which have been responded to or forwarded. Taking this concept a step further, wouldn't it be great if, when you were looking at events on a calendar in Microsoft Outlook or IBM Lotus Notes, you could tell how many people had agreed to attend and how many hadn't responded yet?

Application and object state is best communicated using forms of rich modeless feedback, briefly discussed earlier in this chapter. More detailed examples of rich modeless feedback may be found in Chapter 25.

 DESIGN principle   Avoid unnecessary reporting.

For programmers, it is important to know exactly what is happening in a program. This is necessary to be able to control all the details of the program. For users, it is disconcerting and distracting to know all the details of what is happening. Non-technical people may be alarmed to hear that the database has been modified, for example. It is better for the application to just do what has to be done, issue reassuring clues when all is well, and not burden users with the trivia of *how* it was accomplished.

Many applications are quick to keep users apprised of the details of their progress even though a user has no idea what to make of this information. Applications pop up dialog boxes telling us that connections have been made, that records have been posted, that users have logged on, that transactions were recorded, that data have been transferred, and other useless factoids. To software engineers, these messages are equivalent to the humming of the machinery, the babbling of the brook, the white noise of the waves crashing on the beach: They tell us that all is well. They were, in fact, probably used while debugging the software. To a normal person, however, these reports can be like eerie lights beyond the horizon, like screams in the night, like unattended objects flying about the room.

As discussed before, the application should make clear that it is working hard, but the detailed feedback can be offered in a more subtle way. In particular, reporting information like this with a modal dialog box brings the interaction to a stop with no particular benefit.

It is important that we not stop the proceedings to report normalcy. When some event has transpired that was supposed to have transpired, never report this fact with a dialog box. If you must use them at all, reserve dialogs for events that are outside of the normal course of events.

 **DESIGN principle**   Don't use dialogs to report normalcy.

By the same token, don't stop the proceedings and bother a user with problems that are not serious. If the application is having trouble creating a connection to a server, don't put up a dialog box to report it. Instead, build a status indicator into the application so the problem is clear to the interested user but is not obtrusive to someone who is busy elsewhere.

The key to orchestrating a user interaction is to take a goal-directed approach. You must ask yourself whether a particular interaction moves a person rapidly and directly to his goal. Contemporary applications are often reluctant to take any forward motion without a person directing them in advance. But most people would rather see the application take some "good enough" first step and then adjust it to what is desired. This way, the application has moved a person closer to his goal.

 **DESIGN principle**   Avoid blank slates.

It's easy to assume nothing about what your users want, and rather, ask a bunch of questions up front to help determine what they want. How many applications have you seen that start with a big dialog asking a bunch of questions? But *normal* people — not power users — aren't always capable or comfortable explaining what they want to an interactive product. They would much rather see what the application *thinks* is right and then manipulate that to make it exactly right. In most cases, your application can make a fairly correct assumption based on past experience. For example, when you create a new document in Microsoft Word, the application creates a blank document with preset margins and other attributes rather than opening a dialog that asks you to specify every detail. PowerPoint does a less adequate job, asking you to choose the base style for a new presentation each time you create one. Both applications could do better by remembering frequently and recently used styles or templates, and making those the defaults for new documents.

DESIGN principle   Ask for forgiveness, not permission.

Just because we use the word *think* in conjunction with an interactive product doesn't mean that the software needs to be intelligent (in the human sense) and try to determine the right thing to do by reasoning. Instead, it should simply do something that has a statistically good chance of being correct and then provide a user with powerful tools for shaping that first attempt, instead of merely giving the user a blank slate and challenging him to have at it. This way the application isn't asking for permission to act but rather for forgiveness after the fact.

For most people, a completely blank slate is a difficult starting point. It's so much easier to begin where someone has already left off. A user can easily fine-tune an approximation provided by the application into precisely what he desires with less risk of exposure and mental effort than he would have from drafting it from nothing. As we discuss in Chapter 11, endowing your application with a good memory is the best way to accomplish this.

 DESIGN principle   Differentiate between command and configuration.

Another problem crops up quite frequently whenever functions with many parameters are invoked by users. The problem comes from the lack of differentiation between a function and the *configuration* of that function. If you ask an application to perform a function itself, the application should simply perform that function and not interrogate you about your precise configuration details. To express precise demands to the program, you would request the configuration dialog.

For example, when you ask many applications to print a document, they respond by launching a complex dialog box demanding that you specify how many copies to print, what the paper orientation is, what paper feeder to use, what margins to set, whether the output should be in monochrome or color, what scale to print it at, whether to use PostScript fonts or native fonts, whether to print the current page, the current selection, or the entire document, and whether to print to a file and if so, how to name that file. All those options are useful, but all we wanted was to print the document, and that is all we thought we asked for.

A much more reasonable design would be to have a command to print and another command for print setup. The print command would not issue any dialog but would just go ahead and print, either using previous settings or standard, vanilla settings. The print setup function would offer up all those choices about paper and copies and fonts. It would also be very reasonable to be able to go directly from the configure dialog to printing.

The print control on the Word toolbar offers immediate printing without a dialog box. This is perfect for many people, but for those with multiple printers or printers on a network, it may offer too little information. A user may want to see which printer is selected before he either clicks the control or summons the dialog to change it first. This is a good candidate for some simple modeless output placed on a toolbar or status bar (it is currently provided in the ToolTip for the control, which is good, but the feedback could be better still). Word's print setup dialog is called "Print..." and is available from the File menu. Its name could be more descriptive, although the ellipsis does, according to GUI standards, give some inkling that it will launch a dialog.

There is a big difference between configuring and invoking a function. The former may include the latter, but the latter shouldn't include the former. In general, any user invokes a command ten times for every one time he configures it. It is better to make a user ask explicitly for configuration one time in ten than it is to make a user reject the configuration interface *nine* times in ten.

Microsoft's printing solution is a reasonable rule of thumb. Put immediate access to functions on buttons in the toolbar and put access to function-configuration dialog boxes on menu items. The configuration dialogs are better pedagogic tools, whereas the buttons provide immediate action.

 DESIGN principle   Provide choices, don't ask questions.

Asking questions is quite different from providing choices. The difference between them is the same as that between browsing in a store and conducting a job interview. The individual asking the questions is understood to be in a position superior to the individual being asked. Those with authority ask questions; subordinates respond. Asking users questions makes them feel irritated or inferior.

Dialog boxes (confirmation dialogs in particular) ask questions. Toolbars offer choices. The confirmation dialog stops the proceedings, demands an answer, and it won't leave until it gets what it wants. Toolbars, on the other hand, are always there, quietly and politely offering up their wares like a well-appointed store, giving you the luxury of selecting what you would like with just a flick of your finger.

Contrary to what many software developers think, questions and choices don't necessarily make users feel empowered. More commonly, they make people feel badgered and harassed. *Would you like soup or salad?* Salad. *Would you like cabbage or spinach?* Spinach. *Would you like French, Thousand Island, or Italian?* French. *Would you like lo-cal or regular?* Stop! Just bring me the soup! *Would you like chowder or chicken noodle?*

Users don't like to be asked questions. It cues a user that the application is:

▶ Ignorant

▶ Forgetful

▶ Weak

▶ Lacking initiative

▶ Unable to fend for itself

▶ Fretful

▶ Overly demanding

These are qualities that we typically dislike in people. Why should we desire them in software? The application is not asking us our opinion out of intellectual curiosity or desire to make conversation, the way a friend might over dinner. Rather, it is behaving ignorantly or presenting itself with false authority. The application isn't interested in our opinions; it requires information — often information it didn't really need to ask us in the first place (for more discussion on how to avoid questions, see Chapter 12).

Worse than a single question is a question that is asked repeatedly and unnecessarily. Many ATMs continually ask users what language they prefer: "Spanish, English, or Chinese?" This is not an answer that is likely to change after a person's first use. Interactive products that ask fewer questions appear smarter to users, and more polite and considerate.

In *The Media Equation* (Cambridge University Press, 1996), Stanford sociologists Clifford Nass and Byron Reeves make a compelling case that humans treat and respond to computers and other interactive products *as if they were people*. We should thus pay real attention to the "personality" projected by our software. Is it quietly competent and helpful, or does it whine, nag, badger, and make excuses? We'll discuss more about how to make software more polite and considerate in Chapter 12.

Choices are important, but there is a difference between being free to make choices based on presented information and being interrogated by the application in modal fashion. Users would much rather direct their software the way they direct their automobiles down the street. Automobiles offer drivers sophisticated choices without once issuing a dialog box. Imagine the situation in Figure 10-7.

Figure 10-7 Imagine if you had to steer your car by clicking buttons on a dialog box! This will give you some idea of how normal people feel about the dialog boxes on *your* software. Humbling, isn't it?

Directly manipulating a steering wheel is not only a more appropriate idiom for communicating with your car, but it also puts you in the superior position, directing your car where it should go. No one likes to be questioned like a suspect in a lineup, yet that is exactly what our software often does.

DESIGN principle   Hide the ejector seat levers.

In the cockpit of every jet fighter is a brightly painted lever that, when pulled, fires a small rocket engine underneath the pilot's seat, blowing the pilot, still in his seat, out of the aircraft to parachute safely to earth. Ejector seat levers can only be used once, and their consequences are significant and irreversible.

Just as a jet fighter needs an ejector seat lever, complex desktop applications need configuration facilities. The vagaries of business and the demands placed on the software force it to adapt to specific situations, and it had better be able to do so. Companies that pay millions of dollars for custom software or site licenses for thousands of copies of shrink-wrapped products will not take kindly to a program's inability to adapt to the way things are done in that particular company. The application must adapt, but such adaptation can be considered a one-time procedure, or something done only by the corporate IT staff on rare occasion. In other words, ejector seat levers may need to be used, but they won't be used very often.

Applications must have ejector seat levers so that users can — occasionally — move *persistent objects* (see Chapter 11) in the interface, or dramatically (sometimes irreversibly) alter the function or behavior of the application. The one thing that must never happen is accidental deployment of the ejector seat (see Figure 10-8). The interface design must assure that a user can never inadvertently fire the ejector seat when all he wants to do is make some minor adjustment to the program.

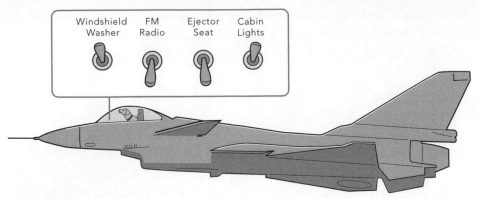

Figure 10-8 Ejector seat levers have catastrophic results. One minute, the pilot is safely ensconced in her jet, and the next she is tumbling end over end in the wild blue yonder, while her jet goes on without her. The ejector seat is necessary for the pilot's safety, but a lot of design work has gone into ensuring that it never gets fired inadvertently. Allowing an unsuspecting user to configure an application by changing permanent objects is comparable to firing the ejection seat by accident. Hide those ejector seat levers!

Ejector seat levers come in two basic varieties: those that cause a significant visual dislocation (large changes in the layout of tools and work areas) in the program and those that perform some irreversible action. Both of these functions should be hidden from inexperienced users. Of the two, the latter variety is by far the more dangerous. In the former, a user may be surprised and dismayed at what happens next, but she can at least back out of it with some work. In the latter case, she and her colleagues are likely to be stuck with the consequences.

By keeping in mind principles of flow and orchestration, your software can keep users engaged at maximum productivity for extended periods of time. Productive users are happy users, and customers with productive, happy users are the goal of any digital product manufacturer. In the next chapter, we further discuss ways to enhance user productivity by eliminating unnecessary barriers to use that arise as a result of implementation-model thinking.

 DESIGN principle   Optimize for responsiveness; accommodate latency.

An application can become slow or unresponsive when it performs a large amount of data processing or when it talks to remote devices like servers, printers, and networks. There isn't much that is more disturbing to a user's sense of flow than staring at a screen waiting for the computer to respond. It's absolutely critical to design your interfaces so that they are sufficiently responsive — all the lush visual style in the world isn't going to impress anyone if the interface moves like molasses because the device is maxed out redrawing the screen.

This is one arena where collaboration with developers is quite important. Depending on the platform and technical environment, different interactions can be quite "expensive" from a latency perspective. You should both advocate for implementation choices that provide the user with appropriately rich interactions with as little latency as possible, and design solutions to accommodate choices that have been made and cannot be revisited. When latency is unavoidable, it's important to clearly communicate the situation to users and provide them the ability to cancel the operation causing the latency and ideally perform other work while they are waiting.

If your application executes potentially time-consuming tasks, make sure that it occasionally checks to see if a person is still out there, banging away on the keyboard or madly clicking on the mouse, whimpering "No, no, I didn't mean to reorganize the *entire* database. That will take 4.3 million years!"

In a number of studies dating back to the late 1960s, it's generally been found that users' perception of response times can be roughly categorized into several buckets.[1]

- ▸ Up to **0.1 seconds**, users perceive the system's response to be **instantaneous.** Here, they feel that they are directly manipulating the user interface and data.

- ▸ Up to about **1 second**, users feel that the system is **responsive**. Users will likely notice a delay, but it is small enough for their thought processes to stay uninterrupted.

- ▸ Up to about **10 seconds**, users clearly notice that the system is slow, and their mind is likely to wander, but they are capable of maintaining some amount of attention on the application. Providing a progress bar is critical here.

- ▸ After about **10 seconds**, you will lose your users' attention. They will wander off and get a cup of coffee or switch to a different application. Ideally, processes that take this long should be conducted offline or in the background, allowing users to continue with other work. In any case, status and progress should be clearly communicated, including estimated time remaining, and a cancel mechanism is absolutely critical.

In summary, creating a successful product requires more than delivering useful functionality. You must also consider how different functional elements are orchestrated to enable users to achieve a sense of flow as they go about their business. The best user interfaces often don't leave users in awe of their beauty, but rather are hardly even noticed because they can be used effortlessly.

Notes

1. Miller, 1968

11

Eliminating Excise

Software too often contains interactions that are top-heavy, requiring extra work for users. Programmers typically focus so intently on the enabling technology that they don't carefully consider the human actions required to operate the technology from a goal-directed point of view. The result is software that charges its users a tax, or **excise**, of cognitive and physical effort every time it is used.

When we decide to drive to the office, we must open the garage door, get in the car, start the motor, back out, and close the garage door before we even begin the forward motion that will take us to our destination. All these actions support the automobile rather than getting to the destination. If we had *Star Trek* transporters instead, we'd dial up our destination coordinates and appear there instantaneously — no garages, no motors, no traffic lights. Our point is not to complain about the intricacies of driving, but rather to distinguish between two types of actions we take to accomplish our daily tasks.

Any large task, such as driving to the office, involves many smaller tasks. Some of these tasks work directly towards achieving the goal; these are tasks like steering down the road towards your office. **Excise tasks,** on the other hand, don't contribute directly to reaching the goal, but are necessary to accomplishing it just the same. Such tasks include opening and closing the garage door, starting the engine, and stopping at traffic lights, in addition to putting oil and gas in the car and performing periodic maintenance.

Excise is the extra work that satisfies either the needs of our tools or those of out-side agents as we try to achieve our objectives. The distinction is sometimes hard to see because we get so used to the excise being part of our tasks. Most of us drive so frequently that differentiating between the act of opening the garage door and the act of driving towards the destination is difficult. Manipulating the garage door is something we do for the car, not for us, and it doesn't move us towards our desti-nation the way the accelerator pedal and steering wheel do. Stopping at red lights is something imposed on us by our society that, again, doesn't help us achieve our true goal. (In this case, it does help us achieve a related goal of arriving *safely* at our offices.)

Software, too, has a pretty clear dividing line between goal-directed tasks and excise tasks. Like automobiles, some software excise tasks are trivial and performing them is no great hardship. On the other hand, some software excise tasks are as obnoxi-ous as fixing a flat tire. Installation leaps to mind here, as do such excise tasks as configuring networks and backing up our files.

The problem with excise tasks is that the effort we expend in doing them doesn't go directly towards accomplishing our goals. Where we can eliminate the need for excise tasks, we make people more effective and productive and improve the usabil-ity of a product, ultimately creating a better user experience. As an interaction designer, you should become sensitive to the presence of excise and take steps to eradicate it with the same enthusiasm a doctor would apply to curing an infection. The existence of excise in user interfaces is a primary cause of user dissatisfaction with software-enabled products. It behooves every designer and product manager to be on the lookout for interaction excise in all its forms and to take the time and energy to see that it is *excised* from their products.

 DESIGN principle   Eliminate excise wherever possible.

GUI Excise

One of the main criticisms leveled at graphical user interfaces by computer users who are accustomed to command-line systems is that users must expend extra effort manipulating windows and menus to accomplish something. With a command line, users can just type in a command and the computer executes it immediately. With windowing systems, they must open various folders to find the desired file or appli-cation before they can launch it. Then, after it appears on the screen, they must stretch and drag the window until it is in the desired location and configuration.

These complaints are well founded. Extra window manipulation tasks like these are, indeed, excise. They don't move a user towards his goal; they are overhead that the applications demand before they deign to assist that person. But everybody knows that GUIs are easier to use than command-line systems. Who is right?

The confusion arises because the real issues are hidden. The command-line interface forces an even more expensive excise budget on users: They must first memorize the commands. Also, a user cannot easily configure his screen to his own personal requirements. The excise of the command-line interface becomes smaller only after a user has invested significant time and effort in learning it.

On the other hand, for a casual or first-time user, the visual explicitness of the GUI helps him navigate and learn what tasks are appropriate and when. The step-by-step nature of the GUI is a great help to users who aren't yet familiar with the task or the system. It also benefits those users who have more than one task to perform and who must use more than one application at a time.

Excise and expert users

Any user willing to learn a command-line interface automatically qualifies as a power user. And any power user of a command-line interface will quickly become a power user of any other type of interface, GUI included. These users will easily learn each nuance of the applications they use. They will start up each application with a clear idea of exactly what they want to do and how they want to do it. To this user, the assistance offered to the casual or first-time user is just in the way.

We must be careful when we eliminate excise. We must not remove it just to suit power users. Similarly, however, we must not force power users to pay the full price for our providing help to new or infrequent users.

Training wheels

One of the areas where software designers can inadvertently introduce significant amounts of excise is in support for first-time or casual users. It is easy to justify adding facilities to a product that will make it easy for newer users to learn how to use it. Unfortunately, these facilities quickly become excise as users become familiar with the product — perpetual intermediates, as discussed in Chapter 3. Facilities added to software for the purpose of training beginners, such as step-by-step wizards, must be easily turned off. Training wheels are rarely needed for extended periods of time, and although they are a boon to beginners, they are a hindrance to advanced users when they are left on permanently.

DESIGN principle   Don't weld on training wheels.

"Pure" excise

Many actions are excise of such purity that nobody needs them, from power users to first-timers. These include most hardware-management tasks that the computer could handle itself, like telling an application which COM port to use. Any demands for such information should be struck from user interfaces and replaced with more intelligent application behavior behind the scenes.

Visual excise

Visual excise is the work that a user has to do to decode visual information, such as finding a single item in a list, figuring out where to begin reading on a screen, or determining which elements on it are clickable and which are merely decoration.

Designers sometimes paint themselves into excise corners by relying too heavily on visual metaphors. Visual metaphors such as desktops with telephones, copy machines, staplers, and fax machines — or file cabinets with folders in drawers — are cases in point. These visual metaphors may make it easy to understand the relationships between interface elements and behaviors, but after users learn these fundamentals, managing the metaphor becomes pure excise (for more discussion on the limitations of visual metaphors, see Chapter 13). In addition, the screen space consumed by the images becomes increasingly egregious, particularly in sovereign posture applications (see Chapter 9 for an extensive discussion of the concept of posture). The more we stare at the application from day to day, the more we resent the number of pixels it takes to tell us what we already know. The little telephone that so charmingly told us how to dial on that first day long ago is now a barrier to quick communication.

Users of transient posture applications often require some instruction to use the product effectively. Allocating screen real estate to this effort typically does not contribute to excise in the same way as it does in sovereign applications. Transient posture applications aren't used frequently, so their users need more assistance understanding what the application does and remembering how to control it. For sovereign posture applications, however, the slightest excise becomes agonizing over time. Another significant source of visual excise is the use of excessively styl-ized graphics and interface elements (see Figure 11-1). The use of visual style should always be primarily in support of the clear communication of information and interface behavior.

Depending on the application, some amount of ornamentation may also be desir-able to create a particular mood, atmosphere, or personality for the product. How-ever, excessive ornamentation can detract from users' effectiveness by forcing them to decode the various visual elements to understand which are controls and critical information and which are mere ornaments. For more about striking the right bal-ance to create effective visual interface designs, see Chapter 14.

Figure 11-1 The home page at Disney.com provides a good example of visual excise. Text is highly stylized and doesn't follow a layout grid. It's difficult for users to differentiate between décor and navigational elements. This requires users to do visual work to interact with the site. This isn't always a bad thing — just the right amount of the right kind of work can be a good source of entertainment (take puzzles, for example).

Determining what is excise

Certain tasks are mainly excise but can be useful for occasional users or users with special preferences. In this case, consider the function excise if it is forced on a user rather than made available at his discretion. An example of this kind of function is windows management. The only way to determine whether a function or behavior such as this is excise is by comparing it to personas' goals. If a significant persona needs to see two applications at a time on the screen in order to compare or transfer information, the ability to configure the main windows of the applications so that they share the screen space is not excise. If your personas don't have this specific goal, the work required to configure the main window of either application is excise.

Stopping the Proceedings

One form of excise is so prevalent that it deserves special attention. In the previous chapter, we introduced the concept of **flow**, whereby a person enters a highly productive mental state by working in harmony with her tools. Flow is a natural state, and people will enter it without much prodding. It takes some effort to break into flow after someone has achieved it. Interruptions like a ringing telephone will do it, as will an error message box. Some interruptions are unavoidable, but most others are easily dispensable. But interrupting a user's flow for no good reason is *stopping the proceedings with idiocy* and is one of the most disruptive forms of excise.

 DESIGN principle   Don't stop the proceedings with idiocy.

Poorly designed software will make assertions that no self-respecting individual would ever make. It states unequivocally, for example, that a file doesn't exist merely because it is too stupid to look for it in the right place, and then it implicitly blames *you* for losing it! An application cheerfully executes an impossible query that hangs up your system until you decide to reboot. Users view such software behavior as idiocy, and with just cause.

Errors, notifiers, and confirmation messages

There are probably no more prevalent excise elements than error message and confirmation message dialogs. These are so ubiquitous that eradicating them takes a lot of work. In Chapter 25, we discuss these issues at length, but for now, suffice it to say that they are high in excise and should be eliminated from your applications whenever possible.

The typical error message box is unnecessary. It either tells a user something that he doesn't care about or demands that he fix some situation that the application can and should usually fix just as well. Figure 11-2 shows an error message box displayed by Adobe Illustrator 6 while a user is trying to save a document. We're not exactly sure what it's trying to tell us, but it sounds dire.

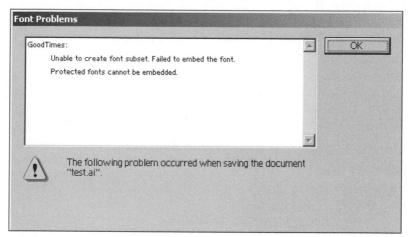

Figure 11-2 This is an ugly, useless error message box that stops the proceedings with idiocy. You can't verify or identify what it tells you, and it gives you no options for responding other than to admit your own culpability with the OK button. This message comes up only when the application is saving; that is, when you have entrusted it to do something simple and straightforward. The application can't even save a file without help, and it won't even tell you what help it needs.

The message stops an already annoying and time-consuming procedure, making it take even longer. A user cannot reliably fetch a cup of coffee after telling the application to save his artwork, because he might return only to see the function incomplete and the application mindlessly holding up the process. We discuss how to eliminate these sorts of error messages in Chapter 25.

Another frustrating example, this time from Microsoft Outlook, is shown in Figure 11-3.

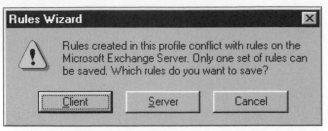

Figure 11-3 Here is a horrible confirmation box that stops the proceedings with idiocy. If the application is smart enough to detect the difference, why can't it correct the problem itself? The options the dialog offers are scary. It is telling you that you can explode one of two boxes: one contains garbage, and the other contains the family dog — but the application won't say which is which. And if you click Cancel, what does that mean? Will it still go ahead and explode your dog?

This dialog is asking you to make an irreversible and potentially costly decision based on no information whatsoever! If the dialog occurs just after you changed some rules, doesn't it stand to reason that you want to keep them? And if you don't, wouldn't you like a bit more information, like exactly what rules are in conflict and which of them are the more recently created? You also don't have a clear idea what happens when you click Cancel. . . . Are you canceling the dialog and leaving the rules mismatched? Are you discarding recent changes that led to the mismatch? The kind of fear and uncertainty that this poorly designed interaction arouses in users is completely unnecessary. We discuss how to improve this kind of situation in Chapter 24.

Making users ask permission

Back in the days of command lines and character-based menus, interfaces indirectly offered services to users. If you wanted to change an item, such as your address, first you explicitly had to ask the application permission to change it. The application would then display a screen where your address could be changed. Asking permission is pure excise, and unfortunately things haven't changed much — if you want to change one of your saved addresses on Amazon.com, you have to click a button and go to a different page. If you want to change a displayed value, you should be able to change it right there. You shouldn't have to ask permission or go to a different room.

DESIGN
principle

Don't make users ask permission.

As in the last example, many applications have one place where the values (such as filenames, numeric values, and selected options) are displayed for output and another place where user input to them is accepted. This follows the implementation model, which treats input and output as different processes. A user's mental model, however, doesn't recognize a difference. He thinks, "There is the number. I'll just click on it and enter a new value." If the application can't accommodate this impulse, it is needlessly inserting excise into the interface. If options are modifiable by a user, he should be able to do so right where the application displays them.

 DESIGN principle   Allow input wherever you have output.

The opposite of asking permission can be useful in certain circumstances. Rather than asking the application to launch a dialog, a user tells a dialog to go away and not come back again. In this way, a user can make an unhelpful dialog box stop badgering him, even though the application mistakenly thinks it is helping. Microsoft now makes heavy use of this idiom. (If a beginner inadvertently dismisses a dialog box and can't figure out how to get it back, he may benefit from another easy-to-identify safety-net idiom in a prominent place: a Help menu item saying, "Bring back all dismissed dialogs," for example.)

Common Excise Traps

You should be vigilant in finding and rooting out each small item of excise in your interface. These myriad little extra unnecessary steps can add up to a lot of extra work for users. This list should help you spot excise transgressions:

- ▶ Don't force users to go to another window to perform a function that affects the current window.

- ▶ Don't force users to remember where they put things in the hierarchical file system.

- ▶ Don't force users to resize windows unnecessarily. When a child window pops up on the screen, the application should size it appropriately for its contents. Don't make it big and empty or so small that it requires constant scrolling.

- ▶ Don't force users to move windows. If there is open space on the desktop, put the application there instead of directly over some other already open program.

- ▶ Don't force users to reenter their personal settings. If a person has ever set a font, a color, an indentation, or a sound, make sure that she doesn't have to do it again unless she wants a change.

▶ Don't force users to fill fields to satisfy some arbitrary measure of completeness. If a user wants to omit some details from the transaction entry screen, don't force him to enter them. Assume that he has a good reason for not entering them. The completeness of the database (in most instances) isn't worth badgering users over.

▶ Don't force users to ask permission. This is frequently a symptom of not allowing input in the same place as output.

▶ Don't ask users to confirm their actions (this requires a robust undo facility).

▶ Don't let a user's actions result in an error.

Navigation Is Excise

The most important thing to realize about navigation is that it is largely excise. Except in the case of games where the *goal* is to navigate successfully through a maze of obstacles, the work that users are forced to do to get around in software and on Web sites is seldom aligned with their needs, goals, and desires. (Though it should be noted that well-designed navigation can be an effective way to instruct users about what is available to them, which is certainly much more aligned with their goals.)

Unnecessary or difficult navigation is a major frustration to users. In fact, in our opinion, poorly designed navigation presents one of the largest and most common problems in the usability of interactive products — desktop, Web-based, or otherwise. It is also the place where the programmer's implementation model is typically made most apparent to users.

Navigation through software occurs at multiple levels:

▶ Among multiple windows, views, or pages

▶ Among panes or frames within a window, view, or page

▶ Among tools, commands, or menus

▶ Within information displayed in a pane or frame (for example: scrolling, panning, zooming, following links)

While you may question the inclusion of some of these bullets as types of navigation, we find it useful to think in terms of a broad definition of navigation: *any action that takes a user to a new part of the interface or which requires him to locate objects, tools, or data.* The reason for this is simple: These actions require people to understand where they are in an interactive system and how to find and actuate what they want. When we start thinking about these actions as navigation, it becomes clear that they are excise and should, therefore, be minimized or eliminated. The following sections discuss each of these types of navigation in more detail.

Navigation among multiple screens, views, or pages

Navigation among multiple application views or Web pages is perhaps the most disorienting kind of navigation for users. It involves a gross shifting of attention that disrupts a user's flow and forces him into a new context. The act of navigating to another window also often means that the contents of the original window are partly or completely obscured. At the very least, it means that a user needs to worry about window management, an excise task that further disrupts his flow. If users must constantly shuttle back and forth between windows to achieve their goals, their disorientation and frustration levels will rise, they will become distracted from the task at hand, and their effectiveness and productivity will drop.

If the number of windows is large enough, a user will become sufficiently disoriented that he may experience **navigational trauma**: He gets lost in the interface. Sovereign posture applications can avoid this problem by placing all main interactions in a single primary view, which may contain multiple independent panes.

Navigation between panes

Windows can contain multiple panes — adjacent to each other and separated by splitters (see Chapters 19 and 20) or stacked on top of each other and denoted by tabs. Adjacent panes can solve many navigation problems because they provide useful supporting functions, links, or data on the screen in close reach of the primary work or display area, thus reducing navigation to almost nil. If objects can be dragged between panes, those panes should be adjacent to each other.

Problems arise when adjacent supporting panes become too numerous or are not placed on the screen in a way that matches users' workflows. Too many adjacent panes result in visual clutter and confusion: Users do not know where to go to find what they need. Also, crowding forces scrolling, which is another navigational hit. Navigation within the single screen thus becomes a problem. Some Web portals, trying to be everything to everyone, have such navigational problems.

In some cases, depending on user workflows, tabbed panes can be appropriate. Tabbed panes include a level of navigational excise and potential for user disorientation because they obscure what was on the screen before the user navigated to them. However, this idiom is appropriate for the main work area when multiple documents or independent views of a document are required (such as in Microsoft Excel; see Figure 11-4).

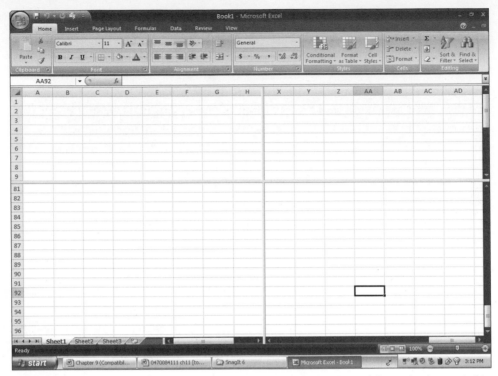

Figure 11-4 Microsoft Excel makes use of tabbed panes (visible in the lower left) to let users navigate between related worksheets. Excel also makes use of splitters to provide adjacent panes for viewing multiple, distant parts of a single spreadsheet without constant scrolling. Both these idioms help reduce navigational excise for Excel users.

Some programmers use tabs to break complex product capabilities into smaller chunks. They reason that using these capabilities will somehow become easier if the functionality is cut into bite-sized pieces. Actually, putting parts of a single facility onto separate panes increases excise and decreases users' understanding and orientation.

The use of tabbed screen areas is a space-saving mechanism and is sometimes necessary to fit all the required information and functions in a limited space. (Settings dialogs are a classic example here. We don't think anyone is interested in seeing all of the settings for a sophisticated application laid bare in a single view.) In most cases, though, the use of tabs creates significant navigational excise. It is rarely possible to describe accurately the contents of a tab with a succinct label. Therefore users must click through each tab to find the tool or piece of information they are looking for.

Tabbed panes can be appropriate when there are multiple supporting panes for a primary work area that are not used at the same time. The support panes can then be stacked, and a user can choose the pane suitable for his current tasks, which is only a single click away. A classic example here involves the color mixer and swatches area in Adobe Illustrator (see Figure 11-5). These two tools are mutually exclusive ways of selecting a drawing color, and users typically know which is appropriate for a given task.

 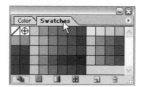

Figure 11-5 Tabbed palettes in Adobe Illustrator allow users to switch between the mixer and swatches, which provide alternate mechanisms for picking a color.

Navigation between tools and menus

Another important and overlooked form of navigation results from users' needs to use different tools, palettes, and functions. Spatial organization of these within a pane or window is critical to minimizing extraneous mouse movements that, at best, could result in user annoyance and fatigue, and at worst, result in repetitive stress injury. Tools that are used frequently and in conjunction with each other should be grouped together spatially and also be immediately available. Menus require more navigational effort on the part of users because their contents are not visible prior to clicking. Frequently used functions should be provided in toolbars, palettes, or the equivalent. Menu use should be reserved only for infrequently accessed commands (we discuss organizing controls again later in this chapter and discuss toolbars in depth in Chapter 23).

Adobe Photoshop 6.0 exhibits some undesirable behaviors in the way it forces users to navigate between palette controls. For example, the Paint Bucket tool and the Gradient tool each occupy the same location on the tool palette; you must select between them by clicking and holding on the visible control, which opens a menu that lets you select between them (shown in Figure 11-6). However, both are fill tools, and both are frequently used. It would have been better to place each of them on the palette next to each other to avoid that frequent, flow-disrupting tool navigation.

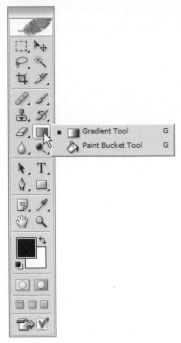

Figure 11-6 In Adobe Photoshop, the Paint Bucket tool is hidden in a combutcon (see Chapter 21) on its tool palette. Even though users make frequent use of both the Gradient tool and the Paint Bucket tool, they are forced to access this menu any time they need to switch between these tools.

Navigation of information

Navigation of information, or of the content of panes or windows, can be accomplished by several methods: scrolling (panning), linking (jumping), and zooming. The first two methods are common: Scrolling is ubiquitous in most software, and linking is ubiquitous on the Web (though increasingly, linking idioms are being adopted in non-Web applications). Zooming is primarily used for visualization of 3D and detailed 2D data.

Scrolling is often a necessity, but the need for it should be minimized when possible. Often there is a trade-off between paging and scrolling information: You should understand your users' mental models and workflows to determine what is best for them.

In 2D visualization and drawing applications, vertical and horizontal scrolling are common. These kinds of interfaces benefit from a thumbnail map to ease navigation. We'll discuss this technique as well as other visual signposts later in this chapter.

Linking is the critical navigational paradigm of the Web. Because it is a visually dislocating activity, extra care must be taken to provide visual and textual cues that help orient users.

Zooming and **panning** are navigational tools for exploring 2D and 3D information. These methods are appropriate when creating 2D or 3D drawings and models or for exploring representations of real-world 3D environments (architectural walkthroughs, for example). They typically fall short when used to examine arbitrary or abstract data presented in more than two dimensions. Some information visualization tools use zoom to mean, "display more attribute details about objects," a logical rather than spatial zoom. As the view of the object enlarges, attributes (often textual) appear superimposed over its graphical representation. This kind of interaction is almost always better served through an adjacent supporting pane that displays the properties of selected objects in a more standard, readable form. Users find spatial zoom difficult enough to understand; logical zoom is arcane to all but visualization researchers and the occasional programmer.

Panning and zooming, especially when paired together, create navigation difficulties for users. While this is improving due to the prevalence of online maps, it is still quite easy for people to get lost in virtual space. Humans are not used to moving in unconstrained 3D space, and they have difficulty perceiving 3D properly when it is projected on a 2D screen (see Chapter 19 for more discussion of 3D manipulation).

Improving Navigation

There are many ways to begin improving (eliminating, reducing, or speeding up) navigation in your applications, Web sites, and devices. Here are the most effective:

- Reduce the number of places to go.
- Provide signposts.
- Provide overviews.
- Provide appropriate mapping of controls to functions.
- Inflect your interface to match user needs.
- Avoid hierarchies.

We'll discuss these in detail below.

Reduce the number of places to go

The most effective method of improving navigation sounds quite obvious: Reduce the number of places to which one must navigate. These "places" include modes, forms, dialogs, pages, windows, and screens. If the number of modes, pages, or screens is kept to a minimum, people's ability to stay oriented increases dramatically. In terms of the four types of navigation presented earlier, this directive means:

▶ Keep the number of windows and views to a minimum. One full-screen window with two or three views is best for many users. Keep dialogs, especially modeless dialogs, to a minimum. Applications or Web sites with dozens of distinct types of pages, screens, or forms are difficult to navigate.

▶ Keep the number of adjacent panes in your window or Web page limited to the minimum number needed for users to achieve their goals. In sovereign applications, three panes is a good thing to shoot for, but there are no absolutes here — in fact many applications require more. On Web pages, anything more than two navigation areas and one content area begins to get busy.

▶ Keep the number of controls limited to as few as your users really need to meet their goals. Having a good grasp of your users via personas will enable you to avoid functions and controls that your users don't really want or need and that, therefore, only get in their way.

▶ Scrolling should be minimized when possible. This means giving supporting panes enough room to display information so that they don't require constant scrolling. Default views of 2D and 3D diagrams and scenes should be such that a user can orient himself without too much panning around. Zooming, particularly continuous zooming, is the most difficult type of navigation for most users, so its use should be discretionary, not a requirement.

Many online stores present confusing navigation because the designers are trying to serve everyone with one generic site. If a user buys books but never CDs from a site, access to the CD portion of the site could be deemphasized in the main screen for that user. This makes more room for that user to buy books, and the navigation becomes simpler. Conversely, if he visits his account page frequently, his version of the site should have his account button (or tab) presented prominently.

Provide signposts

In addition to reducing the number of navigable places, another way to enhance users' ability to find their way around is by providing better points of reference — **signposts**.

In the same way that sailors navigate by reference to shorelines or stars, users navigate by reference to **persistent objects** placed in a user interface.

Persistent objects, in a desktop world, always include the program's windows. Each application most likely has a main, top-level window. The salient features of that window are also considered persistent objects: menu bars, toolbars, and other palettes or visual features like status bars and rulers. Generally, each window of the interface has a distinctive look that will soon become recognizable.

On the Web, similar rules apply. Well-designed Web sites make careful use of persistent objects that remain constant throughout the shopping experience, especially the top-level navigation bar along the top of the page. Not only do these areas provide clear navigational options, but their consistent presence and layout also help orient customers (see Figure 11-7).

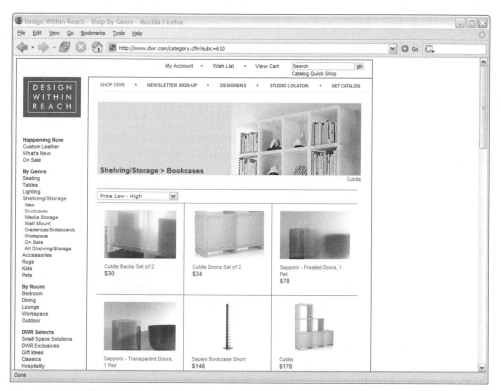

Figure 11-7 The Design Within Reach Web site makes use of many persistent areas on the majority of its pages, such as the links and search field along the top, and the browse tools on the sides. These not only help users figure out where they can go but also help keep them oriented as to where they are.

In devices, similar rules apply to screens, but hardware controls themselves can take on the role of signposts — even more so when they are able to offer visual or tactile feedback about their state. Car radio buttons that, for example, light when selected, even a needle's position on a dial, can provide navigational information if integrated appropriately with the software.

Depending on the application, the contents of the program's main window may also be easily recognizable (especially true in kiosks and small-screen devices). Some applications may offer a few different views of their data, so the overall aspect of their screens will change depending on the view chosen. A desktop application's distinctive look, however, will usually come from its unique combination of menus, palettes, and toolbars. This means that menus and toolbars must be considered aids to navigation. You don't need a lot of signposts to navigate successfully. They just need to be visible. Needless to say, signposts can't aid navigation if they are removed, so it is best if they are permanent fixtures of the interface.

Making each page on a Web site look just like every other one may appeal to marketing, but it can, if carried too far, be disorienting. Certainly, you should use common elements consistently on each page, but by making different rooms look distinct, you will help to orient your users better.

Menus

The most prominent permanent object in an application is the main window and its title and menu bars. Part of the benefit of the menu comes from its reliability and consistency. Unexpected changes to a program's menus can deeply reduce users' trust in them. This is true for menu items as well as for individual menus.

Toolbars

If the application has a toolbar, it should also be considered a recognizable signpost. Because toolbars are idioms for perpetual intermediates rather than for beginners, the strictures against changing menu items don't apply quite as strongly to individual toolbar controls. Removing the toolbar itself is certainly a dislocating change to a persistent object. Although the ability to do so should be there, it shouldn't be offered casually, and users should be protected against accidentally triggering it. Some applications put controls on the toolbar that make the toolbar disappear! This is a completely inappropriate ejector seat lever.

Other interface signposts

Tool palettes and fixed areas of the screen where data is displayed or edited should also be considered persistent objects that add to the navigational ease of the interface. Judicious use of white space and legible fonts is important so that these signposts remain clearly evident and distinct.

Provide overviews

Overviews serve a similar purpose to signposts in an interface: They help to orient users. The difference is that overviews help orient users within the content rather than within the application as a whole. Because of this, the overview area should itself be persistent; its content is dependent on the data being navigated.

Overviews can be graphical or textual, depending on the nature of the content. An excellent example of a graphical overview is the aptly named Navigator palette in Adobe Photoshop (see Figure 11-8).

 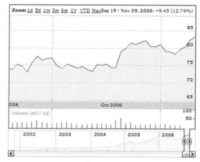

Figure 11-8 On the left, Adobe makes use of an excellent overview idiom in Photoshop: the Navigator palette, which provides a thumbnail view of a large image with an outlined box that represents the portion of the image currently visible in the main display. The palette not only provides navigational context, but it can be used to pan and zoom the main display as well. A similar idiom is employed on the right in the Google Finance charting tool, in which the small graph on the bottom provides a big picture view and context for the zoomed-in view on top.

In the Web world, the most common form of overview area is textual: the ubiquitous breadcrumb display (see Figure 11-9). Again, most breadcrumbs provide not only a navigational aid, but a navigational control as well: They not only show where in the data structure a visitor is, but they give him tools to move to different nodes in the structure in the form of links. This idiom has lost some popularity as Web sites have moved away from strictly hierarchical organizations to more associative organizations, which don't lend themselves as neatly to breadcrumbs.

Figure 11-9 A typical breadcrumb display from Amazon.com. Users see where they've been and can click anywhere in the breadcrumb trail to navigate to that link.

A final interesting example of an overview tool is the **annotated scrollbar**. Annotated scrollbars are most useful for scrolling through text. They make clever use of the linear nature of both scrollbars and textual information to provide location information about the locations of selections, highlights, and potentially many other attributes of formatted or unformatted text. Hints about the locations of these items appear in the "track" that the thumb of the scrollbar moves in, at the appropriate location. When the thumb is over the annotation, the annotated feature of the text is visible in the display (see Figure 11-10). Microsoft Word uses a variant of the annotated scrollbar; it shows the page number and nearest header in a ToolTip that remains active during the scroll.

Figure 11-10 An annotated scrollbar from Microsoft Word 2007 provides useful context to a user as he navigates through a document.

Provide appropriate mapping of controls to functions

Mapping describes the relationship between a control, the thing it affects, and the intended result. Poor mapping is evident when a control does not relate visually or symbolically with the object it affects. Poor mapping requires users to stop and think about the relationship, breaking flow. Poor mapping of controls to functions increases the cognitive load for users and can result in potentially serious user errors.

An excellent example of mapping problems comes from the nondigital world of gas and electric ranges. Almost anyone who cooks has run into the annoyance of a stovetop whose burner knobs do not map appropriately to the burners they control. The typical stovetop, such as the one shown in Figure 11-11, features four burners arranged in a flat square with a burner in each corner. However, the knobs that operate those burners are laid out in a straight line on the front of the unit.

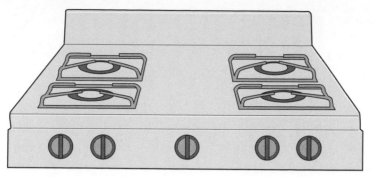

Figure 11-11 A stovetop with poor physical mapping of controls. Does the knob on the far-left control the left-front or left-rear burner? Users must figure out the mapping anew each time they use the stovetop.

In this case, we have a **physical mapping** problem. The *result* of using the control is reasonably clear: A burner will heat up when you turn a knob. However, the *target* of the control — which burner will get warm — is unclear. Does twisting the left-most knob turn on the left-front burner, or does it turn on the left-rear burner? Users must find out by trial and error or by referring to the tiny icons next to the knobs. The unnaturalness of the mapping compels users to figure this relationship out anew every time they use the stove. This cognitive work may become semiconscious over time, but it still exists, making users prone to error if they are rushed or distracted (as people often are while preparing meals). In the best-case scenario, users feel stupid because they've twisted the wrong knob, and their food doesn't get hot until they notice the error. In the worst-case scenario, they might accidentally burn themselves or set fire to the kitchen.

The solution requires moving the physical locations of the stovetop knobs so that they better suggest which burners they control. The knobs don't have to be laid out in exactly the same pattern as the burners, but they should be positioned so that the target of each knob is clear. The stovetop in Figure 11-12 is a good example of an effective mapping of controls.

In this layout, it's clear that the upper-left knob controls the upper-left burner. The placement of each knob visually suggests which burner it will turn on. Donald Norman (1989) calls this more intuitive layout "natural mapping."

Another example of poor mapping — of a different type — is pictured in Figure 11-13. In this case, it is the **logical mapping** of concepts to actions that is unclear.

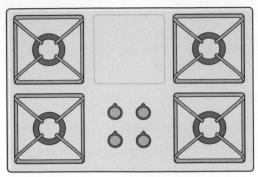

Figure 11-12 Clear spatial mapping. On this stovetop, it is clear which knob maps to which burner because the spatial arrangement of knobs clearly associates each knob with a burner.

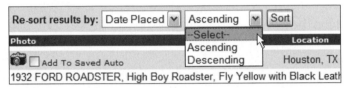

Figure 11-13 An example of a logical mapping problem. If a user wants to see the most recent items first, does he choose Ascending or Descending? These terms don't map well to how users conceive of time.

The Web site uses a pair of drop-down menus to sort a list of search results by date. The selection in the first drop-down determines the choices present in the second. When Re-sort Results by: Date Placed is selected in the first menu, the second drop-down presents the options Ascending and Descending.

Unlike the poorly mapped stovetop knobs, the *target* of this control is clear — the drop-down menu selections will affect the list below them. However, the *result* of using the control is unclear: Which sort order will the user get if he chooses Ascending?

The terms chosen to communicate the date sorting options make it unclear what users should choose if they wish to see the most recent items first in the list. Ascending and Descending do not map well to most users' mental model of time. People don't think of dates as ascending or descending; rather, they think of dates and events as being recent or ancient. A quick fix to this problem is to change the wording of the options to Most Recent First and Oldest First, as in Figure 11-14.

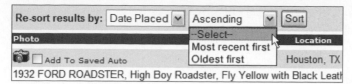

Figure 11-14 Clear logical mapping. Most Recent and Oldest are terms that users can easily map to time-based sorting.

Whether you make appliances, desktop applications, or Web sites, your product may have mapping problems. Mapping is an area where attention to detail pays off — you can measurably improve a product by seeking out and fixing mapping problems, even if you have very little time to make changes. The result? A product that is easier to understand and more pleasurable to use.

Inflect your interface to match user needs

Inflecting an interface means organizing it to minimize typical navigation. In practice, this means placing the most frequently desired functions and controls in the most immediate and convenient locations for users to access them, while pushing the less frequently used functions deeper into the interface, where users won't stumble over them. Rarely used facilities shouldn't be removed from the program, but they should be removed from the everyday workspace.

 DESIGN principle   Inflect the interface for typical navigation.

The most important principle in the proper inflection of interfaces is **commensurate effort**. Although it applies to all users, it is particularly pertinent to perpetual intermediates. This principle merely states that people will willingly work harder for something that is more valuable to get. The catch, of course, is that value is in the eye of the beholder. It has nothing to do with how technically difficult a feature is to implement, but rather has entirely to do with a person's goals.

If a person really wants something, he will work harder to get it. If someone wants to become a good tennis player, for example, he will get out on the court and play very hard. To someone who doesn't like tennis, any amount of the sport is tedious effort. If a user needs to format beautiful documents with multiple columns, several fonts, and fancy headings to impress his boss, he will be highly motivated to explore the recesses of the application to learn how. He will be putting *commensurate effort* into the project. If some other user just wants to print plain old documents in one column and one font, no amount of inducement will get him to learn those more advanced formatting features.

 DESIGN principle   Users make commensurate effort if the rewards justify it.

This means that if you add features to your application that are necessarily complex to manage, users will be willing to tolerate that complexity only if the rewards are worth it. This is why a program's user interface can't be complex to achieve simple results, but it *can* be complex to achieve *complex* results (as long as such results aren't needed very often).

It is acceptable from an interface perspective to make advanced features something that users must expend a little extra effort to activate, whether that means searching in a menu, opening a dialog, or opening a drawer. The principle of commensurate effort allows us to **inflect** interfaces so that simple, commonly used functions are immediately at hand at all times. Advanced features, which are less frequently used but have a big payoff for users, can be safely tucked away where they can be brought up only when needed. Almost any point-and-shoot digital camera serves as a good example of inflection: The most commonly used function — taking a picture — is provided by a prominent button easily accessible at a moment's notice. Less commonly used functions, such as adjusting the exposure, require interaction with onscreen controls.

In general, controls and displays should be organized in an interface according to three attributes: frequency of use, degree of dislocation, and degree of risk exposure.

- ▶ **Frequency of use** means how often the controls, functions, objects, or displays are used in typical day-to-day patterns of use. Items and tools that are most frequently used (many times a day) should be immediately in reach, as discussed in Chapter 10. Less frequently used items, used perhaps once or twice a day, should be no more than a click or two away. Other items can be two or three clicks away.

- ▶ **Degree of dislocation** refers to the amount of sudden change in an interface or in the document/information being processed by the application caused by the invocation of a specific function or command. Generally speaking, it's a good idea to put these types of functions deeper into the interface (see Chapter 10 for an explanation).

▸ **Degree of risk exposure** deals with functions that are irreversible or may have other dangerous ramifications. Missiles require two humans turning keys simultaneously on opposite sides of the room to arm them. As with dislocating functions, you want to make these types of functions more difficult for your users to stumble across. The riskiness of an undesirable can even be thought of as a product of the event's likelihood and its ramifications.

Of course, as users get more experienced with these features, they will search for shortcuts, and you must provide them. When software follows commensurate effort, the learning curve doesn't go away, but it disappears from the user's mind — which is just as good.

Avoid hierarchies

Hierarchies are one of the programmer's most durable tools. Much of the data inside applications, along with much of the code that manipulates it, is in hierarchical form. For this reason, many programmers present hierarchies (the implementation model) in user interfaces. Early menus, as we've seen, were hierarchical. But abstract hierarchies are very difficult for users to successfully navigate, except where they're based on user mental models and the categories are truly mutually exclusive. This truth is often difficult for programmers to grasp because they themselves are so comfortable with hierarchies.

Most humans are familiar with hierarchies in their business and family relationships, but hierarchies are not natural concepts for most people when it comes to storing and retrieving arbitrary information. Most mechanical storage systems are simple, composed either of a single sequence of stored objects (like a bookshelf) or a series of sequences, one level deep (like a file cabinet). This method of organizing things into a single layer of groups is extremely common and can be found everywhere in your home and office. Because it never exceeds a single level of nesting, we call this storage paradigm **monocline grouping**.

Programmers are very comfortable with nested systems where an instance of an object is stored in another instance of the same object. Most other humans have a very difficult time with this idea. In the mechanical world, complex storage systems, by necessity, use different mechanical form factors at each level: In a file cabinet, you never see folders inside folders or file drawers inside file drawers. Even the dissimilar nesting of folder-inside-drawer-inside-cabinet rarely exceeds two levels of nesting. In the current desktop metaphor used by most window systems, you can nest folder within folder ad infinitum. It's no wonder most computer neophytes get confused when confronted with this paradigm.

Most people store their papers (and other items) in a series of stacks or piles based on some common characteristic: The Acme papers go here; the Project M papers go there; personal stuff goes in the drawer. Donald Norman (1994) calls this a *pile cabinet*. Only inside computers do people put the Project M documents inside the Active Clients folder, which, in turn, is stored inside the Clients folder, stored inside the Business folder.

Computer science gives us hierarchical structures as tools to solve the very real problems of managing massive quantities of data. But when this implementation model is reflected in the manifest model presented to users (see Chapter 2 for more on these models), they get confused because it conflicts with their mental model of storage systems. Monocline grouping is the mental model people typically bring to the software. Monocline grouping is so dominant outside the computer that interaction designers violate this model at their peril.

Monocline grouping is an inadequate system for physically managing the large quantities of data commonly found on computers, but that doesn't mean it isn't useful as a *manifest model*. The solution to this conundrum is to render the structure as a user imagines it — as monocline grouping — but to provide the search and access tools that only a deep hierarchical organization can offer. In other words, rather than forcing users to navigate deep, complex tree structures, give them tools to *bring appropriate information to them*. We'll discuss some design solutions that help to make this happen in Chapter 15.

12

Designing Good Behavior

As we briefly discussed in Chapter 10, research performed by two Stanford sociologists, Clifford Nass and Byron Reeves, suggests that humans seem to have instincts that tell them how to behave around other sentient beings. As soon as an object exhibits sufficient levels of interactivity — such as that found in your average software application — these instincts are activated. Our reaction to software as sentient is both unconscious and unavoidable.

The implication of this research is profound: If we want users to like our products, we should design them to behave in the same manner as a likeable person. If we want users to be productive with our software, we should design it to behave like a supportive human colleague. To this end, it's useful to consider the appropriate working relationship between human beings and computers.

 DESIGN principle   The computer does the work and the person does the thinking.

The ideal division of labor in the computer age is very clear: The computer should do the work, and the person should do the thinking. Science fiction writers and computer scientists tantalize us with visions of artificial intelligence: computers that think for themselves. However, humans don't really need much help in the thinking department — our ability to identify patterns and solve complex problems creatively is unmatched in the world of silicon. We *do* need a lot of help with the work of information management — activities like accessing, analyzing, organizing, and visualizing information, but the actual decisions made from that information are best made by us — the "wetware."

Designing Considerate Products

Nass and Reeves suggest that software should be *polite*, but we prefer the term *considerate*. Although politeness could be construed as a matter of manners and protocol — saying "please" and "thank you," but doing little else helpful — being truly *considerate* means being concerned with the needs of others. Above and beyond performing basic functions, considerate software has the goals and needs of its users as a concern.

If an interactive product is stingy with information, obscures its processes, forces users to hunt around for common functions, and is quick to blame people for its own failings, users are sure to have an unpleasant and unproductive experience. This will happen regardless of how polite, cute, visually metaphoric, anthropomorphic, or full of interesting content the software is.

On the other hand, interactions that are respectful, generous, and helpful will go a long way toward creating a positive experience for people using your product.

 DESIGN principle   Software should behave like a considerate human being.

Commonly, interactive products irritate us because they aren't considerate, not because they lack features. Building considerate products is not necessarily substantially more difficult than building rude or inconsiderate products. It simply requires that you envision interactions that emulate the qualities of a sensitive and caring person. None of these characteristics is at odds with more pragmatic goals of functional data processing (which lies at the core of all silicon-enabled products). In fact, behaving more humanely can be the most pragmatic goal of all, and if orchestrated correctly, this kind of dialogue with users can actually contribute to effective functional execution of software.

Humans have many wonderful characteristics that make them considerate, and some of these can be emulated to a greater or lesser degree by interactive products.

We think the following describe some of the most important characteristics of considerate interactive products (and humans):

- Take an interest
- Are deferential
- Are forthcoming
- Use common sense
- Anticipate people's needs
- Are conscientious
- Don't burden you with their personal problems
- Keep you informed
- Are perceptive
- Are self-confident
- Don't ask a lot of questions
- Take responsibility
- Know when to bend the rules

We'll now discuss these characteristics in detail.

Considerate products take an interest

A considerate friend wants to know more about you. He remembers your likes and dislikes so that he can please you in the future. Everyone appreciates being treated according to his or her own personal tastes.

Most software, on the other hand, doesn't know or care who is using it. Little, if any, of the *personal* software on our *personal* computers seems to remember anything *personal* about us, in spite of the fact that we use it constantly, repetitively, and exclusively. A good example of this behavior is the way that browsers such as Firefox and Microsoft Internet Explorer remember information that users routinely enter into forms on Web sites, such as a shipping address or username.

Software should work hard to remember our habits and, particularly, everything that we say to it. From the perspective of the programmer writing an application, it can be tempting to think about gathering a bit of information from a person as similar to gathering a bit of information from a database — every time the information is needed, the product asks the user for it. The application then discards that tidbit, assuming that it might change and that it can merely ask for it again if necessary. Not only are digital products better suited to recording things in memory than humans are, but our products also show they are *inconsiderate* when they forget. Remembering the actions and preferences of humans is one of the best ways to create a positive experience with a software-enabled product. We'll discuss the topic of memory in detail later in this chapter.

Considerate products are deferential

A good service provider defers to her client. She understands the person she is serving is the boss. When a restaurant host shows us to a table in a restaurant, we consider his choice of table to be a suggestion, not an order. If we politely request another table in an otherwise empty restaurant, we expect to be accommodated. If the host refuses, we are likely to choose a different restaurant where *our* desires take precedence over the host's.

Inconsiderate products supervise and pass judgment on human actions. Software is within its rights to express its *opinion* that we are making a mistake, but it is presumptuous for it to judge or limit our actions. Software can *suggest* that we not "submit" our entry until we've typed in our telephone number, and should explain the consequences if we do so, but if we wish to "submit" without the number, we expect the software to do as it is told. The very word *submit* and the concept it stands for are a reversal of the deferential relationship we should expect out of interactive products. Software should submit to users, and any application that proffers a "submit" button is being rude, as well as potentially oblique and confusing.

Considerate products are forthcoming

If you ask a good shop clerk for help locating an item, he will not only answer the question, but also volunteer useful collateral information; for example, the fact that a more expensive, higher-quality item than the one you requested is currently on sale for a similar price.

Most software doesn't attempt to provide related information. Instead, it narrowly answers the precise questions we ask it, and is typically not forthcoming about other information even if it is clearly related to our goals. When we tell our word processor to print a document, it doesn't tell us when the paper supply is low, or when 40 other documents are queued up before us, or when another nearby printer is free. A helpful human would.

Figuring out the right way to offer potentially useful information can require a delicate touch. Microsoft's "Clippy" is almost universally despised for his smarty-pants comments like "It looks like you're typing a letter, can I help?" While we applaud his sentiment, we wish he weren't so obtrusive and could take a hint when it's clear we don't want his help. After all, a good waiter doesn't ask you if you want more water. He just refills your glass when it's empty, and he knows better than to snoop around when it's clear that you're in the middle of an intimate moment.

Considerate products use common sense

Offering inappropriate functions in inappropriate places is a hallmark of poorly designed interactive products. Many interactive products put controls for constantly used functions directly adjacent to never-used controls. You can easily find menus offering simple, harmless functions adjacent to irreversible ejector-seat-lever expert functions. It's like seating you at a dining table right next to an open grill.

Horror stories also abound of customers offended by computer systems that repeatedly sent them checks for $0.00 or bills for $957,142,039.58. One would think that the system might alert a human in the Accounts Receivable or Payable departments when an event like this happens, especially more than once, but common sense remains a rarity in most information systems.

Considerate products anticipate human needs

A human assistant knows that you will require a hotel room when you travel to another city, even when you don't ask explicitly. She knows the kind of room you like and reserves one without any request on your part. She anticipates your needs.

A Web browser spends most of its time idling while we peruse Web pages. It could easily anticipate our needs and prepare for them while we are reading. It could use that idle time to preload all the links that are visible. Chances are good that we will soon ask the browser to examine one or more of those links. It is easy to abort an unwanted request, but it is always time-consuming to wait for a request to be filled. We'll discuss more ways for software to use idle time to our advantage towards the end of this chapter.

Considerate products are conscientious

A conscientious person has a larger perspective on what it means to perform a task. Instead of just washing the dishes, for example, a conscientious person also wipes down the counters and empties the trash because those tasks are also related to the larger *goal*: cleaning up the kitchen. A conscientious person, when drafting a report, also puts a handsome cover page on it and makes enough photocopies for the entire department.

Here's an example: If we hand our imaginary assistant, Rodney, a manila folder and tell him to file it away, he checks the writing on the folder's tab — let's say it reads MicroBlitz Contract — and proceeds to find the correct place in the filing cabinet for it. Under M, he finds, to his surprise, that there is a manila folder already there with the identical MicroBlitz Contract legend. Rodney notices the discrepancy and investigates. He finds that the already filed folder contains a contract for 17 widgets that were delivered to MicroBlitz four months ago. The new folder, on the other hand, is for 32 sprockets slated for production and delivery in the next quarter. Conscientious Rodney changes the name on the old folder to read MicroBlitz Widget Contract, 7/03 and then changes the name of the new folder to read MicroBlitz Sprocket Contract, 11/03. This type of initiative is why we think Rodney is conscientious.

Our former imaginary assistant, Elliot, was a complete idiot. He was not conscientious at all, and if he were placed in the same situation he would have dumped the new MicroBlitz Contract folder next to the old MicroBlitz Contract folder without a second thought. Sure, he got it filed safely away, but he could have done a better job that would have improved our ability to find the right contract in the future. That's why Elliot isn't our imaginary assistant anymore.

If we rely on a word processor to draft the new sprocket contract and then try to save it in the MicroBlitz directory, the application offers the choice of either overwriting and destroying the old widget contract or not saving it at all. The application not only isn't as capable as Rodney, it isn't even as capable as Elliot. The software is dumb enough to make an assumption that because two folders have the same name, I meant to throw the old one away.

The application should, at the very least, mark the two files with different dates and save them. Even if the application refuses to take this "drastic" action unilaterally, it could at least show us the old file (letting us rename *that* one) before saving the new one. There are numerous actions that the application can take that would be more conscientious.

Considerate products don't burden you with their personal problems

At a service desk, the agent is expected to keep mum about her problems and to show a reasonable interest in yours. It might not be fair to be so one-sided, but that's the nature of the service business. An interactive product, too, should keep quiet about its problems and show interest in the people who use it. Because computers don't have egos or tender sensibilities, they should be perfect in this role, but they typically behave the opposite way.

Software whines at us with error messages, interrupts us with confirmation dialog boxes, and brags to us with unnecessary notifiers (Document Successfully Saved! How nice for you, Mr. Software: Do you ever *unsuccessfully* save?). We aren't interested in the application's crisis of confidence about whether or not to purge its Recycle Bin. We don't want to hear its whining about not being sure where to put a file on disk. We don't need to see information about the computer's data transfer rates and its loading sequence, any more than we need information about the customer service agent's unhappy love affair. Not only should software keep quiet about its problems, but it should also have the intelligence, confidence, and authority to fix its problems on its own. We discuss this subject in more detail in Chapter 25.

Considerate products keep us informed

Although we don't want our software pestering us incessantly with its little fears and triumphs, we do want to be kept informed about the things that matter to *us*. We don't want our local bartender to grouse to us about his recent divorce, but we appreciate it when he posts his prices in plain sight and when he writes what time the pregame party begins on his chalkboard, along with who's playing and the current Vegas spread. Nobody is interrupting us to tell us this information: It's there in plain view whenever we need it. Software, similarly, can provide us with this kind of rich modeless feedback about what is going on. Again, we discuss how in Chapter 25.

Considerate products are perceptive

Most of our existing software is not very perceptive. It has a very narrow understanding of the scope of most problems. It may willingly perform difficult work, but only when given the precise command at precisely the correct time. If, for example, you ask the inventory query system to tell you how many widgets are in stock, it will dutifully ask the database and report the number as of the time you ask. But what if, 20 minutes later, someone in the Dallas office cleans out the entire stock of widgets? You are now operating under a potentially embarrassing misconception, while your computer sits there, idling away billions of wasted instructions. It is not being perceptive. If you want to know about widgets once, isn't that a good clue that you probably will want to know about widgets again? You may not want to hear widget status reports every day for the rest of your life, but maybe you'll want to get them for the rest of the week. Perceptive software observes what users are doing and uses those observations to offer relevant information.

Products should also watch our preferences and remember them without being asked explicitly to do so. If we always maximize an application to use the entire available screen, the application should get the idea after a few sessions and always launch in that configuration. The same goes for placement of palettes, default tools, frequently used templates, and other useful settings.

Considerate products are self-confident

Interactive products should stand by their convictions. If we tell the computer to discard a file, it shouldn't ask, "Are you sure?" Of course we're sure; otherwise, we wouldn't have asked. It shouldn't second-guess us or itself.

On the other hand, if the computer has any suspicion that we might be wrong (which is always), it should anticipate our changing our minds by being prepared to undelete the file upon our request.

How often have you clicked the Print button and then gone to get a cup of coffee, only to return to find a fearful dialog box quivering in the middle of the screen asking, "Are you sure you want to print?" This insecurity is infuriating and the antithesis of considerate human behavior.

Considerate products don't ask a lot of questions

As discussed in Chapter 10, inconsiderate products ask lots of annoying questions. Excessive choices quickly stop being a benefit and become an ordeal.

Choices can be offered in different ways. They can be offered in the way that we window shop. We peer in the window at our leisure, considering, choosing, or ignoring the goods offered to us — no questions asked. Alternatively, choices can be forced on us like an interrogation by a customs officer at a border crossing: "*Do you have anything to declare?*" We don't know the consequences of the question. Will we be searched or not? Software should never put users through this kind of intimidation.

Considerate products fail gracefully

When a friend of yours makes a serious faux pas, he tries to make amends later and undo what damage can be undone. When an application discovers a fatal problem, it has the choice of taking the time and effort to prepare for its failure without hurting the user, or it can simply crash and burn.

Many applications are filled with data and settings. When they crash, that information is often just discarded. The user is left holding the bag. For example, say an application is computing merrily along, downloading your e-mail from a server when it runs out of memory at some procedure buried deep in the internals of the application. The application, like most desktop software, issues a message that says, in effect, "You are completely hosed," and terminates immediately after you click OK. You restart the application, or sometimes the whole computer, only to find that the application lost your e-mail and, when you interrogate the server, you find that it has also erased your mail because the mail was already handed over to your application. This is not what we should expect of good software.

In our e-mail example, the application accepted e-mail from the server — which then erased its copy — but didn't ensure that the e-mail was properly recorded locally. If the e-mail application had made sure that those messages were promptly written to the local disk, even before it informed the server that the messages were successfully downloaded, the problem would never have arisen.

Some well-designed software products, such as Ableton Live, a brilliant music performance tool, rely upon the Undo cache to recover from crashes. This is a great example of how products can easily keep track of user behavior, so if some situation causes problems, it is easy to extricate oneself from that situation.

Even when applications don't crash, inconsiderate behavior is rife, particularly on the Web. Users often need to enter detailed information into a set of forms on a page. After filling in 10 or 11 fields, a user might click the Submit button, and, due to some mistake or omission on his part, have the site reject his input and tell him to correct it. The user then clicks the back arrow to return to the page, and lo, the 10 valid entries were inconsiderately discarded along with the single invalid one. Remember Mr. Jones, that incredibly mean geography teacher in junior high school who ripped up your entire report on South America and threw it away because you wrote using a pencil instead of an ink pen? Don't you hate geography to this day? Don't create products like Mr. Jones!

Considerate products know when to bend the rules

When manual information-processing systems are translated into computerized systems, something is lost in the process. Although an automated order-entry system can handle millions more orders than a human clerk can, the human clerk has the ability to *work the system* in a way most automated systems ignore. There is almost never a way to jigger the functioning to give or take slight advantages in an automated system.

In a manual system, when the clerk's friend from the sales force calls on the phone and explains that getting the order processed speedily means additional business, the clerk can expedite that one order. When another order comes in with some critical information missing, the clerk can go ahead and process it, remembering to acquire and record the information later. This flexibility is usually absent from automated systems.

In most computerized systems, there are only two states: nonexistence or full-compliance. No intermediate states are recognized or accepted. In any manual system, there is an important but paradoxical state — unspoken, undocumented, but widely relied upon — of **suspense**, wherein a transaction can be accepted although still not being fully processed. The human operator creates that state in his head or on his desk or in his back pocket.

For example, a digital system needs both customer and order information before it can post an invoice. Whereas the human clerk can go ahead and post an order in advance of detailed customer information, the computerized system will reject the transaction, unwilling to allow the invoice to be entered without it.

The characteristic of manual systems that lets humans perform actions out of sequence or before prerequisites are satisfied is called **fudgeability**. It is one of the first casualties when systems are computerized, and its absence is a key contributor to the inhumanity of digital systems. It is a natural result of the implementation model. Programmers don't see any reason to create intermediate states because the computer has no need for them. Yet there are strong human needs to be able to bend the system slightly.

One of the benefits of fudgeable systems is the reduction of mistakes. By allowing many small temporary mistakes into the system and entrusting humans to correct them before they cause problems downstream, we can avoid much bigger, more permanent mistakes. Paradoxically, most of the hard-edged rules enforced by computer systems are imposed to prevent just such mistakes. These inflexible rules cast the human and the software as adversaries, and because the human is prevented from fudging to prevent big mistakes, he soon stops caring about protecting the software from really colossal problems. When inflexible rules are imposed on flexible humans, both sides lose. It is invariably bad for business to prevent humans from doing what they want, and the computer system usually ends up having to digest invalid data anyway.

In the real world, both missing information and extra information that doesn't fit into a standard field are important tools for success. Information-processing systems rarely handle this real-world data. They only model the rigid, repeatable data portion of transactions, a sort of skeleton of the actual transaction, which may involve dozens of meetings, travel and entertainment, names of spouses and kids, golf games, and favorite sports figures. Maybe a transaction can only be completed if the termination date is extended two weeks beyond the official limit. Most companies would rather fudge on the termination date than see a million-dollar deal go up in smoke. In the real world, limits are fudged all the time. Considerate products need to realize and embrace this fact.

Considerate products take responsibility

Too many interactive products take the attitude: "It isn't my responsibility." When they pass a job along to some hardware device, they wash their hands of the action, leaving the stupid hardware to finish up. Any user can see that the software isn't being considerate or conscientious, that the software isn't shouldering its part of the burden for helping the user become more effective.

In a typical print operation, for example, an application begins sending the 20 pages of a report to the printer and simultaneously puts up a print process dialog box with a Cancel button. If the user quickly realizes that he forgot to make an important change, he clicks the Cancel button just as the first page emerges from the printer. The application immediately cancels the print operation. But unbeknownst to the user, while the printer was beginning to work on page 1, the computer has already sent 15 pages into the printer's buffer. The application cancels the last five pages, but the printer doesn't know anything about the cancellation; it just knows that it was sent 15 pages, so it goes ahead and prints them. Meanwhile, the application smugly tells the user that the function was canceled. The application lies, as the user can plainly see.

The user isn't very sympathetic to the communication problems between the application and the printer. He doesn't care that the communications are one-way. All he knows is that he decided not to print the document before the first page appeared in the printer's output basket, he clicked the Cancel button, and then the stupid application continued printing for 15 pages even though he acted in plenty of time to stop it. It even acknowledged his Cancel command. As he throws the 15 wasted sheets of paper in the trash, he growls at the stupid application.

Imagine what his experience would be if the application could communicate with the print driver and the print driver could communicate with the printer. If the software were smart enough, the print job could easily have been abandoned before the second sheet of paper was wasted. The printer certainly has a Cancel function — it's just that the software was built to be too indolent to use it.

Designing Smart Products

In addition to being considerate, helpful products and people must also be **smart**. Thanks to science fiction writers and futurists, there is some confusion about what it means for an interactive product to be smart. Some naive observers think that smart software is actually capable of behaving intelligently.

While this would certainly be nice, the fact of the matter is that our silicon-enabled tools are still a ways away from delivering on that dream. A more useful understanding of the term (if you're trying to ship a product this decade) is that these products are capable of working hard even when conditions are difficult and even when users aren't busy. Regardless of our dreams of thinking computers, there is a much greater and more immediate opportunity to get our computers to work harder. The remainder of this chapter discusses some of the most important ways that software can work a bit harder to serve humans better.

Putting the idle cycles to work

Because every instruction in every application must pass single-file through the CPU, we tend to optimize our code for this needle's eye. Programmers work hard to keep the number of instructions to a minimum, ensuring snappy performance for users. What we often forget, however, is that as soon as the CPU has hurriedly finished all its work, it waits idle, doing nothing, until the user issues another command. We invest enormous efforts in reducing the computer's reaction time, but we invest little or no effort in putting it to work proactively when it is not busy reacting to the user. Our software commands the CPU as though it were in the army, alternately telling it to hurry up and wait. The hurry up part is great, but the waiting needs to stop.

In our current computing systems, users need to remember too many things, such as the names they give to files and the precise location of those files in the file system. If a user wants to find that spreadsheet with the quarterly projections on it again, he must either remember its name or go browsing. Meanwhile, the processor just sits there, wasting billions of cycles.

Most current software also takes no notice of context. When a user is struggling with a particularly difficult spreadsheet on a tight deadline, for example, the application offers precisely as much help as it offers when he is noodling with numbers in his spare time. Software can no longer, in good conscience, waste so much idle time while users work. It is time for our computers to begin to shoulder more of the burden of work in our day-to-day activities.

Most users in normal situations can't do anything in less than a few seconds. That is enough time for a typical desktop computer to execute at least a *billion* instructions. Almost without fail, those interim cycles are dedicated to idling. The processor does *nothing* except wait. The argument against putting those cycles to work has always been: "We can't make assumptions; those assumptions might be wrong." Our computers today are so powerful that, although the argument is still true, it is frequently irrelevant. Simply put, it doesn't matter if the application's assumptions are wrong; it has enough spare power to make several assumptions and discard the results of the bad ones when the user finally makes his choice.

With Windows and Mac OS X's preemptive, threaded multitasking and multicore, multichip computers, you can perform extra work in the background without significantly affecting the performance most users see. The application can launch a search for a file, and if the user begins typing, merely abandon it until the next hiatus. Eventually, the user stops to think, and the application will have time to scan the whole disk. The user won't even notice. This is precisely the kind of behavior that makes Mac OS X's Spotlight search capabilities vastly superior to that in those windows. Search results are almost instantaneous because the operating system takes advantage of downtime to index the hard drive.

Every time an application puts up a modal dialog box, it goes into an idle waiting state, doing no work while the user struggles with the dialog. This should never happen. It would not be hard for the dialog box to hunt around and find ways to help. What did the user do last time? The application could, for example, offer the previous choice as a suggestion for this time.

We need a new, more proactive way of thinking about how software can help people reach their goals and complete their tasks.

Smart products have a memory

When you think about it, it's pretty obvious that for a person to perceive an interactive product as considerate and smart, that product must have some knowledge about the person and be capable of learning from their behavior. Looking through the characteristics of considerate products presented earlier reinforces this fact: For a product to be truly helpful and considerate it must *remember* important things about the people interacting with it.

Quite often, software is difficult to use because it operates according to rational, logical assumptions that, unfortunately, are very wrong. Programmers and designers often assume that the behavior of users is random and unpredictable, and that users must be continually interrogated to determine the proper course of action. Although human behavior certainly isn't deterministic like that of a digital computer, it is rarely random, and asking silly questions is predictably frustrating for users.

If your application, Web site, or device could predict what a user is going to do next, couldn't it provide a better interaction? If your application could know which selections the user will make in a particular dialog box or form, couldn't that part of the interface be skipped? Wouldn't you consider advance knowledge of what actions your users take to be an awesome secret weapon of interface design?

Well, you *can* predict what your users will do. You *can* build a sixth sense into your application that will tell it with uncanny accuracy exactly what the user will do next! All those billions of wasted processor cycles can be put to great use: All you need to do is give your interface a memory.

When we use the term **memory** in this context, we don't mean RAM, but rather a facility for tracking and responding to user actions over multiple sessions. If your application simply remembers what the user did the last several times (and how), it can use that as a guide to how it should behave the next time.

If we enable our products with an awareness of user behavior, a memory, and the flexibility to present information and functionality based upon previous user actions, we can realize great advantages in user efficiency and satisfaction. We would all like to have an intelligent and self-motivated assistant who shows initiative, drive, good judgment, and a keen memory. A product that makes effective use of its memory is more like that self-motivated assistant, remembering helpful information and personal preferences without needing to ask. Simple things can make a big difference: the difference between a product your users tolerate and one that they *love*. The next time you find your application asking your users a question, make it ask itself one instead.

You might think that bothering with a memory isn't necessary; it's easier to just ask the user each time. Many programmers are quick to pop up a dialog box to request any information that isn't lying conveniently around. But as we discussed in Chapter 10, *people don't like to be asked questions*. Continually interrogating users is not only a form of excise, but also, from a psychological perspective, it is a subtle way of expressing doubt about their authority.

Most software is forgetful, remembering little or nothing from execution to execution. If our applications *are* smart enough to retain any information during and between uses, it is usually information that makes the job easier for the *programmer* and not for the user. The application willingly discards information about the way it was used, how it was changed, where it was used, what data it processed, who used it, and whether and how frequently the various facilities of the application were used. Meanwhile, the application fills initialization files with driver names, port assignments, and other details that ease the programmer's burden. It is possible to use the exact same facilities to dramatically increase the smarts of your software from the perspective of the user.

Task coherence

Predicting what a user will do by remembering what he did last is based on the principle of **task coherence**: the idea that our goals and the way we achieve them (via tasks) is generally similar from day to day. This is not only true for tasks like brushing our teeth and eating our breakfasts, but it also describes how we use our word processors, e-mail applications, cell phones, and enterprise software.

When a consumer uses your product, there is a good chance that the functions he uses and the way he uses them will be very similar to what he did in previous uses of the product. He may even be working on the same documents, or at least the same types of documents, located in similar places. Sure, he won't be doing the exact same thing each time, but his tasks will likely be variants of a limited number of repeated patterns. With significant reliability, you can predict the behavior of your users by the simple expedient of remembering what they did the last several times they used the application. This allows you to greatly reduce the number of questions your application must ask the user.

Sally, for example, though she may use Excel in dramatically different ways than Kazu, will tend to use Excel the same way each time. Although Kazu likes 9-point Times Roman and Sally prefers 12-point Helvetica and uses that font and size with dependable regularity. It isn't really necessary for the application to ask Sally which font to use. A very reliable starting point would be 12-point Helvetica, every time.

Remembering choices and defaults

The way to determine what information the application should remember is with a simple rule: If it's worth the user entering, it's worth the application remembering.

 DESIGN principle   If it's worth the user entering, it's worth the application remembering.

Any time your application finds itself with a choice, and especially when that choice is being offered to a user, the application should remember the information from run to run. Instead of choosing a hard-wired default, the application can use the previous setting as the default, and it will have a much better chance of giving a user what he wanted. Instead of asking a user to make a determination, the application should go ahead and make the same determination a user made last time, and let her change it if it was wrong. Any options users set should be remembered, so that the options remain in effect until manually changed. If a user ignores aspects of an application or turns them off, they should not be offered again. The user will seek them out when and if he is ready for them.

One of the most annoying characteristics of applications without memories is that they are so parsimonious with their assistance regarding files and disks. If there is one place where users need help, it's with files and disks. An application like Word remembers the last place a person looked for a file. Unfortunately, if she always puts her files in a directory called Letters, then edits a document template stored in the Template directory just one time, all her subsequent letters will be stored in the Template directory rather than in the Letters directory. So, the application must remember more than just the last place the files were accessed. It must remember the last place files *of each type* were accessed.

The position of windows should also be remembered, so if you maximized the document last time it should be maximized next time. If you positioned it next to another window, it is positioned the same way the next time without any instruction from the user. Microsoft Office applications now do a good job of this.

Remembering patterns

Users can benefit in several ways from a product with a good memory. Memory reduces excise, the useless effort that must be devoted to managing tools and not doing work. A significant portion of the total excise of an interface is in having to explain things to the application that it should already know. For example, in your word processor, you might often reverse-out text, making it white on black. To do this, you select some text and change the font color to white. Without altering the selection, you then set the background color to black. If the application paid enough attention, it would notice the fact that you requested two formatting steps without an intervening selection option. As far as you're concerned, this is effectively a single operation. Wouldn't it be nice if the application, upon seeing this unique pattern repeated several times, automatically created a new format style of this type — or better yet, created a new Reverse-Out toolbar control?

Most mainstream applications allow their users to set defaults, but this doesn't fit the bill as a memory would. Configuration of this kind is an onerous process for all but power users, and many users will never understand how to customize defaults to their liking.

Actions to remember

Everything that users do should be remembered. There is plenty of storage on our hard drives, and a memory for your application is a good investment of storage space. We tend to think that applications are wasteful because a big application might consume 200 MB of disk space. That is typical usage for an application, but not for user data. If your word processor saved 1 KB of execution notes every time you ran it, it still wouldn't amount to much. Let's say that you use your word processor 10 times every business day. There are approximately 200 workdays per year, so you run the application 2000 times a year. The net consumption is still only 2 MB, and that gives an exhaustive recounting of the entire year! This is probably not much more than the background image you put on your desktop.

File locations

All file-open facilities should remember where the user gets his files. Most users only access files from a few directories for each given application. The application should remember these source directories and offer them on a combo box on the File Open dialog. The user should never have to step through the tree to a given directory more than once.

Deduced information

Software should not simply remember these kinds of explicit facts, but should also remember useful information that can be deduced from these facts. For example, if the application remembers the number of bytes changed in the file each time it is opened, it can help the user with some reasonableness checks. Imagine that the changed-byte-count for a file was 126, 94, 43, 74, 81, 70, 110, and 92. If the user calls up the file and changes 100 bytes, nothing would be out of the ordinary. But if the number of changed bytes suddenly shoots up to 5000, the application might suspect that something is amiss. Although there is a chance that the user has inadvertently done something about which he will be sorry, the probability of that is low, so it isn't right to bother him with a confirmation dialog. It is, however, very reasonable for the application to make sure to keep a milestone copy of the file before the 5000 bytes were changed, just in case. The application probably won't need to keep it beyond the next time the user accesses that file, because the user will likely spot any mistake that glaring immediately, and he would then demand an undo.

Multisession undo

Most applications discard their stack of undo actions when the user closes the document or the application. This is very shortsighted on the application's part. Instead, the application could write the undo stack to a file. When the user reopens the file, the application could reload its undo stack with the actions the user performed the last time the application was run — even if that was a week ago!

Past data entries

An application with a better memory can reduce the number of errors users make. This is simply because users have to enter less information. More of it will be entered automatically from the application's memory. In an invoicing application, for example, if the software enters the date, department number, and other standard fields from memory, the invoicing clerk has fewer opportunities to make typing errors in these fields.

If the application remembers what the user enters and uses that information for future reasonableness checks, the application can work to keep erroneous data from being entered. Contemporary Web browsers such as Internet Explorer and Firefox provide this facility: Named data entry fields remember what has been entered into them before, and allow users to pick those values from a combo box. For security-minded individuals, this feature can be turned off, but for the rest of us, it saves time and prevents errors.

Foreign application activities on application files

Applications might also leave a small thread running between invocations. This little application can keep an eye on the files it worked on. It can track where they go and who reads and writes to them. This information might be helpful to a user when he next runs the application. When he tries to open a particular file, the application can help him find it, even if it has been moved. The application can keep the user informed about what other functions were performed on his file, such as whether or not it was printed or faxed to someone. Sure, this information might not be needed, but the computer can easily spare the time, and it's only bits that have to be thrown away, after all.

Applying memory to your applications

A remarkable thing happens to the software design process when developers accept the power of task coherence. Designers find that their thinking takes on a whole new quality. The normally unquestioned recourse of popping up a dialog box gets replaced with a more studied process, where the designer asks questions of much greater subtlety. Questions like: How *much* should the application remember? Which aspects should be remembered? Should the application remember more than just the last setting? What constitutes a change in pattern? Designers start to imagine situations like this: The user accepts the same date format 50 times in a row, and then manually enters a different format once. The next time the user enters a date, which format should the application use? The format used 50 times or the more recent one-time format? How many times must the new format be specified before it becomes the default? Just because there is ambiguity here, the application still shouldn't ask the user. It must use its initiative to make a reasonable decision. The user is free to override the application's decision if it is the wrong one.

The following sections explain some characteristic patterns in the ways people make choices that can help us resolve these more complex questions about task coherence.

Decision-set reduction

People tend to reduce an infinite set of choices down to a small, finite set of choices. Even when you don't do the exact same thing each time, you will tend to choose your actions from a small, repetitive set of options. People unconsciously perform this **decision-set reduction**, but software can take notice and act upon it.

For example, just because you went shopping at Safeway yesterday doesn't necessarily mean that you will be shopping at Safeway exclusively. However, the next time you need groceries, you will probably shop at Safeway again. Similarly, even though your favorite Chinese restaurant has 250 items on the menu, chances are that you will usually choose from your own personal subset of five or six favorites. When people drive to and from work, they usually choose from a small number of favorite routes, depending on traffic conditions. Computers, of course, can remember four or five things without breaking a sweat.

Although simply remembering the last action is better than not remembering anything, it can lead to a peculiar pathology if the decision set consists of precisely two elements. If, for example, you alternately read files from one directory and store them in another, each time the application offers you the last directory, it will be guaranteed to be wrong. The solution is to remember more than just one previous choice.

Decision-set reduction guides us to the idea that pieces of information the application must remember about the user's choices tend to come in groups. Instead of one right way, several options are all correct. The application should look for more subtle clues to differentiate which one of the small set is correct. For example, if you use a check-writing application to pay your bills, the application may very quickly learn that only two or three accounts are used regularly. But how can it determine from a given check which of the three accounts is the most likely to be appropriate? If the application remembered the payees and amounts on an account-by-account basis, that decision would be easy. Every time you pay the rent, it is the exact same amount! It's the same with a car payment. The amount paid to the electric company might vary from check to check, but it probably stays within 10 or 20% of the last check written to them. All this information can be used to help the application recognize what is going on, and use that information to help the user.

Preference thresholds

The decisions people make tend to fall into two primary categories: important and unimportant. Any given activity may involve hundreds of decisions, but only a few of them are important. All the rest are insignificant. Software interfaces can use this idea of **preference thresholds** to simplify tasks for users.

After you decide to buy that car, you don't really care who finances it as long as the terms are competitive. After you decide to buy groceries, the particular check-out aisle you select may not be important. After you decide to ride the Matterhorn at Disneyland, you don't really care which toboggan they seat you in.

Preference thresholds guide us in our user interface design by demonstrating that asking users for successively detailed decisions about a procedure is unnecessary. After a user asks to print, we don't have to ask him how many copies he wants or whether the image is landscape or portrait. We can make an assumption about these things the first time out, and then remember them for all subsequent invocations. If the user wants to change them, he can always request the Printer Options dialog box.

Using preference thresholds, we can easily track which facilities of the application each user likes to adjust and which are set once and ignored. With this knowledge, the application can offer choices where it has an expectation that a user will want to take control, not bothering him with decisions he won't care about.

Mostly right, most of the time

Task coherence predicts what users will do in the future with reasonable, but not absolute, certainty. If our application relies on this principle, it's natural to wonder about the uncertainty of our predictions. If we can reliably predict what the user will do 80% of the time, it means that 20% of the time we will be wrong. It might seem that the proper step to take here is to offer users a choice, but this means that they will be bothered by an unnecessary dialog 80% of the time. Rather than offering a choice, the application should go ahead and do what it thinks is most appropriate and allow users to override or undo it. If the undo facility is sufficiently easy to use and understand, users won't be bothered by it. After all, they will have to use undo only two times out of ten instead of having to deal with a redundant dialog box eight times out of ten. This is a much better deal for humans.

13

Metaphors, Idioms, and Affordances

Some interface designers speak of finding the right metaphor upon which to base their interface designs. They imagine that filling their interface with images of familiar objects from the real world will give their users a pipeline to easy learning. So, they create an interface masquerading as an office filled with desks, file cabinets, telephones, and address books, or as a pad of paper or a street of buildings. If you, too, search for that magic metaphor, you will be in august company. Some of the best and brightest designers in the interface world consider metaphor selection as one of their first and most important tasks.

We find this very literal approach to be limiting and potentially problematic. Strict adherence to metaphors ties interfaces unnecessarily to the workings of the physical world. One of the most fantastic things about digital products is that the working model presented to users need not be bound by the limitations of physics and the inherent messiness of real three-dimensional space.

User interfaces based on metaphors have a host of other problems as well: There aren't enough good metaphors to go around, they don't scale well, and the ability of users to recognize them is often questionable, especially across cultural boundaries. Metaphors, especially physical and spatial metaphors, have an extremely limited place in the design of most Information-Age, software-enabled products. In this chapter, we discuss the reasons for this, as well as the alternatives to design based on metaphors.

Interface Paradigms

There are three dominant paradigms in the conceptual and visual design of user interfaces: **implementation-centric**, **metaphoric**, and **idiomatic**. The implementation-centric interfaces are based on *understanding* how things actually work under the hood — a difficult proposition. Metaphoric interfaces are based on *intuiting* how things work — a risky method. Idiomatic interfaces, however, are based on *learning* how to accomplish things — a natural, human process.

The field of user-interface design progressed from a heavy focus on technology (implementation) to an equally heavy focus on metaphor. There is ample evidence of all three paradigms in contemporary software design, even though the metaphoric paradigm is the only one that has been named and described. Although metaphors are great tools for humans to communicate with each other (this book is filled with them), they are weak tools for the design of software, and all too often they hamper the creation of truly superior interfaces.

Implementation-centric interfaces

Implementation-centric user interfaces are widespread in the computer industry. These interfaces are expressed in terms of their construction, of how they are built. In order to successfully use them, users must understand how the software works internally. Following the implementation-centric paradigm means user-interface design based exclusively on the implementation model.

The overwhelming majority of software programs today are implementation centric in that they show us, without any hint of shame, precisely how they are built. There is one button per function, one dialog per module of code, and the commands and processes precisely echo the internal data structures and algorithms.

We can see how an implementation model interface ticks by learning how to run its program. The problem is that the reverse is also true: We *must* learn how the program works in order to successfully use the interface.

 DESIGN principle   Most people would rather be successful than knowledgeable.

Clearly, implementation-centric interfaces are the easiest to build — every time a programmer writes a function he slaps on a bit of user interface to test that function. It's easy to debug, and when something doesn't behave properly, it's easy to troubleshoot. Further, engineers like to know how things work, so the implementation-centric paradigm is very satisfying to them. Engineers prefer to see the gears and levers and valves because it helps them understand what is going on inside the machine. That those artifacts needlessly complicate things for users seems a small price to pay. Engineers may want to understand the inner workings, but most users don't have either the time or desire. They'd much rather be successful than be knowledgeable, a preference that is often hard for engineers to understand.

A close relative of the implementation-centric interface worth mentioning is the "org-chart centric" interface. This is the common situation where a product, or most typically, a Web site, is organized, not according to how users are likely to think about information, but by how the company the site represents is structured. On such as site, there is typically a tab or area for each division and a lack of cohesion between these areas. Similar to the implementation-centric product interface, an org-chart-centric Web site requires users to have an intimate understanding of how a corporation is structured to find the information they are interested in.

Metaphoric interfaces

Metaphoric interfaces rely on intuitive connections that users makes between the visual cues in an interface and its function. There is no need to understand the mechanics of the software, so it is a step forward from implementation-centric interfaces, but its power and usefulness has been inflated to unrealistic proportions.

When we talk about metaphors in the context of user interface and interaction design, we really mean visual metaphors: a picture used to represent the purpose or attributes of a thing. Users recognize the imagery of the metaphor and, by extension, can presumably understand the purpose of the thing. Metaphors can range from the tiny images on toolbar buttons to the entire screen on some programs — from a tiny pair of scissors on a button indicating Cut to a full-size checkbook in Quicken. We understand metaphors intuitively, but what does that really mean? Webster's Dictionary defines intuition like this:

> **in·tu·i·tion** \in-'tu-wi-shen\ n 1 : quick and ready insight **2 a** : immediate apprehension or cognition **b** : knowledge or conviction gained by intuition **c** : the power or faculty of attaining to direct knowledge or cognition without evident rational thought and inference

This definition highlights the magical quality of intuition, but it doesn't say *how* we intuit something. Intuition works by inference, where we see connections between disparate subjects and learn from these similarities, while not being distracted by their differences. We grasp the meaning of the metaphoric controls in an interface because we mentally connect them with other things we have already learned. This is an efficient way to take advantage of the awesome power of the human mind to make inferences. However, this method also depends on the idiosyncratic human minds of users, which may not have the requisite language, knowledge, or inferential power necessary to make those connections.

Limitations of metaphors

The idea that metaphors are a firm foundation for user-interface design is misleading. It's like worshipping floppy disks because so much good software once came on them. Metaphors have many limitations when applied to modern, information-age systems.

For one thing, metaphors don't scale very well. A metaphor that works well for a simple process in a simple program will often fail to work well as that process grows in size or complexity. Large file icons were a good idea when computers had floppies or 10 MB hard disks with only a couple of hundred files, but in these days of 250 GB hard disks and tens of thousands of files, file icons become too clumsy to use effectively.

Metaphors also rely on associations perceived in similar ways by both the designer and the user. If the user doesn't have the same cultural background as the designer, it is easy for metaphors to fail. Even in the same or similar cultures, there can be significant misunderstandings. Does a picture of an airplane mean "check flight arrival information" or "make airline reservations?"

Finally, although a metaphor offers a small boost in learnability to first-time users, it exacts a tremendous cost after they become intermediates. By reflecting the physical world of mechanisms, most metaphors firmly nail our conceptual feet to the ground, forever limiting the power of our software. We'll discuss this issue with metaphors later in this chapter.

Our definition of intuition indicates that rational thought is not required in the process of intuiting. In the computer industry, and particularly in the user-interface design community, the word *intuitive* is often used to mean easy-to-use or easy-to-understand. Ease-of-use is obviously important, but it doesn't promote our craft to attribute its success to metaphysics. Nor does it help us to devalue the precise meaning of the word. There are very real reasons why people understand certain interfaces and not others.

Intuition, instinct, and learning

There are certain sounds, smells, and images that make us respond without any previous conscious learning. When a small child encounters an angry dog, she *instinctively* knows that bared fangs signal great danger even without any previous learning. The encoding for such recognition goes deep. Instinct is a hard-wired response that involves no conscious thought. Intuition is one step above instinct because, although it also requires no conscious thought, it is based on a web of knowledge learned consciously.

Examples of instinct in human-computer interaction include the way we are startled and made apprehensive by gross changes in the image on the screen, find our eyes drawn inexorably to the flashing advertisement on a Web page, or react to sudden noises from the computer or the smell of smoke rising from the CPU.

Intuition is a middle ground between having consciously learned something and knowing something instinctively. If we have learned that things glowing red can burn us, we tend to classify all red-glowing things as potentially dangerous until proven otherwise. We don't necessarily know that the particular red-glowing thing is a danger, but it gives us a safe place to begin our exploration.

What we commonly refer to as intuition is actually a mental comparison between a new experience and the things we have already learned. You instantly intuit how to work a wastebasket icon, for example, because you once learned how a real wastebasket works, thereby preparing your mind to make the connection years later. But you didn't *intuit* how to use the original wastebasket. It was just an extremely easy thing to learn. This brings us to the third type of interface, based on the fact that the human mind is an incredibly powerful learning machine that constantly and effortlessly learns new things.

Idiomatic interfaces

Idiomatic design, what Ted Nelson has called "the design of principles," is based on the way we learn and use idioms — figures of speech like "beat around the bush" or "cool." Idiomatic user interfaces solve the problems of the previous two interface types by focusing not on technical knowledge or intuition of function, but rather on the learning of simple, nonmetaphorical visual and behavioral idioms to accomplish goals and tasks.

Idiomatic expressions don't provoke associative connections the way that metaphors do. There is no bush and nobody is beating anything. Idiomatically speaking, something can be both cool and hot and be equally desirable. We understand the idiom simply because we have learned it and because it is distinctive, not because we understand it or because it makes subliminal connections in our minds. Yet, we are all capable of rapidly memorizing and using such idioms: We do so almost without realizing it.

If you cannot intuit an idiom, neither can you reason it out. Our language is filled with idioms that, if you haven't been taught them, make no sense. If we say, "Uncle Joe kicked the bucket," you know what we mean even though there is no bucket or kicking involved. You can't know this by thinking through the various permutations of smacking pails with your feet. You can only learn this from context in something you read or by being consciously taught it. You remember this obscure connection between buckets, kicking, and dying only because humans are good at remembering things like this.

The human mind has a truly amazing capacity to learn and remember large numbers of idioms quickly and easily without relying on comparisons to known situations or an understanding of how or why they work. This is a necessity, because most idioms don't have metaphoric meaning at all, and the stories behind most others were lost ages ago.

Graphical interfaces are largely idiomatic

It turns out that most of the elements of intuitive graphical interfaces are actually visual idioms. Windows, title bars, close boxes, screen-splitters, hyperlinks, and drop-downs are things we learn idiomatically rather than intuit metaphorically. The Macintosh's use of the trashcan to unmount an external FireWire disk before removing it is purely idiomatic (and many designers consider it a poor idiom), despite the visual metaphor of the trash can itself.

The ubiquitous mouse input device is not metaphoric of anything, but rather is learned idiomatically. There is a scene in the movie *Star Trek IV* where Scotty returns to 20th-century Earth and tries to speak into a mouse. There is nothing about the physical appearance of the mouse that indicates its purpose or use, nor is it comparable to anything else in our experience, so learning it is not intuitive. However, learning to point at things with a mouse is incredibly easy. Someone probably spent all of three seconds showing it to you the first time, and you mastered it from that instant on. We don't know or care how mice work, and yet even small children can operate them just fine. That is idiomatic learning.

Ironically, many of the familiar GUI elements that are often thought of as metaphoric are actually idiomatic. Artifacts like resizable windows and endlessly nested file folders are not really metaphoric — they have no parallel in the real world. They derive their strength only from their easy idiomatic learnability.

Good idioms must be learned only once

We are inclined to think that learning interfaces is hard because of our conditioning based on experience with implementation-centric software. These interfaces are very hard to learn because you need to understand how the software works internally to use them effectively. Most of what we know we learn *without* understanding: things like faces, social interactions, attitudes, melodies, brand names, the arrangement of rooms, and furniture in our houses and offices. We don't *understand* why someone's face is composed the way it is, but we *know* that face. We recognize it because we have looked at it and automatically (and easily) memorized it.

 DESIGN principle   All idioms must be learned; good idioms need to be learned only once.

The key observation about idioms is that although they must be learned, they are very easy to learn, and good ones need to be learned only once. It is quite easy to learn idioms like "neat" or "politically correct" or "the lights are on but nobody's home" or "in a pickle" or "take the red-eye" or "grunge." The human mind is capable of picking up idioms like these from a single hearing. It is similarly easy to learn idioms like radio buttons, close boxes, drop-down menus, and combo boxes.

Branding and idioms

Marketing and advertising professionals understand well the idea of taking a simple action or symbol and imbuing it with meaning. After all, synthesizing idioms is the essence of product branding, in which a company takes a product or company name and imbues it with a desired meaning. The golden arches of McDonalds, the three diamonds of Mitsubishi, the five interlocking rings of the Olympics, even Microsoft's flying window are nonmetaphoric idioms that are instantly recognizable and imbued with common meaning. The example of an idiomatic symbol shown in Figure 13-1 illustrates its power.

Figure 13-1 Here is an idiomatic symbol that has been imbued with meaning from its use, rather than by any connection to other objects. For anyone who grew up in the 1950s and 1960s, this otherwise meaningless symbol has the power to evoke a shiver of fear because it represents nuclear radiation. Visual idioms, such as the American flag, can be just as powerful as metaphors, if not more so. The power comes from how we use them and associate them, rather than from any innate connection to real-world objects.

Further Limitations of Metaphors

If we depend on metaphors to create user interfaces, we encounter not only the minor problems already mentioned, but also two more major problems: Metaphors are hard to find, and they constrict our thinking.

Finding good metaphors

It may be easy to discover visual metaphors for physical objects like printers and documents. It can be difficult or impossible to find metaphors for processes, relationships, services, and transformations — the most frequent uses of software. It can be extremely daunting to find a useful visual metaphor for changing channels, purchasing an item, finding a reference, setting a format, changing a photograph's resolution, or performing statistical analysis, yet these operations are precisely the type of processes we use software to perform most frequently.

Computers and digital products are so powerful because of their ability to manage incredibly complex relationships within very large sets of data. Their very utility is based upon the fact that the human mind is challenged by such multidimensional problems, so almost by definition, these processes are not well suited to a simple, physical analog that people "automatically" comprehend.

The problems with global metaphors

The most significant problem with metaphors, however, is that they tie our interfaces to Mechanical Age artifacts. An extreme example of this was Magic Cap, a handheld communicator interface introduced with some fanfare by General Magic in the mid-1990s. It relies on metaphors for almost every aspect of its interface. You access your messages from an inbox or a notebook on a desk. You walk down a hallway that is lined with doors representing secondary functions. You go outside to access third-party services, which as you can see in Figure 13-2, are represented by buildings on a street. You enter a building to configure a service, and so on. The heavy reliance on this metaphor means that you can intuit the basic functioning of the software, but the downside is that, after you understand its function, the metaphor adds significantly to the overhead of navigation. You *must* go back out onto the street to configure another service. You *must* go down the hallway and into the game room to play Solitaire. This may be normal in the physical world, but there is no reason for it in the world of software. Why not abandon this slavish devotion to metaphor and give the user *easy* access to functions? It turns out that a General Magic programmer later created a bookmarking shortcut facility as a kludgy add-on, but alas, too little too late.

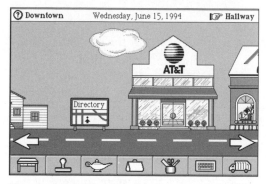

Figure 13-2 The Magic Cap interface from General Magic was used in products from Sony and Motorola in the mid-1990s. It is a tour de force of metaphoric design. All the navigation in the interface, and most other interactions as well, were subordinated to the maintenance of spatial and physical metaphors. It was surely fun to design but was not particularly easy to use after you became an intermediate. This was a shame, because some of the lower-level, nonmetaphoric, data-entry interactions were quite sophisticated and well designed for the time.

General Magic's interface relies on what is called a **global metaphor**. This is a single, overarching metaphor that provides a framework for all the other metaphors in the system. The desktop of the original Macintosh is also a global metaphor.

A hidden problem of global metaphors is the mistaken belief that other lower-level metaphors consistent with them enjoy cognitive benefits by association. The temptation is irresistible to stretch the metaphor beyond simple function recognition: That software telephone also lets us dial with buttons just like those on our desktop telephones. We see software that has address books of phone numbers just like those in our pockets and purses. Wouldn't it be better to go beyond these confining, industrial-age technologies and deliver some of the real power of the computer? Why shouldn't our communications software allow multiple connections or make connections by organization or affiliation, or just hide the use of phone numbers altogether?

It may seem clever to represent your dial-up service with a picture of a telephone sitting on a desk, but it actually imprisons you in a limited design. The original makers of the telephone would have been ecstatic if they could have created a phone that let you call your friends just by pointing to pictures of them. They couldn't because they were restricted by the dreary realities of electrical circuits and Bakelite moldings. On the other hand, today we have the luxury of rendering our communications interfaces in any way we please — showing pictures of our friends is completely reasonable — yet we insist on holding these concepts back with representations of obsolete technology.

There are two snares involved in extending metaphors, one for the user and one for the designer. After the user depends on the metaphor for recognition, he expects consistency of behavior with the real-world object to which the metaphor refers. This causes the snare for the designer, who now, to meet user expectations, is tempted to render the software in terms of the metaphor's Mechanical Age referent. As we discussed in Chapter 2, transliterating mechanical processes onto the computer usually makes them worse than they were before.

Take the example of the ubiquitous file folder in modern computer operating systems. As a mechanism for organizing documents, it is quite easy to learn and understand because of its similarity to a physical file folder in a file cabinet. Unfortunately, as is the case with many metaphoric user interfaces, it functions a bit differently than its real world analog, which has the potential to create cognitive friction on the part of users. For example, in the world of paper, no one nests folders 10 layers deep, which makes it difficult for novice computer users to come to terms with the navigational structures of an operating system.

There are also gravely limiting consequences to the implementation of this mechanism. In the world of paper, it is impossible for the same document to be located in two different places in the filing cabinet, and as a result, filing is executed with a single organization scheme (such as alphabetically by name or numerically by account number). Our digital products are not intrinsically bound by such limitations, but blind adherence to an interface metaphor has drastically limited our ability to file a single document according to multiple organization schemes.

As Brenda Laurel said, "Interface metaphors rumble along like Rube Goldberg machines, patched and wired together every time they break, until they are so encrusted with the artifacts of repair that we can no longer interpret them or recognize their referents." It amazes us that designers, who can finally create that dream-phone interface, give us the same old telephone simply because they were taught that a strong, global metaphor is a prerequisite to good user-interface design. Of all the misconceptions to emerge from Xerox PARC, the global metaphor myth is the most debilitating and unfortunate.

Idiomatic design is the future of interaction design. Using this paradigm, we depend on the natural ability of humans to learn easily and quickly as long as we don't force them to understand how and why. There is an infinity of idioms waiting to be invented, but only a limited set of metaphors waiting to be discovered. Metaphors give first-timers a penny's worth of value but cost them many dollars' worth of problems as they continue to use the software. It is always better to design idiomatically, using metaphors only when a truly appropriate and powerful one falls in our lap.

Use metaphors if you can find them, but don't bend your interface to fit some arbitrary metaphoric standard.

DESIGN principle   Never bend your interface to fit a metaphor.

Macs and metaphors: A revisionist view

In the mid-1970s, the modern graphical user interface (GUI) was invented at Xerox Palo Alto Research Center (PARC). The GUI — as defined by PARC — consisted of many things: windows, buttons, mice, icons, visual metaphors, and drop-down menus. Together they have achieved an unassailable stature in the industry by association with the empirical superiority of the ensemble.

The first commercially successful implementation of the PARC GUI was the Apple Macintosh, with its desktop metaphor: the wastebasket, overlapping sheets of paper (windows), and file folders. The Mac didn't succeed because of these metaphors, however. It succeeded for several other reasons, including an overall attention to design and detail. The interaction design advances that contributed were:

> ▸ It defined a tightly restricted but flexible vocabulary for users to communicate with applications, based on a very simple set of mouse actions.

- ▶ It offered sophisticated, direct manipulation of rich visual objects on the screen.

- ▶ It used square pixels at high resolution, which enabled the screen to match printed output very closely, especially the output of Apple's other new product: the laser printer.

Metaphors helped structure these critical design features and made for good marketing copy but were never the main appeal. In fact, the early years were rather rocky for the Mac as people took time to grow accustomed to the new, GUI way of doing things. Software vendors were also initially gun-shy about developing for such a radically different environment (Microsoft being the exception).

However, people were eventually won over by the *capability* of the system to do what other systems couldn't: WYSIWYG (what you see is what you get) desktop publishing. The combination of WYSIWYG interfaces and high-quality print output (via the LaserWriter printer) created an entirely new market that Apple and the Mac owned for years. Metaphors were but a bit player (no pun intended) in the Mac's success.

Building Idioms

When graphical user interfaces were first invented, they were so clearly superior that many observers credited the success to the interfaces' graphical nature. This was a natural, but incorrect, assumption. The first GUIs, such as the original Mac, were better primarily because the graphical nature of their interfaces required a restriction of the range of vocabulary by which the user interacted with the system. In particular, the input they could accept from the user went from an unrestricted command line to a tightly restricted set of mouse-based actions. In a command-line interface, users can enter any combination of characters in the language — a virtually infinite number. In order for a user's entry to be correct, he needs to know exactly what the program expects. He must remember the letters and symbols with exacting precision. The sequence can be important, and sometimes even capitalization matters.

In modern GUIs, users can point to images or words on the screen with the mouse cursor. Most of these choices migrated from the users' heads to the screen, eliminating any need to memorize them. Using the buttons on the mouse, users can click, double-click, or click and drag. The keyboard is used for data entry, but not typically for command entry or navigation. The number of atomic elements in users' input vocabulary has dropped from dozens (if not hundreds) to just three, even though the range of tasks that can be performed by GUI programs isn't any more restricted than that of command-line systems.

The more atomic elements there are in an interaction vocabulary, the more time-consuming and difficult the learning process is. A vocabulary like that of the English language takes at least 10 years to learn thoroughly, and its complexity requires constant use to maintain fluency, but it can be extraordinarily expressive for a skilled user. Restricting the number of elements in our interaction vocabulary reduces its expressiveness at the atomic level. However, more complex interactions can be easily built from the atomic ones, much the way that letters can be combined to form words, and words to form sentences.

A properly formed interaction vocabulary can be represented by an inverted pyramid. All easy-to-learn communications systems obey the pattern shown in Figure 13-3. The bottom layer contains **primitives**, the atomic elements of which everything in the language is composed. In modern GUIs, these primitives consist of pointing, clicking, and dragging.

The middle layer contains **compounds**. These are more complex constructs created by combining one or more of the primitives. These include simple visual objects such as text display, actions such as double-clicking or clicking-and-dragging, and manipulable objects like pushbuttons, check boxes, hyperlinks, and direct manipulation handles.

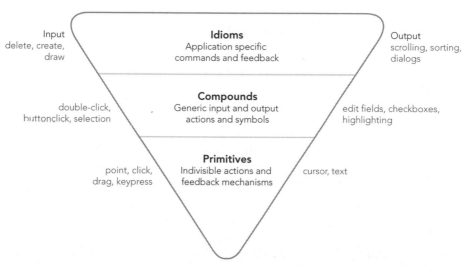

Figure 13-3 One of the primary reasons that GUIs are easy to use is that they enforce a restricted interaction vocabulary that builds complex idioms from a very small set of primitives: pointing, clicking, and dragging. These primitives can build a larger set of simple compounds, which in turn can be assembled into a wide variety of complex, domain-specific idioms, all of which are based on the same small set of easily learned actions.

The uppermost layer contains **idioms**. Idioms combine and structure compounds using **domain knowledge** of the problem under consideration: information related to the user's work patterns and goals, and not specifically to the computerized solution. The set of idioms opens the vocabulary to information about the particular problem the program is trying to address. In a GUI, it includes things like labeled buttons and fields, navigation bars, list boxes, icons, and even groups of fields and controls, or entire panes and dialogs.

Any language that does not follow this form will be very hard to learn. Many effective communications systems outside of the computer world follow similar vocabularies. Street signs in the United States follow a simple pattern of shapes and colors: Yellow triangles are cautionary, red octagons are imperatives, and green rectangles are informative.

Similarly, there is nothing intuitive or metaphoric about text messaging on a phone. The compound interactions involved in tapping numeric buttons in specific sequences to write in alphabetical characters is entirely learned, and when combined with predictive text capabilities, forms an incredibly effective idiom for writing brief notes from a mobile phone.

Manual Affordances

In his seminal book *The Design of Everyday Things*, Donald Norman gave us the term **affordance**, which he defines as "the perceived and actual properties of the thing, primarily those fundamental properties that determine just how the thing could possibly be used."

This concept is absolutely invaluable to the practice of interface design. For our purposes, the definition omits a key connection: *How* do we know what those properties offer to us? If you look at something and understand how to use it — you comprehend its affordances — you must be using some method for making the mental connection.

Therefore, we propose altering Norman's definition by omitting the phrase "and actual." By doing this, affordance becomes a purely cognitive concept, referring to what we *think* the object can do rather than what it can actually do. If a pushbutton is placed on the wall next to the front door of a residence, its affordances are 100% doorbell. If, when we push it, it causes a trapdoor to open beneath us and we fall into it, it turns out that it wasn't a doorbell, but that doesn't change its affordance as one.

So how do we know it's a doorbell? Simply because we have learned about doorbells and door etiquette and pushbuttons from our complex and lengthy socialization and maturation process. We have learned about this class of pushable things by being exposed to electrical and electronic devices in our environs and because — years ago — we stood on doorsteps with our parents, learning how to approach another person's home.

But there is another force at work here, too. If we see a pushbutton in an unlikely place such as the hood of a car, we cannot imagine what its purpose is, but we do recognize it as a finger-pushable object. How do we know this? Undoubtedly, we recognize it because of our tool-manipulating nature. We, as a species, see things that are finger-sized, placed within reach, and we automatically push them. We see things that are long and rounded, and we wrap our fingers around them and grasp them like handles. This is what Norman was getting at with his term **affordance**. For clarity, however, we'll call this instinctive understanding of how objects are manipulated with our hands **manual affordance**. When artifacts are clearly shaped to fit our hands or feet, we recognize that they can be directly manipulated and require no written instructions. In fact, this act of understanding how to use a tool based on the relationship of its shape to our hands is a clear example of intuiting an interface.

Norman discusses at length how [manual] affordances are much more compelling than written instructions. A typical example he uses is a door that must be pushed open using a metal bar for a handle. The bar is just the right shape and height and is in the right position to be grasped by the human hand. The manual affordances of the door scream, "Pull me." No matter how often someone uses this diabolical door, he will always attempt to pull it open, because the affordances are strong enough to drown out any number of signs affixed to the door saying Push.

There are only a few manual affordances. We pull handle-shaped things with our hands or, if they are small, we pull them with our fingers. We push flat plates with our hands or fingers. If they are on the floor we push them with our feet. We rotate round things, using our fingers for small ones — like dials — and both hands on larger ones, like steering wheels. Such manual affordances are the basis for much of our visual user-interface design.

The popular simulated-3D design of systems like Windows, Mac OS, and Motif relies on shading, highlighting, and shadows to make screen images appear more dimensional. These images offer virtual manual affordances in the form of button-like images that say "Push me" to our tool-manipulating brains.

Semantics of manual affordances

What's missing from an unadorned, virtual manual affordance is any idea of what function it performs. We can see that it looks like a button, but how do we know what it will accomplish when we press it? Unlike mechanical objects, you can't figure out a virtual lever's function just by tracing its connections to other mechanisms — software can't be casually inspected in this manner. Instead, we must rely either on supplementary text and images, or, most often, on our previous learning and experience. The affordance of the scrollbar clearly shows that it can be manipulated, but the only things about it that tell us what it does are the arrows, which hint at its directionality. In order to know that a scrollbar controls our position in a document, we either have to be taught or learn through experimentation.

Controls must have text or iconic labels on them to make sense. If the answer isn't suggested by the control, we can only learn what it does by one of two methods: experimentation or training. Either we read about it somewhere, ask someone, or try it and see what happens. We get no help from our instinct or intuition. We can only rely on the empirical.

Fulfilling user expectations of affordances

In the real world, an object does what it can do as a result of its physical form and its connections with other physical objects. A saw can cut wood because it is sharp and flat and has a handle. A knob can open a door because it is connected to a latch. However, in the digital world, an object does what it can do because a programmer imbued it with the power to do something. We can discover a great deal about how a saw or a knob works by physical inspection, and we can't easily be fooled by what we see. On a computer screen, though, we can see a raised, three-dimensional rectangle that clearly wants to be pushed like a button, but this doesn't necessarily mean that it *should* be pushed. It could, literally, do almost anything. We can be fooled because there is no natural connection — as there is in the real world — between what we see on the screen and what lies behind it. In other words, we may not know how to work a saw, and we may even be frustrated by our inability to manipulate it effectively, but we will never be fooled by it. It makes no representations that it doesn't manifestly live up to. On computer screens, canards and false impressions are very easy to create.

When we render a button on the screen, we are making a contract with the user that that button will visually change when she pushes it: It will appear to be depressed when the mouse button is clicked over it. Further, the contract states that the button will perform some reasonable work that is accurately described by its legend. This may sound obvious, but it is frankly astonishing how many programs offer bait-and-switch manual affordances. This is relatively rare for pushbuttons, but all too common for other controls, especially on many Web sites where the lack of affordances can make it difficult to differentiate between controls, content, and ornamentation. Make sure that your program delivers on the expectations it sets via the use of manual affordances.

14

Visual Interface Design

Regardless of how much effort you put into understanding your product's users and crafting behaviors that help them achieve their goals, these efforts will fall short unless significant work is also dedicated to clearly communicating these behaviors to users in an appropriate manner. With interactive products, this communication commonly happens visually, through a display (although in some cases you must communicate product behavior through physical properties such as the shape or feel of a hardware button).

Visual interface design is a frequently misunderstood discipline, largely because of its similarities to visual art and graphic design. It is also commonly mischaracterized as "skinning" the interface; we've even heard people refer to it as "hitting the product with the pretty stick."

In our practice, we've come to recognize that visual interface design is a critical and unique discipline, and it must be conducted in concert with interaction design and industrial design. It has great power to influence the effectiveness and appeal of a product, but for this potential to be fully realized, visual design must not be an afterthought (i.e., "putting lipstick on a pig"), but should be thought of as an essential tool for satisfying user and business needs.

Visual interface design requires several related skills, depending on the product in question. To create an effective and engaging user interface, a designer must have a command of the basic visual properties — color, typography, form, and composition — and must know how they can be used to effectively convey behavior and information and create a mood or visceral response. Interface designers also need a fundamental understanding of the interaction principles and interface idioms that shape the behavior of the product.

In this chapter, we'll talk about effective visual interface design strategies. In Part III, we will provide more detail about specific interaction and interface idioms and principles.

Art, Visual Interface Design, and Other Design Disciplines

Practitioners of fine art and practitioners of visual design share a visual medium. However, while both must be skilled and knowledgeable about that medium, their work serves different ends. The goal of the artist is to produce an observable artifact that provokes an aesthetic response. Art is a means of self-expression on topics of emotional or intellectual concern to the artist and, sometimes, to society at large. Few constraints are imposed on the artist; and the more singular and unique the product of the artist's exertions, the more highly it is valued.

Designers, on the other hand, create artifacts for *people other than themselves*. Whereas the concern of contemporary artists is primarily *self-expression*, visual designers are concerned with clear *communication*. As Kevin Mullet and Darrell Sano note in their excellent book *Designing Visual Interfaces*, "design is concerned with finding the *representation* best suited to the communication of some specific information." Visual interface designers are concerned with finding representations best suited to communicating the specific *behavior* of the interactive product that they are designing. In keeping with a Goal-Directed approach, they should endeavor to present behavior and information in such a way that it is understandable and useful, and supports the branding objectives of the organization as well as the experience goals of the personas.

To be clear, the design of user interfaces should not entirely exclude aesthetic concerns, but rather should place such concerns within a functional framework. While there is always some subjective judgment involved in visual communication, we endeavor to minimize questions of *taste*. We've found that clear articulation of user experience goals and business objectives is invaluable even when it comes to designing the aspects of a visual interface that support brand identity, user experience, and visceral response. (See Chapter 5 for more about visceral processing.)

Graphic design and user interfaces

Graphic design is a discipline that has, until the last 20 years or so, been dominated by the medium of printed ink, as applied to packaging, advertising, and environmental and document design. Traditional graphic designers are not always accustomed to dealing with the demands of pixel-based output. However, a new breed of graphic designer has been trained in digital or "new" media and is more comfortable applying the concepts of traditional graphic design to the new medium.

While graphic designers typically have a strong understanding of visual principles, they usually lack an adequate understanding of the key concepts surrounding software interaction and behavior. Talented, digitally fluent graphic designers excel at providing the sort of rich, aesthetically pleasing, and exciting interfaces we see in Windows Vista, Mac OS X, and the more visually sophisticated computer-game interfaces and consumer-oriented applications. They can create beautiful and appropriate *surfaces* for the interface which establish a mood or connection to a corporate brand. For them, design is first about the tone, style, and framework that communicate a brand experience, then about legibility and readability of information, and finally (if at all) about communicating behavior through affordances (see Chapter 13).

Visual interface designers share some skills with new-media-oriented graphic designers, but they must possess a deeper understanding and appreciation of the role of behavior. Much of their work emphasizes the organizational aspects of the design and the way in which visual cues and affordances communicate behavior to users. They focus on how to match the visual structure of the interface to the logical structure of both the users' mental models and the program's behaviors. Visual interface designers are also concerned with the communication of program states to users (i.e., read-only vs. editable) and with cognitive issues surrounding user perception of functions (layout, visual hierarchy, figure-ground issues, and so on).

Visual information design

Visual *information* designers are concerned with the visualization of data, content, and navigation rather than interactive functions. Their skill set is particularly important in visual interface design, especially as it relates to data-intensive applications and some Web sites, where content outweighs function. The primary focus of information design tends to be on presenting data in a way that promotes proper understanding. This is largely accomplished by controlling the information hierarchy through the use of visual properties such as color, shape, position, and scale. Common examples of information design challenges include charts, graphs, and other displays of quantitative information. Edward Tufte has written several seminal books that cover the topic in detail, including *The Visual Display of Quantitative Information*.

Industrial design

Although it is beyond the scope of this book to discuss industrial design issues in any depth, as interactive appliances and handheld devices become widespread, industrial design is playing an ever-growing role in the creation of new interactive products. Much like the difference in skills between graphic designers and visual interface and information designers, there is a similar split among the ranks of industrial designers. Some are more adept at creating arresting and appropriate forms for objects, whereas others emphasize logical and ergonomic mapping of physical controls in a manner that matches user behaviors and communicates device behaviors. The increase of software-enabled devices that make use of rich visual displays demands a concerted effort on the part of interaction designers, visual designers, and industrial designers in order to produce complete and effective solutions.

The Building Blocks of Visual Interface Design

At its root, interface design is concerned with the treatment and arrangement of visual elements to communicate behavior and information. Every element in a visual composition has a number of properties, such as shape and color, that work together to create meaning. There is rarely an inherent meaning to any one of these properties. Rather, the differences and similarities in the way these properties are applied to each element come together to allow users to make sense of an interface. When two objects share properties, users will assume they are related or similar. When users perceive contrast in these properties, they assume the items are not related, and the items with the greatest contrast tend to demand our attention.

Long before children are capable of using and understanding verbal language, they possess the ability to differentiate between objects with contrasting visual treatments. Just as Sesame Street relies upon this innate human capability with sketches where children are asked, "Which of these things is not like the other? Which of these things doesn't belong?," visual interface design capitalizes on it to create meaning that is far richer than the use of words alone.

When crafting a user interface, consider the following visual properties for each element and group of elements. Each property must be applied with care to create a useful and engaging user interface.

Shape

Is it round, square, or amoeba-like? Shape is the primary way we recognize *what* an object is. We tend to recognize objects by their outlines; a silhouette of a pineapple that's been textured with blue fur still reads as a pineapple. However, distinguishing among different shapes takes a higher level of attention than distinguishing some other properties such as color or size. This means it's not the best property to contrast when your purpose is to capture a user's attention. The weakness of shape as a factor in object recognition is apparent to anyone who's glanced at Apple's OS X dock and mistakenly selected iTunes instead of iDVD, or iWeb instead of iPhoto. While these icons have different shapes, they are of similar size, color, and texture.

Size

How big or small is it in relation to other items on the screen? Larger items draw our attention more, particularly when they're much larger than similar things around them. Size is also an *ordered* and *quantitative* variable, which means that people automatically sequence objects in terms of their size and tend to assign relative quantities to those differences; if we have four sizes of text, we assume relative importance increases with size, and that bold type is more important than regular. This makes size a useful property in conveying information hierarchies. Sufficient distinction in size is also enough to draw our attention quickly. In his classic *The Semiology of Graphics,* Jacques Bertin describes size as a *dissociative* property, which means that when something is very small or very large, it can be difficult to decipher other variables, such as shape.

Value

How light or dark is it? Of course, the idea of lightness or darkness is meaningful primarily in context of the value of the background. On a dark background, dark type is faint, whereas on a light background, dark type is pronounced. Like size, value can be dissociative; if a photo is too dark or light, for example, you can no longer perceive what's in it. Contrasts in value are something people perceive quickly and easily, so value can be a good tool for drawing attention to elements that need to stand out. Value is also an *ordered* variable — for example, lower-value (darker) colors on a map are easy to interpret as deeper water or denser population.

Hue

Is it yellow, red, or orange? Differences in hue draw our attention quickly. In some professions, hue has specific meaning we can take advantage of; for example, an accountant sees red as negative and black as positive, and a securities trader sees blue as "buy" and red as "sell" (in the United States, at least). Colors also take on meaning from the social contexts in which we've grown up. To Westerners who've grown up with traffic signals, red means "stop" and sometimes even "danger," whereas in China, red is the color of good luck. Similarly, white is associated with purity and peace in the West, and with funerals and death in Asia. Unlike size or value, though, hue is not intrinsically ordered or quantitative, so it's less ideal for conveying that sort of data. Also, we don't want to rely on hue as the sole communication vector, since color-blindness is quite common.

Color is best used judiciously. To create an effective visual system that allows users to identify similarities and differences between elements, you should use a limited number of hues — the carnival effect overwhelms users and limits your ability to communicate. Hue is also where the branding needs and communication needs of an interface can collide; it can take a talented visual designer (and skilled diplomat) to navigate these waters.

Orientation

Is it pointing up, down, or sideways? This is a useful variable to employ when you have directional information to convey (up or down, backward or forward). Orientation can be difficult to perceive with some shapes or at small sizes, though, so it's best used as a secondary communication vector. For example, if you want to show the stock market is going down, you might want to use a downward-pointing arrow that's also red.

Texture

Is it rough or smooth, regular or uneven? Of course, elements on a screen don't have real texture, but they can have the appearance of it. Texture is seldom useful for conveying differences or calling attention, since it requires a lot of attention to distinguish. Texture also takes a fair number of pixels to convey. However, it can be an important affordance cue; when we see a textured rubber area on a device, we assume that's where we're meant to grab it. Ridges or bumps on a user-interface (UI) element generally indicate that it's dragable, and a bevel or drop-shadow on a button makes it seem more clickable.

Position

Where is it relative to other elements? Like size, position is both an *ordered* and a *quantitative* variable, which means it's useful for conveying information about hierarchy. We can leverage the reading order of a screen to locate elements sequentially, with the most important or first used in the top and left. Position can also be used to create spatial relationships between objects on the screen and objects in the physical world.

Principles of Visual Interface Design

The human brain is a superb pattern-processing computer, making sense of the dense quantities of visual information that bombard us everywhere we look. Our brains manage the overwhelming amount of data our visual sense provides by discerning visual patterns and establishing a system of priorities for the things we see, which in turn allows us to make sense of the visual world. The ability of the brain's visual system to assemble portions of our visual field into patterns based on visual cues is what allows us to process visual information so quickly and efficiently. For example, imagine manually calculating the trajectory of a thrown baseball in order to predict where it lands. Our eyes and brains together do it in a split second, without conscious effort on our part. To most effectively communicate the behavior and functions of a program to the people that interact with it, visual interface designers must take advantage of this innate visual processing capability.

One chapter is far too little to do justice to the topic of visual interface design. However, there are some important principles that can help make your visual interface more compelling and easier to use. As mentioned earlier in the chapter, Mullet and Sano provide an accessible and detailed analysis of these fundamental principles; we will summarize some of the most important visual interface design concepts here.

Visual interfaces should:

- ▶ Use visual properties to group elements and create a clear hierarchy
- ▶ Provide visual structure and flow at each level of organization
- ▶ Use cohesive, consistent, and contextually appropriate imagery
- ▶ Integrate style and function comprehensively and purposefully
- ▶ Avoid visual noise and clutter

We discuss each of these principles in more detail in the following sections, as well as some general principles governing the appropriate use of text and color in visual user interfaces.

Use visual properties to group elements and provide clear hierarchy

It's usually a good idea to distinguish different logical sets of controls or data by grouping them by using visual properties such as color and dimensional rendering. By consistently applying these visual properties throughout an interface, you can create patterns that your users will learn to recognize. For example, in Windows XP, all buttons are raised with rounded corners and text fields are rectangular, slightly inset, and have a white background and blue border. Because of the consistent application of this pattern, there is no confusion as to what is a button and what is a text field, despite a number of similarities.

 DESIGN principle   A visual interface is based on visual patterns.

In looking at any set of visual elements, users unconsciously ask themselves "What's important here?" followed almost immediately by "How are these things related?" We need to make sure our user interfaces provide answers to both of these questions.

Creating hierarchy

Based on scenarios, determine which controls and bits of data users need to understand instantly, which are secondary, and which are needed only by exception. This ranking informs the visual hierarchy.

Next use hue, saturation, value, size, and position to distinguish levels of hierarchy. The most important elements should be larger, have greater contrast in hue, saturation, and value in relation to the background, and be positioned above or outdented in relation to other items. Items meant to stand out are best rendered in saturated colors. Less important elements should be less saturated, have less value and hue contrast against the background, and should also be smaller, or indented. Desaturated, neutral colors tend to recede.

Of course, adjust these properties with restraint, since the most important element doesn't need to be huge, red, and outdented — often, varying just one of these properties will do the trick. If you find that two items of different importance are competing for attention, it's often a good approach to "turn down" the less important one, rather than "turn up" the more important. This will leave you with more "headroom" to emphasize critical elements. (Think about it this way: If every word on a page is red and bold, do any of them stand out?)

Establishing a clear visual hierarchy is one of the hardest challenges in visual interface design, and takes skill and talent. A good visual hierarchy is almost never noticed by users — it is only the lack of one and an accompanying confusion that tends to jump out at most people.

Establishing relationships

To convey which elements are related, return to your scenarios to determine not only which elements have similar functions but also which elements are used together most often. Elements that tend to be used together should generally be grouped **spatially** to minimize mouse movement, while elements that aren't necessarily used together but have similar functions may be grouped **visually** even if they are not grouped spatially.

Spatial grouping makes it clear to users what tasks, data, and tools relate to each other, and can also imply sequence. Good grouping by *position* takes into account the order of tasks and subtasks and how the eye scans the screen: left to right in Western languages, and generally from top to bottom. (We discuss this in more detail later in the chapter.)

Items in proximity to one another are generally related. In many interfaces, this grouping is done in a heavy-handed fashion with bounding boxes everywhere you look, sometimes even around just one or two elements. In many cases, you can accomplish the same thing more effectively with differences in *proximity*. For example, on a toolbar, perhaps you have four pixels between buttons. To group the file commands, such as open, new, and save, you could simply leave eight pixels between the file command buttons and other groups of buttons.

Group items that are not adjacent by giving them common visual properties, forming a pattern that eventually takes on meaning for users. For example, the use of dimensionality to give the feel of a manual affordance is perhaps the most effective way to distinguish controls from data or background elements (see Chapter 13 for more about affordance). Iconography is a common application of this strategy. Mac OS X uses bright colors for application icons and subdued ones for seldom-used utilities. A green button to start a device can be echoed by a green "running" icon to indicate that it's functioning properly.

After you have decided what the groups are and how best to communicate them visually, begin to adjust the contrast between the groups to make them more or less prominent in the display, according to their importance in context. Emphasize differences between groups, but minimize differences between items within a group.

The squint test

A good way to help ensure that a visual interface design employs hierarchy and relationships effectively is to use what graphic designers refer to as the **squint test**. Close one eye and squint at the screen with the other eye in order to see which elements pop out and which are fuzzy and which items seem to group together. Changing your perspective can often uncover previously undetected issues in layout and composition.

Provide visual structure and flow at each level of organization

It's useful to think of user interfaces as being composed of visual and behavioral elements, which are used in groups, which are then grouped together into panes, which then may, in turn, be grouped into screens, views, or pages. These groupings, as discussed earlier, can be accomplished through spacing or through shared visual properties. There may be several such levels of structure in a sovereign application, and so it is critical that you maintain a clear visual structure so that a user can easily navigate from one part of your interface to another, as his workflow requires. The rest of this section describes several important attributes that help define a crisp visual structure.

Alignment and the grid

Alignment of visual elements is one of the key ways that designers can help users experience a product in an organized, systematic way. Grouped elements should be aligned both horizontally and vertically (see Figure 14-1). In general, every element on the screen should be aligned with as many other elements as possible. The decision not to align two elements or groups of elements should be made judiciously, and always to achieve a specific differentiating effect. In particular, designers should take care to:

- ► **Align labels** — Labels for controls stacked vertically should be aligned with each other; unless labels differ widely in length, left-justification is easier for users to scan than right justification.

- ► **Align within a set of controls** — A related group of check boxes, radio buttons, or text fields should be aligned according to a regular grid.

- ► **Align across control groups and panes** — Groups of controls and other screen elements should all follow the same grid wherever possible.

Figure 14-1 Adobe Lightroom makes very effective use of alignment to a layout grid. Text, controls, and control groups are all tightly aligned, with a consistent atomic spacing grid. It should be noted that the right-alignment of control and control group labels may compromise scanability.

A **grid system** is one of the most powerful tools available to the visual designer. Popularized by Swiss typographers in the years after World War II, the use of a grid provides a uniform and consistent structure to layout, which is particularly important when designing an interface with several levels of visual or functional complexity. After interaction designers have defined the overall framework for the application and its user interface elements (as discussed in Chapter 7), visual interface designers should help regularize the layout into a grid structure that properly emphasizes top-level elements and structures and provides room for lower-level or less important controls.

Typically, the grid divides the screen into several large horizontal and vertical regions (see Figure 14-2). A well-designed grid employs an *atomic grid unit* that represents the smallest spacing between elements. For example, if your atomic unit is four pixels, spacing between screen elements and groups will all be in multiples of four pixels.

Ideally, a grid should also have consistent relationships between the sizes of different screen areas. These relationships are typically expressed as ratios. Commonly used ratios include the celebrated "golden section," or phi (approximately 1.61), which is found frequently in nature and is thought to be particularly harmonious to the human eye; the square root of two (approximately 1:1.14), which is the basis of the international paper size standard (e.g. the A4 sheet); and 4:3, the aspect ratio of most computer displays.

Of course, a balance must be struck between idealized geometric relationships and the specific spatial needs of the functions and information that must be presented on the screen. A perfect implementation of the golden section will do nothing to improve the readability of a screen where things are jammed together with insufficient spacing.

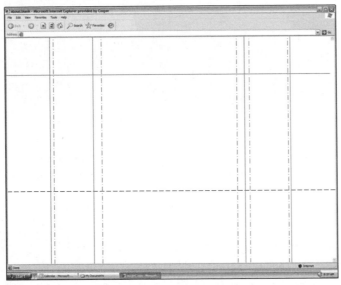

Figure 14-2 This example of a layout grid prescribes the size and position of the various screen areas employed by a Web site. This grid ensures regularity across different screens and reduces both the amount of work that a designer must do to lay out the screens and the work that a user must do to read and understand the screens.

A good layout grid is *modular*, which means that it should be flexible enough to handle necessary variation while maintaining consistency wherever possible. And, as with most things in design, simplicity and consistency are desirable. If two areas of the screen require approximately the same amount of space, make them exactly the same size. If two areas have different requirements, make them substantially different. If the atomic grid unit is too small, the grid will become unrecognizable in its complexity. Slight differences can feel unstable to users (though they are unlikely to know the source of these feelings) and ultimately fail in capitalizing in the potential strength of a strong grid system.

The key is to be decisive in your layout. Almost a square is no good. Almost a double square is also no good. If your layout is close to a simple fraction of the screen, such as a half, third, or fifth, adjust the layout so it is exactly a half, third, or fifth. Make your proportions bold, crisp, and exact.

The use of a grid system in visual interface design provides several benefits:

> ▶ **Usability** — Because grids attempt to regularize positioning of elements, users are able to learn quickly where to find key interface elements. If a screen header is always in precisely the same location, a user doesn't have to think or scan to find it. Consistent spacing and positioning support people's innate visual-processing mechanisms. A well-designed grid greatly improves the readability of the screen.

> ▶ **Aesthetic appeal** — By carefully applying an atomic grid and choosing the appropriate relationships between the various areas of the screen, a design can create a sense of order that feels comfortable to users and invites them to interact with the product.

> ▶ **Efficiency** — Standardizing your layouts will reduce the amount of labor required to produce high quality visual interfaces. We find that definition and implementation of a grid early in design refinement results in less iteration and "tweaking" of interface designs. A well-defined and communicated grid system results in designs that can be modified and extended, allowing developers to make appropriate layout decisions should alterations prove necessary.

Creating a logical path

In addition to precisely following a grid, the layout must also properly structure an efficient **logical path** for users to follow through the interface, taking into account the fact that (in Western languages) the eye will move from top to bottom and left to right (see Figure 14-3).

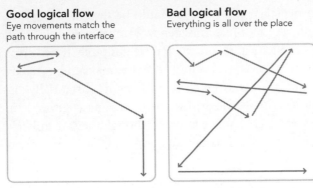

Good logical flow
Eye movements match the
path through the interface

Bad logical flow
Everything is all over the place

Figure 14-3 Eye movement across an interface should form a logical path that enables users to efficiently and effectively accomplish goals and tasks.

Symmetry and balance

Symmetry is a useful tool in organizing interfaces from the standpoint of providing visual balance. Interfaces that don't employ symmetry tend to look unbalanced, as if they are going to topple over to one side. Experienced visual designers are adept at achieving asymmetrical balance by controlling the visual weight of individual elements much as you might balance children of different weights on a seesaw. Asymmetrical design is difficult to achieve in the context of user interfaces because of the high premium placed on white space by screen real-estate constraints. The squint test is again useful for seeing whether a display looks lopsided.

Two types of symmetry are most often employed in interfaces: vertical axial symmetry (symmetry along a vertical line, usually drawn down the middle of a group of elements) or diagonal axial symmetry (symmetry along a diagonal line). Most typical dialog boxes exhibit one or the other of these symmetries — most frequently diagonal symmetry (see Figure 14-4).

Sovereign applications typically won't exhibit such symmetry at the top level (they achieve balance through a well-designed grid), but elements within a well-designed sovereign interface will almost certainly exhibit use of symmetry to some degree (see Figure 14-5).

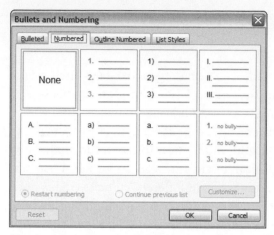

Figure 14-4 Diagonal symmetry in Microsoft Word's Bullets and Numbering dialog. The axis of symmetry runs from lower left to upper right.

Figure 14-5 Vertical symmetry in the Macromedia Fireworks tool palette.

Use cohesive, consistent, and contextually appropriate imagery

Use of icons and other illustrative elements can help users understand an interface, or if poorly executed, can irritate, confuse, or insult. It is important that designers understand both what the program needs to communicate to users and how users think about what must be communicated. A good understanding of personas and their mental models should provide a solid foundation for both the textual and visual language used in an interface. Cultural issues are also important. Designers should be aware of different meanings for colors in different cultures (red is not a warning color in China), for gestures (thumbs up is a terrible insult in Turkey), and for symbols (an octagonal shape means a stop sign in the U.S., but not in many other countries). Also, be aware of domain-specific color coding. In a hospital, yellow means radiation and red usually means something life threatening. On a stock trading desk, red means sell. Make sure you understand the visual language of your users' domains and environments before forging ahead.

Visual elements should also be part of a cohesive and globally applied visual language. This means that similar elements should share visual attributes, such as how they are positioned, their size, line weight, and overall style, contrasting only what is important to differentiate their meaning. The idea is to create a system of elements that integrate together to form a cohesive whole. A design that achieves this seems to fit together perfectly; nothing looks stuck on at the last minute.

In addition to their functional value, icons can play a significant role in conveying the desired brand attributes. Bold, cartoonish icons may be great if you're designing a Web site for kids, whereas precise, conservatively rendered icons may be more appropriate to a productivity application. Whatever the style, it should be consistent — if some of your icons use bold black lines and rounded corners while others use thin, angular lines, the visual style won't hold together.

Icon design and rendering is a craft in and of itself; rendering understandable images at low resolution takes considerable time and practice and is better left to trained visual designers. Icons are a complicated topic from a cognitive standpoint, and we will only highlight a few key points here. For those who want to understand more about what makes usable icons, we highly recommend William Horton's *The Icon Book*. You may find the examples dated, but the principles still hold true.

Function-oriented icons

Designing icons to represent functions or operations performed on objects leads to interesting challenges. The most significant challenge is to represent an abstract concept in iconic, visual language. In these cases, it is best to rely on idioms rather than force a concrete representation where none makes sense and to consider the addition of ToolTips (see Chapter 23) or text labels.

For more obviously concrete functions, some guidelines apply:

▶ Represent both the **action** and an **object** acted upon to improve comprehension. Nouns and verbs are easier to comprehend together than verbs alone (for example, for a Cut command, representing a document with an X through it may be more readily understood than a more metaphorical image of a pair of scissors).

▶ Beware of metaphors and representations that may not have the intended meanings for your target audience. For example, while the thumbs-up hand gesture means "OK" in Western cultures and might strike you as an appropriate icon to communicate "approval," it is quite offensive in Middle Eastern (and other) cultures, and should be avoided in any internationalized application.

▶ Group related functions visually to provide context, either spatially or, if this is not appropriate, using color or other common visual themes.

▶ Keep icons simple; avoid excessive visual detail.

▶ Reuse elements when possible, so users need to learn them only once.

Associating visual symbols to objects

Creating unique symbols for types of objects in the interface supports user recognition. These symbols can't always be representational or metaphoric — they are thus often idiomatic (see Chapter 13 for more information on the strengths of idioms). Such visual markers help users navigate to appropriate objects faster than text labels alone would allow. To establish the connection between symbol and object, use the symbol wherever the object is represented on the screen.

 DESIGN principle   Visually distinguish elements that behave differently.

Designers must also take care to visually differentiate symbols representing different object types. Discerning a particular icon within a screen full of similar icons is as difficult as discerning a particular word within a screen full of words. It's also particularly important to visually differentiate (contrast) objects that exhibit different behaviors, including variants of controls such as buttons, sliders, and check boxes.

Rendering icons and visual symbols

Especially as the graphics capabilities of color screens increase, it is tempting to render icons and visuals with ever-increasing detail, producing an almost photographic quality. However, this trend does not ultimately serve user goals, especially in pro-ductivity applications. Icons should remain simple and schematic, minimizing the number of colors and shades and retaining a modest size. Windows Vista and Mac OS X have taken the step towards more fully rendered icons. Although such icons may look great, they draw undue attention to themselves and render poorly at small sizes, meaning that they must necessarily take up extra real estate to be legible. They also encourage a lack of visual cohesion in the interface because only a small num-ber of functions (mostly those related to hardware) can be adequately represented with such concrete photorealistic images. Photographic icons are like all-capitalized text; the differences between icons aren't sharp and easy to distinguish, so we get lost in the complexity. It's much easier for users to differentiate between icons by shape, but in the case of Mac OS X, the outline of every icon is a similarly indistinct blob. The Mac OS X interface is filled with photorealistic touches that ultimately distract (see Figure 14-6). None of this serves users particularly well.

Figure 14-6 Photorealistic icons in Mac OS X. This level of detail in icons serves only to distract from data and function controls. In addition, although it might, in some instances, make sense to render in detail objects people are familiar with, what is the sense of similarly rendering unfamiliar objects and abstract concepts (for example, a network)? How many users have seen what a naked hard drive looks like (far right)? Ultimately, users must rely on accompanying text to make sense of these icons, unless they are used quite frequently.

Visualizing behaviors

Instead of using words alone to describe the results of interface functions (or worse, not giving any description at all), use visual elements to *show* users what the results will be. Don't confuse this with use of icons on control affordances. Rather, in addi-tion to using text to communicate a setting or state, render an illustrative picture or diagram that communicates the *behavior*. Although visualization often consumes more space, its capability to clearly communicate is well worth the pixels. In recent years, Microsoft has discovered this fact, and the dialog boxes in Microsoft Word, for example, have begun to bristle with visualizations of their meaning in addition to the textual controls. Photoshop and other image-manipulation applications have long shown thumbnail previews of the results of visual-processing operations.

DESIGN
principle

Visually communicate function and behavior.

The Print Preview view in Microsoft Word (see Figure 14-7) shows what a printed document will look like with the current paper size and margin settings. Many users have trouble visualizing what a 1.2-inch left margin looks like; the Preview control shows them. Microsoft could go one better by allowing direct input on the Preview control in addition to output, allowing users to drag the left margin of the picture and watch the numeric value in the corresponding spinner ratchet up and down. The associated text field is still important — you can't just replace it with the visual one. The text shows the precise values of the settings, whereas the visual control accurately portrays the look of the resulting page.

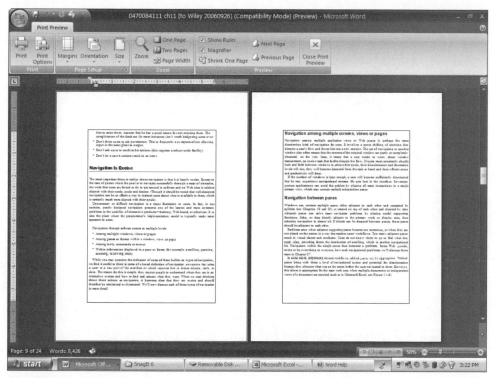

Figure 14-7 Microsoft Word Print Preview is a good example of a visual expression of application functionality. Rather than requiring users to visualize what a 1.2-inch margin might look like, this function allows a user to easily understand the ramifications of different settings.

Integrate style and function comprehensively and purposefully

When designers choose to apply stylistic elements to an interface, it must be from a global perspective. Every aspect of the interface must be considered from a stylistic point of view, not simply as individual controls or other visual elements. You do not want your interface to seem as though someone applied a quick coat of paint. Rather, you need to make sure that the functional aspects of your program's visual interface design are in complete harmony with the visual brand of your product. Your program's behavior is part of its brand, and your user's experience with your product should reflect the proper balance of form, content, and behavior.

Form versus function

Although visual style is a tempting diversion for many stakeholders, the use of stylized visual elements needs to be carefully controlled within an interface — particularly when designing for sovereign applications. The basic shape, behavior, and visual affordance (see Chapter 13) of controls should be driving factors in developing the visual style, and purely aesthetic considerations should not interfere with the meaning of the interface or a user's ability to interact with it.

That said, educational and entertainment applications, especially those designed for children, leave room for a bit more stylistic experimentation. The visual experience of the interface and content are part of the enjoyment of these applications, and a greater argument can also be made for thematic relationships between controls and content. Even in these cases, however, basic affordances should be preserved so that users can, in fact, reach the content easily.

Brand, customer experience, and the user interface

Most successful companies make a significant investment in managing their identity and building brand equity. A company that cultivates substantial brand equity can command a price premium for its products and services, while encouraging greater customer loyalty. Brands indicate the positive characteristics of the product and suggest discrimination and taste in the user.

In its most basic sense, brand value is the sum of all the interactions people have with a given company. Because an increasing number of these interactions are occurring through technology-based channels, it should be no surprise that the emphasis placed on branding user interfaces is greater than ever. If the goal is consistently positive customer interactions, the verbal, visual, and behavioral brand messages must be consistent. For example, if a customer is trying to get pricing for DSL in her area and she finds the phone company's Web site doesn't give her a useful answer after making her do a lot of work, it leaves her with the impression that the phone company itself is an irritating, unhelpful institution, regardless of how stunning the site's visual design is. The same is true of other channels: If she doesn't get the answers she needs, it doesn't matter if the computerized phone voice sounds friendly and accepts voice input in a conversational fashion, or if the human customer service rep says "Have a nice day."

Although companies have been considering the implications of brand as it relates to traditional marketing and communication channels for some time now, many companies are just beginning to address branding in terms of the customer experience. In order to understand branding in the context of the user interface, it can be helpful to think about it from two perspectives: the first impression and the long-term relationship.

Just as with interpersonal relationships, first impressions of a user interface can be exceedingly important. The first five-minute experience is the foundation that long-term relationships are built upon. To ensure a successful first five-minute experience, a user interface must clearly and immediately communicate the brand. Visual design typically plays one of the most significant roles in managing first impressions largely through color and image. By selecting an appropriate color palette and image style that supports the brand, you go a long way towards leveraging the equity of that brand in the form of a positive first impression.

First impressions can also have a significant impact on the usability of a product. This is described as the "Aesthetic-Usability Effect" in Lidwell, Holden, and Butler's eminently useful *Universal Principles of Design*. According to this principle (which is based in research), people perceive more aesthetically pleasing designs as easier to use than less aesthetically pleasing designs, regardless of actual functionality.

After people have developed a first impression, they begin to assess whether the behavior of the interface is consistent with its appearance. You build brand equity and long-term customer relationships by delivering on the promises made during the first impression. Interaction design and the control of behavior are often the best ways to keep the promises that visual branding makes to users.

Avoid visual noise and clutter

Visual noise within an interface is caused by superfluous visual elements that distract from the primary objective of directly communicating software function and behavior. Imagine trying to hold a conversation in an exceptionally crowded and loud restaurant. It can become impossible to communicate if the atmosphere is too noisy. The same is true for user interfaces. Visual noise can take the form of overembellished and unnecessarily dimensional elements, overuse of rules boxes and other visually "heavy" elements to separate controls, insufficient use of white space between controls, and inappropriate or overuse of visual properties, including color, texture, and contrast.

Cluttered interfaces attempt to provide an excess of functionality in a constrained space, resulting in controls that visually interfere with each other. Visually baroque, disorderly, or overcrowded screens raise the cognitive load for the user, causing what Richard Saul Wurman calls "information anxiety," and interfering with users' speed, comprehension, and success.

Keep it simple

In general, interfaces should use simple geometric forms, minimal contours, and a restricted color palette comprised primarily of less-saturated or neutral colors balanced with a few high-contrast accent colors that emphasize important information. Typography should not vary widely in an interface: Typically one or two typefaces, specified to display at just a few sizes, will be sufficient. When multiple design elements (controls, panes, windows) are required for similar or related logical purposes, they should be visually rendered in a consistent fashion to take advantage of the concept of *inheritance*. Inheritance provides the opportunity for an understanding of one element to transfer to other elements that are similar. Elements intended to stand out should be visually contrasted with any regularized elements through adjustment of one or more visual properties, such as size, color, and position.

Unnecessary variation is the enemy of a coherent, usable design. If the spacing between two elements is nearly the same, make that spacing exactly the same. If two typefaces are nearly the same size, adjust them to be the same size. Every visual element and every difference in color, size, or other visual property should be there for a reason. If you can't articulate a good reason why it's there, get rid of it.

Good visual interfaces, like any good visual design, are visually *efficient*. They make the best use out of the minimal set of visual and functional elements. A popular technique used by both graphic designers and industrial designers is to experiment with the removal of individual elements in order to test their contribution to the clarity of the intended message.

 DESIGN principle — Take things away until the design breaks, then put that last thing back in.

As pilot and poet Antoine de Saint Exupery famously said: "Perfection is attained not when there is no longer anything to add, but when there is no longer anything to take away." As you create your interfaces, you should constantly be looking to simplify visually. The more useful work a visual element can accomplish while still retaining clarity, the better. As Albert Einstein suggested, things should be as simple as possible, but no simpler.

Related to the drive for simplicity is the concept of **leverage,** which is where a single interface element is used for multiple, related purposes. For example, in Microsoft Windows XP, an icon is presented next to the title of the window (see Figure 14-8). This icon is used both to visually communicate the contents of the window (for example, whether it is an Explorer window or a Word document) and to provide access to window configuration commands such as Minimize, Maximize, and Close.

In general, interaction designers, not visual designers, are best suited to tackle the assignment of multiple functions to visual elements. Such mapping of elements requires significant insight into the behavior of users in context, the behavior of the software, and programming issues. Don't go overboard in doing this, though — many designers get caught up in the idea of creating a more efficient elegant solution and end up adding too many functions to a control, ultimately confusing users.

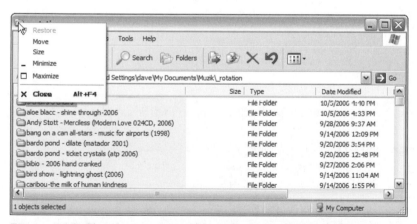

Figure 14-8 The icon in the title bar of windows in Windows XP is a good example of leverage. It both communicates the contents of the window and provides access to window configuration commands.

Text in visual interfaces

Text is a critical component to almost all user interfaces. Written language is capable of conveying dense and nuanced information, but significant care must be taken to use text appropriately, as it also has a great potential to confuse and complicate.

People recognize letters primarily by their shapes. The more distinct the shape, the easier the letter is to recognize, which is why WORDS TYPED IN ALL CAPITAL LETTERS ARE HARDER TO READ than upper/lowercase — the familiar pattern-matching hints are absent in capitalized words, so we must pay much closer attention to decipher what is written. Avoid using all caps in your interfaces.

Recognizing words is also different from *reading*, where we consciously scan the individual words and interpret their meaning in context. Interfaces should try to minimize the amount of text that must be read in order to navigate the interface successfully: After a user has navigated to something interesting, he should be able to read details if appropriate. Using short, easily recognized words facilitates navigation with minimal conscious reading.

Our brains can rapidly differentiate objects in an interface if we represent *what* objects are by using visual symbols and idioms. After we have visually identified the type of object we are interested in, we can read the text to distinguish *which* particular object we are looking at. In this scheme, we don't need to read about types of objects we are not interested in, thus speeding navigation and eliminating excise. The accompanying text only comes into play after we have decided that it is important.

DESIGN principle   Visually show what; textually tell which.

When text must be read in interfaces, the following guidelines apply:

- **Use high contrast text** — Make sure that the text is in high contrast with the background and do not use complementary colors that may affect readability. We aim for 80% contrast as a general rule of thumb.

- **Choose an appropriate typeface and size** — In general, a crisp sans-serif font such as Verdana or Tahoma is your best bet for readability. Serif typefaces such as Times or Georgia can appear "hairy" onscreen, but using a large enough size and font smoothing or appropriate anti-aliasing can often mitigate this issue. Type sizes of less than 10 pixels are difficult to read in most situations, and if you must use small type, it's usually best to go with a sans-serif typeface without anti-aliasing.

▸ **Phrase your text clearly** — Make your text understandable by using the fewest words necessary to clearly convey meaning. Also, try to avoid abbreviations. If you must abbreviate, use standard abbreviations.

Color in visual interfaces

Color is an important aspect of almost all visual interfaces. In these days of ubiquitous color LCDs, users expect color displays even in devices like PDAs and phones. However, color is much more than a marketing checklist item; it is a powerful information and visual interface design tool that can be used to great effect, or just as easily abused.

Color is part of the visual language of an interface, and users will impart meaning to its use. For most applications, color should be used sparingly and integrate well into the other elements of the visual language: symbols and icons, text, and the spatial relationships they maintain in the interface. As discussed earlier in this chapter, when used appropriately, color can draw attention to important items, indicate relationships, and communicate status or other information.

There are a few ways that color can be misused in an interface if you are not careful. The most common of these misuses are:

▸ **Too many colors** — Adding one color to distinguish important items in a set significantly reduces search time. Adding more colors still improves user performance, but at seven or more, search performance degrades significantly. It isn't unreasonable to suspect a similar pattern in any kind of interface navigation, since this number is consistent with how much information we can hold in our short-term memories; when there are too many colors, we spend time trying to remember what the colors mean, so that slows us down.

▸ **Use of saturated complementary colors** — Complementary colors are the inverse of each other in color computation. These colors, when highly saturated and positioned adjacent to each other, can create perceptual artifacts that are difficult to perceive correctly or focus on. A similar effect is the result of **chromostereopsis**, in which colors on the extreme ends of the spectrum "vibrate" when placed adjacent to one another. Just try looking at saturated red text on a saturated blue background and see how quickly you get a headache!

▸ **Excessive saturation** — Highly saturated colors tend to look garish and draw too much attention. Moderately saturated colors can be appropriate in small swatches to capture a user's attention but should always be used sparingly. When multiple saturated colors are used together, chromostereopsis and other perceptual artifacts often occur.

▶ **Inadequate contrast** — When object colors differ from background colors only in hue, but not in saturation or value (brightness), they become difficult to perceive. Objects and background should vary in brightness or saturation, in addition to hue, and color text on color backgrounds should also be avoided when possible.

▶ **Inadequate attention to color impairment** — Roughly 10% of the male population has some degree of color-blindness. Thus care should be taken when using red and green hues (in particular) to communicate important information. Any colors used to communicate should also vary by saturation or brightness to distinguish them from each other. If a grayscale conversion of your color palette is easily distinguishable, color-blind users should be able to distinguish the color version. There are also applications and filters, such as Fujitsu's ColorDoctor, that can be used to see how people with various forms of color-blindness would perceive your product.

Visual interface design for handhelds and other devices

Many of the practices we've discussed in this chapter have their roots in design for the desktop platform and the accompanying large screen size and stationary usage context. Clearly, designing for a handheld or other device such as a mobile phone or medical equipment has its own set of challenges related to a smaller screen size, mobile usage context, and diverse input methods. While this certainly isn't a comprehensive list, it's worth considering the following:

▶ **Onscreen controls should be prominent.** Because handheld devices are used while standing, walking, riding on bumpy trains, and in all sorts of busy medical and industrial environments, onscreen controls must be much more obvious than their desktop counterparts. Different hardware and contexts require different tactics, but as a general rule using high-contrast designs is a good idea. If your hardware limits your ability to do this, you may have to resort to size, color, or line weight to accomplish this.

▶ **Provide visual landmarks.** To accomplish a task, handheld users frequently must traverse several screens. As a result it's important to use visual cues to orient users.

▶ **Onscreen controls should be large if you're using a touch screen.** If you are using a touch screen on your device, controls should be large enough to be touchable by fingers. Styli can get lost, and because of this (and the nerd factor), younger users are often put off by the use of a stylus.

▶ **Use larger, sans-serif fonts.** Serif fonts are hard to read at low resolution; sans-serif fonts should be used for low-resolution handheld displays.

▶ **Clearly indicate when there is more data offscreen.** Many people aren't used to the idea of a small screen with scrolling information. If there is more data than fits on a screen, make sure to boldly indicate that more data is available, ideally with a hint as to how to access it.

Principles of Visual Information Design

Like visual interface design, visual information design also has many principles that the prospective designer can use to his advantage. Information design guru Edward Tufte asserts that good visual design is "clear thinking made visible," and that good visual design is achieved through an understanding of the viewer's "cognitive task" (goal) and a set of design principles.

Tufte claims that there are two important problems in information design:

1. It is difficult to display multidimensional information (information with more than two variables) on a two-dimensional surface.

2. The resolution of the display surface is often not high enough to display dense information. Computers present a particular challenge — although they can add motion and interactivity, computer displays have low information density compared to that of paper.

Although both points are certainly true, the visual interface designer can leverage one capability not available to the print information designer: interactivity. Unlike a print display, which must convey all of the data at once, electronic displays can progressively reveal information as users need more detail. This helps make up, at least in part, for the resolution limitations.

Even with the differences between print and digital media, some universal information design principles — indifferent to language, culture, or time — help maximize the effectiveness of any information display.

In his beautifully executed volume *The Visual Display of Quantitative Information* (1983), Tufte introduces seven "Grand Principles," which we briefly discuss in the following sections as they relate specifically to digital interfaces and content.

Visually displayed information should, according to Tufte:

▶ Enforce visual comparisons

▶ Show causality

- ▶ Show multiple variables

- ▶ Integrate text, graphics, and data in one display

- ▶ Ensure the quality, relevance, and integrity of the content

- ▶ Show things adjacent in space, not stacked in time

- ▶ Not de-quantify quantifiable data

We will briefly discuss each of these principles as they apply to the information design of software-enabled media.

Enforce visual comparisons

You should provide a means for users to compare related variables and trends or to compare before-and-after scenarios. Comparison provides a context that makes the information more valuable and more comprehensible to users (see Figure 14-9 for one example). Adobe Photoshop, along with many other graphics tools, makes frequent use of previews, which allow users to easily achieve before and after comparisons interactively (see Figure 2-2).

Show causality

Within information graphics, clarify cause and effect. In his books, Tufte provides the classic example of the space shuttle Challenger disaster, which could have been averted if charts prepared by NASA scientists had been organized to more clearly present the relationship between air temperature at launch and severity of O-ring failure. In interactive interfaces, modeless visual feedback (see Chapter 25) should be employed to inform users of the potential consequences of their actions or to provide hints on how to perform actions.

Show multiple variables

Data displays that provide information on multiple, related variables should be able to display them all simultaneously without sacrificing clarity. In an interactive display, the user should be able to selectively turn off and on the variables to make comparisons easier and correlations (causality) clearer. Investors are commonly interested in the correlations between different securities, indexes, and indicators. Graphing multiple variables over time helps uncover these correlations (see Figure 14-9).

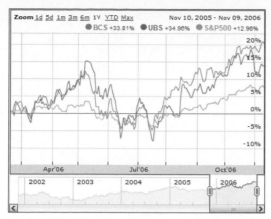

Figure 14-9 This graph from Google finance compares the performance of two stocks with the S&P 500 over a period of time. The visual patterns allow a viewer to see that Barclays Bank (BCS) and UBS are closely correlated to each other and only loosely correlated to the S&P 500.

Integrate text, graphics, and data in one display

Diagrams that require separate keys or legends to decode require additional cognitive processing on the part of users, and are less effective than diagrams with integrated legends and labels. Reading and deciphering diagram legends is yet another form of navigation-related excise. Users must move their focus back and forth between diagram and legend and then reconcile the two in their minds. Figure 14-10 shows an interactive example that integrates text, graphics, and data, as well as input and output: a highly efficient combination for users.

Ensure the quality, relevance, and integrity of the content

Don't show information simply because it's technically possible to do so. Make sure that any information you display will help your users achieve particular goals that are relevant to their context. Unreliable or otherwise poor-quality information will damage the trust you must build with users through your product's content, behavior, and visual brand.

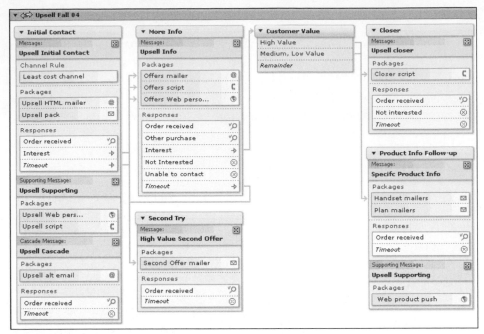

Figure 14-10 This "Communication Plan" is an interface element from a tool for managing outbound marketing campaigns that was designed by Cooper. It provides a visual structure to textual information, which is in turn augmented by iconic representations of different object types. Not only does this tool provide output of the current structure of the Communication Plan, but it also allows a user to modify that structure directly through drag-and-drop interactions.

Show things adjacently in space, not stacked in time

If you are showing changes over time, it's much easier for users to understand the changes if they are shown adjacently in space, rather than superimposed on one another. Cartoon strips are a good example of showing flow and change over time arranged adjacently in space.

Of course, this advice applies to static information displays; in software, **animation** can be used even more effectively to show change over time, as long as technical issues (such as memory constraints or connection speed over the Internet) don't come into play.

Don't de-quantify quantifiable data

Although you may want to use graphs and charts to make perception of trends and other quantitative information easy to grasp, you should not abandon the display of the numbers themselves. For example, in the Windows Disk Properties dialog, a pie chart is displayed to give users a rough idea of their free disk space, but the numbers of kilobytes free and used are also displayed in numerical form.

Consistency and Standards

Many in-house usability organizations view themselves, among other things, as the gatekeepers of consistency in digital product design. **Consistency** implies a similar look, feel, and behavior across the various modules of a software product, and this is sometimes extended to apply across all the products a vendor sells. For at-large software vendors, such as Macromedia and Adobe, who regularly acquire new software titles from smaller vendors, the branding concerns of consistency take on a particular urgency. It is obviously in their best interests to make acquired software look as though it belongs, as a first-class offering, alongside products developed in-house. Beyond this, both Apple and Microsoft have an interest in encouraging their own and third-party developers to create applications that have the look-and-feel of the OS platform on which the program is being run, so that the user perceives their respective platforms as providing a seamless and comfortable user experience.

Benefits of interface standards

User interface standards provide benefits that address these issues when executed appropriately, although they come at a price. According to Jakob Nielsen, relying on a single interface standard improves users' ability to quickly learn interfaces and enhances their productivity by raising throughput and reducing errors. These benefits accrue because users are more readily able to predict program behavior based on past experience with other parts of the interface or with other applications following similar standards.

At the same time, interface standards also benefit software vendors. Customer training and technical support costs are reduced because the consistency that standards bring improves ease of use and learning. Development time and effort are also reduced because formal interface standards provide ready-made decisions on the rendering of the interface that development teams would otherwise be forced to debate during project meetings. Finally, good standards can lead to reduced maintenance costs and improved reuse of design and code.

Risks of interface standards

The primary risk of any standard is that the product that follows it is only as good as the standard itself. Great care must be taken in developing the standard in the first place to make sure, as Nielsen says, that the standard specifies a truly usable interface, and that it is usable by the *developers* who must build the interface according to its specifications.

It is also risky to see interface standards as a panacea for good interfaces. Assuming that a standard is the solution to interface design problems is like saying the *Chicago Manual of Style* is all it takes to write a good novel. Most interface standards emphasize the *syntax* of the interface, its visual look-and-feel, but say little about deeper behaviors of the interface or about its higher-level logical and organizational structure. There is a good reason for this: A general interface standard has no knowledge of context incorporated into its formalizations. It takes into account no specific user behaviors and usage patterns within a context, but rather focuses on general issues of human perception and cognition and, sometimes, visual branding as well. These concerns are important, but they are presentation details, not the interaction framework upon which such rules hang.

Standards, guidelines, and rules of thumb

Although standards are unarguably useful, they need to evolve as technology and our understanding of users and their goals evolve. Some practitioners and programmers invoke Apple's or Microsoft's user interface standards as if they were delivered from Mt. Sinai on a tablet. Both companies publish user interface standards, but both companies also freely and frequently violate them and update the guidelines post facto. When Microsoft proposes an interface standard, it has no qualms about changing it for something better in the next version. This is only natural — interface design is still in its infancy, and it is wrongheaded to think that there is benefit in standards that stifle true innovation. In some respects, Apple's dramatic visual shift from OS 9 to OS X has helped to dispel the notion among the Mac faithful that interface standards are etched in granite.

The original Macintosh was a spectacular achievement precisely because it transcended all Apple's previous platforms and standards. Conversely, much of the strength of the Mac came from the fact that vendors followed Apple's lead and made their interfaces look, work, and act alike. Similarly, many successful Windows programs are unabashedly modeled after Word, Excel, and Outlook.

Interface standards are thus most appropriately treated as detailed *guidelines* or *rules of thumb*. Following interface guidelines too rigidly or without careful consideration of the needs of users in context can result in force-fitting an application's interface into an inappropriate interaction model.

When to violate guidelines

So, what should we make of interface guidelines? Instead of asking if we should *follow* standards, it is more useful to ask: When should we *violate* standards? The answer is when, and only when, we have a very good reason.

 DESIGN principle   Obey standards unless there is a truly superior alternative.

But what constitutes a very good reason? Is it when a new idiom is measurably better? Usually, this sort of measurement can be quite elusive because it can rarely be reduced to a quantifiable factor alone. The best answer is: When an idiom is clearly seen to be significantly better by most people in the target user audience (your personas) who try it, there's a good reason to keep it in the interface. This is how the toolbar came into existence, along with outline views, tabs, and many other idioms. Researchers may have been examining these artifacts in the lab, but it was their useful presence in real-world software that confirmed their success.

Your reasons for diverging from guidelines may ultimately not prove to be good enough and your product may suffer, but you and other designers will learn from the mistake. This is what Christopher Alexander calls the "unselfconscious process," an indigenous and unexamined process of slow and tiny forward increments as individuals attempt to improve solutions. New idioms (as well as new uses for old idioms) pose a risk, which is why careful, Goal-Directed Design and appropriate testing with real users in real working conditions are so important.

Consistency and standards across applications

Using standards or guidelines can involve special challenges when a company that sells multiple software titles decides that all its various products must be completely consistent from a user-interface perspective.

From the perspective of visual branding, as discussed earlier, this makes a great deal of sense, although there are some intricacies. If an analysis of personas and markets indicates that there is little overlap between the users of two distinct products and that their goals and needs are also quite distinct, you might question whether it makes more sense to develop two visual brands that speak specifically to these different customers, rather than using a single, less-targeted look. When it comes to the behavior of the software, these issues become even more urgent. A single standard *might* be important if customers will be using the products together as a suite. But even in this case, should a graphics-oriented presentation application, like PowerPoint, share an interface structure with a text processor like Word? Microsoft's intentions were good, but it went a little too far in enforcing global style guides. PowerPoint doesn't gain much from having a similar menu structure to Excel and Word, and it loses quite a bit in ease of use by conforming to an alien structure that diverges from the user's mental models. On the other hand, the designers did draw the line somewhere, and PowerPoint does have a slide-sorter display, an interface unique to that application.

 DESIGN principle   Consistency doesn't imply rigidity.

Designers, then, should bear in mind that consistency doesn't imply rigidity, especially where it isn't appropriate. Interface and interaction style guidelines need to grow and evolve like the software they help describe. Sometimes you must bend the rules to best serve your users and their goals (and sometimes even your company's goals). When this has to happen, try to make changes and additions that are compatible with standards. The spirit of the law, not the letter of the law, should be your guide.

Part

Designing Interaction Details

15

Searching and Finding: Improving Data Retrieval

One of the most amazing aspects of this new digital world we live in is the sheer quantity of information and media that we are able to access inside applications, on our laptops and devices, and on networks and the Internet. Unfortunately, accompanying the boundless possibilities of this access is a hard design problem: How do we make it easy for people to find what they're looking for, and more importantly, find what they need?

Fortunately, great strides have been made in this area by the likes of Google, with its various search engines, and Apple, with its highly effective Spotlight functionality in Mac OS X (more on these later). However, although these solutions certainly point to effective interactions, they are just a start. Just because Google is a very useful way to find textual or video content on the Web, doesn't mean that the same interaction patterns are appropriate for a more targeted retrieval scenario.

As with almost every other problem in interaction design, we've found that crafting an appropriate solution must start with a good understanding of users' mental models and usage contexts. With this information, we can structure storage and retrieval systems that accommodate specific purposes. This chapter discusses methods of data retrieval from an interaction standpoint and presents some human-centered approaches to the problem of finding useful information.

Storage and Retrieval Systems

A **storage system** is a method for safely keeping things in a repository. It is composed of a container and the tools necessary to put objects in and take them back out again. A **retrieval system** is a method for finding things in a repository according to some associated value, such as name, position, or some other attribute of the contents.

In the physical world, storing and retrieving are inextricably linked; putting an item on a shelf (storing it) also gives us the means to find it later (retrieving it). In the digital world, the only thing linking these two concepts is our faulty thinking. Computers will enable remarkably sophisticated retrieval techniques, if only we are able to break our thinking out of its traditional box.

Digital storage and retrieval mechanisms have traditionally been based around the concept of "folders" (or "directories" in Unix). While it's certainly true that the folder metaphor has provided a useful way to approach a computer's storage and retrieval systems (much as one would approach them for a physical object), as we discussed in Chapter 13, the metaphoric nature of this interaction pattern is limiting. Ultimately, the use of folders or directories as a primary retrieval mechanism requires that users know where an item has been stored in order to locate it. This is unfortunate, since digital systems are capable of providing us with significantly better methods of finding information than those physically possible using mechanical systems. But before we talk about how to improve retrieval, let's briefly discuss how it works.

Storage and Retrieval in the Physical World

We can own a book or a hammer without giving it a name or a permanent place of residence in our houses. A book can be identified by characteristics other than a name — a color or a shape, for example. However, after we accumulate a large number of items that we need to find and use, it helps to be a bit more organized.

Everything in its place: Storage and retrieval by location

It is important that there be a proper place for our books and hammers, because that is how we find them when we need them. We can't just whistle and expect them to find us; we must know where they are and then go there and fetch them. In the physical world, the actual location of a thing is the means to finding it. Remembering where we put something — its address — is vital both to finding it and to putting it away so it can be found again. When we want to find a spoon, for example, we go to the place where we keep our spoons. We don't find the spoon by referring to any inherent characteristic of the spoon itself. Similarly, when we look for a book, we either go to where we left the book, or we guess that it is stored with other books. We don't find the book by association. That is, we don't find the book by referring to its contents.

In this model, the storage system is the same as the retrieval system: Both are based on remembering locations. They are coupled storage and retrieval systems.

Indexed retrieval

This system of *everything in its place* sounds pretty good, but it has a flaw: It's limited in scale by human memory. Although it works for the books, hammers, and spoons in your house, it doesn't work for all the volumes stored in the Library of Congress, for example.

In the world of books and paper on library shelves, we make use of a classification system to help us find things. Using the Dewey Decimal System (or its international offshoot, the Universal Decimal Classification system), every book is assigned a unique "call number" based upon its subject. Books are then arranged numerically (and then alphabetically by author's last name), resulting in a library organized by subject.

The only remaining issue is how to discover the number for a given book. Certainly nobody could be expected to remember every number. The solution is an **index**, or a collection of records that allows you to find the *location* of an item by looking up an **attribute** of the item, such as its name.

Traditional library card catalogs provide lookup by three attributes: author, subject, and title. When the book is entered into the library system and assigned a number, three index cards are created for the book, including all particulars and the Dewey Decimal number. Each card is headed by the author's name, the subject, or the title. These cards are then placed in their respective indices in alphabetical order. When you want to find a book, you look it up in one of the indices and find its number. You then find the row of shelves that contains books with numbers in the same range as your target by examining signs. You search those particular shelves, narrowing your view by the lexical order of the numbers until you find the one you want.

You *physically* retrieve the book by participating in the system of storage, but you *logically* find the book you want by participating in a system of retrieval. The shelves and numbers are the storage system. The card indices are the retrieval system. You identify the desired book with one and fetch it with the other. In a typical university or professional library, customers are not allowed into the stacks. As a customer, you identify the book you want by using only the retrieval system. The librarian then fetches the book for you by participating only in the storage system. The unique serial number is the bridge between these two interdependent systems. In the physical world, both the retrieval system and the storage system may be very labor-intensive. Particularly in older, noncomputerized libraries, they are both inflexible. Adding a fourth index based on acquisition date, for example, would be prohibitively difficult for the library.

Storage and Retrieval in the Digital World

Unlike in the physical world of books, stacks, and cards, it's not very hard to add an index in the computer. Ironically, in a system where easily implementing dynamic, associative retrieval mechanisms is at last possible, we often don't implement *any* retrieval system other than the storage system. If you want to find a file on disk, you need to know its name and its place. It's as if we went into the library, burned the card catalog, and told the patrons that they could easily find what they want by just remembering the little numbers painted on the spines of the books. We have put 100% of the burden of file retrieval on the user's memory while the CPU just sits there idling, executing billions of NOP instructions.

Although our desktop computers can handle hundreds of different indices, we ignore this capability and frequently have no indices at all pointing into the files stored on our disks. Instead, we have to remember where we put our files and what we called them in order to find them again. This omission is one of the most destructive, backward steps in modern software design. This failure can be attributed to the interdependence of files and the organizational systems in which they exist, an interdependence that doesn't exist in the mechanical world.

There is nothing wrong with the disk file storage systems that we have created for ourselves. The only problem is that we have failed to create adequate disk file *retrieval* systems. Instead, we hand the user the storage system and call it a retrieval system. This is like handing him a bag of groceries and calling it a gourmet dinner. There is no reason to change our file storage systems. The Unix model is fine. Our applications can easily remember the names and locations of the files they have worked on, so they aren't the ones who need a retrieval system: It's for us human users.

Digital retrieval methods

There are three fundamental ways to find a document on a digital system. You can find it by remembering where you left it in the file structure, by **positional retrieval**. You can also find it by remembering its identifying name, by **identity retrieval** (and it should be noted that these two methods are typically used in conjunction with each other). The third method, **associative** or **attribute-based retrieval**, is based on the ability to search for a document based on some inherent quality of the document itself. For example, if you want to find a book with a red cover, or one that discusses light rail transit systems, or one that contains photographs of steam locomotives, or one that mentions Theodore Judah, you must use an associative method.

The combination of position and identity provide the basis for most digital storage systems. However, most digital systems do not provide an associative method for storage. By ignoring associative methods, we deny ourselves any attribute-based searching and we must depend on human memory to recall the position and identity of our documents. Users must know the title of the document they want *and* where it is stored in order to find it. For example, to find a spreadsheet in which you calculated the amortization of your home loan, you need to remember that you stored it in the directory called "Home" and that the file was named "amort1." If you can't remember either of these facts, finding the document will be quite difficult.

Attribute-based retrieval systems

For early GUI systems like the original Macintosh, a positional retrieval system almost made sense: The desktop metaphor dictated it (you don't use an index to look up papers on your desk), and there were precious few documents that could be stored on a 144K floppy disk. However, our current desktop systems can easily hold 500,000 times as many documents (and that's not to mention what even a meager local network can provide access to)! Yet, we still use the same old metaphors and retrieval models to manage our data. We continue to render our software's retrieval systems in strict adherence to the implementation model of the storage system, ignoring the power and ease-of-use of a system for *finding* files that is distinct from the system for *keeping* files.

An attribute-based retrieval system enables users to find documents by their contents and meaningful properties (such as when they were last edited). The purpose of such a system is to provide a mechanism for users to express what they're looking for according to the way they think about it. For example, a saleswoman looking for a proposal she recently sent to a client named "Widgetco" could effectively express herself by saying "Show me the Word documents related to 'Widgetco' that I modified yesterday and also printed."

A well-crafted attribute-based retrieval system also enables users to find what they're looking for by synonyms or related topics or by assigning attributes or "tags" to individual documents. A user can then dynamically define sets of documents having these overlapping attributes. Returning to our saleswoman example, each potential client is sent a proposal letter. Each of these letters is different and is naturally grouped with the files pertinent to that client. However, there is a definite relationship between each of these letters because they all serve the same function: proposing a business relationship. It would be very convenient if the saleswoman could find and gather up all such proposal letters, while allowing each one to retain its uniqueness and association with its particular client. A file system based on place — on its single storage location — must necessarily store each document by a single attribute (client or document type) rather than by multiple characteristics.

A retrieval system can learn a lot about each document just by keeping its eyes and ears open. If it remembers some of this information, much of the burden on users is made unnecessary. For example, it can easily remember such things as:

- The application that created the document
- Contents and format of the document
- The application that last opened the document
- The size of the document, and if the document is exceptionally large or small
- If the document has been untouched for a long time
- The length of time the document was last open
- The amount of information that was added or deleted during the last edit
- If the document was created from scratch or cloned from another
- If the document is frequently edited
- If the document is frequently viewed but rarely edited
- Whether the document has been printed and where
- How often the document has been printed, and whether changes were made to it each time immediately before printing
- Whether the document has been faxed and to whom
- Whether the document has been e-mailed and to whom

Spotlight, the search function in Apple's OS X, provides effective attribute-based retrieval (see Figure 15-1). Not only can a user look for documents according to meaningful properties, but they can save these searches as "Smart Folders," which enables them to see documents related to a given client in one place, and all proposals in a different place (though a user would have to put some effort into identifying each proposal as such — Spotlight can't recognize this). It should be noted that one of the most important factors contributing to the usefulness of Spotlight is the speed at which results are returned. This is a significant differentiating factor between it and the Windows search functionality, and was achieved through purposeful technical design that indexes content during idle time.

Figure 15-1 Spotlight, the search capability in Apple's OS X, allows users to find a document based upon meaningful attributes such as the name, type of document, and when it was last opened.

While an attribute-based retrieval system can find documents for users without users ever having to explicitly organize documents in advance, there is also considerable value in allowing users to **tag** or manually specify attributes about documents. Not only does this allow users to fill in the gaps where technology can't identify all the meaningful attributes, but it allows people to define de facto organizational schemes based upon how they discuss and use information. The retrieval mechanism achieved by such tagging is often referred to as a "folksonomy," a term credited to information architect Thomas Vander Wal. Folksonomies can be especially useful in social and collaborative situations, where they can provide an alternative to a globally defined taxonomy if it isn't desirable or practical to force everyone to adhere to and think in terms of a controlled vocabulary. Good examples of the use of tagging to facilitate information retrieval include Flickr, del.icio.us, and LibraryThing (see Figure 15-2), where people are able to browse and find documents (photos and links, respectively) based upon user-defined attributes.

Figure 15-2 LibraryThing is a Web application that allows users to catalog their own book collections online with a tag-based system. The universe of tags applied to all the books in all the collections has become a democratic organizational scheme based upon the way the user community describes things.

Relational Databases versus Digital Soup

Software that uses database technology typically makes two simple demands of its users: First, users must define the form of the data in advance; second, users must then conform to that definition. There are also two facts about human users of software: First, they rarely can express what they are going to want in advance, and second, even if they could express their specific needs, more often than not they change their minds.

Organizing the unorganizable

Living in the Internet age, we find ourselves more and more frequently confronting information systems that fail the relational database litmus: We can neither define information in advance, nor can we reliably stick to any definition we might conjure up. In particular, the two most common components of the Internet exemplify this dilemma.

The first is electronic mail. Whereas a record in a database has a specific identity, and thus belongs in a table of objects of the same type, an e-mail message doesn't fit this paradigm very well. We can divide our e-mail into incoming and outgoing, but that doesn't help us much. For example, if you receive a piece of e-mail from Jerry about Sally, regarding the Ajax Project and how it relates to Jones Consulting and your joint presentation at the board meeting, you can file this away in the "Jerry" folder, or the "Sally" folder, or the "Ajax" folder, but what you really want is to file it in all of them. In six months, you might try to find this message for any number of unpredictable reasons, and you'll want to be able to find it, regardless of your reason.

Second, consider the Web. Like an infinite, chaotic, redundant, unsupervised hard drive, the Web defies structure. Enormous quantities of information are available on the Internet, but its sheer quantity and heterogeneity almost guarantee that no regular system could ever be imposed on it. Even if the Web could be organized, the method would likely have to exist on the outside, because its contents are owned by millions of individuals, none of whom are subject to any authority. Unlike records in a database, we cannot expect to find a predictable identifying mark in a record on the Internet.

Problems with databases

There's a further problem with databases: All database records are of a single, predefined type, and all instances of a record type are grouped together. A record may represent an invoice or a customer, but it never represents an invoice *and* a customer. Similarly, a field within a record may be a name or a social security number, but it is never a name *and* a social security number. This is the fundamental concept underlying all databases — it serves the vital purpose of allowing us to impose order on our storage system. Unfortunately, it fails miserably to address the realities of retrieval for our e-mail problem: It is not enough that the e-mail from Jerry is a record of type "e-mail." Somehow, we must also identify it as a record of type "Jerry," type "Sally," type "Ajax," type "Jones Consulting," and type "Board Meeting." We must also be able to add and change its identity at will, even after the record has been stored away. What's more, a record of type "Ajax" may refer to documents other than e-mail messages — a project plan, for example. Because the record format is unpredictable, the value that identifies the record as pertaining to Ajax cannot be stored reliably within the record itself. This is in direct contradiction to the way databases work.

Databases do provide us with retrieval tools with a bit more flexibility than matching simple record types. They allow us to find and fetch a record by examining its contents and matching them against search criteria. For example, we search for invoice number "77329" or for the customer with the identifying string "Goodyear Tire and Rubber." Yet, this *still* fails for our e-mail problem. If we allow users to enter the keywords "Jerry," "Sally," "Ajax," "Jones Consulting," and "Board Meeting" into the message record, we must define such fields in advance. But as we've said, defining things in advance doesn't guarantee that a user will follow that definition later. He may now be looking for messages about the company picnic, for example. Besides, adding a series of keyword fields leads you into one of the most fundamental and universal conundrums of data processing: If you give users 10 fields, someone is bound to want 11.

The attribute-based alternative

So, if relational database technology isn't right, what is? If users find it hard to define their information in advance as databases require, is there an alternative storage and retrieval system that might work well for them?

Once again, the key is separating the storage and retrieval systems. If an *index* were used as the retrieval system, the storage technique could still remain a database. We can imagine the storage facility as a sort of **digital soup** where we could put our records. This soup would accept any record we dumped into it, regardless of its size, length, type, or contents. Whenever a record was entered, the program would return a token that could be used to retrieve the record. All we have to do is give it back that token, and the soup instantly returns our record. This is just our storage system, however; we still need a retrieval system that manages all those tokens for us.

Attribute-based retrieval thus comes to our rescue: We can create an index that stores a key value along with a copy of the token. The real magic, though, is that we can create an infinite number of indices, each one representing its own key and containing a copy of the token. For example, if our digital soup contained all our e-mail messages, we could establish an index for each of our old friends, "Jerry," "Sally," "Ajax," "Jones Consulting," and "Board Meeting." Now, when we need to find e-mail pertinent to the board meeting, we don't have to paw manually and tediously through dozens of folders. Instead, a single query brings us everything we are looking for.

Of course, someone or something must fill those indices, but that is a more mundane exercise in interaction design. There are two components to consider. First, the system must be able to read e-mail messages and automatically extract and index information such as proper names, Internet addresses, street addresses, phone numbers, and other significant data. Second, the system must make it very easy for a user to add ad hoc pointers to messages. He should be able to explicitly specify that a given e-mail message pertains to a specific value, whether or not that value is quoted verbatim in the message. Typing is okay, but selecting from picklists, clicking-and-dragging, and other more advanced user interface idioms can make the task almost painless.

Significant advantages arise when the storage system is reduced in importance and the retrieval system is separated from it and significantly enhanced. Some form of digital soup will help us to get control of the unpredictable information that is beginning to make up more and more of our everyday information universe. We can offer users powerful information-management tools without demanding that they configure their information in advance or that they conform to that configuration in the future. After all, they can't do it. So why insist?

Natural Language Output: An Ideal Interface for Attribute-Based Retrieval

In the previous sections of this chapter, we discussed the merits of attribute-based retrieval. This kind of a system, to be truly successful, requires a front end that allows users to very easily make sense of what could be quite complex and interrelated sets of attributes.

One alternative is to use natural language processing, where a user can key in his request in English. The problem with this method is that it is not possible for today's run-of-the-mill computers to effectively understand natural language queries in most commercial situations. It might work reasonably in the laboratory under tightly controlled conditions, but not in the real world, where it is subject to whim, dialect, colloquialism, and misunderstanding. In any case, the programming of a natural language recognition engine is beyond the capabilities and budget of your average programming team.

A better approach, which we've used successfully on numerous projects, is a technique we refer to as **natural language output**. Using this technique, the program provides an array of bounded controls for users to choose from. The controls line up so that they can be read like an English sentence. The user chooses from a grammar of valid alternatives, so the design is in essence a self-documenting, bounded query facility. Figure 15-3 shows how it works.

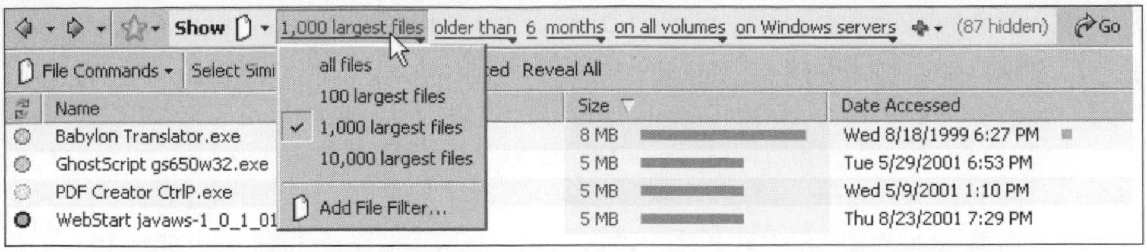

Figure 15-3 An example of a natural language output interface to an attribute-based retrieval engine, part of a Cooper design created for Softek's Storage Manager. These controls produce natural language as output, rather than attempting to accept natural language as input, for database queries. Each underlined phrase, when clicked, provides a drop-down menu with a list of selectable options. The user constructs a sentence from a dynamic series of choices that always guarantees a valid result.

A natural language output interface is also a natural for expressing everything from queries to plain old relational databases. Querying a database in the usual fashion is very hard for most people because it calls for Boolean notation and arcane database syntax, à la SQL. We discussed the problems with Boolean notation in Chapter 2. We determined that just because the program needs to understand Boolean queries, users shouldn't be forced to as well.

English isn't Boolean, so the English clauses aren't joined with AND and OR, but rather with English phrases like "all of the following apply" or "not all of the following apply." Users find that choosing among these phrases is easy because they are very clear and bounded, and they can read it like a sentence to check its validity.

The trickiest part of natural language output from a programming perspective is that choosing from controls on the left may, in many circumstances, change the content of the choices in controls to the right of them, in a cascading fashion. This means that in order to effectively implement natural language output, the grammars of the choices need to be well mapped out in advance, and that the controls need to be dynamically changeable or hideable, depending on what is selected in other controls. It also means the controls themselves must be able to display or, at least, load data dynamically.

The other concern is localization. If you are designing for multiple languages, those with very different word orders (for example, German and English) may require different grammar mappings.

Both attribute-based retrieval engines and natural language output interfaces require a significant design and programming effort, but users will reap tremendous benefits in terms of the power and flexibility in managing their data. Because the amount of data we all must manage is growing at an exponential rate, it makes sense to invest now in these more powerful, Goal-Directed tools wherever data must be managed.

16

Understanding Undo

Undo is the remarkable facility that lets us reverse a previous action. Simple and elegant, the feature is of obvious value. Yet, when we examine current implementations and uses of Undo from a Goal-Directed point of view, we see considerable variation in purpose and method. Undo is critically important for users, and it's not quite as simple as it may appear at first glance. In this chapter, we explore different ways that users think about Undo and the different uses for such a facility.

Users and Undo

Undo is the facility traditionally thought of as the rescuer of users in distress; the knight in shining armor; the cavalry galloping over the ridge; the superhero swooping in at the last second.

As a computational facility, Undo has no merit. Mistake-free as they are, computers have no need for Undo. Human beings, on the other hand, make mistakes all the time, and Undo is a facility that exists for their exclusive use. This singular observation should immediately tell us that of all the facilities in a program, Undo should be modeled the least like its construction methods — its implementation model — and the most like the user's mental model.

Not only do humans make mistakes, they make mistakes as part of their everyday behavior. From the standpoint of a computer, a false start, a misdirected glance, a pause, a sneeze, some experimentation, an "uh," and a "you know" are all errors. But from the standpoint of a person, they are perfectly normal. Human "mistakes" are so commonplace that if you think of them as "errors" or even as abnormal behavior, you will adversely affect the design of your software.

User mental models of mistakes

Users generally don't believe, or at least don't want to believe, that they make mistakes. This is another way of saying that the persona's mental model typically doesn't include error on his part. Following a persona's mental model means absolving him of blame. The implementation model, however, is based on an error-free CPU. Following the implementation model means proposing that all culpability must rest with the user. Thus, most software assumes that it is blameless, and any problems are purely the fault of the user.

The solution is for the user-interface designer to completely abandon the idea that the user can make a mistake — meaning that everything the user does is something he or she considers to be valid and reasonable. Most people don't like to admit to mistakes in their own minds, so the program shouldn't contradict this mindset in its interactions with users.

Undo enables exploration

If we design software from the point of view that nothing users do should constitute a mistake, we immediately begin to see things differently. We cease to imagine the user as a module of code or a peripheral that drives the computer, and we begin to imagine him as an explorer, probing the unknown. We understand that exploration involves inevitable forays into blind alleys and down dead ends. It is natural for humans to experiment, to vary their actions, to probe gently against the veil of the unknown to see where their boundaries lie. How can they know what they can do with a tool unless they experiment with it? Of course, the degree of willingness to experiment varies widely from person to person, but most people experiment at least a little bit.

Programmers, who are highly paid to think like computers, view such behavior only as errors that must be handled by the code. From the implementation model — necessarily the programmer's point of view — such gentle, innocent probing represents a continuous series of "mistakes." From a humanistic perspective based on our users' mental models, these actions are natural and normal. An application has the choice of either rebuffing those perceived mistakes or assisting users in their explorations. Undo is thus a primary tool for supporting exploration in software user interfaces. It allows users to reverse one or more previous actions if they decide to change their mind.

A significant benefit of Undo is purely psychological: It reassures users. It is much easier to enter a cave if you are confident that you can get back out of it at any time. The Undo function is that comforting rope ladder to the surface, supporting a user's willingness to explore further by assuring him that he can back out of any dead-end caverns.

Curiously, users often don't think about Undo until they need it, in much the same way that homeowners don't think about their insurance policies until a disaster strikes. Users frequently charge into the cave half prepared, and only start looking for the rope ladder — for Undo — after they have encountered trouble.

Designing an Undo Facility

Although users need Undo, it doesn't directly support any particular goal that underlies their tasks. Rather, it supports a necessary condition — trustworthiness — on the way to a real goal. It doesn't contribute positively to attaining users' goals, but keeps negative occurrences from spoiling the effort.

Users visualize the Undo facility in different ways, depending on the situation and their expectations. If a user is very computer-naive, he might see it as an unconditional panic button for extricating himself from a hopelessly tangled misadventure. A more experienced computer user might visualize Undo as a storage facility for deleted data. A really computer-sympathetic user with a logical mind might see it as a stack of procedures that can be undone one at a time in reverse order. To create an effective Undo facility, we must satisfy as many of these mental models as we expect our personas will bring to bear.

The secret to designing a successful Undo system is to make sure that it supports typically used tools and avoids any hint that Undo signals (whether visually, audibly, or textually) a failure by a user. It should be less a tool for reversing errors and more one for supporting exploration. Errors are generally single, incorrect actions. Exploration, by contrast, is a long series of probes and steps, some of which are keepers and others that must be abandoned.

Undo works best as a global, programwide function that undoes the last action regardless of whether it was done by direct manipulation or through a dialog box. One of the biggest problems in current implementations of Undo functionality is when users lose the ability to reverse their actions after they save the document (in Excel, for example). Just because a user has saved her work to avoid losing it in a crash doesn't necessarily mean that she wants to commit to all the changes she has made. Furthermore, with our large disk drives, there is no reason not to save the Undo buffer with the document.

Undo can also be problematic for documents with embedded objects. If a user makes changes to a spreadsheet embedded in a Word document, clicks on the Word document, and then invokes Undo, then the most recent Word action is undone instead of the most recent spreadsheet action. Users have a difficult time with this. It forces them to abandon their mental model of a single unified document and forces them to think in terms of the implementation model — that there is one document embedded within another, and each has a separate editor with a separate Undo buffer.

Types and Variants of Undo

As is so common in the world of software, there is no adequate terminology to describe the different types of Undo that exist — they are uniformly referred to as "Undo" and left at that. This language gap contributes to the lack of innovation to produce new and better variants of Undo. In this section, we define several Undo variants and explain their differences.

Incremental and procedural actions

Undo operates on a user's actions. A typical user action in a typical application has a procedure component — what the user did — and often a data component — what information was affected. When the user requests an Undo function, the procedure component of the action is reversed, and if the action had a data component — resulting in the addition, modification, or deletion of data — that data will be modified appropriately. Cutting, pasting, drawing, typing, and deleting are all actions that have a data component, so undoing them involves removing or replacing the affected text or image parts. Those actions that include a data component are called **incremental actions**.

Many undoable actions are data-free transformations such as a paragraph reformatting operation in a word processor or a rotation in a drawing program. Both of these operations act on data but neither of them add, modify, or delete data (from the perspective of the database, though a user may not share this view). Actions like these (with only a procedure component) are **procedural actions**. Most existing Undo functions don't discriminate between procedural and incremental actions but simply reverse the most recent action.

Blind and explanatory Undo

Normally, Undo is invoked by a menu item or toolbar control with an unchanging label or icon. Users know that triggering the idiom undoes the last operation, but there is no indication of what that operation is. This is called a **blind Undo**. On the other hand, if the idiom includes a textual or visual description of the particular operation that will be undone, it is an **explanatory Undo**.

If, for example, a user's last operation was to type in the word **design**, the Undo function on the menu says Undo Typing **design**. Explanatory Undo is, generally, a much more pleasant feature than blind Undo. It is fairly easy to put on a menu item, but more difficult to put on a toolbar control, although putting the explanation in a ToolTip is a good compromise (see Chapter 23 for more about toolbars and ToolTips).

Single and multiple Undo

The two most familiar types of Undo in common use today are single Undo and multiple Undo. **Single Undo** is the most basic variant, reversing the effects of the most recent user action, whether procedural or incremental. Performing a single Undo twice usually undoes the Undo and brings the system back to the state it was in before the first Undo was activated.

This facility is very effective because it is so simple to operate. The user interface is simple and clear, easy to describe and remember. A user gets precisely one free lunch. This is by far the most frequently implemented Undo, and it is certainly adequate, if not optimal, for many programs. For some users, the absence of this simple Undo is sufficient grounds to abandon a product entirely.

A user generally notices most of his command mistakes right away: Something about what he did doesn't feel or look right, so he pauses to evaluate the situation. If the representation is clear, he sees his mistake and selects the Undo function to set things back to the previously correct state; then he proceeds.

Multiple Undo can be performed repeatedly in succession — it can reverse more than one previous operation, in reverse temporal order. Any program with simple Undo must remember the user's last operation and, if applicable, cache any changed data. If the program implements multiple Undo, it must maintain a stack of operations, the depth of which may be set by the user as an advanced preference. Each time Undo is invoked, it performs an incremental Undo; it reverses the most recent operation, replacing or removing data as necessary and discarding the restored operation from the stack.

Limitations of single Undo

The biggest limitation of single-level, functional Undo occurs when a user accidentally short-circuits the capability of the Undo facility to rescue him. This problem crops up when a user doesn't notice his mistake immediately. For example, assume he deletes six paragraphs of text, then deletes one word, and then decides that the six paragraphs were erroneously deleted and should be replaced. Unfortunately, performing Undo now merely brings back the one word, and the six paragraphs are lost forever. The Undo function has failed him by behaving literally rather than practically. Anybody can clearly see that the six paragraphs are more important than the single word, yet the program freely discarded those paragraphs in favor of the one word. The program's blindness caused it to keep a quarter and throw away a fifty-dollar bill, simply because the quarter was offered last.

In some applications, any click of the mouse, however innocent of function it might be, causes the single Undo function to forget the last meaningful thing the user did. Although multiple Undo solves these problems, it introduces some significant problems of its own.

Limitations of multiple Undo

The response to the weaknesses of single-level Undo has been to create a multiple-level implementation of the same, incremental Undo. The program saves each action a user takes. By selecting Undo repeatedly, each action can be undone in the reverse order of its original invocation. In the previous scenario, a user can restore the deleted word with the first invocation of Undo and restore the precious six paragraphs with a second invocation. Having to redundantly redelete the single word is a small price to pay for being able to recover those six valuable paragraphs. The excise of the one-word redeletion tends to not be noticed, just as we don't notice the cost of ambulance trips: Don't quibble over the little stuff when lives are at stake. But this doesn't change the fact that the Undo mechanism is built on a faulty model, and in other circumstances, undoing functions in a strict LIFO (last in, first out) order can make the cure as painful as the disease.

Imagine again our user deleting six paragraphs of text, then calling up another document and performing a global find-and-replace function. In order to retrieve the missing six paragraphs, the user must first unnecessarily Undo the rather complex global find-and-replace operation. This time, the intervening operation was not the insignificant single-word deletion of the earlier example. The intervening operation was complex and difficult and having to Undo it is clearly an unpleasant, excise effort. It would sure be nice to be able to choose which operation in the queue to Undo and to be able to leave intervening — but valid — operations untouched.

The model problems of multiple Undo

The problems with multiple Undo are not due to its behavior as much as they are due to its manifest model. Most Undo facilities are constructed in an unrelentingly function-centric manner. They remember what a user does function by function and separate her actions by individual function. In the time-honored way of creating manifest models that follow implementation models, Undo systems tend to model code and data structures instead of user goals. Each click of the Undo button reverses precisely one function-sized bite of behavior. Reversing on a function-by-function basis is a very appropriate mental model for solving most simple problems that arise when a user makes an erroneous entry. The mistake is noticed right away and the user takes action to fix it right away, usually by the time he's taken two or three actions. However, when the problem grows more convoluted, the incremental, multiple-step Undo model doesn't scale very well.

You bet your LIFO

When a user goes down a logical dead end (rather than merely mistyping data), he can often proceed several complex steps into the unknown before realizing that he is lost and needs to get a bearing on known territory. At this point, however, he may have performed several interlaced functions, only some of which are undesirable. He may well want to keep some actions and nullify others, not necessarily in strict reverse order. What if he entered some text, edited it, and then decided to Undo the entry of that text but not Undo the editing of it? Such an operation is problematic to implement and explain. Neil Rubenking offers this pernicious example: Suppose that a user did a global replace changing *tragedy* to *catastrophe* and then another changing *cat* to *dog*. To Undo the first without undoing the second, can the program reliably fix all the *dogastrophes*?

In this more complex situation, the simplistic representation of the Undo as a single, straight-line, LIFO stack doesn't satisfy the way it does in simpler situations. The user may be interested in studying his actions as a menu and choosing a discontinuous subset of them for reversion, while keeping some others. This demands an explanatory Undo with a more robust presentation than might otherwise be necessary for a normal, blind, multiple Undo. Additionally, the means for selecting from that presentation must be more sophisticated. Representing the operation in the queue to show the user what he is actually undoing is a more difficult problem.

Redo

The **Redo** function came into being as the result of the implementation model for Undo, wherein operations must be undone in reverse sequence, and in which no operation may be undone without first undoing all of the valid intervening opera-tions. Redo essentially undoes the Undo and is easy to implement if the program-mer has already gone to the effort to implement Undo.

Redo prevents a diabolical situation in multiple Undo. If a user wants to back out of a half-dozen or so operations, he clicks the Undo control a few times, waiting to see things return to the desired state. It is very easy in this situation to press Undo one time too many. He immediately sees that he has undone something desirable. Redo solves this problem by allowing him to Undo the Undo, putting back the last good action.

Many programs that implement single Undo treat the last undone action as an undoable action. In effect, this makes a second invocation of the Undo function a minimal Redo function.

Group multiple Undo

Microsoft Word has what has unfortunately become a somewhat typical facility — a variation of multiple Undo we will call **group multiple Undo**. It is multiple level, showing a textual description of each operation in the Undo stack. You can exam-ine the list of past operations and select some operation in the list to Undo; how-ever, you are not undoing that one operation, but rather all operations back to that point, inclusive (see Figure 16-1). This style of multiple Undo is also employed by many Adobe products.

Figure 16-1 With Microsoft Office's Undo/Redo facility, you can Undo multiple actions, but only as a group; you can't choose to Undo only the thing you did three actions ago. Redo works in the same manner.

As a result, you cannot recover your six missing paragraphs without first reversing all the intervening operations. After you select one or more operations to Undo, the list of undone operations becomes available in reverse order in the Redo control. Redo works exactly the same way as Undo works. You can select as many operations to redo as desired and all operations up to that specific one will be redone.

The program offers two visual cues to this fact. If the user selects the fifth item in the list, that item and all four items before it in the list are selected. Also, the text legend says "Undo 5 actions." The fact that the designers had to add that text legend tells me that, regardless of how the programmers constructed it, the users were applying a different mental model. The users imagined that they could go down the list and select a single action from the past to Undo. The program didn't offer that option, so the signs were posted. This is like a door with a pull handle that has been pasted with Push signs — which everybody still pulls on anyway. While multiple Undo is certainly a very useful mechanism, there's no reason not to finish the job and use our ample computing resources to allow users to Undo just the undesirable actions, instead of everything that has happened since them.

Other Models for Undo-Like Behavior

The manifest model of Undo in its simplest form — single Undo — conforms to the user's mental model: "I just did something I now wish I hadn't done. I want to click a button and Undo that last thing I did." Unfortunately, this manifest model rapidly diverges from the user's mental model as the complexity of the situation grows. In this section, we discuss models of Undo-like behavior that work a bit differently from the more standard Undo and Redo idioms.

Comparison: What would this look like?

Besides providing robust support for the terminally indecisive, the paired Undo-Redo function is a convenient comparison tool. Say that you'd like to compare the visual effect of ragged-right margins against justified right margins. Beginning with ragged-right, you invoke Justification. Now you click Undo to see ragged-right and now you press Redo to see justified margins again. In effect, toggling between Undo and Redo implements a **comparison** or **what-if?** function; it just happens to be represented in the form of its implementation model. If this same function were to be added to the interface following a user's mental model, it might be manifested as a comparison control. This function would let you repeatedly take one step forward or backward to compare two states.

Some TV remote controls include a function labeled Jump, which switches between the current channel and the previous channel — very convenient for viewing two programs concurrently. The jump function provides the same utility as the Undo-Redo function pair with a single command — a 50% reduction in excise for the same functionality.

When used as comparison functions, Undo and Redo are really one function and not two. One says "Apply this change," and the other says "Don't apply this change." A single Compare button might more accurately represent the action to users.

Although we have been describing this tool in the context of a text-oriented word processing program, a compare function might be most useful in a graphic manipulation or drawing program, where users are applying successive visual transformations on images. The ability to see the image *with* the transformation and quickly and easily compare it to the image *without* the transformation would be a great help to the digital artist. Many products address this with small thumbnail "preview" images.

Doubtlessly, the Compare function would remain an advanced function. Just as the jump function is probably not used by a majority of TV users, the Compare button would remain one of those niceties for frequent users. This shouldn't detract from its usefulness, however, because drawing programs tend to be used very frequently by those who use them. For programs like this, catering to the frequent user is a reasonable design choice.

Category-specific Undo

The Backspace key is really an Undo function, albeit a special one. When a user mistypes, the Backspace key "undoes" the erroneous characters. If a user mistypes something, then enters an unrelated function such as paragraph reformatting, then presses the Backspace key repeatedly, the mistyped characters are erased and the reformatting operation is ignored. Depending on how you look at it, this can be a great flexible advantage giving users the ability to Undo discontiguously at any selected location. You could also see it as a trap for users because they can move the cursor and inadvertently backspace away characters that were not the last ones keyed in.

Logic says that this latter case is a problem. Empirical observation says that it is rarely a problem for users. Such discontiguous, incremental Undo — so hard to explain in words — is so natural and easy to use because everything is visible: Users can clearly see what will be backspaced away. Backspace is a classic example of an incremental Undo, reversing only some data while ignoring other, intervening actions. Yet if you imagined an Undo facility that had a pointer that could be moved and that could Undo the last function that occurred where the pointer points, you'd probably think that such a feature would be patently unmanageable and would confuse a typical user. Experience tells us that Backspace does nothing of the sort. It works as well as it does because its behavior is consistent with a user's mental model of the cursor: Because it is the source of added characters, it can also reasonably be the locus of deleted characters.

Using this same knowledge, we could create different categories of incremental Undo, like a format-Undo function that would Undo only preceding format commands and other types of **category-specific Undo** actions. If a user entered some text, changed it to italic, entered some more text, increased the paragraph indentation, entered some more text, and then clicked the Format-Undo button, only the indentation increase would be undone. A second click of the Format-Undo button would reverse the italicize operation. Neither invocation of the format-Undo would affect the content.

What are the implications of category-specific Undo in a nontext program? In a drawing program, for example, there could be separate Undo commands for pigment application tools, transformations, and cut-and-paste. There is really no reason that we couldn't have independent Undo functions for each particular class of operation in a program.

Pigment application tools include all drawing implements — pencils, pens, fills, sprayers, brushes — and all shape tools — rectangles, lines, ellipses, arrows. Transformations include all image-manipulation tools — shear, sharpness, hue, rotate, contrast, and line weight. Cut-and-paste tools include all lassos, marquees, clones, drags, and other repositioning tools. Unlike the Backspace function in the word processor, undoing a pigment application in a draw program would be temporal and would work independently of selection. That is, the pigment that is removed first would be the last pigment applied, regardless of the current selection. In text, there is an implied order from the upper left to the lower right. Deleting from the lower right to the upper left maps to a strong, intrinsic mental model, so it seems natural. In a drawing, no such conventional order exists so any deletion order other than one based on entry sequence would be disconcerting to users.

A better alternative might be to Undo within the current selection only. A user selects a graphic object, for example, and requests a transformation-Undo. The last transformation to have been applied to that *selected object* would be reversed.

Most software users are familiar with the incremental Undo and would find a category-specific Undo novel and possibly disturbing. However, the ubiquity of the Backspace key shows that incremental Undo is a learned behavior that users find to be helpful. If more programs had modal Undo tools, users would soon adapt to them. They would even come to expect them the way they expect to find the Backspace key on word processors.

Deleted data buffers

As a user works on a document for an extended time, she may desire a repository of deleted text. Take for example, the six missing paragraphs. If they are separated from her by a couple of complex search-and-replaces, they can be as difficult to reclaim by Undo as they are to rekey. Our user is thinking, "If the program would just remember the stuff I deleted and keep it in a special place, I could go get what I want directly."

What the user is imagining is a repository of the data components of her actions, rather than merely a LIFO stack of procedurals — a **deleted data buffer**. The user wants the missing text without regard to which function elided it. The usual manifest model forces her not only to be aware of every intermediate step but to reverse each of them, in turn. To create a facility more amenable to our user, we can create, in addition to the normal Undo stack, an independent buffer that collects all deleted text or data. At any time, she can open this buffer as a document and use standard cut-and-paste or click-and-drag idioms to examine and recover the desired text. If the entries in this deletion buffer are headed with simple date stamps and document names, navigation would be very simple and visual.

Users can then browse the buffer of deleted data at will, randomly, rather than sequentially. Finding those six missing paragraphs would be a simple, visual procedure, regardless of the number or type of complex, intervening steps she had taken. A deleted data buffer should be offered in addition to the regular, incremental, multiple Undo because it complements it. The data must be saved in a buffer, anyway. This feature would be quite useful in most programs, too, whether spreadsheet, drawing program, or invoice generator.

Versioning and reversion

Users occasionally want to back up long distances, but when they do, the granular actions are not terrifically important. The need for an incremental Undo remains, but discerning the individual components of more than the last few operations is overkill in most cases. **Versioning** (as we'll discuss more in Chapter 17) simply makes a copy of the entire document the way a camera snapshot freezes an image in time. Because versioning involves the entire document, it is typically implemented by direct use of the file system. The biggest difference between versioning and other Undo systems is that the user must explicitly request the version — recording a copy or snapshot of the document. After he has done this, he can safely modify the original. If he later decides that his changes were undesirable, he can return to the saved copy — a previous version of the document.

Many tools exist to support the milestoning concept in source code, but this concept is just emerging in the world outside of programming. 37signals' Writeboard, for example, automatically creates versions of a collaborative text document, and allows users to compare versions, and of course, to revert to any previous version (see Figure 16-2).

Critical to the effectiveness of a versioning facility is the behavior of the "revert" command. It should provide a list of the available saved versions of the document in question, along with some information about each one, such as the time and day it was recorded, the name of the person who recorded it, the size, and some optional user-entered notes. A user should be able to understand the differences among versions and ultimately choose to revert to any one of these versions, in which case, the current state of the document should be saved as another version that can be reverted to.

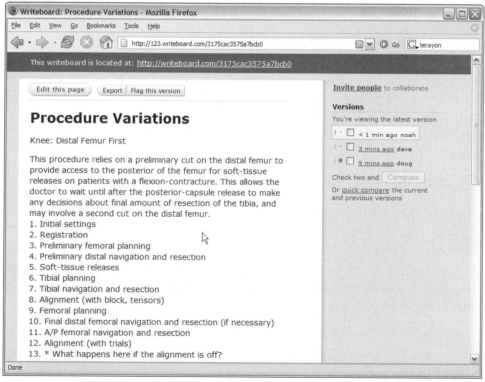

Figure 16-2 37signals' Writeboard allows multiple people to collaborate on a single document. It creates a new version every time a user saves changes to the document, and allows users to compare the different versions. This can be quite useful as it allows collaboration to take its course without worry that valuable work will be overwritten.

Freezing

Freezing, the opposite of milestoning, involves locking the data in a document so that it cannot be changed. Anything that has been entered becomes unmodifiable, although new data can be added. Existing paragraphs are untouchable, but new ones can be added between older ones.

This method is much more useful for a graphic document than for a text document. It is much like an artist spraying a drawing with fixative. All marks made up to that point are now permanent, yet new marks can be made at will. Images already placed on the screen are locked down and cannot be changed, but new images can be freely superimposed on the older ones. Corel Painter offers a similar feature with its Wet Paint and Dry Paint commands.

Undo-Proof Operations

Some operations simply cannot be undone because they involve some action that triggers a device not under the direct control of the program. For example, after an e-mail message has been sent, there is no undoing it. Many operations, however, masquerade as Undo-proof, but they are really easily reversible. For example, when you save a document for the first time in most programs, you can choose a name for the file. But almost no program lets you rename that file. Sure, you can Save As under another name, but that just makes *another* file under the new name, leaving the old file untouched under the old name. Why isn't a filename Undo provided? Because it doesn't fall into the traditional view of what Undo is for; programmers generally don't provide a true Undo function for changing a filename.

There are also situations where we're told that it's not possible to Undo an action because of business rules or institutional polices. Examples here include records of financial transactions, or entries in a medical record. In these cases, it may very well be true that "Undo" isn't an appropriate function, but you can still better support human goals and mental models by providing a way to reverse or adjust the action while leaving an audit trail.

Spend some time looking at your own application and see if you can find functions that seem as if they should be undoable, but currently aren't. You may be surprised by how many you find.

17

Rethinking Files and Save

In the world of digital technology, the place where implementation-model thinking most strikingly rears its ugly head is the management of files and the concept of "save." If you have ever tried to teach your mother how to use a computer, you will know that *difficult* doesn't really do the problem justice. Things start out all right: You start up the word processor and type a couple sentences. She's with you all the way — it's like writing on paper. But when you click the Close button, up pops a dialog box asking "Do you want to save changes?" You and Mom hit a wall together. She looks at you and asks, "What does this mean? Is everything okay?"

This problem is caused by software that forces people to think like computers by unnecessarily making them confront the internal mechanisms of data storage. This isn't just a problem for your mother; even sophisticated computer users can easily become confused or make mistakes. People spend thousands of dollars on hardware and software just to confront impertinent questions like "Do you really want me to save this document that you've been working on all afternoon?" and must remember to use to the Save As... command when what they really want to do is work on a copy of the document.

In our experience, people find computer file systems — the facilities that store application and data files on disk — very difficult to use and understand. This is one of the most critical components of computers, and errors here have significant consequences. The difference between main memory and disk storage is not clear to most people, but unfortunately, the way we've historically designed software forces users — even your mom — to know the difference and to think about their documents in terms of the way a computer is constructed.

The popularization of Web applications and other database-driven software has been a great opportunity to abandon this baggage of computer file system implementation-model thinking. Unfortunately, a similar problem has arisen there — every time a user makes a change to a document or setting, she is typically required to click a Submit or Save Changes button, once again forcing her to think about how the system works — in this case in terms of a client-server architecture.

This chapter provides a different way of presenting interactions involving files and saving — one that is more in harmony with the mental models of the people who use your products. Thankfully, we are not the only ones thinking in this way.

What's Wrong with Saving Changes to Files?

Every running application exists in two places at once: in memory and on disk. The same is true of every open file. For the time being, this is a necessary state of affairs — our technology has different mechanisms for accessing data in a responsive way (memory) and storing that data for future use (disks). This, however, is not what most people think is going on. Most of our mental models (aside from programmers) are of a single document that we are directly creating and making changes to.

When that Save Changes dialog box, shown in Figure 17-1, opens, users suppress a twinge of fear and confusion and click the Yes button out of habit. A dialog box that is always answered the same way is a redundant dialog box that should be eliminated.

Figure 17-1 This is the question Word asks when you close a file after you have edited it. This dialog is a result of the programmer inflicting the implementation-model of the disk file system on the hapless user. This dialog is so unexpected by new users that they often choose No inadvertently.

The Save Changes dialog box is based on a poor assumption: That saving and not saving are equally probable behaviors. The dialog gives equal weight to these two options even though the Yes button is clicked orders of magnitude more frequently than the No button. As we discussed in Chapter 10, this is a case of confusing possibility and probability. The user might say no, but the user will almost always say yes. Mom is thinking, "If I didn't want those changes, why would I have closed the document with them in there?" To her, the question is absurd.

There's something else a bit odd about this dialog: Why does it only ask about saving changes when you are all done? Why didn't it ask when you actually made them? The connection between closing a document and saving changes isn't all that natural, even though power users have gotten quite familiar with it.

The application issues the Save Changes dialog box when the user requests Close or Quit because that is the time when it has to reconcile the differences between the copy of the document in memory and the copy on the disk. The way the technology actually implements the facility associates saving changes with Close and Quit, but the user sees no connection. When we leave a room, we don't consider discarding all the changes we made while we were there. When we put a book back on the shelf, we don't first erase any comments we wrote in the margins.

As experienced users, we have learned to use this dialog box for purposes for which it was never intended. There is no easy way to undo massive changes, so we use the Save Changes dialog by choosing No. If you discover yourself making big changes to the wrong file, you use this dialog as a kind of escape valve to return things to the status quo. This is handy, but it's also a hack: There are better ways to address these problems (such as a Revert function).

So what is the real problem? The file systems on modern personal computer operating systems, like Windows XP, Vista, or Mac OS X, are technically excellent. The problem Mom is having stems from the simple mistake of faithfully rendering that excellent implementation model as an interface for users.

In actuality, many applications need not even concern themselves with document or file management. Apple's iPhoto and iTunes both provide rich and easy-to-use functionality that allows a typical user to ignore the fact that a file even exists. In iTunes, a playlist can be created, modified, shared, put onto an iPod, and persist for years, despite the fact that a user has never explicitly saved it. Similarly, in iPhoto, image files are sucked out of a camera into the application and can be organized, shown, e-mailed, and printed, all without users ever thinking about the file system.

Problems with the Implementation Model

The computer's file system is the tool it uses to manage data and applications stored on disk. This means the large hard drives where most of your information resides, but it also includes your flash (or "thumb") drives, CD-Rs, DVD-Rs, and the hard drives of the servers on your network. The Mac OS Finder and Windows Explorer graphically represent the file system in all its glory.

 DESIGN principle   Managing disks and files is not a user goal.

Even though the file system is an internal facility that shouldn't be the concern of users, it pervasively influences the user interface of most applications. It's all too easy to revert to implementation-model thinking because there are difficult problems facing interaction designers looking to improve the experience of dealing with the file system. The implementation details of the file system directly affect our ability to construct useful and meaningful interactions around versions of documents, relationships between documents, and even the procedural framework of our applications. This influence is likely to continue indefinitely unless we make a concerted effort to stop it.

Currently, most software applications treat the file system in much the same way that the operating system does. This is tantamount to making you deal with your car in the same way a mechanic does. Although this approach is unfortunate from an interaction perspective, it is a de facto standard, and there is considerable resistance to improving it.

Closing documents and removing unwanted changes

Those of us who have been using computers for a long time have been conditioned to think that the document Close function is the appropriate way to abandon unwanted changes if we make an error or are simply noodling around. This is not correct; the proper time to reject changes is when the changes are made. We even have a well-established idiom to support this: The Undo function.

Save As

When you save a document for the first time or choose the Save As command from the File menu, many applications then present you with the Save As dialog box. A typical example is shown in Figure 17-2.

Functionally, this dialog offers two things: It lets users name a file, and it lets them choose which directory to place it in. Both of these functions demand that users have intimate knowledge of the file system and a fair amount of foresight into how they'll need to retrieve the file later. Users must know how to formulate an acceptable and memorable filename and understand the hierarchical file directory. Many users who have mastered the name portion have completely given up on trying to understand the directory tree. They put their documents on their Desktop or in the directory that the application chooses for a default. Occasionally, some action will cause the application to forget its default directory, and these users must call in an expert to find their files for them.

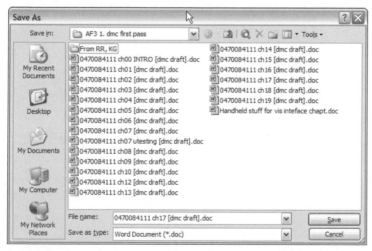

Figure 17-2 The Save As dialog provides two functions: It lets you name your file and it lets you place it in a directory you choose. Users, however, don't have a concept of **saving**, so the title of the dialog does not match their mental models of the function. Furthermore, if a dialog allows you to name and place a document, you might expect it would allow you to *rename* and *replace* a document as well. Unfortunately, our expectations are confounded by poor design.

The Save As dialog needs to decide what its purpose truly is. If it is to name and place files, then it does a very poor job. After a user has named and placed a file for the first time, he cannot change its name or its directory without creating a new document — at least not with this dialog, which purports to offer naming and placing functions — nor can he with any other tool in the application itself. In fact, in Windows XP, he can rename other files using this dialog, but not the ones he is currently working on. Huh? Beginners are out of luck, but experienced users learn the hard way that they can close the document, launch Windows Explorer, rename the file, return to the application, summon the Open dialog from the File menu, and reopen the document.

Forcing the user to go to Explorer to rename the document is a minor hardship, but therein lies a hidden trap. The bait is that Windows easily supports several applications running simultaneously. Attracted by this feature, the user tries to rename the file in the Explorer without first closing the document in the application. This very reasonable action triggers the trap, and the steel jaws clamp down hard on his leg. He is rebuffed with a rude error message box shown in Figure 17-3. Trying to rename an open file is a sharing violation, and the operating system rejects it with a patronizing error message box.

The innocent user is merely trying to rename his document, and he finds himself lost in operating system arcana. Ironically, the one entity that has both the authority and the responsibility to change the document's name while it is still open — the application itself — refuses even to try.

Figure 17-3 If a user attempts to rename a file using the Explorer while Word is still editing it, the Explorer is too stupid to get around the problem. It is also too rude to be nice about it and puts up this patronizing error message. Rebuffed by both the editing application and the OS, it is easy for a new user to imagine that a document cannot be renamed at all.

Archiving

There is no explicit function for making a copy of, or archiving, a document. Users must accomplish this with the Save As dialog, and doing so is as clear as mud. If a user has already saved the file as "Alpha," she must explicitly call up the Save As dialog and change the name. Alpha is closed and put away on disk, and New Alpha is left open for editing. This action makes very little sense from a single-document viewpoint of the world, and it also offers a really nasty trap for the user.

Here is a completely reasonable scenario that leads to trouble: Let's say that our user has been editing Alpha for the last 20 minutes and now wishes to make an archival copy of it on disk so she can make some big but experimental changes to the original. She calls up the Save As dialog box and changes the filename to "New Alpha." The application puts Alpha away on disk leaving her to edit New Alpha. But Alpha was never saved, so it gets written to disk without any of the changes she made in the last 20 minutes! Those changes only exist in the New Alpha copy that is currently in memory — in the application. As she begins cutting and pasting in New Alpha, trusting that her handiwork is backed up by Alpha, she is actually modifying the sole copy of this information.

Everybody knows that you can use a hammer to drive a screw or pliers to bash in a nail, but any skilled craftsperson knows that using the wrong tool for the job will eventually catch up with you. The tool will break or the work will be hopelessly ruined. The Save As dialog is the wrong tool for making and managing copies, and it is the user who will eventually have to pick up the pieces.

Implementation Model versus Mental Model

The implementation model of the file system runs contrary to the mental model almost all users bring to it. Most users picture electronic files like printed documents in the real world, and they imbue them with the behavioral characteristics of those real objects. In the simplest terms, users visualize two salient facts about all documents: First, there is only one document, and second, it belongs to them. The file system's implementation model violates both these rules: When a document is open, there are two copies of the document, and they both belong to the application they are open in.

As we've discussed, every data file, every document, and every application, while in use by the computer, exists in two places at once: on disk and in main memory. A user, however, imagines his document as a book on a shelf. Let's say it is a journal. Occasionally, it comes down off the shelf to have something added to it. There is only one journal, and it either resides on the shelf or it resides in the user's hands. On the computer, the disk drive is the shelf, and main memory is the place where editing takes place and is equivalent to the user's hands. But in the computer world, the journal doesn't come off the shelf. Instead a copy is made, and that copy is what resides in computer memory. As the user makes changes to the document, he is actually making changes to the copy in memory, while the original remains untouched on disk. When the user is done and closes the document, the application is faced with a decision: whether to replace the original on disk with the changed copy from memory, or to discard the altered copy. From the programmer's point of view, equally concerned with all possibilities, this choice could go either way. From the software's implementation-model point of view, the choice is the same either way. However, from the user's point of view, there is no decision to be made at all. He made his changes, and now he is just putting the document away. If this were happening with a paper journal in the physical world, the user would have pulled it off the shelf, penciled in some additions, and then replaced it on the shelf. It's as if the shelf suddenly were to speak up, asking him if he really wants to keep those changes!

Dispensing with the Implementation Model

Right now, serious programmer-type readers are beginning to squirm in their seats. They are thinking that we're treading on holy ground: A pristine copy on disk is a wonderful thing, and we'd better not advocate getting rid of it. Relax! There is nothing terribly wrong with the implementation of our file systems (although we do look forward to greater support for indexing in Windows). We simply need to hide its existence from users. We can still offer users all the advantages of that extra copy on disk without exploding their mental model.

If we begin to render the file system according to users' mental models, we can achieve several significant advantages. First, all users will become more effective. If they aren't forced to spend effort and mental energy managing their computer's file system, they're going to be more focused on the task at hand. And of course, they won't have to redo hours of work lost to a mistake in the complex chess game of versioning in contemporary operating systems.

Second, we can all teach Mom how to really use computers well. We won't have to answer her pointed questions about the inexplicable behavior of the interface. We can show her applications and explain how they allow her to work on the document, and, upon completion, she can store the document on the disk as though it were a journal on a shelf. Our sensible explanation won't be interrupted by that Save Changes? dialog. And Mom is representative of the mass-market of computer buyers, who may own and use computers, but don't like them, trust them, or use them effectively.

Another big advantage is that interaction designers won't have to incorporate clumsy file system awareness into their products. We can structure the commands in our applications according to the goals of users instead of according to the needs of the operating system. We no longer need to call the leftmost menu the File menu. This nomenclature is a bold reminder of how technology currently pokes through the facade of our applications. We'll discuss some alternatives later in this chapter.

Changing the name and contents of the File menu violates an established, though unofficial, standard. But the benefits will far outweigh any dislocation the change might cause. There will certainly be an initial cost as experienced users get used to the new idioms, but it will be far less than you might suppose. This is because these power users have already shown their ability and tolerance by learning the implementation model. For them, learning the better model will be no problem, and there will be no loss of functionality. The advantage for new users will be immediate and significant. We computer professionals forget how tall the mountain is after we've climbed it, but every day newcomers approach the base of this Everest of computer literacy and are severely discouraged. Anything we can do to lower the heights they must scale will make a big difference, and this step will tame some of the most perilous peaks.

Designing with a Unified File Model

Properly designed software should treat a document as a single thing, never as a copy on disk and a copy in memory. In this **unified file model**, users should never be forced to confront the internal mechanisms of the computer — it is the file system's job to manage writing data between the disks and memory.

The established standard suite of file management for most applications includes Open, Save, and Close commands, and the related Save As, Save Changes, and Open dialogs. Collectively, these dialogs are, as we've shown, confusing for some tasks and completely incapable of performing other tasks. The following is a different approach to document management that better supports most users' mental model.

Besides presenting a document as a single entity, there are several goal-directed functions that a user may need to perform on a document; each one should have its own corresponding function.

- ▶ Automatically saving
- ▶ Creating a copy
- ▶ Creating a version
- ▶ Naming and renaming
- ▶ Placing and repositioning in the file system
- ▶ Specifying the document format
- ▶ Reversing changes
- ▶ Reverting to a different version

Automatically saving

One of the most important functions every computer user must learn is how to **save** a document. Invoking this function means taking whatever changes a user has made to the copy in computer memory and writing them onto the disk copy of the document. In the unified model, we abolish all user interface recognition of the two copies, so the Save function disappears completely from the mainstream interface. That *doesn't* mean that it disappears from the application; it is still a very necessary operation.

 DESIGN principle   Save documents and settings automatically.

Applications should automatically save documents. For starters, when a user is done with a document and requests the Close function, the application should go ahead and write the changes out to disk without stopping to ask for confirmation with the Save Changes dialog box.

In a perfect world, this would be sufficient, but computers and software can crash, power can fail, and other unpredictable, catastrophic events can conspire to erase your work. If the power fails before you save, all your changes are lost as the memory containing them scrambles. The original copy on disk will be all right, but hours of work can still be lost. To prevent this from happening, the application must also save the document at intervals during the user's session. Ideally, the application will save every single little change as soon as the user makes it, in other words, after each keystroke. For most applications, this is quite feasible. Another approach is to keep track of small changes in memory and write them to the disk at reasonable intervals.

It's important that this automatic save function be performed in such a way as to not affect the responsiveness of the user interface. Saving should either be a background function, or should be performed when the user has stopped interacting with the application. Nobody types continuously. Everybody stops to gather his thoughts, or flip a page, or take a sip of coffee. All the application needs to do is wait until the user stops typing for a couple of seconds and then save.

Automatic save will be adequate for almost everybody. However, people who have been using computers for a long time are so paranoid about crashes and data loss that they habitually press Ctrl+S after every paragraph, and sometimes after every sentence. All applications should have manual save controls, but users should not be required to invoke manual saves.

Creating a copy

There should be an explicit function called Create a Copy. The copy will be identical to the original, but not tied to the original in any way. That is, subsequent changes to the original will have no effect on the copy. The new copy of a file named "Alpha" should automatically be given a name with a standard form like Alpha Copy. If there is already a document with that name, the new copy should be named "Alpha Copy #2." (Another reasonable form would be "Copy of Alpha" and "Second Copy of Alpha," but the problem with this approach is that copies and originals would not be adjacent to each other in the default alphabetically sorted file directory.) The copy should be placed in the same directory as the original.

It is very tempting to envision the dialog box that accompanies this command, but there should be no such interruption. The application should take its action quietly, efficiently, and sensibly, without badgering the user with silly dialogs like "Are you sure you want to make a Copy?" In the user's mind it is a simple command. If there are any anomalies, the application should make a constructive decision on its own authority.

Naming and renaming

The name of the document should be shown on the application's title bar. If the user decides to rename the document, he should be able to click on the title to edit it in place. What could be simpler and more direct than that?

Placing and moving

Most often when someone uses an application to edit a document, that document already exists. Documents are typically opened rather than created from scratch. This means that their position in the file system is already established. Although we think of establishing the home directory for a document at the moment of creation or when we first save it, neither of these events is meaningful outside of the implementation model. The new file should be put somewhere reasonable where the user can find it again (such as the Desktop).

DESIGN
principle   Put files where users can find them.

The specific appropriate location should depend on your users and the posture of the product you are designing. For complex sovereign applications that most people use daily, it is sometimes appropriate to define an application-specific document location, but for transient applications or sovereign applications that are used less frequently, don't hide your users' files in your own special corner of the file system.

If a user wants to place the document somewhere else, he can request this function from the menu. A Move dialog would then appear with the current document highlighted. In this dialog (an appropriately named relative of the Save As dialog), the user can move the file to any location. The application thus places all files automatically, and this dialog is used only to move them elsewhere.

Specifying the stored format

At the bottom of the current Save As dialog shown in Figure 17-2, a combo box allows a user to specify a file format. This function should not be located here. By tying the format to the act of saving, users are confronted with additional, unnecessary complexity added to saving. In Word, if a user innocently changes the format, both the save function and any subsequent close action are accompanied by a frightening and unexpected confirmation box. Overriding the format of a file is a relatively rare occurrence. Saving a file is a very common occurrence. These two functions should not be combined.

From a user's point of view, the format of the document — whether it is rich text, plain text, or Word format, for example — is a characteristic of the document rather than of the disk file. Specifying the format shouldn't be associated with the act of saving the file to disk. It belongs more properly in a Document Properties dialog, accessible from a mechanism near the display of the document's filename.

This dialog box should have significant cautions built into its interface to make it clear to the user that the function could involve significant data loss.

In the case of some drawing applications, where saving image files to multiple formats is desirable, an Export dialog (which some drawing applications already support) is appropriate for this function.

Reversing changes

If a user inadvertently makes changes to the document that must be reversed, the tool already exists for correcting these actions: Undo (see Chapter 16 for more on Undo behaviors). The file system should not be called in as a surrogate for Undo. The file system may be the mechanism for supporting the function, but that doesn't mean it should be rendered to users in those terms. The concept of going directly to the file system to undo changes merely undermines the Undo function.

The version function described later in this chapter shows how a file-centric vision of Undo can be implemented so that it works well with the unified file model.

Abandoning all changes

While it's not the most common of tasks, we certainly want to allow a user to discard all the changes she has made after opening or creating a document, so this action should be explicitly supported. Rather than forcing the user to understand the file system to achieve her goal, a simple Abandon Changes function on the main menu would suffice. A similarly useful way to express this concept is Revert to version, which is based upon a version system described in the next section. Because Abandon Changes involves significant data loss, the user should be protected with clear warning signs. Making this function undoable would also be relatively easy to implement and highly desirable.

Creating a version

Creating a **version** is very similar to using the Copy command. The difference is that this copy is managed by the application and presented to users as the single document instance after it is made. It should also be clear to users that they can return to the state of the document at each point that a version was made. Users should be able to see a list of versions along with various statistics about them, like the time each was recorded and its size or length. With a click, a user can select a version and, by doing so, he also immediately selects it as the active document. The document that was current at the time of the version selection will be created as a version itself. Also, since disk space is hardly a scarce resource these days, it makes sense to create versions regularly, in case it doesn't occur to your users.

A new File menu

Our new File menu now looks like the one shown in Figure 17-4, and functions as described below:

- ▶ New and Open function as before.
- ▶ Close closes the document without a dialog box or any other fuss, after automatically saving changes.
- ▶ Rename/Move brings up a dialog that lets the user rename the current file or move it to another directory.
- ▶ Create a Copy creates a new file that is a copy of the current document.
- ▶ Print collects all printer-related controls in a single dialog.
- ▶ Create Version is similar to Copy, except that the application manages these copies by way of a dialog box summoned by the Revert to Version menu item.
- ▶ Abandon Changes discards all changes made to the document since it was opened or created.
- ▶ Document Properties opens a dialog box that lets the user change the physical format of the document.
- ▶ Exit behaves as it does now, closing the document and application.

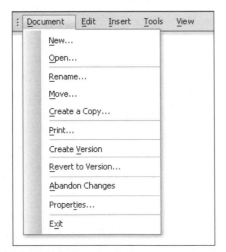

Figure 17-4 The revised file menu now better reflects the user's mental model, rather than the programmer's implementation model. There is only one file, and the user owns it. If she wants, she can make tracked or one-off copies of it, rename it, discard any changes she's made, or change the file format. She no longer needs to understand or worry about the copy in RAM versus the copy on disk.

A new name for the File menu

Now that we are presenting a unified model of storage instead of the bifurcated implementation model of disk and RAM, we no longer need to call the leftmost application menu the File menu — a reflection on the implementation model, not the user's model. There are two reasonable alternatives.

We could label the menu after the type of documents the application processes. For example, a spreadsheet application might label its leftmost menu Sheet. An invoicing application might label it Invoice.

Alternatively, we can give the leftmost menu a more generic label such as Document. This is a reasonable choice for applications like word processors, spreadsheets, and drawing applications, but may be less appropriate for more specialized niche applications.

Conversely, those few applications that do represent the contents of disks as files — generally operating system shells and utilities — should have a File menu because they are addressing files as files.

Communicating status

If the file system is going to show a user a file that cannot be changed because it is in use by another application, the file system should indicate this to the user. Showing the filename in red or with a special symbol next to it would be sufficient. A new user might still get an error message as shown in Figure 17-3, but at least some visual clues would show the reason the error cropped up.

Not only are there two copies of all data files in the current model, but when they are running, there are two copies of all applications. When a user goes to the Windows taskbar's Start menu and launches his word processor, a button corresponding to Word appears on the taskbar. But if he returns to the Start menu, Word is still there! From the user's point of view, he has pulled his hammer out of his toolbox only to find that there is still a hammer in there.

This should probably not be changed; after all, one of the strengths of the computer is its capability to have multiple copies of software running simultaneously. But the software should help users understand this very unintuitive action. The Start menu could, for example, make some reference to the already running application.

Are Disks and File Systems a Feature?

From a user's point of view, there is no reason for disks to exist. From the hardware engineer's point of view, there are three:

- ▶ Disks are cheaper than solid-state memory.
- ▶ Once written to, disks don't forget when the power is off.
- ▶ Disks provide a physical means of moving information from one computer to another.

The second and third reasons are certainly useful, but they are also not the exclusive domains of disks. Other technologies work as well or better. There are varieties of RAM that don't forget their data when the power is turned off. Some types of solid-state memory can retain data with little or no power. Networks and phone lines can be used to transport data to other sites, often more easily than with removable disks.

Reason number one — cost — is the real reason disks exist. Nonvolatile solid-state memory is a lot more expensive than disk drives are. Unfortunately, disk drives have many drawbacks compared to RAM. Disk drives are much slower than solid-state memory is. They are much less reliable, too, because they depend on moving parts. They generally consume more power and take up more space, too. But the biggest problem with disks is that the computer, the actual CPU, can't directly read or write to them! Its helpers must first bring data into solid-state memory before the CPU can work with it. When the CPU is done, its helpers must once again move the data to the disk. This means that processing that involves disks is necessarily orders of magnitude slower and more complex than working in plain RAM.

 DESIGN principle   Disks are a hack, not a design feature.

The time and complexity penalty for using disks is so severe that nothing short of an enormous cost differential could compel us to rely on them. Disks do not make computers better, more powerful, faster, or easier to use. Instead, they make computers weaker, slower, and more complex. They are a compromise, a dilution of the solid-state architecture of digital computers. If computer designers could have economically used RAM instead of disks they would have done so without hesitation — and in fact they do, in the newest breeds of handheld communicators and PDAs that make use of Compact Flash and similar solid-state memory technologies.

Wherever disk technology has left its mark on the design of our software, it has done so for implementation purposes only, and not in the service of users or any goal-directed design rationale.

Time for Change

Only two arguments can be mounted in favor of application software implemented in the file system model: Our software is already designed and built that way, and users are used to it.

Neither of these arguments is valid. The first one is irrelevant because new applications written with a unified file model can freely coexist with the older implementation-model applications. The underlying file system doesn't change at all. In much the same way that toolbars quickly invaded the interfaces of most applications in the last few years, the unified file model could also be implemented with similar success and user acclaim.

The second argument is more insidious, because its proponents place the user community in front of them like a shield. What's more, if you ask users themselves, they will reject the new solution because they abhor change, particularly when that change affects something they have already worked hard to master — like the file system. However, users are not always the best predictors of design successes, especially when the designs are different from anything they've already experienced.

In the '80s, Chrysler showed consumers early sketches of a dramatic new automobile design: the minivan. The public gave a uniform thumbs down to the new design. Chrysler went ahead and produced the Caravan anyway, convinced that the design was superior. They were right, and the same people who initially rejected the design have not only made the Caravan one of the bestselling minivans, but also made the minivan the most popular new automotive archetype since the convertible.

Users aren't interaction designers, and they cannot be expected to visualize the larger effects of interaction paradigm shifts. But the market has shown that people will gladly give up painful, poorly designed software for easier, better software even if they don't understand the explanations behind the design rationale.

18

Improving Data Entry

In Chapter 12, we discussed how interactive products should be designed to behave like considerate and intelligent people. One of the ways in which products are least capable in this regard is when the user is required to enter data. Some unfortunate artifacts of implementation-model thinking prevent people from working in the way they find most natural. In this chapter, we'll discuss problems with existing ways of dealing with data entry and some possible strategies for making this process more focused on human needs and less focused on the needs of the database.

Data Integrity versus Data Immunity

One of the most critical requirements for properly functioning software is clean data. As the aphorism says, "garbage in, garbage out." As a result, programmers typically operate according to a simple imperative regarding data entry and data processing: Never allow tainted, unclean data to touch an application. Programmers, thus, erect barriers in user interfaces so that bad data can never enter the system and compromise the pure internal state that is commonly called **data integrity**.

The imperative of data integrity posits that there is a world of chaotic information out there, and before any of it gets inside the computer it must be filtered and cleaned up. The software must maintain a vigilant watch for bad data, like a customs official at a border crossing. All data is validated at its point of entry. Anything on the outside is assumed to be suspect, and after it has run the gauntlet and been allowed inside, it is assumed to be pristine. The advantage is that once data is inside the database, the code doesn't have to bother with successive, repetitive checks on its validity or appropriateness.

The problem with this approach is that it places the needs of the database before those of its users, subjecting them to the equivalent of a shakedown every time they enter a scrap of data into the system. You don't come across this problem often with most personal productivity software: PowerPoint doesn't know or care if you've formatted your presentation correctly. But as soon as you deal with a large corporation — whether you are a clerk performing data entry for an enterprise management system or a Web surfer buying DVDs online — you come face to face with the border patrol.

People who fill out lots of forms every day as part of their jobs know that data isn't typically provided to them in the pristine form that their software demands. It is often incomplete, and sometimes wrong. Furthermore, they may break from the strict demands of a form to expedite processing of this data to make their customers happy. But when confronted with a system that is entirely inflexible in such matters, these people must either grind to a halt or find some way to subvert the system to get things done. If, however, the software recognized these facts of human existence and addressed them directly with an appropriate user interface, everyone would benefit.

Efficiency aside, there is a more insidious aspect to this problem: When software shakes down data at the point of entry, it makes a very clear statement that the user is insignificant and the application is omnipotent — that the user works for the good of the application and not vice versa. Clearly, this is not the kind of world we want to create with our technological inventions. We want people to feel empowered, and make it clear that computers work for us. We must return to the ideal division of digital labor: The computer does the work, while the human makes the decisions.

Happily, there's more than one way to protect software from bad data. Instead of keeping it out of the system, the programmer needs to make the system *immune* to inconsistencies and gaps in the information. This method involves creating much smarter, more sophisticated applications that can handle all permutations of data, giving the application a kind of **data immunity**.

Data immunity

To implement this concept of data immunity, our applications must be built to look before they leap and to ask for help when they need it. Most software blindly performs arithmetic on numbers without actually examining them first. The application assumes that a number field must contain a number — data integrity tells it so. If a user enters the word "nine" instead of the number "9," the application will barf, but a human reading the form wouldn't even blink. If the application simply looked at the data before it acted, it would see that a simple math function wouldn't do the trick.

We must design our applications to believe that a user will enter what he means to enter, and if a user wants to correct things, he will do so without paranoid insistence. But applications can look elsewhere in the computer for assistance. Is there a module that knows how to make numeric sense of alphabetic text? Is there a history of corrections that might shed some light on a user's intent?

If all else fails, an application must add annotations to the data so that when — and if — a user comes to examine the problem, he finds accurate and complete notes that describe what happened and what steps the application took.

Yes, if a user enters "asdf" instead of "9.38" the application won't be able to arrive at satisfactory results. But stopping the application to resolve this *right now* is not satisfactory either; the entry process is just as important as the end report. If a user interface is designed correctly, the application provides visual feedback when a user enters "asdf," so the likelihood of a user entering hundreds of bad records is very low. Generally, users act stupidly only when applications treat them stupidly.

When a user enters incorrect data, it is often *close* to being correct; applications should be designed to provide as much assistance in correcting the situation as possible. For example, if a user erroneously enters "TZ" for a two-letter state code, and also enters "Dallas" for a city name, it doesn't take a lot of intelligence or computational resources to figure out how to correct the problem.

What about missing data?

It is clearly counter to the goals of users — and to the utility of the system — if crucial data is omitted. The data-entry clerk who fails to key in something as important as an invoice amount creates a real problem. However, it isn't necessarily appropriate for the application to stop the clerk and point out this failure. Think about your application like a car. Your users won't take kindly to having the steering wheel lock up because the car discovered it was low on windshield-washer fluid.

Instead, applications should provide more flexibility. Users may not immediately have access to data for all the required fields, and their workflow may be such that they first enter all the information they have on hand and then return when they have the information needed to fill in the other fields. Of course, we still want our users to be *aware* of any required fields that are missing information, but we can communicate this to them through *rich modeless feedback*, rather than stopping everything to let them know something they may be well aware of.

Take the example of a purchasing clerk keying invoices into a system. Our clerk does this for a living and has spent thousands of hours using the application. He has a sixth sense for what is happening on the screen and wants to know if he has entered bad data. He will be most effective if the application notifies him of data-entry errors by using subtle visual and audible cues.

The application should also help him out: Data items, such as part numbers, that *must* be valid shouldn't be entered through free text fields, but instead should be entered via type-ahead (auto-completion) fields or bounded controls such as drop-downs. Addresses and phone numbers should be entered more naturally into smart text fields that can parse the data. The application should provide unobtrusive modeless feedback on the status of his work. This will enable our clerk to take control of the situation, and will ultimately require less policing by the application.

Most of our information-processing systems *are* tolerant of missing information. A missing name, code, number, or price can almost always be reconstructed from other data in the record. If not, the data can always be reconstructed by asking the various parties involved in the transaction. The cost is high, but not as high as the cost of lost productivity or technical support centers. Our information-processing systems can work just fine with missing data. Some of the programmers who develop these systems may not like all the extra work involved in dealing with missing data, so they invoke data integrity as an unbreakable law. As a result, thousands of clerks must interact with rigid, overbearing software under the false rubric of keeping databases from crashing.

It is obviously counterproductive to treat workers like idiots to protect against those few who are. It lowers everyone's productivity, encourages rapid, expensive, and error-causing turnover, and decreases morale, which increases the unintentional error rate of the clerks who want to do well. It is a self-fulfilling prophecy to assume that your information workers are untrustworthy.

The stereotypical role of the data-entry clerk mindlessly keypunching from stacks of paper forms while sitting in a boiler room among hundreds of identical clerks doing identical jobs is rapidly evaporating. The task of data entry is becoming less a mass-production job and more of a productivity job: a job performed by intelligent, capable professionals and, with the popularization of e-commerce, directly by customers. In other words, the population interacting with data-entry software is increasingly less tolerant of being treated like unambitious, uneducated, unintelligent peons.

Users won't tolerate stupid software that insults them, not when they can push a button and surf for another few seconds until they find another vendor who presents an interface that treats them with respect.

Data entry and fudgeability

If a system is too rigid, it can't model real-world behaviors. A system that rejects the reality of its users is not helpful, even if the net result is that all its fields are valid. Which is more important, the database or the business it is trying to support? The people who manage the database and create the data-entry applications that feed it are often serving only the CPU. This is a significant conflict of interest that good interaction design can help resolve.

Fudgeability can be difficult to build into a computer system because it demands a considerably more capable interface. Our clerk cannot move a document to the top of the queue unless the queue, the document, and its position in the queue can be easily seen. The tools for pulling a document out of the electronic stack and placing it on the top must also be present and obvious in their functions. Fudgeability also requires facilities to hold records in suspense, but an Undo facility has similar requirements. A more significant problem is that fudging admits the potential for abuse.

The best strategy to avoid abuse is using the computer's ability to record a user's actions for later examination, if warranted. The principle is simple: Let users do what they want, but keep very detailed records of those actions so that full accountability is possible.

Auditing versus Editing

Many programmers believe it is their duty to inform users when they make errors entering data. It is certainly an application's duty to inform *other applications* when they make an error, but this rule shouldn't extend to users. The customer is always right, so an application must accept what a user tells it, regardless of what it does or doesn't know. This is similar to the concept of data immunity because whatever a user enters should be acceptable, regardless of how incorrect the application believes it to be.

This doesn't mean that the application can wipe its hands and say, "All right, he doesn't want a life preserver, so I'll just let him drown." Just because the application must act as though a user is always right, doesn't mean that a user actually *is* always right. Humans are always making mistakes, and your users are no exception. User errors may not be your application's fault, but they are its responsibility. How are you going to fix them?

 DESIGN principle   An error may not be your fault, but it's your responsibility.

Applications can provide warnings — as long as they don't stop the proceedings with idiocy — but if a user chooses to do something suspect, the application can do nothing but accept the fact and work to protect that user from harm. Like a faithful guide, it must follow its client into the jungle, making sure to bring along a rope and plenty of water.

Warnings should clearly and modelessly inform users of what they have done, much as the speedometer silently reports our speed violations. It is not reasonable, however, for the application to stop the proceedings, just as it is not right for the speedometer to cut the gas when we edge above 65 miles per hour. Instead of an error dialog, for example, data-entry fields can highlight any user input the application evaluates as suspect.

When a user does something that the application thinks is wrong, the best way to protect him (unless real disaster is imminent) is to make it clear that there may be a problem, but to do this in an unobtrusive way that ultimately relies on the user's intelligence to figure out the best solution. If the application jumps in and tries to fix it, it may be wrong and end up subverting the user's intent. Further, this approach fails to give the user the benefit of learning from the situation, ultimately compromising his ability to avoid the situation in the future. Our applications should, however, remember each of the user's actions, and ensure that each action can be cleanly reversed, that no collateral information is lost, and that a user can figure out where the application thinks the problems might be. Essentially, we maintain a clear audit trail of his actions. Thus the principle: Audit, don't edit.

 **DESIGN principle**   Audit, don't edit.

Microsoft Word has an excellent example of auditing, as well as a nasty counterexample. This excellent example is the way it handles real-time spell checking: As you type, red wavy underlines identify words that the application doesn't recognize (see Figure 18-1). Right-clicking on these words pops up a menu of alternatives you can choose from — but you don't have to change anything, and you are not interrupted by dialogs or other forms of modal idiocy.

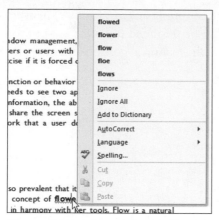

Figure 18-1 Microsoft Word's automatic spelling checker audits misspelled words with a wavy red underline, providing modeless feedback to users. Right-clicking on an underlined word pops open a menu of possible alternatives to choose from.

Word's AutoCorrect feature, on the other hand, can be a little bit disturbing at first. As you type, it silently changes words it thinks are misspelled. It turns out that this feature is incredibly useful for fixing minor typos as you go. However, the corrections leave no obvious audit trail, so a user has no idea that what he typed has been changed. It would be better if Word could provide some kind of mark that indicates it has made a correction on the off chance that it has miscorrected something (which becomes much more likely if you are, for instance, writing a technical paper heavy in specialized terminology and acronyms).

More frightening is Word's AutoFormat feature, which tries to interpret user behaviors like use of asterisks and numbers in text to automatically format numbered lists and other paragraph formats. When this works, it seems magical, but frequently the application does the wrong thing, and once it does so, there is not always a straightforward way to undo the action. AutoFormat is trying to be just a bit too smart; it should really leave the thinking to the human. Luckily, this feature can be turned off (though it's hard to determine how). Also, more recent versions of Word provide a special in-place menu that allows users to adjust AutoFormat assumptions.

In the real world, humans accept partially and incorrectly filled-in documents from each other all the time. We make a note to fix the problems later, and we usually do. If we forget, we fix it when we eventually discover the omission. Even if we never fix it, we somehow survive. It's certainly reasonable to use software to improve the efficiency of our data collection efforts, and in many cases it is consistent with human goals to do so. (No one wants to enter the wrong shipping address for an expensive online purchase.) However, our applications can be designed to better accommodate the way humans think about such things — the technical goal of data integrity should not be our users' problem to solve.

19

Pointing, Selecting, and Direct Manipulation

Modern graphical user interfaces are founded on the concept of direct manipulation of graphical objects on the screen: buttons, sliders, and other function controls, as well as icons and other representations of data objects. The ability to choose and modify objects on the screen is fundamental to the interfaces we design today. But to perform these manipulations, we also require input mechanisms that give us the flexibility to do so. This chapter discusses both the basics of direct manipulation and the various devices that have been employed to make such manipulation possible.

Direct Manipulation

In 1974, Ben Shneiderman coined the term *direct manipulation* to describe an interface design strategy consisting of three important components:

- ▶ Visual representation of the objects that an application is concerned with

- ▶ Visible and gestural mechanisms for acting upon these objects (as opposed to text commands)

- ▶ Immediately visible results of these actions

A less rigorous definition would say that direct manipulation is clicking and dragging things, and although this is true, it can easily miss the point that Shneiderman subtly makes. Notice that two of his three points concern the visual feedback the program offers to users. It might be more accurate to call it "visual manipulation" because of the importance of what users see during the process. Unfortunately, many attempts at direct-manipulation idioms are implemented without adequate visual feedback, and these interactions fail to effectively create an experience of direct manipulation.

 DESIGN principle   Rich visual feedback is the key to successful direct manipulation.

Another important consideration is that users can directly manipulate only things that are displayed by the application. In other words, it must be visible to manipulate it. If you want to create effective direct-manipulation idioms in your software, you must take care to render data, objects, controls, and cursors with a certain amount of rich graphic detail.

Direct manipulation is simple, straightforward, easy to use, and easy to remember. However, when most users are first exposed to a given direct-manipulation idiom, they do not immediately intuit or discover how to use it. Direct manipulation idioms often must be taught, but their strength is that teaching them is easy, and once taught, they are seldom forgotten. It is a classic example of idiomatic design. Because the visible and direct nature of these interactions bears such similarity to interactions with the objects in the physical world, we are well suited to remember these skills.

With regard to direct manipulation, Apple's classic *Human Interface Style Guide* says, "Users want to feel that they are in charge of the computer's activities." The Macintosh user interface itself makes it clear that Apple believes in direct manipulation as a fundamental tenet of good user-interface design. However, user-centered design guru Don Norman says "Direct manipulation, first-person systems have their drawbacks. Although they are often easy to use, fun, and entertaining, it is often difficult to do a really good job with them. They require the user to do the task directly, and the user may not be very good at it." Whom should we believe?

The answer, of course, is both of them. Direct manipulation is an extremely powerful tool; but it can require skill development for users to become effective. Many direct manipulation idioms require motor coordination and a sense of purpose. For example, even moving files between folders in Windows Explorer can be a complicated task requiring dexterity and foresight. Keep these challenges in mind as you design direct manipulation idioms — some amount of direct manipulation is usually a good thing, but depending on the skills and usage contexts of your personas, it's also possible to go overboard. You should always consider what users need to manipulate themselves, and what the application can help them with, more indirectly.

Most direct manipulation interaction idioms fall into one of seven categories:

- ▶ Pointing
- ▶ Selection
- ▶ Drag and drop
- ▶ Control manipulation
- ▶ Palette tools
- ▶ Object manipulation (such as positioning, shaping, and resizing)
- ▶ Object connection

We discuss each of these as we progress through the chapter, starting with the fundamentals of pointing devices (such as the mouse), the input methods that are used to drive modern graphical user interfaces.

Pointing Devices

Direct manipulation of objects on a screen is made possible through the use of a **pointing device**. Clearly, the best way to point to something is with your fingers. They're always handy; you probably have several nearby right now. The only real drawback they have is that their ends are too blunt for precisely pointing at high-resolution screens, and most high resolution screens also can't recognize being pointed at. Because of this limitation, we use a variety of other pointing devices, the most popular of which is a mouse.

As you roll the mouse around on your desktop, you see a visual symbol, the cursor, move around on the computer screen in the same way. Move the mouse left and the cursor moves left; move the mouse up and the cursor moves up. As you first use the mouse, you immediately get the sensation that the mouse and cursor are connected, a sensation that is extremely easy to learn and equally hard to forget.

This is good, because perceiving how the mouse works by inspection is nearly impossible. In a scene from the movie *Star Trek IV: The Voyage Home*, Scotty (one of the best engineers from the 24th century) comes to 20th-century Earth and tries to work a computer. He picks up the mouse, holds it to his mouth, and speaks into it. This scene is funny and believable: The mouse has no visual affordance that it is a pointing device. However, as soon as we are shown how the movements of the mouse and the cursor are related, understanding is instantaneous. As we've said, all idioms must be learned, but good idioms need be learned only once. The mouse is certainly a good idiom in that regard.

Of course, there are several other options for pointers that a designer should take into consideration, including trackballs, touchpads (or trackpads), tablets, and touch screens. It's worth considering that while the first two basically behave like mice (with different ergonomic factors), tablets and touch screens are a bit different.

Although the mouse is a relative pointing device — moving the mouse moves the cursor *based upon the current cursor position* — tablets usually absolute pointing devices — each location on the tablet *maps directly to a specific location on the screen*. If you pick up the pen from the top-left corner and put it down in the bottom-right corner, the cursor immediately jumps from the top-left to the bottom-right of the screen. The same is true of touch screens.

Using the mouse

When you mouse around on the screen, there is a distinct dividing line between near motions and far motions: Your destination is either near enough that you can keep the heel of your hand stationary on your desktop, or you must pick up your hand. When the heel of your hand is down and you move the cursor from place to place, you use the fine motor skills of the muscles in your fingers. When you lift the heel of your hand from the desktop to make a larger move, you use the gross motor skills of the muscles in your arm. Transitioning between gross and fine motor skills is challenging. It involves coordinating two muscle groups that require dexterity to use together, which typically requires time and practice for computer users to master. (It's actually similar to drawing, another skill that requires practice to do well.) Touch-typists dislike anything that forces them to move their hands from the home position on the keyboard because it requires a transition between their muscle groups. Similarly, moving the mouse cursor across the screen to manipulate a control forces a change from fine to gross and back to fine motor skills. Don't force users to do this continually.

Clicking a mouse button also requires fine motor control — without it, the mouse and cursor will inadvertently move, botching the intended action. A user must learn to plant the heel of his hand and go into fine motor control mode to position the cursor in the desired location, then he must maintain that position when he clicks. Further, if the cursor starts far away from the desired control, the user must first use gross motor control to move the cursor near the control before shifting to fine motor control to finish the job. Some controls, such as scrollbars, compound the problem by forcing users to switch back and forth between fine and gross motor skills several times to complete an interaction (see Figure 19-1).

It is absolutely critical that designers pay significant attention to users' aptitudes, skills, and usage contexts and make a conscious decision about how much complex motor work using an interface should require. This is a delicate balancing act between reducing complexity and user effort and providing useful and powerful tools. It's almost always a good idea for things that are used together to be placed together.

Not only do the less manually dexterous find the mouse problematic, but also many experienced computer users, particularly touch-typists, find the mouse difficult at times. For many data-intensive tasks, the keyboard is superior to the mouse. It is frustrating to have to pull your hands away from the keyboard to reposition a cursor with the mouse, only to have to return to the keyboard again. In the early days of personal computing, it was the keyboard or nothing, and today, it is often the mouse or nothing. Programs should fully support both the mouse and the keyboard for all navigation and selection tasks.

Figure 19-1 The familiar scrollbar, shown on the left, is one of the more difficult-to-use GUI controls. To go between scrolling up and scrolling down, a user must transition from the fine motor control required for clicking the up button to the gross motor control needed to move her hand to the bottom of the bar, and back to fine motor control to accurately position the mouse and click the down button. If the scrollbar were modified only slightly, as in the center, so that the two buttons were adjacent, the problem would go away. (Macintosh scrollbars can be similarly configured to place both arrow buttons at the bottom.) The scrollbar on the right is a bit visually cluttered, but has the most flexible interaction. Scroll wheels on the input device are also a great solution to the problem. For more on scrollbars, see Chapter 21.

DESIGN principle   Support both mouse and keyboard use for navigation and selection tasks.

A significant portion of computer users have some trouble using a mouse, so if we want to be successful, we must design our software in sympathy with them as well as with expert mouse users. This means that for each mouse idiom there should be at least one non-mouse alternative. Of course, this may not always be possible — it would be ridiculous to try to support drawing interactions without a mouse. However, most enterprise and productivity software lends itself pretty well to keyboard commands.

Mouse buttons

The inventors of the mouse tried to figure out how many buttons to put on it, and they couldn't agree. Some said one button was correct, whereas others swore by two buttons. Still others advocated a mouse with several buttons that could be clicked separately or together so that five buttons could yield up to 32 distinct combinations. Ultimately, though, Apple settled on one button for its Macintosh, Microsoft went with two, and the Unix community (Sun Microsystems in particular) went with three. Apple's extensive user testing determined that the optimum number of buttons for beginners was one, thereby enshrining the single-button mouse in the pantheon of Apple history. This was unfortunate, as the right mouse button usually comes into play soon after a person graduates from beginner status and becomes a perpetual intermediate. A single button sacrifices power for the majority of computer users in exchange for simplicity for beginners. Recently, Apple has admitted the importance of right-click contextual menus and Macintoshes now come with two-button mice.

The left mouse button

In general, the left mouse button is used for all the primary direct-manipulation functions, such as triggering controls, making selections, drawing, and so on. The most common meaning of the left mouse button is activation or selection. For standard controls, such as buttons or check boxes, clicking the left mouse button means pushing the button or checking the box. If you are clicking in data, the left mouse button generally means selecting. We'll discuss selection idioms later in the chapter.

The right mouse button

The right mouse button was long treated as nonexistent by Microsoft and many others. Only a few brave programmers connected actions to the right mouse button, and these actions were considered to be extra, optional, or advanced functions. When Borland International used the right mouse button as a tool for accessing a dialog box that showed an object's properties, the industry seemed ambivalent towards this action although it was, as they say, critically acclaimed. This changed with Windows 95, when Microsoft finally followed Borland's lead. Today the right mouse button serves an important and extremely useful role: enabling direct access to properties and other context-specific actions on objects and functions.

The middle mouse button

Generally speaking, you can't count on users having a mouse with a middle button, unless they are using specialized tools that are so important that they will buy any hardware that is required to use the product. As a result, most applications use only the middle button as a shortcut. In its style guide, Microsoft states that the middle button "should be assigned to operations or functions already in the interface," a definition it once reserved for the right mouse button. We have some friends who swear by the middle button. They use it as a shortcut for double-clicking with the left mouse button — which is enabled by configuring the mouse driver.

The scroll wheel

One of the most useful innovations in pointing devices is the scroll wheel. There are several variations, but it is typically a small wheel embedded in the mouse under the user's middle finger. Rolling the wheel forward scrolls the window up, and rolling it backwards scrolls the window down. The fantastic thing about the scroll wheel is it allows users to avoid dealing with the challenges of interacting with scrollbars (see Figure 19-1).

Meta-keys

Using **meta-keys** in conjunction with a mouse can extend direct manipulation idioms. Meta-keys include the Ctrl key, the Alt key, the Command key (on Apple Computers), and the Shift keys.

Commonly, these keys are used to modify the functions of selection and drag-and-drop interactions. For example, in Windows Explorer, holding the Ctrl key while dragging and dropping a file turns the function from a Move into a Copy. These keys are also commonly used to adjust mouse behavior — holding Shift while dragging often constrains cursor movement to a single direction (either up/down or right/left). We'll discuss more about these conventions later in the chapter.

Apple has had a history of well-articulated standards for use of meta-keys in combination with a mouse, and there tends to be a fair amount of consistency in their usage. In the Windows world, no single voice articulated user-interface standards in the same way, but some conventions (often rather similar to Apple's) have emerged.

Using cursor hinting to dynamically show the meanings of meta-keys is a good idea. While the meta-key is pressed, the cursor should change to reflect the new function of the idiom.

DESIGN principle   Use cursor hinting to show the meanings of meta-keys.

Pointing and clicking with a mouse

At its most basic, there are two atomic operations you can perform with a mouse: You can move it to point at different things, and you can click the buttons. Any further mouse actions beyond pointing and clicking will be made up of a combination of one or more of those actions. The complete set of mouse actions (that can be accomplished without using meta-keys) is summarized in the following list. For the sake of discussion, we have assigned a short name to each of the actions (shown in parenthesis).

- ▶ Point (Point)
- ▶ Point, click left button, release (click)
- ▶ Point, click right button, release (right-click)
- ▶ Point, click left button, drag, release (click and drag)
- ▶ Point, click left button, release, click left button, release (double-click)
- ▶ Point, click left button, click right button, release, release (chord-click)
- ▶ Point, click left button, release, click, drag, release (double-drag)

An expert mouse user may perform all seven actions, but only the first five items on the list are within the scope of normal users.

Pointing

This simple operation is a cornerstone of the graphical user interface and is the basis for all mouse operations. A user moves the mouse until the onscreen cursor is pointing to, or placed over, the desired object. Objects in the interface can take notice of when they are being pointed at, even when they are not clicked. Objects that can be directly manipulated often change their appearance subtly to indicate this attribute when the mouse cursor moves over them. This property is called **pliancy** and is discussed in detail later in this chapter.

Clicking

While a user holds the cursor over a target, he clicks the button down and releases it. In general, this action is defined as triggering a state change in a control or selecting an object. In a matrix of text or cells, the click means, "Bring the selection point over here." For a pushbutton control, a state change means that while the mouse button is down and directly over the control, the button will enter and remain in the pushed state. When the mouse button is released, the button is triggered, and its associated action occurs.

 DESIGN principle   Single-click selects data or an object or changes the control state.

If, however, the user, while still holding the mouse button down, moves the cursor off the control, the pushbutton control returns to its unpushed state (though input focus is still on the control until the mouse button is released). When the user releases the mouse button, input focus is severed, and nothing happens. This provides a convenient escape route if a user changes his mind or inadvertently clicks the wrong button. The mechanics of mouse-down and mouse-up events in clicking are discussed in more detail later in this chapter.

Clicking and dragging

This versatile operation has many common uses including selecting, reshaping, repositioning, drawing, and dragging and dropping. We'll discuss all of these in this chapter and the rest of the book.

As with clicking, it's often important to have an escape hatch for users who become disoriented or have made an error. The Windows scrollbar provides a good example of this: It allows users to scroll successfully without having the mouse directly over the scrollbar (imagine how hard it would be to use if it behaved like a button). However, if a user drags too far from the scrollbar, it resets itself to the position it was in before being clicked on. This behavior makes sense, since scrolling over long distances requires gross motor movements that make it difficult to stay within the bounds of the narrow scrollbar control. If the drag is too far off base, the scrollbar makes the reasonable assumption that the user didn't mean to scroll in the first place. Some programs set this limit too close, resulting in frustratingly temperamental scroll behavior.

Double-clicking

If double-clicking is composed of single-clicking twice, it seems logical that the first thing double-clicking should do is the same thing that a single-click does. This is indeed its meaning when the mouse is pointing at data. Single-clicking selects something; double-clicking selects something and then takes action on it.

 DESIGN principle   Double-click means single-click plus action.

This fundamental interpretation comes from the Xerox Alto/Star by way of the Macintosh, and it remains a standard in contemporary GUI applications. The fact that double-clicking is difficult for less dexterous users — painful for some and impossible for a few — was largely ignored. The solution to this accessibility problem is to include double-click idioms but ensure that their functions have equivalent single-click idioms.

Although double-clicking on file and application icons is well defined, double-clicking on most controls has no meaning, and the extra click is discarded. Or, more often, it will be interpreted as a second, independent click. Depending on the control, this can be benign or problematic. If the control is a toggle button, you may find that you've just returned it to the state it started in (rapidly turning it on, then off). If the control is one that goes away after the first click, like the OK button in a dialog box, for example, the results can be quite unpredictable — whatever was directly below the pushbutton gets the second button-down message.

Chord-clicking

Chord-clicking means clicking two buttons simultaneously, although they don't really have to be clicked or released at precisely the same time. To qualify as a chord-click, the second mouse button must be clicked before the first mouse button is released.

There are two variants to chord-clicking. The first is the simplest, whereby the user merely points to something and clicks both buttons at the same time. This idiom is very clumsy and has not found much currency in existing software, although some creative and desperate programmers have implemented it as a substitute for a Shift key on selection.

The second variant is using chord-clicking to cancel a drag. The drag begins as a simple, one-button drag, then the user adds the second button. Although this technique sounds more obscure than the first variant, it actually has found wider acceptance in the industry. It is well suited for canceling drag operations, and we'll discuss it in more detail later in the chapter.

Double-clicking and dragging

This is another expert-only idiom. Faultlessly executing a double-click and drag can be like patting your head and rubbing your stomach at the same time. Like triple-clicking, it is useful only in specialized, sovereign applications. Use it as a variant of selection extension. In Microsoft Word, for example, you can double-click text to select an entire word; so, expanding that function, you can extend the selection word by word by double-dragging.

In a big sovereign application that has many permutations of selection, idioms like this one are appropriate. But for most products, we recommend that you stick with more basic mouse actions.

Mouse-up and mouse-down events

Each time the user clicks a mouse button, the program must deal with two discrete events: the mouse-down event and the mouse-up event. How these events are interpreted varies from platform to platform and product to product. Within a given product (and ideally a platform), these actions should be made rigidly consistent.

When selecting an object, the selection should always take place on mouse-down. The button click may be the first step in a dragging sequence, and you can't drag something without first selecting it.

 DESIGN principle   Mouse-down over an object or data should select the object or data.

On the other hand, if the cursor is positioned over a control rather than selectable data, the action on the mouse-down event is to *tentatively* activate the control's state transition. When the control finally sees the button-up event, it then commits to the state transition (see Figure 19-2).

 DESIGN principle   Mouse-down over controls means propose action; mouse-up means commit to action.

This mechanism allows users to gracefully bow out of an inadvertent click. After clicking a button, for example, a user can just move the mouse outside of the button and release the mouse button. For a check box, the meaning is similar: On mouse-down the check box visually shows that it has been activated, but the check doesn't actually appear until the mouse-up transition. This idiom is called "pliant response hinting" and is further described in the section on object hinting.

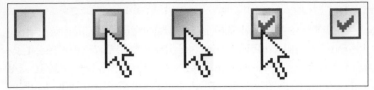

Figure 19-2 These images depict feedback and state change of a check box in Windows XP. The first image shows an unselected check box, the second is the mouseover state (or hover), the third shows the feedback to the click (or mouse-down), the fourth shows what happens when the button is released (mouse-up) but with a hover, and the final image shows the selected state of the check box without a hover. Notice that while there is visual feedback to the click, the check box control doesn't register a state change until the mouse-up or release.

Pointing and the Cursor

The cursor is the visible representation of the mouse's position on the screen. By convention, it is normally a small arrow pointing diagonally up and left, but under program control it can change to any shape as long as it stays relatively small (32 x 32 pixels in Windows XP). Because the cursor frequently must resolve to a single pixel in order to point at small things, there must be some way for the cursor to indicate precisely which pixel is the one pointed to. This is accomplished by designating one single pixel of any cursor as the actual locus of pointing, called the **hotspot**. For the standard arrow, the hotspot is, logically, the tip of the arrow. Regardless of the shape the cursor assumes, it always has a single hotspot pixel.

As discussed, the key to successful direct manipulation is rich visual feedback. It should be obvious to users which aspects of the interface are manipulable, which are informational, and which are décor. Especially important for creating effective interaction idioms is attention to mouse cursor feedback.

Pliancy and hinting

Returning to Norman's concept of affordance (see Chapter 13), it's absolutely critical to communicate visually how various interface elements may be used. We use the term **pliant** to refer to objects or screen areas that may be manipulated by a user. For example, a button control is pliant because it can be "pushed" by the mouse cursor. Any object that can be picked up and dragged is pliant, and every cell in a spreadsheet and every character in a word processor document is pliant.

In most cases, the fact that an object is pliant should be communicated to users. The only situation where this isn't true is when you are concerned with presenting rich, complex functionality solely to expert users with no concern about their ability to learn and use the application. In these cases, the screen real estate and visual attention that would otherwise be devoted to communicating pliancy may be more appropriately used elsewhere. Do not make the decision to take this route lightly.

DESIGN
principle   Visually communicate pliancy.

There are three basic ways to communicate — or hint at — the pliancy of an object to users: by creating static visual affordances of the object itself, by dynamically changing visual affordances of the object, or by changing the visual affordances of the cursor as it passes over and interacts with the object.

Object hinting

Static object hinting is when the pliancy of an object is communicated by the static rendering of the object itself. For example, the three-dimensional sculpting of a button control is static visual hinting because it provides manual affordance for pushing (see Figure 19-3).

For interfaces with a lot of objects and controls, static object hinting can require an impractical amount of rendered screen elements. If everything has a three-dimensional feel to provide affordance, your interface can start to look like a sculpture garden. Also, static hinting requires that objects be large enough to accommodate the creation of affordance. These impracticalities call for dynamic visual hinting.

Dynamic visual hinting works like this: When the cursor passes over a pliant object, it changes its appearance (see Figure 19-3). This action occurs before any mouse buttons are clicked and is triggered by cursor fly-over only, and is commonly referred to as a "rollover." A good example of this is behavior of **butcons** (iconlike buttons) on toolbars: Although there is no persistent buttonlike affordance of the butcon, passing the cursor over any single butcon causes the affordance to appear. The result is a powerful hint that the control has the behavior of a button, and the elimination of the persistent affordance dramatically reduces visual clutter on the toolbar.

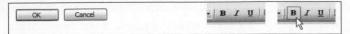

Figure 19-3 The buttons on the left are an example of static visual hinting: Their "clickability" is suggested by the dimensional rendering. The toolbar butcons on the right demonstrate dynamic visual hinting: While the Bold toggle doesn't appear to be a button at first glance, passing the mouse cursor over it causes it to change, thereby creating affordance.

Pliant response hinting should occur if the mouse is clicked (but not released) while the cursor is inside a control. The control must visually show that it is poised to undergo a state change (see Figure 19-2). This action is important and is often neglected by those who create their own controls.

A pushbutton needs to change from a visually raised state to a visually indented state; a check box should highlight its box but not show a check just yet. Pliant response is an important feedback mechanism for any control that either invokes an action or changes its state, letting the user know that some action is forthcoming if she releases the mouse button. The pliant response is also an important part of the cancel mechanism. When the user clicks down on a button, that button responds by becoming indented. If the user moves the mouse away from that button while still holding the mouse button down, the onscreen button should return to its quiescent, raised state. If the user then releases the mouse button, the onscreen button will not be activated (which is consistent with the lack of pliant response).

Cursor hinting

Cursor hinting communicates pliancy by changing the appearance of the cursor as it passes over an object or screen area. For example, when the cursor passes over a window's frame, the cursor changes to a double-ended arrow showing the axis in which the window edge can be stretched. This is the only visual affordance that the frame can be stretched.

 DESIGN principle   Use cursor hinting to indicate pliancy.

Cursor hinting should first and foremost make it clear to users that an object is pliant. It is also often useful to indicate what type of direct-manipulation action is possible.

Generally speaking, controls should offer static or dynamic visual hinting, whereas *pliant* (manipulable) data more frequently should offer cursor hinting. For example, it is difficult to make dense tabular data visually hint at pliancy without disturbing its clear representation, so cursor hinting is the most effective method. Some controls are small and difficult for users to spot as readily as a button, and cursor hinting is vital for the success of such controls. The column dividers and screen splitters in Microsoft Excel are good examples, as you can see in Figure 19-4.

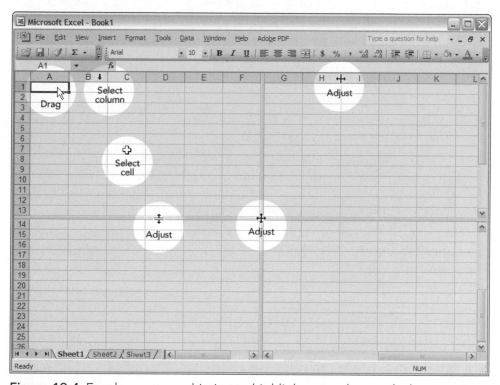

Figure 19-4 Excel uses cursor hinting to highlight several controls that are not obviously pliant by themselves. The width of the individual columns and height of rows can be set by dragging on the short vertical lines between each pair of columns, so the cursor changes to a two-headed horizontal arrow both hinting at the pliancy and indicating the permissible drag direction. The same is true for the screen-splitter controls. When the mouse is over an unselected editable cell, it shows the plus cursor, and when it is over a selected cell, it shows the drag cursor.

Wait cursor hinting

There is a variant of cursor hinting called **wait cursor hinting** that is often used when an application is doing something that causes it to be unresponsive — like performing calculation-intensive functions or opening a file. Here, the cursor is used to visually indicate that the application has become unresponsive. In Windows, this image is the familiar hourglass. Other operating systems have used wristwatches, spinning balls, and steaming cups of coffee.

When this idiom was introduced in GUIs, if one application became unresponsive then the cursor would change for all applications. This was confusing and misleading. Modern, multithreaded operating systems no longer feature this shortcoming, but it is important to provide as much context as possible about the source of any latency or lack of responsiveness.

Selection

The act of choosing an object or a control is referred to as **selection**. This is a simple idiom, typically accomplished by pointing and clicking on the item in question (though there are other keyboard- and button-actuated means of doing this). Selection is often the basis for more complex interactions — once a user has chosen something, she is then in the appropriate context for performing an action on that thing. The sequence of events implied by such an idiom is called **object verb ordering**.

Command ordering and selection

At the foundation of every user interface is the way in which a user can express commands. Almost every command has a **verb** that describes the action and an **object** that describes what will be acted upon (in more technical parlance, these are the operation and the operands, respectively).

If you think about it, you can express a command in two ways: With the verb first, followed by the object; or with the object first, followed by the verb. These are commonly called **verb-object** and **object-verb** orders, respectively. Modern user interfaces use both orders.

Verb-object ordering is consistent with the way that commands are formed in English. As a result, it was only logical that command-line systems mimic this structure in their syntax (for example, to delete a file in Unix, one must type "rm filename.txt".

When graphical user interfaces first emerged, it became clear that verb-object ordering created a problem. Without the rigid, formal structures of command-line idioms, graphical interfaces must use the construct of *state* to tie together different interactions in a command. If a user chooses a verb, the system must then enter a state — a mode — to indicate that it is waiting for the user to select an object to act on. In the simple case, the user will then choose a single object, and all will be well. However, if a user wants to act on more than one object, the system can only know this if the user tells it in advance how many operands he will enter, or if the user enters a second command indicating that has completed his object list. These are both very clumsy interactions and require users to express themselves in a very unnatural manner that is difficult to learn. What works just fine in a highly structured linguistic environment falls apart completely in the looser universe of the graphical user interface.

With an object-verb command order, we don't need to worry about termination. Users select which objects will be operated upon and then indicate which verb to execute on them. The application then executes the indicated function on the selected data. A benefit of this is that users can easily execute a series of verbs on the same complex selection. A second benefit is that when a user chooses an object, the application can then show only appropriate commands, potentially reducing the user's cognitive load and reducing the amount of visual work required to find the command (in a visual interface, all commands should be visually represented).

Notice that a new concept has crept into the equation — one that doesn't exist, and isn't needed in a verb-object world. That new concept is called **selection**. Because the identification of the objects and the verb are not part of the same user interaction, we need a mechanism to indicate which operands are selected.

The object-verb model can be difficult to understand in the abstract, but selection is an idiom that is very easy to grasp and, once shown, is rarely forgotten (clicking an e-mail in Outlook and deleting it, for example, quickly becomes second nature). Explained through the linguistic context of the English language, it doesn't sound too useful that we must choose an object first. On the other hand, we use this model frequently in our nonlinguistic actions. We pick up a can, and then use a can opener on it.

In interfaces that don't employ direct manipulation, such as some modal dialog boxes, the concept of selection isn't always needed. Dialog boxes naturally come with one of those object-list-completion commands: the OK button. Here, users may choose a function first and one or more objects second.

While object-verb orderings are more consistent with the notion of direct manipulation, there are certainly cases where the verb-object command order is more useful or usable. These are cases where it isn't possible or reasonable to define the objects up front without the context of the command. An example here is mapping software, where a user probably can't always select the address he wants to map from a list (though we should allow this for his address book); instead, it is most useful for him to say "I want to create a map for the following address. . . ."

Discrete and contiguous selection

Selection is a pretty simple concept, but there are a couple of basic variants worth discussing. Because selection is typically concerned with objects, these variants are driven by two broad categories of selectable data.

In some cases, data is represented by distinct visual objects that can be manipulated independently of other objects. Icons on the Desktop and vector objects in drawing applications are examples. These objects are also commonly selected independently of their spatial relationships with each other. We refer to these as **discrete data**, and their selection as **discrete selection**. Discrete data is not necessarily homogeneous, and discrete selection is not necessarily contiguous.

Conversely, some applications represent data as a matrix of many small contiguous pieces of data. The text in a word processor or the cells in a spreadsheet are made up of hundreds or thousands of similar little objects that together form a coherent whole. These objects are often selected in contiguous groups, and so we call them **contiguous data,** and selection within them **contiguous selection**.

Both contiguous selection and discrete selection support single-click selection and click-and-drag selection. Single-clicking typically selects the smallest useful discrete amount and clicking and dragging selects a larger quantity, but there are other significant differences.

There is a natural order to the text in a word processor's document — it consists of contiguous data. Scrambling the order of the letters destroys the sense of the document. The characters flow from the beginning to the end in a meaningful continuum and selecting a word or paragraph makes sense in the context of the data, whereas random, disconnected selections are generally meaningless. Although it is theoretically possible to allow a discrete, discontiguous selection — several disconnected paragraphs, for example — the user's task of visualizing the selections and avoiding inadvertent, unwanted operations on them is more trouble than it is worth.

Discrete data, on the other hand, has no inherent order. Although many meaningful orders can be imposed on discrete objects (such as sorting a list of files by their modification dates), the lack of a single inherent relationship means that users are likely to want to make discrete selections (for example, Ctrl+clicking multiple files that are not listed adjacently). Of course, users may also want to make contiguous selections based upon some organizing principle (such as the old files at the bottom of that chronologically ordered list). The utility of both approaches is evident in a vector drawing application (such as Illustrator or PowerPoint). In some cases, a user will want to perform a contiguous selection on objects that are close to each other, and in other cases, she will want to select a single object.

Mutual exclusion

Typically, when a selection is made, any previous selection is unmade. This behavior is called **mutual exclusion**, as the selection of one excludes the selection of the other. Typically, a user clicks on an object and it becomes selected. That object remains selected until the user selects something else. Mutual exclusion is the rule in both discrete and contiguous selection.

Some applications allow users to deselect a selected object by clicking on it a second time. This can lead to a curious condition in which nothing at all is selected, and there is no insertion point. You must decide whether this condition is appropriate for your product.

Additive selection

Mutual exclusion is often appropriate for contiguous selection because users cannot see or know what effect their actions will have if selections can readily be scrolled off the screen. Selecting several independent paragraphs of text in a long document might be useful, but it isn't easily controllable, and it's easy for users to get into situations where they are causing unintended changes because they cannot see all of the data that they are acting upon. Scrolling, not the contiguous selection, creates the problem, but most programs that manage contiguous data are scrollable.

However, if there is no mutual exclusion for interactions involving discrete selection, a user can select many independent objects by clicking on them sequentially, in what is called **additive selection**. A list box, for example, can allow users to make as many selections as desired and to deselect them by clicking them a second time. After the user has selected the desired objects, the terminating verb acts on them collectively.

Most discrete-selection systems implement mutual exclusion by default and allow additive selection only by using a meta-key. In Windows, the Shift meta-key is used most frequently for this in contiguous selection; the Ctrl key is frequently used for discrete selection. In a draw program, for example, after you've clicked to select one graphical object, you typically can add another one to your selection by Shift-clicking.

While interfaces employing contiguous selection generally should not allow additive selection (at least without an overview mechanism to make additive selections manageable), contiguous-selection interfaces do need to allow selection to be *extended*. Again, meta-keys should be used. In Word, the Shift key causes everything between the initial selection and the Shift+click to be selected.

Some list boxes, as well as the file views in Windows (both examples of discrete data), do something a bit strange with additive selection. They use the Ctrl key to implement "normal" discrete additive selection, but then they use the Shift key to *extend* the selection, as if it were contiguous, not discrete data. In most cases this mapping adds confusion, because it conflicts with the common idiom for discrete additive selection.

Group Selection

The click-and-drag operation is also the basis for group selection. For contiguous data, it means "extend the selection" from the mouse-down point to the mouse-up point. This can also be modified with meta-keys. In Word, for example, Ctrl+click selects a complete sentence, so a Ctrl+drag extends the selection sentence by sentence. Sovereign applications should rightly enrich their interaction with these sorts of variants as appropriate. Experienced users will eventually come to memorize and use them, as long as the variants are manually simple.

In a collection of discrete objects, the click-and-drag operation generally begins a drag-and-drop move. If the mouse button is clicked in an area between objects, rather than on any specific object, it has a special meaning. It creates a **drag rectangle**, shown in Figure 19-5.

A drag rectangle is a dynamically sizable rectangle whose upper-left corner is the mouse-down point and whose lower-right corner is the mouse-up point. When the mouse button is released, any and all objects enclosed within the drag rectangle are selected as a group.

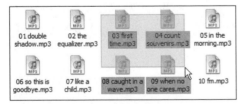

Figure 19-5 When the cursor is not on any particular object at mouse-down time, the click-and-drag operation normally creates a drag rectangle that selects any object wholly enclosed by it when the mouse button is released. This is a familiar idiom to users of drawing programs and many word processors. This example is taken from Windows Explorer. The rectangle has been dragged from the upper left to the lower right.

Insertion and replacement

As we've established, selection indicates on which object subsequent actions will operate. If that action involves creating or pasting new data or objects (via keystrokes or a PASTE command), they are somehow added to the selected object. In discrete selection, one or more discrete objects are selected, and the incoming data is handed to the selected discrete objects, which process the data in their own ways. This may cause a **replacement** action, where the incoming data replaces the selected object. Alternatively, the selected object may treat the incoming data in some predetermined way. In PowerPoint, for example, when a shape is selected, incoming keystrokes result in a text annotation of the selected shape.

In contiguous selection, however, the incoming data always replaces the currently selected data. When you type in a word processor or text-entry box, you replace what is selected with what you are typing. Contiguous selection exhibits a unique quirk: The selection can simply indicate a location *between* two elements of contiguous data, rather than any particular element of the data. This in-between place is called the **insertion point**.

In a word processor, the **caret** (usually a blinking vertical line that indicates where the next character will go) indicates a position between two characters in the text, without actually selecting either one of them. By pointing and clicking anywhere else, you can easily move the caret, but if you drag to extend the selection, the caret disappears and is replaced by the contiguous selection of text.

Spreadsheets also use contiguous selection but implement it somewhat differently than word processors do. The selection is contiguous because the cells form a contiguous matrix of data, but there is no concept of selecting the space between two cells. In the spreadsheet, a single-click will select exactly one whole cell. There is currently no concept of an insertion point in a spreadsheet, although the design possibilities are intriguing (that is, select the line between the top and bottom of two vertically adjacent cells and start typing to insert a row and fill a new cell in a single action).

A blend of these two idioms is possible as well. In PowerPoint's slide-sorter view, insertion-point selection is allowed, but single slides can be selected, too. If you click on a slide, that slide is selected, but if you click in between two slides, a blinking insertion-point caret is placed there.

If a program allows an insertion point, objects must be selected by clicking and dragging. To select even a single character in a word processor, the mouse must be dragged across it. This means that the user will be doing quite a bit of clicking and dragging in the normal course of using the program, with the side effect that any drag-and-drop idiom will be more difficult to express. You can see this in Word, where dragging and dropping text involves first a click-and-drag operation to make the selection, then another mouse move back into the selection to click and drag again for the actual move. To do the same thing, Excel makes you find a special pliant zone (only a pixel or two wide) on the border of the selected cell. To move a discrete selection, the user must click and drag on the object in a single motion. To relieve the click-and-drag burden of selection in word processors, other direct manipulation shortcuts are also implemented, like double-clicking to select a word.

Visual indication of selection

Selected objects must be clearly, boldly indicated as such to users. The selected state must be easy to spot on a crowded screen, must be unambiguous, and must not obscure normally visible details of the object.

 DESIGN principle   The selection state should be visually evident and unambiguous.

You must ensure that, in particular, users can easily tell which items are selected and which are not. It's not good enough just to be able to see that the items are different. Keep in mind that a significant portion of the population is color-blind, so color alone is insufficient to distinguish between selections.

Historically, inversion has been used to indicate selection (e.g., making the white pixels black and black pixels white). Although this is visually bold, it is not necessarily very readable, especially when it comes to full-color interfaces. Other approaches include colored backgrounds, outlines, pseudo-3D depression, handles, and animated marquees.

In drawing, painting, animation, and presentation programs, where users deal with visually rich objects, it's easy for selections to get lost. The best solution here is to add selection indicators to the object, rather than merely indicating selection by changing any of the selected object's visual properties. Most drawing programs take this approach, with **handles**: little boxes that surround the selected object, providing points of control.

With irregularly shaped selections (such as those in a image-manipulation program like Adobe Photoshop), handles can be confusing and get lost in the clutter. There is, however, one way to ensure that the selection will always be visible, regardless of the colors used: Indicate the selection by movement.

One of the first programs on the Macintosh, MacPaint, had a wonderful idiom where a selected object was outlined with a simple dashed line, except that the dashes all moved in synchrony around the object. The dashes looked like ants in a column; thus, this effect earned the colorful sobriquet **marching ants**. Today, this is commonly called a **marquee**, after the flashing lights on old cinema signs that exhibited a similar behavior.

Adobe PhotoShop uses this idiom to show selected regions of photographs, and it works extremely well (expert users can toggle it off and on with a keystroke so that they can see their work without visual distraction). The animation is not hard to do, although it takes some care to get it right, and it works regardless of the color mix and intensity of the background.

Drag-and-Drop

Of all the direct-manipulation idioms, nothing defines the GUI more than the drag-and-drop operation: clicking and holding the button while moving some object across the screen and releasing in a meaningful location. Surprisingly, drag-and-drop isn't used as widely as we'd like to think, and it certainly hasn't lived up to its full potential.

In particular, the popularity of the Web and the myth that Web-like behavior is synonymous with superior ease of use have set back the development of drag-and-drop on the desktop, as developers mistakenly emulated the crippled interactions of Web browsers in other, far less appropriate contexts. Luckily, as Web technology has been refined, programmers have been able to provide rich drag-and-drop behavior in the browser, and while this is still somewhat challenging, it seems that there is a resurgence in rich, expressive command idioms for all platforms.

We might define **drag-and-drop** as "clicking on an object and moving it to a new location," although that definition is somewhat narrow in scope for such a broad idiom. A more accurate description of drag-and-drop is "clicking on some object and moving it to imply a transformation."

The Macintosh was the first successful system to offer drag-and-drop. It raised a lot of expectations with the idiom that were never fully realized for two simple reasons. First, drag-and-drop wasn't a systemwide facility, but rather an artifact of the Finder, a single program. Second, as the Mac was at the time a single-tasking computer, the concept of drag-and-drop between applications didn't surface as an issue for many years.

To Apple's credit, they described drag-and-drop in their first user-interface standards guide. On the other side of the fence, Microsoft not only failed to put drag-and-drop aids in its early releases of Windows but didn't even describe the procedure in its programmer documentation. However, Microsoft eventually caught up and even pioneered some novel uses of the idiom, such as movable toolbars and dockable palettes.

While we generally use the term "direct manipulation" to refer to all kinds of GUI interaction idioms, when it comes to drag-and-drop, there are two levels of directness. First we have the true direct manipulation idioms where dragging-and-dropping represents putting the object somewhere, such as moving a file between two directories, opening a file in a specific application (by dropping a file icon on an application icon), or arranging objects on a canvas in drawing programs.

The second type of drag-and-drop idiom is little more indirect: A user drags the object to a specific area or onto another object in order to perform a function. These idioms are less popular but can be very useful. A good example of this can be found in the Mac OS X Automator (see Figure 19-6).

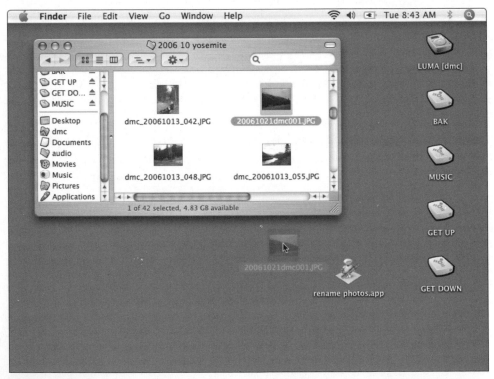

Figure 19-6 Apple's Automator tool in Mac OS X allows users to set up common workflows, such as renaming an image, that are then represented as an icon. Users can then drag and drop files or folders onto the workflow icon to perform the function. While this isn't, strictly speaking, direct manipulation, it does provide a reasonably direct way to invoke a command.

Visual feedback for drag-and-drop

As we've discussed, an interface should visually hint at its pliancy, either statically, in the way it is drawn, or actively, by animating as the cursor passes over it. The idea that an object can be dragged is easily learned idiomatically. While it is difficult for a user to forget that an icon, selected text, or other distinct object can be directly manipulated after learning the behavior, he may forget the details of the action, so feedback is very important *after* the user clicks on the object and starts dragging. The first-timer or very infrequent user will probably also require some additional help to get them started (e.g., textual hints built into the interface). Forgiving interactions and Undo encourage users to try direct manipulation without trepidation.

As soon as a user clicks the mouse button with the cursor on an object, that object becomes the source object for the duration of the drag-and-drop. As the user moves the mouse around with the button held down, the cursor passes over a variety of objects. It should be obvious which of these objects are meaningful drop targets. Until the button is released, these are called **drop candidates**. There can only be one source and one target in a drag, but there may be many drop candidates.

The only task of each drop candidate is to visually indicate that the hotspot of the captive cursor is over it, meaning that it will accept the drop — or at least comprehend it — if the user releases the mouse button. Such an indication is, by its nature, active visual hinting.

DESIGN principle   Drop candidates must visually indicate their receptivity.

The weakest way to offer the visual indication of receptivity to being dropped upon is by changing the cursor. It is the primary job of the cursor to represent what is being dragged. It is best to leave indication of drop candidacy to the drop candidate itself.

DESIGN principle   The drag cursor must visually identify the source object.

It is important that these two visual functions not be confused. Unfortunately, Microsoft seems to have done so in Windows, with its use of cursor hinting to indicate that something *is not* a drop target. This decision was likely made more for the ease of coding than for any design considerations. It is much easier to change the cursor than it is to highlight drop candidates to show their drop receptivity. The role of the cursor is to represent the master, the dragged object. It should not be used to represent the drop candidate.

As if that wasn't bad enough, Microsoft performs cursor hinting using the detestable circle with a bar sinister, the universal icon for Not Permitted. This symbol is an unpleasant idiom because it tells users what they can't do. It is negative feedback. A user can easily construe its meaning to be, "Don't let go of the mouse now, or you'll do some irreversible damage," instead of "Go ahead and let go now and nothing will happen." Adding the Not Permitted symbol to cursor hinting is an unfortunate combination of two weak idioms and should be avoided, regardless of what the Microsoft style guide says.

After a user finally releases the mouse button, the current drop candidate becomes the **target**. If the user releases the mouse button in the interstice between valid drop candidates, or over an invalid drop candidate, there is no target and the drag-and-drop operation ends with no action. Silence, or visual inactivity, is a good way to indicate this termination. It isn't a cancellation, exactly, so there is no need to show a cancel indicator.

Indicating drag pliancy

Active cursor hinting to indicate drag pliancy is a problematic solution. In an increasingly object-oriented world, more things can be dragged than not. A cursor flicking and changing rapidly can be more visual distraction than help. One solution is to just assume that things can be dragged and let users experiment. This method is reasonably successful in the Windows Explorer and Macintosh Finder windows. Without cursor hinting, drag pliancy can be a hard-to-discover idiom, so you might consider building some other indication into the interface, maybe a textual hint or a ToolTip-style pop-up.

After the source object is picked up and the drag operation begins, there must be some visual indication of this. The most visually rich method is to fully animate the drag operation, showing the entire source object moving in real time. This method can be hard to implement, can be annoyingly slow, and may introduce too much visual complexity into the interface. The problem is that a drag-and-drop operation can require a pretty precise pointer. For example, the source object may be 6-centimeters square, but it must be dropped on a target that is 1-centimeter square. The source object must not obscure the target, and because the source object is big enough to span multiple drop candidates, we need to use a cursor hotspot to precisely indicate which candidate it will be dropped on. What this means is that dragging a transparent outline or a thumbnail of the object may be much better than actually dragging an exact image of the source object or data. It also means that the dragged object can't obscure the normal arrow cursor. The tip of the arrow is needed to indicate the exact hotspot.

Dragging an outline also is appropriate for most repositioning, as the outline can be moved relative to the source object, still visible in its original position.

Indicating drop candidacy

As the cursor traverses the screen, carrying with it an outline of the source object, it passes over one drop candidate after another. These drop candidates must visually indicate that they are aware of being considered as potential drop targets. By visually changing, the drop candidate alerts users that they can do something constructive with the dropped object. (Of course, this requires that the software be smart enough to identify meaningful source-target combinations.)

A point, so obvious that it is difficult to see, is that the only objects that can be drop candidates are ones that are currently visible. A running application doesn't have to worry about visually indicating its readiness to be a target if it isn't visible. Usually, the number of objects occupying screen real estate is very small — a couple of dozen at most. This means that the implementation burden should not be overwhelming.

Insertion targets

In some applications, the source object can be dropped in the spaces between other objects. Dragging text in Word is such an operation, as are most reordering operations in lists or arrays. In these cases, a special type of visual hinting is drawn on the background "behind" the GUI objects of the program or in its contiguous data: an **insertion target**.

Rearranging slides in PowerPoint's slide-sorter view is a good example of this type of drag-and-drop. A user can pick up a slide and drag it into a different place in the presentation. As our user drags, the insertion target (a vertical black bar that looks like a big text edit caret) appears between slides. Word, too, shows an insertion target when you drag text. Not only is the loaded cursor apparent, but you also see a vertical gray bar showing the precise location, in between characters, where the dropped text will land.

Whenever something can be dragged and dropped on the space between other objects, the program must show an insertion target. Like a drop candidate in source-target drag-and-drop, the program must visually indicate where the dragged object can be dropped.

Visual feedback at completion

If the source object is dropped on a valid drop candidate, the appropriate operation then takes place. A vital step at this point is visual feedback that the operation has occurred. For example, if you're dragging a file from one directory to another, the source object must disappear from its source and reappear in the target. If the target represents a function rather than a container (such as a print icon), the icon must visually hint that it received the drop and is now printing. It can do this with animation or by otherwise changing its visual state.

Other drag-and-drop interaction issues

When we are first exposed to the drag-and-drop idiom, it seems simple, but for frequent users and in some special conditions, it can exhibit problems and difficulties that are not so simple. As usual, the iterative refinement process of software design has exposed these shortcomings, and in the spirit of invention, clever designers have devised equally clever solutions.

Auto-scrolling

What action should the program take when the selected object is dragged beyond the border of the enclosing application? Of course, the object is being dragged to a new position, but is that new position inside or outside of the enclosing application?

Take Microsoft Word, for example. When a piece of selected text is dragged outside the visible text window, is the user saying "I want to put this piece of text into another program" or is he saying "I want to put this piece of text somewhere else in this same document, but that place is currently scrolled off the screen"? If the former, we proceed as already discussed. But if the user desires the latter, the application must automatically scroll (**auto-scroll**) in the direction of the drag to reposition the selection at a distant, not currently visible location in the same document.

Auto-scroll is a very important adjunct to drag-and-drop. Wherever the drop target can possibly be scrolled offscreen, the program needs to auto-scroll.

 DESIGN principle   Any scrollable drag-and-drop target must auto-scroll.

In early implementations, auto-scrolling worked if you dragged outside of the application's window. This had two fatal flaws. First, if the application filled the screen, how could you get the cursor outside of the app? Second, if you want to drag the object to another program, how can the app tell the difference between that and the desire to auto-scroll?

Microsoft developed an intelligent solution to this problem. Basically, it begins auto-scrolling just *inside* the application's border instead of just *outside* the border. As the drag cursor approaches the borders of the scrollable window — but is still inside it — a scroll in the direction of the drag is initiated. If the drag cursor comes within about 30 pixels of the bottom of the text area, Word begins to scroll the window's contents upward. If the drag cursor comes equally close to the top edge of the text area, Word scrolls down.

Thankfully, in recent times developers have commonly implemented a variable auto-scroll rate as shown in Figure 19-7, where the automatic scrolling increases in speed as the cursor gets closer to the window edge. For example, when the cursor is 30 pixels from the upper edge, the text scrolls down at one line per second. At 15 pixels, the text scrolls at two lines per second, and so on. This gives the user sufficient control over the auto-scroll to make it useful in a variety of situations.

Another important detail required by auto-scrolling is a time delay. If auto-scrolling begins as soon as the cursor enters the sensitive zone around the edges, it is too easy for a slow-moving user to inadvertently auto-scroll. To cure this, auto-scrolling should begin only after the drag-cursor has been in the auto-scroll zone for some reasonable time cushion — about a half-second.

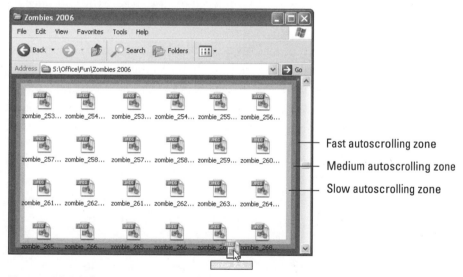

Figure 19-7 This image expresses the concept of variable-speed auto-scroll, as it could be applied to Windows Explorer. Unfortunately, in Windows XP, auto-scroll scrolls at a single speed that is impossible to control. It would be better if the auto-scroll went faster the closer the cursor gets to the edge of the window (though it's also important to have a speed limit — it doesn't help anyone if it goes too fast). To their credit, Microsoft's idea of auto-scrolling as the cursor approaches the *inside* edges of the enclosing scrollbox, rather than the outside, is very clever indeed.

If a user drags the cursor completely outside of the Word's scrollable text window, no auto-scrolling occurs. Instead, the repositioning operation will terminate in a program other than Word. For example, if the drag cursor goes outside of Word and is positioned over PowerPoint, when the user releases the mouse button, the selection will be pasted into the PowerPoint slide at the position indicated by the mouse. Furthermore, if the drag cursor moves within three or four millimeters of any of the borders of the PowerPoint Edit window, PowerPoint begins auto-scrolling in the appropriate direction. This is a very convenient feature, as the confines of contemporary screens mean that we often find ourselves with a loaded drag cursor and no place to drop its contents.

Avoiding drag-and-drop twitchiness

When an object can be either selected or dragged, it is vital that the mouse be biased towards the selection operation. Because it is so difficult to click on something without inadvertently moving the cursor a pixel or two, the frequent act of selecting something must not accidentally cause the program to misinterpret the action as the beginning of a drag-and-drop operation. Users rarely want to drag an object only one or two pixels across the screen. (And even in cases where they do, such as in drawing programs, it's useful to require a little extra effort to do so, in order to prevent frequent accidental repositioning.)

In the hardware world, controls like pushbuttons that have mechanical contacts can exhibit what engineers call **bounce**, which means that the tiny metal contacts of the switch literally bounce when someone presses them. For electrical circuits like doorbells, the milliseconds the bounce takes aren't meaningful, but in modern electronics, those extra clicks can be significant. The circuitry backing up such switches has special logic to ignore extra transitions if they occur within a few milliseconds of the first one. This keeps your stereo from turning back off a thousandth of a second after you've turned it on. This situation is analogous to the oversensitive mouse problem, and the solution is to copy switch makers and **debounce** the mouse.

To avoid inadvertent repositioning, programs should establish a **drag threshold**, in which all mouse-movement messages that arrive after the mouse-down event are ignored unless the movement exceeds a small threshold amount, such as three pixels. This provides some protection against initiating an inadvertent drag operation. If a user can keep the mouse button within three pixels of the mouse-down point, the entire click action is interpreted as a selection command, and all tiny, spurious moves are ignored. As soon as the mouse moves beyond the three-pixel threshold, the program can confidently change the operation to a drag. This is shown in Figure 19-8. Whenever an object can be selected and dragged, the drag operation should be debounced.

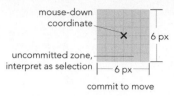

Figure 19-8 Any object that can be both selected and dragged must be debounced. When the user clicks on the object, the action must be interpreted as a selection rather than a drag, even if the user accidentally moves the mouse a pixel or two between the click and the release. The program must ignore any mouse movement as long as it stays within the uncommitted zone, which extends three pixels in each direction. After the cursor moves more than three pixels away from the mouse-down coordinate, the action changes to a drag, and the object is considered "in play." This is called a drag threshold.

 DESIGN principle   Debounce all drags.

Some applications may require more complex drag thresholds. Three-dimensional applications often require drag thresholds that enable movement in three projected axes on the screen. Another such example arose in the design of a report generator for one of our clients. A user could reposition columns on the report by dragging them horizontally; for example, he could put the First Name column to the left of the Last Name column by dragging it into position from anywhere in the column. This was, by far, the most frequently used drag-and-drop idiom. There was, however, another, infrequently used, drag operation. This one allowed the values in one column to be interspersed *vertically* with the values of another column — for example, an address field and a state field (see Figure 19-9).

We wanted to follow the persona's mental model and enable him to drag the values of one column on top of the values of another to perform this stacking operation, but this conflicted with the simple horizontal reordering of columns. We solved the problem by differentiating between horizontal drags and vertical drags. If a user dragged the column left or right, it meant that he was repositioning the column as a unit. If the user dragged the column up or down, it meant that he was interspersing the values of one column with the values of another.

Name	Address	City
1 Ginger Beef	342 Easton Lane	Waltham
2 C. U. Lator	339 Disk Drive	Borham
3 Justin Case	68 Elm	Albion
4 Creighton Barrel	9348 N. Blenheim	Five Island
5 Dewey Decimal	1003 Water St.	Freeport

Name	Address/City
1 Ginger Beef	342 Easton Lane Waltham
2 C. U. Lator	339 Disk Drive Borham
3 Justin Case	68 Elm Albion
4 Creighton Barrel	9348 N. Blenheim Five Island
5 Dewey Decimal	1003 Water St. Freeport

Figure 19-9 This report-generator program offered an interesting feature that enabled the contents of one column to be interspersed with the contents of another by dragging and dropping it. This direct-manipulation action conflicted with the more frequent drag-and-drop action of reordering the columns (like moving City to the left of Address). We used a special, two-axis drag threshold to accomplish this.

Because the horizontal drag was the predominant user action, and vertical drags were rare, we biased the drag threshold towards the horizontal axis. Instead of a square uncommitted zone, we created the spool-shaped zone shown in Figure 19-10. By setting the horizontal-motion threshold at four pixels, it didn't take a big movement to commit users to the normal horizontal move, while still insulating users from an inadvertent vertical move. To commit to the far less frequent vertical move, the user had to move the cursor eight pixels on the vertical axis without deviating more than four pixels left or right. The motion is quite natural and easily learned.

This axially nonsymmetric threshold can be used in other ways, too. Visio implements a similar idiom to differentiate between drawing a straight and a curved line.

Fine scrolling

The weakness of the mouse as a precision pointing tool is readily apparent, particularly when dragging objects around in drawing programs. It is darned hard to drag something to the exact desired spot, especially when the screen resolution is 72 pixels per inch and the mouse is running at a six-to-one ratio to the screen. To move the cursor one pixel, you must move the mouse about 1/500th of an inch. Not easy to do.

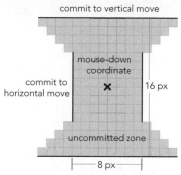

Figure 19-10 This spool-shaped drag threshold allowed a bias towards horizontal dragging in a client's program. Horizontal dragging was, by far, the most frequently used type of drag in this application. This drag threshold made it difficult for a user to inadvertently begin a vertical drag. However, if the user really wanted to drag vertically, a bold move either up or down would cause the program to commit to the vertical mode with a minimum of excise.

This is solved by adding a **fine scrolling** function, whereby users can quickly shift into a mode that allows much finer resolution for mouse-based manipulation of objects. During a drag, if a user decides that he needs more precise maneuvering, he can change the ratio of the mouse's movement to the object's movement on the screen. Any program that might demand precise alignment must offer a fine scrolling facility. This includes, at a minimum, all drawing and painting programs, presentation programs, and image-manipulation programs.

 DESIGN principle   Any program that demands precise alignment must offer a vernier.

There are several variants of this idiom. Commonly, using a meta-key while dragging puts the mouse into vernier mode. In vernier mode, every 10 pixels of mouse movement will be interpreted as a single pixel of object movement.

Another effective method is to make the arrow keys active during a drag operation. While holding down the mouse button, a user can manipulate the arrow keys to move the selection up, down, left, or right — one pixel at a time. The drag operation is still terminated by releasing the mouse button.

The problem with such a vernier is that the simple act of releasing the mouse button can often cause a user's hand to shift a pixel or two, causing the perfectly placed object to slip out of alignment just at the moment of acceptance. The solution to this is, upon receipt of the first vernier keystroke, to **desensitize** the mouse. This is accomplished by making the mouse ignore all subsequent movements under some reasonable threshold, say five pixels. This means that a user can make the initial gross movements with the mouse, then make a final, precise placement with the arrow keys, and release the mouse button without disturbing the placement. If the user wants to make additional gross movements after beginning the vernier, he simply moves the mouse beyond the threshold, and the system shifts back out of vernier mode.

If the arrow keys are not otherwise spoken for in the interface, as in a drawing program, they can be used to control vernier movement of the selected object. This means that a user does not have to hold the mouse button down. Adobe Illustrator and Photoshop do this, as does PowerPoint. In PowerPoint, the arrow keys move the selected object one step on the grid — about 2 millimeters using the default grid settings. If you hold the Alt key down while using the arrow keys, the movement is one pixel per arrow keystroke.

Control Manipulation

Controls are the fundamental building blocks of the modern graphical user interface. While we discuss the topic in detail in Chapter 21, in our current discussion of direct manipulation it is worth addressing the mouse interactions required by several controls.

Many controls, particularly menus, require the moderately difficult motion of a click-and-drag rather than a mere click. This direct-manipulation operation is more demanding of users because of its juxtaposition of fine motions with gross motions to click, drag, and then release the mouse button. Although menus are not used as frequently as toolbar controls, they are still used very often, particularly by new or infrequent users. Thus, we find one of the more intractable conundrums of GUI design: The menu is the primary control for beginners, yet it is one of the more difficult controls to physically operate.

There is no solution to this problem other than to provide additional idioms to accomplish the same task. If a function is available from the menu, and it is one that will be used more than just rarely, make sure to provide idioms for invoking the function that don't require a click-and-drag operation, such as a toolbar button.

One nice feature in Windows, which Mac OS has also adopted, is the capability to work its menus with a series of single clicks rather than clicking and dragging. You click on the menu, and it drops down. You point to the desired item, click once to select it and close the menu. Microsoft further extended this idea by putting programs into a sort of **menu mode** as soon as you click once on any menu. When in this mode, all the top-level menus in the program and all the items on those menus are active, just as though you were clicking and dragging. As you move the mouse around, each menu, in turn, drops down without your having to use the mouse button at all. This can be disconcerting if you are unfamiliar with it, but after the initial shock has worn off, the behavior is a definite improvement over having to hold the mouse button down, mostly because it is easier on the wrist.

Palette Tools

In many drawing and painting programs, when a user selects a tool from a palette the cursor changes so that it will perform specific functions upon clicking and dragging. Palette tools have their own unique behaviors, which are worthy of separate mention here. There are two basic variants of palette tool behavior: modal tools and charged cursor tools.

Modal tools

With **modal tools**, the user selects a tool from a list or specialized toolbar, usually called a toolbox or palette. The display area of the program is then completely in that tool's mode: It will only do that one tool's job. The cursor usually changes to indicate the active tool.

When a user clicks and drags with the tool on the drawing area, the tool does its thing. If the active tool is a spray can, for example, the program enters Spray Can mode and it can only spray. The tool can be used over and over, spraying as much ink as the user desires until he clicks on a different tool. If the user wants to use some other tool on the graphic, like an eraser, he must return to the toolbox and select the eraser tool. The program then enters Eraser mode and on the canvas, the cursor will only erase things until the user chooses another tool. There is usually a selection-cursor tool on the palette to let the user return the cursor to a selection-oriented pointer, as in Adobe Photoshop, for example.

Modal tools work for tools that perform **actions** on drawings — such as an eraser — or for **shapes** that can be drawn — such as ellipses. The cursor can become an eraser tool and erase anything previously entered, or it can become an ellipse tool and draw any number of new ellipses. The mouse-down event anchors a corner or center of the shape (or its bounding-box), the user drags to stretch out the shape to the desired size and aspect, and the mouse-up event confirms the draw.

Modal tools are not bothersome in a program like Paint, where the number of drawing tools is very small. In a more advanced drawing program, such as Adobe

Photoshop, however, the modality is very disruptive because, as users get more facile with the cursor and the tools, the percentage of time and motion devoted to selecting and deselecting tools — the excise — increases dramatically. Modal tools are excellent idioms for introducing users to the range of features of such a program, but they don't usually scale well for intermediate users of more sophisticated programs. Luckily, Photoshop makes extensive use of keyboard commands for power users.

The difficulty of managing a modal tool application isn't caused by the modality as much as it is by the sheer quantity of tools. More precisely, the efficiencies break down when the quantity of tools in a user's working set gets too large. A working set of more than a handful of modal tools tends to get hard to manage. If the number of necessary tools in Adobe Illustrator could be reduced from 24 to 8, for example, its user interface problems might diminish below the threshold of user pain.

To compensate for the profusion of modal tools, products like Adobe Illustrator use meta-keys to modify the various modes. The Shift key is commonly used for constrained drags, but Illustrator adds many nonstandard meta-keys and uses them in nonstandard ways. For example, holding down the Alt key while dragging an object drags away a *copy* of that object, but the Alt key is also used to promote the selector tool from single vertex selection to object selection. The distinction between these uses is subtle: If you click something, then press the Alt key, you drag away a copy of it. Alternately, if you press the Alt key and *then* click on something, you select all of it, rather than a single vertex of it. But then, to further confuse matters, you must *release* the Alt key or you will drag away a copy of the entire object. To do something as simple as selecting an entire object and dragging it to a new position, you must press the Alt key, point to the object, click and hold the mouse button without moving the mouse, release the Alt key, and then drag the object to the desired position! What were these people thinking?

Admittedly, the possible combinations are powerful, but they are very hard to learn, hard to remember, and hard to use. If you are a graphic arts professional working with Illustrator for eight hours a day, you can turn these shortcomings into benefits in the same way that a race car driver can turn the cantankerous behavior of a finely tuned automobile into an asset on the track. The casual user of Illustrator, however, is like the average driver behind the wheel of an Indy car: way out of his depth with a temperamental and unsuitable tool.

Charged cursor tools

With **charged cursor** tools, users again select a tool or shape from a palette, but this time, rather than the cursor switching permanently (until the user switches again) to the selected tool, the cursor becomes loaded — or **charged** — with a single instance of the selected object.

When a user clicks once in the drawing area, an instance of the object is created on the screen at the mouse-up point. The charged cursor doesn't work too well for functions (though Microsoft uses it ubiquitously for its Format Painter function), but it is nicely suited for graphic objects. PowerPoint, for example, uses it extensively. A user selects a rectangle from the graphics palette, and the cursor then becomes a modal rectangle tool charged with exactly one rectangle.

In many charged cursor programs like PowerPoint, a user cannot always deposit the object with a simple click but must drag a bounding rectangle to determine the size of the deposited object. Some programs, like Visual Basic, allow either method. A single click of a charged cursor creates a single instance of the object in a default size. The new object is created in a state of selection, surrounded by **handles** (which we'll discuss in the next section), and ready for immediate precision reshaping and resizing. This dual mode, allowing either a single-click for a default-sized object or dragging a rectangle for a custom-sized object, is certainly the most flexible and discoverable method that will satisfy most users.

Sometimes charged cursor programs forget to change the appearance of the cursor. For example, although Visual Basic changes the cursor to crosshairs when it's charged, Delphi doesn't change it at all. If the cursor has assumed a modal behavior — if clicking it somewhere will create something — it is important that it visually indicate this state. A charged cursor also demands good cancel idioms. Otherwise, how do you harmlessly discharge the cursor?

Object Manipulation

Like controls, data objects on the screen, particularly graphical objects in drawing and modeling programs, can be manipulated by clicking and dragging. Objects (other than icons, which were discussed earlier in this chapter) depend on click-and-drag motions for three main operations: repositioning, resizing, and reshaping.

Repositioning

Repositioning is the simple act of clicking on an object and dragging it to a new location. The most significant design issue regarding repositioning is that it usurps the place of other direct-manipulation idioms. The repositioning function demands the click-and-drag action, making it unavailable for other purposes.

The most common solution to this conflict is to dedicate a specific physical area of the object to the repositioning function. For example, you can reposition a window in Windows or on the Macintosh by clicking and dragging its title bar. The rest of the window is not pliant for repositioning, so the click-and-drag idiom is available for functions within the window, as you would expect. The only hints that the window can be dragged are its color and slight dimensionality of the title bar, a subtle visual hint that is purely idiomatic. (Thankfully, the idiom is very effective.)

In general, however, you should provide more explicit visual hinting of an area's pliancy. For a title bar, you could use cursor hinting or a gripable texture as a pliancy hint.

To move an object, it must first be selected. This is why selection must take place on the mouse-down transition: The user can drag without having to first click and release on an object to select it, then click and drag it to reposition it. It feels so much more natural to simply click it and then drag it to where you want it in one easy motion.

This creates a problem for moving contiguous data. In Word, for example, Microsoft uses this clumsy click-wait-click operation to drag chunks of text. You must click and drag to select a section of text, wait a second or so and click, then drag to move it. This is unfortunate, but there is no good alternative for contiguous selection. If Microsoft were willing to dispense with its meta-key idioms for extending the selection, those same meta-keys could be used to select a sentence and drag it in a single movement, but this still wouldn't solve the problem of selecting and moving arbitrary chunks of text.

When repositioning, a meta-key (such as Shift) is often used to constrain the drag to a single dimension (either horizontal or vertical). This type of drag is called a **constrained drag.** Constrained drags are extremely helpful in drawing programs, particularly when drawing neatly organized diagrams. The predominant motion of the first five or ten pixels of the drag determines the angle of the drag. If a user begins dragging on a predominantly horizontal axis, for example, the drag will henceforth be constrained to the horizontal axis. Some applications interpret constraints differently, letting users shift angles in mid-drag by dragging the mouse across a threshold.

Another way to assist users as they move objects around onscreen is by providing **guides.** In the most common implementations (such as in Adobe Illustrator), they are special lines that a user may place as references to be used when positioning objects. Commonly, a user may tell the application to "snap" to the guides, which means that if an object is dragged within a certain distance of the guide, the application will assume that it should be aligned directly with the guide. Typically this can be overridden with a keyboard nudge.

A novel and useful variation on this concept is OmniGraffle's Smart Guides, which provide dynamic visual feedback and assistance with the positioning of objects, based upon the (very reasonable) assumption that users are likely to want to align objects to each other and to create evenly spaced rows and columns of these aligned objects. Google's SketchUp (described at greater length later in the chapter) provides similar help with three-dimensional sketches.

Resizing and reshaping

When it comes to windows in a GUI, there isn't really any functional difference between resizing and reshaping. A user can adjust a window's size and aspect ratio at the same time by dragging a control on the lower-right corner of a window. It is also possible to drag on any window edge. These interactions are typically supported by clear cursor hinting.

Such idioms are appropriate for resizing windows, but when the object to be resized is a graphical element (as in a drawing or modeling program), it is important to communicate clearly which object is selected, and where a user must click to resize or reshape the object. A resizing idiom for graphical objects must be visually bold to differentiate itself from parts of the drawing, especially the object it controls, and it must not obscure the user's view of the object and the area around it. The resizer must also not obscure the resizing action.

A popular idiom accomplishes these goals; it consists of eight little black squares positioned one at each corner of a rectangular object and one centered on each side. These little black squares, shown in Figure 19-11, are called **resize handles** (or, simply, **handles**).

Handles are a boon to designers because they can also indicate selection. This is a naturally symbiotic relationship because an object must usually be selected to be resizable.

The handle centered on each side moves only that side, while the other sides remain motionless. The handles on the corners simultaneously move both the sides they touch, an interaction that is quite visually intuitive.

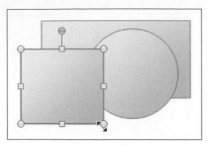

Figure 19-11 The selected object has eight handles, one at each corner and one centered on each side. The handles indicate selection and are a convenient idiom for resizing and reshaping the object. Handles are sometimes implemented with pixel inversion, but in a multicolor universe they can get lost in the clutter. These handles from Microsoft PowerPoint 2007 feature a small amount of dimensional rendering to help them stand out on the slide.

Handles tend to obscure the object they represent, so they don't make very good permanent controls. This is why we don't see them on top-level resizable windows (although windows in some versions of Sun's Open Look GUI come close). For that situation, frame or corner resizers are better idioms. If the selected object is larger than the screen, the handles may not be visible. If they are hidden offscreen, not only are they unavailable for direct manipulation, but they are also useless as indicators of selection.

As with dragging, a meta-key is often used to constrain the direction of a resize interaction. Another example of a constrained drag idiom, Shift is again used to force the resize to maintain the original aspect ratio of the object. This can be quite useful. In some cases, it's also useful to constrain the resize to either a vertical, horizontal, or locked aspect ratio.

Notice that the assumption in this discussion of handles is that the object in question is rectangular or can be easily bounded by a rectangle. If a user is creating an organization chart this may be fine, but what about reshaping more complex objects? There is a very powerful and useful variant of the resize handle: a **vertex handle**.

Many programs draw objects on the screen with **polylines**. A **polyline** is a graphics programmer's term for a multisegment line defined by an array of vertices. If the last vertex is identical to the first vertex, it is a closed form and the polyline forms a polygon. When the object is selected, the program, rather than placing eight handles as it does on a rectangle, places one handle on top of every vertex of the polyline. A user can then drag any vertex of the polyline independently and actually change one small aspect of the object's internal shape rather than affecting it as a whole. This is shown in Figure 19-12.

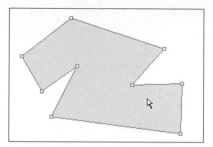

Figure 19-12 These are vertex handles, so named because there is one handle for each vertex of the polygon. The user can click and drag any handle to reshape the polygon, one segment at a time. This idiom is primarily useful for drawing programs.

Freeform objects in PowerPoint are rendered with polylines. If you click on a freeform object, it is given a bounding rectangle with the standard eight handles. If you right-click on the freeform object and choose Edit Points from the context menu, the bounding rectangle disappears and vertex handles appear instead. It is important that both these idioms are available, as the former is necessary to scale the image in proportion, whereas the latter is necessary to fine-tune the shape.

If the object in question is curved, rather than a collection of straight lines, the best mechanism to allow for reshaping is the Bézier handle. Like a vertex of a polyline, it expresses a point on the object, but it also expresses the shape of the curve at the point. Bézier curves require a good deal of skill to operate effectively and are probably best reserved for specialized drawing and modeling applications.

3D object manipulation

Working with precision on three-dimensional objects presents considerable interaction challenges for users equipped with 2D input devices and displays. Some of the most interesting research in UI design involves trying to develop better paradigms for 3D input and control. So far, however, there seem to be no real revolutions but merely evolutions of 2D idioms extended into the world of 3D.

Most 3D applications are concerned either with precision drafting (for example, architectural CAD) or with 3D animation. When models are being created, animation presents problems similar to those of drafting. An additional layer of complexity is added, however, in making these models move and change over time. Often, animators create models in specialized applications and then load these models into different animation tools.

There is such a depth of information about 3D-manipulation idioms that an entire chapter or even an entire book could be written about them. We will, thus, briefly address some of the broader issues of 3D object manipulation.

Display issues and idioms

Perhaps the most significant issue in 3D interaction on a 2D screen is that surrounding lack of parallax, the binocular ability to perceive depth. Without resorting to expensive, esoteric goggle peripherals, designers are left with a small bag of tricks with which to conquer this problem. Another important issue is one of occlusion: near objects obscuring far objects. These navigational issues, along with some of the input issues discussed in the next section, are probably a large part of the reason virtual reality hasn't yet become the GUI of the future.

Multiple Viewpoints

Use of **multiple viewpoints** is perhaps the oldest method of dealing with both of these issues, but it is, in many ways, the least effective from an interaction standpoint. Nonetheless, most 3D modeling applications present multiple views on the screen, each displaying the same object or scene from a different angle. Typically, there is a top view, a front view, and a side view, each aligned on an absolute axis, which can be zoomed in or out. There is also usually a fourth view, an orthographic or perspective projection of the scene, the precise parameters of which can be adjusted by the user. When these views are provided in completely separate windows, each with its own frame and controls, this idiom becomes quite cumbersome: Windows invariably overlap each other, getting in each other's way, and valuable screen real estate is squandered with repetitive controls and window frames. A better approach is to use a multipane window that permits one-, two-, three-, and four-pane configurations (the three-pane configuration has one big pane and two smaller panes). Configuration of these views should be as close to single-click actions as possible, using a toolbar or keyboard shortcut.

The shortcoming of multiple viewpoint displays is that they require users to look in several places at the same time to figure out the position of an object. Forcing a user to locate something in a complex scene by looking at it from the top, side, and front, and then expecting him to triangulate in his head in real time is a bit much to expect, even from modeling whizzes. Nonetheless, multiple viewpoints *are* helpful for precisely aligning objects along a particular axis.

Baseline grids, depthcueing, shadows, and poles

Baseline grids, depthcueing, shadows, and poles are idioms that help get around some of the problems created by multiple viewpoints. The idea behind these idioms is to allow users to successfully perceive the location and movement of objects in a 3D scene projected in an orthographic or perspective view.

Baseline grids provide virtual floors and walls to a scene, one for each axis, which serve to orient users. This is especially useful when (as is usually the case) the camera viewpoint can be freely rotated.

Depthcueing is a means by which objects deeper in the field of view appear dimmer. This effect is typically continuous, so even a single object's surface will exhibit depthcueing, giving useful clues about its size, shape, and extent. Depthcueing, when used on grids, helps disambiguate the orientation of the grid in the view.

One method used by some 3D applications for positioning objects is the idea of **shadows** — outlines of selected objects projected onto the grids as if a light is shining perpendicularly to each grid. As the user moves the object in 3D space, she can track, by virtue of these shadows or silhouettes, how she is moving (or sizing) the object in each dimension.

Shadows work pretty well, but all those grids and shadows can get in the way visually. An alternative is the use of a single **floor grid** and a **pole**. Poles work in conjunction with a horizontally oriented grid. When a user selects an object, a vertical line extends from the center of the object to the grid. As she moves the object, the pole moves with it, but the pole remains vertical. The user can see where in 3D space she is moving the object by watching where the base of the pole moves on the surface of the grid (x- and y-axes), and also by watching the length and orientation of the pole in relation to the grid (z-axis).

Guidelines and other rich visual hints

The idioms described in the previous section are all examples of rich visual modeless feedback, which we will discuss in detail in Chapter 25. However, for some applications, lots of grids and poles may be overkill. For example, Google's SketchUp is an architectural sketching program where users can lay down their own drafting lines using tape measure and protractor tools and, as they draw out their sketches, get color-coded hinting that keeps them oriented to the right axes. Users can also turn on a blue-gradient sky and a ground color to help keep them oriented. Because the application is focused on architectural sketching, not general-purpose 3D modeling or animation, the designers were able to pull off a spare, powerful, and simple interface that is easy to both learn and use (see Figure 19-13).

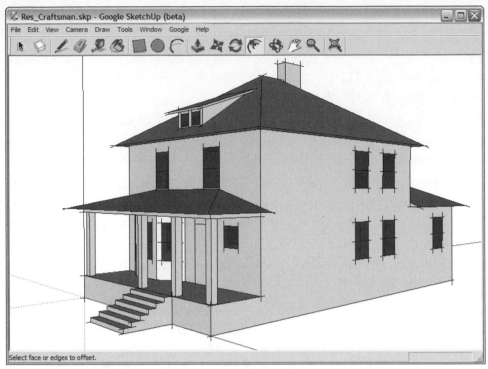

Figure 19-13 Google's SketchUp is a gem of an application that combines powerful 3D architectural sketching capability with smooth interaction, rich feedback, and a manageable set of design tools. Users can set sky color and real-world shadows according to location, orientation, and time of day and year. These not only help in presentation but also help orient users. Users also can lay down 3D grid and measurement guides just as in a 2D sketching application. Camera rotate and zoom functions are cleverly mapped to the mouse scroll wheel, allowing fluid access while using other tools. ToolTips provide textual hints that assist in drawing lines and aligning objects.

Wire frames and bounding boxes

Wire frames and **bounding boxes** solve problems of object visibility. In the days of slower processors, all objects needed to be represented as wire frames because computers weren't fast enough to render solid surfaces in real time. It is fairly common these days for modeling applications to render a rough surface for selected objects, while leaving unselected objects as wire frames. Transparency would also work, but is still very computing-intensive. In highly complex scenes, it is sometimes necessary or desirable, but not ideal, to render only the bounding boxes of unselected objects.

Input issues and idioms

3D applications make use of many idioms such as drag handles and vertex handles that have been adapted from 2D to 3D. However, there are some special issues surrounding 3D input.

Drag thresholds

One of the fundamental problems with direct manipulation in a 2D projection of a 3D scene is the problem of translating 2D motions of the cursor in the plane of the screen into a more meaningful movement in the virtual 3D space.

In a 3D projection, a different kind of drag threshold is required to differentiate between movement in three, not just two, axes. Typically, up and down mouse movements translate into movement along one axis, whereas 45-degree-angle drags are used for each of the other two axes. SketchUp provides color-coded hinting in the form of dotted lines when the user drags parallel to a particular axis, and it also hints with ToolTips. In a 3D environment, rich feedback in the form of cursor and other types of hinting becomes a necessity.

The picking problem

The other significant problem in 3D manipulation is known as the **picking problem**. Because objects need to be in wire frame or otherwise transparent when assembling scenes, it becomes difficult to know which of many overlapping items a user wants to select when she mouses over it. Locate highlighting can help but is insufficient because the object may be completely occluded by others. Group selection is even trickier.

Many 3D applications resort to less direct techniques, such as an object list or object hierarchy that users can select from outside of the 3D view. Although this kind of interaction has its uses, there are more direct approaches.

For example, hovering over a part of a scene could open a ToolTip-like menu that lets users select one or more overlapping objects (this menu wouldn't be necessary in the simple case of one unambiguous object). If individual facets, vertices, or edges can be selected, each should hint at its pliancy as the mouse rolls over it.

Although it doesn't address the issue directly, a smooth and simple way to navigate around a scene can also ameliorate the picking problem. SketchUp has mapped both zoom and **orbit** functions to the mouse scroll wheel. Spin the wheel to zoom in towards or away from the central zero point in 3D space; press and hold the wheel to switch from whatever tool you are using to orbit mode, which allows the camera to circle around the central axes in any direction. This fluid navigation makes manipulation of an architectural model almost as easy as rotating it in your hand.

Object rotation, camera movement, rotation, and zoom

One more issue specific to 3D applications is the number of spatial manipulation functions that can be performed. Objects can be repositioned, resized, and reshaped in three axes. They can also be rotated in three axes. Beyond this, the camera viewpoint can be rotated in place or revolved around a focal point, also in three axes. Finally, the camera's field of view can be zoomed in and out.

Not only does this mean that assignment of meta-keys and keyboard shortcuts is critical in 3D applications, there is another problem: It can be difficult to tell the difference between camera transformations and object transformations by looking at a camera viewpoint, even though the actual difference between the two can be quite significant. One way around this problem is to include a thumbnail, absolute view of the scene in a corner of the screen. It could be enlarged or reduced as needed, and could provide a reality check and global navigation method in case the user gets lost in space (note that this kind of thumbnail view is useful for navigating large 2D diagrams as well).

Object Connection

A direct-manipulation idiom that can be very powerful in some applications is **connection**, in which a user clicks and drags from one object to another, but instead of dragging the first object onto the second, a connecting line or arrow is drawn from the first object to the second one.

If you use project management or organization chart programs, you are undoubtedly familiar with this idiom. For example, to connect one task box in a project manager's network diagram (often called a PERT chart) with another, you click and drag an arrow between them. In this case the direction of the connection is significant: The task where the mouse button went down is the *from* task, and the task where the mouse button is released is the *to* task.

As a connection is dragged between objects, it provides visual feedback in the form of **rubber-banding**: The arrow forms a line that extends from the first object to the current cursor position. The line is animated, following the movement of the cursor with one end, while remaining anchored at its other end. As a user moves the cursor over connection candidates, cursor hinting should suggest that the two objects may be connected. After the user releases the mouse button over a valid target, the program draws a more permanent line or arrow between the two objects. In some applications, it also links the objects logically. As with drag-and-drop, it's vital to provide a convenient means of canceling the action, such as the Esc key or chord-clicking.

Connections can also be full-fledged objects themselves, with reshape handles and editable properties. This sort of implementation would mean connections could be independently selected, moved, and deleted as well. For programs where connections between objects need to contain information (such as in a project-planning application), it makes sense for connections to be first-class citizens.

Connection doesn't require as much cursor hinting as other idioms do because the rubber-banding effect is so clearly visible. However, it would be a big help in programs where objects are connected logically, to show which currently pointed-to objects are valid targets for the arrow. In other words, if the user drags an arrow until it points to some icon or widget on the screen, how can he tell if that icon or widget can legally be connected to? The answer is to have the potential target object engage in some active visual hinting. This hinting for potential targets can be quite subtle, or even eschewed completely when all objects in the program are equally valid targets for any connection. Target objects should always highlight, however, when a connection is dragged over them, in order to indicate willingness to accept the connection.

20

Window Behaviors

Any book on user interface design must discuss windows (with a lowercase w), a hallmark of the modern graphical user interface. While windowing systems provide modularity and flexibility to user interfaces, they can be horribly abused. In this chapter, we'll first place these omnipresent rectangles in some historical perspective and then discuss important design considerations for the use of windows in applications.

PARC and the Alto

Modern GUIs all derive their appearance from the Xerox Alto, an experimental desktop computer system developed in the mid-1970s at Xerox's Palo Alto Research Center (PARC), now PARC, Inc. PARC's Alto was the first computer with a graphical interface and was designed to explore the potential of computers as desktop business systems. The Alto was designed as a networked office system where documents could be composed, edited, and viewed in WYSIWYG (what you see is what you get) form, stored, retrieved, transferred electronically between workstations, and printed. The Alto system contributed many significant innovations to the vernacular of desktop computing that we now regard as commonplace: The mouse, the rectangular window, the scrollbar, the pushbutton, the "desktop metaphor," object-oriented programming, drop-down menus, Ethernet, and laser printing.

PARC's effect on the industry and contemporary computing was profound. Both Steve Jobs and Bill Gates, chairmen of Apple Computer and Microsoft, respectively, saw the Alto at PARC and were indelibly impressed.

Xerox tried to commercialize the Alto itself, and later a derivative computer system called the Star, but both were expensive, complex, agonizingly slow, and commercial failures. It was widely felt that executive management at Xerox, then primarily a copy machine company, didn't have the vision or the gumption to put a concerted effort behind marketing and selling the "paperless office." The brain trust at PARC, realizing that Xerox had blown an opportunity of legendary proportions, began an exodus that greatly enriched other software companies, particularly Apple and Microsoft.

Steve Jobs and his PARC refugees immediately tried to duplicate the Alto/Star with the Lisa. In many ways they succeeded, including copying the Star's failure to deal with reality. The Lisa was remarkable, accessible, exciting, too expensive ($9995 in 1983), and frustratingly slow. Even though it was a decisive commercial failure, it ignited the imagination of many people in the small but booming microcomputer industry.

Meanwhile, Bill Gates was less impressed by the sexy "graphicalness" of the Alto/Star than he was by the advantages of an object-oriented presentation and communication model. Software produced by Microsoft in the early 1980s, notably the spreadsheet Multiplan (the forerunner of Excel), reflected this thinking.

Steve Jobs wasn't deterred by the failure of the Lisa. He was convinced that PARC's vision of a truly graphical personal computer was an idea whose time had come. He added to his cadre of PARC refugees by raiding Apple's various departments for skilled and energetic individuals, then set up a skunk works to develop a commercially viable incarnation of the Alto. The result was the legendary Macintosh, a machine that has had enormous influence on our technology, design, and culture. The Mac single-handedly brought an awareness of design and aesthetics to the industry. It not only raised the standards for user-friendliness, but it also enfranchised a whole population of skilled individuals from disparate fields who were previously locked out of computing because of the industry's self-absorption in techno-trivia.

The almost-religious aura surrounding the Macintosh was also associated with many aspects of the Mac's user interface. The drop-down menus, metaphors, dialog boxes, rectangular overlapping windows, and other elements all became part of the mystique. Unfortunately, because its design has acquired these heroic proportions, its shortcomings go unexamined.

PARC's Principles

The researchers at PARC, in addition to developing a revolutionary set of hardware and software technologies to create the Alto, also pioneered many of the concepts held as gospel today in the world of GUI design and development.

Visual metaphors

One of the ideas that emerged from PARC was the *visual metaphor*. At PARC, the global visual metaphor was considered critical to a user's ability to understand the system, and thus critical to the success of the product and its concept. As we discussed in Chapter 13, the use of metaphor in interaction design can be severely limiting. It isn't surprising, though, that early interface designers found the approach compelling in the face of a potential user population largely unfamiliar with computers.

Avoiding modes

Another principle associated with the modern GUI is the notion that modes should be avoided. A **mode** is a state the program can enter where the effects of a user's action changes from the norm — essentially a behavioral detour.

For example, older programs demanded that you shift into a special state to enter records, and then shift into another state to print them out. These behavioral states are modes, and they can be extremely confusing and frustrating. Larry Tesler, former PARC researcher and former Chief Scientist at Apple, was an early advocate of eliminating modes from software and was pictured in an influential magazine wearing a T-shirt with the bold legend "Don't mode me in." His license plate read, "NOMODES." In a command-line environment, modes are indeed poisonous. However, in the object-verb world of a GUI, they aren't inherently evil, although *poorly designed* modes can be terribly frustrating. Unfortunately, the don't-mode-me-in principle has become an unquestioned part of our design vernacular.

Arguably, the most influential program on the Macintosh was MacPaint, a program with a thoroughly modal interface. This program enabled users to draw pixel-by-pixel on the computer screen. A user selected one tool from a palette of a dozen or so and then drew on the screen with it. Selecting a tool is entering a mode because, when a tool is selected, the behavior of the program conforms to the attributes of that tool. The program can only behave in one way.

The PARC researchers weren't wrong, just misunderstood. The user-interface benefits of MacPaint, when compared with contemporary programs, were great, but they didn't accrue from its imagined modelessness. Rather, they resulted from the ease with which the user could see which mode the program was in and the effortlessness of changing that mode.

Overlapping windows

Another Mac fundamental that emerged from PARC (and which has metastasized in Microsoft Windows) is the idea of overlapping rectangular windows. The rectangular theme of modern GUIs is so dominating and omnipresent that it is often seen as vital to the success of visual interaction.

There are good reasons for displaying data in rectangular panes. Probably the least important of these is that it is a good match for our display technology: CRTs and LCDs have an easier time with rectangles than with other shapes. More important is the fact that most data output used by humans is in a rectangular format: We have viewed text on rectangular sheets since Gutenberg, and most other forms, such as photographs, film, and video also conform to a rectangular grid. Rectangular graphs and diagrams are also the easiest for us to make sense of. There's something about rectangles that just seems to work cognitively for humans. Rectangles are also quite space-efficient.

Overlapping windows demonstrated clearly that there are better ways to transfer control between concurrently running programs other than typing in obscure commands. They were initially intended to represent overlapping sheets of paper on a user's desktop. Okay, but why? The answer again goes back to the global metaphor of the desktop. Your desk, if it is like ours, is covered with papers; when you want to read or edit one, you pull it out of the pile, lay it on top, and get to work. The problem is that this works only as well as it does on a real desktop and that isn't particularly well, especially if your desk is covered with papers and is only 21 inches across diagonally.

The overlapping window *concept* is good, but its execution is impractical in the real world. The overlapping-sheets-of-paper metaphor starts to suffer when you get three or more applications and documents on the screen — it just doesn't scale up well. The idiom has other problems, too. A user who misclicks the mouse a couple of pixels in the wrong direction can find his program disappearing, to be replaced by another one. User testing at Microsoft showed that a typical user might launch the same word processor several times in the mistaken belief that he has somehow "lost" the program and must start over. Problems like these prompted Microsoft to introduce the taskbar and Apple to invent Exposé, which is an attractive and usable way to keep track of open windows (though its lack of integration with applications minimized to the Dock is more than a bit problematic).

Another part of the confusion regarding overlapping windows comes from several other idioms that are also implemented using an overlapping window. The familiar dialog box is one, as are menus and floating tool palettes. Such overlapping within a single application is completely natural and a well-formed idiom. It even has a faint but resonant metaphoric trace: that of someone handing you an important note.

Microsoft and Tiled Windows

In the grand tradition of focusing on the most visible aspect of the new PARC GUI, Bill Gates hastily cobbled together a response to the Macintosh's success and named it "Windows."

The first version of Microsoft Windows diverged somewhat from the pattern established by Xerox and Apple. Instead of using overlapping rectangular windows to represent the overlapping sheets of paper on one's desktop, Windows 1.0 relied on what was called **tiling** to allow users to have more than one application onscreen at a time. Tiling meant that applications would divide up the available pixels in a uniform, rectilinear tessellation, evenly parsing out the available space to running programs. Tiling was invented as an idealistic means to solve the orientation and navigation problems caused by overlapping windows. Navigation between tiled windows is much easier than between overlapped windows, but the cost in pixels is horrendous. And besides, as soon as the user moves neatly tiled windows, he is thrust right back into overlapping window **excise** (see Chapter 11). Tiling died as a mainstream idiom, although it can still be found in the most interesting places: Try right-clicking on the current Windows taskbar.

Full-Screen Applications

Overlapping windows fail to make it easy to navigate between multiple, running programs; so other vendors continue to search for new ways to achieve this. The **virtual desktop** of session managers on some Unix-based platforms extends the desktop to six times the size of the visible window. (Apple has recently introduced something similar in Mac OS X.) In a corner of the screen are small, superimposed, thumbnail images of all six desktop spaces, all of which can be running different things simultaneously and each of which can have many open windows. You switch between these virtual desktops by clicking on the one you want to make active. In some versions, you can even drag tiny window thumbnails from one desktop to another.

Microsoft braved a double-barreled, breach-of-contract and patent-infringement lawsuit from Apple in order to add overlapping to Windows 2.0. In all this controversy, the basic problem seemed to have been forgotten: How can a user easily navigate from one program to another? Multiple windows sharing a small screen — whether overlapping or tiled — is not a good general solution (although it certainly may have its occasional uses). We are moving rapidly to a world of full-screen programs. Each application occupies the entire screen when it is "at bat." A tool like the taskbar borrows the minimum quantity of pixels from the running application to provide a visual method of changing the lineup. (Amusingly, this concept is similar to the early days of the Mac with its Switcher, which would toggle the Mac display between one full-screen application and another.) This solution is much more pixel-friendly, less confusing to users, and highly appropriate when an application is being used for an extended period of time. In Mac OS X and Windows XP and Vista, users have the choice of making their applications full-screen or overlapping.

Contemporary software design often begins with the assumption that the user interface will consist of a series of overlapping windows, without modes, informed by a global metaphor. The PARC legacy is a strong one. Most of what we know about modern graphical user interface design came from these origins, whether right or wrong. But the well-tempered designer will push the myths aside and approach software design from a fresh viewpoint, using history as a guide, not as a mandate.

Multipaned Applications

It turns out that there is an idiom that takes the best elements of tiled windows and provides them within a sovereign, full-screen application — the idiom of **multipaned windows**. Multipaned windows consist of independent views or **panes** that share a single window. **Adjacent panes** are separated by fixed or movable dividers or **splitters.** (We discuss splitters more in Chapter 21.) The classic example of a multipaned application is Microsoft Outlook, where separate panes are used to display the list of mailboxes, contents of the selected mailbox, a selected message, and upcoming appointments and tasks, all on one screen (see Figure 20-1).

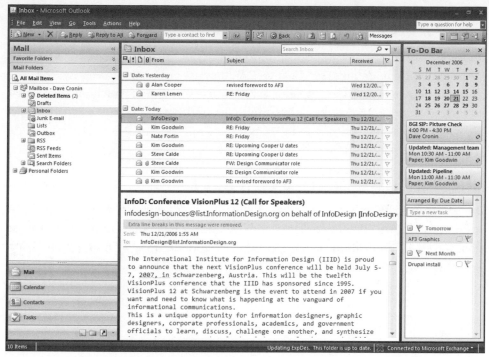

Figure 20-1 Microsoft Outlook 2007 is a classic example of a multipaned application. The far-left pane includes a list of mailboxes, as well as providing the ability to switch between views such as Mail and Calendar. The top-center pane shows all the messages in the selected mailbox, while the pane below it shows the contents of the selected message. The pane on the right shows the next three appointments and upcoming tasks.

The advantage of multipaned windows is that independent but related information can be easily displayed in a single, sovereign screen in a manner that reduces navigation and window management excise to almost nil. For a sovereign application of any complexity, adjacent pane designs are practically a requirement. Specifically, designs that provide navigation and/or building blocks in one pane and allow viewing or construction of data in an adjacent pane seem to represent an efficient pattern that bears repeating.

The concept of adjacent panes was also adopted on the Web in the form of **frames**, but thanks to a poorly designed implementation out of the gate and a standards war between then preeminent Netscape and Microsoft, frames have been tainted as awkward and complex. Hopefully, as Web technologies progress and highly interactive Web applications become more prevalent, the concept behind frames will reemerge inside the browser (the browsers themselves *already* make use of multiple panes). To some extent, current client-side technology approaches (such as AJAX and Flash) and can already deliver pane-like behaviors.

Another form of multiple panes are **stacked panes** or **tabs**. Although these are seen most frequently in dialogs (see Chapter 24), they are also sometimes useful in sovereign windows. A good example of this is Microsoft Excel, which allows related spreadsheets to be accessible via inverted tabs at the bottom of the screen. Excel makes use of stacked panes with its "Sheets."

Designing with Windows

Our programs are constructed of two kinds of windows: main windows and subordinate windows (like documents and dialog boxes). Determining how to use windows in an application is an important aspect of defining a Design Framework (see Chapter 7).

Unnecessary rooms

If we imagine our application as a house, each window is a separate room. The house itself is represented by the application's main window, and each room is a pane, document window, or dialog box. We don't add a room to our house unless it has a purpose that cannot be served by other rooms. Similarly, we shouldn't add windows to our application unless they have a purposes that can't or shouldn't be served by existing windows.

It's important to think through this question of purpose from prospective users' goals and mental models. The way we think about it, saying that a room has a **purpose** implies that using it is associated with a goal, but not necessarily with a particular task or function.

 DESIGN principle   A dialog box is another room; have a good reason to go there.

For example, in Adobe Photoshop, if you'd like to change the brightness and contrast of a photo, you must go to the Image menu, select the Adjustments submenu, and then select the Brightness/Contrast command. This triggers a dialog box, where you can make your adjustments (see Figure 20-2). This sequence is so commonplace that it is completely unremarkable, and yet it is undeniably poor design. Adjusting the image is the primary task in a photo editing program. The image is in the main window, so that's where the tools that affect it should be also. Changing the brightness and contrast isn't a tangential task but one quite integral to the purpose of the application.

Putting functions in a dialog box emphasizes their separateness from the main task. Putting the brightness and contrast adjustment in a dialog box works just fine, but it creates an awkward interaction. From a programmer's point of view, adjusting brightness and contrast is a single function, independent of many other functions, so it seems natural to segregate it into its own container. From a user's point of view, however, it is integral to the job at hand and should be obvious in the main window.

Things have improved considerably in Adobe Lightroom. The application is divided into views or "rooms," each concerned with a specific purpose: Library, Develop, Slideshow, Print, and Web. In Develop, brightness and contrast adjustment are presented in a pane on the right side of the main window, along with every other imaginable way of adjusting an image (see Figure 20-3).

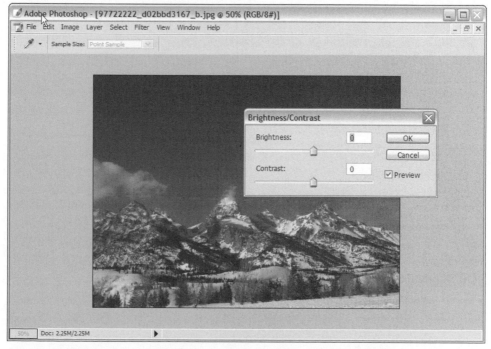

Figure 20-2 One of Adobe Photoshop's many rooms: Brightness & Contrast. We're all used to the fact that we have to invoke a dialog to perform a basic function, so we hardly notice it. But this creates unnecessary work for users, and of course the dialog obscures the most important thing on the screen — the image.

Figure 20-3 Adobe Lightroom shows vast improvements over Photoshop. Critical tools are grouped by purpose and presented directly in the main window, adjacent to the image being adjusted.

DESIGN principle

Provide functions in the window where they are used.

This is one of the most frequently violated principles in user-interface design. Programmers often work by breaking down the application into discrete functions, and the user interface is often constructed in close parallel. Combine this with the incredible ease with which programmers can implement a dialog box, and the obvious result is one dialog box per function. Our modern GUI-building tools tend to make dialogs easy to create, but adding controls to the surface of a document window or creating direct-manipulation idioms is generally not supported by these handy tools. The developer who wants to create a better user interface often must build his own without much help from the tool vendors.

Necessary rooms

When you want to go swimming, it would be odd if you were offered a living room full of people as a place to change your clothes. Decorum and modesty are excellent reasons for you to want a separate room in which to change. It is entirely appropriate to provide a separate room when one is needed.

When users perform a function outside their normal sequence of events, it's usually desirable to provide a special place in which to perform it. For example, purging a database is not a normal activity. It involves setting up and using features and facilities that are not part of the normal operation of the database program. The more prosaic parts of the application support daily tasks like entering and examining records, but erasing records en masse is not an everyday occurrence. The purge facility correctly belongs in a separate dialog box. It is entirely appropriate for the program to lead a user into a separate room — a window or dialog — to handle that function.

Using goal-directed thinking, we can examine each function to good effect. If someone is using a graphics program to develop a drawing, his goal is to create an appealing and effective image. All the drawing tools are directly related to this goal, but the pencils and paintbrushes and erasers are the most tightly connected functions. These tools should be intimately integrated into the workspace itself in the same way that the conventional artist arranges his tools on his drawing board, close at hand. They are ready for immediate use without his having to reach far, let alone having to get up and walk into the next room. In the program, drawing tools should be arrayed on the edges of the drawing space, available with a single click of the mouse. Users shouldn't have to go to the menu or to dialog boxes to access these tools.

For example, Corel Painter arranges artists' tools in trays, and lets you move the things that you use frequently to the front of the tray. Although you can hide the various trays and palettes if you want, they appear as the default and are part of the main drawing window. They can be positioned anywhere on the window, as well. And if you create a brush that is, for example, thin charcoal in a particular shade of red that you're going to need again, you simply "tear it off" the palette and place it wherever you want on your workspace — just like laying that charcoal in the tray on your easel. This tool selection design closely mimics the way we manipulate tools while drawing.

If, on the other hand, you decide to import a piece of clip art, although the function is related to the goal of producing a good drawing, the tools used are not immediately related to drawing. The clip art directory is clearly not congruent with the user's goal of drawing — it is only a means to an end. The conventional artist probably does not keep a book of clip art right on his drawing board, but you can expect that it is close by, probably on a bookshelf immediately adjacent to the drawing board and available without even getting up. In the drawing application, the clip art facility should be very easy to access but, because it involves a whole suite of tools that aren't normally needed, it should be placed in a separate facility: a dialog box.

When you're done creating the artwork, you've achieved your initial goal of creating an effective image. At this point, your goals change. Your new goal is to preserve the picture, protect it, and communicate through it. The need for pens and pencils is over. The need for clip art is over. Leaving these tools behind now is no hardship. The conventional artist would now unpin the drawing from his board, take it into the hall and spray it with fixative, then roll it up and put it in a mailing tube. He purposely leaves behind his drawing tools — he doesn't want them affected by fixative overspray and doesn't want accidents with paint or charcoal to mar the finished work. Mailing tubes are used infrequently and are sufficiently unrelated to the drawing process, so he stores them in a closet. In the software equivalent of this process, you end the drawing program, put away your drawing tools, find an appropriate place on the hard drive to store the image, and send it to someone else via electronic mail. These functions are clearly separated from the drawing process by goals and motivations.

By examining users' goals, we are naturally guided to an appropriate form for the application. Instead of merely putting every function in a dialog box, we can see that some functions shouldn't be enclosed in a dialog at all. Others should be put into a dialog that is integral to the main body of the interface, and still other functions should be completely removed from the program.

Windows pollution

Some designers take the approach that each dialog box should embody a single function. What they end up with is **windows pollution**.

Achieving many user goals involves executing a series of functions. If there is a single dialog box for each function, things can quickly get visually crowded and navigationally confusing. CompuServe Navigator, shown in Figure 20-4, is the case in point.

Adding a squirt of oil to a bicycle makes it pedal more easily, but that doesn't mean that dumping a gallon of oil on it will make it pedal itself. The designer of Navigator was on a mission to put more windows in our lives, perhaps in the mistaken belief that windows are inherently good.

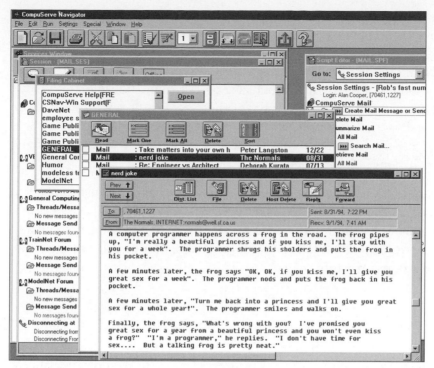

Figure 20-4 Version 1.0 of CompuServe's Navigator suffered from tragic windows pollution. Normal downloading of e-mail required three windows to be opened. To examine a filed message required three more windows. Examining mail is one integral activity and should occupy a single, integrated window. But the worst is yet to come: Users had to put every window away individually, in the reverse order of opening them.

DESIGN
principle

The utility of any interaction idiom is context-dependent.

Another possibility is that Navigator was the result of a large team of programmers working without an integrated framework for the design. Thus each module of functionality is expressed in a window or dialog, simply because it's easier than trying to fit them cleanly together ex post facto: the classic implementation model. This example was presented in the first edition of About Face in 1995, and we wish we could say things have improved. But one need only look at America Online's interface today to see how little things have changed. AOL, despite the disservice it does to its huge user base in terms of excise and confusion, continues to be one of the worst windows polluters on the planet.

There is no way to show the connections between lots of windows, so don't create lots of windows. This is a particularly annoying problem with Visual Basic (VB) where it is easy to create **forms**. Forms are independent, top-level windows. In terms of behavior, they are the same as modeless dialog boxes. Creating applications as collections of several modeless dialog boxes is a questionable strategy that was never very common until VB made it easy to do. Just because it's easy to do doesn't mean it is good design. Each window added contributes more to users' burden of window management excise. This overhead can grow to obnoxious and painful proportions if the program is used daily.

A VB programmer once explained that his program was especially difficult to design because it had 57 forms. No program with 57 forms can be used effectively. Each form may be excellent in its own right, but collectively, it's simply too many. It's like saying you're going to taste 57 bottles of vintage Bordeaux at a sitting or test drive 57 sports cars on Saturday.

Window States

Programmers typically call an application's primary window its **top-level window**. Each top-level window can be in one of three states (in Windows, Mac OS X, and some Unix GUI platforms), depending on how they are programmed. Oddly, only two of these three states have been given names by Microsoft: **minimized** and **maximized**.

In Unix GUIs like Motif, and on pre-95 versions of Windows, **minimized** windows were shrunk to boxy icons (usually larger than normal desktop icons) that stacked on the desktop. Starting with Windows 95, minimizing a window collapses the window into the button that represents it on the taskbar. In Mac OS X, minimizing a window collapses it into the Dock.

Maximized windows fill the entire screen, covering up whatever is beneath them. Apple refers to the button that activates this state as the Zoom button, but doesn't seem to have a term for the actual state. Microsoft and Apple both somehow manage to avoid directly referring to the third state, and the only hint of a name is on the Microsoft system menu (click the upper-left corner of the title bar to see it) where the verb **Restore** describes how to get to it. This function restores a maximized top-level window to that *other* state. In the interests of sanity, we will call this third state **pluralized**, although it has also been called **restored**.

The pluralized state is that in-between condition where the window is neither an icon nor maximized to cover the entire screen. When a window is pluralized, it shares the screen with icons and other pluralized windows. Pluralized windows can be either tiled or overlapping.

Back in the days of Windows 1.0, the states of minimization and maximization were called **iconized** and **zoomed**, terms that were more descriptive and certainly more engaging. IBM, then enjoying a cozy relationship with Microsoft, demanded the change to corporate-speak in the mistaken impression that America's executives would feel more comfortable. The weaker appellations have stuck.

The normal state for a sovereign application is the maximized state. There is little reason for such a program to be pluralized, other than to support switching between programs or dragging and dropping data between programs or documents (the latter could be cleverly accomplished using a toolbar control instead). Some transient applications, like Windows Explorer, the calculator, and iTunes are appropriately displayed in a pluralized window.

MDI versus SDI

About 20 years ago, Microsoft began proselytizing a new method for organizing the functions in a Windows application. The company called this the **multiple document interface**, or **MDI**. It satisfied a need apparent in certain categories of applications, namely those that handled multiple instances of a single type of document simultaneously. Notable examples were Excel and Word.

Microsoft backed up its new standard with code built into the operating system, so the emergence of MDI as a standard was inevitable. For a time in the late 1980s and early 1990s, MDI was regarded by some at Microsoft as a kind of cure-all patent medicine for user interface ills. It was prescribed liberally for all manner of ailments.

These days, Microsoft has turned its back on MDI and embraced **single document interface**, or **SDI**. It seems that MDI didn't fix all the problems after all.

If you want to copy a cell from one spreadsheet and paste it to another, opening and closing both spreadsheets, in turn, is very tedious. It would be much better to have two spreadsheets open simultaneously. Well, there are two ways to accomplish this: You can have one spreadsheet program that can contain two or more spreadsheet instances inside of it. Or you can have multiple instances of the entire spreadsheet program, each one containing a single instance of a spreadsheet. The second option is technically superior but it demands higher-performance equipment.

In the early days of Windows, Microsoft chose the first option for the simple, practical reason of resource frugality. One program with multiple spreadsheets (documents) was more conservative of bytes and CPU cycles than multiple instances of the same program, and performance was a serious issue then.

Unfortunately, the one-instance-multiple-documents model violated a fundamental design rule established early on in Windows: Only one window can be active at a time. What was needed was a way to have one program active at a time along with one document window active at a time within it. MDI was the hack that implemented this solution.

Two conditions have emerged in the years since MDI was made a standard. First, well-meaning but misguided programmers tragically abused the facility. Second, our computers have gotten much more powerful — to the point where multiple instances of programs, each with a single document, are very feasible. Thus, Microsoft has made it clear that MDI is no longer politically correct, if not actually doomed.

The winds of change at Microsoft notwithstanding, MDI is actually reasonable enough, as long as it is not abused. In particular, it is useful when users need to work on multiple related views of information in a single environment. While it's not terribly inconvenient to switch between instances of Word to go back and forth between different documents, you wouldn't want a purchasing agent to have to switch between multiple instances of his enterprise system to look at an invoice and the billing history for a vendor. These things may be used together for a single purpose, in which case, they should be presented together.

Of course, this can be abused. The CompuServe Navigator program offered a dozen or more different types of document windows, making it very difficult to understand what was going on (and AOL still does this today). To accomplish a goal in SAP's R3 ERP system, a user may have to open 10 windows. Confusion sets in as functions lose their sharp edges, and navigation becomes oppressive. As document windows of different types are selected, the menus must change to keep up. Users depend on the permanency of menus to help keep them oriented on the screen. Changing the menus bleeds away this reliability. Further, everything described in our earlier discussion about minimizing, maximizing, and pluralizing windows goes double for document windows inside an MDI application. Users are forced to manage little windows inside a big window, a truly heinous example of excise. It can be much better to go cleanly from one window to the next. Going from one fully maximized spreadsheet to another fully maximized spreadsheet is powerful and effective.

Today there is little effective difference between MDI and SDI, as Microsoft implements them. In most Microsoft applications, you can go either to the Window menu or the taskbar to change from spreadsheet to spreadsheet, and you can go to the taskbar to change from Excel to Word.

21

Controls

Controls are manipulable, self-contained screen objects through which people interact with digital products. Controls (otherwise known as widgets, gadgets, and gizmos) are the primary building blocks for creating a graphical user interface.

Examined in light of users' goals, controls come in four basic flavors: **imperative controls**, used to initiate a function; **selection controls**, used to select options or data; **entry controls**, used to enter data; and **display controls**, used to directly manipulate the program visually. Some controls combine one or more of these flavors.

Most of the controls that we are familiar with are those that come standard with Windows, the Mac OS, and other common windowing interfaces. This set of canned controls has always been very limited in scope and power.

Avoiding Control-Laden Dialog Boxes

The easiest thing to build in most windowing systems is a dialog box. The dialog box facility offers automatic tools for specifying how and where controls will be placed. Unfortunately, it's quite easy for developers to create user interfaces composed mostly of control-laden dialog boxes. It's much more difficult to create a visual interface with direct manipulation idioms that are consistent with user mental models and workflows. As a result, most existing literature covers the canned-control world reasonably well, while ignoring other approaches. However, control-laden dialog boxes are *not* the key to successful user-interface design. (For more about the strengths of a user interface based around direct manipulation, see Chapter 19. For more about dialogs boxes, see Chapter 24.)

 DESIGN principle   A multitude of control-laden dialog boxes doth not a good user interface make.

To be clear, we're not suggesting the elimination of standard controls. However, while using these controls in your designs may guarantee ease of implementation, it absolutely won't guarantee ease of use. Controls must be used appropriately and judiciously, like all elements of a good user interface.

We'll now look at each of the four types of controls — imperative, selection, entry, and display — in more detail.

Imperative Controls

In the interaction between humans and computers, there is a language of nouns (sometimes called objects), verbs, adjectives, and adverbs. When we issue a command, we are specifying the verb — the action of the statement. When we describe what the action will affect, we are specifying the noun of the sentence. Sometimes we choose a noun from an existing list, and sometimes we enter a new one. We can modify both the noun and the verb with adjectives and adverbs, respectively.

The control type that corresponds to a verb is called the **imperative control** because it commands immediate action. Imperative controls take action, and they take it immediately. Menu items (which we discuss in Chapter 22) are also imperative idioms. In the world of controls, the quintessential imperative idiom is the button; in fact, it is the only one, although it comes in numerous guises. Click the button and the associated action — the verb — executes immediately.

Buttons

Buttons are most often identified by their simulated-3D raised aspect (see Figure 21-1). If the control is rectangular (or sometimes oval) and appears raised (due to its shadow on the right and bottom and highlight on the top and left), it has the visual affordance of an imperative. It will execute as soon as a user clicks and releases it with the mouse cursor. In dialogs, a default button is often highlighted to indicate the most reasonable typical action for a user to take.

Figure 21-1 Standard buttons from Microsoft Windows (on the left) and Apple OS X (on the right). The use of shading and highlights suggest dimensionality, which gives these buttons affordance or clickability.

The button is arguably the most visually compelling control in the designer's toolkit. It isn't surprising that it has evolved with such diversity across the user interface. The manipulation affordances of contemporary faux three-dimensional buttons have prompted their widespread use. It's a good thing — so why *not* use it a lot?

Part of the affordance of a button is its visual pliancy, which indicates its "press-ability." When a user points to it and clicks the mouse button, the button onscreen visually changes from raised to indented, indicating that it is activated. This is an example of dynamic visual hinting, as discussed in Chapter 19. Poorly designed programs and many Web sites contain buttons that are painted on the screen but don't actually move when clicked. This is cheap and easy for the developer to do (especially on the Web), but it is very disconcerting for users, because it generates a mental question: "Did that actually do something?" Users expect to see the button move — the pliant response — and you must satisfy those expectations.

Butcons

With the release of Windows 3.0 came the introduction of the **toolbar** (which we discuss at length in Chapter 23), an idiom that has grown into a de facto standard as familiar as the menu bar. To populate the toolbar, the button was adapted from its traditional home on the dialog box. On its way, it expanded significantly in function, role, and visual aspect.

On dialog boxes, the button is rectangular (with rounded edges on the Mac) and exclusively labeled with text. When it moved to the toolbar, it became square, lost its text, and acquired a pictograph, an iconic legend. Thus was born the **butcon**: half button, half icon (see Figure 21-2). In Windows 98, the butcon, or toolbar button, continued to develop, losing its raised affordance except when used — a move to reduce visual clutter in response to the overcrowding of toolbars. Unfortunately, this makes it more difficult for newcomers to understand the idiom; starting with Windows 2000, the toolbar butcon now reveals its button affordance only when pointed at.

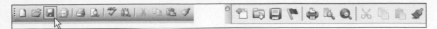

Figure 21-2 Butcons from Microsoft Office 2003. On the left are examples in Office for Windows, and on the right are the same examples in Office for OS X. Notice how each item isn't rendered as a distinct button until the mouse cursor passes over it.

Butcons are, in theory, easy to use: They are always visible and don't demand as much time or dexterity as a drop-down menu does. Because they are constantly visible, they are easy to memorize, particularly in sovereign applications. The advantages of the butcon are hard to separate from the advantages of the toolbar — the two are inextricably linked. The consistently annoying problem with the butcon derives not from its button part but from its icon part. Most users have no problem understanding the visual affordance. The problem is that the image on the face of the butcon is seldom that clear.

Most icons are difficult to decipher with certainty upon first glance, but ToolTips can help with this. It takes a skilled and talented visual designer to be able to create an icon that is sufficiently recognizable and memorable that users aren't required to rely upon ToolTips *every time* they look for a butcon. A good icon will be learned and remembered when users return to that function frequently. This is the type of behavior we typically see from intermediate and advanced users.

However, even the best icon designer in the world will be hard pressed to devise an icon system that will be usable without text labels by novice users. Of course, ToolTips will help them, but it is terribly awkward to move a mouse cursor over each icon and wait for the ToolTip for every butcon. In these cases, menus with their explicit wording are a much better command vector. For more about menus, see Chapter 22. We'll speak more about butcons, toolbars, and ToolTips in Chapter 23.

Hyperlinks

Hyperlinks, or **links**, are a Web convention that have found their way into all sorts of different applications. Typically taking the form of underlined text (though of course, images can be linked too), a link is an imperative control used for navigation. This is a simple, direct, and useful interaction idiom. If a user is interested in an underlined word, she may click on it and will be brought to a new page with more information.

Unfortunately, the idiom's success and utility have given many designers the wrong idea: They believe that replacing more common imperative controls such as buttons or butcons with underlined words will automatically result in a more usable and successful user interface. By and large this is not the case. Because most users have learned that links are a navigational idiom, they will be confused and disoriented if clicking a link results in the execution of an action. In general, you should use links for navigation through content, and buttons or butcons for other actions and functions.

 DESIGN principle   Use links for navigation, and buttons or butcons for action.

Selection Controls

Because the imperative control is a verb, it needs a noun upon which to operate. Selection and entry controls are the two controls used to define nouns (in addition to direction manipulation idioms). A **selection control** allows the user to choose this noun from a group of valid choices. Selection controls are also used to configure actions — in the case of a direct manipulation idiom, the noun may be defined and the selection control is used to define an adjective or adverb. Common examples of selection controls include check boxes, list boxes, and drop-down lists.

Traditionally, selection controls do not directly result in actions — they require an imperative control to activate. This is no longer always the case. In some situations, such as the use of a drop-down list as a navigation control on a Web page, this can be disorientating to users. In other cases, such as using a drop-down to adjust type size in a word processor, this can seem quite natural.

As in many things in interaction design, there are advantages and disadvantages to both approaches. In cases where it is desirable to allow a user to make a series of selections before committing to the action, there should be an explicit imperative control (i.e., button). In cases where users would benefit from seeing the immediate impact of their actions, and those actions are easy to undo, it is completely reasonable for the selection control to double as an imperative control.

Check boxes

The **check box** was one of the earliest visual control idioms invented, and it is the favorite for presenting a single, binary choice (see Figure 21-3). The check box has a strong visual affordance for clicking; it appears as a pliant area because of a mouseover highlight or a 3D "recessed" visual treatment. After a user clicks on it and sees the checkmark appear, he has learned all he needs to know to make it work at will: Click to check; click again to uncheck. The check box is simple, visual, and elegant.

Figure 21-3 These are standard check boxes from Microsoft Windows (on the left) and Apple OS X (on the right). Again, the use of shading and highlights suggest dimensionality, which gives the check boxes affordance or clickability. Notice how the Windows check boxes feature the more typical recessed look, whereas those from OS X are raised.

The check box is, however, primarily a text-based control. The check box is a familiar, effective idiom, but it has the same strengths and weaknesses as menus. Well-written text can make check boxes unambiguous. However, this exacting text forces users to slow down to read it, and takes a considerable amount of real estate.

Traditionally, check boxes are square. Users recognize visual objects by their shape, and the square check box is an important standard. There is nothing inherently good or bad about squareness; it just happens to have been the shape originally chosen and many users have already learned to recognize this shape. There is no good reason to deviate from this pattern. Don't make them diamond-shaped or round, regardless of what the marketing or graphic arts people say.

However, it is possible to implement a more graphical approach to the check box function by expanding on the butcon. The button evolved into the butcon by replacing its text with an icon, then migrating onto the toolbar. Once there, the metamorphosis of the button continued by the simple expedient of allowing it to stay in the recessed — or pushed-in — state when clicked, then returning to the raised aspect when it is clicked again, a **latching butcon** or **toggle** (see Figure 21-4). The state of the toggle is no longer momentary, but rather locks in place until it is clicked again. The character of the control has changed sufficiently to move it into an entirely different category: from imperative to selection control.

Figure 21-4 These images depict toggle butcons in their flat, mouseover, clicked, and selected states in Microsoft Office 2003.

The toggle button is widely superseding the check box as a single-selection idiom and is especially appropriate in modeless interactions that do not require interruption of a user's flow to make a decision. Latching butcons are more space efficient than check boxes are: They are smaller because they can rely on visual recognition instead of text labels to indicate their purpose. Of course, this means that they exhibit the same problem as imperative butcons: the inscrutability of the icon. We are saved once again by ToolTips. Those tiny, pop-up windows give us just enough text to disambiguate the butcon without permanently consuming too many pixels.

Flip-flop buttons: A selection idiom to avoid

Flip-flop buttons are an all-too-common control variant used to save interface real estate. Unfortunately, this savings comes at the cost of considerable user confusion. The verb on the flip-flop button is always one of multiple states that the control can be in. A classic example here is collapsing play and pause onto the same button on an audio player, where it contains the universal play triangle icon until you click it, and then it contains the universal pause icon of two vertical bars.

The control suggests that you can click it, so when it displays the play icon it intends to mean that by clicking it music will start. The button then changes to display the pause icon to indicate that clicking it again will pause playback. The problem with this approach is that the control could be interpreted to serve as an indicator of the state of the player (paused or playing). This means that there are two very reasonable and contradictory interpretations of the icons on the button. The control can either serve as a state indicator or as a state-switching selection control, but not both (see Figure 21-5).

The solution to this one is to either spell it out on the button as a verb or verb phrase — Play or Pause — or better yet, to use some other technique entirely, such as replacing it with two buttons. The downside is that this consumes more screen real estate.

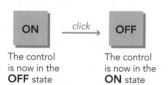

Figure 21-5 Flip-flop button controls are very efficient. They save space by controlling two mutually exclusive options with a single control. The problem with flip-flop controls is that they fail to fulfill the second duty of every control — to inform users of their current state. If the button says ON when the state is off, it is unclear what the setting is. If it says OFF when the state is off, however, where is the ON button? Don't use them.

Radio buttons

Similar in appearance to the check box is the **radio button** (see Figure 21-6). The name says it all. When radios were first put in automobiles, we all discovered that manually tuning an analog radio with a rotating knob while driving was dangerous to your health. So automotive radios were offered with a newfangled panel consisting of a half-dozen chrome-plated buttons, each of which would twist the tuner to a preset station. Now you could tune to your favorite station, without taking your eyes off of the road, just by pushing a button. The idiom is a powerful one, and it still has many practical uses in interaction design.

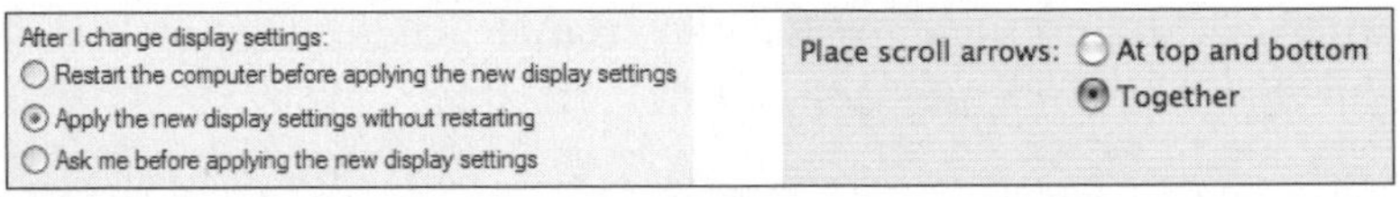

After I change display settings:
○ Restart the computer before applying the new display settings
◉ Apply the new display settings without restarting
○ Ask me before applying the new display settings

Place scroll arrows: ○ At top and bottom
◉ Together

Figure 21-6 The image on the left shows radio buttons from Microsoft Windows XP. On the right are radio buttons from Macintosh OS X.

The behavior of radio buttons is **mutually exclusive**, which means that when one option is selected, the previously selected option automatically deselects. Only one button can be selected at a time.

In consequence of mutual exclusion, radio buttons always come in groups of two or more, and one radio button in each group is always selected. A single radio button is undefined — it must act like a check box instead. (You should use a check box or similar nonmutual selection control in this instance.)

Radio buttons can consume even more screen real estate than check boxes. They use the same amount of space as check boxes, but radio buttons are only meaningful in groups, so their use of space is always multiplied. In some cases, the space is justified, particularly where it is important to show users the full set of available choices at all times. Radio buttons are well suited to a teaching role, which means that they can be justified in infrequently used dialog boxes, but drop-down list boxes are often a better choice on the surface of a sovereign application which must cater to daily users.

For the same reason that check boxes are traditionally square — that's how we've always done it — radio buttons are round (except in the case of Motif, where radio buttons were diamonds, but this seems not to have caught on).

As you might imagine, the butcon has also done to the radio button what it did to the check box: replaced it on the surface of an application. If two or more latching butcons are grouped together and mux-linked — so that only one of them at a time can be latched — they behave in exactly the same way as radio buttons. They form a **radio butcon**.

They work just like radio buttons: One is always selected — latched down — and whenever another one is pressed, the first one returns to its normal — raised — position. The alignment controls on Word's toolbar are an excellent example of a radio butcon, as shown in Figure 21-7.

Figure 21-7 Word's alignment controls are a radio butcon group, acting like radio buttons. One is always selected, and when another is clicked, the first one returns to its normal, raised position. This variant is a very space-conservative idiom that is well suited for frequently used options.

Just as in all butcon idioms, these are very efficient consumers of space, letting experienced users rely on pattern recognition to identify them and letting infrequent users rely on ToolTips to remind users of their purpose. First-time users will either be clever enough to learn from the ToolTips or will learn more slowly, but just as reliably, from other, parallel, pedagogic command vectors.

Combutcons

A variant of the radio butcon is a drop-down version. Because of its similarity to the combo box control, we call this a **combutcon** (see Figure 21-8). Normally, it looks like a single button with a small down-arrow to its right (in Windows), but if you click the arrow, it drops down a menu of several butcons, which users may choose among. The selected butcon now appears on the toolbar next to the arrow. Clicking on the button itself actuates the imperative indicated by the selected state. Like menus, the butcons should also activate if the user clicks and holds on the arrow, drags and then releases over the desired selection.

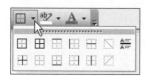

Figure 21-8 This combutcon from Microsoft Office 2003 is a group of latching butcons that behave like a combo box.

Variations on combutcons include drawing a small, downward- or right-pointing triangle in the lower-right corner of the combutcon icon in place of the separate down arrow that is seen in Microsoft toolbars. Adobe products make use of this variant in their palette controls; this variant also requires a click and hold on the butcon itself to bring up the menu (which, in Adobe palette controls, unfolds to the right rather than down, as shown in Figure 21-9). You can vary this idiom quite a bit, and creative software designers are doing just that in the never-ending bid to cram more functions onto screens that are always too small.

You can see a Microsoft variant in Word, where the butcon for specifying the colors of highlights and text show combutcon menus that look more like little palettes than stacks of butcons. As you can see from Figure 21-9, these menus can pack a lot of power and information into a very compact control. This facility is definitely for frequent users, particularly mouse-heavy users, and not at all for first-timers. However, for a user who has at least a basic familiarity with the available tools, the idiom is instantly clear after it is discovered or demonstrated. This is an excellent control idiom for sovereign-posture programs with which users interact for long hours. It demands sufficient manual dexterity to work a menu with relatively small targets, but it is much faster than going to the menu bar, pulling down a menu, selecting an item, waiting for the dialog box to deploy, selecting a color on the dialog box, and then clicking the OK button.

Figure 21-9 These combutcons taken from Adobe Photoshop (left) and Mozilla Firefox (right) show the diversity of applications of the idiom. In Photoshop, the combutcon is used to switch between various modal cursor tools, whereas in Firefox it is used to select a previously visited Web page to return to. In the first example, it is used to configure the user interface, whereas in the second it is used to perform an action.

List controls

List controls allow users to select from a finite set of text strings, each representing a command, object, or attribute. These controls are sometimes called **picklists** because they offer lists of items from which the user can pick a selection; they are also known as **list boxes** or **listviews**, depending on which platform and which control variant you are talking about. Like radio buttons, list controls are powerful tools for simplifying interaction because they eliminate the possibility of making an invalid selection.

List controls are small text areas with a vertical scrollbar on the right-hand edge (see Figure 21-9). The application displays objects as discrete lines of text in the box, and the scrollbar moves them up or down. A user can select a single line of text at a time by clicking on it. A list control variant allows multiple selection, where a user can select multiple items at one time, usually by pressing the Shift or Ctrl key while clicking with the mouse.

The **drop-down** is a variant of the list control. These ubiquitous controls show only the selected item in a single row, until the arrow button is pressed, which reveals other available choices (also illustrated in Figure 21-10).

Figure 21-10 On the right is a standard list control from Windows. The images on the left show a drop-down list control in its closed and open states.

Early list controls handled only text. Unfortunately, that decision often affects their behavior to this day. A list control filled with line after line of text unrelieved by visual symbols is a dry desert indeed. However, starting with Windows 95, Microsoft has allowed each line of text in a **listview control** to be preceded with an icon (without need of custom coding). This can be quite useful — there are many situations in which users benefit from seeing a graphical identifier next to important text entries (see Figure 21-11). A newer convention is to use the list items in a drop-down or other listview control as a preview facility. This is commonly used in cases where the control is doubling as a selection control and an imperative control, such as the selection of a style in Microsoft Word (also see Figure 21-11).

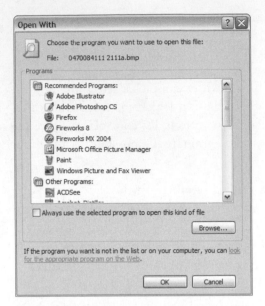

Figure 21-11 On the left is a list control with icons from Windows XP that allows users to visually identify the application they are looking for. On the right is the style drop-down list from Office 2007. Here, the items in the list provide a preview for the effects of their selection.

  Distinguish important text items in lists with graphic icons.

Listviews are, true to their name, good for displaying lists of items and allowing users to select one or more of them. They are also good idioms for providing a source of draggable items (though clearly not with the drop-down variant). If the items are draggable within the listview itself, it makes a fine tool for enabling the user to put items in a specific order (see the "Ordering lists" section later in this chapter).

Earmarking

Generally speaking, users select items in a list control as input to some function, such as selecting the name of a desired font from a list of several available fonts. Selection in a list control is conventional, with keyboard equivalents, focus rectangles, and selected items shown in highlighted colors.

Occasionally, however, list controls are used to select multiple items, and this can introduce complications. The selection idiom in list controls is very well suited for single selection but much weaker for multiple selection. In general, the multiple selection of discrete objects works adequately if the entire playing field is visible at once, like the icons on a desktop. If two or more icons are selected at the same time, you can clearly see this because all the icons are visible.

But if the pool of available discrete items is too large to fit in a single view and some of it must be scrolled offscreen, the selection idiom immediately becomes unwieldy. This is the normal state of affairs for list controls. Their standard mode of selection is mutual exclusion, so when you select one thing, the previous selected thing is deselected. It is thus far too easy, in the case of multiple selection, for users to select an item, scroll it into invisibility, and then select a second item, forgetting that they have now *deselected* the first item because they can no longer see it.

The alternative is equally unpalatable: The list control is programmed to disable the mutual-exclusion behavior of a standard list control in its selection algorithm, allowing users to click on as many items as they like with them all remaining selected. Things now work absolutely perfectly (sort of): A user selects one item after another, and each one stays selected. The fly in the ointment is that there is no visual indication that selection is behaving differently from the norm. It is just as likely that a user will select an item, scroll it into invisibility, then spot a more desirable second item and select it *expecting the first — unseen — item to automatically be deselected* because the control is mutually exclusive. You get to choose between offending the first half of your users or the second half. Bad idea.

When objects can scroll off the screen, multiple selection requires a better, more distinct idiom. The correct action is to use a different idiom from simple selection, one that is visually distinct. But what is it?

It just so happens we already have another well-established idiom to indicate that something is selected — the check box. Check boxes communicate their purposes and their settings quite clearly and, like all good idioms, are extremely easy to learn. Check boxes are also very clearly disassociated from any hint of mutual exclusion. If we were to add a check box to every item in our problematic list control, the user would not only clearly see which items were selected and which were not, he would also clearly see that the items were not mux-linked, solving both of our problems in one stroke. This check box alternative to multiple selection is called **earmarking**, an example of which is shown in Figure 21-12.

Figure 21-12 Selection is normally a mutually exclusive operation. When the need arises to discard mutual exclusivity in order to provide multiple selection, things can become confusing if some of the items can be scrolled out of sight. Earmarking is a solution to this. Put check boxes next to each text item and use them instead of selection to indicate the user's choices. Check boxes are a clearly non–mutually exclusive idiom and a very familiar GUI idiom. Users grasp the workings of this idiom right away.

Dragging and dropping from lists

List controls can be treated as palettes of goodies to use in a direct-manipulation idiom. If the list were part of a report-writing program, for example, you could click on an entry and drag it to the surface of the report to add a column representing that field. It's not selection in the usual sense, because it is a completely captive operation. Without a doubt, many programs would benefit if they made use of list controls that supported dragging and dropping.

Such draggable items can help users gather items into a set. Providing two adjacent list controls, one showing available items and the other showing chosen items, is a common GUI idiom. One or sometimes a bidirectional pair of buttons placed between them allows items to be selected and transferred from one box to the other, as shown in Figure 21-13. It is so much more pleasant when the idiom is buttressed with the capability to just click and drag the desired item from one box to another without having to go through the intermediate steps of selection and function invocation.

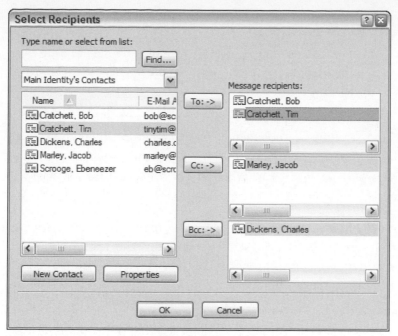

Figure 21–13 This dialog from Microsoft Outlook Express would benefit from the capability to drag a contact from the list at the left into the To, Cc, and Bcc lists at the right. Also notice the unfortunate use of horizontal scrollbars in all list fields. In the left-hand field, in particular, ToolTips could show the full row of information in the left-hand box. (Alternately, the dialog could be expanded. There's no practical reason to limit it to this size.)

Ordering lists

Sometimes the need arises to drag an item from a list control to another position in the same list control. (Actually, this need arises far more often than most interaction designers seem to think.) Many programs offer automatic sort facilities for important lists. Windows Explorer, for example, allows sorting files by name, by type, by modification date, and by size. That's nice, but wouldn't it be even better if users could order them by importance? Algorithmically, the program could order them by frequency of user access, but that won't always get the right results. Adding in a factor of how recently files were accessed, as well, would get closer but still wouldn't be exactly right. (Microsoft does this with its font picker in some applications, and it works pretty well for this purpose.) Why not let users move what's important to them to a region at the top, and sort those things separately (in alphabetical or whatever order), in addition to sorting the full directory below? For example, you might want to rearrange a list of the people in your department in descending order by where they sit. There is no automatic function that will do this;

you just have to drag them until it's right. Now, this is the kind of customizing that an experienced user wants to do after long hours of familiarization with an application. It takes a lot of effort to fine-tune a directory like this, and the program *must* remember the exact settings from session to session — otherwise, the capability to reorder things is worthless.

Being able to drag items from one place to another in a list control is powerful, but it demands that auto-scrolling be implemented (see Chapter 19). If you pick up an item in the list but the place you need to drop it is currently scrolled out of view, you must be able to scroll the listview without putting down the dragged object.

Horizontal scrolling

List controls normally have a vertical scrollbar for moving up and down through the list. List controls can also be made to scroll horizontally. This feature allows the programmer to put extra-long text into the list controls with a minimum of effort. However, it offers nothing to users but a major pain.

Scrolling text horizontally is a terrible thing, and it should *never, ever* be done, except in large tables such as spreadsheets where locked row and column headers can provide context for each column. When a text list is scrolled horizontally, it hides from view one or more of the first letters of every single line of text showing. This makes *none* of the lines readable and the continuity of the text is utterly destroyed.

DESIGN principle   Never scroll text horizontally.

If you find a situation that seems to call for horizontal scrolling of text, search for alternative solutions. Begin by asking yourself why the text in your list is so long. Can you shorten the entries? Can you wrap the text to the next line to avoid that horizontal length? Can you allow the user to enter aliases for the longer entries? Can you use graphical entries instead? Can you use ToolTips? Ideally, you should alternatively be asking yourself if there is some way to widen the control. Can you rearrange things on the window or dialog to expand horizontally?

Absent the ability to widen the control, the best answer will usually be to wrap the text onto the next line, indenting it so it is visually different from other entries. This means that you now have a list control with items of variable height, but this is still better than horizontal scrolling.

Remember, we're just talking about *text*. For graphics or large tables, there is nothing wrong with horizontal scrollbars or horizontally scrollable windows in general.

But providing a text-based list with a required horizontal scrollbar is like providing a computer with a required pedal-powered electrical generator — bad news.

Entering data into a list

Little work has been done historically to enable users to make direct text entry into an item in a list control. Of course, the need to enter text where text is output is widespread, and much of the kludginess of dialog box design can be directly attributed to programmers trying to dodge the bullet of having to write edit-in-place code.

However, modern list and tree controls in Windows and other platforms offer an edit-in-place facility. Windows Explorer uses both of these controls, and you can see how they work by renaming a file or directory. To rename a file in the Mac OS or in Windows 95, you click twice — but not too quickly (lest it be interpreted as a double-click and open the object in question) — on the desired name. You then enter whatever changes are desired. (This changed a bit in Windows XP, so that in some views you need to select Rename from a right-click menu to get into Rename mode — is this progress?) Items that are editable in other circumstances should, when displayed in list controls, be editable there as well.

The edge case that makes edit-in-place a real problem is adding a new entry to the list. Most designers use other idioms to add list items: Click a button or select a menu item and a new, blank entry is added to the list and the user can then edit-in-place its name. It would be more sensible if you could, say, double-click in the space between existing entries to create a new, blank entry right there, or at least have a perpetual open space at the beginning or end of the list with a Click to Add Entry label on it to make it discoverable. Another solution to this problem is the combo box, which we'll talk about next.

Combo boxes

Windows 3.0 introduced a new control called the **combo box**. It is — as its name suggests — a combination of a list box and an edit field (see Figure 21-14). It provides an unambiguous method of data entry into a list control. As with normal list boxes, there is a drop-down variant that has a reduced impact on screen real estate.

Combo boxes clearly differentiate between the text-entry part and the list-selection part, minimizing user confusion. For single selection, the combo box is a superb control. The edit field can be used to enter new items, and it also shows the current selection in the list. When the current selection is showing in the edit field, a user can edit it there — sort of a poor man's edit-in-place.

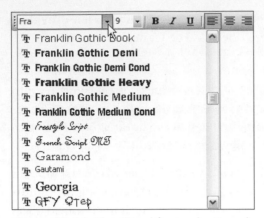

Figure 21-14 The Word font selection drop-down combo box allows users to make a font selection from the drop-down list, or to simply type the name of the desired font into the text field.

Because the edit field of the combo box shows the current selection, the combo box is by nature a single-selection control. There is no such thing as a multiple-selection combo box. Single selection implies mutual exclusion, which is one of the reasons why the combo box is fast replacing groups of radio buttons for selection amongst mutually exclusive options. (The Mac OS had pop-up menus before Windows had the combo box, and these served to replace large banks of radio buttons on that platform. The Mac versions didn't have the combo box's edit feature, however.) The other reasons include its space efficiency and its capability to add items dynamically, something that radio buttons cannot do.

When the drop-down variants of the combo box are used, the control shows the current selection without consuming space to show the list of choices. Essentially, it becomes a list-on-demand, much like a menu provides a list of immediate commands on demand. A combo box is a pop-up list control.

The screen efficiency of the drop-down combo box allows it to do something remarkable for a control of such complexity: It can reasonably reside permanently on a program's main screen. It can even fit comfortably on a toolbar. It is a very effective control for deployment on a sovereign-posture application. Using combo boxes on the toolbar is more effective than putting the equivalent functions on menus, because the combo boxes display their current selection without requiring any action on the user's part, such as pulling down a menu to see the current status.

If drag-and-drop is implemented in list controls, it should also be implemented in combo boxes. For example, being able to open a combo box, scroll to a choice, and then drag the choice onto a document under construction is a very powerful idiom. Drag-and-drop functionality should be a standard part of combo boxes.

Tree controls

Mac OS 7 and Windows 95 both brought us general-purpose tree controls, which had already been in use in the Unix world for some time. Tree controls are listviews that can present hierarchical data. They display a sideways tree, with icons for each entry. The entries can be expanded or collapsed the way that many outline processors work. Programmers tend to like this presentation. It is often used as a file system navigator, and is a highly effective way to present inherently hierarchical information.

Unfortunately, hierarchical trees are one of the most inappropriately used controls in the toolbox. They can be highly problematic for users; many people have difficulty thinking in terms of hierarchical data structures. We have seen countless interfaces where programmers have forced nonhierarchical data into a tree control with the rationale that trees are "intuitive." While they certainly are intuitive for programmers (and other people are certainly becoming more accustomed to them), the big problem is that they do not allow users to capitalize on other, more interesting relationships between objects other than a strict hierarchy.

In general, it only makes sense to use a treeview (no matter how tempting it may be) in the case where what is being represented is "naturally" thought of as a hierarchy (such as a family tree). Using a treeview to represent arbitrary objects organized in an arbitrary fashion at the whim of a programmer is asking for big trouble when it comes to usability.

Entry Controls

Entry controls enable users to enter new information into an application, rather than merely selecting information from an existing list.

The most basic entry control is a text edit field. Like selection controls, entry controls represent nouns to the program. Because a combo box contains an edit field, some combo box variants qualify as entry controls, too. Also, any control that lets users enter a numeric value is an entry control. Controls such as spinners, gauges, sliders, and knobs fit in this category.

Bounded and unbounded entry controls

Any control that restricts the available set of values that a user can enter is a **bounded entry control**. A slider that moves from 1 to 100, for example, is bounded. Regardless of a user's actions, no number outside those specified by the program can be entered with a bounded control. It is thus impossible for users to enter an invalid value with bounded entry controls.

Conversely, a simple text field can accept any alphanumeric data a user keys into it. This open-ended entry idiom is an example of an **unbounded entry control**. With an unbounded entry control, it is easy for users to enter invalid values. The program may subsequently reject it, of course, but users can still enter it.

Simply put, bounded controls should be used wherever bounded values are needed. If the program needs a number between 7 and 35, presenting users with a control that accepts any numeric value from −1,000,000 to +1,000,000 is not doing anyone any favors. People would much rather be presented with a control that embodies 7 as its bottom limit and 35 as its upper limit (clearly indicating these limits is also useful). Users are smart, and they will immediately comprehend and respect the limits of their sandbox.

It is important to understand that we mean a quality of the entry control and not of the data. To be a bounded control, it needs to clearly communicate, preferably visually, the acceptable data boundaries to the user. A text field that rejects a user's input *after* he has entered it is *not* a bounded control. It is simply a *rude* control.

DESIGN principle   Use bounded controls for bounded input.

Most quantitative values needed by software are bounded, yet many programs allow unbounded entry with numeric fields. When a user inadvertently enters a value that the program cannot accept, the program issues an error message box. This is cruelly teasing the user with possibilities that aren't. "What would you like for dessert? We've got everything," we say. "Ice cream," you respond. "Sorry, we don't have any," we say. "How about pie?" you innocently ask. "Nope," we say. "Cookies?" "Nope." "Candy?" "Nope." "Chocolate?" "Nope." "What, then?" you scream in anger and frustration. "Don't get mad," we say indignantly. "We have plenty of fruit compote." This is how users feel when we put up a dialog box with an unbounded edit field when the valid values are bounded. A user types 17, and we reward this innocent entry with an error message box that says "You can only enter values between 4 and 8." This is poor user-interface design; a much better scheme is to use a bounded control that automatically limits the input to 4, 5, 6, 7, or 8. If the bounded set of choices is composed of text rather than numbers, you can still use a slider of some type, or a combo box, or list box. Figure 21-15 shows a bounded slider used by Microsoft in the Windows Display Settings dialog. It works like a slider or scrollbar, but has four discrete positions that represent distinct resolution settings. Microsoft could easily have used a noneditable combo box in its place, too. In many cases, a slider is a nice choice because it telegraphs the range of valid entries. A combo box isn't much smaller but it keeps its cards hidden until clicked — a less friendly stance.

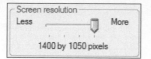

Figure 21-15 A bounded control lets users enter only valid values. It does *not* let them enter invalid values, only to reject them when then try to move on. This figure shows a bounded slider control from the Display Settings dialog in Windows XP. The little slider has four discrete positions. As you drag the slider from left to right, the legend underneath it changes from "800 by 600 pixels" to "1024 by 768 pixels" to to "1280 by 1024" to "1400 by 1050 pixels."

If a user must express a choice that requires a numeric value within specific boundaries, give her a control that intrinsically communicates those limits and prevents her from entering a value outside of the boundaries. The slider control does this. Although sliders have significant drawbacks, they are exemplary in one area: They allow users to enter quantitative information by analogy. Sliders allow users to specify numeric values in relative terms, rather than by directly keying in a number. That is, a user moves the sliding thumb to indicate, by its relative position, a proportional value for use inside the program. Sliders are less useful for entering precise numbers, though many programs use them for that purpose. Controls such as spinners are better for entering exact numbers.

Spinners

Spinner controls are a common form of numeric entry control that permit data entry using either the mouse or keyboard. Spinners contain a small edit field with two half-height buttons attached, as shown in Figure 21-16. Spinners blur the difference between bounded and unbounded controls.

Spinners blur the difference between bounded and unbounded controls. Using either of the two small arrow buttons enables a user to change the value in the edit window in small, discrete steps. These steps are bounded — the value won't go above the upper limit set by the program or below the lower limit. If a user wants to make a large change in one action or to enter a specific number, he can do so by clicking in the edit window portion and directly entering keystrokes into it, just like entering text into any other edit field. Unfortunately, the edit window portion of this control is unbounded, leaving users free to enter values that are out of bounds or even unintelligible garbage. In the page setup dialog box in the figure, if a user enters an invalid value, the program behaves like most other rude programs, issuing an error message box explaining the upper and lower boundaries (sometimes) and requiring the user to click the OK button to continue.

Figure 21-16 The Page Setup dialog from MS Word makes heavy use of the spinner control. On the left side of the dialog, you see a stack of seven of these controls. By clicking on either of the small, arrowed buttons, a user may increase or decrease the specific numeric value in small, discrete steps. If the user wants to make a large change in one action or to enter a precise setting, he can use the edit field portion for direct text entry. The arrow button portion of the control embodies bounding, whereas the edit field portion does not. Does that make this a bounded control?

Overall, the spinner is an excellent idiom and can be used in place of plain edit fields for most bounded entry. In Chapter 25, we will discuss ways to improve control error handling.

Dials and Sliders

Dials and **sliders** are idioms borrowed directly from Mechanical-Age metaphors of rotating knobs and sliding levers. Dials are very space efficient, and both can do a nice job of providing visual feedback about settings (see Figure 21-17).

Figure 21-17 Native Instruments' Reaktor, a modular software synthesizer, makes heavy use of dials and sliders. These are effective interface elements, not only because musicians and producers are familiar with them from hardware, but more importantly because they provide users with more visual and easy-to-comprehend feedback about parameter settings than a long list of numbers, which aren't that exciting to look at while making music.

Improperly implemented, dials can be extremely difficult to manipulate. Sometimes programmers erroneously force users to trace a circular arc with their mouse, which can be quite challenging. Proper implementation of a dial should allow linear input in two dimensions: clicking on the dial and moving up or right should increase the value of the dial, and moving down or left should decrease the value. Of course, this idiom must be learned by users (otherwise, they may be inclined to try to mouse in an arc), so dials are best suited for specialized applications where users become accustomed to the idiom. Sliders are often a better option, because they visually suggest the fact that movement is along just one axis. Because of their compact size and visual qualities (not to mention heritage), they are popular in audio software.

Although sliders and dials are primarily used as bounded entry controls, they are sometimes used and misused as controls for changing the display of data. For most purposes, scrollbars do a better job of *moving* data in a display because the scrollbars can easily indicate the magnitude of the scrolling data, which sliders can't do as well. However, sliders are an excellent choice for zooming interactions, such as adjusting the scale of a map or the size of photo thumbnails.

Thumbwheels

The **thumbwheel** is a variant of the dial, but one that is much easier to use. Onscreen thumbwheels look rather like the scroll wheel on a mouse, and behave in much the same way. They are popular with some 3D applications because they are a compact, unbounded control, which is perfect for certain kinds of panning and zooming. Unlike a scrollbar, they need not provide any proportional feedback because the range of the control is infinite. It makes sense to map a control like this to unbounded movement in some direction (like zoom), or movement within data that loops back on itself.

Other bounded entry controls

Breaking free from the heritage of traditional GUI controls and the baggage of mechanical analogs, a new generation of more experimental user interfaces allows more visual and gestural idioms. These range from a simple two-dimensional box where a click at any point defines the values for two input mechanisms (the vertical and horizontal coordinates each drive the value of a parameter), to more complex direct manipulation interfaces (see Figure 21-18 for examples). These controls are typically bounded, as their implementation requires careful thought about the relationship between gesture and function. Such control surfaces often provide a mechanism for visual feedback. These controls are also most appropriate for situations where users are attempting to express themselves in regards to a number of variables, and are willing to spend some effort developing proficiency with a challenging idiom.

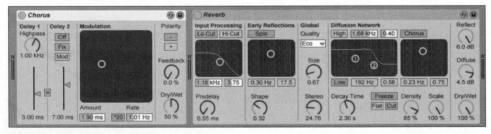

Figure 21-18 Ableton Live, a computer-based music production and performance tool, employs a variety of two-dimensional bounded input controls. These provide good visual feedback, allow users to adjust multiple parameters from a single control, and support more expressive gestural user interactions. Their bounded nature also provides users with context about how the current settings fit within the allowable ranges, and eliminates the chance that a user will make an invalid entry (because no musician wants to be stopped by an error dialog).

Unbounded entry: Text edit controls

The primary unbounded entry control is the **text edit control**. This simple control allows users to key in any alphanumeric text value. Edit fields are often small areas where a word or two of data can be entered by a user, but they can also be fairly sophisticated text editors. Users can edit text within them using the standard tools of contiguous selection (as discussed in Chapter 19) with either the mouse or the keyboard.

Text edit controls are often used either as data-entry fields in database applications (including Web sites connected to databases), as option entry fields in dialog boxes, or as the entry field in a combo box. In all these roles, they are frequently called upon to do the work of a bounded entry control. However, if the desired values are finite, the text edit control should not be used. If the acceptable values are numeric, use a bounded numeric entry control such as a slider, instead. If the list of acceptable values is composed of text strings, a list control should be used so users are not forced to type.

Sometimes the set of acceptable values is finite but too big to be practical for a list control. For example, a program may require a string of any 30 alphabetic characters excluding spaces, tabs, and punctuation marks. In this case, a text edit control is probably unavoidable even though its use is bounded. If these are the only restrictions, however, the text edit control can be designed to reject nonalphabetic characters and similarly disallow more than 30 characters to be entered into the field. This, however, brings up interaction issues surrounding validation.

Validation

In cases where an unbounded text-entry field is provided, but the field may only accept entries of a certain form, it may be necessary to help users to construct a "valid" entry. Typically, this is done by evaluating a user's entry after she has finished entering it, and throwing up an error message if it is invalid. Obviously, this can be irritating for users, and ultimately undermine their effectiveness.

As we've been alluding to, the best solution to this problem is to use bounded controls to make invalid entries impossible. (A common example of this is providing a drop-down list of months, rather than requiring a user to properly spell "February.")

In other cases, this isn't immediately practical (a serial number on a registration screen, for example). Programmers have dealt with this dilemma by creating **validation controls**, or a type of unbounded text-entry control with built-in validation and feedback. Many data-entry types are commonplace, including formats such as dates, phone numbers, zip codes, and Social Security numbers. Specialized text edit controls are commercially available; you can purchase variants of the text-entry control that will only allow numbers or letters or phone numbers, or reject spaces and tabs, for example.

Although the validation control is a very widespread idiom, most such controls can be improved. The key to successfully designing a validation control is to give users generous feedback. An entry control that merely refuses to accept input is just plain rude and will guarantee an angry and resentful user.

One fundamental improvement is based on the design principle: *Visually distinguish elements that behave differently* (Chapter 14). Make validation controls visually distinct from nonvalidation controls, whether through the typeface used in the text edit field, the border color, or the background color for the field itself.

However, the primary way to improve validation controls is to provide rich feedback to users. Unfortunately, the text edit control, as we know it today, provides virtually no built-in support for feedback of any kind. Designers must specify such mechanisms in detail, and programmers will likely need to implement them as custom controls.

Active and Passive Validation

Some controls reject users' keystrokes as they are entered. When a control actively rejects keystrokes during the entry process, this is an example of **active validation**. A text-only entry control, for example, may accept only alphabetic characters and refuse to allow numbers to be entered. Some controls reject any keystrokes other than the numeric digits 0 through 9. Other controls reject spaces, tabs, dashes, and other punctuation in real time. Some variants can get pretty intelligent and reject some numbers based on live calculations, for example, unless they pass a checksum algorithm.

When an active validation control rejects a keystroke, it must make it clear to the user that it has done so. It should also alert the user as to why it made the rejection. If an explanation is offered, users will be less inclined to assume the rejection is arbitrary (or the product of a defective keyboard). They will also be in a better position to give the application what it wants.

Sometimes the range of possible data is such that the program cannot validate it until the user has completed his entry (rather than at each individual keystroke). The validation then takes place only when the control loses focus, that is, when a user is done with the field and moves on to the next one. The validation step must also take place if a user closes the dialog — or invokes another function if the control is not in a dialog box (for example, clicks "Place Order" on a Web page). If the control waits until a user finishes entering data before it edits the value, this is **passive validation**.

The control may wait until an address is fully entered, for instance, before it interrogates a database to see if it is recognizable as a valid address. Each character is valid by itself, yet the whole may not pass muster. The program could attempt to verify the address as each character is entered but could introduce some undesirable latency with the extra workload. Besides, while the program would know at any given instant whether the address was valid, the user could still move on while the name was in an invalid state.

A way to address this is by maintaining a countdown timer in parallel with the input and reset it on each keystroke. If the countdown timer ever hits zero, do your validation processing. The timer should be set to something around half a second. The effect of this is that as long as a user is entering a keystroke faster than once every half a second, the system is extremely responsive. If the user pauses for more than half a second, the program reasonably assumes that he has paused to think (something that takes months in CPU terms) and goes ahead and performs its analysis of the input so far.

To provide rich visual feedback, the entry field could change colors to reflect its estimate of the validity of the entered data. The field could show in shades of pink until the program judged the data valid, when it would change to white or green.

Clue Boxes

Another good solution to the validation control problem is the **clue box**. This little pop-up window looks and behaves just like a ToolTip (but could be made distinguishable from a ToolTip by background color). Its function is to explain the range of acceptable data for a validation control, either active or passive. Whereas a ToolTip appears when the cursor sits for a moment on a control, a clue box would appear as soon as the control detects an invalid character (it might also display unilaterally just like a ToolTip if the cursor sits unmoving on the field for a second or so). If a user enters, for example, a non-numeric character in a numeric-only field, the program would put up a clue box near the point of the offending entry, yet without obscuring it. It would say, for example, 0–9. Short, terse, but very effective. Yes, the user is rejected, but he is not also ignored. The clue box also works for passive validation, as shown in Figure 21-19.

Figure 21-19 The ToolTip idiom is so effective that it could easily be extended to other uses. Instead of yellow ToolTips offering fly-over labels for butcons, we could have pink ones offering fly-over hints for unbounded edit fields. These clue boxes could also help eliminate error message boxes. In this example, if a user enters a value lower than allowable, the program could replace the entered value with the lowest allowable value and display the cluebox that modelessly explains the reason for the substitution. The user can enter a new value or accept the minimum without being stopped by an error dialog.

Handling out of bounds data

Typically, an edit field is used to enter a numeric value needed by the program, such as the point size of a font. A user can enter anything he wants, from 5 to 500, and the field will accept it and return the value to the owning program. If a user enters garbage, the control must make some kind of decision. In Microsoft Word, for example, if you enter **asdf** as a font point size, the program issues an error message box informing you: This is not a valid number. It then reverts the size to its previous value. The error dialog is rather silly, but the summary rejection of my meaningless input is perfectly appropriate. But what if you had keyed in the value **nine**? The program rejects it with the same curt error message box. If instead the control were programmed to think of itself as a numeric entry control, it could perhaps behave better. It doesn't bother me if the program converts the **nine** into a 9, but it certainly is incorrect when it says that **nine** is not a valid number. Without a doubt, it is valid, and the program has put its foot in its mouth.

Units and measurements

It's nice when a text edit control is smart enough to recognize appropriate units. For example, if a program is requesting a measurement, and a user enters "5i" or "5in" or "5 inches," the control should not only report the result as five, but it should report inches as well. If a user enters "5mm," the control should report it as five millimeters. SketchUp, an elegant architectural sketching application, supports this type of feedback. Similarly, well-designed financial analytics applications should know that "5mm" means five million.

Say that the field is requesting a column width. A user can enter either a number or a number and an indicator of the measurement system as described above. Users could also be allowed to enter the word "default" and the program would set the column width to the default value for the program. A user could alternately enter "best fit" and the program would measure all the entries in the column and choose the most appropriate width for the circumstances. There is a problem with this scenario, however, because the words *default* and *best fit* must be in the user's head rather than in the program somewhere. This is easy to solve, though. All we need to do is provide the same functionality through a combo box. The user can drop down the box and find a few standard widths and the words *default* and *best fit*. Microsoft uses this idea in Word, as shown in Figure 21-20.

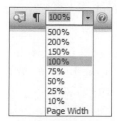

Figure 21–20 The drop-down combo box makes an excellent tool for bounded entry fields because it can accommodate entry values other than numbers. The user doesn't have to remember or type words like Page Width or Whole Page because they are there to be chosen from the drop-down list. The program interprets the words as the appropriate number, and everyone is satisfied.

The user can pull down the combo box, see items like Page Width or Whole Page, and choose the appropriate one. With this idiom, the information has migrated from the user's head into the program where it is visible and choosable.

Insert and overtype entry modes

In most text editors there is a user-settable option toggling between insert mode, where text following the insertion point is preserved by sliding it out of the way as new text is added, and overtype mode, where text following the insertion point is lost as the user types over it. These two modes are omnipresent in the world of word processors and, like FORTRAN, never seem to die. Insert and overtype are modes that cause a significant change in the behavior of an interface, with no obvious indication until after a user has interacted, and there is no clear way into or out of these modes (at least in Windows) except by means of a rather obscure keystroke.

Today, with modern GUI word processors, it's hard to imagine anyone using overtype mode, but undoubtedly such people are out there. But for edit fields of a single line, adding controls beyond simple insert-mode entry and editing is foolish — the potential for trouble is far greater than the advantages. Of course, if you are designing a word processor, the story is different.

Using text edit controls for output: A bad idea

The text edit control, with its familiar system font and visually articulated white box, encourages data entry. Yet software developers frequently use the text edit control for read-only output fields. The edit control certainly works as an output field, but to use this control for output only is like pulling a bait and switch on your user, and he will not be amused. If you have text data to output, use a text display control and not a text *edit* control. If you want to show the amount of free space on disk, for example, don't use a text edit field, because users are likely to think that they can get more free space by entering a bigger number. At least, that is what the control is telling them with its equivalent of body language.

If you are going to output editable information, go ahead and output it in a fully editable text control and wire it up internally so that it works exactly as it will appear. If not, stick to display controls, described in the next section.

DESIGN principle   Use noneditable (display) controls for output-only text.

Display Controls

Display controls are used to display and manage the *visual presentation of information* on the screen. Typical examples include scrollbars and screen-splitters. Controls that manage the way objects are displayed visually on the screen fall into this category, as do those that display static, read-only information. These include paginators, rulers, guidelines, grids, group boxes, and those 3D lines called dips and bumps. Rather than discuss all of these at length, we focus on a few of the more problematic controls.

Text controls

Probably the simplest display control is the **text control**, which displays a written message at some location on the screen. The management job that it performs is pretty prosaic, serving only to label other controls and to output data that cannot or should not be changed by users.

The only significant problem with text controls is that they are often used where edit controls should be (and vice versa). Most information stored in a computer can be changed by users. Why not allow them to change it at the same point the software displays it? Why should the mechanism to input a value be different from the mechanism to output that value? In many cases, it makes no sense for the program to separate these related functions. In almost all cases where the program displays a value that could be changed, it should do so in an editable field so a user can click on it and change it directly. Special edit modes are almost always examples of excise.

For years, Adobe Photoshop insisted on opening a dialog box in order to create formatted text in an image. Thus, a user could not see exactly how the text was going to look in the image, forcing her to repeat the procedure again and again to get things right. Finally Adobe fixed the problem, letting users edit formatted text directly into an image layer, in full WYSIWYG fashion — as it should be.

Scrollbars

Scrollbars serve a critical need in the modern GUI — they enable smallish rectangles (i.e., windows or panes) to meaningfully contain large amounts of information. Unfortunately, they are also typically quite frustrating, difficult to manipulate, and wasteful of pixels. The scrollbar is, without a doubt, both overused and underexamined. In its role as a window content and document navigator — a display control — its application is appropriate.

The singular advantage of the scrollbar — aside from its near universal availability — is that it provides useful context about where you are in the window. The scrollbar's **thumb** is the small, draggable box that indicates the current position, and, often, the scale of the "territory" that can be scrolled.

Many scrollbars are quite parsimonious in doling out information to users. The best scrollbars use thumbs that are proportionally sized to show the percentage of the document that is currently visible, as well as:

- How many pages there are in total
- The page number (record number, graphic) as we scroll with the thumb
- The first sentence (or item) of each page as we scroll with the thumb

Additionally, many scrollbar implementations are stingy with functions. To better help us manage navigation within documents, they should give us powerful tools for going where we want to go quickly and easily, such as:

- Buttons for skipping ahead by pages/chapters/sections/keywords
- Buttons for jumping to the beginning and end of the document
- Tools for setting bookmarks that we can quickly return to

Recent versions of Microsoft Word make use of scrollbars that exhibit many of these features.

Shortcomings in contextual information aside, one of the biggest problems with scrollbars is that they demand a high degree of precision with the mouse. Scrolling down or up in a document is generally much easier than scrolling down *and* up in a document. You must position the mouse cursor with great care, taking your attention away from the data you are scrolling. Some scrollbars replicate both their up and down nudge arrows at each end of the scrollbar; for windows that will likely stretch across most of the screen, this can be helpful; for smaller windows, such replication of controls is probably overkill and simply adds to screen clutter (see Chapter 19 and Figure 19-1 for more discussion of this idiom).

The ubiquity of scrollbars has unfortunately resulted in some unfortunate misuse. Most significant here is their shortcomings in navigating time. Without getting too philosophical or theological, we can all hopefully agree that time has no meaningful beginning or end (at least within the perception of the human mind). What, then, is the meaning of dragging the thumb to one end of a calendar scrollbar? (See Figure 21-21).

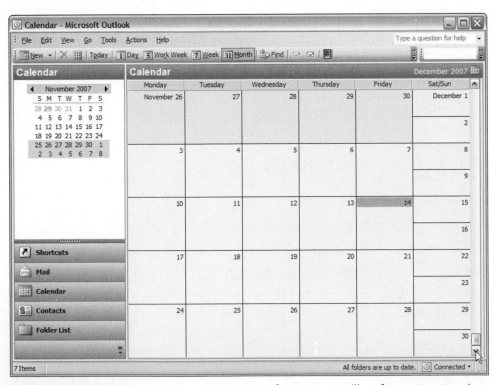

Figure 21-21 This image shows a limitation of using a scrollbar for navigating the endless stream of time. Dragging the thumb all the way to the end of the scrollbar brings a user one year into the future. This seems a bit arbitrary and limiting.

There are some viable alternatives to scrollbars. One of the best is the **document navigator**, which uses a small thumbnail of the entire document space to provide direct navigation to portions of the document (see Figure 21-22). Many image editing applications (such as Photoshop) utilize these for navigating around a document when zoomed in. These can also be very useful when navigating time-based documents, such as video and audio. Critical to the success of such idioms is that it is possible to meaningfully represent the big picture of the document in visual form. For this reason, they aren't necessarily appropriate for long text documents. In these cases, the structure of the document itself (in outline form) can provide a useful alternative to scrollbars. A basic example of this can be seen in Microsoft Word's Document Map (which is well intended, but of only limited utility — it deems only first- and second-level headers worth displaying).

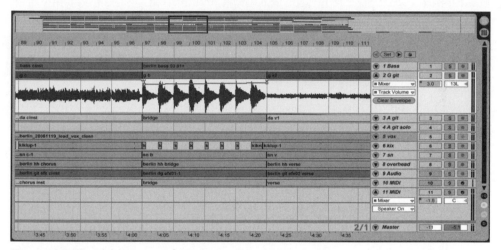

Figure 21-22 Ableton Live features a document navigator on the top of the arrangement screen that provides an overview of the entire song. The black rectangle denotes part of the song that the work area below is zoomed in on. The navigator both provides context in a potentially confusing situation and simultaneously provides a direct navigation idiom where a user may move the rectangle to focus on a different part of the song.

Splitters

Splitters are useful tools for dividing a sovereign application into multiple, related panes in which information can be viewed, manipulated, or transferred. Movable splitters should always advertise their pliancy with cursor hinting. Though it is easy and tempting to make all splitters movable, you should exercise care in choosing which ones to make movable. In general, a splitter shouldn't be able to be moved in such a way that makes the contents of a pane completely unusable. In cases where panes need to collapse, a drawer may be a better idiom.

Drawers and levers

Drawers are panes in a sovereign application that can be opened and closed with a single action. They can be used in conjunction with splitters if the amount that the drawer opens is user configurable. A drawer is usually opened by clicking on a control in the vicinity of the drawer. This control needs to be visible at all times and should either be a latching button/butcon or a **lever**, which behaves similarly, but typically swivels to indicate an open or closed state.

Drawers are a great place to put controls and functions that are less frequently used but are most useful in context of the main work area of the application. Drawers have the benefit of not covering up the main work area the way a dialog does. Property details, searchable lists of objects or components, and histories are perfect candidates for putting in drawers.

Although the big-picture principles discussed throughout this book can provide enormous leverage in creating products that will please and satisfy users, it's always important to remember that the devil is in the details. Frustrating controls can lead to a constant low-level annoyance, even if an overall product concept is excellent. Be sure to dot your i's and cross your t's, and ensure that your controls are well behaved.

22

Menus

Menus are perhaps the oldest idioms in the GUI pantheon — revered and surrounded by superstition and lore. Most designers, programmers, and users accept without question that traditional menu design is correct — there are so many existing programs that attest to its excellence. But this belief is like snapping your fingers to keep the tigers away. There aren't any tigers here, you say? See, it works! That said, a well-designed menu can be a very useful way to provide access to application functionality in certain contexts. We start this chapter with a brief history of menus and then discuss some problems with menus and how to use them appropriately.

A Bit of History

While the modern GUI with its drop-down menus and dialog boxes has only been mainstream since the Macintosh's introduction in 1984, it is now so ubiquitous that it's easy to take for granted. Before diving into the details of contemporary menu idioms, it's useful to look back and examine the path we've taken in the development of modern interaction idioms as a basis for our understanding of menus' strengths and potential pitfalls.

The command-line interface

If you wanted to talk to an IBM mainframe computer in the 1970s, you had to manually keypunch a deck of computer cards, use an obscure language called JCL (Job Control Language), and submit this deck of cards to the system through a noisy, mechanical card reader. Each line of JCL or program had to be punched on a separate card. Even the first microcomputers, small, slow, and stupid, running a primitive operating system called CP/M, had a much better conversational style than those hulking dinosaurs in their refrigerated glass houses. You could communicate directly with microcomputers running CP/M merely by typing commands into a standard keyboard. What a miracle! The program issued a prompt on the computer screen that looked like this:

```
A>
```

You could then type in the names of programs, which were stored as files, as commands and CP/M would run them. We called it the **command-line** interface, and it was widely considered a great leap forward in man-machine communications.

The only catch is that you had to know what to type. For frequent users, who at that time were mostly programmers, the command-line prompt was very powerful and effective because it offered the quickest and most efficient route to getting the desired task done. With his hands on the keyboard in the best tradition of touch typists, a user could rip out `copy a:*.* b:`, and the disk was copied. Even today, for users who have mastered the command set, the command line is still considerably faster (and often more powerful) than using a mouse for many operations.

The command-line interface really separated the men (and women) from the nerds. As software got more powerful and complex, however, the memorization demands that the command-line interface made on users were just too great, and it had to give way to something better.

Sequential hierarchical menus

Finally, sometime in the late-1970s, some very clever programmer came up with the idea of offering users a list of choices. You could read the list and select an item from it the way that you choose a dish at a restaurant by reading the menu. The appellation stuck, and the age of the **sequential hierarchical menu** began.

The sequential hierarchical menu enabled users to forget many of the commands and option details required by the command-line interface. Instead of keeping the details in his head, a user could read them off the screen. Another miracle! Circa

1979, your program was judged heavily on whether or not it was menu-based. Those vendors stuck in the command-line world fell by the wayside in favor of the more modern paradigm.

Although the paradigm was called *menu-based* at the time, we refer to these menus as *sequential* and *hierarchical* to differentiate them from the menus in widespread use today. The old pre-GUI menus were deeply hierarchical: After you made a selection from one menu, it would be replaced by another, then another, drilling down into a tall tree of commands.

Because only one menu at a time could be placed on the screen and because software at that time was still heavily influenced by the batch style of mainframe computing, the hierarchical menu paradigm was sequential in behavior. Users were presented with a high-level menu for choosing between major functions, for example:

```
1. Enter transactions
2. Close books for month
3. Print Income Statement
4. Print Balance Sheet
5. Exit
```

After a user chose a function, say 1. Enter transactions; he would then be prompted with another menu, subordinate to his choice from the first one, such as:

```
1. Enter invoices
2. Enter payments
3. Enter invoice corrections
4. Enter payment corrections
5. Exit
```

A user would choose from this list and, most likely, be confronted with a couple more such menus before the actual work would begin. Then, the Exit option would take him up only one level in the hierarchy. This meant that navigating through the menu tree was a real chore.

Once a user made his selection, it was set in concrete — there was no going back. People, of course, made mistakes all the time, and the more progressive developers of the day added confirmation menus. The program would accept the user's choice as before, then issue another menu to enquire: Press the Escape Key to Change Your Selection, Otherwise Press Enter to Proceed. This was an incredible pain, because regardless of whether you had made a mistake or not, you needed to answer this awkward and confusing meta-question, which could lead you to make exactly the kind of mistake you were hoping to avoid.

Such menu-based interfaces would be terrible judged by today's standards. Their chief failing was that with such a limited command vector, the hierarchies became quite deep. They also demonstrated a striking lack of flexibility and clarity in communicating with people. Still, they were better than command lines, where you had to remember a sometimes complex command syntax, as well as the exact spelling of every operand you wanted to act upon. Sequential hierarchical menus lightened the amount of memory work required of users, but forced them to laboriously navigate a maze of confusing choices and options. They, too, had to give way to something better. (Though it doesn't take much looking to find current-day devices and kiosks that fall back on these idioms — take most ATMs, for example.)

The Lotus 1-2-3 interface

The next great advance in user-interface technology came in 1979 from Lotus Corporation with the original 1-2-3 spreadsheet program. 1-2-3 was still controlled by a deeply hierarchical menu interface, but Lotus added its own twist — the **visible hierarchical menu.** This helped make it the most successful piece of software ever sold at that point.

In 1979, a computer screen offered exactly 2000 characters per screen (see Figure 22-1), arranged in 25 horizontal rows of 80 characters each. 1-2-3 presented its menu horizontally along the top of the screen, where it consumed only two rows out of the 25 available. This meant that the menu could coexist on the screen with the actual spreadsheet program. Unlike the hierarchical menu programs that came before it, a user didn't have to leave a productive screen to see a menu. He could enter a menu command right where he was working in the program.

Figure 22-1 The original Lotus 1-2-3, which first shipped in 1979, exhibited a remarkable new menu structure that actually coexisted with the working screen of the program. All other menu-based programs at that time forced you to leave the working screen to make menu selections.

Lotus used its new menu idiom with great abandon, creating a hierarchical menu structure of remarkable proportions. There were dozens of nodes in the menu tree and several hundred individual choices available. Each one could be found by looking at the top line of the screen and tabbing over and down to the desired selection. The program differentiated between data for the spreadsheet and a command for the menu by detecting the presence of a backslash character (\). If a user typed a slash, the keystrokes that followed were interpreted as menu commands rather than data. To select an item on the menu, all you had to do was read it and type in its first letter preceded by a slash. Submenus then replaced the main menu on the top line.

Frequent users quickly realized that the patterns were memorable, and they didn't necessarily have to read the menu. They could just type /-s to save their work to disk. They could just type /-c-g-x to add up a column of numbers. They could, in essence, bypass the use of the menu entirely. They became power users, memorizing the letter commands and gloating over their knowledge of obscure functions.

It may seem silly now, but it illustrates a very powerful point: A good user interface enables users to move in an ad hoc, piecemeal fashion from beginner to expert. A given power user of 1-2-3 may have been on intimate terms with a couple of dozen functions, while simultaneously being completely ignorant of several dozen others. If he had memorized a particular slash-key sequence, he could go ahead and access it immediately. Otherwise, he could read the menu to find those less frequently used ones that he hadn't committed to memory. We discuss the significance of menus as a means of discovering and learning the functions of an application at length later in this chapter.

But 1-2-3's hierarchical menu was hideously complex. There were simply too many commands, and every one of them had to fit into the single hierarchical menu structure. The program's designers bent over backwards to make logical connections between functions in an attempt to justify the way they had apportioned the commands in the hierarchy. In the delirium of revolutionary success and market dominance, such details were easily ignored.

As you might imagine, because of 1-2-3's success, the mid-1980s were a time of widespread 1-2-3 cloning. The always visible, hierarchical menu found its way into numerous programs, but the idiom was really the last gasp of the character-based user interface in the same way that the great, articulated steam locomotives of the late 1940s were the final, finest expression of a doomed technology. As surely as diesel locomotives completely eliminated all steam power within the span of a decade, the GUI eliminated the 1-2-3-style hierarchical menu within a few short years.

Drop-down and pop-up menus

Many concepts and technologies had to come together to make the GUI possible: the mouse, memory-mapped video, powerful processors, and pop-up windows. A pop-up window is a rectangle on the screen that appears, overlapping and obscuring the main part of the screen, until it has completed its work, whereupon it disappears, leaving the original screen behind, untouched. The pop-up window is the mechanism used to implement **drop-down menus** (also called pull-down menus) and dialog boxes.

In modern GUIs, menus are visible across the top row of a screen or window in a **menu bar**. A user points and clicks on a menu bar and its immediately subordinate list of options appears in a small window just below it. A variant of the drop-down menu is a menu that "pops up" when you click (or more frequently, right-click) on an object, even though it has no menu title: a **pop-up menu**.

After the menu is open, a user makes a single choice by clicking once or by dragging and releasing. There's nothing remarkable about that, except that the menus most frequently go no deeper than this. The selection a user makes on the menu either takes immediate effect or calls up a dialog box. The hierarchy of menus has been flattened down until it is only one level deep. In many cases, especially when optimizing interactions for novice users, flattening the organization of user choices (whether they be among commands or objects) can greatly improve the scanability of the user interface.

Arguably the most significant advance of the GUI menu was this retreat from the hierarchical form into monocline grouping. The dialog box, another use of the pop-up window, was the tool that simplified the menu. The dialog box enabled the software designer to encapsulate all the subchoices of any menu item within a single, interactive container. With dialogs, menu hierarchies could flatten out considerably, gathering all the niggling details further down the menu tree into a single dialog window. The deeply hierarchical menu was a thing of the past.

With the higher resolution of GUI displays, enough choices could be displayed on the menu bar to organize all the program's functions into about a half-dozen meaningful groups, each group represented by a one-word menu title. The menu for each group was also roomy enough to include all its related functions. The need to go to additional levels of menus was made almost superfluous.

(Of course, Philistines and reprobates are always with us, and they have created methods for turning pull-down menus back into hierarchical menus. They are called **cascading menus**, and although they are occasionally useful, more often they merely tempt the weaker souls in the development community to gum up their menus for little gain. We discuss this in more detail later in this chapter.)

Menus Today: The Pedagogic Vector

As the modern GUI evolved, two idioms fundamentally changed the role of the menu in the user interface: direct manipulation and toolbars. The development of direct-manipulation idioms has been a slow and steady progression from the first days of graphical user interfaces. Conversely, the toolbar was an innovation that swept the industry around 1989. Within a couple of years, virtually every Windows program had a toolbar filled with butcons. A few years before, nobody had seen a toolbar.

In the same way that a stranger to town may take a roundabout route to her destination while a native will always proceed on the most economical path, experienced users of a program will commonly invoke a function with the most immediate command rather than one that requires intermediate steps. As a result, the most frequently used commands in a program are often invoked by butcons on the toolbar. Ultimately, menus are commonly needed less and less for functions that are used on a daily basis, and instead become a way of learning about infrequently used tools.

The butcons and other controls on the toolbar are usually redundant with commands on the menu. Butcons are immediate, whereas menu commands remain relatively slow and hidden. Menu commands have a great advantage, however, in their verbal descriptions of functions. This makes them amongst the most useful interaction techniques for the purpose of teaching users about the capabilities of the product. In other words, menus provide a **pedagogic vector**.

For people to best learn how to use an interactive product, they should be able to examine and experiment without fear of commitment or causing irreparable harm. The Undo function and Cancel button on each dialog box supports this function well. Contrary to user-interface paradigms of 20 years ago, menus and dialog boxes shouldn't be the main method by which normal users perform everyday functions. Many programmers and designers haven't yet realized this fact, and they continue to confuse the purpose of the menu command vector. Its primary role should be to teach new users, to remind those who have forgotten, and to provide a way to access infrequently used functions.

DESIGN
principle   Use menus to provide a pedagogic vector.

When a user looks at an application for the first time, it is often difficult to size up what that application is capable of. An excellent way to get an impression of the power and purpose of an application is to glance at the set of available functions by way of its menus and dialogs. We do this in the same way we look at a restaurant's menu posted at its entrance to get an idea of the type of food, the presentation, the setting, and the price.

Understanding the scope of what a program can and can't do is one of the fundamental aspects of creating an atmosphere conducive to learning. Many otherwise easy-to-use programs put users off because there is no simple, unthreatening way for them to find out just what the program is capable of doing.

Toolbars and direct-manipulation idioms can be too inscrutable for a first-time user to understand, but the textual nature of the menus serves to explain the functions. Reading the words "Format Gallery" (see Figure 22-2) is more enlightening to the new user than trying to interpret a butcon that looks like this (although ToolTips obviously help).

Figure 22-2 A menu item reading Format Gallery is likely to be more enlightening to new users than a butcon like this one. But after they become intermediates, it's a different story altogether.

For an infrequent user who is somewhat familiar with an application, the menu's main task is as an index to tools: A place to look when he knows there is a function but can't remember where it is or what it's called. This works the same way as its namesake, the restaurant menu, which permits him to rediscover that delightful fish curry thing he ordered a year ago, without having to remember its precise name. The drop-down menu lets him rediscover functions whose names he's forgotten. He doesn't have to keep such trivia in his head, but can depend on the menu to keep it for him, available when he needs it.

If the main purpose of menus were to execute commands, terseness would be a virtue. But because the main justification of their existence is to teach us about what is available, how to get it, and what shortcuts are available, terseness is really the exact opposite of what we need. Our menus have to explain what a given function does, not just where to invoke it. Because of this it behooves us to be more verbose in our menu item text. Menus shouldn't say "Open...," but rather "Open Report..."; not "Auto-arrange," but rather "Auto-arrange icons." We should stay away from jargon, as our menu's users won't yet be acquainted with it.

Many applications also use the status bar that goes across the bottom of their main window to display an even longer line of explanatory text associated with the currently selected menu item. This idiom can enhance the teaching value of the command vector — if a user knows to look for it. The location ensures that such information will often go unnoticed.

To provide a good pedagogic vector, menus must be complete and offer a full selection of the actions and facilities available in the application. A scan of the menus should make clear the scope of the program and the depth and breadth of its various facilities.

Another teaching purpose is served by providing hints pointing to other command vectors in the menu itself. Repeating button icons next to menu commands and including hints that describe keyboard equivalents teach users about quicker command methods that are available (we discuss this further later in this chapter). By putting this information right in the menu, the user may register it subconsciously. It won't intrude upon his conscious thoughts until he is ready to learn it, and then he will find it readily available and already familiar.

Standard menus for desktop applications

Almost every GUI these days has at least a File and an Edit menu in (or near) its two leftmost positions and a Help menu to the right (Mac OS X has a menu named after the in-focus application in the furthest left position — followed by File and Edit). The Windows, Macintosh, and even the Motif style guides state that these File, Edit, and Help menus are standard. It is tempting to think that this de facto cross-platform standard is a strong indication of the proven correctness of the idiom. Wrong! It is a strong indication of the development community's willingness to blithely accept mediocre design, changing it only when the competition forces us to do better. The File menu's name is the result of implementation model thinking about how our operating systems work, the Edit menu is based on a very weak clipboard, and the Help menu is frequently not terribly helpful and often only contains a single item that is actually directly related to helping users.

These menu conventions can trap us into designing weak user interfaces. The menus on most of our programs may be familiar, but are they good ways to organize functions? Selections like View, Insert, Format, Tools, and Options sound like tools and functions, not goals. Why not organize the facilities in a more goal-directed way?

Can't you hear the programmers shouting, "How can you change something that has become a standard? People *expect* the File menu!" The reply is simple: People may get used to pain and suffering, but that is no reason to perpetuate them. Users will adapt just fine if we change the File menu so that it delivers a *better, more meaningful* model. The key to figuring out a reasonable menu structure goes back to understanding users' mental models. How do they think about what they are doing? What terms make the most sense to them? If your users are computer-savvy, and you're designing a productivity application, it might make sense to stick to recognizable standards, at least at the top level (and then again, it might not). If, however, you're designing a specialized and purposeful application, the structure might very well need to be different.

All that said, there is obviously still a place for the standard menu structures. In the many situations where it is not appropriate to restructure an application's menu structure, much good can be done merely by making good choices about how menu standards are applied.

File (or document)

Most users only think of files when they're forced to understand the implementation model. A much more Goal-Directed term for the menu is "Document." If your application deals with one primary document or object type, it's worth considering whether it makes sense to use that for the menu name. For example, in a music sequencer, "Song" would be a much more user-friendly term than "File." We assure you, there's nothing worse to be thinking about when making music than a computer's file system.

In Chapter 17 we described a better File (or Document) menu. One useful feature we didn't mention there is the Most Recently Used list on Microsoft applications (see Figure 22-3).

Edit

The Edit menu contains facilities for selecting, cutting, pasting, and making modifications to selected objects (though if there are a lot of functions to do this, they should be grouped in a separate Modify or Format menu). Don't use the Edit menu as a catch-all for functions that don't seem to fit anywhere else.

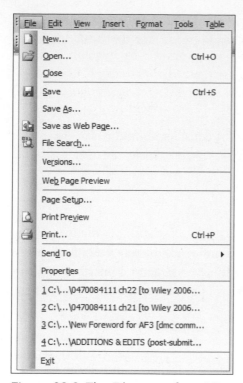

Figure 22-3 The File menu from Microsoft Word shows off the excellent Most Recently Used (MRU) list. In Chapter 17, you saw how to reconstruct the first six items so that they better reflect the user's mental model, rather than following the technically faithful implementation model as shown here.

Windows

The Windows menu is for arranging, viewing, and switching between multiple windows opened by the program. It can also offer tools for laying out multiple documents onscreen simultaneously. Nothing else should go on this menu. It should be noted that unless you have a multiple document interface (MDI), this menu is seldom necessary.

Help

Today's Help menus tend to reflect poorly designed and implemented help systems. We talk much more about help in general in Chapter 25, but suffice to say, this menu should contain a variety of methods for helping people learn to use your application. One thing sorely lacking on most Help menus is an item labeled Shortcuts that explains how to go beyond relying on the menus. It could offer pointers on more powerful idioms such as accelerators, toolbar buttons, and direct-manipulation idioms.

Optional Menus

The following menus are commonly used, but considered optional in most style guides. An application of moderate complexity is likely to make use of at least some of these menus.

View

The View menu should contain all options that influence the way a user looks at the program's data. Additionally, any optionally displayed structural interface elements such as rulers, toolbars, grids, drawers, sidebars, or palettes should be controlled here.

Insert

The Insert menu provides the facility to introduce new objects in a document. In a word processor, appropriate examples include inserting tables, graphs, and symbols. In a music sequencer, appropriate examples include inserting new instruments, effects, and key changes.

Settings

If you have a Settings menu in your application, you are making a commitment to a user that anytime he wants to alter a setting in the program he will easily find the way to do it here. Don't offer up a settings menu and then scatter other setting items or dialogs on other menus. This includes printer settings, which are often erroneously found on the File menu.

Format

The Format menu is one of the weakest of the optional menus because it deals almost exclusively with properties of visual objects and not functions. In a more object-oriented world, properties of visual objects are controlled by more visual direct-manipulation idioms, not by functions. The menu serves its pedagogic purpose, but you might consider omitting it entirely if you've implemented a more object-oriented format property scheme.

The page setup commands that typically reside on the File menu should be placed here. (Notice that page setup is very different from printer setup.)

Tools

The Tools menu, sometimes less clearly called the Options menu, is where big, powerful functions go. Functions like spell checkers and goal finders are considered tools. Also, the Tool menu is where the **hard-hat items** should go.

Hard-hat items are the functions that should only be used by real power users. These include various advanced settings. For example, a client-server database program has easy-to-use, direct-manipulation idioms for building a query, while behind the scenes the program is composing the appropriate SQL statement to create the report. Giving power users a way to edit the SQL statement directly is most definitely a hard-hat function! Functions like these can be dangerous or dislocating, so they must be visually set off from the more benign tools available. Another possible approach is to place them in an Expert or Advanced menu, to the right of the more benign Tools menu, which Apple has done in iPhoto, for example, though some of the functions there may be improperly placed.

Menu Idioms

Over the years, simple menus have been embellished with new and more complex behavioral idioms. Some have their uses, and others simply get in the way. This section discusses these idioms and their appropriate uses.

Cascading menus

One variant of the standard drop-down menu provides a secondary menu when a user selects certain items in the primary menu. This mechanism, called a **cascading menu** (see Figure 22-4), presents some serious issues for ease of use.

Where standard drop-down menus provide clear, easy-to-navigate monocline grouping, cascading menus move us into the complex territory of nesting and hierarchies. They not only make it much more difficult for users to locate items, but they also require well-coordinated mouse movements in two dimensions to navigate them smoothly. (If you trace the path required to select an item in a multilevel cascading menu [such as the Windows Start menu], you will notice that it quite literally takes the form of a path through a maze).

However, cascading menus are not entirely without worth. They also allow menus to contain much larger command sets, and they provide a hierarchical method of organizing these command sets. As useful as this may sound, please pay close attention to your users before choosing to employ this idiom.

It should be clear that cascading menus should only be employed in sophisticated sovereign applications for rarely used functions or as a secondary command vector for something more directly provided in the interface. Also, if you implement cascading menus, be sure to allow for a wide threshold in mouse movement, so the submenu doesn't disappear.

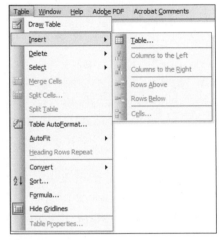

Figure 22-4 This is an example of a cascading menu from Microsoft Word 2003. Cascading menus make it difficult for users to find and browse the command set, but they do allow menus to usefully contain much larger command sets.

Menus

With Office 2000, Microsoft introduced **adaptive menus**, which display only those items accessed most frequently by a specific user (see Figure 22-5). This menu idiom was enabled by default in Office 2000 and 2003, but Office 2007 marked a departure from this approach (and menus in general) in favor of the ribbon bar, which we discuss below and in Chapter 23.

With adaptive menus, Microsoft attempted to make their products seem simpler and easier by hiding those items that a user never accesses. To see the hidden menu items, users are required to click or hover on an icon at the bottom of the menu. When displayed, the previously hidden items are interspersed with the originally shown items.

The adaptive menu is well intended, and we certainly applaud the attempt to customize a user interface based upon usage behavior. Unfortunately, the idiom is annoying and severely compromises user effectiveness. Adaptive menus significantly increase the amount of work performed by users as the idiom runs contrary to the two primary roles of a menu system: to teach users about the breadth and depth of application functionality and to provide access to less-frequently used functions.

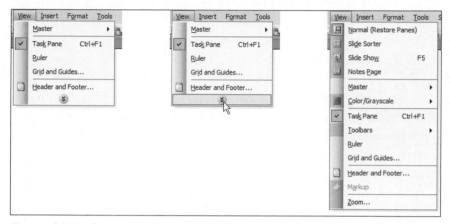

Figure 22-5 These images show an expanding menu from PowerPoint 2003. On the left is the menu in its default state, showing a subset of commands based upon usage patterns. The middle image shows the hover state, and on the right is the full menu that is displayed after clicking the expand button.

It's worth noting that usability studies support this assessment. In a 1989 study, subjects took a significantly longer time to complete tasks with adaptive menus than with static menus, and 81% reported preferring static menus to adaptive menus.[1] We would caution readers about interpreting these findings to mean that users will never feel well supported by adaptive interfaces. Rather, we suggest that this particular application of adaptability was directly at odds with the purpose of menus.

The ribbon

In Office 2007, Microsoft introduced a new command control — the **ribbon**, a tabbed panel at the top of the application window that combines the menus and toolbars into a single unified structure (see Figure 22-6). The idea behind the ribbon is to combine the visually expressive and pliant characteristics of toolbar buttons and buttons with the verbose and more explicit and comprehensive depiction of functionality of a menu system.

Figure 22-6 This is the ribbon from Microsoft PowerPoint 2007. This new interface idiom is a combination between a menu system's hierarchical organization and the more direct and visual presentation of a toolbar.

Unlike adaptive menus, the ribbon appears to have been designed with the strengths and uses of both menus and toolbars. As with a menu, clicking through the tabs of the ribbon provides a good overview of the capabilities of an application (though the visual complexity and the fact that some items are vertically stacked somewhat compromises its scanability). Like a toolbar, the ribbon provides fairly direct and visual access to functions, though a user is sometimes required to change tabs to find the right button. This is somewhat mitigated by the fact that a contextual toolbar is provided immediately next to a selected item in the document workspace (more on this in Chapter 23), and the tabs are meant to change automatically to provide access to appropriate tools. While the ribbon idiom is appealing and intriguing, it seems that this is not entirely effective in initial releases of Office 2007. After repeated use, we find ourselves continually hunting for commonly used functions. Perhaps this will improve — at the time of writing, Office 2007 has only been available for six months.

Bang menus

In the early days of the Mac and Windows, some applications featured a menu variant that has, for good reason, fallen out of favor: the **immediate** menu or **bang menu**. In programmer's jargon, an exclamation mark is a **bang**, and, by convention, top-level immediate menu items were always followed with a bang.

As the name implies, it is a menu *title* — directly on the menu bar next to other menu titles — that behaves like a menu *item*. Rather than displaying a drop-down menu for subsequent selection, the bang menu causes a function to execute right away! For example, a bang menu title for printing would be called Print!.

This behavior is so unexpected that it generates instant disorientation (and sometimes even anger). The bang menu title has virtually no instructional value (except perhaps through shock value). It is dislocating and disconcerting. The same immediacy on a toolbar button or butcon bothers nobody, though. The difference is that butcons on a toolbar advertise their immediacy because they are known by convention to be *imperative controls*. This is a classic example where breaking from standard and convention without sufficient cause can result in serious cognitive friction for users. Immediate commands belong in toolbars.

Disabled menu items

An important menu convention is to disable (make nonfunctional) menu items when they are unavailable in a given state or not relevant to the selected data object or item. The disabled state is typically indicated by lightening or "graying out" the text for the item in the menu. This is a useful and expected idiom — it helps the menu become an even better teaching tool, as users can better understand the context in which certain commands are applicable.

 DESIGN principle Disable menu items when they are not applicable.

Checkmark menu items

Checkmarks next to menu items are usually used for enabling and disabling aspects of the program's interface (such as turning toolbars on and off) or adjusting the display of data objects (such as wire frame versus fully rendered images). This is an idiom easily grasped by users and is effective because it not only provides a functional control but also indicates the state of that control.

This idiom is probably best used in programs with fairly simple menu structures. If the application is more complex and sophisticated, the menu space will be sorely needed, and opening and scrolling through a menu to find the right item may become laborious. If the attributes in question are frequently toggled, they should also be accessible from a toolbar. If they are infrequently accessed and menu space is at a premium, all similar attributes could be gathered in a dialog box that would provide more instruction and context (as is commonly required for infrequently used functionality).

A checkmark menu item is vastly preferable to a **flip-flop menu item** that alternates between two states, always showing the one currently *not* chosen. The problem with the flip-flop menu is the same issue we identified with flip-flop buttons in Chapter 21 — namely that users can't tell if it is offering a choice or describing a state. If it says Display Toolbar, does that mean tools are now being displayed or does it mean that by selecting the option you can begin displaying them? By making use of a single checkmark menu item instead (Status bar is either checked or unchecked), you can make the meaning unambiguous.

Icons on menus

Visual symbols next to text items help users recognize them without having to read, so they can be identified faster. They also provide a helpful visual connection to other controls that do the same task. In order to create a strong visual language, a menu item should show the same icon as the corresponding toolbar butcon.

 DESIGN principle   Use consistent visual symbols on parallel command vectors.

Windows provides powerful tools for putting graphics in menus. Too few programs take full advantage of this opportunity for providing an easy, visual learning trick. For example, the applications in Microsoft's Office suite all use an icon depicting a blank sheet of paper to indicate the New Document function on their toolbars. The same icon is used in the File menu to the left of the New... menu item. Users soon make the connection, probably without even thinking about it. Microsoft Office applications have done an excellent job incorporating graphics into their menus, as shown in Figure 22-3.

Accelerators

Accelerators or "keyboard shortcuts" provide an easy way to invoke functions from the keyboard. These are commonly function keys (such as F9) or combinations involving meta-keys (e.g., Ctrl, Alt, Option, and Command). By convention, they are shown to the right of drop-down menu items to allow users to learn them as they continue to access a menu item. There are standards defined for Windows, Mac OS X, and other platforms, but their implementation is up to the individual designer, and they are too often forgotten.

There are three tips for successfully creating good accelerators:

1. Follow standards.
2. Provide for their daily use.
3. Show how to access them.

Where standard accelerators exist, use them. In particular, this refers to the standard editing set as shown on the Edit menu. Users quickly learn how much easier it is to type Ctrl+C and Ctrl+V than it is to remove their mouse hands from the home row to pull down the Edit menu, select Copy, then pull it down again and select

Paste. Don't disappoint them when they use your program. Don't forget standards like Ctrl+P for print and Ctrl+S for save.

Identifying the set of commands that will be needed for daily use is the tricky part. You must select the functions that are likely to be used frequently and ensure that those menu items are given accelerators. The good news is that this set won't be large. The bad news is that it can vary significantly from user to user.

The best approach is to perform a triage operation on the available functions. Divide them into three groups: Those that are definitely part of everyone's daily use, those that are definitely not part of anyone's daily use, and everything else. The first group must have accelerators and the second group must not. The final group will be the toughest to configure, and it will inevitably be the largest. You can perform a subsequent triage on this group and assign the best accelerators, like F2, F3, F4, and so on, to the winners in this group. More obscure accelerators, like Alt+7, should go to those least likely to be part of someone's everyday commands.

Don't forget to show the accelerator in the menu. An accelerator isn't going to do anyone any good if they have to go to the manual or online help to find it. Put it to the right of the corresponding menu item, where it belongs. Users won't notice it at first, but eventually they will find it, and they will be happy to make the discovery as perpetual intermediates (see Chapter 3). It will give them a sense of accomplishment and a feeling of being an insider. These are both feelings well worth encouraging in your customers.

Some programs offer user-configurable accelerators, and there are many instances where this is a good idea, and even a necessity, especially for expert users. Allowing users to customize accelerators on the sovereign applications that they use most of the time really lets them adapt the software to their own style of working. Be sure to include a Return to Defaults control along with any customization tools.

Access keys

Access keys or **mnemonics** are another Windows standard (they are also seen in some Unix GUIs) for adding keystroke commands in parallel to the direct manipulation of menus and dialogs.

The Microsoft style guide covers **access keys** and accelerators in detail, so we will simply stress that they should not be overlooked. Mnemonics are accessed using the Alt key, arrow keys, and the underlined letter in a menu item or title. Pressing the Alt key places the application into mnemonic mode, and the arrow keys can be used to navigate to the appropriate menu. After it opens, pressing the appropriate letter key executes the function. The main purpose of mnemonics is to provide a keyboard equivalent of each menu command. For this reason, mnemonics should be complete, particularly for text-oriented programs. Don't think of them as a convenience so much as a pipeline to the keyboard. Keep in mind that your most experienced users will rely heavily on their keyboards; so to keep them loyal, ensure that the mnemonics are consistent and thoroughly thought out. Mnemonics are not optional.

Menus on other platforms

Most of the preceding discussion is based in pattern and convention for traditional desktop software platforms. Of course, things change a bit when you consider other platforms. On devices such as mobile phones and palmtops, menus must often be relied upon as a primary command vector. While applications on handhelds typically do provide some functions in the form of buttons, due to screen real-estate limitations, toolbars and more direct idioms are not always possible, so the only way to provide access to the vast majority of functions is through a menu system.

PalmOS and Windows Mobile feature drop-down menus much like those found on modern desktop GUIs, complete with accelerators. This is, by and large, a useful translation, but it's worth considering that some idioms don't work as well with smaller screens, styluses, and four-way rocker switches. First of all, cascading menus are to be avoided at all costs. It is next to impossible to fit two adjacent open menus on the screen, and having one overlay another can cause serious confusion and dislocation for a mobile user. Second, due to space constraints, it may not be feasible to include icons on menus, despite the fact that they may be of great utility to a walking user who may find an icon easier to identify than a word.

Mobile phones and other small-screened devices (such as blood glucose meters) are typically even a generation behind drop-down menus and provide interaction idioms much in the vein of the sequential hierarchical menu (which you'll recall from earlier in the chapter). When designing for such a platform, you have little to work with, so every decision really counts. In applications where choices are mapped to the numeric keypad (and some choices may be relegated to the "More" submenu), it is of utmost importance to make sure the most frequently used functions are mapped to the number keys. Similarly, the sequence of functions should provide both cognitive guidance (by locating similar functions next to each other) and the most commonly used functions at the top of the list.

Notes

1. Mitchell, J., & Shniederman, B., 1989

23

Toolbars

Ubiquitous, toolbars are actually a relatively recent GUI development. Unlike so many GUI idioms that were popularized on the Apple Macintosh, Microsoft was the first to introduce these to mainstream user interfaces. An important complement to a menu system, the toolbar has proven to be an effective mechanism for providing persistent, direct access to functions. Whereas menus are complete toolsets with the main purpose of teaching, toolbars are for frequently used commands and offer little help to new users.

In this chapter, we'll discuss the merits and shortcomings of the toolbar command idiom. We'll also talk about ToolTips and toolbar variants such as the ribbon.

Toolbars: Visible, Immediate Commands

The typical toolbar is a collection of butcons (icons that serve as buttons), usually without text labels, in a horizontal slab positioned directly below the menu bar or in a vertical slab attached to the side of the main window (see Figure 23-1). Essentially, a toolbar is a single row (or column) of visible, immediate, graphical, functions.

Figure 23-1 This image shows the Standard and Formatting toolbars in Microsoft Word 2003. Notice how the toolbar is made up of butcons without static hinting, rather than buttons. This saves space and improves readability.

Great ideas in user-interface design often seem to spring from many sources simultaneously. The toolbar is no exception. It appeared on many programs at about the same time, and nobody can say who invented it first. What is clear is that its advantages were immediately apparent to all. In a stroke, the invention of the toolbar solved the problems of the pull-down menu. Toolbar functions are always plainly visible, and users can trigger them with a single mouse click.

Toolbars versus Menus

Toolbars are often thought of as just a speedy version of the menu. The similarities are hard to avoid: They offer access to the program's functions, and they usually form a horizontal row across the top of the screen. It seems that some designers imagine that toolbars, beyond being a command vector in parallel to menus, are an *identical* command vector to menus. They think that the functions available on toolbars should be the same as those available on menus.

In fact, in many cases, toolbars should serve a different purpose than menus do. Toolbars and their controls should be designed to provide immediate access to functions frequently accessed by users who are already familiar with the application's basics. Because of their concise nature, toolbars are typically not an ideal way for beginners to understand an application's capabilities and operation (though ToolTips alleviate this to some extent). Menus provide a much more comprehensive and descriptive view of an application, and are often more appropriate as the pedagogic vector for beginners.

 DESIGN principle   Toolbars provide experienced users fast access to frequently used functions.

The great strength of menus is their completeness and verbosity. Everything a user needs can be found somewhere on the program's menus. Of course, this very richness means that menus can get big and cumbersome. To avoid consuming too many pixels, these big menus have to be folded away most of the time and only popped-up on request. The act of popping up excludes menus from the ranks of visible and immediate commands. The trade-off with menus is thoroughness and power in exchange for a small but uniform dose of clunkiness applied at every step. The butcons on toolbars, on the other hand, are incomplete and inscrutable; but they are undeniably visible, immediate, and very space-efficient compared to menus.

Toolbars and Toolbar Controls

The toolbar gave birth to the **butcon**, a happy marriage between a button and an icon. As a visual mnemonic of a function, butcons are excellent. They can be hard for newcomers to interpret, but then, they're not *for* newcomers.

Icons versus text on toolbars

If the butcons on a toolbar act the same as the items on a drop-down menu, why are the menu items almost always shown with text and the toolbar buttons almost always shown with little images? There are good reasons for the difference, although we almost certainly stumbled on them accidentally.

Text labels, like those on menus, can be very precise and clear — they aren't always, but precision and clarity is their basic purpose. To achieve this, they demand that a user take the time to focus on them and read them. As we discussed in Chapter 14, reading is slower and more difficult than recognizing images. In their pedagogic role, menus must offer precision and clarity — a teacher who isn't precise and clear is a bad teacher. Taking the extra time and effort is a reasonable trade-off in order to teach.

On the other hand, well-designed pictorial symbols are easy for humans to recognize, but they often lack the precision and clarity of text. Pictographs can be ambiguous until you learn their meaning. However, once you learn it, you don't easily forget it, and your recognition remains lightning fast (whereas you still have to read the text every time).

Because toolbars are primarily for providing quick access to frequently used tools, their identifiers must elicit quick recognition from experienced users. The pictorial imagery of symbols suits that role better than text does. Butcons have the pliancy of buttons, along with the fast-recognition capability of images. They pack a lot of power into a very small space, but their great strength is also their great weakness: the icon.

Relying on pictographs to communicate is reasonable as long as the parties have agreed in advance what the icons mean. They must do this because the meaning of an icon of any kind is by nature ambiguous until it is learned. Many designers think that they must invent visual metaphors for butcons that adequately convey meaning to first-time users. This is a Quixotic quest that not only reflects a misunderstanding of the purpose of toolbars but also reflects the futile hope for magical powers in metaphors, which we discussed in Chapter 13.

The image on the button doesn't need to teach users its purpose; it merely needs to be easily recognizable. Users should have help learning its purpose through other means. This is not to say that the designer shouldn't strive to achieve both ends, but don't fool yourself: It can't be done very often. It's a lot easier to find images that represent *things* than it is to find images that represent actions or relationships. A picture of a trash can, printer, or chart is somewhat easy to interpret, but it's much more difficult to convey "apply style," "connect," or "convert." And when it comes down to it, perhaps a user will find himself wondering what a picture of a printer means. It could mean "find a printer," "change the printer's settings," or "report on the status of the printer." Of course, after he learns that the little printer means "print one copy of the current document on the default printer now," he won't have trouble with it again.

The problem with labeling butcons

It might seem like a good idea to label butcons with both text and images. There is not only logic to this argument but precedent, too. The original icons on the Macintosh desktop had text subtitles, as did the icon controls on some older Web browsers. Icons are useful for allowing quick classification, but beyond that, we need text to tell us *exactly* what the object is for.

The problem is that using both text and images is very expensive in terms of pixels. Except in rare circumstances, screen space is far too valuable to use this way. Designers who choose to label their icons are trying to satisfy two groups of users with different needs: One wants to learn in a gentle, forgiving environment; the other knows where the sharp edges are but sometimes needs a brief reminder. ToolTips provide an effective way to bridge the gap between these two classes of users.

Explaining Toolbar Controls

The biggest problem with toolbars is that although their controls are fast and quickly memorable, they are not initially decipherable. How is a new user supposed to learn what butcons and other toolbar controls do?

Balloon help: A first attempt

Apple was the first to attempt a solution with the introduction of **balloon help** in the System 7 OS, which provided comic-book-style speech balloons describing the purpose and operation of whatever a user's mouse cursor passed over (this is called a **fly-over**, **rollover**, or **mouseover** facility).

Despite good intentions, balloon help was ill-received. Because there was no lag between when the cursor passed over an object and when the balloon was displayed, it rendered the application largely unusable when balloon help was enabled. As a result, it was basically a modal help system. Users had to choose between learning about the application and using the application, and it hardly needs to be pointed out that this is not consistent with the way people learn most effectively. Of course, experienced users would usually keep balloon help off. Then, when they had to use a part of the application they weren't familiar with, they had to go up to the Help menu, pull it down, turn balloon help on, point to the unknown object, read the balloon, go back to the menu, and turn balloon help off. What a pain.

Needless to say, balloon help never really caught on, and developers typically created content only for the most obvious and well-known functions, ultimately undermining its usefulness. Mac OS X marked the death of balloon help in favor of a ToolTip mechanism similar to that popularized in Microsoft products.

ToolTips

Though not historically known for inventive user interfaces, Microsoft created a variant of balloon help called ToolTips that is one of the cleverest and most effective user-interface idioms we've ever seen (see Figure 23-2). At first, ToolTips may seem similar to balloon help, but on closer inspection you can see the minor physical and behavioral differences that have a huge effect from a user's point of view. First of all, ToolTips have a well-timed lag that displays the helpful information only after a user has dwelled on the item for a second or so. This is just enough time for a user to point to and select the function without getting the ToolTip. This ensures that users aren't barraged by little pop-ups as they move the mouse across the toolbar trying to do actual work. It also means that if a user forgets what a rarely used butcon is for, she only need to invest a half-second to find out.

Figure 23-2 This ToolTip from Microsoft Word 2003 helps users who have forgotten the meaning of the icon without using a lot of real estate on text labels.

ToolTips typically contain a single word or a very short phrase that describes the function. They don't traditionally attempt to explain in prose how the object is used; they assume that you will get the rest from context. This illustrates the difference in design intent between Microsoft and Apple. Apple wanted their bubbles to *teach* things to first-time users. Microsoft figured that first-timers would just have to learn how things work through "F1 Help" or by reading the manual and that ToolTips would merely act as a memory jogger for frequent users.

Super ToolTips in Microsoft Office 2007 now integrate help content into the ToolTip, in a manner very similar to balloon help. While it remains to be seen how this is received, there's no reason why it shouldn't be effective, provided that it doesn't get in the way of experienced users. By taking advantage of the inherent context sensitivity of ToolTips, better integration with other help mechanisms can only serve to reduce the excise involved in learning an application.

ToolTips make the controls on the toolbar much more accessible for intermediate users, which has allowed the toolbar to evolve beyond simply providing alternative access to menu commands. As a result, toolbars were able to take the lead as the main idiom for issuing commands to sovereign applications. This has allowed the menu to recede into the background as a command vector for beginners and for invoking advanced or occasionally used functions. The natural order of butcons as the primary idiom, with menus as a backup, makes sovereign applications much easier to use. In fact, this trajectory has continued into Microsoft Office 2007 with its Ribbon control, which replaces the menu altogether with a visually and textually expressive tabbed toolbar. We further discuss the ribbon later in this chapter.

 DESIGN principle   Use ToolTips with all toolbar and iconic controls.

Disabling toolbar controls

Toolbar controls should become disabled if they are not applicable to the current selection. They must not offer a pliant response: The butcon must not depress, for example, and controls should also gray themselves out to make matters absolutely clear.

Some programs make disabled toolbar controls disappear altogether, which can have undesirable effects. Users remember toolbar layouts by position. If butcons disappear, the trusted toolbar becomes a skittish, tentative idiom that scares the daylights out of new users and disorients even those more experienced.

Evolution of the Toolbar

After people started to regard the toolbar as something more than just an accelerator for the menu, its growth potential became more apparent. Designers began to see that there was no reason other than habit to restrict the controls on toolbars to butcons. Soon designers began to invent new idioms expressly for the toolbar. With the advent of these new constructions, the toolbar truly came into its own as a primary control device, separate from — and in many cases superior to — menus.

After the butcon, the next control to find a home on the toolbar was the combo box, as in Microsoft Word's Style, Font, and Font Size controls. It is perfectly natural that these selectors be on the toolbar. They offer the same functionality as those on the drop-down menu, but they also show the current style, font, and font size as a property of the current selection. The idiom delivers more information in return for less effort by users.

After combo boxes were admitted onto the toolbar, the precedent was set, and all kinds of idioms appeared, as we have already discussed in Chapter 21. Some of these toolbar idioms are shown in Figure 23-1.

State-indicating toolbar controls

This variety of controls contributed to a broadening use of the toolbar. When it first appeared, the toolbar was merely a place for fast access to frequently used *functions*. As it developed, controls on it began to reflect the *state* of the program's data. Instead of a butcon that simply changed a word from plain to italic text, the butcon now began to indicate — by its state — whether the currently selected text was already italicized. The butcon not only controlled the application of the style, but it also represented the status of the selection with respect to the style.

Menus on toolbars

As the variety of controls on the toolbar grows, we find ourselves in the ironic position of adding menus to it. The Word toolbar shown in Figure 23-3 shows the Undo drop-down. Sophisticated and powerful idioms such as this are pushing the old-fashioned menu bar further into the background as a secondary command vector.

Figure 23-3 Toolbars now contain drop-down menus such as the Undo menu shown here. This provides a compact way to provide powerful functionality.

Movable toolbars

Microsoft has done more to develop the toolbar as a user-interface idiom than any other software publisher. This is reflected in the quality of its products. In its Office suite, all the toolbars are very customizable. Each program has a standard battery of toolbars that users can choose to make visible or invisible. If they are visible, they can be dynamically positioned in one of five locations. They can be attached — or **docked** — to any of the four sides of the program's main window. If a user drags the toolbar away from the edge, it configures itself as a floating toolbar, complete with a mini title bar, as shown in Figure 23-4.

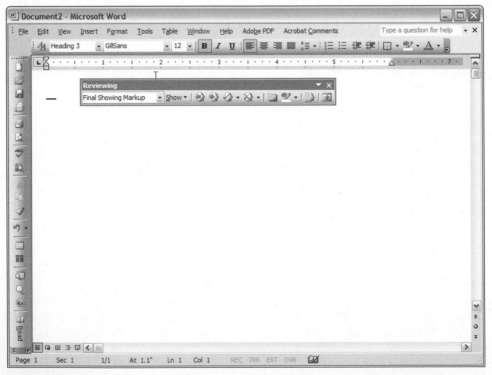

Figure 23-4 Toolbars can be docked horizontally (top), vertically (left), and dragged off the toolbar to form free-floating palettes.

Allowing users to move toolbars around also provided the possibility for users to obscure parts of toolbars with other toolbars. Microsoft handily addresses this problem with an expansion combutcon or drop-down menu that appears only when a toolbar is partly obscured, and provides access to hidden items via a drop-down menu, as shown in Figure 23-5.

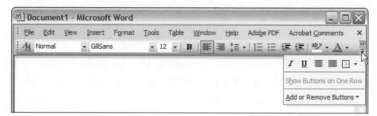

Figure 23-5 Microsoft's clever way of allowing users to overlap toolbars but still get at all their functions. This provides a very lightweight kind of customization; power users would more likely perform full toolbar customization to address similar needs via the Customize . . . item at the bottom of the drop-down menu. It's also important to note that these toolbars do have a default anchored location — users aren't forced to move them around without good reason, which would be pure excise.

Customizable toolbars

Microsoft has clearly seen the dilemma that arises because toolbars represent the frequently used functions for all users, but at least a few of those functions are different for each user. Microsoft apparently arrived at this solution: Ship the program with the best guess at what typical users' daily-use controls are, and let the others customize this. This solution has been diluted somewhat, however, by the addition of non-daily-use functions. For example, the Word toolbar's default butcon suite contains functions that certainly are not frequently used. Controls like Insert Autotext or Insert Excel Spreadsheet seem more like feature checklist items than practical, daily options for the majority of users. Although they may be useful at times, most users do not *frequently* use them. The use of personas and scenarios is a useful tool for sorting out situations such as these (see Chapters 5 and 6).

Word gives more advanced users the ability to customize and configure the toolbars to their hearts' content. There is a certain danger in providing this level of customizability to the toolbars, as it is possible for a reckless user to create a really unrecognizable and unusable toolbar. However, it takes some effort to totally wreck things. People generally won't invest much effort into creating something that is ugly and hard to use. More likely, they will make just a few custom changes and enter them one at a time over the course of months or years. Microsoft has extended the idiom so that you can create your own completely new, completely custom toolbars. The feature is certainly overkill for normal users, but there are those who appreciate such flexibility.

The ribbon

As we discussed earlier in this chapter and in Chapter 22, Microsoft introduced a new GUI idiom with Office 2007: The ribbon (see Figure 23-6). In essence, it is a tabbed toolbar with textual labels for groups of functions, as well as a heterogeneous presentation of butcons and textual commands. The tabs provide groupings similar to those used in menus (such as Home, Insert, Page Layout, References, Mailings, Review, and View in Word 2007).

Figure 23-6 The ribbon in Microsoft Word 2007 replaces the menu system with what is essentially a tabbed toolbar. While it does provide a more visual way to access functions than a traditional menu, its lack of text labels may limit its effectiveness as a pedagogical mechanism.

Aside from creating a more visually structured way of presenting a considerable number of functions, which is certainly of value, it isn't clear that the ribbon is quite as innovative as Microsoft suggests. (And although positioned differently, it also seems quite similar to Apple's "Inspectors." For example, iWeb has a tool palette that changes contents based on selection of a tool at the top. It is not represented as a tab, but it behaves as one.)

In fact, the near abandonment of text commands as found in traditional menus (which users have to go to Options to turn on) in favor of butcons may have grave implications for users learning to use the products. At the time of writing, this idiom has only been in widespread use for a few months, and it is too early to assess its success.

Contextual toolbars

A truly useful evolution of the toolbar idiom is the contextual toolbar. Similar to a right-click contextual menu, it provides a small group of butcons adjacent to the mouse cursor. In some implementations, the specific butcons presented are dependent on the object selected: If text is selected, the buttons provide text-formatting options; if a drawing object is selected, the buttons enable users to change object properties. A variation of this idiom was also popularized with Microsoft Office 2007 (where it is called the "Mini Toolbar"), though similar idioms have been used in several applications, including Adobe Photoshop (where the toolbar is docked) and Apple's Logic music production environment (where the toolbar is a modal cursor palette).

24

Dialogs

As we discussed in Chapter 21, the hallmark of bad interaction design is a user interface that consists primarily of control-laden modal dialog boxes. It is very difficult to create fluid interactions by forcing users through a maze of dialogs. If a user is the chef, and the application is the kitchen, then a dialog box is the pantry. The pantry plays a secondary role, as should dialog boxes. They are supporting actors rather than lead players, and although they may ratchet the action forward, they should not be the engines of motion.

Appropriate Uses for Dialog Boxes

Dialogs are superimposed over the main window of the application. A dialog engages users in a conversation by offering information and requesting some input. When a user has finished viewing or changing the information presented, he has the option of accepting or rejecting his changes. The dialog then disappears and returns the user to the main application window.

Unfortunately, many users and programmers have come to think of dialog boxes as the primary user-interface idiom of the GUI (this is largely a result of the ease with which dialogs can be implemented). Many applications use dialogs to provide the main method of interaction with the program (and we're not talking about simple applications that are composed of just a single dialog box; in those cases, the dialog assumes the role of a main window). In most applications, users are forced to bounce back and forth between the main window and its dialog boxes, inevitably leading to fatigue and frustration.

 DESIGN principle   Put primary interactions in the primary window.

When an application presents a dialog box, it temporarily moves the action out of the primary flow, abandoning a user's main focus of attention to introduce a secondary issue. If you asked your dinner party guests to temporarily abandon their soup and step into the pantry, the smooth flow of conversation would be broken, which is clearly to be avoided unless you have a darn good reason for dragging them in there. In the same way, a dialog box breaks the smooth flow of rapport between a user and the program. Dialogs, for good or ill, interrupt the interaction and make users react to the program instead of driving it.

It's sometimes useful to take users out of their flow to force them to focus on particular interactions. Dialogs are appropriate for functions or features that are out of the mainstream: Anything that is confusing, dangerous, or rarely used can usefully be placed in a dialog box. This is particularly true for dislocating actions that make immediate and gross changes to the application state. Such changes can be visually disturbing to users and should be cordoned off from users unfamiliar with them. For example, a function that allows wholesale reformatting of a document should be considered a dislocating action. The dialog helps prevent this feature from being invoked accidentally by assuring that a big, friendly Cancel button is always present, and also by providing the space to show more protective and explanatory information along with the risky controls. The dialog can graphically show users the potential effects of the function with a thumbnail picture of what the changes will look like (and of course, on a separate topic, a robust Undo function should be provided for such actions).

 DESIGN principle   Dialogs are appropriate for functions that are out of the main interaction flow.

Dialog boxes are also good for presenting infrequently used functions and settings. A dialog box serves to isolate these operations from more frequently used functions and settings. A dialog box is generally a roomier setting for presenting controls than other primary control venues are; you have more space for explanatory labels than you do in a toolbar, for example.

Dialog boxes are also well suited for concentrating information related to a single subject, such as the properties of a domain object — an invoice or a customer, for example. They can also gather together all information relevant to a function performed by a program — such as printing reports. This has obvious benefits to users: with all the information and controls related to a given subject in a single place, users don't have to search around the interface as much for a given function, and navigation excise is reduced.

 DESIGN principle   Dialogs are appropriate for organizing controls and information about a single domain object or application function.

Similar to menus, dialog boxes can be effective command vectors for users who are still learning an application. Because dialog boxes can be more verbose and structured, they can provide an alternate, pedagogic vector for functions that are also accessible through direct manipulation in the main application window. An example of this can be seen in tab definition in Microsoft Word. A user proficient in the application's idioms can define tab stops by directly manipulating the small thumbs in the document ruler. This idiom is not terribly easy to discover, so Microsoft designers had the foresight to provide a Tabs command in the Format menu, as well, which gives more guidance to users (though it should be said that this dialog unfortunately does little to teach users how to use the ruler idiom).

Dialog boxes serve two masters: The frequent user who is familiar with the program and uses them to control its more advanced or dangerous facilities, and the infrequent user who is unfamiliar with the scope and use of the program and who is using dialogs to learn the basics. This dual nature means that dialog boxes must be compact and powerful, speedy and smooth, and yet be clear and self-explanatory. These two goals may seem to contradict each other, but they can actually be useful complements. A dialog's speedy and powerful nature can contribute directly to its power of self-explanation.

Dialog Box Basics

Most dialogs contain a combination of informative text, interactive controls, and associated text labels. Although there are some rudimentary conventions, the diverse applications of the idiom mean that there are few hard and fast rules. It is important to create dialog boxes in accordance with good visual interface design practices and ensure that they use GUI controls appropriately. In particular, a dialog should exhibit a strong visual hierarchy, visual groupings based upon similarities in subject, and a layout based on the conventional reading order (left to right and top to bottom for Western cultures). For more details about these visual interface design practices, see Chapter 14. For more about the appropriate use of standard GUI controls, see Chapter 21.

When instantiated, a dialog box should always initially appear on the topmost visual layer, so it is obvious to the user who requested it. Subsequent user interactions may obscure the dialog with another dialog or application, but it should always be obvious how to restore the dialog to prominence.

A dialog should always have a title that clearly identifies its purpose. If the dialog box is a function dialog, the title bar should contain the function's *action* — the verb, if you will. For example, if you request Break from the Insert menu in Word, the title bar of the dialog should say Insert Break. What are we doing? We are *inserting a break*! We are not breaking, so the title bar should not say Break. A word like that could easily scare or confuse someone.

DESIGN principle   Use verbs in function dialog title bars.

If the dialog box is used to define the properties of an object, the title bar should contain the name or description of that object. The properties dialogs in Windows work this way. When you request the Properties dialog for a directory named Backup, the title bar says Backup Properties. Similarly, if a dialog box is operating on a selection, it can be useful to reflect a truncated version of the selection in the title in order to keep users oriented.

DESIGN principle   Use object names in property dialog title bars.

Most conventional dialog boxes have at least one **terminating command**, a control that, when activated, causes the dialog box to shut down and go away. Most modal dialogs offer at least two pushbuttons as terminating commands, OK and Cancel, although the Close box in the upper-right corner is also a terminating command idiom.

It is technically possible for dialogs not to have terminating commands. Some dialogs are unilaterally erected and removed by the program — for reporting on the progress of a time-consuming function, for example — so their designers may have omitted terminating commands. This is poor design for a variety of reasons, as we will see.

Modal Dialog Boxes

There are two types of dialog boxes: modal and modeless. **Modal dialogs boxes** are, by far, the most common variety. After a modal dialog opens, the owner application cannot continue until the dialog box is closed. It stops all proceedings in their tracks. Clicking on any other window belonging to the program will only get a user a rude "beep" for his trouble. All the controls and objects on the surface of the owner application are deactivated for the duration of the modal dialog box. Of course, a user can activate *other* programs while a modal dialog box is up, but the dialog box will stay there indefinitely. When the user goes back to the program, the modal dialog box will still be there waiting.

In general, modal dialogs are the easiest for users (and designers) to understand. The operation of a modal dialog is quite clear, saying to users, "Stop what you are doing and deal with me now. When you are done, you can return to what you were doing." The rigidly defined behavior of the modal dialog means that, although it may be abused, it will rarely be misunderstood. There may be too many modal dialog boxes and they may be weak or stupid, but their purpose and scope will usually be clear to users.

Some modal dialogs operate on the entire application or on the entire active document. Others operate on the current selection, in which case, a user can't change the selection after summoning the dialog. This is the most important difference between modal and modeless dialogs.

Actually, because modal dialog boxes only stop their owning applications, they are more precisely named **application modal**. It is also possible to create a **system modal** dialog box that brings every program in the system to a halt. In most cases, applications should never have one of these. Their only purpose is to report truly catastrophic occurrences (such as the hard disk melting) that affect the entire system or a real-world process.

Modeless Dialog Boxes

The other variety of dialog box is called **modeless**. Modeless dialogs are less common than their modal siblings.

After the modeless dialog opens, the parent program continues without interruption. It does not stop the proceedings, and the application does not freeze. The various facilities and controls, menus, and toolbars of the main program remain active and functional. Modeless dialogs have terminating commands, too, although the conventions for them are far weaker and more confusing than for modal dialogs.

A modeless dialog box is a much more difficult beast to use and understand, mostly because the scope of its operation is unclear. It appears when you summon it, but you can go back to operating the main program while it stays around. This means that you can change the selection while the modeless dialog box is still visible. If the dialog acts on the current selection, you can select, change, select, change, select, and change all you want. For example, Microsoft Word's Find and Replace dialog allows you to find a word in text (which is automatically selected), make edits to that word, and then pop back to the dialog, which has remained open during the edit.

In some cases, you can also drag objects between the main window and a modeless dialog box. This characteristic makes them really effective as tool or object palettes in drawing programs.

Modeless dialog issues

Many modeless dialogs are implemented awkwardly. Their behavior is inconsistent and confusing. They are visually very similar to modal dialog boxes, but they are functionally very different. There are few established behavioral conventions for them, particularly with respect to terminating commands.

Much of the confusion creeps into the situation because users are so familiar with the behavior of modal dialogs. A modal dialog can adjust itself for the current selection at the instant it was summoned. It can do this with assurance that the selection won't change during its lifetime. Conversely, the selection is quite likely to change during the lifetime of a modeless dialog box. Then what should the dialog do? For example, if a modeless dialog box modifies text, what should it do if we now select some nontext object on the main window? Should gizmos on the dialog box gray out? Change? Disappear? Questions such as this require refined design practices, as well as close examination of persona needs, goals, and mental models. Consequently, modeless dialogs can be much more challenging to design and implement than modal dialogs, which avoid these issues by freezing application state.

Two solutions for better modeless dialogs

We offer two design strategies for improving modeless dialogs. The first one is easy to swallow, a stopgap for common predicaments. The second one is more radical; an evolutionary step forward. The first solution is less thorough and effective than the second one. As you might guess, we prefer the evolutionary step. (Luckily, as you will see, in recent years, many other designers have already generated some momentum in this direction.)

A stopgap solution

If you have limited time and resources to deal with interaction design issues, we recommend leaving modeless dialog boxes pretty much the way they are, but adopting two guiding principles and applying them consistently to all modeless dialog boxes.

 DESIGN principle   Visually differentiate modeless dialogs from modal dialogs.

If a programmer uses the standard modeless dialog box facility in the Windows API, the resultant dialog is visually indistinguishable from a modal one. We must break this habit. The designer must assure that all modeless dialog boxes are rendered with a clearly noticeable visual difference. Possible methods include using a different background, making the controls visually distinct, or using a different color title bar or icon. Whatever method you choose, you must consistently stick with it.

The second principle says that we must adopt consistent and correct conventions for the terminating commands. It seems that each vendor, sometimes each programmer, uses a different technique on each individual dialog box. There isn't any reason for this cacophony of methods. Some dialogs say Close, some say Apply, some use Done, while others use Dismiss, Accept, Yes, and even OK. The variety is endless. Still others dispense with terminating buttons altogether and rely only upon the Close box in the title bar. Terminating a modeless dialog box should be a simple, easy, consistent idiom, very similar — if not exactly the same — from program to program.

 DESIGN principle   Use consistent terminating commands for modeless dialog boxes.

One particularly obnoxious construction is the use of terminating buttons that change their legends from Cancel to Apply, or from Cancel to Close, depending on whether a user has taken an action within the modeless dialog box. This dynamic change is, at best, disconcerting and hard to interpret and, at worst, frightening and inscrutable. These legends should *never* change. If a user hasn't selected a valid option but clicks OK anyway, the dialog box should assume the user means, "Dismiss the box without taking any action," for the simple reason that that is what the user actually did. Modal dialog boxes offer us the ability to cancel our actions directly, with the Cancel button. Modeless dialogs don't usually allow this direct idiom — we must resort to Undo — so changing the legends to warn users just confuses things.

DESIGN principle   Don't dynamically change the labels of terminating buttons.

The cognitive strength of *modal* dialog boxes is in their rigidly consistent OK and Cancel buttons. In modal dialogs, the OK button means, "Accept my input and close the dialog." The problem is that there is no equivalent for modeless dialog boxes. Because the controls on a modeless dialog box are always live, the equivalent concept is clouded in confusion. A user doesn't conditionally configure changes in anticipation of a terminal Execute command as he does for a modal dialog box. In modal dialogs, the Cancel button means, "Abandon my input and close the dialog." But because the changes made from a modeless dialog box are immediate — occurring as soon as an activating button is clicked — there is no concept of "Cancel all of my actions." There may have been dozens of separate actions on a number of selections. The proper idiom for this is the Undo function, which resides on the toolbar or Edit menu and is active application-wide for all modeless dialog boxes. This all fits together logically, because the Undo function is unavailable if a modal dialog box is up, but is still usable with modeless ones.

The only consistent terminating action for modeless dialog boxes is Close. Every modeless dialog box should have a Close button placed in a consistent location such as the lower-right corner. It must be consistent from dialog to dialog, in the exact same place and with the exact same caption. This button should never be disabled. Further, if the Close button actuates a function in addition to shutting the dialog, you have created a modal dialog box that should follow the conventions for the modal idiom instead.

Modeless dialog boxes frequently have several buttons that immediately invoke various functions. The dialog box should not close when one of these function buttons is clicked. It is modeless because it stays around for repetitive use and should close only when the single, consistently placed Close button is clicked.

Modeless dialog boxes must also be incredibly conservative of pixels. They will be staying around on the screen, occupying the front and center location, so they must be extra careful not to waste pixels on anything unnecessary. For this reason, especially in the context of floating palettes, the Close box in the title bar may be the best solution for a sole terminating control.

Taking an evolutionary step

The previous recommendations add up to a modest solution. Following them will surely improve some otherwise rough interactions, but the results will still leave something to be desired. There is a more radical solution that delivers us from modeless dialog maladies.

There have traditionally been two modeless tool idioms in common use. The modeless dialog box is the older of the two. The other modeless idiom is a relative newcomer on the user-interface scene but has been largely successful: namely, the toolbar. The toolbar idiom has been demonstrably effective and convenient. Most importantly, users really seem to understand that the toolbar state reflects what is selected, and that interactions with the widgets in a toolbar have a direct and immediate impact on the selection or application.

Here's where we see an opening for a new approach to modeless interactivity. Toolbars are modeless, but they don't introduce the conundrums that modeless dialogs do. They also offer two characteristics that modeless dialog boxes don't: They are visually different from dialog boxes, and there is no need to worry about dismissing them because they are omnipresent — thus there is no need for terminating controls. They solve other problems, too. Toolbars are incredibly efficient in screen space, particularly compared to dialog boxes, *and they don't cover up what they are operating on*!

Modeless dialogs are conventionally free-floating windows, which allows users to position them on the screen wherever they like, but it also results in window-management excise. It is no user's goal to reposition windows — all work done in the service of this is excise. **Docking toolbars** point us in the direction of a good solution (see Chapter 23 for more about them). You can click and drag on a docking toolbar, pull it away from the edge of the program, and it will instantly convert into a **floating palette** (also called a palette window). You can leave it this way or drag it to any edge of the program's main window, where it will convert back to a toolbar and become **docked** against the edge.

The palette takes the idea of the docking toolbar and extends to allow for even more interactivity. In fact, modern toolbars commonly contain all the control widgets that you might need for a highly interactive palette. The minor leap from a toolbar to a palette is really mostly one of changing the layout and allocation of vertical space.

Palettes are popular in graphics applications, where modeless access to tools is absolutely critical for users to maintain a productive flow. Adobe Photoshop was among the first to provide a good deal of functionality modelessly through palettes. With a growing number of palettes, it has become necessary to give them a more permanent home. Adobe Fireworks MX and other applications originally developed by Macromedia were among the first to provide a more robust docking structure to minimize screen management excise (see Figure 24-1). Recent versions of Photoshop have taken up the idiom.

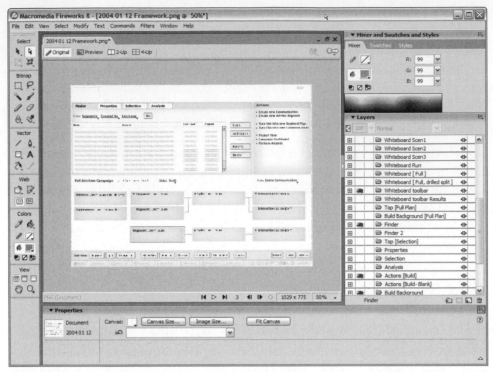

Figure 24-1 The docked palettes in Adobe Fireworks MX provide similar interactivity as modeless dialog boxes, but don't require users to spend as much effort and attention invoking, moving, and dismissing dialogs. It doesn't take a lot of imagination to see that these are really quite similar to toolbars in the sense that they use standard controls and widgets to provide application functionality directly, visibly, and persistently in the user interface.

The final step in the evolution of this new modeless command idiom has been the introduction of the **sidebar** or **task pane** — a pane in the application window dedicated to providing the kind of functions that were formerly delivered through dialog boxes. One of the first applications to do this was Autodesk's 3ds Max, a 3D modeling application that provides the ability to adjust object parameters modelessly through a sidebar. Mainstream applications that feature sidebars include Microsoft Windows Explorer and Internet Explorer, with their Explorer Bars, Mozilla Firefox with its Side Bar, Apple's uLife applications with their Inspectors, and Microsoft Office through its Task Pane. Adobe Lightroom has perhaps adopted this approach the most wholeheartedly — almost all of the application's functionality is provided modelessly through sidebars (see Figure 24-2).

Figure 24-2 Sidebars in Adobe Lightroom replace the need for dozens of dialog boxes. This approach is similar to the palette approach shown in Figure 24-1, but unlike palettes, the sidebar doesn't require users to position it on the screen and doesn't allow users to undock or dismiss it individually (though the entire sidebar may be hidden). This further reduces screen management excise and represents a significant improvement over using dialog boxes to present application functions.

Sidebars holds a lot of promise as an interaction idiom — they are featured prominently in many Cooper designs, and they need not be limited to the sides of the screen. A commonly employed pattern is the dedicated properties area below a document pane or "workspace." This modelessly provides the ability to modify a selected domain object while minimizing confusion and screen management excise (see Figure 24-3). This idiom may even be usefully employed for functions that must be submitted. Among other applications, we've used inline dialogs as mechanisms for defining orders for financial markets.

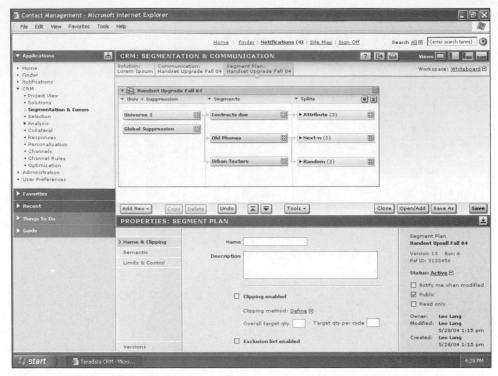

Figure 24-3 This design by Cooper for a customer-relationship management (CRM) application features dedicated properties. When a user selects an object in the workspace (top half of the screen, on the left), its properties are displayed below, thereby retaining the users context and minimizing screen management excise.

Four Different Purposes for Dialogs

The concepts of modal and modeless dialogs are derived from programmers' terms. They affect our design, but we must also examine dialogs from a goal-directed point of view. In that light, there are four fundamental types of information that are useful to convey with a dialog box: property, function, process, and bulletin.

Property dialog boxes

A **property dialog box** allows users to view and change settings or attributes of a selected object. Sometimes the attributes may relate to the entire application or document, rather than just one object.

The Font dialog box in Word, shown in Figure 24-4, is a good example. A user selects some text in the main window and then requests the dialog box from the Format menu. The dialog enables users to change font-related attributes of the selected characters. You can think of property dialogs as control panels with exposed configuration controls for the selected object. Property dialog boxes can be either modal or modeless. A properties dialog box generally controls the current selection. This follows the object-verb form: A user selects the object, then, via the property dialog, picks new settings for the selection.

Figure 24-4 The Font dialog box in Microsoft Word 2003 is a classic example of a properties dialog. A user selects text in a document, invokes the dialog with a menu command, and is then presented with a tabbed modal dialog containing all of the Font settings relevant to that text. This is one of the most common operations in a word processor. Why should a user have to go to another room to do this?

Function dialog boxes

Function dialog boxes are usually summoned from a menu. They are most frequently modal dialog boxes, and they control a single function such as printing, modifying large numbers of database records, inserting objects, or spell checking.

Function dialog boxes not only allow users to initiate an action, but they often also enable users to configure the details of the action's behavior. In many applications, for example, when a user wants to print, she uses the Print dialog to specify which pages to print, the number of copies to print, which printer to output to, and other settings directly relating to the print function. The terminating OK button on the dialog not only confirms the settings and closes the dialog but also executes the print operation.

This technique, though common, combines two functions into one: Configuring the function and invoking it. Just because a function *can* be configured, however, doesn't necessarily mean that a user will *want* to configure it before every invocation. It's often better to make these two functions separately accessible (though clearly they should also be seamlessly linked).

Many functions available from modern software are quite flexible and have a number of options. If you don't segregate configuration and actuation, users can be forced to confront considerable complexity, even if they want to perform a routine task in a simple manner.

Process dialog boxes

Process dialog boxes are launched at an application's discretion rather than at a user's request. They indicate that the application is busy with some internal function and that performance in other areas is likely to degrade.

When an application begins a process that will take perceptible quantities of time, it must make clear that it is busy, but that everything is otherwise normal. If the program does not indicate this, a user will interpret it as rudeness at best; at worst, he will assume the program has crashed and that drastic action must be taken.

DESIGN principle

Inform the user when the application is unresponsive.

As we discussed in Chapter 19, many programs currently rely on active wait-cursor hinting, turning the cursor into an hourglass. A better, more informative solution is a process dialog box (we'll discuss an even better solution later in this chapter).

Each process dialog box has four requirements:

▶ Make clear to users that a time-consuming process is happening

▶ Make clear to users that things are completely normal

▶ Make clear to users how much more time the process will take

▶ Provide a way for users to cancel the operation and regain control of the program

The mere presence of the process dialog box satisfies the first requirement, alerting users to the fact that some process is occurring. Satisfying the third requirement can be accomplished with a **progress meter** of some sort, showing the relative percentage of work performed and how much is yet to go. Satisfying the second requirement is the tough one. The application can crash and leave the dialog box up, lying mutely to the user about the status of the operation. The process dialog box must continually show, via time-related movement, that things are progressing normally. The meter should show the progress relative to the total *time* the process will consume rather than the total size of the process. Fifty percent of one process may be radically different in time from 50% of the next process.

A user's mental model of the computer executing a time-consuming process will quite reasonably be that of a machine cranking along. A static dialog box that merely announces that the computer is Reading Disk may *tell* users that a time-consuming process is happening, but it doesn't *show* that this is true. The best way to show the process is by using animation in the dialog box. In Windows, when files are moved, copied, or deleted, a process dialog box shows a small animated cartoon of papers flying from one folder to another folder or the wastebasket (see Figure 24-5). The effect is remarkable: Users get the sense that the computer is really *doing* something. The sensation that things are working normally is visceral rather than cerebral, and users — even expert users — are reassured.

Microsoft's progress meter satisfies — barely — the third requirement by hinting at the amount of time remaining in the process. There is one dialog box per operation, but the operation can affect many files. The dialog should also show an animated countdown of the number of files in the operation (for example, "12 out of 37 files remaining"). Right now, the meter shows only the progress of the single file currently being transferred (interestingly, the standard Windows install process *does* use a meter that indicates how many documents there are to go).

Notice that the copy dialog in Figure 24-5 also has a Cancel button. Ostensibly, this satisfies requirement number four, that there be a way to cancel the operation. A user may have second thoughts about the amount of time the operation will take and decide to postpone it, so the Cancel button enables him to do so. However, if the user realizes that he issued the wrong command and wishes to cancel the operation, he will not only want the operation to stop but will want all traces of the operation to be obliterated.

Figure 24-5 Microsoft got this one mostly right. For any move, copy, or delete operation in this Explorer, they show this reasonably well-designed process dialog box. It provides a hint of the time remaining in the operation, and the dialog uses animation to show paper documents flying out of the folder on the left into the folder (or wastebasket) on the right. Many users' mental models are of things moving inside the computer, and this little gem actually shows things moving. It is refreshing to see the outside of the computer reflect the inside of the computer in users' terms. The one thing missing is a countdown of the number of files left to move, which would provide even better feedback about the process at hand.

If a user drags 25 files from directory Alpha to directory Bravo, and halfway through the move realizes that he really wanted them placed in directory Charlie, he will try clicking the Cancel button. Unfortunately, all that does is *stop* the move at its current state and abandons the remainder of the moves. In other words, if a user clicks the Cancel button after 10 files have been copied, the remaining 15 files are still in directory Alpha, but the first 10 are now in directory Bravo. This is *not* what the user wants. If the button says Cancel, it should mean *cancel*, and that means, "I don't want any of this to happen." If the button were to accurately represent its action, it would say Stop Move or Stop Copy. Instead, it says Cancel, so cancel is what it should do. This may mean some significant buffering is needed, and the cancel operation could easily take more time than the original move, copy, or delete. But isn't this rare event one when the extra time required is easily justified? In Windows Explorer, the program can completely undo a copy, move, or delete, so there is no reason why the Cancel button can't also undo the portion that has already been performed.

A good alternative would be to have two buttons on the dialog, one labeled Cancel and other labeled Stop. Users could then choose the one they really want.

Eliminating process dialogs

Because a dialog is a separate room, we must ask whether the process reported by the dialog is a function separate from that on the main window. If the function is an integral part of what is shown on the main window, the status of that function should be shown on the main window. For example, the Windows flying pages dialog that was shown in Figure 24-5 is attractive and appropriate, but isn't copying a file fundamental to what the Explorer does? The animation, in this case, could have been built right into the main Explorer window. The little pages could fly across the status bar, or they could fly directly across the main window from directory to directory.

Process dialogs are, of course, much easier to program than building animation right into the main window of a program. They also provide a convenient place for the Cancel button, so it is a very reasonable compromise to fling up a process dialog for the duration of a time-consuming task. But don't lose sight of the fact that, by doing this, we are still going to another room for a this-room function. It is an easy solution, but not the correct solution. Web browsers such as Mozilla Firefox and Microsoft Internet Explorer provide a much more elegant solution. Because loading Web pages is so intrinsic to their operation, the progress indicator is displayed in the status bar itself (see Figure 24-6).

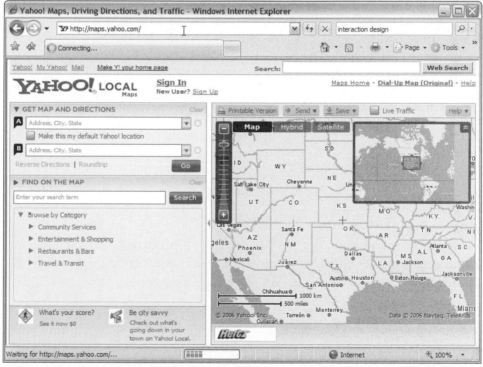

Figure 24-6 Web browsers such as Internet Explorer don't throw up a process dialog every time they load a page. Rather, a progress indicator is displayed in the status bar on the bottom of the window. This allows users to easily understand what's going on without obscuring their view of the partially loaded Web page in front of them (which in this case is quite usable). Consider whether this would be appropriate for your users before you assume that process dialogs are the correct solution.

Bulletin dialog boxes

The **bulletin dialog box** is a simple, devilish little artifact that is arguably the most abused element of any graphical user interface. Like the process dialog, it is launched, unrequested, by the program.

The ubiquitous error message box best characterizes the bulletin dialog. Normally, the application's name is shown in the caption bar, and a very brief text description of the problem is displayed in the body. A graphic icon that indicates the class or severity of the problem, along with an OK button, usually completes the ensemble. Sometimes a button to summon online help is added. An example from Word is shown in Figure 24-7.

Figure 24-7 Here's a typical bulletin dialog box. It is never requested by the user but is always issued unilaterally by the program when the program fails to do its job or when it just wants to brag about having survived the procedure. The program decides that it is easier to blame the user than it is to go ahead and solve the problem. Users interpret this as saying, "The measurement must be between -22 inches and 22 inches, and you are an incredible buffoon for not knowing that basic, fundamental fact. You are so stupid, in fact, that I'm not even going to change it for you!"

The familiar message box is normally an application modal dialog that stops all further progress of the program until a user issues a terminating command — like clicking the OK button. This is called a **blocking bulletin** because the program cannot continue until the user responds.

It is also possible for a program to put up a bulletin dialog and then unilaterally take it down again. This type is a **transitory bulletin** because the dialog disappears and the program continues without user intervention.

Transitory bulletins are sometimes used for error reporting. A program that launches an error message to report a problem may correct the problem itself or may detect that the problem has disappeared via some other agency. Some programmers will issue an error or notifier bulletin merely as a warning — Your disk is getting full — and take it down again after it has been up for, say, 10 seconds. This type of behavior is fraught with usability problems.

An error or confirmation message *must* stop the program. If it doesn't, a user may not be able to read it fully, or if he is looking away, he either won't see it or worse yet, see only a fleeting glimpse out of the corner of his eye. He will be justifiably suspicious that he has missed something important, something that will come back to haunt him later. He will now begin to worry: What did I miss? Was that an important bit of intelligence that I will regret not knowing? Is the system unstable? Is it about to crash? This is true even if the problem has gone away by itself.

If a thing is worth saying with a dialog box, it's worth ensuring that a user definitely gets the message. A transitory bulletin can't make that guarantee. It should never be used in the role of error reporting or confirmation gathering.

 DESIGN principle   Never use transitory dialogs as error messages or confirmations.

Property and function dialog boxes are intentionally requested by users — they serve users. The application, however, issues bulletin dialogs — they serve the application, at users' expense. Error, notification (alert), and confirmation messages are blocking bulletin dialogs. As we shall see, even these can and should be avoided in most circumstances.

Managing Content in Dialog Boxes

Even if you are conscientious about the use and organization of dialogs, they can easily become quite crowded with properties, options, and the like. There are a couple of common strategies for managing this crowding so your dialogs maintain their usefulness.

Tabbed dialogs

A number of years back, **tabbed dialogs** quickly became an established standard in the world of commercial software. The idiom, while quite useful at times, has also become an unfortunately convenient way for programmers to jam a whole pile of vaguely related functions into a dialog box.

On a positive note, many domain or application objects with numerous properties can now have correspondingly rich property dialog boxes without making those boxes excessively large and crowded with controls (see Figure 24-8 for an example). Many function dialogs that were previously jam-packed with controls now make better use of their space. Before tabbed dialogs, the problem was often clumsily solved with expanding and cascading dialogs, which we'll discuss shortly.

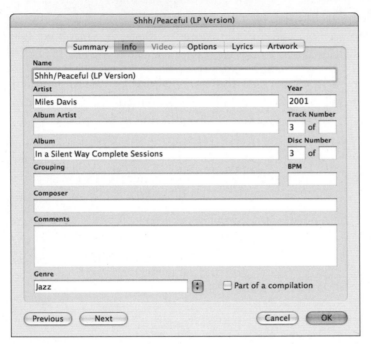

Figure 24-8 This is a tabbed dialog box from iTunes. Combining the different properties of a song in one dialog box is effective for users because they have a single place to go to find such things. Note that the terminating controls are correctly placed outside the tabbed pane, in the lower right.

A tabbed dialog allows programmers to cram more controls into a single dialog box, but more controls won't necessarily mean that users will find the interface easier to use or more powerful. The contents of the various tabs must have a meaningful rationale for being together, otherwise this capability is just another way to build a product according to what is easy for programmers, rather than what is good for users.

The tabs in a dialog should be organized to provide either increased depth or increased breadth on a well-defined topic. To organize for breadth, each tab should cover parallel, alternate aspects of the primary topic, the way song properties from iTunes, shown in Figure 24-8, addresses a variety of properties and settings for the song that would be unwieldy in a single pane. In the case of organizing for more depth, each tab should probe the same aspect of one topic in greater depth. The commonly employed Advanced tab is an example of this strategy.

Tabs are successful because the idiom follows many users' mental model of how things are normally stored. The various controls are grouped in several parallel panes, one level deep. But this idiom is often abused.

Because it's easy to cram so many controls into a tabbed dialog, the temptation is great to add more and more tabs to a dialog. The Options dialog in Microsoft Word, shown in Figure 24-9, is a clear example of this problem. The 10 tabs are far too numerous to show in a single line, so they are stacked two deep. The problem with this idiom, called **stacked tabs**, is that a user has to do a fairly significant amount of work to find the single option she wants to change. While the labels of the tabs may give her some help, she is still forced to scan the contents of several tabs while switching between them. And if that isn't enough, when she clicks on a tab in the back row, the entire row of tabs moves forward, shunting the other two rows to the back. Very few users seem to be happy with this — it's disconcerting to click on a tab and then have it move out from under the mouse.

 DESIGN principle   All interaction idioms have practical limits.

Stacked tabs illustrate the following axiom of user-interface design: All idioms, regardless of their merits, have practical limits. A group of 5 radio buttons may be excellent, but a group of 50 of them is ridiculous. Five or six tabs in a row are fine, but adding enough tabs to require stacking greatly reduces the usefulness of the idiom.

A better alternative would be to use several separate dialogs with fewer tabs on each. In this example, Options is just too broad a category, and lumping all this functionality in one place isn't doing users any favors. There is little connection among the 12 panes, so there is little need to move among them. This solution may lack a certain programming elegance, but it is much better for users.

Figure 24-9 The Options dialog in Word is an abuse of the tabbed dialog idiom. The problem is that users have to do quite a lot of work to find the option that they're looking for.

 Don't stack tabs.

Expanding dialogs

Expanding dialog boxes were big around 1990 but have declined in popularity since then, largely due to the ubiquity of toolbars and tabbed dialogs. You can still find them in many mainstream applications, such as the Find dialog in Word.

Expanding dialogs unfold to expose more controls. The dialog shows a button marked More or Expand, and when a user clicks it, the dialog box grows to occupy more screen space. The newly added portion of the dialog box contains added functionality, usually for advanced users or more complex, but related, operations. The Find dialog in Microsoft Word is a familiar example of this idiom and is shown in Figure 24-10.

Figure 24-10 The Microsoft Word Find dialog is an example of an expanding dialog. The image on the left shows it in its original state; the one on the right is what happens after the More button is pressed.

Expanding dialog boxes allow infrequent or first-time users the luxury of not having to confront the complex facilities that more frequent users don't find confusing or overwhelming. Think of the dialog as being in either beginner or advanced mode. However, these types of dialogs must be designed with care. When a program has one dialog for beginners and another for experts, it all too often simultaneously insults the beginners and hassles the experts. It's usually a good idea for the dialog to remember what mode it was used in the last time it was invoked. Of course, this means you should always remember to include a Shrink or Less command to return the dialog to simple beginner mode (as you can see in the Find dialog in Figure 24-10).

Cascading dialogs

Cascading dialogs are a diabolical idiom whereby controls, usually pushbuttons, in one dialog box summon up another dialog box in a hierarchical nesting. The second dialog box usually covers up the first one. Sometimes the second dialog can summon up yet a third one. What a mess! Thankfully, cascading dialogs have been falling from grace, but examples can still be found. Figure 24-11 shows an example taken from Windows Vista.

It is simply hard to understand what is going on with cascading dialogs. Part of the problem is that the second dialog covers up at least part of the first. That isn't the big issue — after all, combo boxes and pop-up menus do that, and some dialogs can be moved. The real confusion comes from the presence of a second set of terminating buttons. What is the scope of each Cancel? What are we OKing?

Figure 24-11 You can still find cascading dialogs in Windows. Each dialog box offers a set of terminating buttons. The resulting excise and ambiguity are not helpful.

The strength of tabbed dialogs is handling breadth of complexity, while cascading dialogs are better suited for depth. The problem is that excessive depth is a prime symptom of too much complexity in an interface. If you find your program requiring cascading dialogs for anything other than really obscure stuff that your users won't generally need, you should take another look at your interaction framework — you may find some severe structural flaws.

Dialogs can become useful assistants that help your users accomplish their goals, instead of dreaded roadblocks that confound them at every step. By keeping your dialogs manageable, and invoking them only when their functions are truly those that belong in another room, you will go far towards maintaining your users' flow and ensuring their success and gratitude.

25

Errors, Alerts, and Confirmation

In Chapter 24, we discussed the bulletin dialog, commonly issued by applications when they have problems or confront decisions they don't feel capable of making, or really any time they have something to notify users about. In other words, these dialog boxes are used for error messages, alerts, and confirmations, three of the most abused components of modern GUI design. With proper design, these dialogs can all but be eliminated. In this chapter, we explore how and why.

Error Dialogs

There is probably no user-interface idiom more abused than the error dialog. They are typically poorly written, unhelpful, rude, and worst of all, are never in time to prevent the error in the first place. Users never *want* error messages. Users want to avoid the *consequences* of making errors. This is very different from saying that they want error messages — it's like saying that people want to abstain from skiing when what they really want to do is avoid breaking their legs. As usability heavyweight Donald Norman points out, users frequently blame themselves for errors in product design. Just because you aren't getting complaints from your users doesn't mean that they are happy getting error messages.

The idea that an application doesn't have the right — even the duty — to reject a user's input is so heretical that many practitioners dismiss it summarily. Yet, we'd like to suggest that if you examine this assertion rationally and from a user's point of view, it is not only possible, but quite reasonable.

Why we have so many error messages

The first computers were undersized, underpowered, and expensive, and didn't lend themselves easily to software sensitivity. The operators of these machines were white-lab-coated scientists who were sympathetic to the needs of the CPU and weren't offended when handed an error message. They knew how hard the computer was working. They didn't mind getting a core dump, a bomb, an "Abort, Retry, Fail?" or the infamous "FU" message (File Unavailable). This is how the tradition of software treating people like machines began. Ever since the early days of computing, programmers have accepted that the proper way for software to interact with humans was to demand input and to complain when the human failed to achieve the same perfection level as the CPU.

Examples of this approach exist wherever software demands that users do things its way instead of the software adapting to the needs of humans. Nowhere is it more prevalent, though, than in the omnipresence of error messages.

What's wrong with error messages

Error messages stop the proceedings with a modal dialog box. Many designers and programmers imagine that their error message boxes are alerting users to serious problems. This is a widespread misconception. Most error message boxes are informing users of the inability of the program to work flexibly and are an admission of real stupidity on the application's part. In other words, to most users, error message boxes are seen not just as the program stopping the proceedings but as *stopping the proceedings with idiocy*. We can significantly improve the quality of our interfaces by eliminating error message boxes.

 DESIGN principle   Error message boxes stop the proceedings with idiocy and should be avoided.

People hate error messages

Humans have emotions and feelings: Computers don't. When one chunk of code rejects the input of another, the sending code doesn't care; it doesn't scowl, get hurt, or seek counseling. Humans, on the other hand, get angry when they are flatly told they are stupid.

When a user sees an error message box, it is as if another person has told her that she is stupid. Users hate this (see Figure 25-1). Despite the inevitable user reaction, most programmers just shrug their shoulders and put error message boxes in anyway. They don't know how else to create reliable software.

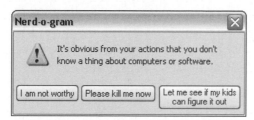

Figure 25-1 No matter how nicely your error messages are phrased, this is how they will be interpreted.

Many programmers and user-interface designers labor under the misconception that people need to be told when they are wrong. This assumption is false in several ways. First of all, it ignores human nature. Very few people wish to hear from a machine that they're wrong. You may call it denial, but it is true, and users will blame the messenger before they blame themselves.

The assumption that users *need* to know when they are wrong is similarly false. How important is it for you to know that you requested an invalid type size? Most programs can make a reasonable substitution.

We consider it very impolite to tell people when they have committed some social *faux pas*. Telling someone they have a bit of lettuce sticking to their teeth or that their fly is open is equally embarrassing for both parties. Sensitive people look for ways to bring the problem to the attention of the victim without letting others notice. Yet programmers assume that a big, bold box in the middle of the screen that stops all the action and emits a bold "beep" is the appropriate way to behave.

Whose mistake is it, anyway?

Conventional wisdom says that error messages tell users when they have made a mistake. Actually, most error bulletins report when the *computer* gets confused. Users make far fewer substantive mistakes than imagined. Typical "errors" consist of a user inadvertently entering an out-of-bounds number, or entering a space where the computer doesn't allow it. When a user enters something unintelligible by the computer's standards, whose fault is it? Is it a user's fault for not knowing how to use the program properly, or is it the fault of the program for not making the choices and effects clearer?

Information that is entered in an unfamiliar sequence is usually considered an error by software, but people don't have this difficulty with unfamiliar sequences. Humans know how to wait, to bide their time until the story is complete. Software usually jumps to the erroneous conclusion that out-of-sequence input means wrong input, so it issues an evil error message box.

When, for example, a user creates an invoice for a customer without an ID number, most applications reject the entry. They stop the proceedings with the idiocy that the user must enter a valid customer number *right now*. Alternatively, the application could accept the transaction with the expectation that a customer number will eventually be entered, or that a user may even be trying to create a new customer. The program could provide a little modeless feedback that the number isn't recognized, then watch to make sure the user enters the necessary information to make that customer number valid before the end of the session, or even the end of the month book closing. This is the way most humans work. They don't usually enter "bad" codes. Rather, they enter codes in a sequence that the software isn't prepared to accept.

If a person forgets to fully explain things to the computer, the computer can, after some reasonable delay, provide more insistent signals to the user. At day's or week's end, the program can make sure that irreconcilable transactions are apparent to the user. The application doesn't have to bring the proceedings to a halt with an error message. After all, the application will remember the transactions, so they can be tracked down and fixed. This is the way it worked in manual systems, so why can't computerized systems do at least this much? Why stop the entire process just because something is missing? As long as users remain well informed throughout, there shouldn't be a problem. The trick is to inform without stopping the proceedings. We'll discuss this idea more later in the chapter.

If the application were a human assistant and it staged a sit-down strike in the middle of the Accounting Department because we handed it an incomplete form, we'd be pretty upset. If we were the bosses, we'd consider finding a replacement for this uptight, petty, sanctimonious clerk. Just take the form, we'd say, and figure out the missing information. The authors have used Rolodex programs that demand you enter an area code with a phone number even though the person's address has already been entered. It doesn't take a lot of intelligence to make a reasonable guess at the area code. If you enter a new name with an address in Menlo Park, the program can reliably assume that the area code is 650 by looking at the other 25 people in your database who also live in Menlo Park and have 650 as their area code. Sure, if you enter a new address for, say, Boise, Idaho, the program might be stumped. But how tough is it to access a directory on the Web, or even keep a list of the 1,000 biggest cities in America along with their area codes?

Programmers may now protest: "The program might be wrong. It can't be sure. Some cities have more than one area code. It can't make that assumption without approval of the user!" Not so.

If we asked an assistant to enter a client's phone contact information into our Rolodex, and neglected to mention the area code, he would accept it anyway, expecting that the area code would arrive before its absence was critical. Alternatively, he could look the address up in a directory. Let's say that the client is in Los Angeles so the directory is ambiguous: The area code could be either 213 or 310. If our human assistant rushed into the office in a panic shouting "Stop what you're doing! This client's area code is ambiguous!" we'd be sorely tempted to fire him and hire somebody with a greater-than-room-temperature IQ. Why should software be any different? A human might write *213/310?* into the area code field in this case. The next time we call that client, we'll have to determine which area code is correct, but in the meantime, life can go on.

Again, squeals of protest: "But the area code field is only big enough for three digits! I can't fit 213/310? into it!" Gee, that's too bad. You mean that rendering the user interface of your program in terms of the underlying implementation model — a rigidly fixed field width — forces you to reject natural human behavior in favor of obnoxious, computer-like inflexibility supplemented with demeaning error messages? Not to put too fine a point on this, but error message boxes come from a failure of applications to behave reasonably, not from any failure of users.

Error messages don't work

There is a final irony to error messages: *They don't prevent users from making errors.* We imagine that users are staying out of trouble because our trusty error messages keep them straight, but this is a delusion. What error messages really do is prevent the *program* from getting into trouble. In most software, the error messages stand like sentries where the program is most sensitive, not where users are most vulnerable, setting into concrete the idea that the program is more important than users. Users get into plenty of trouble with our software, regardless of the quantity or quality of the error messages in it. All an error message can do is keep me from entering letters in a numeric field — it does nothing to protect me from entering the wrong numbers — which is a much more difficult design task.

Eliminating error messages

We can't eliminate error messages by simply discarding the code that shows the actual error message dialog box and letting the program crash if a problem arises. Instead, we need to redesign applications so that they are no longer susceptible to the problem. We must replace the error message with more robust software that prevents error conditions from arising, rather than having the program merely complain when things aren't going precisely the way it wants. Like vaccinating it against a disease, we make the program immune to the problem, and then we can toss the message that reports it. To eliminate the error message, we must first reduce the possibility of users making errors. Instead of assuming error messages are normal, we need to think of them as abnormal solutions to rare problems — as surgery instead of aspirin. We need to treat them as an idiom of last resort.

Every good programmer knows that if module A hands invalid data to module B, module B should clearly and immediately reject the input with a suitable error indicator. Not doing this would be a great failure in the design of the interface between the modules. But human users are not modules of code. Not only should software not reject the input with an error message, but the software designer must also reevaluate the entire concept of what "invalid data" is. When it comes from a human, the software must assume that the input is correct, simply because the human is more important than the code. Instead of software rejecting input, it must work harder to understand and reconcile confusing input. A program may understand the state of things inside the computer, but only a user understands the state of things in the real world. Remember, the real world is more relevant and important than what the computer thinks.

Making errors impossible

Making it impossible for users to make errors is the best way to eliminate error messages. By using bounded widgets (such as spinners and drop-down list boxes) for data entry, we can prevent users from entering bad numbers. Instead of forcing a user to key in his selection, present him with a list of possible selections from which to choose. Instead of making a user type in a state code, for example, let him choose from a list of valid state codes or even from a picture of a map. In other words, make it impossible for the user to enter a bad state.

 DESIGN principle   Make errors impossible.

Another excellent way to eliminate error messages is to make the application smart enough that it no longer needs to make unnecessary demands. Many error messages say things like "Invalid input. User must type xxxx." Why can't the program, if it knows what the user must type, just enter xxxx by itself and save the user the tongue-lashing? Instead of demanding that a user find a file on a disk, introducing the chance that the user will select the wrong file, the program should remember which files it has accessed in the past and allow a selection from that list. Another example is designing a system that gets the date from the internal clock instead of asking for input from users.

Undoubtedly, all these solutions will cause more work for programmers. However, it is the programmer's job to satisfy users and not vice versa. If the programmer thinks of the user as just another input device, it is easy to forget the proper pecking order in the world of software design.

Users of computers aren't sympathetic to the difficulties faced by programmers. They don't see the technical rationale behind an error message box. All they see is the unwillingness of the program to deal with things in a human way. They see all error messages as some variant of the one shown in Figure 25-2.

Figure 25-2 This is how most users perceive error message dialog boxes. They see them as Kafkaesque interrogations with each successive choice leading to a yet blacker pit of retribution and regret.

One of the problems with error messages is that they are usually *ex post facto* reports of failure. They say, "Bad things just happened, and all *you* can do is acknowledge the catastrophe." Such reports are not helpful. And these dialog boxes always come with an OK button, requiring the user to be an accessory to the crime. These error message boxes are reminiscent of the scene in old war movies where an ill-fated soldier steps on a landmine while advancing across the rice paddy. He and his buddies clearly hear the click of the mine's triggering mechanism and the realization comes over the soldier that although he's safe now, as soon as he removes his foot from the mine, it will explode, taking some large and useful part of his body with it. Users get this feeling when they see most error message boxes, and they wish they were thousands of miles away, back in the real world.

Positive feedback

One of the reasons why software is so hard to learn is that it so rarely gives positive feedback. People learn better from positive feedback than they do from negative feedback. People want to use their software correctly and effectively, and they are motivated to learn how to make the software work for them. They don't need to be slapped on the wrist when they fail. They do need to be rewarded, or at least acknowledged, when they succeed. They will feel better about themselves if they get approval, and that good feeling will be reflected back to the product.

Advocates of negative feedback can cite numerous examples of its effectiveness in guiding people's behavior. This evidence is true, but almost universally, the context of effective punitive feedback is getting people to refrain from doing things they want to do but shouldn't: things like not driving over 55 mph, not cheating on their spouses, and not fudging their income taxes. But when it comes to *helping* people do what they want to do, positive feedback is best. If you've ever learned to ski, you know that a ski instructor who yells at you isn't helping the situation.

 DESIGN principle   Users get humiliated when software tells them they failed.

Keep in mind that we are talking about the drawbacks of negative feedback from a computer. Negative feedback by another person, although unpleasant, can be justified in certain circumstances. One can say that a coach is helping your mental toughness for competition, and the imperious professor is at least preparing you for the vicissitudes of the real world. But to be given negative feedback by a machine is an insult. The drill sergeant and professor are at least human and have bona fide experience and merit. But to be told by software that you have failed is humiliating and degrading. There is nothing that takes place inside a computer that will be helped by humiliating or degrading a human user. We only resort to negative feedback out of habit.

Aren't there exceptions?

As our technological powers grow, the portability and flexibility of our computer hardware grows, too. Modern computers can be connected to and disconnected from networks and peripherals without having to first power down. This means that it is now normal for hardware to appear and disappear ad hoc. Printers, modems, and file servers can come and go like the tides. With the development of wireless networks such as WiFi and Bluetooth, our computers can frequently connect and disconnect from networks. Is it an error if you move between two wireless networks? Is it an error if you print a document, only to find that no printers are connected? Is it an error if the file you are editing normally resides on a drive that is no longer reachable?

None of these occurrences should be considered as errors. If you open a file on the server and begin editing it, then wander out to a restaurant for lunch, taking your notebook with you, the program should see that the normal home of the file is no longer available and do something intelligent. It could use a wireless network and VPN to log on to the server remotely, or it could just save any changes you make locally, synchronizing with the version on the server when you return to the office from lunch. In any case, it is normal behavior, not an error, and you shouldn't have to tell the computer what it should do every single time it encounters the situation.

Almost all error message boxes can be eliminated. If you examine the situation from the point of view that the error message box must be eliminated and that everything else is subject to change in search of this objective, you will see the truth of this assertion. You will also be surprised by how little else needs to be changed in order to achieve it. In those rare cases where the rest of the program must be altered too much, that is the time to compromise with the real world and go ahead and use an error message box. But programmers need to start thinking of this compromise as an admission of failure on their part, as a solution of last resort.

All this said, there are certainly some time-critical situations where users must be notified in an obtrusive, attention-demanding manner. For example, if during market hours, an investment manager sets up some trades to be executed by the end of the day, and then sends them down to the trading desk after market close, she should be interrupted from whatever else she's working on to be warned that the trades can't be executed until the market opens tomorrow, at which point she may no longer want to make the trades.

Improving error messages: The last resort

In the case that it is truly infeasible to redesign your application to eliminate the need for error dialogs, we offer you some ways to improve the quality of error message boxes. Use these recommendations only as a last resort, when you run out of other reasonable options for actually eliminating the error dialog.

An error dialog should always be *polite*, *illuminating*, and *helpful*. Never forget that an error dialog is the application's way of reporting on *its* failure to do its job, and that it is interrupting the user to do this. The error message box must be unfailingly polite. It must never even hint that the user caused this problem, because that is simply not true from the user's perspective.

The error message box must illuminate the problem for the user. This means that it must give him the information he needs to make an appropriate plan to solve the program's problem. It needs to make clear the scope of the problem, what the alternatives are, what the program will do as a default, and what information was lost, if any.

It is wrong, however, for the program to just dump the problem on a user's lap and wipe its hands of the matter. It should directly offer to implement at least one suggested solution right there on the error message box. It should offer buttons that will take care of the problem in various ways. If a printer is missing, the message box should offer options for deferring the printout or selecting another printer. If the database is hopelessly trashed and useless, it should offer to rebuild it to a working state, including telling the user how long that process will take and what side effects it will cause.

Figure 25-3 shows an example of a reasonable error message. Notice that it is polite, illuminating, and helpful. It doesn't even hint that the user's behavior is anything but impeccable.

Figure 25-3 In the case that you must use an error dialog, it should look something like this. It politely and clearly illuminates the problem and proposes a good solution. The action buttons and resulting effects are also clearly described.

Alert Dialogs: Announcing the Obvious

Like error dialogs, alerts and confirmations stop the proceedings, often with idiocy. Alerts and confirmations do not report malfunctions. An **alert** notifies a user of the program's action, whereas a **confirmation** also gives a user the authority to override that action. These dialogs pop up like weeds in most programs and should, like error dialogs, be eliminated in favor of more useful idioms.

Alerts usually violate one of our basic design principles: *A dialog box is another room; you should have a good reason to go there* (see Chapter 20). Even if a user must be informed about an action taken by the application, why go into another room to do it?

When it comes down to it, an application should either have the courage of its convictions or it should not take action without a user's direct instruction. If the application, for example, saves a user's file to disk automatically, it should have the confidence to know that it is doing the right thing. It should provide a means for users to find out what the application did, but it doesn't have to stop the proceedings to do so. If the application really isn't sure that it should save the file, it shouldn't save the file but should leave that operation up to the user.

Conversely, if a user directs the program to do something — dragging a file to the trash can, for example — it doesn't need to stop the proceedings with idiocy to announce that the user just dragged a file to the trashcan. The program should ensure that there is adequate visual feedback regarding the action, and if the user has actually made the gesture in error, the program should unobtrusively offer him a robust Undo facility so he can backtrack.

The rationale for alerts is to keep users informed. This is a great objective, but it need not come at the expense of smooth interaction flow.

The alert shown in Figure 25-4 is an example of how alerts are more trouble than help. The Find dialog (the one underneath) already forces a user to click Cancel when the search is completed, but the superimposed alert box adds another flow-breaking button. To return to his work, a user must first click the OK button on the alert, then the Cancel button on the Find dialog. If the information provided by the alert were built into the main Find dialog, the user's burden would be reduced by half.

Figure 25-4 A typical alert dialog box. It is unnecessary, inappropriate, and stops the proceedings with idiocy. Word has finished searching the document. Should reporting that fact be a different facility than the search mechanism itself? If not, why does it use a different dialog?

Alerts are so numerous because they are so easy to create. Most programming languages offer some form of message box facility in a single line of code. Conversely, building an animated status display into the face of a program might require a thousand or more lines of code. Programmers cannot be expected to make the right choice in this situation. They have a conflict of interest, so designers must be sure to specify precisely where information is reported on the surface of an application. The designers must then follow up to be sure that the design wasn't compromised for the sake of rapid coding. Imagine if the contractor on a building site decided unilaterally not to add a bathroom because it was just too much trouble to deal with the plumbing. There would be consequences.

Of course, software must keep users informed of its actions. It should have visual indicators built into its main screens to make such status information immediately available to users, should they desire it. Launching an alert to announce an unrequested action is bad enough. Putting up an alert to announce a *requested* action is pathological.

Software should be flexible and forgiving, but it doesn't need to be fawning and obsequious. The dialog box shown in Figure 25-5 is a classic example of an alert that should be put out of our misery. It announces that the application successfully completed a synchronization — its sole reason for existence. This occurs a few seconds after we told it to synchronize. It stops the proceedings to announce the obvious. It's as though the application wants approval for how hard it worked. If a person interacted with us like this, we'd find it uncomfortable and him overbearing. Of course some feedback is appropriate, but is another dialog that must be dismissed really necessary?

Figure 25-5 This dialog, from AirSet Desktop Sync, is unnecessarily obsequious. We tell it to synchronize and are promptly stopped in our tracks by this important message. Do we really need the program to waste our time demanding recognition that it managed to do its job?

Confirmation Dialog

When an application does not feel confident about its actions, it often asks a user for approval with a dialog box, like the one shown in Figure 25-6. This is called a **confirmation**. Sometimes a confirmation is offered because the application second-guesses one of the user's actions. Sometimes the program feels that is not competent to make a decision it faces and uses a confirmation to give the user the choice instead. Confirmations always come from the program and never from the user. This means that they are often a reflection of the implementation model and are not representative of user goals.

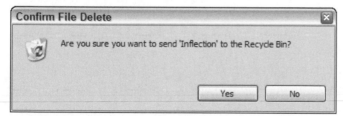

Figure 25-6 Every time we delete a file in Windows, we get this confirmation dialog box asking if we're sure. Yes, we're sure. We're always sure. And if we're wrong, we expect Windows to be able to recover the file for us. Windows lives up to that expectation with its Recycle Bin. So, why does it still issue the confirmation message? When a confirmation box is issued routinely, users get used to approving it routinely. So, when it eventually reports an impending disaster to the user, he goes ahead and approves it anyway, because it is routine. Do your users a favor and never create another confirmation dialog box.

Revealing the implementation model to users is a surefire way to create an unpleasant and inferior product. This means that confirmation messages are inappropriate. Confirmations get written into software when a programmer arrives at an impasse in her coding. Typically, she realizes that she is about to direct the program to take some bold action and feels unsure about taking responsibility for it. Sometimes the bold action is based on some condition the program detects, but more often it is based on a command the user issues. Typically, the confirmation will be launched after the user issues a command that is either irrecoverable or whose results might cause undue alarm.

Confirmations pass the buck to users. Users trust the application to do its job, and the application should both do it and ensure that it does it right. The proper solution is to make the action easily reversible and provide enough modeless feedback so that users are not taken off-guard.

As a program's code grows during development, programmers detect numerous situations where they don't feel that they can resolve issues adequately. Programmers will unilaterally insert buck-passing code in these places, almost without noticing it. This tendency needs to be closely watched, because programmers have been known to insert dialog boxes into the code even after the user-interface specification has been agreed upon. Programmers often don't consider confirmation dialogs to be part of the user interface, but they are.

The dialog that cried "Wolf!"

Confirmations illustrate an interesting quirk of human behavior: They only work when they are unexpected. That doesn't sound remarkable until you examine it in context. If confirmations are offered in routine places, users quickly become inured to them and routinely dismiss them without a glance. Dismissing confirmations thus becomes as routine as issuing them. If, at some point, a truly unexpected and dangerous situation arises — one that *should* be brought to a user's attention — he will, by rote, dismiss the confirmation, exactly because it has become routine. Like the fable of the boy who cried "Wolf," when there is finally real danger, the confirmation box won't work because it cried too many times when there was no danger.

For confirmation dialog boxes to work, they must only appear when a user will almost definitely click the No or Cancel button, and they should *never* appear when a user is likely to click the Yes or OK button. Seen from this perspective, they look rather pointless, don't they?

Eliminating confirmations

Three design principles provide a way to eliminate confirmation dialog boxes. The best way is to obey the simple dictum: Do, don't ask. When you design your software, go ahead and give it the force of its convictions (backed up, of course, by user research, as discussed in Chapter 4). Users will respect its brevity and its confidence.

 DESIGN principle   Do, don't ask.

Of course, if an application confidently does something that a user doesn't like, it must have the capability to reverse the operation. Every aspect of the program's action must be undoable. Instead of asking in advance with a confirmation dialog box, on those rare occasions when the program's actions were out of turn, let the user issue the Stop-and-Undo command.

Most situations that we currently consider unprotectable by Undo can actually be protected fairly well. Deleting or overwriting a file is a good example. The file can be moved to a directory where it is kept for a month or so before it is physically deleted. The Recycle Bin in Windows uses this strategy, except for the part about automatically erasing files after a month: Users still have to take out the garbage.

 DESIGN principle   Make all actions reversible.

Even better than acting in haste and forcing users to rescue the program with Undo, you can make sure that applications offer users adequate information so that they never issue a command (or omit a command) that leads to an undesirable result. Applications should use rich visual feedback so that users are constantly kept informed, the same way the instruments on dashboards keep us informed of the state of our cars.

 DESIGN principle   Provide modeless feedback to help users avoid mistakes.

Occasionally, a situation arises that really can't be protected by Undo. Is this a legitimate case for a confirmation dialog box? Not necessarily. A better approach is to provide users with protection the way we give them protection on the freeway: with consistent and clear markings. You can often build excellent, modeless warnings right into the interface. For instance, look at the dialog from Adobe Photoshop in

Figure 25-7, telling us that our document is larger than the available print area. Why has the program waited until now to inform us of this fact? What if guides were visible on the page at all times (unless a user hid them) showing the actual printable region? What if those parts of the picture outside the printable area were highlighted when a user moused over the Print button in the toolbar? Clear, modeless feedback (see the next section) is the best way to address these problems.

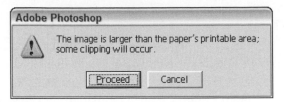

Figure 25-7 This dialog provides too little help too late. What if the program could display the printable region right in the main interface as dotted guides? There's no reason for users to be subjected to dialogs like these.

Much more common than honestly irreversible actions are those actions that are easily reversible but still uselessly protected by routine confirmation boxes. The confirmation in Figure 25-6 is an excellent specimen of this species. There is no reason whatsoever to ask for confirmation of a move to the Recycle Bin. The sole reason the Recycle Bin exists is to implement an undo facility for deleted files.

Replacing Dialogs: Rich Modeless Feedback

Most computers (and many devices) come with high-resolution displays and high-quality audio systems. Yet, very few applications (outside of games) even scratch the surface of using these facilities to provide useful information about the status of the program, the users' tasks, and the system and its peripherals in general. An entire toolbox is available to express information to users, but designers and programmers have stuck to using the same blunt instrument — the dialog — to communicate information. Needless to say, this means that subtle status information is simply *never* communicated to users at all, because even the most clueless designers know that you don't want dialogs to pop up *constantly*. But constant feedback is exactly what users need. It's simply the channel of communication that needs to be different.

In this section, we'll discuss **rich modeless feedback**, information that can be provided to users in the main displays of your application, which doesn't stop the flow and can all but eliminate pesky dialogs.

Rich visual modeless feedback

Perhaps the most important type of modeless feedback is **rich visual modeless feedback** (RVMF). This type of feedback is *rich* in terms of giving in-depth information about the status or attributes of a process or object in the current application. It is *visual* in that it makes idiomatic use of pixels on the screen (often dynamically), and it is *modeless* in that this information is always readily displayed, requiring no special action or mode shift on the part of a user to view and make sense of the feedback.

For example, in Microsoft Outlook 2007, a small icon next to an e-mail sender's name visually indicates whether that person is available for a chat session or a phone call, if it turns out that a real-time conversation is preferable to an e-mail exchange. This small icon (as well as the ability to start a chat session from a right-click menu), means that users don't have to open their chat client and find the sender's name to see if that person happens to be available. This is so easy and convenient that a user literally does not have to think about it. Another example of the strategy, as designed for a Cooper client, can be seen in Figure 25-8.

Here's another example, this time from the Mac: When you download a file from the Internet, the downloading file appears on the desktop as an icon with a small dynamically updating progress bar, indicating visually what percentage has downloaded.

A final example of RVMF is from the computer gaming world: Sid Meier's Civilization. This game provides dozens of examples of RVMF in its main interface, which is a map of the historical world that you, as a leader of an evolving civilization, are trying to build and conquer. Civilization uses RVMF to indicate a half-dozen things about a city, all represented visually. If a city is more advanced, its architecture is more modern. If it is larger, the icon is larger and more embellished. If there is civil unrest, smoke rises from the city. Individual troop and civilian units also show status visually, by way of tiny meters showing unit health and strength. Even the landscape has RVMF: Dotted lines marking spheres of influence shift as units move and cities grow. Terrain changes as roads are laid, forests are cleared, and mountains are mined. Although dialogs exist in the game, much of the information needed to understand what is going on is communicated clearly with no words or dialogs whatsoever.

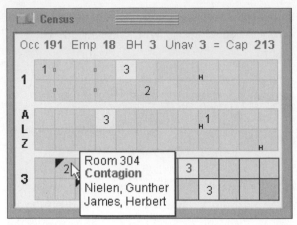

Figure 25-8 This pane from a Cooper design for a long-term health-care information system is a good example of RVMF. The diagram is a representation of all the rooms in the facility. Color-coding indicates male, female, empty, or mixed-gender rooms; numbers indicate empty beds; tiny boxes between rooms indicate shared bathrooms. Black triangles indicate health issues, and a tiny "H" means a held bed. This RVMF is supplanted with ToolTips, which show room number and names of the occupants of the room, and highlight any important notices about the room or the residents. A numeric summary of rooms, beds, and employees is given at the top. This display has a short learning curve. Once mastered, it allows nurses and facility managers to understand their facility's status at a glance.

Imagine if all the objects that had pertinent status information on your desktop or in your application were able to display their status in this manner. Printer icons could show how near they were to completing your print job. Disks and removable media icons could show how full they were. When an object was selected for drag and drop, all the places that could receive it would visually highlight to announce their receptiveness.

Think about the objects in your application, what attributes they have — especially dynamically changing ones — and what kind of status information is critical for your users. Figure out how to create a representation of this. After a user notices and learns this representation, it tells him what is going on at a glance. (There should also be a way to get fully detailed information if the user requests it.) Put this information into main application windows in the form of RVMF and see how many dialogs you can eliminate from routine use!

One important point does need to be made about rich modeless visual feedback. It isn't for beginners. Even if you add ToolTips to textually describe the details of any visual cues you add (which you should), it requires users to perform work to discover it and decode its meaning. RVMF is something that users will begin to use over time. When they do, they'll think it's amazing; but, in the meantime, they will need support of menus and dialogs to find what they're looking for. This means that RVMF used to replace alerts and warnings of serious trouble must be extraordinarily clear to users. Make sure that this kind of status is visually emphasized over less critical, more informational RVMF.

Audible feedback

In data-entry environments, clerks sit for hours in front of computer screens entering data. These users may well be examining source documents and typing by touch instead of looking at the screen. If a clerk enters something erroneous, he needs to be informed of it via both auditory and visual feedback. The clerk can then use his sense of hearing to monitor the success of his inputs while he keeps his eyes on the document.

The kind of auditory feedback we're proposing is *not* the same as the beep that accompanies an error message box. In fact, it isn't a beep at all. The auditory indicator we propose as feedback for a problem is *silence*. The problem with much current audible feedback is the still prevalent idea that, rather than positive audible feedback, negative feedback is desirable.

Negative audible feedback: Announcing user failure

People frequently counter the idea of audible feedback with arguments that users don't like it. Users are offended by the sounds that computers make, and they don't like to have their computer beeping at them. Despite the fact that Microsoft and Apple have tried to improve the quality of alert sounds by hiring sound designers (including the legendary Brian Eno for Windows 95), all the warm ambience in the world doesn't change the fact that they are used to convey negative, often insulting messages.

Emitting noise when something bad happens is called **negative audible feedback**. On most systems, error message boxes are normally accompanied by a shrill beep, and audible feedback has thus become strongly associated them. That beep is a public announcement of a user's failure. It explains to all within earshot that you have done something execrably stupid. It is such a hateful idiom that most software developers now have an unquestioned belief that audible feedback is bad and should never again be considered as a part of interface design. Nothing could be further from the truth. It is the negative aspect of the feedback that presents problems, not the audible aspect.

Negative audible feedback has several things working against it. Because the negative feedback is issued at a time when a problem is discovered, it naturally takes on the characteristics of an alarm. Alarms are designed to be purposefully loud, discordant, and disturbing. They are supposed to wake sound sleepers from their slumbers when their house is on fire and their lives are at stake. They are like insurance: We hope that they will never be heard. Unfortunately, users are constantly doing things that programs can't handle, so these actions have become part of the normal course of interaction. Alarms have no place in this normal relationship, the same way we don't expect our car alarms to go off whenever we accidentally change lanes without using our turn indicators. Perhaps the most damning aspect of negative audible feedback is the implication that success must be greeted with silence. Humans like to know when they are doing well. They *need* to know when they are doing poorly, but that doesn't mean that they like to hear about it. Negative feedback systems are simply appreciated less than positive feedback systems.

Given the choice of no noise versus noise for negative feedback, people will choose the former. Given the choice of no noise versus soft and pleasant noises for positive feedback, however, many people will choose the feedback. We have never given our users a chance by putting high-quality, positive audible feedback in our programs, so it's no wonder that people associate sound with bad interfaces.

Positive audible feedback

Almost every object and system outside the world of software offers sound to indicate success rather than failure. When we close the door, we know that it is latched when we hear the click, but silence tells us that it is not yet secure. When we converse with someone and they say, "Yes" or "Uh-huh," we know that they have, at least minimally, registered what was said. When they are silent, however, we have reason to believe that something is amiss. When we turn the key in the ignition and get silence, we know we've got a problem. When we flip the switch on the copier and it stays coldly silent instead of humming, we know that we've got trouble. Even most equipment that we consider silent makes some noise: Turning on the stovetop returns a hiss of gas and a gratifying "whoomp" as the pilot ignites the burner. Electric ranges are inherently less friendly and harder to use because they lack that sound — they require indicator lights to tell us of their status.

When success with our tools yields a sound, it is called **positive audible feedback**. Our software tools are mostly silent; all we hear is the quiet click of the keyboard. Hey! That's positive audible feedback. Every time you press a key, you hear a faint but positive sound. Keyboard manufacturers could make perfectly silent keyboards, but they don't because we depend on audible feedback to tell us how we are doing. The feedback doesn't have to be sophisticated — those clicks don't tell us much — but they must be consistent. If we ever detect silence, we know that we have failed to press the key. The true value of positive audible feedback is that its absence is an extremely effective problem indicator.

The effectiveness of positive audible feedback originates in human sensitivity. Nobody likes to be told that they have failed. Error message boxes are negative feedback, telling the user that he has done something wrong. Silence can ensure that the user knows this without actually being told of the failure. It is remarkably effective, because the software doesn't have to insult the user to accomplish its ends.

Our software should give us constant, small, audible cues just like our keyboards. Our applications would be much friendlier and easier to use if they issued barely audible but easily identifiable sounds when user actions are correct. The program could issue a reassuring click every time the user enters valid input to a field, and an affirming tone when a form has been successfully completed. If an application doesn't understand some input, it should remain silent, subtly informing the user of the problem, allowing her to correct the input without embarrassment or ego-bruising. Whenever a user starts to drag an icon, the computer could issue a low-volume sound reminiscent of sliding as the object is dragged. When it is dragged over pliant areas, an additional percussive tap could indicate this collision. When the user finally releases the mouse button, he is rewarded with a soft, cheerful "plonk" from the speakers for a success or with silence if the drop was not meaningful.

As with visual feedback, computer games tend to excel at positive audio feedback. Mac OS X also does a good job with subtle positive audio feedback for activities like document saves and drag and drop. Of course, the audible feedback must be at the right volume for the situation. Windows and the Mac offer a standard volume control, so one obstacle to beneficial audible feedback has been overcome, but audible feedback should also not overpower music playing on the computer.

Rich modeless feedback is one of the greatest tools at the disposal of interaction designers. Replacing annoying, useless dialogs with subtle and powerful modeless communication can make the difference between a program users will despise and one they will love. Think of all the ways you might improve your own applications with RVMF and other mechanisms of modeless feedback!

26

Designing for Different Needs

As we discussed in Part I, personas and scenarios help us focus our design efforts on the goals, behaviors, needs, and mental models of real users. In addition to the specific focus that personas can give a design effort, there are some consistent and generalizable patterns of user needs that should inform the way our products are designed. In this chapter, we'll explore some strategies for serving these well-known needs.

Command Vectors and Working Sets

Two concepts are particularly useful in sorting out the needs of users with different levels of experience: Command vectors and working sets. **Command vectors** are distinct techniques for allowing users to issue instructions to the program. Direct manipulation handles, drop-down and pop-up menus, toolbar controls, and keyboard accelerators are all examples of command vectors.

Good user interfaces provide **multiple command vectors**, where critical application functions are provided in the form of menu commands, toolbar commands, keyboard accelerators, and direct manipulation controls, each with the parallel capability to invoke a particular command. This redundancy enables users of different skill sets and attitudes to command the program according to their abilities and inclinations.

Immediate and pedagogic vectors

Direct manipulation controls, like pushbuttons and toolbar controls, are **immediate vectors**. There is no delay between clicking a button and seeing the results of the function. Direct manipulation also has an immediate effect on the information without any intermediary. Neither menus nor dialog boxes have this immediate property. Each one requires an intermediate step, sometimes more than one.

Some command vectors offer more support to new users. Typically, menus and dialog boxes offer the most, which is why we refer to them as **pedagogic vectors**. Beginners avail themselves of the pedagogy of menus as they get oriented in a new program, but perpetual intermediates often want to leave them behind to find more immediate and efficient vectors.

Working sets and personas

Because each user unconsciously memorizes commands that are used frequently, perpetual intermediates memorize a moderate subset of commands and features, a **working set**. The commands that comprise any user's working set are unique to that individual, although it will likely overlap significantly with the working sets of other users who exhibit similar use patterns. In Excel, for example, almost every user will enter formulas and labels, specify fonts, and print; but Sally's working set might include graphs, whereas Elliot's working set includes linked spreadsheets.

Although, strictly speaking, there is no such thing as a standard working set that will cover the needs of all users, research and modeling of users and their use patterns can yield a smaller subset of functions that designers can be reasonably confident are accessed frequently by most users. This **minimal working set** can be determined via Goal-Directed Design methods: by using scenarios to discover the functional needs of your personas. These needs translate directly to the contents of the minimal working set.

The commands in any person's working set are those they most often use. Users want those commands to be especially quick and easy to invoke. This means that the designer must, at least, provide immediate command vectors for the minimal working set of the most likely users of the application.

Although a program's minimal working set is almost certainly part of each user's full working set, individual user preferences and job requirements will dictate which additional features are included. Even custom software written for corporate operations can offer a range of features from which each user can pick and choose. This means that the designer must, while providing immediate access to the minimal working set, also provide means for promoting other commands to immediate vectors. Similarly, immediate commands also require more pedagogic vectors to enable beginners to learn the interface. This implies that most functions in the interface should have multiple command vectors.

There is an exception to the rule of multiple vectors: Dangerous commands (like Erase All, Clear, Abandon Changes, and so on) should not have easy, parallel command vectors. Instead, they need to be protected within menus and dialog boxes (in keeping with our design principle from Chapter 10: *Hide the ejector seat levers*).

Graduating Users from Beginners to Intermediates

Donald Norman provides another useful perspective on command vectors. In *The Design of Everyday Things*, Norman uses the phrases, **information in the world** and **information in the head** to refer to different ways that users access information. When he talks about information in the world, Norman refers to situations in which there is sufficient information available in an environment or interface to accomplish something. A kiosk showing a printed map of downtown, for example, is information in the world. We don't have to bother remembering exactly where the Transamerica Building is, because we can find it by reading a map. Opposing this is information in your head, which refers to knowledge that you have learned or memorized, like the back-alley shortcut that isn't printed on any map. Information in your head is much faster and easier to use than information in the world, but you are responsible for ensuring that you learn it, that you don't forget it, and that it stays up to date. Information in the world is slower and more cumbersome, but very dependable.

World vectors and head vectors

A pedagogic vector is necessarily filled with information in the world, which is why it is a **world vector**. Conversely, keyboard accelerators constitute a **head vector** because using them requires a user to have filled his head with information about the functions and their keyboard equivalents. World vectors are required by beginners and by more experienced users accessing advanced or seldom-used functions. Head vectors are used extensively by intermediates and even more so by experts.

For example, when you first moved into your neighborhood, you probably had to use a map — a world vector. After living there a couple of days, you abandoned the map because you had learned how to get home — a head vector. On the other hand, even though you know your house intimately, when you have to adjust the temperature setting on the water heater, you need to read the instructions — a world vector — because you didn't bother to memorize them when you moved in.

Our relationship to our software works the same way. We find ourselves easily memorizing facilities and commands that we use frequently and ignoring the details of commands that we use only rarely. This means that any vector that is used frequently will automatically become a candidate for a head vector. After daily use, for example, we no longer really read the menus, but find what we need by recognizing patterns: Pull down the second menu and select the bottom-most item in the next-to-last section. Pattern recognition is much faster for the human mind than reading is. We read only to verify our choices.

Memorization vectors

New users are happy with world vectors, but as they progress to become perpetual intermediates they begin to develop their working sets, and the (pedagogic) world vectors will start to seem tedious. Users like to find more immediate head vectors for the contents of their working sets. This is a natural and appropriate user desire and, if our software is to be judged easy to use, we must satisfy it. The solution consists of two components. First, we must provide a head vector in parallel to the world vector, and second, we must provide a path by which a user can learn the head vector corresponding to each world vector. This path is a vector itself: a **memorization vector**.

There are several ways to provide memorization vectors for users. The least effective method is to mention the vector only in the user documentation. The slightly better, but still ineffective, method is to mention it in the program's main online help system. These methods put the onus of finding the memorization vector on users and also leave it up to users to realize that they need to find it in the first place.

Superior memorization vectors are built right into the interface, or are at least offered in an application's interface by way of its own world vectors. The latter can be minimally implemented just by adding a menu item to the standard Help menu called Shortcuts. This item takes users directly to a section of help that describes available shortcuts. This method has the benefit of being explicit and, therefore, pedagogic. New users can see that multiple command vectors exist and that there is an easy-to-find resource for learning them. All programs should have this Shortcut item.

DESIGN principle   Offer shortcuts from the Help menu.

Integrating memorization vectors directly into the main interface is less problematic than it sounds. There are already two on the menus of most programs. As defined by Microsoft, a typical Windows application has two keyboard head vectors: mnemonics and accelerators. In Microsoft Word, for example, the mnemonic for Save is Alt+F+S. The memorization vector for this mnemonic is achieved visually by underlining the F and S in the menu title and the menu item, respectively. The accelerator for Save is Ctrl+S. Ctrl+S is noted explicitly on the right side of the menu on the same line as the Save item, which acts as a memorization vector.

Neither of these vectors intrudes on a new user. He may not even notice their existence until he has used the program for some time — that is, until he becomes an intermediate user. Eventually, he will notice these visual hints and will wonder about their meaning. Most reasonably intelligent people — most users — will get the accelerator connection without any help. The mnemonic is slightly tougher, but once a user is clued into the use of the Alt meta-key, either by direction or accident, the idiom is extremely easy to remember and use wherever it occurs.

As you'll recall from Chapter 23, **butcons** are an excellent technique whereby small icons are used to provide memorization vectors for transitioning from menus to toolbar. The icon identifying each function or facility should be shown on every artifact of the user interface that deals with it: each menu, each butcon, each dialog box, every mention in the help text, and every mention in the printed documentation. A memorization vector formed of visual symbols in the interface is the most effective technique, yet it remains underexploited in the industry at large.

Personalization and Configuration

Interaction designers often face the conundrum of whether to make their products user-customizable. It is easy to be torn between some users' need to have things done their way, and the clear problem this creates when the program's navigation suffers due to familiar elements being moved or hidden. The solution is to cast the problem in a different light.

People like to change things around to suit themselves. Even beginners, not to mention perpetual intermediates, like to put their own personal stamps on a program, changing it so that it looks or acts the way they prefer, uniquely suiting their tastes. People will do this for the same reason they fill their identical cubicles with pictures of their spouses and kids, plants, favorite paintings, quotes, and Dilbert cartoons.

Decorating the persistent objects — the walls — gives them individuality without removing them. It also allows you to recognize a hallway as being different from dozens of identical hallways because it is the one with the M. C. Escher poster hanging in it. The term **personalization** describes the decoration of persistent objects.

Personalization makes the places in which we work more likable and familiar. It makes them more human and pleasant to be in. The same is true of software, and giving users the ability to decorate their personal applications is both fun and useful as a navigational aide.

On the other hand, moving persistent objects *themselves* can hamper navigation. If the facilities people come into your office over the weekend and rearrange all the cubicles, Dilbert cartoons notwithstanding, finding your office again on Monday morning will be tough (persistent objects and their importance to navigation are discussed in Chapter 11).

Is this an apparent contradiction? Not really. Adding decoration to persistent objects helps navigation, whereas moving the persistent objects hinders navigation. The term **configuration** describes moving, adding, or deleting persistent objects.

Configuration is desirable for more experienced users. Perpetual intermediates, after they have established a working set of functions, will want to configure the interface to make those functions easier to find and use. They will also want to tune the program itself for speed and ease, but in all cases, the level of custom configuration will be light to moderate.

Configuration is a necessity for expert users. They are already beyond the need for more traditional navigation aids because they are so familiar with the product. Experts may use the program for several hours every day; in fact, it may be the main application for accomplishing the bulk of their jobs.

Moving controls around on the toolbar is a form of personalization. However, the three leftmost toolbar controls on many programs, which correspond to File New, File Open, and File Save, are now so common that they can be considered persistent objects. A user who moves these around is *configuring* his program as much as he is personalizing it. Thus, there is a gray boundary between configuration and personalization.

Changing the color of objects on the screen is clearly a personalization task. Windows has always been very accommodating in this respect, allowing users to independently change the color of each component of the windows interface, including the color and pattern of the desktop itself. Windows gives users a *practical* ability to change the system font, too. Personalization is **idiosyncratically modal** (discussed a bit later in the chapter); people either love it or they don't. You must accommodate both categories of users.

Tools for personalizing must be simple and easy to use, giving users a visual preview of their selections. Above all, they must be easy to undo. A dialog box that lets users change colors should offer a function that returns everything to the factory settings.

Most end users won't squawk if they can't configure your program as long as it does its job well. Some really expert users may feel slighted, but they will still use and appreciate your program if it works the way they expect. In some cases, however, flexibility is absolutely critical. If you're designing for a rapidly evolving workflow, it's of utmost importance that the software used to support the workflow can evolve as quickly as the state of the art.

Also, corporate IT managers value configuration. It allows them to subtly coerce corporate users into practicing common methods. They appreciate the ability to add macros and commands to menus and toolbars that make the off-the-shelf software work more intimately with established company processes, tools, and standards. Many IT managers base their buying decisions on the configurability of programs. If they are buying ten or twenty thousand copies of a program, they rightly feel that they should be able to adapt it to their particular style of work. It is, thus, not on a whim that Microsoft Office applications are among the most configurable shrink-wrapped software titles available.

Idiosyncratically Modal Behavior

Many times user testing indicates that a user population divides relatively equally on the effectiveness of an idiom. Half of the users clearly prefer one idiom, whereas the other half prefers another. This sort of clear division of a population's preferences into two or more large groups indicates that their preferences are **idiosyncratically modal**.

Development organizations can become similarly emotionally split on issues like this. One group becomes the menu-item camp, while the rest of the developers are the butcon camp. They wrangle and argue over the relative merits of the two methods, although the real answer is staring them in the face: Use both!

When the user population splits on preferred idioms, the software designers *must* offer both idioms. Both groups must be satisfied. It is no good to satisfy one-half of the population while angering the other half, regardless of which particular group you or your developers align yourselves with.

Windows offers an excellent example of how to cater to idiosyncratically modal desires in its menu implementation. Some people like menus that work the way they did on the original Macintosh. You click the mouse button on a menu bar item to make the menu appear; then — while still holding down the button — you drag down the menu and release the mouse button on your choice. Other people find this procedure difficult and prefer a way to accomplish it without having to hold the mouse button down while they drag. Windows neatly satisfies this by letting users click and release on the menu bar item to make the menu appear. Then users can move the mouse — button released — to the menu item of choice. Another click and release selects the item and closes the menu. A user can also still click and drag to select a menu item. The brilliance of these idioms is that they coexist quite peacefully with each other. Any user can freely intermix the two idioms, or stick consistently with one or the other. The program requires no change. There are no preferences or options to be set; it just works.

Starting in Windows 95, Microsoft added a third idiosyncratically modal idiom to the menu behavior: The user clicks and releases as before, but now he can drag the mouse along the menu bar and the other menus are triggered in turn. Amazingly, now all three idioms are accommodated seamlessly. The Mac now, too, supports all three of these idioms.

Localization and Globalization

Designing applications for use in different languages and cultures presents some special challenges to designers. Here again, however, consideration of command vectors can provide guidance.

Immediate vectors such as direct manipulation and toolbar butcons are idiomatic (see Chapter 20) and visual rather than textual. They are, therefore, capable of being globalized with considerable ease. It is, of course, important for designers to do their homework to ensure that colors or symbols chosen for these idioms do not have particular meanings in different cultures that the designer would not intend. (In Japan, for example, an X in a check box would likely be interpreted as *de*selection rather than selection.) However, nonmetaphorical idioms should, in general, be fairly safe for globalized interfaces.

The pedagogic vectors such as menu items, field labels, ToolTips, and instructional hints are language dependent, and thus must be the subject of localization via translation to appropriate languages. Some issues to bear in mind when creating interfaces that must be localized include:

> ► In some languages, words and phrases tend to be longer than in others (German text labels, for example, are significantly longer than those in English on average).

- ▶ Words in some languages, Asian languages in particular, can be difficult to sort alphabetically.

- ▶ Ordering of day-month-year and the use of 12- or 24-hour notation for time vary from country to country.

- ▶ Decimal points in numbers and currency are represented differently (some countries use periods and commas the opposite of the way they are used in the U.S.).

- ▶ Some countries make use of week numbers (for example, week 50 is in mid-December), and some countries make use of calendars other than the Gregorian calendar.

Menu items and dialogs, when they are translated, need to be considered holistically. It is important to make sure that translated interfaces remain coherent as a whole. Items and labels that translate straightforwardly in a vacuum may become confusing when grouped with other independently translated items. Semantics of the interface need to be preserved at the higher level as well as at the detail level.

Galleries and Templates

Not all users of document-creation applications are capable of building documents completely from scratch. Most programs, however, offer users atomic tools: the equivalent of hammers, saws, and chisels. That is fine for some users, but others require more: the equivalent of an unfinished table or chair that they can then sand and paint.

For example, consider a program that lets you configure your own personalized newspaper from information on the Internet. Some users will really appreciate being able to put sports at the top of page one. Most users, however, will probably want a more traditional view, with world news at the top and sports at the back. Even these more-traditional users will appreciate the fact that they can add their local news and news concerning topics of particular personal interest. They should be able to pick a premade newspaper and then make the few small changes needed to get their custom version. Constructing a whole newspaper from a blank slate would be an unpleasant task for all but the closet journalists among us.

In other words, users should be allowed to choose a starting design or document structure in any application from a gallery of possible designs, if they don't have the need or desire to create one from scratch.

DESIGN principle   Offer users a gallery of ready-to-use templates.

Some programs already offer galleries of predesigned templates, but more should do the same. Blank slates intimidate most people, and users shouldn't have to deal with one if they don't want to. A gallery of basic designs is a fine solution.

Help

Online help is just like printed documentation, a reference tool for perpetual intermediates. While good online help is critical, it should never be a crutch for your product. Good design should greatly reduce your users' reliance on help.

A complex program with many features and functions should come with a reference document: a place where users who wish to expand their horizons can find definitive answers. This document can be a printed manual or it can be online help. The printed manual is comfortable, browsable, friendly, and can be carried around. The online help is searchable, semi-comfortable, very lightweight, and cheap.

The index

Because you don't read a manual like a novel, the key to a successful and effective reference document is the quality of the tools for finding what you want in it. Essentially, this means the index. A printed manual has an index in the back that you use manually. Online help has an automatic index search facility.

We suspect that few online help facilities were indexed by a professional indexer. However many entries are in your program's index, you could probably double the number. What's more, the index needs to be generated by examining the program and all its features, not by examining the help text. This is not easy, because it demands that a highly skilled indexer be intimately familiar with all the features of the program. It may be easier to rework the interface to improve it than to create a really good index.

The list of index entries is arguably more important than the text of the entries themselves. A user will forgive a poorly written entry with more alacrity than he will forgive a missing entry. The index must have as many synonyms as possible for topics. Prepare for it to be huge. A user who needs to solve a problem will be thinking "How do I turn this cell black?" not "How can I set the *shading* of this cell to 100%?" If the entry is listed under shading, the index fails the user. The more goal-directed your thinking is, the better the index will map to what might possibly pop into a user's head when he is looking for something. An index model that works is the one in *The Joy of Cooking* by Irma S. Rombaur and Marion Rombaur Becker. That index is one of the most complete and robust of any we have used.

Shortcuts and overview

One of the features missing from almost every help system is a **shortcuts** option. It is an item in the Help menu that, when selected, shows in digest form all the tools and keyboard commands for the program's various features. It is a very necessary component of any online help system because it provides what perpetual intermediates need the most: access to features. They need the tools and commands more than they need detailed instructions.

The other missing ingredient from online help systems is **overview**. Users want to know how the Enter Macro command works, and the help system explains uselessly that it is the facility that lets you enter macros into the system. What we need to know is scope, effect, power, upside, downside, and why we might want to use this facility both in absolute terms and in comparison to similar products from other vendors.

Not for beginners

Many help systems assume that their role is to provide assistance to beginners. This is not strictly the case. While it's important that there be a "quick start guide" for beginners, online help should be focused on people who are already successfully using the product, but who want to expand their horizons: the perpetual intermediates.

Modeless and interactive help

ToolTips are modeless online help, and they are incredibly effective. Standard help systems, on the other hand, are implemented in a separate program that covers up most of the program for which it is offering help. If you were to ask a human how to perform a task, he would use his finger to point to objects on the screen to augment his explanation. A separate help program that obscures the main program cannot do this.

Wizards

Wizards are an idiom unleashed on the world by Microsoft, and they have rapidly gained popularity among programmers and user-interface designers. A wizard attempts to guarantee success in using a feature by stepping users through a series of dialog boxes. These dialogs parallel a complex procedure that is "normally" used to manage a feature of the program. For example, a wizard helps a user create a presentation in PowerPoint.

Programmers like wizards because they get to treat users like peripheral devices. Each of the wizard's dialogs asks users a question or two, and in the end the application performs whatever task was requested. They are a fine example of interrogation tactics on the program's part, and violate the design principle: *Provide choices, don't ask questions* (see Chapter 10).

Wizards are written as step-by-step procedures, rather than as informed conversations between user and program. The user is like the conductor of a robot orchestra, swinging the baton to set the tempo but otherwise having no influence on the proceedings. In this way, wizards rapidly devolve into exercises in confirmation messaging. The user learns that he merely clicks the Next button on each screen without critically analyzing why. The worst thing about wizards is that they often still ask obscure questions. A user who doesn't know what an IP address is in a normal dialog will be equally mystified by it in a wizard.

A better way to create a wizard is to make a simple, automatic function that asks no questions of users but that just goes off and does the job. If it creates a presentation, for example, it should create it, and then let the user have the option, later, using standard tools, to change the presentation. The interrogation tactics of the typical wizard are not friendly, reassuring, or particularly helpful. The wizard often doesn't explain what is going on.

Wizards were purportedly designed to improve user interfaces, but they are, in many cases, having the opposite effect. They are giving programmers license to put raw implementation model interfaces on complex features with the bland assurance that: "We'll make it easy with a wizard." This is all too reminiscent of the standard abdication of responsibility to users: "We'll be sure to document it in the manual."

"Intelligent" agents

Perhaps not much needs to be said about Clippy and his cousins, since even Microsoft has turned against their creation in its marketing of Windows XP (not that it has actually *removed* Clippy from XP, mind you). Clippy is a remnant of research Microsoft did in the creation of BOB, an "intuitive" real-world, metaphor-laden interface remarkably similar to General Magic's Magic Cap interface, discussed briefly in Chapter 13. BOB was populated with anthropomorphic, animated characters that conversed with users to help them accomplish things. It was one of Microsoft's most spectacular interface failures. Clippy is a descendant of these help agents and is every bit as annoying as they were.

A significant issue with "intelligent" animated agents is that by employing animated anthropomorphism, the software is upping the ante on user expectations of the agent's intelligence. If it can't deliver on these expectations, users will quickly become furious, just as they would with a sales clerk in a department store who claims to be an expert on his products, but who, after a few simple questions, proves to be clueless.

These constructs soon become cloying and distracting. Users of Microsoft Office are trying to accomplish something, not be entertained by the antics and pratfalls of the help system. Most applications demand more direct, less distracting, and more trustworthy means of getting assistance.

Afterword: On Collaboration

We think of the Goal-Directed method as consisting of four *p*'s: processes, patterns, principles, and practices. This book mostly concerns itself with the first three. In closing, we'd like to share a few thoughts about the *practice* of interaction design.

Interaction design is largely a difficult and messy affair (which is not to say that we don't love it). Interaction designers are often asked to help imagine and define something that has never been seen before, using new technology on an ambitious timeline. They must develop a sophisticated understanding of a complex domain, balance competing priorities, and understand the limitations and opportunities associated with the technology at their disposal and the business context of the project at hand.

The vertigo caused by these struggles and challenges has motivated us to take a very methodical approach. When we work according to the processes described in Part I, we know that we will have the benefit of the appropriate information to answer the right questions at the right time, a sense of predictability and an audit trail for design decisions back through requirements, scenarios, personas, and research. Patterns and principles are useful because they help us avoid wasted effort of continually examining first assumptions and reinventing the wheel.

But ultimately, these things are not enough. Process, patterns, and principles are necessary, but not sufficient, for a successful interaction design project. As much as these tools help, designers must still have the spark of inventiveness to imagine a new reality, and the experience and judgment to know if it's good. There is no recipe for creative vision and good design judgment. And even when you believe you have the right concept, it takes considerable hard work, diligence, and skill to execute it well. One of the most challenging, chaotic — but ultimately rewarding — aspects of this hard work is collaboration with the rest of the product and business team.

As we've discussed, interaction design needs input from and has implications for business decision makers, marketers, technologists, business analysts, and a potentially huge cast of product fabrication, quality assurance, support, and installation people, among others. If interaction design is done in a vacuum, the product team will lack common direction and the expertise and intelligence of its members will not provide benefit to the design. As we described in Chapter 4, designers must develop an understanding of the goals, vision, and constraints of the different constituencies during stakeholder interviews early in the Research phase. However, it is also necessary to involve key stakeholders throughout the design process to provide visibility and opportunities for input and feedback, and to create buy-in for the design.

In particular, we'd to highlight three important groups with which interaction designers should collaborate. First, there are the business decision makers, who, as we discussed in the Introduction, are ultimately responsible for the profitability and success of the product and commonly fund the interaction design effort. It is important to work with these people closely at project inception to understand product vision and define user research focus, and then throughout the Requirements Definition and Framework Definition phases (see Chapters 6 and 7) to define and agree upon the product definition. Business decision makers are also important to involve in Design Refinement discussions, because the trade-offs between different solutions may involve making decisions about the development budget and timeline.

Second, interaction designers must collaborate quite closely with programmers and other technologists (such as mechanical and electrical engineers for physical products). Without the talents and abilities of these people, even the best design solutions are completely worthless. The purpose of this collaboration is to make sure that design and implementation are in perfect alignment: that designs accommodate technical and cost constraints, capitalize on technological opportunities, and are effectively communicated to programmers. Also, it is often the case that a technologist's expertise can point in the direction of new possibilities that designers weren't aware of.

Finally, interaction designers must collaborate with all the other people on the project team whose work impacts the overall user experience. Depending on the project, this may include design strategists, user and market researchers, industrial designers, visual designers, user documentation writers, packaging designers, and possibly even store and point-of-sale designers. The purpose of this collaboration is to ensure that all aspects of the user experience are in harmony with each other, and not working at cross-purposes or using different design languages that could ultimately confuse the user or muddy the product's message.

Involvement of these three critical groups best happens in two venues: at formal checkpoints that correspond to the end of each phase in the process, and at frequent, informal working meetings where new ideas are explored, evaluated, and elaborated on. Working meetings are particularly important for the second group, technologists, once the design has begun to gel, and are critical for the third group in the early stages of ideation as well as later in the process. We briefly discussed the relationship between visual, industrial, and interaction designers in Chapters 4–7.

We once believed that all design work should be completed before coding begins. Experience has taught us that this is not a practical reality due to aggressive development schedules and, most importantly, the need to prove the feasibility of proposed design solutions. We do believe, though, that *all aspects of a product should be designed before they are built.* By this we mean that, even in a highly iterative process, informed planning of the user experience should always precede construction, but that it is also possible to effectively sequence work so that construction can begin on some aspects of the product while others are still being designed. This is unfortunately a much messier reality than the neat sequential compartmentalization of design and construction. To accommodate it, we've learned that it is critical for technologists, designers, and business decision makers to continually collaborate around the prioritization of both design and implementation activities.

Ultimately, the successful delivery of a product that meets people's needs requires the careful coordination of the efforts of a large number of people. We've found that to be effective, interaction designers must ultimately assume considerable responsibility for orchestrating a fine balance between the numerous forces pushing and pulling on a product. We hope that the tools provided to you in this book will help you to create great digital products that truly satisfy your users and customers.

Design Principles

Chapter 1

> ▶ Interaction design is not guesswork.

Chapter 2

> ▶ User interfaces should be based on user mental models rather than implementation models.
>
> ▶ Goal-directed interactions reflect user mental models.
>
> ▶ Users don't understand Boolean logic.
>
> ▶ Don't replicate Mechanical-Age artifacts in user interfaces without Information-Age enhancements.
>
> ▶ Significant change must be significantly better.

Chapter 3

> ▶ Nobody wants to remain a beginner.
>
> ▶ Optimize for intermediates.
>
> ▶ Imagine users as very intelligent but very busy.

Chapter 5

> ▶ Don't make the user feel stupid.
>
> ▶ Focus the design for each interface on a single primary persona.

Chapter 6

- ▶ Define *what* the product will do before you design *how* the product will do it.

- ▶ In early stages of design, pretend the interface is magic.

Chapter 7

- ▶ Never show a design approach that you're not happy with; stakeholders just might like it.

- ▶ There is only one user experience — form and behavior must be designed in concert with each other.

Chapter 9

- ▶ Decisions about technical platform are best made in concert with interaction design efforts.

- ▶ Optimize sovereign applications for full-screen use.

- ▶ Sovereign interfaces should feature a conservative visual style.

- ▶ Sovereign applications should exploit rich input.

- ▶ Maximize document views within sovereign applications.

- ▶ Transient applications must be simple, clear, and to the point.

- ▶ Transient applications should be limited to a single window and view.

- ▶ A transient application should launch to its previous position and configuration.

- ▶ Kiosks should be optimized for first-time use.

Chapter 10

- ▶ No matter how cool your interface is, less of it would be better.

- ▶ Well-orchestrated user interfaces are transparent.

- ▶ Follow users' mental models.

- ▶ Less is more.

- ▶ Enable users to direct, don't force them to discuss.

- ▶ Keep tools close at hand.

- ▶ Provide modeless feedback.

- ▶ Design for the probable; provide for the possible.

- ▶ Contextualize information.

- ▶ Provide direct manipulation and graphical input.

- ▶ Reflect object and application status.

- ▶ Avoid unnecessary reporting.
- ▶ Don't use dialogs to report normalcy.
- ▶ Avoid blank slates.
- ▶ Ask for forgiveness, not permission.
- ▶ Differentiate between command and configuration.
- ▶ Provide choices; don't ask questions.
- ▶ Hide the ejector seat levers.
- ▶ Optimize for responsiveness; accommodate latency.

Chapter 11

- ▶ Eliminate excise wherever possible.
- ▶ Don't weld on training wheels.
- ▶ Don't stop the proceedings with idiocy.
- ▶ Don't make users ask for permission.
- ▶ Allow input wherever you have output.
- ▶ Inflect the interface for typical navigation.
- ▶ Users make commensurate effort if the rewards justify it.

Chapter 12

- ▶ The computer does the work and the person does the thinking.
- ▶ Software should behave like a considerate human being.
- ▶ If it's worth the user entering, it's worth the application remembering.

Chapter 13

- ▶ Most people would rather be successful than knowledgeable.
- ▶ All idioms must be learned; good idioms need to be learned only once.
- ▶ Never bend your interface to fit a metaphor.

Chapter 14

- ▶ A visual interface is based on visual patterns.
- ▶ Visually distinguish elements that behave differently.
- ▶ Visually communicate function and behavior.
- ▶ Take things away until the design breaks, then put that last thing back in.
- ▶ Visually show what; textually tell which.

- ▶ Obey standards unless there is a truly superior alternative.
- ▶ Consistency doesn't imply rigidity.

Chapter 17

- ▶ Managing disks and files is not a user goal.
- ▶ Save documents and settings automatically.
- ▶ Put files where users can find them.
- ▶ Disks are a hack, not a design feature.

Chapter 18

- ▶ An error may not be your fault, but it's your responsibility.
- ▶ Audit, don't edit.

Chapter 19

- ▶ Rich visual feedback is the key to successful direct manipulation.
- ▶ Support both mouse and keyboard use for navigation and selection tasks.
- ▶ Use cursor hinting to show the meanings of meta-keys.
- ▶ Single-click selects data or an object or changes the control state.
- ▶ Mouse-down over an object or data should select the object or data.
- ▶ Mouse-down over controls means propose action; mouse-up means commit to action.
- ▶ Visually communicate pliancy.
- ▶ Use cursor hinting to indicate pliancy.
- ▶ The selection state should be visually evident and unambiguous.
- ▶ Drop candidates must visually indicate their receptivity.
- ▶ The drag cursor must visually identify the source object.
- ▶ Any scrollable drag-and-drop target must auto-scroll.
- ▶ Debounce all drags.
- ▶ Any program that demands precise alignment must offer a vernier.

Chapter 20

- ▶ A dialog box is another room; have a good reason to go there.
- ▶ Provide functions in the window where they are used.
- ▶ The utility of any interaction idiom is context-dependent.

Chapter 21

- ▶ A multitude of control-laden dialog boxes doth not a good user interface make.
- ▶ Use links for navigation, and buttons or butcons for action.
- ▶ Distinguish important text items in lists with graphic icons.
- ▶ Never scroll text horizontally.
- ▶ Use bounded controls for bounded input.
- ▶ Use noneditable (display) controls for output-only text.

Chapter 22

- ▶ Use menus to provide a pedagogic vector.
- ▶ Disable menu items when they are not applicable.
- ▶ Use consistent visual symbols on parallel command vectors.

Chapter 23

- ▶ Toolbars provide experienced users fast access to frequently used functions.
- ▶ Use ToolTips with all toolbar and iconic controls.

Chapter 24

- ▶ Put primary interactions in the primary window.
- ▶ Dialogs are appropriate for functions that are out of the main interaction flow.
- ▶ Dialogs are appropriate for organizing controls and information about a single domain object or application function.
- ▶ Use verbs in function dialog title bars.
- ▶ Use object names in property dialog title bars.
- ▶ Visually differentiate modeless dialogs from modal dialogs.
- ▶ Use consistent terminating commands for modeless dialog boxes.
- ▶ Don't dynamically change the labels of terminating buttons.
- ▶ Inform the user when the application is unresponsive.
- ▶ Never use transitory dialogs as error messages or confirmations.
- ▶ All interaction idioms have practical limits.
- ▶ Don't stack tabs.

Chapter 25

- ▶ Error message boxes stop the proceedings with idiocy and should be avoided.
- ▶ Make errors impossible.

- ► Users get humiliated when software tells them they failed.
- ► Do, don't ask.
- ► Make all actions reversible.
- ► Provide modeless feedback to help users avoid mistakes.

Chapter 26

- ► Offer shortcuts from the Help menu.
- ► Offer users a gallery of ready-to-use templates.

Bibliography

Alexander, Christopher. 1964. *Notes on the Synthesis of Form*. Harvard University Press.

Alexander, Christopher. 1977. *A Pattern Language*. Oxford University Press.

Alexander, Christopher. 1979. *The Timeless Way of Building*. Oxford University Press.

Bertin, Jacques. 1983. *Semiology of Graphics*. University of Wisconsin Press.

Beyer, Hugh, and Holtzblatt, Karen. 1998. *Contextual Design*. Morgan Kaufmann Publishers.

Borchers, Jan. 2001. *A Pattern Approach to Interaction Design*. John Wiley and Sons.

Borenstein, Nathaniel S. 1994. *Programming As If People Mattered*. Princeton University Press.

Buxton, Bill. 1990. "The 'Natural' Language of Interaction: A Perspective on Non-Verbal Dialogues." Laurel, Brenda, ed. *The Art of Human-Computer Interface Design*. Addison-Wesley.

Carroll, John M. ed. 1995. *Scenario-Based Design*. John Wiley and Sons.

Carroll, John M. 2000. *Making Use: Scenario-based Design of Human-Computer Interactions*. The MIT Press.

Constantine, Larry L., and Lockwood, Lucy A. D. 1999. *Software for Use*. Addison-Wesley.

Constantine, Larry L., and Lockwood, Lucy A. D. 2002. *forUse Newsletter* #26, October.

Cooper, Alan. 1999. *The Inmates Are Running the Asylum*. SAMS/Macmillan.

Crampton Smith, Gillian, and Tabor, Philip. 1996. "The Role of the Artist-Designer." Winograd, Terry, ed. *Bringing Design to Software*. Addison-Wesley.

Csikszentmihalyi, Mihaly. 1991. *Flow: The Psychology of Optimal Experience*. HarperCollins.

DeMarco, Tom, and Lister, Timothy R. 1999. *Peopleware*. Dorset House.

Dillon, Andrew. "Beyond Usability: Process, Outcome and Affect in Human Computer Interaction." Paper presented at the Lazerow Lecture at the Faculty of Information Studies, University of Toronto, March 2001. Retrieved from www.ischool.utexas.edu/~adillon/publications/beyond_usability.html.

Gamma, Erich, et al. 1995. *Design Patterns: Elements of Reusable Object-Oriented Software*, Addison-Wesley Professional.

Garrett, Jesse James. 2002. *The Elements of User Experience*. New Riders Press.

Gellerman, Saul W. 1963. *Motivation and Productivity*. Amacom Press.

Goodwin, Kim. 2001. "Perfecting Your Personas." *Cooper Newsletter*, July/August.

Goodwin, Kim. 2002. "Getting from Research to Personas: Harnessing the Power of Data." User Interface 7 West Conference.

Goodwin, Kim. 2002a. Cooper U Interaction Design Practicum Notes. Cooper.

Grudin, J., and Pruitt, J. 2002. "Personas, Participatory Design and Product Development: An Infrastructure for Engagement." *PDC'02: Proceedings of the Participatory Design Conference*.

Heckel, Paul. 1994. *The Elements of Friendly Software Design*. Sybex.

Horn, Robert E. 1998. *Visual Language*. Macro Vu Press.

Horton, William. 1994. *The Icon Book: Visual Symbols for Computer Systems and Documentation*. John Wiley & Sons.

Johnson, Jeff. 2000. *GUI Bloopers*. Morgan Kaufman Publishers.

Jones, Matt, and Marsden, Gary. 2006. *Mobile Interaction Design*. John Wiley & Sons.

Kobara, Shiz. 1991. *Visual Design with OSF/Motif*. Addison-Wesley.

Korman, Jonathan. 2001. "Putting People Together to Create Good Products." *Cooper Newsletter*, September.

Krug, Steve. 2000. *Don't Make Me Think!* New Riders Press.

Kuniavsky, Mike. 2003. *Observing the User Experience*. Morgan Kaufmann Publishers, an Imprint of Elsevier.

Kuutti, Kari. 1995. "Work Processes: Scenarios as a Preliminary Vocabulary." Carroll, John M., ed. *Scenario-based Design*. John Wiley and Sons, Inc.

Laurel, Brenda. 1991. *Computers as Theatre*. Addison-Wesley.

Lidwell, William; Holden, Kritina; Butler, Jill. 2003. *Universal Principles of Design*. Rockport Publishers.

MacDonald, Nico. 2003. *What Is Web Design?* Rotovision.

McCloud, Scott. 1994. *Understanding Comics.* Kitchen Sink Press.

Mikkelson, N., and Lee, W. O. 2000. "Incorporating user archetypes into scenario-based design." *Proceedings of UPA 2000*.

Miller, R. B. 1968. Response time in man-computer conversational transactions. *Proc. AFIPS Fall Joint Computer Conference* Vol. 33, 267–277.

Mitchell, J. and Shneiderman, B. (1989). Dynamic versus static menus: An exploratory comparison. *SIGCHI Bulletin*, Vol. 20 No. 4, 33–37.

Moggridge, Bill. 2007. *Designing Interactions*. The MIT Press.

Morville, Peter. 2005. *Ambient Findability*. O'Reilly Media.

Mulder, Steve, and Yaar, Ziv. 2006. *The User Is Always Right*. New Riders Press.

Mullet, Kevin, and Sano, Darrell. 1995. *Designing Visual Interfaces*. Sunsoft Press.

Nelson, Theodor Holm. 1990. "The Right Way to Think about Software Design." Laurel, Brenda, ed. *The Art of Human-Computer Interface Design*. Addison-Wesley.

Newman, William M., and Lamming, Michael G. 1995. *Interactive System Design*. Addison-Wesley.

Nielsen, Jakob. 1993. *Usability Engineering*. Academic Press.

Nielsen, Jakob. 2000. *Designing Web Usability*. New Riders Press.

Nielsen, Jakob. 2002. UseIt.com (Web site).

Norman, Donald. 1989. *The Design of Everyday Things*. Currency Doubleday.

Norman, Donald. 1994. *Things That Make Us Smart*. Perseus Publishing.

Norman, Donald A. 1998. *The Invisible Computer*. The MIT Press.

Norman, Donald. 2005. *Emotional Design*. Basic Books.

Papanek, Victor. 1984. *Design for the Real World*. Academy Chicago Publishers.

Perfetti, Christine, and Landesman, Lori. 2001. "The Truth About Download Times" UIE.com.

Pinker, Stephen. 1999. *How the Mind Works*. W. W. Norton & Company.

Preece, Jenny; Rogers, Yvonne and Sharp, Helen. 2007. *Interaction Design*. John Wiley & Sons.

Raskin, Jeff. 2000. *The Humane Interface*. Addison-Wesley Professional.

Reimann, Robert M. 2001. "So You Want to Be an Interaction Designer." *Cooper Newsletter*, June.

Reimann, Robert M. 2002. "Bridging the Gap from Research to Design." Panel Presentation, IBM Make IT Easy Conference.

Reimann, Robert. 2002. "Perspectives: Learning Curves." *edesign Magazine*, Dec.

Reimann, Robert. 2005. "Personas, Scenarios, and Emotional Design". UXMatters.com.

Reimann, Robert M., and Forlizzi, Jodi. 2001. "Role: Interaction Designer." Presentation to AIGA Experience Design 2001.

Rheinfrank, John, and Evenson, Shelley. 1996. "Design Languages." Winograd, Terry, ed. *Bringing Design to Software*. Addison-Wesley.

Rombaur, Irma S., and Becker, 1975. Marion Rombaur. *The Joy of Cooking*. Scribner.

Rosenfeld, Louis, and Morville, Peter. 1998. *Information Architecture*. O'Reilly.

Rudolf, Frank. 1998. "Model-Based User Interface Design: Successive Transformations of a Task/Object Model." Wood, Larry E., ed. *User Interface Design: Bridging the Gap from User Requirements to Design*. CRC Press.

Saffer, Dan. 2006. *Designing for Interaction*. Peachpit Press.

Schön, D., and Bennett, J. 1996. "Reflective Conversation with Materials." Winograd, T., ed. *Bringing Design to Software*. Reading, MA: Addison-Wesley.

Schumann, J., Strothotte, T., Raab, A., and Laser, S. 1996. *Assessing the Effect of Non-Photorealistic Rendered Images in CAD*, CHI 1996 Papers, pp. 35–41.

Shneiderman, Ben. 1998. *Designing the User Interface*. Addison-Wesley.

Simon, Hebert. 1996. *The Sciences of the Artificial*. The MIT Press.

Snyder, Carolyn. 2003. *Paper Prototyping*. Morgan Kaufmann Publishers, an Imprint of Elsevier.

SRI Consulting Business Intelligence. 2002. "Welcome to VALS." SRI-BC.com

Tidwell, Jennifer. 2006. *Designing Interfaces,* O'Reilly Media.

Tufte, Edward. 1983. *The Visual Display of Quantitative Information*. Graphic Press.

Van Duyne, Douglas K., Landay, James A., Hong, Jason I. 2002. *The Design of Sites*. Addison-Wesley.

Veen, Jeffrey. 2000. *The Art and Science of Web Design*. New Riders Press.

Verplank, B., Fulton, J., Black, A., and Moggridge, B. 1993. "Observation and Invention: Use of Scenarios in Interaction Design." Tutorial Notes, InterCHI'93, Amsterdam.

Weiss, Michael J. 2000. *The Clustered World: How We Live, What We Buy, and What It All Means About Who We Are*. Little Brown & Company.

Winograd, Terry, ed. 1996. *Bringing Design to Software*. Addison-Wesley.

Wirfs-Brock, Rebecca. 1993. "Designing Scenarios: Making the Case of a Use Case Framework." *SmallTalk Report*, November/December.

Wixon, Dennis, and Ramey, Judith, eds. 1996. *Field Methods Casebook for Software Design*. John Wiley and Sons.

Wood, Larry E. 1996. "The Ethnographic Interview in User-Centered Task/Work Analysis."

Style Guides

Apple Computer. 1992. *Macintosh Human Interface Guidelines*. Addison–Wesley.

Apple Computer. 2002. *Aqua Human Interface Guidelines*. Apple Developer Website.

Microsoft. 1999. *Windows User Experience Guidelines*. Microsoft Press.

Sun MicroSystems. 1990. *Open Look Graphical User Interface Application Style Guidelines*. Addison-Wesley.

Index

R

cooper

Research
Innovation
Design
Training
Consulting

→ www.cooper.com

Did you like this book? There's more good stuff where this came from! Read more at **www.cooper.com**